Marketing Operations 1999–2000

The Chartered Institute of Marketing/Butterworth-Heinemann Marketing Series is the most comprehensive, widely used and important collection of books in marketing and sales currently available worldwide.

As the CIM's official publisher, Butterworth-Heinemann develops, produces and publishes the complete series in association with the CIM. We aim to provide definitive marketing books for students and practitioners that promote excellence in marketing education and practice.

The series titles are written by CIM senior examiners and leading marketing educators for professionals, students and those studying the CIM's Certificate, Advanced Certificate and Postgraduate Diploma courses. Now firmly established, these titles provide practical study support to CIM and other marketing students and to practitioners at all levels.

The Chartered
Institute of Marketing

Formed in 1911, The Chartered Institute of Marketing is now the largest professional marketing management body in the world with over 60,000 members located worldwide. Its primary objectives are focused on the development of awareness and understanding of marketing throughout UK industry and commerce and in the raising of standards of professionalism in the education, training and practice of this key business discipline.

Marketing Operations 1999–2000

Mike Worsam

Published on behalf of
The Chartered Institute of Marketing

OXFORD AUCKLAND BOSTON JOHANNESBURG MELBOURNE NEW DELHI

This book is for my best friend and wife – Patricia

Butterworth-Heinemann
Linacre House, Jordan Hill, Oxford OX2 8DP
225 Wildwood Avenue, Woburn, MA 01801-2041
A division of Reed Educational and Professional Publishing Ltd

ℛ A member of the Reed Elsevier plc group

First published 1999

British Library Cataloguing in Publication Data
A catalogue record for this book is available from the British Library

ISBN 0 7506 4362 5

Illustrations by Jane Jones, Bill Piggins and Charles Whelan

Composition by Genesis Typesetting, Laser Quay, Rochester, Kent
Printed and bound in Italy

Contents

A quick word from the Chief Examiner   vii

Acknowledgements   ix

How to use your CIM workbook   x

1   Marketing planning – audit and analysis   1

2   Marketing planning – implementation and control   29

3   Marketing relationships   64

4   Promotional operations – communications   97

5   Promotional operations – tools   117

6   Product operations   138

7   Pricing operations   157

8   Place operations   173

9   Services marketing   191

10   Charity and not-for-profit marketing   222

11   Industrial/business-to-business marketing   248

12   International marketing   277

13   Focus on the examination   310

Appendix Syllabus   362

Glossary   365

Further reading   371

Index   373

A quick word from the Chief Examiner

I am delighted to recommend to you the new series of CIM workbooks. All of these have been written by authors involved with examining and marking for the CIM.

Preparing for the CIM Exams is hard work. These workbooks are designed to make that work as interesting and illuminating as possible, as well as providing you with the knowledge you need to pass. I wish you success.

Trevor Watkins
CIM Chief Examiner,
Deputy Vice Chancellor,
South Bank University

Acknowledgements

Writing a book is often thought of as a solitary process and, insofar as there is considerable focus on the word processor to the exclusion of the outside world, it is. There is, however, considerable interaction with the support team primarily but also with academics, students and the 'real world'.

This is a workbook, and so it needs to be both current and user-friendly. The one requires support from the marketing and management environments, the other a friendly critic who will review and improve each unit as it is drafted and re-worked.

Support has come from the academic community indirectly, through published materials, and directly, through contacts that have ranged from specific requests for aid to general conversations. A major source of support and encouragement has been, as always, the students of management and marketing who have been exposed to much of the thinking and methodology as part of their learning experiences – I do so hate that phrase – as part of their coming to grips with the practical needs of the career marketer as well as of the marketing student. There is life after study!

Critical review has been the responsibility of my best friend (and wife) who has the knack of being able to put herself in the position of a student coming fresh to the material. She is also a very good proof-reader and so I am happy to give her full credit for picking up the unintentional errors of grammar and spelling. I suppose that I must say I take responsibility for errors that creep through, authors always do this, but I don't believe it! Errors of fact are mine and mine alone. As for any others, well you be the judge.

It is difficult to select individuals for special mention when so many have been involved, but Paul Cook of CCN Marketing (MOSAIC) must be singled out for special thanks. Karina Mellinger of CACI provided ACORN data and the Chartered Institute of Marketing's INFOLINK service researched background. Sally Dibb, as Chief Examiner, influenced the shape of the book as well as being most supportive. Debbie Clewes, on taking over from Sally has also helped considerably.

Every effort has been made to trace and acknowledge ownership of copyright. The publishers will be glad to hear from any copyright holders whom it has not been possible to contact.

In the interests of clear communication the masculine pronoun is used unless there is clear reason to do otherwise. This stems solely from a desire for clarity and to avoid ugly and cumbersome language. No discrimination, prejudice or bias is intended nor should any be implied.

Remember that as a marketing student you need to master not only the subject, but also the technique needed to get your examination passes. This workbook is targeted on helping you to do both. It has been fun to write, I hope you will find it fun to work with.

A bientôt.

Mike Worsam
Marseillan, France

How to use your CIM workbook

The authors have been careful to structure your book with the exams in mind. Each unit, therefore, covers an essential part of the syllabus. You need to work through the complete workbook systematically to ensure that you have covered everything you need to know.

This workbook is divided into thirteen units. Each unit contains the following standard elements:

Objectives tell you what part of the syllabus you will be covering and what you will be expected to know having read the unit.

Study guides tell you how long the unit is and how long its activities take to do.

Questions are designed to give you practice – they will be similar to those you get in the exam.

Answers give you a suggested format for answering exam questions. *Remember* there is no such thing as a model answer – you should use these examples only as guidelines.

Activities give you the chance to put what you have learnt into practice.

Exam tips are hints from the Senior Examiner or Examiner which are designed to help you avoid common mistakes made by previous candidates.

Definitions are used for words you must know to pass the exam.

Extending knowledge sections are designed to help you use your time most effectively. It is not possible for the workbook to cover *everything* you need to know to pass. What you read here needs to be supplemented by your classes, practical experience at work and day-to-day reading.

Summaries cover what you should have picked up from reading the unit.

A glossary is provided at the back of the book to help define and underpin understanding of the key terms used in each unit.

Unit 1 Marketing planning – audit and analysis

Objectives

In this unit you will:

- ❑ Focus on the purpose of your study.
- ❑ Establish the CIM Examiner's requirements.
- ❑ Meet the key planning tools.

By the end of this unit you will:

- ❑ Have established a personal action plan.
- ❑ Understand planning's key role within an organization.
- ❑ Understand the terms used in management planning.
- ❑ Appreciate the need for a planning structure.
- ❑ Be able to work with the key planning tools.
- ❑ Be able to segment a market.

Study Guide

You should start out with a clear idea of your needs – which should be to learn the subject *and* to pass your examination.

The one is different from, but dependent upon, the other. Subject knowledge is vital to success in your career, and in the examination. But subject knowledge has to be conveyed to the examiner if you are to secure a pass. Thus examination technique is extremely important. As we progress you will find a series of Examination Hints to help you come to grips with the techniques needed, and Activities will give you opportunities to practise.

Unfortunately some students do not accept (or understand) the need to master examination technique – and so fail even though they have an excellent command of the subject.

Because of its importance the first part of this unit focuses on what the Examiner requires. Plan your learning so that you develop subject knowledge and practise exam skills side-by-side. You will need both to secure a pass.

Definitions and explanations

All the key technical terms that you will need to understand are grouped in a Glossary. Definitions are given, and explained where necessary. Remember that you are expected to use technical terms correctly at work, but especially in your examinations.

Passing your examination

To do well in marketing you need:

- Command of marketing theories.
- Understanding of how theories are applied in real-life marketing.
- Ability to apply theory and understanding to given situations.
- Ability to effectively communicate decisions and recommendations.

To do well in examinations you need:

- Command of the examination process.
- Understanding of the examiner's needs.
- Ability to plan answers that match requirement.
- Ability to effectively communicate with the examiner.

Examiner's requirements

The Senior Examiner has specified the requirements.

A good answer will:

- Address each part of each specific question.
- Use the question to provide a clear structure for the answer.
- Display a good understanding of the relevant principles and theories.
- Make reference to relevant writers.
- Apply theory by using effective and interesting real-life examples.
- Adopt the specified answer format.

  Note: This may be a report, an article, a training programme or notes for a presentation.

  An essay will *not* be required.

A good answer paper will:

- Be well presented.
- Use diagrams and models to communicate.
- Use white space, underlining, bullet points, etc. to add clarity.
- Be written clearly and legibly.
- Reflect good time management skills. (By submitting full answers to all four questions.)

The key faults reported – time and again – are:

- Failure to comply with the above points.
- Not reading the question carefully and so not answering it specifically.
- Submitting generalized answers.
- Reproducing textbook material rather than applying principles.
- Failure to adopt the specified format.
- Failure to use examples or to explain them in a meaningful way.
- Too much time spent on Part A, causing the Part B answers to be rushed.

These key faults are all easily avoidable. All that is needed is the ability to plan, and to write in a variety of Business English formats.

Practice

As we progress you will be offered opportunities to develop your examination skills. You will also find, in the last unit, a detailed guide to examination success, and two actual examination papers with specimen answers.

Many students report that it is best to work through Unit 13 now. They find it helps to provide a focus into which to slot their learning and, of course, it applies across any other subjects that you may be studying.

If you do turn forwards, be sure *not* to read through the examination papers. You will need to come to them fresh as part of your active revision. It is a good idea to staple the relevant pages together to maintain confidentiality.

Action plan

Planning underpins all successful endeavours. We will be covering marketing planning: remember to apply exactly the same process to your own needs.

- *Time* Determine the best use of your time between now and your examination. You need to divide your time into two major elements:
  - A period for careful study of the materials in this Workbook, and to complete all the Activities.
  - A period of active revision ahead of the examination.
- *Review* Plan periods of active review into your learning. This simply means a skim through of your notes to keep them fresh in your mind. Leave them for several months and they are far harder to understand when revision time comes around. The key is: on-going revision.
- *Space* You need space in which to study. No distractions, no interruptions. This does *not* mean that you can't work with the radio, a tape or even the TV. Some people can. But there is a body of thought which says you can retrieve learning better in conditions similar to those in which you learned. You can't take a radio into the exam, so you are perhaps better doing without. Your choice.
- *Personalize* Study how best it suits you. Some people operate best in the early morning; others at night. There is no single 'best time', nor 'best way'. Listen to others but don't mimic them unless their way is also the best for you.

Study Tips

- Organize
  It is far easier to study and to review if you have a structure to your materials:
  - Index by topic and separate with file dividers.
  - Note the reference (the source) of materials you add to the notes.
  - File relevant materials and articles with your notes.
  - Incorporate past questions, summary and revision notes as you complete each section of your studies.

- Personalize
  You will find it much easier to remember if you personalize your notes. Reading through materials is far less effective than paraphrasing them in your own words. The Activities in this workbook are designed to help you personalize but you should take the process further by making supplementary notes that rephrase the key issues. Why? Because reading is a passive activity. Writing is active. You have to read, translate into your own words, instruct your muscular system to write and check what you have written. The same material is processed at least five times actively, instead of once passively.

Passive  Active

Figure 1.1
Passive reading and active learning

- Illustrate
  Look out for relevant articles and current examples. These will add interest to your studies and you will need current examples in the exam room. In these ways your files will be complete and ready for easy revision when exam time comes.

  Never use examples from textbooks, or from this workbook. The examiners are impressed by a candidate who shows evidence of current awareness and there are so many live examples for a marketer to use that falling back on Coca-Cola and McDonald's can be perceived as a sign of laziness!

- Revise

  Set up for your revision as you learn. Page after page of notes are not memorable – they all look the same. Help your memory by laying out your notes so that the key points are easily found. Set up flash cards as you go, and flick through them in every learning session. (See the *Effective Management for Marketing* Workbook for details on how to maximize your learning.)

Marketing planning

User centred – consumer focused

Those at the cutting edge of marketing have always known that the product or service is doomed unless it is bought, paid for, used, re-purchased and established in a repeat use – re-purchase pattern.

It has also long been known that people buy Benefits. Smirnoff Vodka only became established in the US market when they stopped selling liquor, stopped selling vodka and came up with:

Smirnoff: It takes your breath away.

and

Smirnoff: It leaves you breathless.

If interest comes from features, then desire comes from benefits. Why, then, do we work with a marketing mix comprised of either the 4 or 7Ps?

Philip Kotler said, in 1990, that the 4Ps were an internal approach to marketing, that by their use marketing could be seen as an extension of the Production Concept.

Following this argument it can be seen that the Ps are product centred – internally focused. A C approach helps a marketer to more correctly focus on what needs to be provided. Customers and consumers value the benefits to them – not the functions identified in the Ps. A product offer, for example, is judged as value-in-use by a customer. The number of features is not important. The criterion of choice is *What is the benefit to me?*

Marketers do well to start their thinking process from a C viewpoint, simply by translating the Ps into Cs:

Product	–	Customer value
Price	–	Cost
Place	–	Convenience
Promotion	–	Communication
Physical evidence	–	Confirmation
People	–	Consideration
Process	–	Co-ordination.

Activity 1.1

Take a recent purchase (or attempt to purchase). Analyse it carefully from the C perspective.

- How is the C approach of more value to you as a shopper?
- What does this mean to you as a marketer?

(**See**: Debriefing at the end of the unit.)

Marketing's evolving role

Remember that a Decision Making Unit (DMP) and a Decision Making Process (DMP) are present within every transaction. It is a key marketing task to identify and provide for customer and consumer needs. How can this be done without first understanding what they actually want, and what they perceive they need?

Marketing has evolved from advertising and selling, but these functions were created to sell what the organization produced. The concept of Brand and Product Managers allowed the development of an active link between customer/consumer and the organization – but usually at a tactical, functional level.

Marketing's strategic role

Marketing has a major contribution to make to corporate-level strategic management. Alongside the other key functions of finance, production, personnel and distribution, marketers must take the needs of the organization as a whole into account.

At senior level the marketer is a manager within the organization as a whole. The individual functions are vital, of course, and skilled practitioners are needed in each – but at senior level the management need is for an overview.

Functional strategies must fit within corporate strategy – as we shall see – and each functional manager therefore has a responsibility to achieve functional objectives in order that corporate objectives may be met.

Planning

Marketing plans fit within the corporate plan, just as do the financial, production, personnel and distribution plans. The net result of the planning process should be a budget which guides the entire organization and helps to ensure synergy.

With an effective system of budgetary control every sub-unit within an organization knows exactly what has to be achieved, and by when. If all meet their identified budgets, then the organization will achieve its corporate objectives. The control aspect of budgeting ensures that progress against each budget is monitored and deviation(s) reported in time for action to be taken.

Budgets are to be achieved, not beaten. They are set as the result of a planning process that aims to achieve the optimum result for the organization. Therefore if one manager under-achieves it follows that others must compensate. (A shortfall in production, for example, must be reported in time for the sales force to stop selling. Similarly, an abundant demand must not result in an excess of orders unless and until production can be increased to meet the demand.)

Activity 1.2

Profit achievement through market success

Organizations of all types are concerned to generate profits from a market place. The basic marketing concept – Exchange of Value for Mutual Satisfaction – sees 'profit' as a far wider concept than purely financial.

Take 15 minutes to identify the markets served by different organizations and the 'profit' sought in each:

Organization	Markets	'Profit'
1 A hospital	_____	_____
	_____	_____
	_____	_____
2 A charity	_____	_____
	_____	_____
	_____	_____
3 A tax office	_____	_____
	_____	_____
	_____	_____

(**See**: Debriefing at the end of the unit.)

The planning hierarchy

A hierarchy of planning levels is necessary if synergy is to be achieved. Not every organization has adopted budgetary control but all have some form of planning hierarchy.

At the top of the organization the manager's concern is with long-term issues; middle managers are responsible for the achievement of strategies that help achieve long-term success; operational managers deal with the day-to-day achievement of individual activities which, taken as a whole, enable strategies to be achieved.

Thus a corporate level manager (or director) is like the admiral commanding a fleet who has a mission to ensure that his ships are in all respects ready for a given task. He or she has to take the major strategic decisions about:

- Levels of performance to be achieved by a time sufficiently ahead of commitment to action.
- The overall battle plan.
- Logistical support so that committed units are supplied with the necessary stores and ammunition.
- Physical and psychological support so that individuals in the command are motivated to succeed.

Captains of individual ships have similar responsibilities to their admiral but their sphere of responsibility is limited to their ship. Each captain can set his or her own strategies but these must be within the overall strategies determined by the admiral. In other words, the admiral has set policies, and determined corporate strategies.

Heads of departments within each ship have clear guidelines (policies) set by their captain and dictated by the admiral's overall plan. They can set their own strategies to ensure that the ship's objectives are met.

Junior officers and senior petty officers each have a limited area of responsibility but still a degree of freedom of action. A limited ability to select the best course of action.

Rank and file seamen are strictly concerned with tactical issues. They ensure that the equipment is working, relay messages and service equipment, but if any one fails it can have a ripple effect that extends upwards and outwards through the hierarchy.

For example, when an aircraft is catapulted from an aircraft carrier one person has the task of checking that the nose wheel is locked. If it is not, the launch will fail. The immediate result can be the loss of two irreplaceable aircrew and an aircraft worth £30 m. It can delay subsequent launches and an attack may have to be aborted, or go forward under strength. Failure to hit the target may result in a land force facing heavier than expected opposition, many lives may be lost unnecessarily and the objective may not be taken.

Planning terminology

Be careful to use terms correctly and to communicate effectively your use:

- *Objectives* – the keystones of all planning. Objectives are needed so that everybody knows exactly what is required. In Unit 1 we turned some generalized statements into quantified objectives as a first step towards helping you acquire the skills unconsciously to apply objectives to all situations.

  Evaluate your draft objectives to ensure that they are SMART: Specific, Measurable, Achievable, Relevant, Timed. Re-draft until they are!

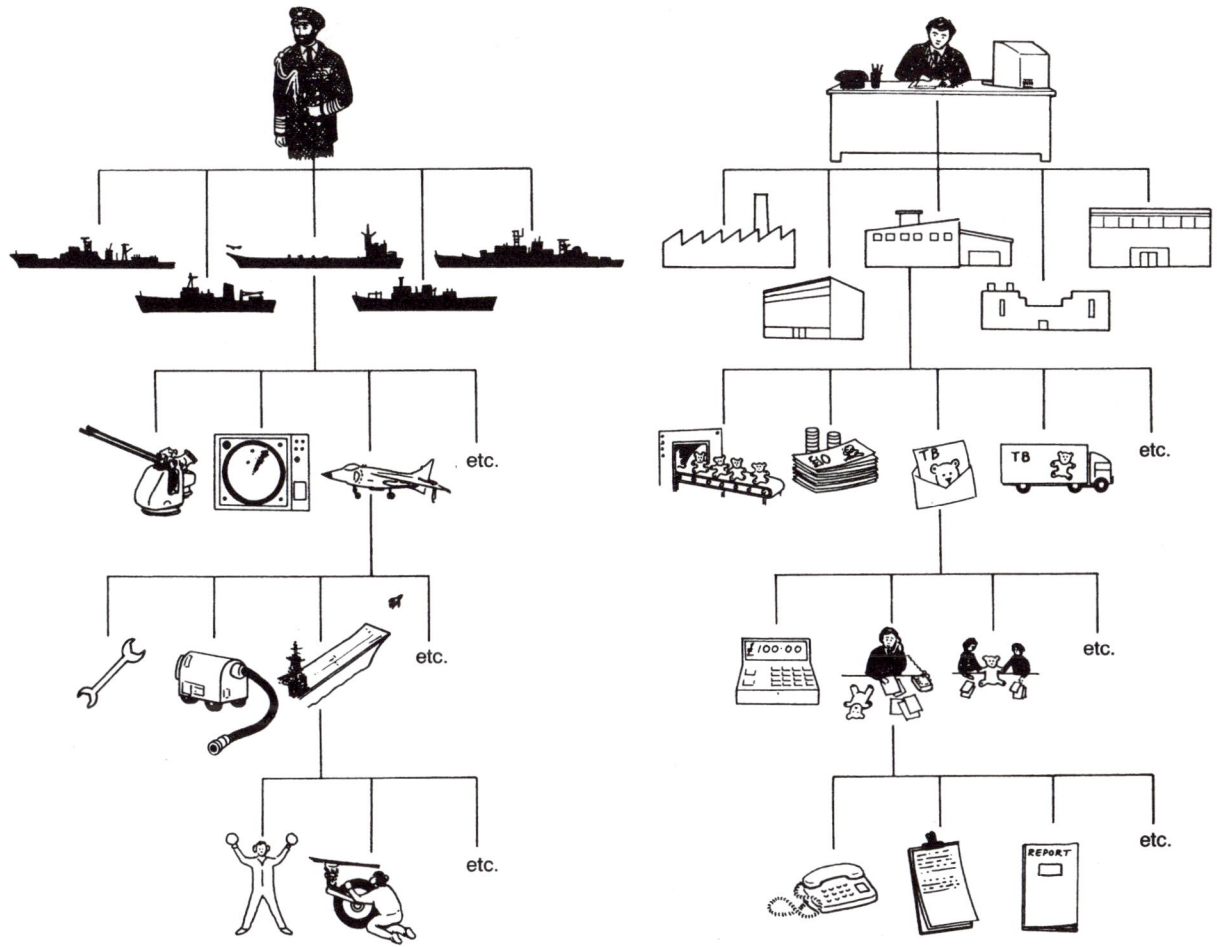

Figure 1.2 Planning hierarchy

- *Mission* – the purpose of a mission statement is to encapsulate the central purpose and rationale of the organization. It is not expressed in objective terms but all policies and strategies must be consistent with it. Mission statements are adopted at board level and are intended to provide long-term guidance. An organization's strategies can change dramatically but must always remain within the mission.
- *Policies* – are extracted from the mission as general principles to guide behaviour and direct action. A typical policy statement could be: 'It is our policy to attract the best staff by paying the highest wages on the high street'. Note the difference between this and the aim of 'Being a good employer of high-quality staff.'

  Policies provide a clarity of purpose which guides the thinking and actions of managers at all levels in an organization.
- *Aims and goals* – aims are broad statements of general intention. They are not quantified and are used generally to describe a future intention. A chief executive may well use a series of aims at an Annual General Meeting to illustrate intention.

  Goals are quantified objectives. Thus a goal may be: 'To achieve a 40 per cent share of the energy market in Great Britain by the year 2010.' This could be expressed as an aim: 'To become a major player in the energy market.'
- *Corporate objectives* – also known as goals it is the role of corporate objectives to set clear objectives to be achieved by the organization overall. A corporate objective may be: 'To achieve a consistent 12 per cent Return on Capital Employed (ROCE).' (**Note**: ROCE levels vary across industries and sectors.) The ROCE objective pays no attention to how it is to be achieved, although managers will have written it in the knowledge that certain actions will be necessary and are achievable.

  Corporate objectives will be produced for each area of organizational activity. They will be consistent with each other and set the expectation levels for achievement throughout the organization.

Because corporate objectives are necessarily broad brush they have to be broken down into strategic objectives for each functional department or section within the organization. Thus financial strategies, production strategies, marketing strategies, etc. all have to be devised and cross-checked to ensure that in synergy they will ensure that the corporate objectives are met.

- *Strategies* – strategies are concerned with the best route to take to achieve specific results. Each level of management is concerned with a level of strategy, each fitting into the strategy of the next most senior manager and each cross-referencing to other functions and departments. For example, if the need is to increase profit by 2 per cent there is little point in sales deciding to drive for new accounts whilst credit control is tightening down on evaluative criteria to improve cash flow and production is cutting back on overtime. All three managers are taking sensible action, but it is uncoordinated and the result will be destructive at operational level.

- *Strategic objectives* – are strategies quantified in SMART terms.

- *Tactics* – short-term achievements are needed if strategies are to be achieved. A whole series of tactical (or operational) decisions have to be made, implemented and followed through. There is no actual requirement for a tactical operator to know anything of the corporate plan: his or her focus can be extremely time limited. A sales person, for example, is concerned with one sales call at a time and, within each call, with tactical achievement of objectives relating to issues such as order taking, credit control, delivery scheduling, competitive activity, and so on.

- *Control* – SMART objectives provide for evaluation of achievement against intention. Evaluation, however, is passive. Control provides for the evaluation results to be fed back to managers who need to know so that action(s) can be taken if necessary.

It follows that effective control provides for the fast feedback of information in a form that makes it easy to understand and act upon.

Effective control, and remedial action(s) are vital to on-going success since marketing works in a rapidly changing environment and managers have to be willing to make modifications in the light of experience and new information.

COMMUNICATION HINT

Clarity is essential and yet, unfortunately, the usage of standard terms varies slightly between organizations. To ensure that you communicate what you intend, associate level with description. Thus use terms such as 'Corporate Strategy', 'Marketing Strategy' and 'Sales Tactics.'

Similarly the terms short-, medium- and long-term vary with industry. Clarity can be ensured by stating the time periods when the terms are first used. 'Short-term (two years) strategies are . . .'

'In the medium-term (5 years) we shall . . .' 'Our long-term (25 years) plans incorporate . . .'

Figure 1.3 shows how the mission statement centres all planning activities and how Strategic and Tactical Plans are derived from Strategic and Tactical Objectives.

It is important to note that all planning is interlinked. Note also that the control feedback has been incorporated in this simplified overview of the process.

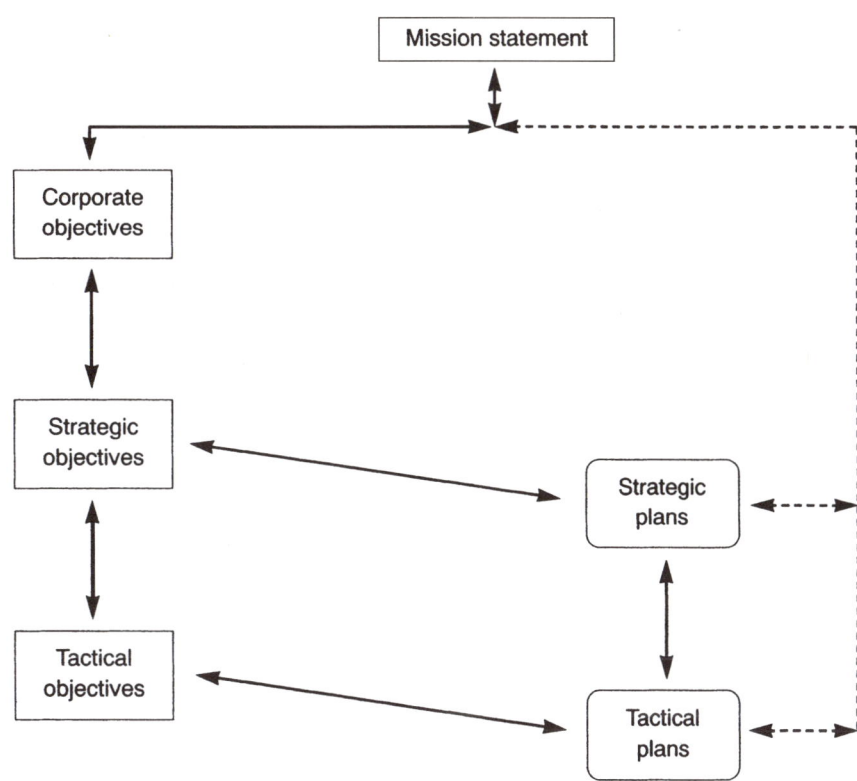

Figure 1.3
Planning relationships

Planning in action
Take 15 minutes to match the form of statement with its description.

A	To become market leader.	1	A corporate objective.
B	To increase the orders-to-calls ratio to 65 per cent within three months.	2	A sales force strategy.
C	To increase repeat sales by using 45 per cent of the promotional budget below the line.	3	A mission statement.
D	To achieve an order of value £10 000 from this account within the next 30 minutes.	4	A corporate aim.
E	To reduce the days of debt by 10 per cent within three months.	5	A sales tactical objective.
F	To increase revenue by opening new accounts.	6	A financial strategic objective.
G	To report automatically any variance that is +/−5 per cent from budget.	7	A marketing strategy.
H	To deliver at a minimum of 95 per cent efficiency within 24 hours of order receipt.	8	A sales force strategic objective.
I	To embrace the highest quality standards throughout our organization so that we become recognized as the foremost quality provider in every market in which we operate.	9	A control.
J	To site posters immediately facing the entrances to all Central London Underground Stations in Period 4.	10	A strategic marketing objective.
K	To achieve a minimum market share of 15 per cent in every market in which we operate within 12 months.	11	A promotional strategy.
L	To win market share through extensive distribution.	12	An advertising tactic.

(**See**: Debriefing at the end of the unit.)

The corporate plan

The corporate plan is, as has been said, the basis for all other planning within an organization. It is not created without considerable discussion, nor is it imposed by senior management. The best corporate plans are produced by joint efforts that involve all functional divisions . . .

Draft plans will be produced and tested for compatibility and to see that they are likely to achieve the intended results. An effective corporate plan is detailed enough to allow cash-flow projections to be made, and for projected P&L accounts and Balance Sheets to be prepared.

Corporate objectives are always formulated to achieve a return on investment, even if this investment is sometimes a mixture of finance and personal effort as in not-for-profit organizations. The planning process will continue until the desired return can be achieved from acceptable resource investment.

Only when an acceptable series of functional plans can be matched to a corporate plan will the corporate plan be finalized.

Only when the corporate plan is finalized can marketing and other functional plans be finalized.

Think of any plan as made of glass, never stone, or rubber. Glass allows the process to be seen but is strong enough to contain activities and channel them in a given direction. Once the pressures become too great, however, a glass conduit will break. Rubber will merely bend, but continue to hold the same material. Stone will resist great stress until environmental forces either wear it away or shatter it.

We can see when a plan in 'glass' needs review

PLANS

Note that while basic frameworks exist for all forms of plan there is no universal given or required format (as there is for financial accounts).

Individual organizations have their preferred planning formats and, if they contain all the needed information and are crisp and clear communication tools, they will achieve what they set out to do: 'to formulate or organize a method by which a thing should be done'.

The planning formats in this workbook should be treated as frameworks, to be adapted to need and circumstances.

There is no excuse for going into the Marketing Operations examination without the ability to reproduce routinely the frameworks for the marketing plans and programmes that will be covered in later units.

The headings for a typical corporate plan follow. Note that there can be overlap between the contents of a corporate and a marketing plan since both draw on the same background information. It is a matter of judgement to determine how much, if any, of the corporate plan should be included in a marketing plan. Remember that the audiences are different.

A corporate plan is a classified internal document. A marketing plan is a more open document which is broken down into sections to provide strategic guidance to operational marketers. Some parts of the plan are, in some circumstances, shared with managers external to the organization, most notably with promotional agency management.

Management accounts are highly confidential and so detailed financial information will only be revealed to very senior management. For operational purposes a notional level of costs can be provided which is sufficient to allow effective management yet does not reveal the true profitability of the organization.

Corporate plan framework

The basic framework has six sections:

1 *Background* – an overview of the situation, including environmental threats and opportunities.
2 *Mission* – clarification of positioning.
3 *Corporate objectives* – quantified in financial terms.
4 *Corporate strategies* – established to provide clarity for each functional division.
5 *Budget* – a detailed coverage of budgetary expectations.
6 *Control* – clear indications of how success is to be evaluated.

Naturally each major heading will sub-divide and a typical corporate plan is a substantial document. As with all such plans much will be background information and it is usual to find a plan opening with an Executive Summary which contains all the key provisions. The corporate plan is strictly strategic; tactical plans are never included.

Fortunately you do not have to deal with corporate plans in the Marketing Operations examination but you must be familiar with the process since it provides the background against which the marketing plan is set. We shall move on to Marketing Planning in Unit 2.

Key planning tools

The key planning tools have to do with Analysis and Decision, with Control issues always of concern.

- *Analysis* – because there is crucial need to discover not only where one is starting from but also what it is feasible to plan to achieve. Plans need to be realistic, never optimistic, or pessimistic.
- *Decision* – because only one route can be taken and there is usually more than one available. Plans must make decisions clear and the expected results must be worked through in advance. Managers are risk takers, they are not gamblers, in other words, they minimize the element of luck through pre-thinking and careful planning.
- *Control* – because without knowing progress against intention it is impossible to make any adjustments in time for them to be effective.

There should always be a concern for control, even in the preliminary planning stages. If the objectives contained in a plan cannot be controlled there can be no effective feedback. On occasion no control mechanism will exist: it is therefore necessary to budget for one to be created.

SWOT

The SWOT technique has become the fundamental tool of analysis. You will find that it can be applied across a range of situations, large or small, business or domestic, commercial or not-for-profit.

SWOT analysis is a technique that provides a framework to assist you in analysing and assessing a particular situation. 'SWOT' is an acronym which stands for:

- Strengths ⎤ Internal
- Weaknesses ⎦ analysis

- Opportunities ⎤ External
- Threats ⎦ analysis

Using these four categories to examine a situation will focus your attention on the critical aspects and:

- Provide a snapshot of the scenario you are considering.
- Summarize the key facts.
- Focus the issues where action is needed.
- Allow you to see relationships.

SWOT analysis soon becomes a routine way in which to come to grips with a situation – but it takes time and practice to become fully proficient. At first you will come up with a basic list in each of the four quadrants. With practice you will acquire the ability to allow one thought to spark off another. Those proficient at brainstorming and/or mind mapping will more quickly be able to produce detailed SWOT analyses. (See the *Effective Management for Marketing* Workbook.)

Always remember that SWOT and similar techniques allow you to visualize a situation. They do not indicate relative importance, nor do they list factors in any order of priority.

The basic framework is of four segments, that share relationships:

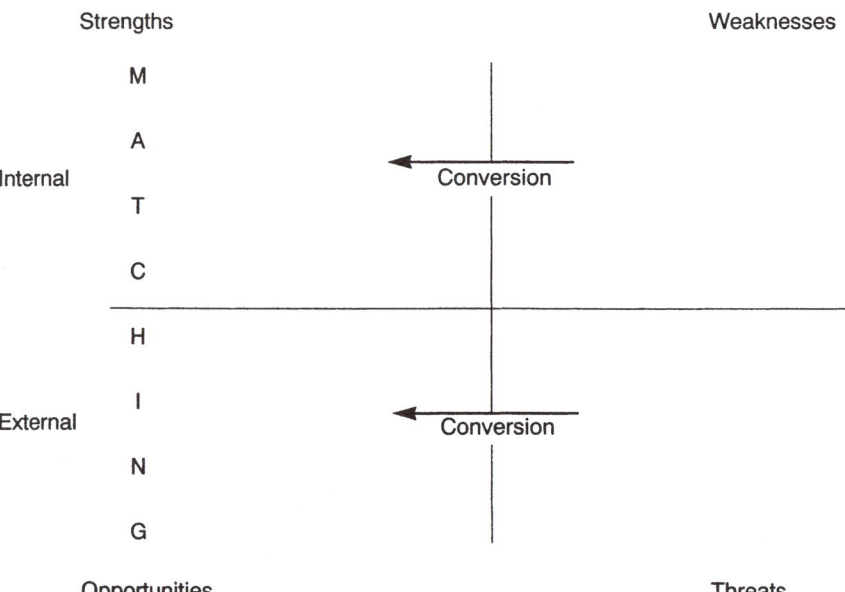

Figure 1.4
SWOT frame

- *Internal factors* – are classified as strengths and weaknesses because they have to do with the organization and its abilities. They are therefore *controllable* – they are factors which management can directly influence.

The main internal areas to consider include:

- *Financial resources:*
  - How well capitalized is the organization?
  - Is it showing a profit?
  - Is the cash flow healthy?
  - How committed are the financial resources, are they tied up or available?
- *Human resources:*
  - Management – how skilled and committed?
  - What is the overall morale and motivation?

- How skilled is the workforce? How adaptable?
- How easy is it to recruit, and retain, staff?
- What are the wage costs?
- What training and development programme is in place?
- *Production:*
  - Technologically capable? Advanced?
  - Capacity – how far utilized?
  - Age and condition of equipment?
  - Quality control?
- *Research & Development:*
  - Actively seeking new opportunities?
  - Quality control?
- *Marketing:*
  - Strategies?
  - The marketing mix(es)?
  - Customer/consumer understanding?
- *Operations:*
  - An active, alert organization?
  - Budgetary control effective?
  - Monitoring of effectiveness and efficiency?

Note that what is a strength at one time or place may be judged a weakness in other circumstances. An individual may be judged a strength by one organization but a weakness by another. The qualities and activities needed to launch a project vary considerably from those needed to maintain and manage in the longer term. Often a strength is matched by a compensating weakness, e.g. where good credit control (Strength) restricts the flow of orders (Weakness).

- *External factors* – are opportunities or threats because any organization has to justify its existence in an environment which is fluid and where the basic laws of nature apply. Any person or organization which cannot justify its existence is very soon forced out by those who are tougher and more useful to the environment of their time.

Macro- and micro-environmental factors

To identify the areas in which opportunities can be found, and where threats originate, one needs to audit both the macro and micro environments.

The macro environment exists outside the organization and is covered by the STEEPLE acronym.

Macro-environmental factors:
The macro-environmental headings are:

S – Social/Cultural
T – Technological/Product Innovation
E – Economic/Market Competition
E – Education/Training/Employment
P – Political
L – Legal
E – Environmental Protection

- *S – Social and Cultural Influences*
  Language, culture, attitudes and behaviour are particular to each society. Studies of societal influences can aid the development of marketing plans, strategies and lead to the markets of tomorrow.

- *T – Technological and Product Innovation*
  Managers have a sad history of clinging on to existing and proven technology whilst competitors are developing new. Then they find they are in a declining sector, whilst the market is moving on. It is essential to be active and open minded in searching for details of advanced research and to search for opportunities rather than seeing change as threatening.

- *E – Economics and Market Competition (E1)*
  Issues such as the business cycle, inflation rates, patterns of energy costs, investment and exchange-rate fluctuations make differences to economic levels of activity in each country.
  Of particular concern are the:
    - Demographic profile.
    - Customer buying habits.
    - Currency value and inflation rate.
    - Business cycle.
    - Unemployment, levels of training and of retraining.
    - Income levels, disposable income, savings.
    - Availability of resources.
    - Resources and competitive forces within an economy.

- *E – Education, Training and Employment (E2)*
  The long-term capability of the economy is dependent on the levels of achievement by school pupils, college and university students, early learners and trainees in industry, as well as on programmes of on-going training and continuing professional development.
  Lower levels of literacy and shorter attention spans may well have an effect on the quality of service and require organizations to re-think their recruitment, selection and training policies.

- *P – Political*
  National and local government have a direct effect on organizations and individuals. Other bodies such as the professional institutes use self-regulation and codes of conduct to influence the way their members behave.

- *L – Legal*
  Control over such issues as competition, unfair trading practices and consumer protection exists as legislation in most countries. A wise marketing manager relies upon an experienced lawyer or legal department to ensure that actions taken comply with regulations.

- *E – Environmental Protection (E3)*
  Growing international concern with global environmental protection, air, water and land usage is leading organizations to establish 'good neighbour' policies but there is considerable difficulty in securing agreement on detailed action from individual governments. The 'green movement' is extremely active on an international basis to encourage governments, organizations and individuals to introduce and enforce strict measures to protect the environment.

STEEPLE was developed from PEST, through SLEPT and SLEPT/C, where the C refers to customers. It is suggested that customers fit better within the micro environment since they are likely to be of more immediate concern to the practising marketer. Where they are located is of less importance than that they not be overlooked. (Worsam and Wright in *Marketing in Management*, 1995.)

Micro-environmental factors

The range of micro-environmental factors will be specific to each organization. The key micro factors will become clear as we progress. For the moment, note that they include such issues as:

- Market size and trends.
- Customer location, size, trend.
- Competitors.
- Suppliers.
- Distributors.
- Market opportunities.

You will find that you quickly become familiar with the key internal and environmental factors, and that the acronyms are extremely helpful in ensuring that you do not miss out a key area.

Activity 1.4

SWOT analysis
Take 10 minutes to produce a SWOT analysis of the following scenario, which we shall also be using as the Unit Activity.

Stanza Limited

Since 1908 Stanza Limited has been a UK wholly owned subsidiary of an Italian international tyre conglomerate. Today the company accounts for 8 per cent of all UK passenger car tyre sales with an annual turnover exceeding £100 m.

Historically Stanza was associated with high-performance tyres retailing at up to £400 each. The company's renowned position in the specialist low profile tyre segment continues but product development now positions Stanza tyres also for the family car market.

Technological development in tyre production has more than doubled the life of the average tyre in terms of mileage. Hence the annual market in the UK remains static at 15 m units. However, within this overall market the low profile, high performance tyre market seemed set to grow fast as a result of the launch of performance saloon cars by motor-car manufacturers. Unfortunately, the effects of the recession have restricted sales but demand definitely exists and there is every reason to believe that, in time, the market will take off.

Within the next five years Stanza believes that the low profile segment will account for over 30 per cent of the UK market from a current position of 19 per cent. The potential demand for Stanza low profile tyres, which offer a relatively high mark-up to the trade, within this segment is substantial.

Consumers, as owners of high performance saloon cars, purchase a vehicle with low-profile tyres fitted as original equipment and the company feels there is low interest in the product. They also believe that replacement of car tyres is often a distress purchase rather than a planned one.

(Adapted from the CIM Practice of Marketing exam, December 1992.)

(**See:** Debriefing at the end of the unit.)

Ansoff matrix

The Ansoff matrix is beautifully simple, yet you will find yourself using it almost as routinely as SWOT. It is an ideal tool to develop creative thinking and to indicate how a marketing situation can be developed over time. It is a very effective tool of communication as well as of analysis.

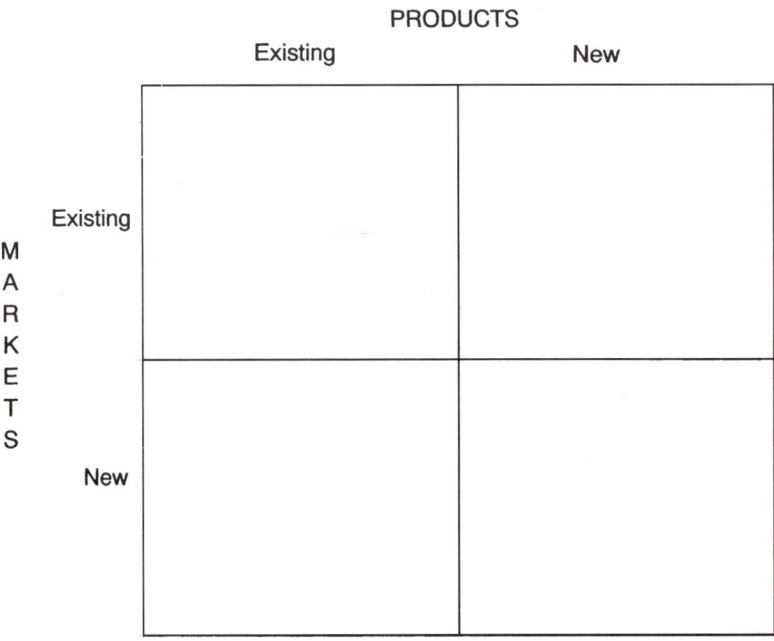

Figure 1.5
Ansoff matrix

No organization can afford to stand still:

> *To stand still on the summit of reflection is difficult, and in the natural course of things, who cannot go forward steps back.*

Gauss Velleius Paterculus (20 BC to AD 30)

Ansoff realized that there are only two areas within which an organization can move. Those of product and of market.

Knowing where one starts from:	current product(s), current market(s).
Enables the alternatives to be explored:	new product(s) into current market(s), current products into new market(s).
The fourth alternative, highest in risk, is:	new product(s) into new market(s).

A fundamental maxim of successful operations is to consolidate and then move from strength in a well-planned move with irresistible force. Striking positively, and with sufficient power, provides a breakthrough which should then be exploited and consolidated before moving on again. This technique, which closely parallels military principles, requires meticulous planning, and determined commitment to succeed.

It is not good to 'fight' on two or more fronts, hence Ansoff's clarity in helping us to identify and then choose from the alternatives that are or can be made available. The four quadrants indicate, broadly, the strategic options of Market Penetration, Product or Market Development and Diversification.

The Ansoff matrix can be used passively simply by noting the alternatives in each quadrant. It is far more powerful, however, as a dynamic tool.

Ansoff used dynamically

When Ansoff is used as a dynamic tool of planning and/or communication it is possible to show intention very clearly. The matrix in Figure 1.6 is taken from analysis done on a CIM mini-case. The company has two products: drain cleaning and restoration. Resources are limited. What are the alternatives open to them?

The matrix clearly shows, even without knowing the case, that the distant large commercial customers can be added to those existing locally. Also that the current local authority business can be extended to a distance. Two existing products into new markets.

There is an opportunity to add diagnostic services to the drain-cleaning operation and thus help clients to prevent blocked drains altogether. An attractive proposition. Finally, because the company is small and cannot hope for national cover in the medium-term (five to eight years) there is the opportunity to franchise. With no experience it would indeed be a high risk activity to convert existing product to a franchise package as a new product and then insert it into a new market!

Note that the Ansoff matrix facilitated the original thinking and then allowed the alternatives to be displayed visually.

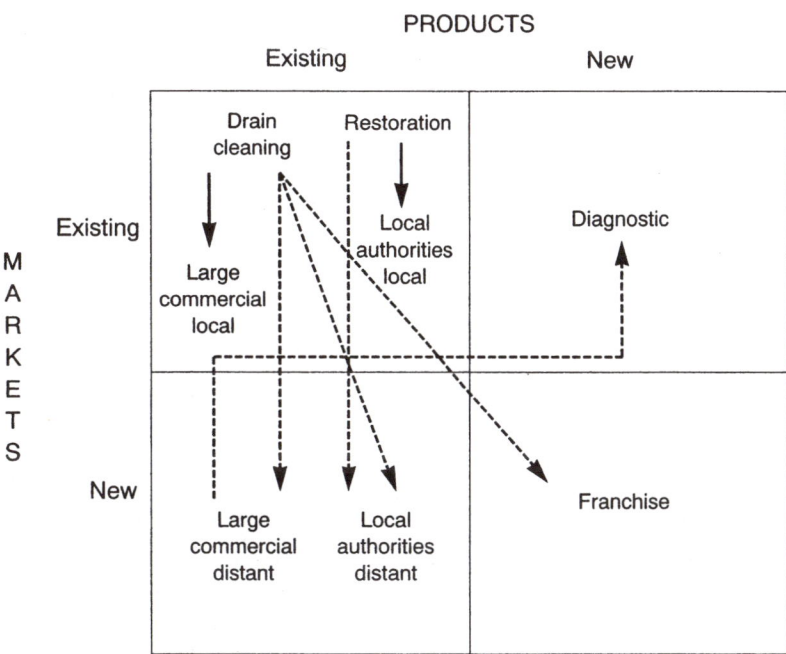

Figure 1.6
Ansoff dynamic

Segmentation, targeting and positioning

Today's most effective marketing relies heavily on the linked concepts of:

- *Segmentation* – where markets are broken into smaller groups, each requiring a separate marketing mix.
- *Targeting* – where individual segments are selected from those available as the focus for specific marketing activity.
- *Positioning* – where a concept, product, brand, etc., is established in the minds of individuals within the targeted segment.

Kotler has established that a segment has to be:

- *Measurable* – so that its size and characteristics can be determined.
- *Substantial* – it must be large enough to be worthwhile to the specific organization at a specific time.

17

- *Accessible* – both promotion and product must be able to reach the individual members of the targeted segment.
- *Actionable* – of a size where an organization can effectively tackle it.

There are many potential segments that currently fail Kotler's criteria. In theory, makers of hair-grooming products can target by sex and by age and by colouring: blondes, brunettes, redheads; those with greying hair; those with white hair. Hair colours, sex and age can be cross-referenced with characteristics such as thick or thin hair; dry or greasy hair, to produce a multi-dimensional matrix of potential targets (for example, female blondes aged 30 to 39 with thick, greasy hair; male blonds aged 30 to 39 with thin and dry hair, etc.).

Unfortunately there is no way accurately to identify and count the number who have each colour of hair, or of how many have each hair type. Nor can individuals with certain types of hair be reached by any media targeted on them or their interests. Thus a manufacturer may feel certain that there is a large market for a specific product but be unable precisely to identify the segment.

The only solution is to offer a range of hair-grooming products and evaluate the numbers who need each by the sales and sales promotional responses. This is an undifferentiated marketing approach, which cannot be as cost effective as a tightly targeted (differentiated) marketing plan.

In industrial and business-to-business marketing it is often possible to segment by individuals. There are fewer buying points, and each is likely to be more significant than a typical single consumer.

Extending Your Knowledge

Get to grips with segmentation, targeting and positioning by developing the habit of analysing the media, products and brands in which you come into contact.

- Who is that newspaper targeted at?
- How do you think they have defined their segment?
- What position do they have?

Note: A good test of positioning is to use a title, brand, etc., as a descriptor. If 'She is a Volvo driver but he is more of an Escort person' means anything then both brands are positioned in your mind. If you can use this form of descriptor to communicate – 'We need to target the BMW drivers' – then the product is positioned in your and your audience's minds.

Consider how well, if at all, products and brands from markets you are not interested in are positioned in your mind. Tightly-targeted products are positioned in the minds of their targets: individuals not in the target segment may not even know they exist. Unless you are a fly fisherman what do you know about the equipment that is in routine use and promoted through targeted media and sold through specialized channels? What do you need to know? What a waste of resources to promote fishing equipment in non-specialist media.

Chanel No. 5 is perhaps the best known perfume in the world. It has deliberately been positioned as a product to be used by women but bought by both sexes. It is positioned as a highly-desirable gift, both to give and to receive. Thus men, who are not users of the product and not experienced in the ways of perfume, know they can safely give Chanel No. 5 as a gift that will be welcomed by a female friend.

Forms of segmentation

The marketer's imagination is the only limit to the number and type of bases which can be used to segment markets. That, and the availability of the technology to open up new segmentation possibilities.

Commonly used bases are:

Consumer	Industrial
Demographics	Demographics
Socio-economic	Geographic
Geographic	Purchasing organization
Personality and lifestyle	User status
Purchase occasion	Usage rate
User status	Benefits sought
Usage rate	
Benefits sought	

Individual organizations commonly devise their own segmentation: Levi Strauss have used five segments, which they refer to as Q1, Q2, etc. Consultancies come up with novel approaches to segmentation. One segments by the attitudinal and behavioural information on a wide range of products from BMRB's Target Group Index to produce an overview of the alcoholic drinks market. The result is fourteen strongly differentiated segments. Another works from first names on the basis that names indicate both age and social background. The key to successful segmentation, however, is not the base(s) used. It is the accuracy, clarity and reliability with which each segment is defined.

The traditional socio-economic system was first used by the research company RSL after the Second World War. The major failure with this system was the classifying, all in a household, by the data applicable to the 'head of the household' who was normally reckoned to be the husband in the family. Thus a professional wife and graduate children would all be classified C2 if the father happened to be a blue-collar worker. This has to some extent been corrected with head of the household replaced by 'chief income earner' who is defined as 'the person with the largest income, whether from employment, pension, state benefits, investments or any other source'. Unfortunately, this places the blue-collar father in the same segment as his brain-surgeon wife!

This imprecision is joined by a second factor to account for the decline in the use of socio-economic segmentation. Segment size is far too unwieldy for differentiated marketing. In 1990 the five segments accounted for:

Segment	Percentage of UK population
A/B	16
C1	27
C2	26
D	19
E	12

The only valid use today is as a general descriptor along the lines of 'We have more of an AB than a D product.'

Personality, motives and lifestyle segmentation

Three commonly used bases for segmentation take consumer behavioural characteristics into account rather than mechanical factors such as age, sex and location. These behavioural characteristics can, of course, be used in combination with other factors to sub-divide (segment) a market.

Personality characteristics are useful when a product is similar to many competitive products and consumer needs are not significantly affected by other segmentation variables. Although this method has the promise of working most effectively it has, unfortunately, been shown that there is a comparatively weak correlation between personality, lifestyle and product choice. Personality is, of course, extremely difficult to evaluate but work is progressing to develop more accurate and useful methods of determining personality characteristics in a way that will make them useful to the marketing planner.

Motive based segmentation uses the rationale behind the purchase as the segmentation variable. The consumer's reasons for making a purchase must

ACORN Categories	% of population	ACORN groups	% of population	ACORN types	% of population
A **THRIVING**	19.8	1 Wealthy Achievers, Suburban Areas	15.1	1.1 Wealthy Suburbs, Large Detached Houses 1.2 Villages with Wealthy Commuters 1.3 Mature Affluent Home Owning Areas 1.4 Affluent Suburbs, Older Families 1.5 Mature, Well-Off Suburbs	2.6 3.2 2.7 3.7 3.0
		2 Affluent Greys, Rural Communities	2.3	2.6 Agricultural Villages, Home Based Workers 2.7 Holiday Retreats, Older People, Home Based Workers	1.6 0.9
		3 Prosperous Pensioners, Retirement Areas	2.3	3.8 Home Owning Areas, Well-Off Older Residents 3.9 Private Flats, Elderly People	2.1 0.3
B **EXPANDING**	11.6	4 Affluent Executives, Family Areas	3.7	4.10 Affluent Working Families with Mortgages 4.11 Affluent Working Couples with Mortgages, New Homes 4.12 Transient Workforces, Living at their Place of Work	2.6 3.0 2.2
		5 Well-Off Workers, Family Areas	7.8	5.13 Home Owning Family Areas 5.14 Home Owning Family Areas, Older Children 5.15 Families with Mortgages, Younger Children	1.5 2.6 1.9
C **RISING**	7.5	6 Affluent Urbanites, Town & City Areas	2.2	6.16 Well-Off Town & City Areas 6.17 Flats & Mortgages, Singles & Young Working Couples 6.18 Furnished Flats & Bedsits, Younger Single People	1.1 0.8 0.4
		7 Prosperous Professionals, Metropolitan Areas	2.1	7.19 Apartments, Young Professional Singles & Couples 7.20 Gentrified Multi-Ethnic Areas	1.1 1.0
		8 Better-Off Executives, Inner City Areas	3.2	8.21 Prosperous Enclaves, Highly Qualified Executives 8.22 Academic Centres, Students & Young Professionals 8.23 Affluent City Centre Areas, Tenements & Flats 8.24 Partially Gentrified Multi-Ethnic Areas 8.25 Converted Flats & Bedsits, Single People	0.7 0.5 0.4 0.7 0.9
D **SETTLING**	24.1	9 Comfortable Middle Agers, Mature Home Owning Areas	13.4	9.26 Mature Established Home Owning Areas 9.27 Rural Areas, Mixed Occupations 9.28 Established Home Owning Areas 9.29 Home Owning Areas, Council Tenants, Retired People	3.3 3.4 4.0 2.6
		10 Skilled Workers, Home Owning Areas	10.7	10.30 Established Home Owning Areas, Skilled Workers 10.31 Home Owners in Older Properties, Younger Workers 10.32 Home Owning Areas with Skilled Workers	4.5 3.1 3.1
E **ASPIRING**	13.7	11 New Home Owners, Mature Communities	9.8	11.33 Council Areas, Some New Home Owners 11.34 Mature Home Owning Areas, Skilled Workers 11.35 Low Rise Estates, Older Workers, New Home Owners	3.8 3.1 2.9
		12 White Collar Workers, Better-Off Multi-Ethnic Areas	4.0	12.36 Home Owning Multi-Ethnic Areas, Young Families 12.37 Multi-Occupied Town Centres, Mixed Occupations 12.38 Multi-Ethnic Areas, White Collar Workers	1.1 1.8 1.1
F **STRIVING**	22.8	13 Older People, Less Prosperous Areas	3.6	13.39 Home Owners, Small Council Flats, Single Pensioners 13.40 Council Areas, Older People, Health Problems	1.9 1.7
		14 Council Estate Residents, Better-Off Homes	11.6	14.41 Better-Off Council Areas, New Home Owners 14.42 Council Areas, Young Families, Some New Home Owners 14.43 Council Areas, Young Families, Many Lone Parents 14.44 Multi-Occupied Terraces, Multi-Ethnic Areas 14.45 Low Rise Council Housing, Less Well-Off Families 14.46 Council Areas, Residents with Health Problems	2.4 3.0 1.6 0.8 1.8 2.0
		15 Council Estate Residents, High Unemployment	2.7	15.47 Estates with High Unemployment 15.48 Council Flats, Elderly People, Health Problems 15.49 Council Flats, Very High Unemployment, Singles	1.3 1.1 1.2
		16 Council Estate Residents, Greatest Hardship	2.8	16.50 Council Areas, High Unemployment, Lone Parents 16.51 Council Flats, Greatest Hardship, Many Lone Parents	1.9 0.9
		17 People in Multi-Ethnic, Low-Income Areas	2.1	17.52 Multi-Ethnic, Large Families, Overcrowding 17.53 Multi-Ethnic, Severe Unemployment, Lone Parents 17.54 Multi-Ethnic, High Unemployment, Overcrowding	0.6 1.0 0.5

Figure 1.7 AreaData ACORN profile

be determined and such factors as product durability, economy, convenience and status are typical motivations. Remember that motivation is an internal force which is unique to each individual. Not all react in the same way to given situations. Thus motive based segmentation attempts to group consumers by the way in which they react – to differentiate those motivated to buy coffee, say, for economy from those buying for status. Some households have everyday and best coffees and ground coffee has a higher status than even the best instants. Of key interest is the determination of associated purchases. Does the economy buyer of groceries also use economy as a motive in other types of purchase situations?

Lifestyle segmentation groups individuals according to how they choose to use their time, the values they place upon belongings and their beliefs about themselves. Their activities, interests and opinions are cross-referenced to achieve unique segmentation of value to individual marketers.

Personalized systems

Systems of segmentation must be personalized within an organization, usually on the basis of a detailed segmentation framework selected from a research consultancy. Geodemographic systems came available in the 1970s and outside of industrial and similar marketing are becoming virtually mandatory. As database marketing spreads so the geodemographic frames will increase in importance.

Geodemographic segmentation

ACORN (A Classification of Residential Neighbourhoods) was the first geodemographic segmentation classification. It came on to the UK market in 1978 and was based on the 1971 Census of Population. It is re-classified following each full Census. The most recent is, of course, based on 1991 data, updated in 1996.

ACORN takes as its basic premise that like people live close together. Its overall classification is generally linked through a PC system so that the other databases can be cross-referenced. The result is a combined geographic and demographic (geodemographic) segmentation which has proved over time to be extremely reliable and effective.

CACI, who supply ACORN, say that: 'ACORN classifies the people in your trading areas and on your customer databases into distinct types so you can understand more about their likely characteristics.'

The ACORN geodemographic classification is a targeting tool which enables you to sell to your customers more accurately, plan for them more effectively and find other consumers like them more quickly.

CACI uses the Census to build ACORN because it is the only data source which provides a complete picture across the country. For any local area you need to look at, the Census gives a comprehensive overview of who is living there. Because it is so complete, Census data does not suffer from any bias to a particular product, region or social group. It gives equally good coverage throughout the country. This means that it will give the most accurate definition of your database.

The ACORN classifications currently identify 54 types which are classified into 17 groups and 6 categories. You will see that no type accounts for more than 4.5 per cent of the population, and that many target down to 1 per cent or less.

If you are scanning for new sites for a family leisure venue, you may only want a general overview of customer characteristics, where can you find areas which are predominantly Category B: Expanding Family Areas.

If you are a discount DIY retailer planning a highly targeted mailing, you may want to isolate a very specific selection of people such as Type 41 Better-Off Council Areas, New Home Owners.

ACORN classifications can be described by their category, group and type, e.g. Category F, Group 14, Type 41. For this categorization ACORN have established the profile shown in Figure 1.8.

Type 41 Better-Off Council Areas, New Home Owners

These family, blue collar neighbourhoods, are located all over Britain, although they tend to be found more in Scotland. Also, they tend to be found outside the major conurbations. This ACORN Type includes most of the New Towns of the 1960s – Cumbernauld, Stevenage, Redditch, Harlow, East Kilbride. These are relatively affluent areas where spending takes precedence over saving.

DEMOGRAPHICS
ACORN Type 41 has a youthful age profile, with above average proportions of children and young people. Almost 50% of households have dependent children and the proportion having 3 or more children is nearly double the national average. The proportion of households with 6 or more members is also much higher than average. There are 91% more than average single parent households.

SOCIO-ECONOMIC PROFILE
The unemployment rate is 15% above average. The proportion of women in couples who work is high. The proportion of adults working in the manufacturing sector is 21% above average. The proportions of skilled manual, semi-skilled and unskilled workers are all higher than average.

HOUSING
61% of homes are terraced houses, a level over twice the national average. Of the remainder, half are semi-detached homes. The tenure profile is split roughly equally between buying, accounting for 43% of homes, and council renting which accounts for

40% of homes. Many council tenants bought their homes during the 1980s.

FOOD AND DRINK
Over 75% of grocery shopping trips are made by car. The proportion of people doing grocery shopping on a daily basis is 90% above average. Although freezer ownership is just average usage of freezer centres and consumption of some frozen foods, such as fish fingers, are high. These people are very heavy consumers of a wide range of food products, partly because household sizes are large. Products which are particularly popular are fresh and dried pasta, fresh meat, crisps and snacks, colas and cigarettes. Alcoholic drinks which are more popular here than average are draught lager and vodka.

DURABLES
Car ownership levels are modest – the proportion of households owning one car is 13% above average, but rates of multiple car ownership are much lower than average. Cars tend to be much older and there are very few expensive cars. A wide range of durables are purchased much more frequently than average – computer games and games systems, home computers, keep fit equipment, video cameras, electric cookers and fridge freezers. There are high levels of home improvement activity, with 42% more homes than average installing new central heating and 78% more than average fitting new secondary glazing.

FINANCIAL
Incomes in these neighbourhoods peak in the range of £15–30,000 per annum. Savings account ownership and opening levels are low. Although

ownership of National Savings Certificates is slightly above average, share ownership is low as is plastic card ownership. Mortgages from lenders other than building societies are 50% more common than nationality.

MEDIA
The penetration of cable television is 86% above average, while ownership of satellite television is slightly above average. The *Daily Record* is read by 3.3 times more people than average, while readership of *The Sun* is 70% above average. Scottish Sunday papers are very popular, but the most widely read Sunday paper is *The News of the World*. Both ITV viewing and commercial radio listening are heavy.

LEISURE
Slightly fewer than average people go on holiday. On the whole, they do not tend to patronise pubs and restaurants frequently, though they are more likely than average to visit licensed clubs regularly. Participation rates in sporting activities are generally fairly low. Activities which are more popular than average are darts, snooker and visiting zoos.

ATTITUDES
People in ACORN Type 41 are less concerned than average about keeping fit and healthy with diet and exercise. They are much less likely than average to be vegetarian. They tend to be careful with money when shopping and to look for the lowest possible prices, although they are often tempted to buy new brands. They are more likely than average to respond to direct mail, but no more or less likely than average to respond to other forms of advertising.

Figure 1.8

A major strength of ACORN is its ability to profile an organization's customer database. Thus a unique segmentation, tailored to specific need is easily achieved. Profiling with the combined databases provides new dimensions to the information held on file and enables far greater proactivity in analysing and understanding who is responding to promotion and who is buying.

Campaign costs can be optimized because applying the appropriate ACORN profiles to new lists will generate whatever you need:

- A complete mailing list of your selected targets.
- Door-to-door campaigns that are targeted only on households that you want to reach.
- Response evaluation that leads to tighter targeting.

Profiling

The ability to identify and reach individuals within a defined segment is crucial to marketing success. The tighter a promotional campaign can be structured, the less waste and the more refined the database becomes.

Profiling is a major tool of marketing today and it is essential that marketing students develop the ability routinely to think of target customers in profiling terms, as a necessary part of the segmentation, targeting and positioning processes.

MOSAIC is a rival geodemographic system which is marketed by CCN Marketing. It is based upon the same form of data input to powerful computer modelling.

Costs

Geodemographic systems are cost-effective wherever a differentiated approach is taken to the consumer market. They have less to offer in undifferentiated marketing but marketers are rapidly inventing ways to transform all marketing to differentiated. Industrial and business-to-business marketing normally can be tightly targeted on an individual basis but the potential in not-for-profit marketing is considerable providing there is sufficient budget to fund the beginning of the necessary cycle of profile, control and tighten profile.

The costs of a project involving ACORN analysis are very variable and reflect the wide variety of applications for which ACORN profiling may be used. A simple report giving an ACORN profile of an area on paper or disk costs as little as £150; Insite, CACI's PC-based market analysis system, which provides a facility for in-house data analysis including ACORN profiles, will cost from £20 000 upwards.

MOSAIC costings depend on the number of customer records and the type of service required. Between £5 000 and £10 000 per annum is needed for data directories used to append MOSAIC codes to client databases. A complete PC system can cost from £20 000 to £50 000. Reports and maps through a Bureau start at about £150 for a basic Area Analysis report and £300 for Census reports. Area maps start at about £120 for an A4 map.

Most MOSAIC-based products are sold either as PC systems or on a bureau basis. One product on-line is the coding of customer records by MOSAIC. The main area of use is in credit decisions as part of a credit application scorecard. The cost is approximately five pence per record.

ACORN or MOSAIC?

Both systems offer essentially the same service. Both are operated by highly reputable firms. The only way to choose between them is to specify a need and then call upon each to analyse that need and provide recommendations and a quotation for achievement of your requirements. Enter into a contract with care because, once committed to a system, it is unlikely to be cost effective to leave it and switch to the other.

Positioning and targeting

Establishing a concept, product, brand, etc., in the minds of individuals within a target market requires dedicated and long-term marketing planning. The promotional tools are of major importance, of course, but everything about the product offering must be consistent with the selected position. Thus a new product must have its positioning characteristics designed into it, the channels of distribution and pricing must be consonant with the overall image and the promotional plan must feature the characteristics to which the target consumers will respond.

Re-positioning an existing product involves a planned move from one position to another. This may be executed as a series of steps over a long period of time, with each step sequential and designed to be as unobtrusive as possible. Thus the image of HP brown sauce was changed from an old fashioned to a sharp modern product in four stages over nearly three years. The reputation that HP had earned over many years was retained, as were their existing older customers, but the new youthful and active positioning was one to which new, younger consumers also responded.

Re-launching requires the effective withdrawal of a product so that it can be positioned where it is now required. To some extent this is akin to a new product launch except that there will be a residue of consumer reaction to the product which will be related to its old position. In the case of Lucozade this was judged beneficial because it had strong positive image as a tonic drink for invalids recovering from illness and operations. Bedside cupboards in hospitals were incomplete without their bottle of Lucozade. The decision was taken to reposition the product as an energy drink for the youth market, and it was successfully relaunched. It was not re-positioned in stages because it needed to be introduced to a new segment as a new product. Obviously it is still available for its original purpose but is no longer targeted upon that segment.

Segmentation, positioning and targeting are always considered together since any change in one factor inevitably affects the others. We shall develop practical skills in this area as we progress through this workbook.

Exam Hint

Time planning

Three hours may not seem very long . . . but that is the time you will have in each examination to convince the examiner that you merit a pass.

Management of the time resource requires just as much care as the management of any other resource, especially in an examination where you are chasing deadlines just as you chase copy dates. You will need to complete answers to four questions within the three hours if you are to impress. There is no excuse for not completing the last question, nor for submitting your answer as notes.

Practice is the only answer. Take notice of the advice given, especially in Unit 13, and start to develop your question answering skills well ahead of the exam. You need to have them developed to a routine so that you can concentrate intellectually. That way both the *content* and *context* of your answers will be up to standard.

Unit Activity

Allow 45 minutes.

Revisit your work on Stanza Limited but this time adopt a role as the marketing manager responsible for the low-profile tyres. You had confidently expected that your product would be eating into the UK tyre market but your sales are conditioned by the sales of cars needing your tyres and by the mileage covered before replacement is needed. Cars sales have slowed and research shows that usage is being restricted by drivers due to the high running costs of performance cars.

You need to review the situation, and make recommendations for action.

1   Gain a perspective on the market by carrying out a SWOT analysis from the viewpoint of a major competitive tyre manufacturer.
2   In note form set out the actions and key points you want to bring to your manager's attention.

(**See:** Debriefing at the end of the unit.)

Summary

In this unit we have seen that:

- Advanced Certificate subjects are not exclusively knowledge-based study programmes.
- Consumer focus is the driving force for a marketing-oriented organization.
- Interest comes from features, desire comes from benefits.
- The 7Cs are a better base than the 7Ps to guide today's marketers.
- Marketing is a significant part of the strategic planning process in addition to its role as a functional activity alongside finance, production, procurement, etc.
- Marketing plans fit within the corporate plan.
- Budgetary control allows every sub-unit to know what it has to achieve, and by when, and ensures that achievement against budget is reported in time for action.
- Communicate clearly by associating level with description, i.e. Marketing Strategy.
- Unleash your creativity with the dynamic use of models.
- The corporate plan is produced as a joint effort. It goes through a process of drafting at the same time as functional plans are drafted.
- Basic frameworks exist for business plans but there is no single required format.
- Planning tools have to do with analysis and decision, with control always in mind.
- Time planning is crucial to success.
- Build your studies into your everyday life.
- A well prepared candidate has nothing to fear from a CIM examination.

Debriefing

Activity 1.1

Assuming that you wanted a new hi-fi unit your purchase process may have gone something like this:

1. Assumed need – possibly from Communication in the form of advertising on the radio, TV or in the press. Perhaps through a recommendation from a friend (word-of-mouth).
2. Choice of outlet(s) from Communication – the store's promotion. Also from the ease with which you could access them (Convenience). The store(s) that were located close to you had a better chance of selection.
3. Confirmation of your choice began as you went into the store. Was the ambience right for the product you wanted to buy? Were the staff Considerate? Was the buying process Co-ordinated and straightforward? Was the product range well displayed, clean, clearly labelled?
4. Were prices shown, and was the Cost acceptable? Was there a Special Offer? Could you buy on terms and so spread the cost? Was this suggested? Explained?
5. Was the proposed purchase value for your money? Would it function as claimed? How good was the store's after-market service?
6. Overall, how satisfied were you, short- and long-term? What have you learned about the brand – of the hi-fi and of the store? Will you buy the brand again? Will you use the store again? If you were the manufacturer of the hi-fi you would need your marketing people to meet the C needs of the target customers. You would want them to: build in value, select a channel of distribution, train store staff, provide special offers and/or finance deals, position the offer and select appropriate communication channels.

Note: Although the 7Ps/7Cs are 'extended for services' from the 4Ps/Cs, it should be apparent that all seven apply to some extent in all transactions.

Activity 1.2

Profit to a commercial organization normally means a financial surplus of revenue over costs. But, as the 7Cs show, we have to be concerned with issues such as value which are only partially financial in nature. Even commercial organizations are concerned with non-financial issues, and need to make a 'profit' from non-financial exchange.

Organization	Markets	'Profit'
1 A hospital	Patients	Personnel's satisfaction from caring. Reputation for efficiency, effectiveness and consideration and concern.
	Relatives	Personnel's satisfaction from caring.
	'Profit' from both	Recommendation and word-of-mouth promotion leading to goodwill from the community leading to tangible assistance, for example donations and/or petitions to keep open.
	Local doctors	Flow of patients. Support in Ethical and Funding Committees.
	Government	Continued or extended funding.
2 A charity	Clients	Personnel's satisfaction from caring. Reputation for efficiency, effectiveness and consideration and concern.
	Donors	Funding, gifts in kind and legacies.
3 A tax office	Tax payers	Effective collection of taxes due. Personnel's satisfaction from correct assessments and from ensuring fairness.
	Head Office	Continued or extended funding.

Note: It is individual personnel who appreciate the benefits, not the organizations which are comprised of individuals. Also note that each organization has several markets with which to deal. The marketing mix should vary in accordance with the requirements of the individuals who comprise each target audience.

Activity 1.3

You would probably have found it much harder to complete this activity if the bare terms strategy, tactic, etc., had been used. Adding a descriptor considerably enhances the effectiveness of the communication.

The correct matches are:

A	4	B	8	C	11
D	5	E	6	F	2
G	9	H	10	I	3
J	12	K	1	L	7

Activity 1.4

You will have analysed the mini-case from your perspective so evaluate your results for style and completeness rather than attempting to exactly duplicate the analysis that follows (see Figure 1.9).

Most of the SWOT factors come directly from the mini-case, others have been deduced from general market awareness. The company is long

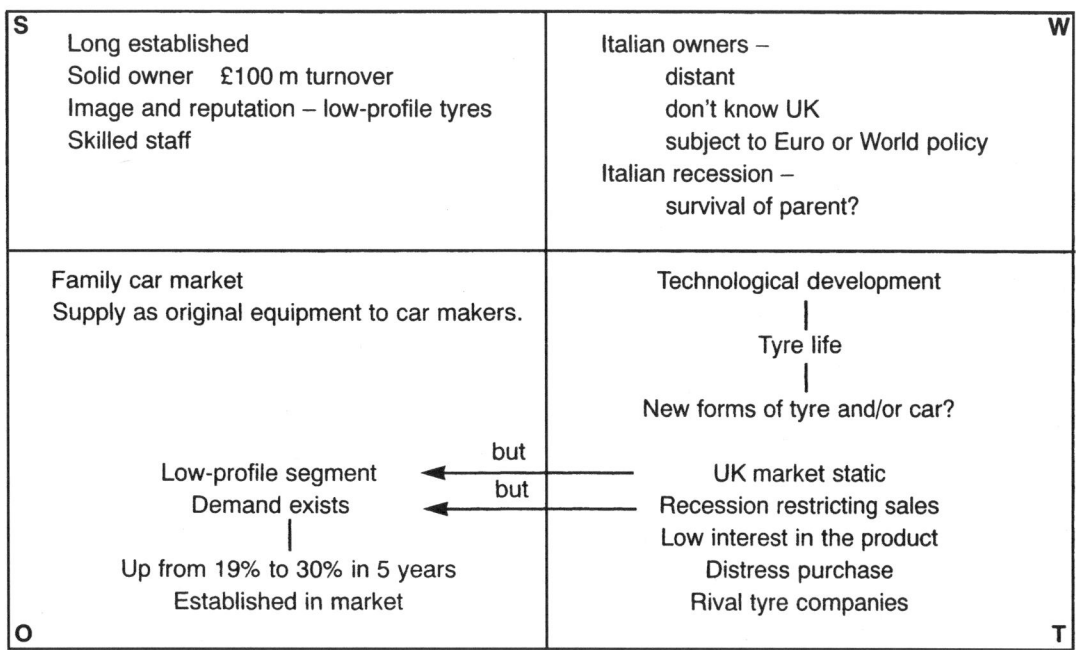

S
Long established
Solid owner   £100 m turnover
Image and reputation – low-profile tyres
Skilled staff
	W
	Italian owners –
	  distant
	  don't know UK
	  subject to Euro or World policy
	Italian recession –
	  survival of parent?

Family car market
Supply as original equipment to car makers.
 	
                                    but
Low-profile segment   ←
                                    but
Demand exists   ←
                    |
Up from 19% to 30% in 5 years
Established in market
O
	Technological development
	|
	Tyre life
	|
	New forms of tyre and/or car?
	
	UK market static
	Recession restricting sales
	Low interest in the product
	Distress purchase
	Rival tyre companies
	T

Figure 1.9 SWOT – Stanza Limited

established (1908) which means that it has expertise and contacts in the UK. Channels of distribution will be well known and have the necessary agents in place.

Skilled staff can be assumed, given we are not told anything to the contrary, but with a market slowdown the staff may be feeling insecure. This may be heightened by the parent company's Italian base. Italy has a weak economy in the EU and is politically unstable. What actions might be forced on the company by the Italian situation? Will they even survive?

In any case they are distant. We don't know how much autonomy Stanza UK has. Perhaps it has to follow Euro or even world policies set in Italy?

Opportunities exist, but they are 'jam tomorrow'. The need is for survival until the market picks up but that is possibly five years away. In the meantime will competitors emerge? Will technology change in the tyre market and/or the car market? Will today's product still be dominant in five years time?

There is low interest in the product: no brand identity and no brand loyalty. We don't know, but can assume, that Stanza are not supplying the original tyres. This could be a major opportunity but only for new models since those coming through would have been contracted for their tyres in their design stages.

We don't know anything about the new family car tyres but the market must be an opportunity, although a tough one since it will already be saturated.

Unit activity

Always personalize where you can. We have taken Dunlop as our major competitor (see Figure 1.10). There is little information for the strengths box apart from general belief in Dunlop's positioning and none at all for the weaknesses quadrant. But the issues are in the uncontrollable quadrants.

Dunlop probably have contracts with car manufacturers to supply original tyres. (Somebody does!) They could build on this to tie down new models coming through and Stanza ought to compete hard to get their share of the new business. They could also work to turn the distress purchase into a branded purchase by well-planned and targeted

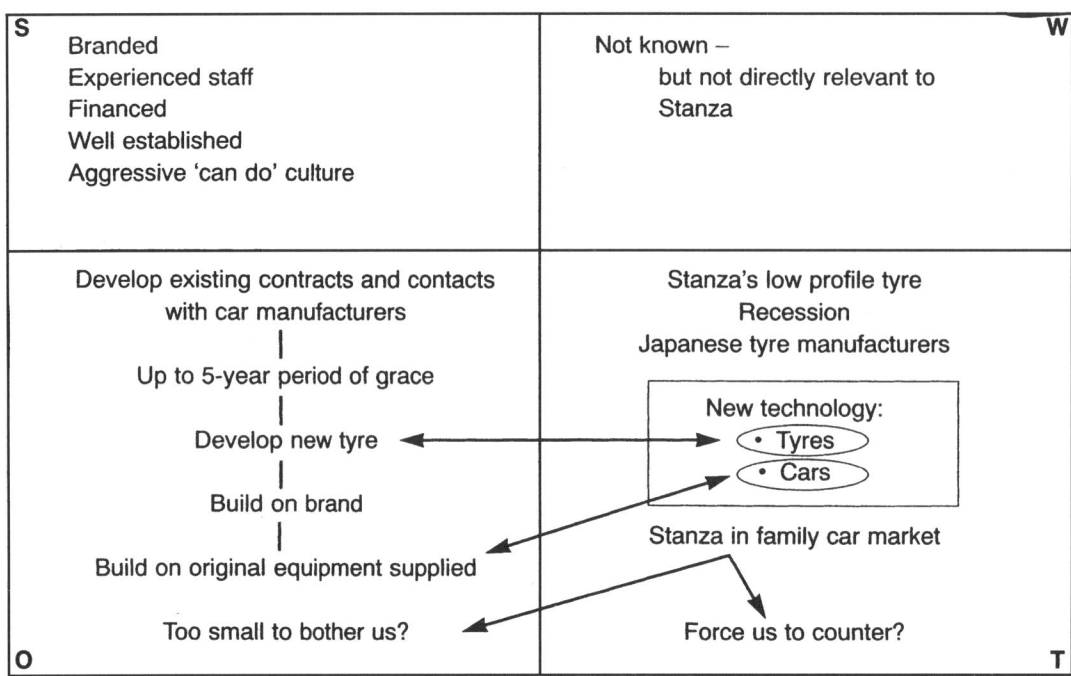

Figure 1.10 SWOT matrix, complete

promotion which could well include direct marketing if names and addresses of new car owners can be secured. Stanza can't do that as they haven't the car manufacturer contacts.

The recession is really bad news for the marketing team. Instead of having an immediately open market they have to wait for it to pick up. Thus the competitors have time – a period of grace – to analyse Stanza's products and marketing policies and to catch up and, possibly, move ahead!

The new family tyre market could present problems to Dunlop if Stanza are aggressive, but may well be hard work for little gain if there is not sufficient support to break into this already saturated market. Is it good policy for Stanza actively to market the family car tyres at this time? It would mean diverting resources from their leading product and the opportunities seem to be limited at best.

Could Stanza be better off concentrating on securing car manufacturer contracts, developing a brand awareness for their low profile tyres and devising a way to segment the users of the cars that need their leading product? Probably.

Note: This is a mini-case with limited information but you should by now appreciate how you can blend common sense, general market and marketing knowledge, and come up with a scenario that follows key marketing principles – even though you do not have all the information you would like.

The notes for your manager would, of course, be constructed around the issues, and include your clear recommendations for action. 'Notes' indicates that they are intended as an *aide-memoire* for a conversation you will be having. There is no requirement for a written communication.

Unit 2 · Marketing planning – implementation and control

Objectives

In this unit you will:

- ❏ Examine the planning process.
- ❏ Develop an understanding of the need for strategies.
- ❏ Identify the requirement for specific objectives.
- ❏ Discover the need for effective and efficient management information.
- ❏ Consider how a marketing function may be organized.

By the end of the unit you will:

- ❏ Have begun to practise the use of key planning tools.
- ❏ Be aware of the importance of an effective management information system.
- ❏ Be able to write SMART objectives.
- ❏ Understand the operation of budgeting and budgetary control.
- ❏ Be able to write an outline marketing plan.

Study Guide

Several short bursts of study time are much more valuable than long unbroken stretches. Regular breaks are an essential part of effective learning because they allow your brain to relax and absorb what it has just been given. Try to take at least one active break in every session. Get out for a short walk even if it is just down the garden. This exercise refreshes you physically and is in total contrast to the mental activity to which you are going to return. Plan your study sessions:

- Identify clearly what you are going to do in each.
- Set yourself clear objectives.
- Allocate time to each activity.
- Vary the type of study method that you use.
- Plan at least three breaks in a two-hour session.
- Do not go near an active TV in any break!

This workbook is designed to encourage active learning, so do work through the activities. They are intended both to reinforce your learning and to extend your abilities. Do not skip activities, do not simply read and re-read textbooks and other study material. You have to take the content out of the material and establish it in your head. It is the process of *doing* that reinforces learning. Make your own notes, undertake the activities, practise question answering and, above all, put what you are learning to use in your 'real life'.

Expect to take about two hours to work through this unit and up to four hours to complete the specified activities.

You are studying to improve your personal abilities and to enhance your career potential. It follows that you have to be able to impress both your employers and your examiners. Employers see the results of your work over a period of time and have your CV to show what you have achieved throughout your career. Examiners see you through a three-hour window and can judge only from written submissions. Obviously the approach you must take to examiners differs from that you can take with employers.

The key differences can be summarized as:

Factor	'Real life'	Examination
Information	Considerable	Restricted
Research	Possible	Not possible
Clarification	Possible	Not possible
Assistance	Possible	Not possible
Drafting	Several drafts possible	One outline only
Presentation	Word processed	Handwritten
Background	Required	Not practical
Completeness	Fully complete	Outline or section only

Examiners are, of course, aware of these major differences but experienced in making fair judgements about a candidate's abilities. They do not attempt to judge a candidate in the round, as can an employer. Instead they present a candidate with a situation as a scenario or mini-case and ask that a real life approach be taken to that scenario.

There are three devices adopted by examiners to confirm ability. One is to ask how a task would be performed, i.e. a 'process' question. Another is to ask for an 'outline' answer, i.e. the major headings and the key points within each *in context to the scenario*. The third option is to ask for a detailed response in one part of a report.

These questioning techniques, in combination, check how able a candidate is in finding and keeping to a focus; if he or she knows what to do in a given situation; if he or she can identify the key points and can broadly suggest how to tackle them; if a candidate has detailed marketing ability.

Student or candidate?
Take 10 minutes to consider the major differences between a student and a candidate. Then consider what the differences mean to you as you prepare for your examination.

(**See:** Debriefing at the end of the unit.)

The planning process

Whatever the organization, whatever the industry or the sector, however large or small the organization, the planning process remains constant. It will be adapted by organizations and terminology may change but the process itself cannot change if planning is to be effective. (Less effective planning muddles through the process, taking the steps out of order. Ineffective planning has no structure and usually results in disaster. See Figure 2.1 on page 31.

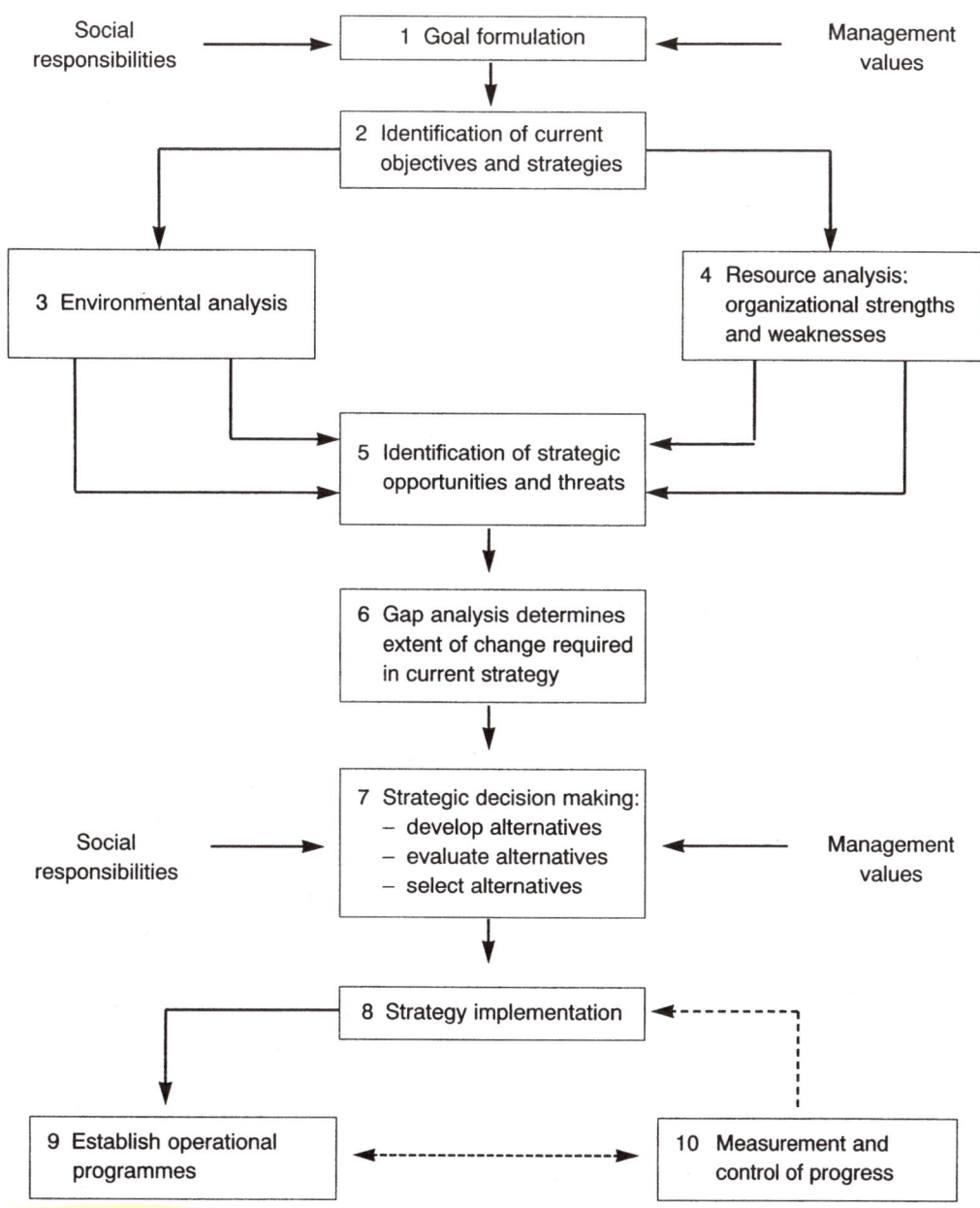

Figure 2.1 The formal planning process. (Source: adapted from *Management*, Stoner and Freeman, Prentice-Hall International, 1992.)

The logical flow of the planning process is easy to understand if we translate each of the stages into a simple question or statement:

1. What do we want?
2. What are we doing at the moment to get what we want?
3. What is 'out there' that we ought to know about?
4. What are we able to do?
5. What could we do?
6. Will continuing as we are take us to where we want to be?
7. This is what we shall do.
8. Let's get it done.
9. Prepare the detailed programmes to ensure nothing is missed.
10. Check frequently to ensure we are doing it right. Evaluate what has been learned so we can do it better next time.

This planning process applies to the corporate planning of a multinational, the marketing planning of an SBU, the strategic planning of a marketing manager, the tactical planning of a sales manager, and the planning of a holiday by an individual. The difference is of degree, not of process.

For example, an individual going on holiday has to deal with all ten steps:

1 Do I want relaxation or activity, sea and sand, cities, mountains?
2 What do I usually do? What am I happiest doing?
3 What holiday destinations are available at the time I want them? Who offers packages, transportation, etc.? What problems might there be in terms of personal safety, health, visa restrictions, etc.?
4 How much can I afford? Do I have the skills/abilities/determination to benefit from certain types of holiday?
5 What issues directly impact on me to condition my choice? Which maximize the return on my investment. What actual and potential threats can I identify?
6 Shall I be contented to do again what I have done before? Can I afford, financially and psychologically, to make a change?
7 Now I can create a short list and choose my preferred holiday.
8 Make the booking.
9 Plan the details of the trip, go and return.
10 Continuous checking on progress in time for amendment if possible.

Final evaluation: what have I learned about the whole process, about the holiday provider, the destination, the focus of the holiday. How will I improve my future planning?

Extending Your Knowledge

The concept of strategy can be viewed from two perspectives: what an organization intends to do and what an organization actually does. Effective organizations set out their strategies clearly in advance, ineffective ones, even those which go into liquidation, can be seen with hindsight to have followed one or more strategies. The strategies may have led to disaster but they can be seen to have existed. Organisms, a term which includes organizations, cannot survive without strategies because without a destination or a purpose there can be no movement.

Planning, as has been said above, follows a staged process no matter whether the planner is working at corporate or tactical level. The degree of analysis will vary with the volume and complexity of the data but it is impossible to avoid taking each stage in turn if an effective plan is to be achieved.

1 Goal formulation

The organization's mission is a statement of values and purpose which is intended to serve long-term as a clear beacon to guide the managers through the alternative actions that they identify. It is not, however, to be carved in stone. Circumstances change and missions have to be reviewed if organizational survival is to be ensured. All the major oil suppliers have reviewed their missions and are going into the 21st Century as energy providers, thus opening the way for research and development of alternative energy sources which was denied them by their previous concentration on oil.

The values that managers hold will affect the kinds of goals they select. They must consider such issues as:

- Social and ethical considerations.
- Preferred size of the organization.
- The type of consumer need(s) they want to satisfy.
- Desire to produce or procure.
- Preferred style of operation.

When placed into context with market need and opportunity the value combination will condition the approach a particular group of senior managers takes and thus affects the decisions and subsequent actions.

Senior managers sometimes fail to challenge the status quo of the mission statement, yet unless it is challenged at regular intervals it cannot be shown to still be valid. The most common reasons for failure to test the mission are:

- Unwillingness to risk giving up on an existing situation.
- Concern that a revised mission will fail.
- Fear of endangering their self-esteem and/or status and/or respect and/or job security.
- Lack of sufficient knowledge of the organization and/or the environment.
- Lack of self-confidence.

Activity 2.2

Establishing strategies

Take 20 minutes to analyse a small business that you have experience of as a customer; perhaps a general store in a village or suburb, or a petrol filling station that offers breakdown recovery and mechanical repairs.

Consider how far the business has reached its present state through planned action and how much through chance. Attempt to distinguish the major areas of business and to determine their relative importance.

What would you recommend as the major areas to concentrate upon to secure medium-term profitable survival.

Use this matrix to aid your thinking:

Where are we heading?	
Do we want to go there?	
What is our business?	
What should it be?	
Who are our customers?	
Who should they be?	
What are our major areas of competence?	
What should they be?	
What competitive advantages do we enjoy?	
What could they be?	
What major threats can we identify?	
What can we do about them?	
What opportunities can we identify?	
What can we do about them?	

(**See:** Debriefing at the end of the unit.)

---

2 Identification of current objectives and strategy

Where are we starting from? This key question must never be ignored, nor must assumptions be made that what was laid down is actually taking place!

In an organization with a formal planning process installed and operating effectively there will be little problem at this stage since any deviation from intention will have been picked up by the control feedback and either accepted and built into the (revised) plan or rejected and the original plan reinstated.

When starting the process for the first time there may be need to distinguish what is actually happening and then to refine that into a valid set of strategic objectives which represent the current situation.

> Unless managers know where they are starting from they cannot reasonably expect to get to where they want to be.

3 Environmental analysis

Organizations must survive within the environment as it is not as it ought to be and certainly not as it used to be. They must also take the necessary steps to predict environmental changes so that they can prepare to make any necessary adaptation. In many cases an organization will want to actively participate in bringing about environmental modification and to this end will specifically devote resources.

The STEEPLE factors covered in Unit 1 provide the necessary headings to ensure that every aspect of the macro-environment is covered but note that a full environmental audit is a vast undertaking only possible for major undertakings. Even for multi-nationals the costs of a fully detailed review outweigh the benefits and so it is for management to determine the specific areas for analysis and, for each, the depth and thoroughness of the work.

Obviously priorities differ. Each organization must specify the range of information that is *needed* in order to adequately inform their decision making. Within this information need the items which are critical to environmental understanding should be identified and given priority.

Information gathered in this stage of the process is vital to the success of the subsequent stages and especially to the success of forecasting. Needed is an awareness not only of environmental issues that impact directly onto the organization but also those which can, or may, impact indirectly. Thus a beef farmer must be concerned with direct competitors such as lamb and pork producers and also with threats from new technology (e.g. Quorn, a meat substitute), from behavioural change (such as a move towards vegetarianism), from legislative changes (e.g. a potential EU policy to reduce beef output) and from climate changes (e.g. global warming and its long-term effects on what he can most effectively produce). Add to these such concerns as a national road building programme which may take part or all of his land, local government changes, national or international regulations affecting his form of farming, the containment of disease. It can be seen that a farmer cannot afford just to sit on his land and produce beef cattle.

Stakeholder reaction is included as part of the environmental analysis, an especially important part since final approval of actions will be reflected in stakeholder response. It is becoming recognized that specific contact is needed with stakeholders to inform and educate them to understand, accept and support the actions that the organization is taking.

4 Resource analysis

The Strengths and Weaknesses quadrants of the SWOT matrix. Concern should not be with inward-looking analysis, although that is the natural course that most managers will attempt to adopt. Instead the concern should be with *relative* strengths and weaknesses.

Relative strengths and relative weaknesses relate an organization's situation against its competitors. If there are no competitors then whatever is offered, however it is presented, must be a strength. There will be a compensating weakness, however, since a poor service, badly presented, will attract competition. Therefore the relative nature of both strengths and weaknesses must be against both present and potential competition.

The question is not 'What do we do well?', it is 'What are we doing better or worse than anyone else?'

The supplementary questions then become:

- How much better/worse than who?
- What are they likely to do to change their offering?
- Where we are weak, what must we do as a minimum to attain a competitive advantage?
- Where we are strong, what must we do as a minimum to maintain our advantage?

Relative strength, of course, refers to what an organization is planning to do. It is counter productive to build strengths in a market that one is planning to leave; it is foolish to attempt market entry without marked differential or distinctive advantages that will be well promoted.

Finally note that the rose-coloured spectacles syndrome is likely to apply. Managers are not the best people to critically evaluate their own performance against competition. They are too used to majoring on the strengths and talking down the opposition. Strengths and weaknesses analysis above all must be objective. It must report things as they are perceived to be from the customers' viewpoint.

Extending Your Knowledge	Insurance brokers in the UK were operating quite contentedly on the high street. Offering friendly personal service, they saw no need to change. Many, in fact, refused to accept that change was possible.
	It came as a major blow, therefore, when a new concept was invented by a person who looked at the current and future environments and decided there was a substantial market opportunity.
	Direct Writers (of insurance) were established using 0500 and 0800 (free) numbers to provide a heavily discounted insurance service. To the surprise of the high street brokers, many of their clients proved quite happy to negotiate insurance over the telephone. The insurance market changed beyond recognition – within a decade the market leaders were all direct writers and the high street brokers had virtually ceased to exist.

5 Identification of strategic opportunities and threats

Opportunities and threats can arise from a very wide range of factors. Can the production line be extended without the lease being renewed? If the office set up is now too extensive can it be split and part re-packaged as a new product? Perhaps as a facilitator for the increasing number of companies offering freephone service and needing their calls answered effectively and efficiently? Lyons Maid used to take their ice cream delivery fleet off the road each autumn. Walls kept theirs active, and earning, by sub-contracting to extend Cadbury's delivery fleet over the peak Christmas and Easter fancy chocolate delivery periods.

Technological changes are normally flagged well ahead of their commercial impact and so there is little excuse for an organization to be caught out in old technology, yet it happens regularly.

To succeed in these quadrants of the SWOT matrix there is need for flair and imagination. Far better to identify too many opportunities and threats, and then to whittle them down through careful analysis, than to take a conservative approach on the assumption that everybody else moves slowly and in straight lines too!

6 Gap analysis

Given that existing strategies continue, the organization will make certain achievements. We also know the goals that have been determined as corporate objectives in Stage 1. Any variation in these two key achievements is referred to as a *performance gap*.

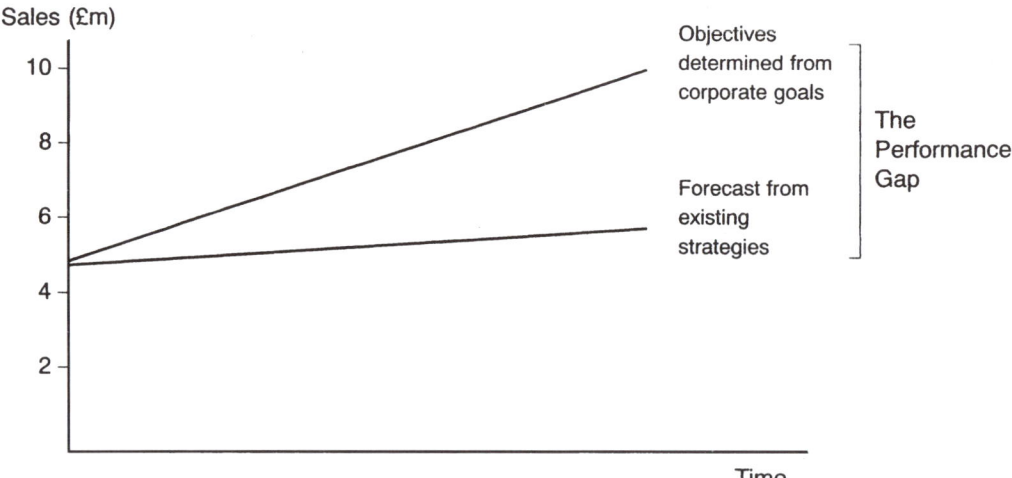

Figure 2.2
Performance gap

Performance gaps arise when organizations choose different objectives and/or when competitors become more or less aggressive and/or when environmental conditions change. They should be identified whilst still potential gaps and appropriate actions taken.

<table>
<tr><td>**Activity 2.3**</td><td>*SWOT*
Take 20 minutes to conduct an objective SWOT analysis of an organization that you know well. The college or last school that you attended will do fine. Be tightly objective from a client's perspective when in the S & W quadrants. Extend your creative thinking as widely as possible to pull in as many opportunities and threats as you can. Pay particular attention to how potential threats may be turned into opportunities, and how potential opportunities may bring threats along with them.

(**See:** Debriefing at the end of the unit.)</td></tr>
</table>

7 Strategic decision making

Decision making is possibly the single most important management attribute. No decisions, no action! Stages 1 to 6 provide the strategic manager with the needed information on which to act. It is then necessary to:

7.1 Identify the strategic alternatives

Search out and identify as many as possible of the strategic alternatives that are open or could be opened. This stage is identification only, it never implies a commitment and so one should not be restricted by any negative feelings such as 'We don't work in that market' or 'We've tried that and it didn't work'. Mind maps are excellent tools for loosening the constrictions of logical thinking. There will be plenty of time (and need) for logic later. The aim at this stage is to identify as many options as possible.

Note that strategic alternatives apply internally as well as externally. Perhaps profitability can be improved even in the face of a market contraction if two production units were to be amalgamated. Could the distribution function be sub-contracted?

7.2 Evaluation of strategic alternatives

Take the alternatives that have been identified and delete all that are obviously inappropriate. From those that remain, select for evaluation the ones that appear to best match the needs of the current situation. Hold the others in reserve for use if necessary and for submission to R&D as potential ways forward.

Evaluate each alternative for:

- *Consistency* – throughout the identified strategy and the supporting strategies that will be needed. This consistency should extend down into the needed tactics and, of course, consistency with corporate mission is essential.
- *Focus* – of resources on to the identified critical issues.
  - 'Doability' – it should be possible to achieve the strategy within the organization's available range of skills, expertise and resources.
  - *Practicality* – the strategy should be capable of producing the intended results. (It is very easy to become carried away with a brilliant new idea only to find out, too late, that it doesn't deliver what was intended.)

Target tightly on to a particular product offering, its marketplace and its competition. A strategy that does not create and/or exploit an organization's advantages over competition should be reworked or rejected.

7.3 Selection of strategic alternatives

It is always best to work outwards from strengths, and to acquire new skills and experience ahead of need. Therefore one should look for those alternatives which:

- Best suit the organization's capabilities.
- Require the least reorganization and/or redesign.
- Have the lowest levels of calculated risk.

Alternatives which call for new capabilities in equipment and/or personnel require time for successful implementation and so are usually best suited to a medium-term strategy where they can be developed with care over sufficient time. Alternatives which call for diversification – into Ansoff's fourth quarter of new market and new product – should only be undertaken by organizations that are solidly established in their home markets and see this extension as a necessary part of their long-term planning.

Activity 2.4

Objectives
Take 15 minutes to consider these statements. Each is a statement of intention yet none is an objective. What is needed to turn them into objectives against which performance can be evaluated?

1 Thanks for your enquiry. Our Sales Manager will contact you as soon as possible.
2 The Trade Debtor Collection Period is extending. We intend to get it back under control.
3 I'm going to get an order from this customer.
4 It is our intention to increase sales of the Acme Dishwasher and we are therefore taking on additional sales staff and increasing our marketing budget.

(**See:** Debriefing at the end of the unit.)

Extending Your Knowledge

An error made by many organizations in the boom times of the late 1960s and early 1970s was to diversify by acquisition. The giant Lyons group was brought to its knees by such a policy. The three errors which they made have become classics and, in retrospect, it is hard to see how professional businessmen could have exhibited such poor judgement. Their errors were:

1 They acquired a company making a product of which they had no knowledge.

2 Their acquisition was of an American company that traded only in the US, and they had no US market knowledge.
3 They left the existing management in place. Thus the errors which had opened the company to take-over were continued, but now funded by Lyons new finance.

The group pulled out, and suffered enormous losses from which it never fully recovered when the dollar moved unfavourably against the pound leaving them hopelessly over-exposed.

8 Strategy implementation

Each selected strategy must be implemented if it is to be successful. This may appear a truism not worthy of inclusion, but it is a sad truth that many organizations have excellent planners, but lack the ability to translate those plans into terms that are meaningful to those who must carry them out.

Strategy implementation requires far more than the simple issuing of orders. Of far greater importance is securing the commitment of those who must make the strategy work. They have to believe in it, they must see the benefits to themselves as well as to the organization, they must be encouraged to contribute their skills and expertise to improve the basic strategic plan so that the completed strategy is a shared result of planners and operational managers.

9 Establish operational programmes

Strategy establishes a desired end result. Tactical (operational) programmes are needed to provide the necessary momentum. Tactical planning is a highly detailed process but without each tactical cog in place and running smoothly, no strategy can succeed.

Tactical planning is carried out at operational level and co-ordinated across functions to ensure synergy. Given that all are working to the same strategy there should be no problems, yet there are options at tactical as well as strategic level. A process of tactical alternative identification, evaluation and selection must be carried through and co-ordinated with the other tactical functions that will be effected before operational programming can be completed.

10 Measurement and control of progress

As the operational programmes are being made so the control mechanisms can be put into place. For each objective there needs to be a control which records progress and reports back to the appropriate manager(s) in time for any needed action. When working under budgetary control the control system reports only exceptions to expectation and so prevents the need for managers to wade through masses of data to identify areas where action may be needed.

The Management Information System (see page 43) incorporates an effective control system and is an essential part of modern management.

Objectives

Without clear objectives it is impossible to maintain any form of control. It is essential to always set objectives that are unambiguous and express intention against time. Test your objectives to see that they are SMART:

S Specific   – objectives must deal with one thing at a time, and not be ambiguous.

M Measurable – it must be possible to measure achievement against objective in either quantity or quality terms.

A Achievable   – it is demotivational to set an 'objective' that is not attainable.

R Relevant   – the objective must be relevant to the task in hand.

T Timed   – a time for achievement must be specified or control is impossible.

Budgetary control

Given that all managers should be setting SMART objectives it should be possible to evaluate progress against each rather than wait for historical information until after the period has ended.

Waiting for historical information ensures accuracy (if the necessary systems are effectively and efficiently in place) but by the time it comes to hand a manager is already well into the next period. Thus any corrective measures can only be taken on the basis of hindsight into a period that has passed and which may have no relevance to the current period.

Controls are concerned with the measurement of performance and the isolation of variances. Effective and efficient control brings relevant information to the appropriate manager in a form that facilitates decision. We know that managers often need to revisit their decisions since as new information comes to hand it becomes easier to identify the appropriate action.

Budgetary control therefore exists to:

- Encourage (force) managers to plan ahead.
- Provide information on progress against objectives.
- Maximize the probability that individual decisions are refined and improved whilst there is still time for such refinement to have meaning.
- Assist managers to make better decisions in subsequent planning/budgetary cycles.

Control information must:

- Follow organizational lines.
- Cover short-time periods.
- Be concerned with financial and non-financial data.
- Be historical.
- Be very detailed.

A computer is therefore an ideal vehicle to manage a system of budgetary control, the more so since it allows easy and fast manipulation of data to provide managers at different levels with the information they actually need.

Budgets

Budgets are needed if there is to be effective control. They are constructed well in advance of the period which they will cover. A brand or market manager in a blue-chip company can be many management levels away from the point of decision, and have to work several months ahead in order that the budget can be approved in sufficient time.

Figure 2.3(a) shows the first stage of budgeting for a marketing-oriented organization. From market surveys an outline sales estimate will be prepared for the budget period. This will show anticipated sales for each of, usually, 12 months or 13 four-week periods. As each sales and marketing manager produces estimates for his tactical area they are brought together, adjusted as necessary, and approved by the Marketing Director. This Sales Budget provides the basis for all other departmental budgets.

Figure 2.3(b) shows how, when sales expectations are converted to output requirements, it is possible to produce a production budget. It also indicates how sales expense and other principal budgets need to be prepared. (The sales expense budget is a part of the consolidated sales budget, but is of no concern to production.)

Note that production will be making product well ahead of sales, and that purchasing will be committing the organization even further ahead and so the budgetary process is critical.

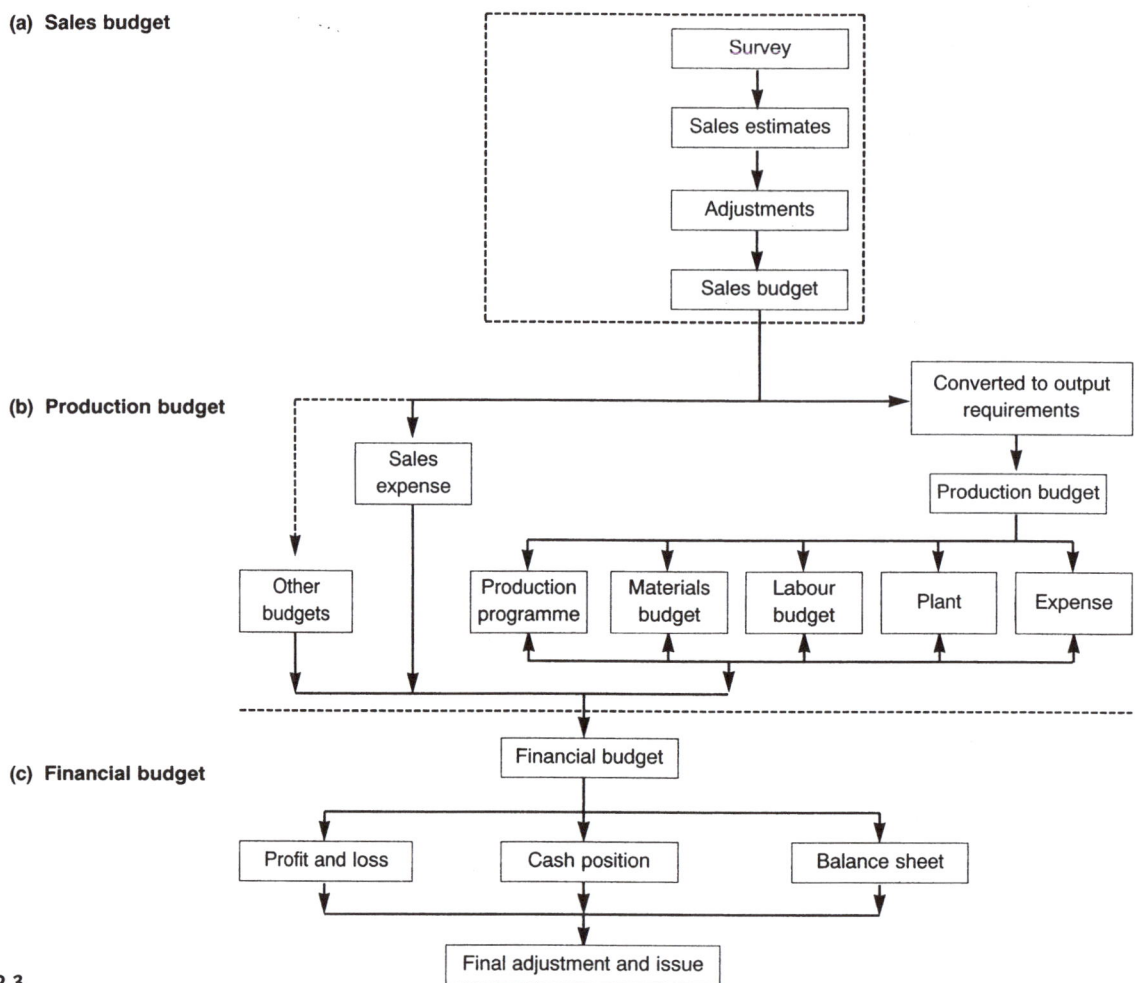

(a) Sales budget

(b) Production budget

(c) Financial budget

Figure 2.3

Just as the production budget can be derived from the sales budget, so can every other functional departmental budget. Distribution can calculate the warehouse space and delivery systems needed and when they will be under pressure and when slack; finance can determine when they will have cash surplus, and when they will be needing to secure short-term funds, etc. It will be appreciated that sales achievement is only part of cash flow. The raw material for the goods has often to be bought well before they are sold, and the costs of production and distribution have to be absorbed as well. Only when the customers pay – a major activity for credit control is seeing that credit limits are not exceeded and that customers pay to time – is the business transaction complete.

Figure 2.3(c) shows how the Financial Budget, complete with projected Profit and Loss statement, Cash Flow projection and Balance Sheet, can be produced from budgeted figures.

From an effective budgeting system it is possible to produce projected figures for any part of the organization at any time covered by the budget. As time passes, and experience is gathered, these forecasts will tend to become ever more reliable. The projected cash position is of particular importance because it can be highly beneficial to secure funds in advance to cover any projected shortfall, and to plan to make short-term surpluses available to the money market.

It is necessary to appoint a Budget Officer who may hold the job part time in a small organization. A Budget Department may be required in a large organization for there is much co-ordination needed if budgetary control is to be effective.

Control of costs and of revenue
Once an organization has ensured that the managers have a balanced budget it is necessary for individual managers to hit their budgets. If every

manager hits budget, then the whole budget will be secure; any who miss will set up ripples that if severe enough, or allowed to proceed uncorrected, will effect every other department. For example:

- If a salesperson oversells budget by 5 per cent it may be compensated for by another who undersells. Thus the sales manager's budget will be achieved.
- If the sales manager's budget is 5 per cent over-achieved it will mean that customers will be disappointed since production will have made to budget, and there will be no stocks to meet this extra demand.

If the tendency to exceed budget is noted in time there are two possible solutions: sales efforts can be reduced or production increased. One or the other must happen if customers are to be supplied with goods ordered in good faith. It is the function of budgetary control to ensure that managers are appraised of the situation in time for remedial action. It is, as always, for managers to decide upon the action.

Documentation

An organization is concerned only to achieve budget. Previous results have been taken into account when constructing the budget and so a comparison to 'last year', is meaningless. There is no way to use historical data as part of a control process.

- *Financial accounts* will show a comparison of this year's results with historical data.
- *Management accounts* will compare achievement to budget.

This is excellent psychology since it prevents the complacency, and the potential excuse, that can come from an excess over last year even if budget is not met: 'No, I didn't meet budget, but I am 5 per cent up on last year.' The need to be *more than 5 per cent up* was taken into account at time of budget construction and so the only valid comparison is with budget.

Variance analysis

No news is good news. (Proverb)

Variance analysis is at the heart of an effective budgetary control system. Through well-planned variance analysis it is possible to provide each manager with a brief statement showing exactly which budget items are outside agreed limits. The system ignores everything that is within limits and so removes the need for managers to sift through a mass of data to find the information they must have.

An upper and lower control limit is required for each objective. These must be fixed with the needs of individuals in mind – a tactical manger needs details of his function, a senior manager needs overall results from a range of individuals. Variances should be flagged as *favourable* or *unfavourable*. The unfavourable ones take priority in the reporting hierarchy.

Extending Your Knowledge

Marks & Spencer
M & S used to have an exhibition in a conference room in their Baker Street headquarters. It showed the differences brought about by a change to MBE. On three walls they just managed to squeeze a copy of every form that every branch had previously submitted each week as a report on achievement. On the fourth wall – an end wall with a large door in it – they had room and more to show the minimal paper that was now in use.

They had accepted that there was no need for a manager to report when things were going according to plan. Therefore they adopted a system of MBE, supported by what we now call budgetary control.

The result of selecting a range of control measures – and although we are using a sales example the principle applies to every operational area – is that management can become overwhelmed with information. Corrective action is only possible if managers can quickly see where intervention is needed. Thus variance analysis must be coupled with the principle of management by exception (MBE). If *tolerance limits* are established for each control measure it becomes only necessary to report instances that are outside those limits.

Corrective action

Budgetary control is not focused on error, its purpose is to help managers achieve their budgets by providing them with information on progress in a form and at a time when corrective action is possible. If a sales budget cannot be achieved the corrective action must firstly be internal. Procurement, Production and Distribution are Operational Divisions that are immediately affected, with Finance and Personnel concerned as well. Revisions to the budget must be made, issued and acted upon quickly. A production problem may require a redirection of sales effort, and so on, for every operating area.

The decision on sales budget achievement will normally have been made only after individual sales managers had worked with sales people to improve results, but the temptation to delay reporting the inevitable on the grounds that 'it will improve tomorrow' is tempered with the knowledge that actual results are being reported simultaneously throughout the organization and management performance is judged on decisive action, not upon prevarication.

Activity 2.5

Sales management

As a Sales Manager with nine sales people covering the North of England and Scotland you can spend a working day per month with each sales person. You have just received a control statement for your area which ranks the team in order of their overall variance from a range of criteria. What immediate communication will you have with your team members and how will you plan your field trips for the coming month?

(**See:** Debriefing at the end of the unit.)

Organizational considerations

In order for any system of control to be effective the organization must be clearly structured so that responsibility and authority are delegated. Every item must be the responsibility of an identified person and each person must unambiguously know their role and be involved in the budgeting process. Without commitment to the budget there will be little commitment to results and therefore to control.

Individuals are concerned to know what has happened; why it has happened and what to do about it.

- *What has happened* is feedback of results against budget. This should be a straightforward budgetary control performance statement and should be a routine and regular event.
- *Why it has happened* is not normally for the control system to determine. The root causes of a variation may be outside an individual's control. The source of the problem must be located, of course. Otherwise it can only be reacted to – not dealt with.
- *What to do about it* is for management to determine. The purpose of the control system is to alert management to the need to determine 'Why?' and then to take appropriate action.

Flexible budgets

Given that most budgets cannot be hit on the nose every time there will be a constant flow of revisions. Flexible budgeting provides accurate information on the actual state of affairs so that managers do not have to work with historical data.

The true value of variance analysis is in allowing management to quickly understand where action is required in a complex set of circumstances. It is therefore better to show on the one statement all of the factors which may have contributed to the achieved result.

Working in a dynamic environment with control information coming forward promptly usually makes it possible to revise plans to take into account the actuality of the situation.

Risk

Risk is a 'hazard or chance' where the probability of loss is known. Thus managers who take decisions in uncertain conditions are taking risks. They are not gambling, where the outcome is left to chance. All managers, therefore, are risk managers.

A major aim is to reduce the amount of risk implicit in every decision, but not to attempt to eradicate it altogether. Eradication is either impossible, or will cost far more than going ahead with a known amount of risk.

Organizational culture will vary from the risk-taking to the risk-averse. The true risk-averse organization cannot survive for long since the time and effort spent in attempting to eradicate risk will leave no time to actually trade!

It follows that every manager will make mistakes. Senior managers should recognize this and not penalize a junior for taking a quantified risk that was within his level of authority. Criticism for errors of judgement will only result in the manager avoiding decisions in the future.

Information systems

Management information system (MIS)

Information is the life blood of management decision making. Without a constant flow of accurate, reliable, current and measurable information a manager is either completely unaware of events or has, at best, a curtailed understanding of a situation.

Note that *information* is required. We know that a vast amount of data flows in any organization; the key is to extract the information which is pertinent to any given situation and have it available in usable form when it is needed.

Figure 2.4 shows how management's information needs change depending upon role. Whilst in planning mode the manager needs information that enables him to set objectives, formulate strategy and decide amongst alternatives. In control mode the needs are to measure performance, isolate variances and aid in replanning.

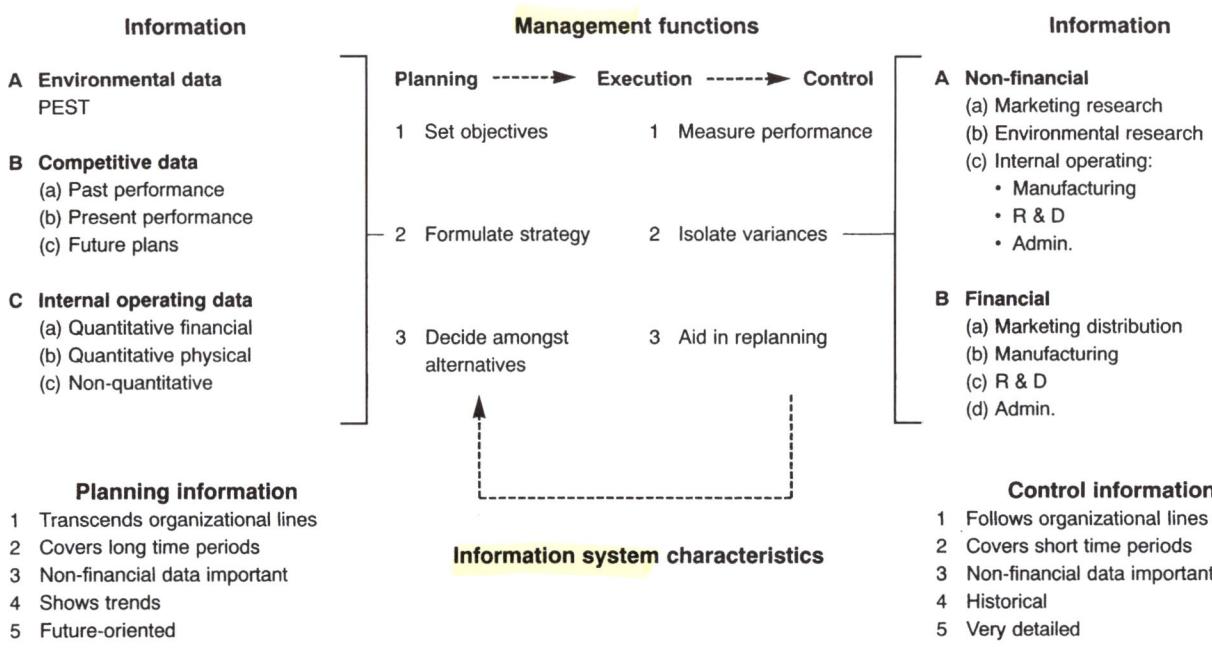

Figure 2.4 The anatomy of management information. (Source: *Strategic Marketing Management,* Wilson, Gilligan and Pearson (1992), Butterworth-Heinemann.)

Thus the information stream must be managed in such a way that the appropriate information is presented in a user-friendly way, at the time it is needed.

Note also how planning information must transcend organizational lines, cover long-time periods, show trends and be future oriented. By contrast, control information must follow organizational lines, cover short-time periods, be historical and very detailed. Both forms of information must draw on non-financial data.

A fully effective MIS is proactive and will carry out secondary and primary searches of the macro- and micro-environments with particular regard to overall, long-term information needs. Essentially, however, a MIS is now the entry point to the information superhighway which is linking data users world-wide. Thus the concept of the data being gathered and retained in a single system has passed. No longer is it possible. What is now required is specialist understanding of what data is available, from where, and at what cost. The management of information is set to become a major speciality and effective information managers will be highly valued.

The overall purpose of a MIS is to translate all relevant data into pertinent information and then to disseminate that information to managers that need it in time for it to be of value. Thus a MIS will inform, in a general way, but also alert individuals as key information comes to hand.

A fully integrated system will incorporate all the data within an organization under a system of password protection so that levels of access are protected.

Only major organizations can afford to maintain a fully integrated MIS but every organization should take steps to regulate their manager's scanning of the environment.

Marketing information system (MkIS)

All marketers have some form of MkIS, even if it is contained between their ears! Marketers must have a constant flow of fresh, reliable and accurate information about the marketplace whether they are preparing next period's forecast or monitoring current results. For many this

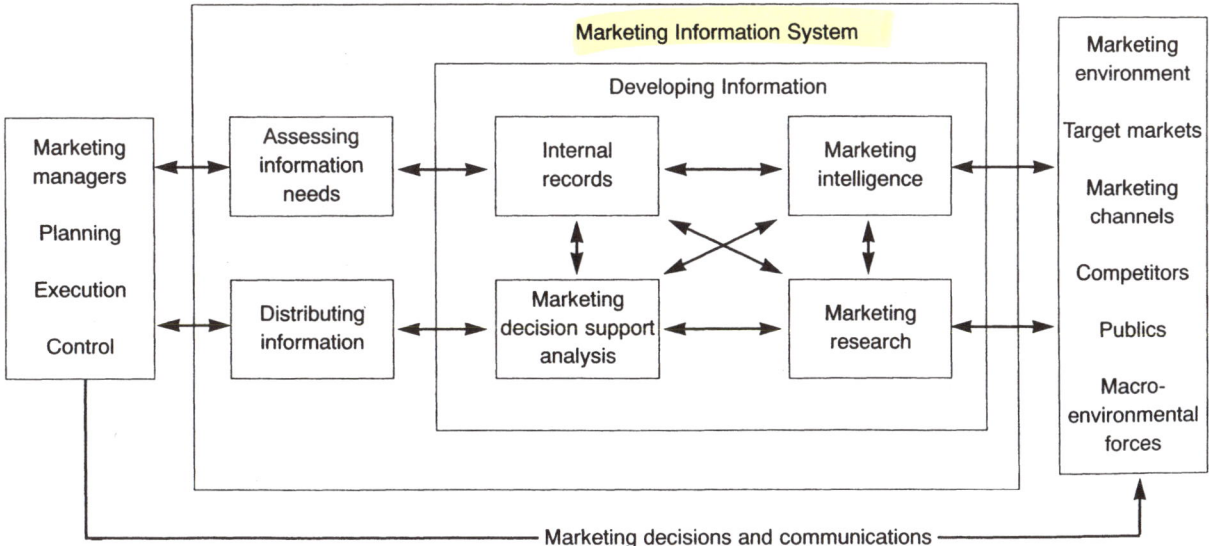

Figure 2.5 Marketing information system. (Adapted from Kotler: *Marketing Management – Analysis Planning, Implementation and Control*, Prentice-Hall, 1991.)

information flow is spasmodic because it is generated by the urgency of short-term need. Thus the marketer becomes a 'fire fighter' rushing from one minor conflagration to another, rather than having the time to manage effectively.

All Management Information Systems have a MkIS within them but a MkIS can stand alone. As a self-standing system it concentrates solely upon the requirements of the marketers and so is targeted to their needs. In essence it is a MIS which is restricted to marketing needs.

In Figure 2.5, Kotler shows that the MkIS is a contained system which uses decision support analysis to develop information from internal records, marketing intelligence and marketing research.

Marketing plans

Strategic marketing planning

We have seen that marketing strategy can only follow from corporate strategy, that all functional strategies are derived from corporate strategies which, in turn, relate back to the Mission Statement. We have also seen how the MIS and MkIS exist to actively search all relevant environments to secure data and then to process this into information of direct value to specific management need.

Marketing strategies provide clear direction, in SMART terms. They set the parameters which guide the tactical decision makers.

The components of strategic marketing planning are shown in Figure 2.6.

Marketing programme

This is a term sometimes used to describe the combination of marketing strategies but it is more usual simply to call them 'marketing strategies' and to present them as part of a marketing plan. The term is also sometimes used to describe the range of tactical plans which are needed, within the marketing plan, in order that strategic intention is fulfilled. Again, it is better to directly refer to tactical marketing plans.

Marketing plan

The marketing plan is of major significance to any organization since it is a fully detailed document which itemizes the actions that must be taken to achieve the marketing strategies.

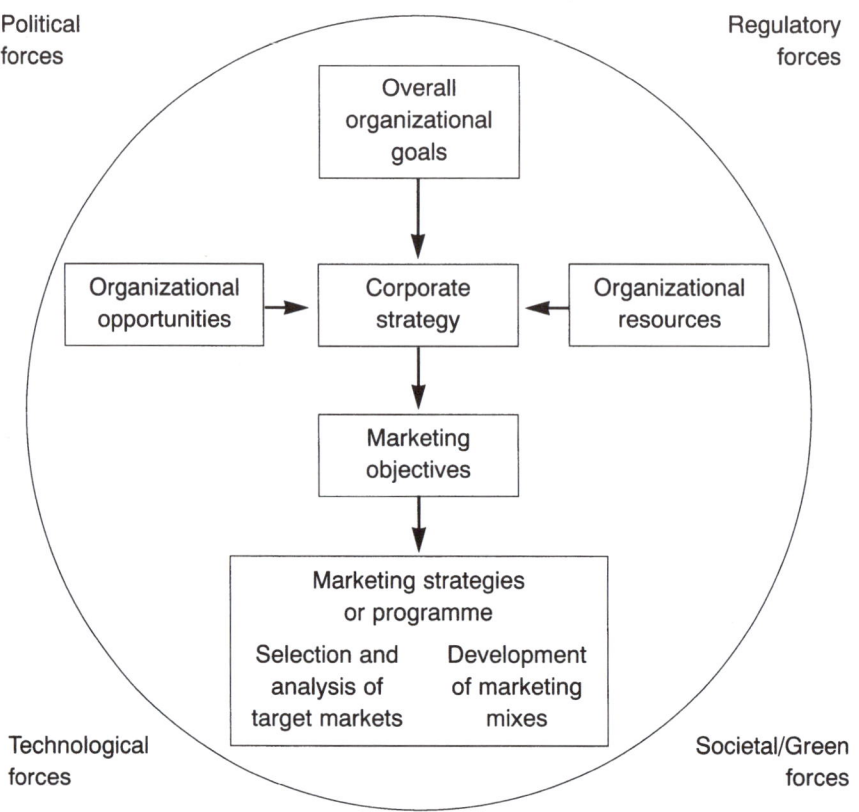

Political
forces

Regulatory
forces

Technological
forces

Societal/Green
forces

Overall
organizational
goals

Organizational
opportunities

Corporate
strategy

Organizational
resources

Marketing
objectives

Marketing strategies
or programme

Selection and
analysis of
target markets

Development
of marketing
mixes

Figure 2.6
Components of strategic marketing planning. (Source: *Marketing Concepts and Strategies*, Dibb, Simkin, Pride and Ferrell, 1994.)

A full marketing plan contains the Tactical Marketing Plans which enable strategies to be achieved. Because tactical marketing needs are either current or in the very near future they must be worked through in considerable detail. They are concerned with the whole of the marketing mix and must contain detailed scheduling to ensure that all the needed activities take place to time so that strategies are achieved.

It can be seen that the marketing plan is a major enterprise which must be dynamic and flexible because marketing must adapt to the changing environments in which the organization exists. Where budgetary control is effective and efficient it is routine to flex budgets and therefore to flex the whole planning process. In fact the budgetary and the marketing planning processes exist in a kind of symbiosis, with each dependent upon the other.

Because a full marketing plan is such a major undertaking it is normal for examiners to call for an *Outline Marketing Plan*. Outline plans are also used in organizations to present the key information without the need for the readers to wade through all the supporting evidence and background information. Detailed tactics are not included since the target audiences for an outline plan are:

- *Other senior managers* – for information.
- *Tactical marketers* – for creation and implementation of tactical plans.
- *The budgetary process* – to establish the parameters of marketing's intentions.
- *Examiners* – to demonstrate marketing management credibility.

Note: Outline marketing plans cannot be written without an awareness of how each strategy is to be achieved. In other words, just inventing a strategy without regard for its implementation is counter productive in examinations just as it is in work.

Contents of a marketing plan

There is no set form which must be followed (as there is for financial accounts). The key is to produce a plan which is sufficiently documented to meet the needs of the organization. This, of course, means to meet the needs of the managers who must understand and approve the plan as well as those who will subsequently have to understand and work with it. Each organization therefore produces a document which is unique to their needs.

The most extensive marketing plan will include the items shown in Figure 2.7 but note that the split of information between sections and supporting appendices will be determined by the level of knowledge and need of the targeted recipients. Background information such as SWOT and market analyses will usually be summarized in the body of the plan but covered extensively in the appendices for those who need to refer to the detailed information.

Time requirements

Always indicate the time span over which the plan extends. A Marketing Plan can be for a limited period, commonly one year, or it can extend into the medium and long term.

The general descriptions, short, medium and long term, must be given specific meaning within the context of the organization. Fast-moving sectors such as pop-music and fashion tend to have shorter planning horizons, the large and slow moving conglomerates plan over a longer period and industries such as energy are looking decades ahead.

---

1 Executive or Management Summary

2 Objectives
- Organization's mission statement.
- Detailed organization's objectives.
- Product/group goals.

3 Product/Market Background
- Product range and explanation.
- Market overview and sales summary.

4 Situation or SWOT Analysis
- Performance of current marketing strategies.
- Greatest challenges or threats.
- Opportunity analysis.

5 Marketing Analyses
- Marketing environment and trends.
- Customers' needs and segments.
- Competition and competitors' strategies.

6 Marketing Strategies
- Core target markets (segments).
- Basis for competing/differential advantage.
- Desired product/brand positioning.

7 Statement of Expected Sales Forecasts and Results

8 Marketing Programmes for Implementation
- Marketing mixes.
- Tasks and responsibilities.

9 Controls and Evaluation: Monitoring of Performance

10 Financial Implications/Required Budgets
- Delineation of costs.
- Expected returns on investment for implementing the marketing plan.

11 Operational Considerations
- Personnel and internal communications.
- Research and development/production needs.
- Marketing information system.

12 Appendices
- SWOT analysis details.
- Background data and information.
- Marketing research findings.

Figure 2.7
Components of a full Marketing Plan. (Source: *Marketing Concepts and Strategies*, Dibb, Simkin, Pride and Ferrell, 1994.)

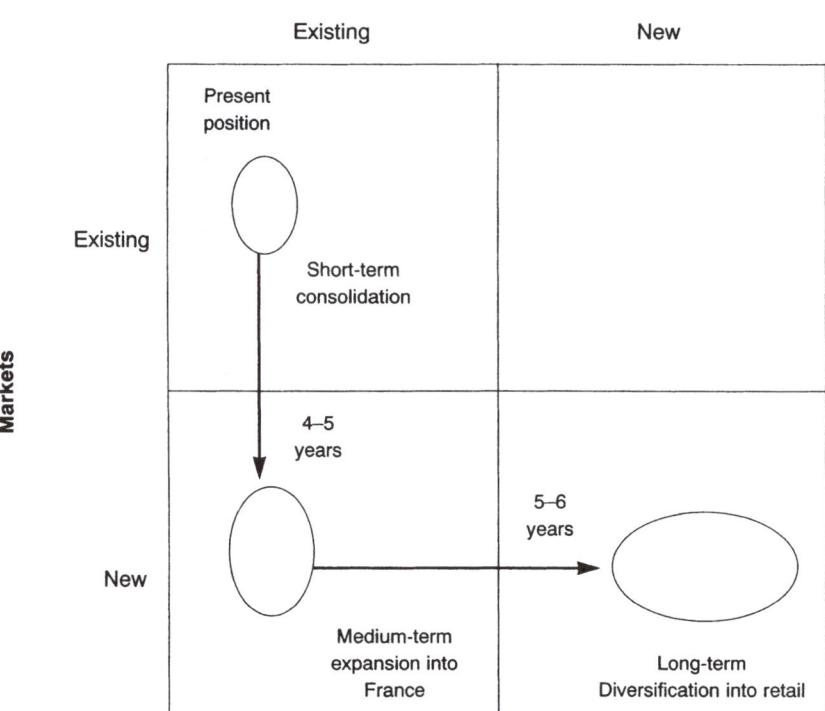

Products

| | Existing | New |

Figure 2.8
The Ansoff matrix used to communicate strategy.
(Source: Worsam.)

As a broad rule-of-thumb:

- *Short term*   Anything up to three years but usually refers to the next one-year plan.
- *Medium term* Usually two to three years; up to five years.
- *Long term*   More than five years.

The rule is to always specify the time periods the first time they are used in a document, e.g. Short-term (Year to 30 June, 20xx).

When adding the time dimension to your planning remember that nothing remains static. It follows that your strategy for the medium and long term can only be expressed in general terms.

Using schematics such as the Ansoff matrix is an effective way of communicating strategy over time.

The marketing planning cycle

Marketing is a dynamic and continuing process and so a marketing plan will already be in operation unless a new organization is starting up. It may not be called a marketing plan, it may not even be documented, but no functioning organization can exist without an interface with the environment. By definition this interface requires the use of marketing skills.

Such 'interface skills' may be seriously inadequate or they may be developed intuitively by managers trained in other disciplines.

The marketer therefore will face three broad possibilities:

1 *Marketing planning is not formalized.*
   The need is for formulation and for serious internal marketing to demonstrate the value of an organized approach.

2 *Marketing is bureaucratized.*
   The process has become so set within the established bureaucracy that initiative and creativity are subjugated to the needs of the system. The need is to break free – probably not easy – since fettered marketing is ineffective.

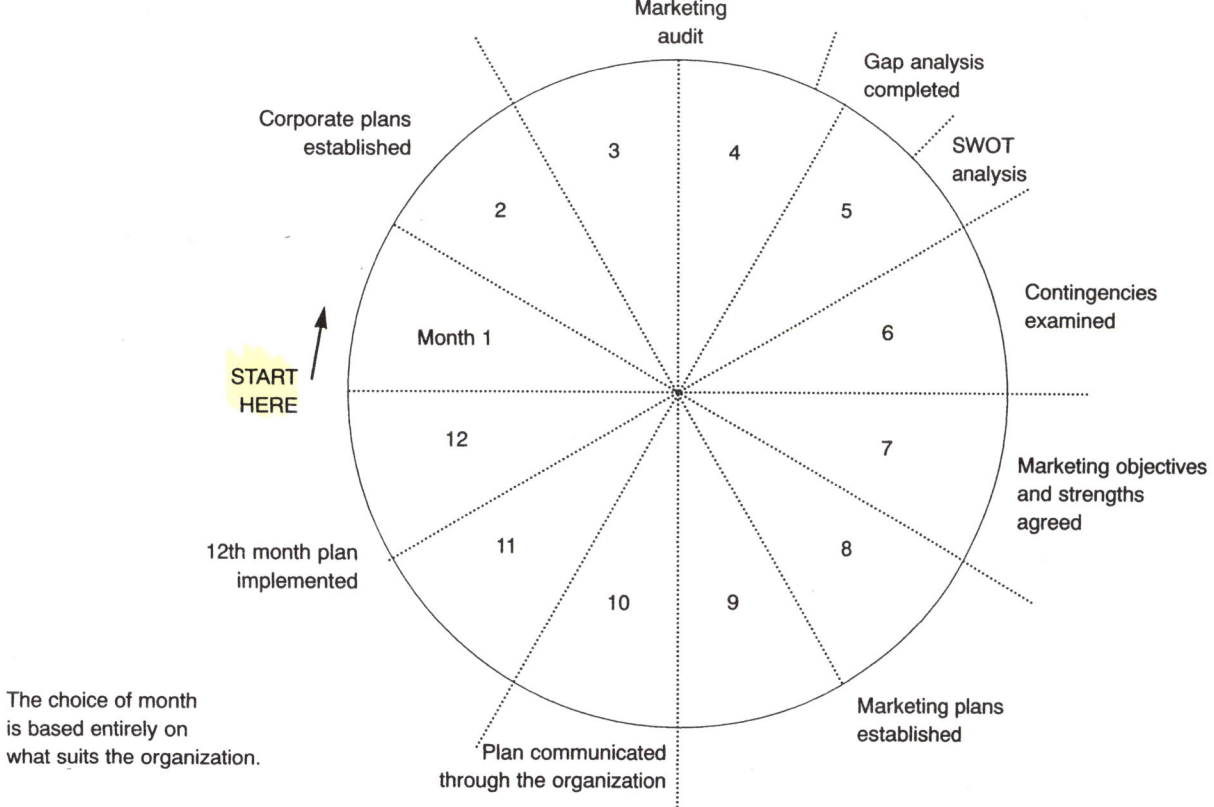

Figure 2.9 Implementing the marketing planning system. (Source: *The Marketing Audit*, McDonald and Leppard, 1993.)

3 *Marketing planning is in place and operating smoothly.*
Never take an existing situation as perfect, be prepared to modify to meet need, but *never* make changes without a good and valid reason.

The marketing planning system

A full marketing plan is the product of considerable analysis and decision carried through over a lengthy period of time. In major organizations the process can take an entire twelve months, with marketers fully active for perhaps two-thirds of that time. Figure 2.9 shows a typical planning year for a major organization.

The marketing planning system will normally follow the organization's financial year. This makes for a very tidy arrangement but is not obligatory. Systems should provide for the needs of management, never force management to abide by a bureaucratic insistence on neatness for its own sake.

Obviously the marketing planning process fits into the overall corporate planning needs and yet, because of its need for continuous monitoring and adjustment, is actually never ending. All marketers are involved with three short-term plans at the same time:

● *Last year's plan* Evaluation.
● *Current plan* Implementation
● *Next year's plan* Analysis, decision and recommendations.

The marketing planning process is shown in Figure 2.10

1 *Development or revision of marketing objectives relative to performance.*
This involves the re-appraisal of the current marketing objectives for the short, medium and long term. Under a system of budgetary control the performance relative to objectives will be assessed routinely, but many organizations have yet to introduce effective control systems. It is vital that all plans are reviewed to evaluate the achieved level of success. This stage of the planning cycle is of fundamental importance.

49

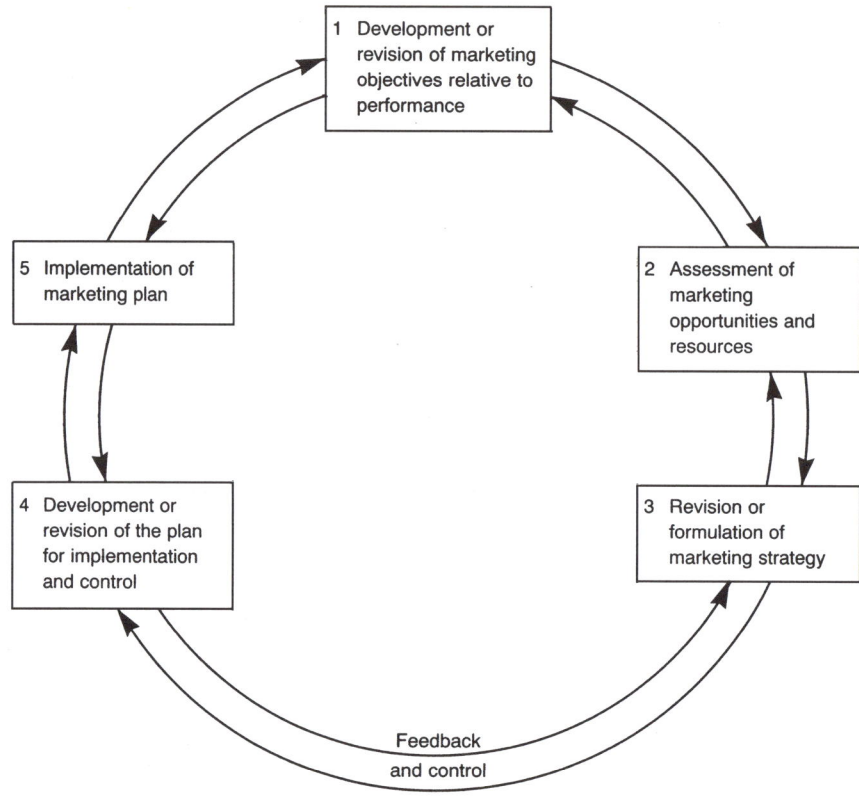

Figure 2.10
The marketing planning cycle.
(Source: *Marketing Concepts and Strategies*, Dibb, Simkin, Pride and Ferrell, 1994.)

2   *Assessment of marketing opportunities and resources.*
Opportunities occur continuously for those who are actively seeking them. They come about from a variety of sources ranging from the advent of new technology to a competitor having difficulty making deliveries in one area.

Opportunities exist to be exploited. But only if it is in the organization's best interests to do so, and only if the resources exist to take advantage of the opening. A contingency sum should be built into every budget to allow flexibility to deal with unexpected crises and to exploit opportunities.

Activity 2.6	*Multi-SWOT*

Select an organization with which you are familiar and carry through a SWOT analysis. Then take up a role as a major competitor and carry out another SWOT of the market situation from their perspective. Finally, take a role as a major provider, supplier or customer and SWOT again.

Examine the results of your three SWOTs, and identify how far they have extended your knowledge and understanding of the market situation.

(**See:** Debriefing at the end of the unit.)

3   *Revision or formulation of marketing strategy.*
It is most likely that strategies will need to be revised. Most will need to be slightly amended but in some cases a complete overhaul will be necessary. If it is needed, do it! Holding on to out-dated strategies is a recipe for disaster.
4   *Development or revision of the plan for implementation and control.*
Note that this stage requires the implementation plans to be developed and revised. It also calls for the control systems to be reviewed and improved where necessary. Remember that SMART objectives have their control issues built in and it is inexcusable for there to be no effective system of reporting back on progress.

5 *Implementation of marketing plan.*

No plan is of any value until it is implemented. Too often a team of corporate planners work from a sheltered environment deep in Group Headquarters and produce complex plans which have little relationship to the needs of the strategic and tactical managers who have to implement them. The result is that the managers in touch with events adapt the plans whilst the corporate planners busy themselves in meetings to analyse and discuss the reams of print-out coming from their computer systems.

Note: this view is only slightly exaggerated. It results from many years experience operating at the front end of marketing in multi-national conglomerates.

Marketing strategies

Marketing strategies are based on three key issues:

- Segmentation of profiled target markets.
- Positioning.
- Differential advantage.

We have covered segmentation and profiling in Unit 1. Positioning and differential advantage will be covered later. For now, simply note that positioning is establishing the product offer clearly in the minds of target audience members. Differential advantage is creating a difference that sets a given product offer apart from its competitors.

Critical success factors

Within any given market there are critical success factors for winning the business, such as: reliable delivery; acceptable design; low running costs and high volume turnover.

There are also internal CSFs which influence how well the organization performs: there will be a lead time on procurement and production; in a bureaucracy the proper forms must be completed ahead of time, and so on.

It is essential to identify the applicable CSFs, and to evaluate how the organization compares with the competition when measured against these factors. Naturally it is necessary to judge CSFs from the viewpoint of those targeted by marketing because it is their needs and perceptions that must be taken into account.

A full marketing audit is a major activity that cannot be completed in the short term. It is necessary to obtain very detailed information from across the range of marketing's activities and to process this information so that it is readily usable. In fact the auditing process should be routine and continuous. The MkIS should be fed with data on all issues within the audit's remit and information processing should be routinized.

Day-to-day adjustments to plans will be made in the light of current information which, of course, is actually a part of the on-going audit process.

It is necessary, however, to review the entire audit annually as part of the marketing planning process.

Marketing organization

The standard management hierarchy that everybody knows is based on the military model that we met in Unit 1. Business did not create an organization suited to its needs – it simply adopted the one that was easily available.

Today's managers need a more flexible structure – one that motivates and facilitates the achievement of specified objectives. There is also need for a hierarchy – but in the background as a way to take care of personnel administration.

Alternative structures

Management are concerned with how best to get the work done – how to meet corporate objectives. Today's thinking is based on three factors:

- Leadership need not equate with rank.
- Structures need not be permanent.
- Communications allows more flexible approaches to work.

Leadership does not equate with rank. Changing circumstances may mean that different members of a team are better suited to leading at different stages of a task.

Structures need not be permanent, providing there is an underpinning hierarchy to keep track of individuals. Teams can be set up to achieve specific objectives and then disbanded when the task is done. Individuals can be in several teams at the same time, and have different roles in each.

- *Functional team-work* is a concept of Gerald Fisher, who suggests there are three functional areas:
  - *Process* functions include all that must be controlled with time as a major element. Thus product design, purchasing, manufacturing, marketing, credit control, sales, distribution and invoicing are all included. This creates a functional unit concerned with the movement of a product from concept to invoicing.
  - *Resources* functions include all resources, human, physical and monetary.
  - *Relations* functions can be summed up as communications. Both internal and external communications are included.
  Functional team-work divides responsibilities into clearly defined areas of responsibility. The structure encourages team-work.

- *Task force organization* is more limited in its approach but does not require the major reorganization of functional team-work. A task force is established to achieve a specific task or objective, and is a tightly knit unit under the control of one manager who usually has broad powers of authority. It will work against a deadline and those who make up the team will come from a wide variety of backgrounds.
  Each task force can draw members from functional areas without affecting the current organizational structure. Task forces can be 'part-time' in nature, with the members devoting only part of their time to it.

Communication channels now allow many to work away from their desks, away from their offices, and still be able to communicate. Electronics allow virtually instant contact with anybody in the world – it is becoming impossible to be out of touch.

With individuals networked and able to make instant contact with colleagues there is no way that individuals can (or will) constantly refer to higher authority. Thus today's junior staff are taking decisions that a decade ago would have been referred to a higher authority.

The move to flatter structures

Organizations are rapidly moving to flatter structures. With the lateral channels opened up by electronics there is no longer a need for a series of managers in the chain between senior and junior.

The implications of this on staff selection and training and on management style, expectation and training are immense – but the process seems irreversible.

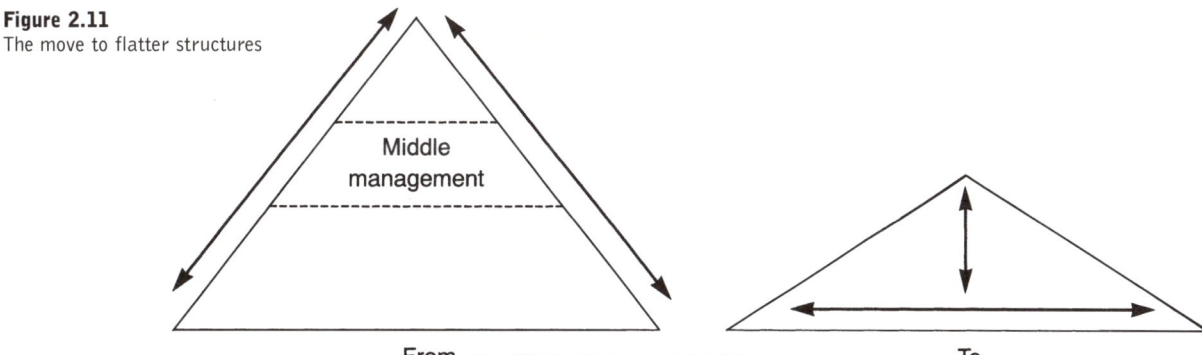

Figure 2.11
The move to flatter structures

From .... To

Matrix structure

Organizing by matrix facilitates the flexibility which modern organizations require. They allow individuals to contribute from their strengths and specialities regardless of rank.

To understand their value, consider the problems of structuring a major food manufacturing company. Should it organize around its markets: grocery, catering, vending and so on? Or around its products: coffee, milks and creams, biscuits, etc.? Or perhaps around its brands?

On the one hand there will be people experienced in a product, but not in the different market needs. On the other will be people expert in each market, but without specialized product understanding. If operating via brands there may be several quite different products marketed under the one brand identity – and this has to extend across product and market management.

An answer is to use a matrix approach. The matrix in Figure 2.12 is deliberately simplistic, but shows the principle. It can be seen that individuals can share expertise and that task forces can be made up of several different specialists. Note carefully that any one individual can hold a place on both axes. A brand manager may also be a catering market specialist and could also manage one of the products. Thus the one person could contribute from three areas of expertise.

Place and role

The place of marketing within a structure will vary depending on the overall needs of the organization. Its role will not change, but the way it achieves its objectives will be affected by the form and degree of rigidity in the organizational structure.

Subjects	Maths					
	Art					
	etc.					
School secretary						
Librarian						
Senior administrator						
etc.						

Figure 2.12
School matrix

53

An audit is the systematic collection of data and information about a given subject. In the case of marketing this involves the external environment and the organization's operations.

A marketing oriented organization will have a hierarchy that shows marketing to be an important and separate function. But where that function is located will depend upon corporate decisions concerning the organization itself.

Figures 2.13, 2.14 and 2.15 show departmentalism by function, by territory and by product.

- *Functional* organization is traditional, safe, expected. It provides excellently for the hygiene needs and is easy to understand. It does, however, force a vertical approach to communication unless lateral contacts are formally approved and made to work.
- *Territory* organization is useful when there is a wide area to cover with very similar activities. Sales departments are habitually organized on a territorial basis, often within organizations that are basically structured by function.
- *Product* or *brand* organization is adopted by organizations who have need for specialist attention to a range of differing product offerings. An organization such as Philips has world-wide interests in electrics, electronics, radio and television and telecommunications. Each area is sub-divided into discrete products appealing to a range of specific markets from the housewife to the radiologist, but not all products are offered in each country where Philips has a presence.

  Their organizational structure is likely to be complex, using a variety of the three basic types, but with a core focus on product or brand groupings since this is focus for the key technical skills of production and marketing. Note that this shows the inwards looking approach that characterized the first three decades of organized marketing in the UK.
- *Market* organization is beginning to replace product-based structure in some organizations as they move to a 4Cs or 7Cs approach and away from the traditional Ps. Many argue that marketing should always have been outward focused and that it is now about time that it is finally beginning to happen.

It is less important, however, to worry about hierarchical structure. What matters is the facility with which the organization fulfils its key tasks. We have established that structure can restrict. It is important for management to ensure that sufficient freedom exists for key objectives to be fulfilled, and for efficient and effective control to be exercised to the maximum benefits of employees and with the minimum constraints on their actions.

Marketing in operation

In many organizations the marketing team is very small in number compared to the other functions. A multi-national such as Nestlé UK, for example, may have fewer than 50 people in their marketing team, yet their entire effort is founded on the activities of these few. It follows that marketers are very influential and can be individually known throughout the organization. The high-profile role cannot be avoided given the importance of the marketing process. It is, in fact, often one of the keys to marketing's success.

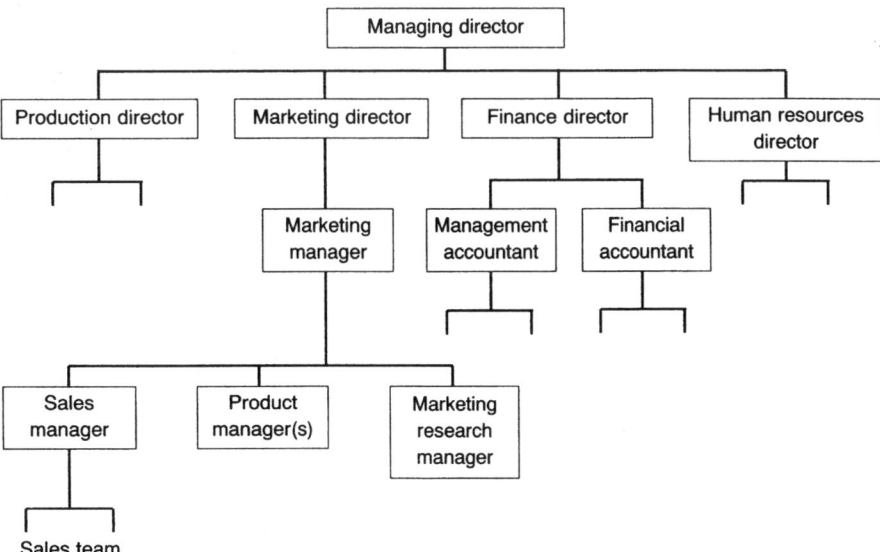

Figure 2.13
Departmentalism by function

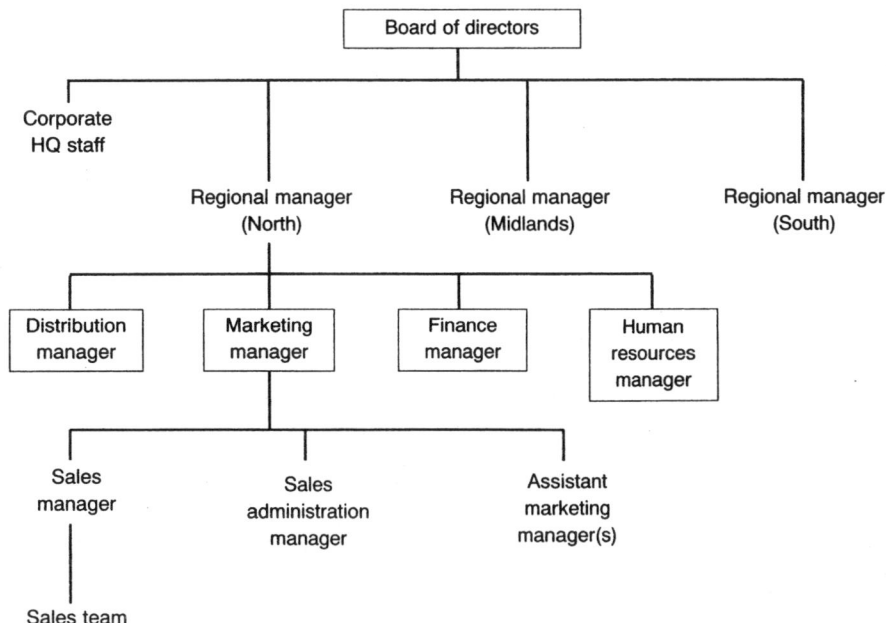

Figure 2.14
Departmentalism by territory

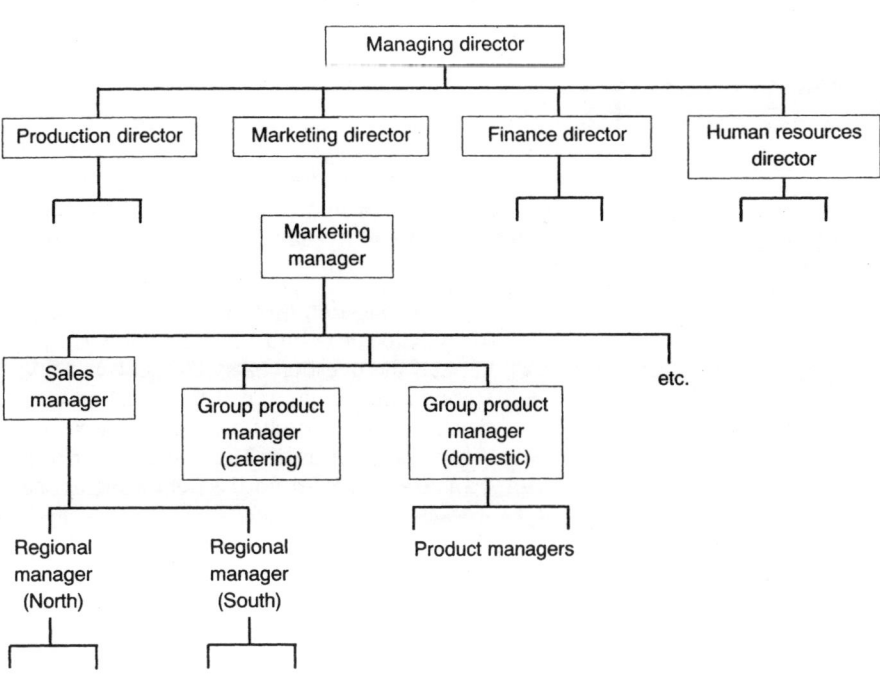

Figure 2.15
Departmentalism by product

Process questions are increasingly being used throughout the CIM Advanced Certificate and Diploma and you can be certain that they will feature strongly in your examination. They require you to show that you know how to do a particular thing, how to achieve a given task. They are testing your theoretical and practical understanding of the process of marketing management.

Hints on answering process questions:

- Answer practically and directly. The examiner is looking for a crisp resume of actions that could be taken, not an essay which sets out possibilities.
- Use marketing and management theory to support your recommendations; only explain it if you are using it in an unusual or specially creative way. If you are using the correct theory in context the examiner will appreciate that you understand it.
- Quantify your recommendations. Even if you cannot include a budget make it clear that you know a budget is needed. You can transmit this message in a variety of ways:
  - *Budget: Recommendations will follow in the light of our discussions.*
  - *Budget: It is not possible to include a detailed budget at this time but preliminary costings show that the recommendations in this report are cost-effective.*
  - *Budget: Detailed budget figures are dependent on the selection of methodology.*
- Recommendations must be realistic and credible in the context of the scenario: don't recommend a full MIS with links to the IT superhighway for a start-up business with £50000 capitalization. (Don't laugh: candidates regularly do this sort of thing!)
- Use report format to provide clear headings and sub-headings as an easy-to-follow path of recommended actions.
- Wherever possible illustrate your answer with a diagram or model. If you can reduce wordage by the use of an illustration do so. The examiner will be impressed and pleased because you are making his job easier.
- Add a time frame, where appropriate, through the use of Gantt charts and timetables.
- Ensure that everything to do within your answer book is crisply professional. This means taking care in every aspect of your presentation. Therefore illustrations must be drawn with a ruler and correctly titled and labelled.

Unit Activity

This activity is a single question from the CIM's pilot question paper. It is therefore exactly the type of question that you can expect to meet in the examination room. Remember that the examination timing allows you a maximum of 36 minutes to complete this question. At this stage of your studies you will probably find this too tight for a complete answer. Therefore:

- Read the question through the day before you plan to answer it.
- Allow it to settle into your unconscious overnight.
- Re-read the question early the next morning.
- Throughout the day recall the question and using appropriate headings check that you are up to speed on the given market.
- When ready set aside 36 minutes to write a full answer.
- Compare your work to the Debriefing at the end of the unit.

Question
Assume that you are the Marketing Manager for an international airline. In order to take advantage of marketing opportunities your company needs to have a sound understanding of its internal capabilities and the marketing environment in which it operates.

Your company's board of directors has already assessed the organization's internal capabilities and now wishes to become better informed about the marketing environment. You have been given the task of preparing a document for the board, which identifies the elements of the marketing environment that your company needs to understand and explains why each is of importance.

(**See:** Debriefing at the end of the unit.)

Summary

In this unit we have seen that:

- Several bursts of study time are more valuable than long stretches.
- 'Real-life' marketing must be adapted to meet examiners needs.
- The planning process is a staged development which underpins effective decision taking.
- It is essential to define (determine) where one is starting from if a plan is to be effective.
- Budgetary control provides managers with key information in time for remedial action.
- Management by exception presents variances from budgeted expectation in such a way as to facilitate management decision making.
- Management decision making should be reserved for important and relevant issues.
- Quantify risk – never gamble.
- Management information systems provide management with needed information in appropriate form and at the appropriate time.
- Marketing information systems can be within the MIS, or free standing.
- All marketers have a MkIS – for many it is informal.
- Structure provides the framework against which actions are taken.
- A hierarchy is needed to control administration, but more flexible structures allow clearer focus on achieving functional and corporate objectives.

Debriefing

Activity 2.1

A student is concerned to take in knowledge, to acquire new skills and abilities. It is traditionally a passive role that requires the student to listen and to learn. There is a continuing role for traditional teaching but it should be only one of a range of techniques designed to help learners acquire the needed knowledge and skills as expeditiously as possible.

A candidate has to bring out the appropriate knowledge, and illustrate it with the best examples. A candidate has to work under time pressure knowing that he or she gets only one chance to prove capability.

There is little point being an excellent student, a sponge that absorbs and retains a mass of knowledge. To pass the examination you have to be able to select, bring forward and use the knowledge that is appropriate to a given situation.

We examined the differences between passive reading and active note taking in Unit 1. The same principles apply to the student/candidate transformation.

Obviously you are a student while you are learning any new subject, hopefully a student who uses activities to help cement understanding through use. When you are on the run-in to the examination, however, it is necessary to deliberately switch to candidate mode.

In candidate mode you are no longer learning the subject. You are practising the skills needed to pass the examination. This means taking past questions and working out answer plans. It means writing full answers against the clock; it means working up the ability to routinely take a three-hour exam and effectively manage your time and your effort.

You must practise your role as a candidate! Would you learn to play chess from a book and then enter a tournament and expect to do well? Would you study a street map of a city and expect to find your way round as easily as a city dweller? Of course not.

Activity 2.2

Businesses such as general stores and privately owned filling stations are often set up in response to a need and then continually add bits and pieces to their total offering as new opportunities come along. It is unusual to find one that has been audited and restructured to focus on current opportunities. Many are forced out of business by larger and more aggressive organizations that offer improved services, often at lower cost, but usually without the warmth of personal service. Many eke out an existence because they fail to appreciate that stock turn is crucial and that 'the profit is in the last dozen'.

Note that 'the profit is in the last dozen' refers to the fact that when buying a case of 48 cans no profit is earned until their cost has been recovered, traditionally out of 75 per cent sales volume. Thus retailers who meet customer demand by stocking a new line have to be confident that it will not have only short-term appeal. They cannot afford to have stocks lying unsold on their shelves. Incidentally, this need to clear stocks explains why sale or return is often demanded of suppliers bringing new products to market.

As an unbiased observer you should be able to classify the business you have selected into categories, and then determine which are taking effort for little or no return and which ought to be concentrated upon.

Finally, ask yourself if the broad areas of strategy are so clear to you, why is the trader continuing as he is? Will he have or has he the ability to see the need for change and the determination to bring the needed changes about?

Activity 2.3

Your SWOT will be personal and only you can judge how effective it has been. If you are not satisfied that you have penetrated deeply enough then you should take the time to rework the SWOT. It is crucially important that you master this essential marketing management skill.

You should find that you have, on a single sheet of paper, the key issues on which the management of the College or School should be taking action. What do you think ought to be done? How do you rate the chances of its being done? What will prevent the needed action?

Activity 2.4

To turn these statements of intention into Objectives it is necessary to quantify the requirement, and set a time limit for achievement.

1 'Thanks for your enquiry. Our Sales Manager will contact you as soon as possible.'
   'As soon as possible' is today used in place of 'at once', but it actually means 'as soon as possible', i.e. as soon as we can do it. Today, tomorrow, sometime.
   An Objective reply would be: 'Thanks for your enquiry. Will you be available to take a call from our Sales Manager between 11.00 and 12.00 tomorrow morning?'
2 The Trade Debtor Collection Period is extending. We intend to get it back under control.

How far has it extended? What does 'under control' mean? Are we willing to accept that in conditions of recession a slightly-extended period is needed? What happens if some sales people read this to mean 'Crack down and demand the money', whilst others read it as 'Don't let it slip any further'? How can the actions of Credit Control be reconciled with what the various members of the sales team believe this to mean?

An Objective statement would be: 'Our Debtor Days have extended from 46 to 49 to 55 in succeeding months. Our objectives are:

1   Immediately: To stabilize at 55 days.
2   Within 3 months: To reduce to 52 days.
3   Within 6 months: To reduce to 50 days.
4   Thereafter: To hold at 50 days.'

3   I'm going to get an order from this customer.

Any order will do. No matter how small or how big. Sometimes a salesperson is congratulated for an excellent sales-to-call ratio when closer examination would show that the individual orders were small and for low-profit routine items. Another person may have a worse sales-to-call ratio, but be selling large quantities of high-profit goods.

An Objective statement would be: 'I'm going to take 30 minutes on this call and achieve an order for at least £10 000 of high-profit goods.'

4   It is our intention to increase sales of the Acme Dishwasher and we are therefore taking on additional sales staff and increasing our marketing budget.

This is a general statement (an aim) the kind of thing a Company Chairman will say at an Annual General Meeting. How large an increase in sales is planned? How many sales people are needed? How much extra budget? By when are the new people to be in place and by when effective?

Of course this *management* information will not be publicly released, it is highly confidential. Only the minimum possible should be revealed to the competition. Internally, however, there will be a need for a marketing plan that specifies the sales volume objective, the personnel objectives and the budgetary objectives. We shall become involved in this type of detailed planning later in the workbook.

Activity 2.5

Immediate action

1   Isolate the positive achievements of each team member, as well as noting their unfavourable variances. Check back to individual statements to pick up examples to illustrate your points.
2   Confirm diary availability and plan to see sales people in order of their need. This will normally be to visit those with the least favourable results as soon as possible but you may feel that to visit a very successful sales person may provide current information that you can pass on in person.
3   Contact each team member by telephone to congratulate them on the positive work done and then to ascertain their views on the overall control document. Make specific dates to visit, and arrange these so as to coincide with areas in which each person is having problems. In other words, visit a successful small customer sales person when large customers are scheduled for visits.
4   Leave each sales person confidently looking forward to your visit.

Note: It is important to contact all. The least good first, then the best, finally those in the middle of the range.

Activity 2.6

The Australian Tourist Commission exists to foster and encourage people to visit Australia. They are funded by the Australian Government and are established under an Act of Parliament.

A SWOT from the perspective of their Regional Director responsible for Europe – a market of 350 million people – could easily be:

STRENGTHS	WEAKNESSES
Australia is a 'great place'. It is safe. Olympics 2000 (Sydney). Joint Marketing Agreements with States and Territories. High desire to travel among target customers. Single European Market de-regulations. Established by Government.	Internal organization geared to promotion, not to marketing. Distance from Head Office (Sydney). Time difference (communications). Lack of current market information. Budget reduction threatened. Poor management of distribution channels.
To segment geodemographically because of privileged access to data (visa applications, landing cards, etc.). Olympics – 1997 to 2000. Create new products, e.g. eco-tourism. Develop modular packages for visitors to mix and match from. Exploit the Conference and Incentive markets.	Visas are needed. Aircraft capacity is limited. Hotel capacity is limited. Australia's poor image – uncouth. Recession. European languages other than English. Long-haul travel unwelcome. Increased competition from other countries.
OPPORTUNITIES	THREATS

Note:
1 In this outline SWOT the internal focus is on ATC/Australia.
2 The Olympics appears twice because it is an internal strength in the argument for funding, etc., and a major opportunity to attract visitors.

A SWOT from the perspective of the United States Travel Director may be:

STRENGTHS	WEAKNESSES
Olympics 1996 and their overall effect on the promotion of the USA. Large budget. Large market share. Relative distance from Europe. Deregulated air access. Visa waiver programme. Easy access. Good infrastructure. Wider product range. US culture spread by film, video, music, etc.	USA not seen as a safe place. Dollar fluctuations. Racial problems.
Exchange rate – now. Exciting destinations. Diversification by adding product packages. New/emerging markets across the world. Wide range: skiing, theatre, theme parks, eco-tourism, etc. Proximity to Canada and Mexico. Wide range of language and cultural variation. Perceived as an easy flight – no longer long haul.	Exchange rate – future? Olympics 2000, Sydney. Australian Tourist Commission becoming better organized. Australian/UK cultural links. Increased competition from other countries. European Union as an internal holiday destination.
OPPORTUNITIES	THREATS

A SWOT from the perspective of a major customer, Thomas Cook Limited, may be:

STRENGTHS	WEAKNESSES
Up market destination.	Information hard to come by.
High price – high profit.	Training not focused.
Training programme to help us sell.	Cultural image is negative.
Broad product range.	Visa needed and often delayed in
No language/cultural barriers.	issue.
Need to visit friends and relatives	High price.
who have emigrated.	Confused product offering.
Improve retail training.	System bureaucracy.
Incentivize retailers at PoS and overall.	Medium/short haul destinations.
Olympics 2000.	Not perceived as unique – what are
Offer flexible packages.	the product benefits?
Waive Visa need for EU citizens.	Better servicing by competitive
Co-operate with 'on-route'	countries.
destinations, e.g. joint package with	
Singapore.	
OPPORTUNITIES	THREATS

Now consider the effects of these (and your) alternative SWOTs on the (and your) original thinking. You should find that you have new insights into the situation. Within reason the more alternative views you can identify to SWOT from the greater your awareness will become. Excellent viewpoints to take are: your own; your managing director's; your production director's; a major supplier's; a major customer's; a major competitor. Select the perspectives which have the greatest relevance to any given situation.

Unit activity

You will have noticed two things about this examination question that apply across the whole paper:

1 The examiner expects you to have everyday knowledge about major markets. Without working in the airline industry you are expected to have enough general knowledge about it to be able to answer this question.
2 Process is also expected to be firmly grasped. You are expected to pull out the STEEPLE factors and apply them as routine which is exactly what a marketing practitioner is required to do.

Note: in the answer guidelines that follow, the examiner has used different headings to PEST, SLEPT, SLEPT/C and STEEPLE. This is because the acronyms exist as *aide mémoires*, not as frameworks. Build the appropriate framework most suitable to an organization within its industry at a particular time.

Note: the call is for exploration of the exterior marketing environment. Marks as well as valuable time would be lost by candidates who dealt with internal factors and who described or defined an MIS and/or MkIS. It is essential to answer the question that has been asked!

Economic: The state of the economy fluctuates in different countries. These fluctuations affect the forces of supply and demand, buying power, willingness to spend and the intensity of competitive situations. Traditionally, the business cycle is said to comprise four stages: prosperity (unemployment is low and total income is relatively high), recession (decline in buying power and more price conscious consumers), depression (very high unemployment, low wages and disposable income) and recovery (unemployment falls and disposable income rises).

Competitive: Most organizations are subject to the effects of other firms competing for the customers' spending power. In different markets different competitive situations exist: monopoly (the company's product has no close substitutes), oligopoly (few sellers control supply of a large proportion of the product – governments have acted to try to avoid this happening with air travel), monopolistic competition (firms with many potential competitors attempt to develop a marketing edge to build up market share – most similar to the airline's situation) and perfect competition (large numbers of sellers each of which has no significant influence on price or supply).

In order to compete effectively in its competitive environment, the airline will need to avail itself of a number of competitive tools such as route availability, price, service quality or perhaps by focusing on a particular market segment. In general, the company will compete with those firms that provide comparable transport services within a similar geographic area.

Not all elements of the environment will have the same level of impact on the international airline. In recent times political and economic issues, such as wars, terrorism and the recession have played a particularly important role. These considerations need to be made when showing the link between marketing opportunities and the environment. For example, during the recent world recession, buying power has declined and stifled both consumer and business spending. This, in turn, has resulted in a more price conscious customer base, a factor which needs to be considered when the organization makes marketing decisions.

Useful tips
Answers should be presented in a format which would be suitable for presentation to a board of directors. Short, concise report format, with a clear introduction and summary, making use of headings and subheadings, which guide the reader to the key points, would be particularly appropriate.

Approach
This question acknowledges the importance of internal capabilities and the external marketing environment in assessing different marketing opportunities. The question assumes that the internal capabilities are already understood and requires that the different elements of the organization's marketing environment are explored. The answer should clearly identify each of the relevant areas and show why these are relevant to the international airline. In addition, the answer should demonstrate how an understanding of these elements helps in the identification of opportunities.

Introduction
In order to take advantage of available marketing opportunities it is necessary to have a clear picture of an organization's particular competencies and weaknesses. To be meaningful, this needs to be combined with an understanding of the state of the external marketing environment.

This understanding of internal and external factors plays an important role in helping organizations choose between different opportunities and make more informed decisions about future marketing actions.

Marketing environment
The marketing environment is concerned with political, legal, regulatory, societal (cultural), technological, economic and competitive issues. Each of these broad elements needs to be considered in relation to the international airline.

Political, legal and regulatory: These three areas of the marketing environment are closely linked. Civil servants and those holding political office create legislation which is enacted by legal and regulatory bodies. The laws and regulations which are established tend to reflect the current political outlook and have the potential to affect marketing activities. Marketers therefore need to maintain good relationships with political forces where possible. In addition, the airline will inevitably be subject from time to time to the effect of terrorist activity and war.

Marketing decisions are subject to a host of laws and regulatory forces which govern what can and cannot be done. These include pro-competitive legislation such as that covered by the European Community's competition policy and the Monopolies and Mergers Commission as well as the Financial Services Act, Restrictive Trade Practices Act, etc. The activities of airlines have frequently been curtailed by such laws. Consumer protection legislation, which aims to protect the interests of consumers is another important area. A host of laws from the Fair Trading and Trade Descriptions Acts through to the Sales of Goods and Supply of Goods and Services Acts must be considered by airlines when marketing their services.

A number of regulatory bodies also exists which exert control over organizations. For example, airlines may need to consider regulations put in place by government departments such as Transport and Trade and Industry as well as local authorities and non-governmental agencies.

Societal: These are forces which relate to the structure and dynamics of individuals and groups and the issues in which they are involved. The level of concern which society has about the actions of marketers tends to increase when those actions have dubious or negative consequences. Society expects that marketers will provide a high standard of living (offering more than basic necessities) and protect the overall quality of life. In relation to airlines, consumers have an expectation that the transport provided will be as safe as possible, readily available and not damaging to the environment. For instance, the consumer movement, a diverse collection of individuals, groups and organizations which seeks to protect consumer rights increasingly has expectations about the types of fuel used in transport situations, the environmental friendliness of manufacturing processes and the recyclability of material used in them.

Technological: These factors relate to knowledge about how to accomplish tasks and goals. Changes in technology have been rapid over recent years and have an important effect on how customer needs are met. In general, technological change can impact on consumers and society in general as well as influencing how, when and where products and services are marketed. For the international airline, technological change can lead to more efficient and safer air travel and could potentially lead to more frequent and simpler transport.

Marketing relationships

In this unit you will:

- ❑ Establish the relationships which facilitate effective and efficient operation.
- ❑ Identify the outside resources with which marketing must be concerned.
- ❑ Examine the managerial needs in relation to external resources.
- ❑ Understand the need to operate within legal, ethical and moral frameworks.

By the end of the unit you will be able to:

- ❑ Identify the needs of those with whom marketing interrelates.
- ❑ Determine when to use external resources.
- ❑ Brief, review and control external suppliers.
- ❑ Set up effective and efficient customer relations procedures.
- ❑ Use internal marketing to provide a shared focus.

Study Guide

Traditionally organizations maintained most of their primary and secondary operations in-house. The drive towards greater efficiency and effectiveness has brought about an understanding that specialism adds value. Thus we have seen the extremely rapid growth of specialist support services.

You should monitor the quality and trade press for examples of how organizations are reorganizing to become leaner and fitter . . . and what effects this trend is having on the organizations, their workforces, their suppliers and their customers.

Remember – you need current, practical examples to add life to your examination answers.

Plan to take about three hours to work through this unit and its activities.

Relationships

Relationships are about transactions, and not about transfers.

- *Transactions* are about building a series of psychological contracts. About the development of exchange relationships.
- *Transfers* are about one-way contact.

Thus organizations operating within the Marketing Concept work to achieve transactions, whereas those with a Sales Concepts focus on transfers.

Relating to customers and consumers

Kotler specifies five levels of relating to customers:

- *Basic* the simple Sales Concept, aiming for a transfer.
- *Reactive* encourages a buyer to call if there are problems.
- *Accountable* contact with a buyer shortly after sale to check that the product is meeting expectations.
- *Proactive* contacts with customers with suggestions about improved product use or helpful new products.
- *Partnership* working continuously with customers to discover ways to effect customer savings or help the customer to perform better.

Relationship marketing adds a sixth level – one which works to build on-going psychological contracts with customers and consumers.

Relating to the wider public and society

In recent times managements have come to realize not only that their organizations occupy a place within their local, national and the global environments, but also that they have a duty to act as good neighbours within those environments. Thus the relationship approach must extend beyond relationships with customers to include all those with whom the organization interrelates.

This overriding need to foster good relationships has been encapsulated within the concept of *Quality.*

Quality

The achievement of quality in product offering and in relationships has become a corporate objective in an ever-increasing number of organizations. Managements have come to appreciate the importance of the opinions of those with whom the organization relates to the on-going success of the organization. A psychological contract needs to be developed with all who are in any form of contact. (Another way of putting this is to say that organizations are adopting *corporate branding* and marketing themselves to meet the needs of each identified target audience.)

The *quality chain* shows the series of relationships needed to ensure customer and consumer satisfaction. A similar series of chains is required to create and cement relationships with each target group, from shareholders to consultancies.

The quality chain (see Figure 3.1) shows the dependence of each link if total quality is to be provided at the point of use. Customer satisfaction, it is realized, depends on every individual having a quality focus.

The concept of internal customers and suppliers has developed from the concept of cost centres which were themselves converted to profit centres.

Under the profit centred approach each unit within the chain is responsible for its own costs, and is required to achieve an agreed level of profit. This has a tendency to encourage a self-centred approach with each responsible manager concerned to buy and sell where he can achieve the best results for his unit. Thus goods or services can be outsourced because the internal supplier is too expensive. Internal services may be too busy with outside work to meet an internal demand.

In the short term a profit-centred approach looks attractive. In practice, if it is taken too literally, it is damaging to the long-term interests of the organization overall.

Total quality management

TQM has its origins in Japan in the period immediately following the Second World War. With its economy devastated Japan needed to rebuild and were highly influenced and motivated by two Americans, W. Edwards Deming and J. M. Duran.

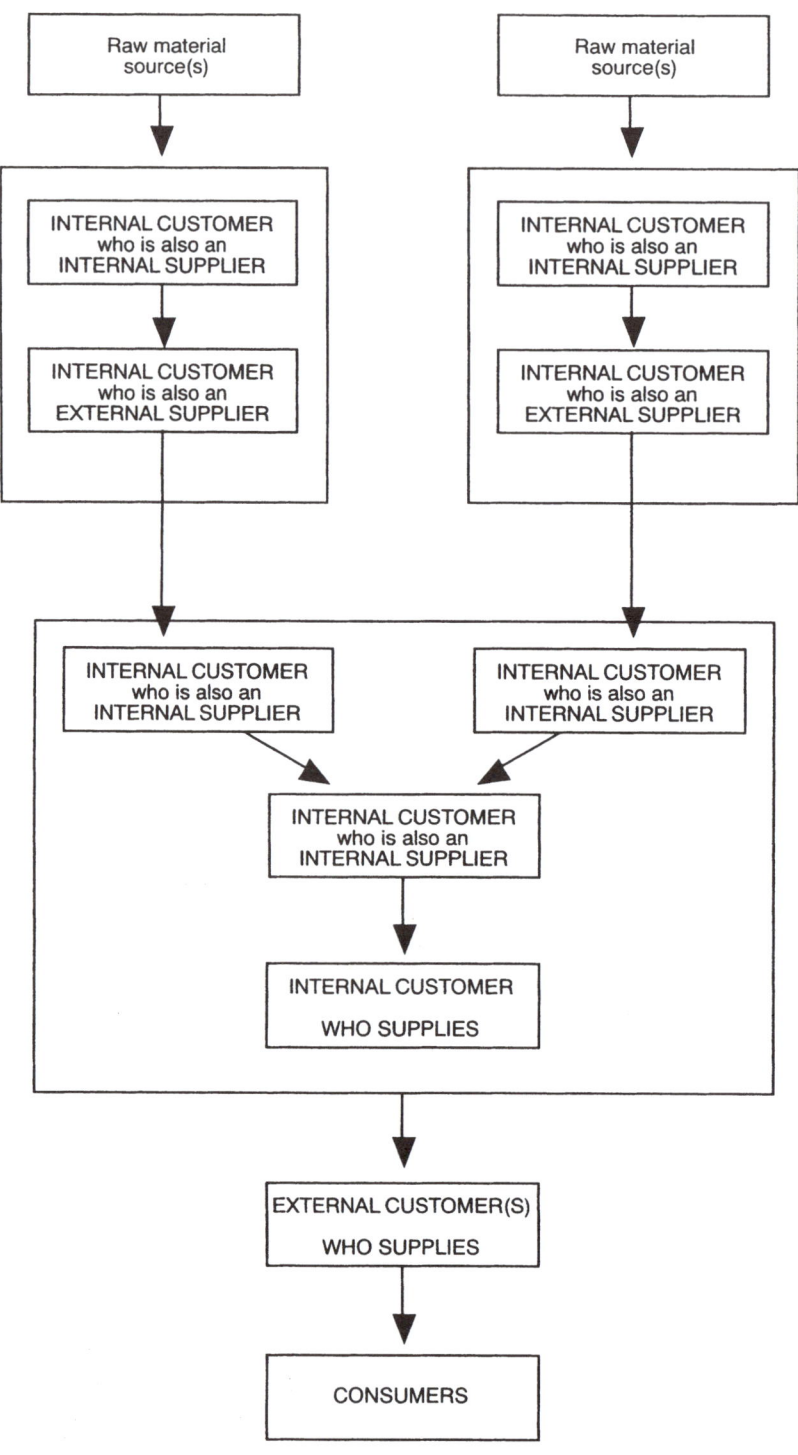

Figure 3.1
Quality chain. (Adapted from *Total Quality Management*, Oakland.)

One of Duran's key ideas was to define quality as 'fitness for use', which can only mean fitness as defined by the user. Organizations adopting Duran's thinking are therefore forced to cease internal judgements of suitability and subject their product concepts to the rigorous and often unpredictable demands of the marketplace.

Deming felt that perhaps as many as 85 per cent of quality problems stemmed from faults in manufacturing and not from errors by production workers. He introduced statistical quality control and this, coupled with his other thinking, turned round product quality in just a few years.

Deming's 14 points are the foundation of modern TQM and, whilst they are a mixture of objective and subjective, goals and objectives, they stand together as of key importance.

1	Create consistency of purpose towards improvement of product and service, with the aim of becoming competitive to stay in business and to provide jobs.
2	Adopt the new philosophy: We are in a new economic age, created by Japan. Transformation of Western style of management is necessary to halt the continued decline of industry.
3	Cease dependence on mass inspection to achieve quality. Eliminate the need for inspection on a mass basis by building quality into the product in the first place.
4	End the practice of awarding business on the basis of the price tag. Purchasing must be combined with design of product, manufacturing with sales, to work with the chosen supplier. The aim is to minimize total cost, not merely initial cost.
5	Improve constantly and forever every activity in the company, to improve quality and productivity and thus constantly decrease costs.
6	Institute training and education on the job, including management.
7	Institute supervision. The aim of supervision should be to help people and machines do a better job.
8	Drive out fear, so that everyone may work effectively for the company.
9	Break down barriers between departments. People in research, design, sales and production must work as a team to foresee problems of production and in use that may be encountered with the product or service.
10	Eliminate slogans, exhortations, and targets for the work force asking for zero defects and new levels of productivity. Such exhortations only create adversarial relationships, since the bulk of the causes of low productivity lie beyond the power of the workforce.
11	Eliminate work standards that prescribe numerical quotas for the day. Substitute aids and helpful persuasion.
12a	Remove the barriers that rob the hourly worker of his pride of workmanship. The responsibility of the supervisor must be changed from sheer numbers to quality.
12b	Remove the barriers that rob people in management and engineering of their right to pride of workmanship. This means abolishment of the annual or merit rating and of management by objectives.
13	Institute a vigorous programme of education and retraining. New skills are required for changes in techniques, materials and service.
14	Put everybody in the company in teams to accomplish the transformation.

Figure 3.2
Deming's points. (Source: *Out of the Crisis:* W. Edwards Deming, MIT Centre for Advanced Engineering Study, 1986.)

TQM and marketing

It can readily be seen that the essence of the quality approach is identical to the pure marketing concept. It is ironic that marketing identified the need to focus on the customers and consumers but it took an engineering based approach to achieve the totality of depth of understanding, involvement and action to achieve the consumer/quality focus.

Building in quality from the design stage is a fundamental concept, as is the development of a culture that expects to achieve quality in everything it does and which rewards all employees in terms of Herzberg's motivators.

Such issues as Quality Circles, about which we hear so much, are techniques of achievement. They will be useless in an organization which has not adopted TQM as its central driving force.

Just in time

Just in Time (JIT) stock control is only possible in conditions of total quality and excellent relationships.

It exemplifies the need for today's organizations to think simultaneously rather than sequentially. Instead of regarding a process as a series of separate steps it is necessary to conceive of it as a seamless operation, despite the fact that several departments in each of several organizations have their part to play.

Quality management allowed suppliers to contract to supply only perfect parts and removed the need for inward quality control, returns, credits and/or exchanges. JIT is a development of this process which removes (or at least considerably lessens) the need for stock storage at point of use.

JIT stock control operates on a pull basis with the initial pull coming from the market. Rather than product being manufactured and moved forward 'just in case', the members of the quality chain now respond immediately to market need. Its success is dependent on perfect synchronization between chain members which, in turn, depends on the free and speedy flow of information.

Ethical, moral and legal issues

Impacting on the planning process at every level, the issues of social responsibilities and management values are of crucial importance. Issues of ethics and morality impact on organizations just as they do on individuals. A major, and technical, difference is that individuals can attempt to hide behind the shelter of the corporate existence: 'It wasn't me, I just followed policy'.

This so-called defence is not tenable when exposed to the full glare of a media spotlight but, unfortunately, some individuals allow themselves to become subjugated to the corporate entity to the point where they disguise, often from themselves, immoralities which they may condemn in others.

When individual survival is threatened, in the very real sense of long-term career and short-term pay cheque, it takes a brave person to stand against what may be perceived as immoral behaviour. It is difficult to know what action(s) any individual may take until he is faced with the decision.

John Winkler, in *Pricing for Results*, asks the question:

You are the marketing manager in a pharmaceutical company in South Africa. You make a life-support drug. Once people are treated with it, they must stay on it continuously to survive. It has been outdated by a machine which now treats new patients. So gradually your market is eroding. You sell very little of the drug, which is costly to produce. There is no national health service so patients pay for the drugs they use. Which pricing technique would you use?

(a)   Cost-plus.
(b)   What the market will bear.
(c)   A morality-based price.
(d)   To match the competition.

(*The answers are shown below.)

Morality-based pricing is, of course, based on a system of social responsibility, management value, and a personal value system. How can one reconcile the three possibly conflicting forces, each of which is a complex web of interactions?

Ethics in management

A major breakthrough in marketing understanding came about when Peter Drucker asked: 'What business are you in?' It remains, and will forever remain, one of the most pertinent questions. One that every marketing director should be constantly answering.

A question that is less often asked is 'What do you stand for?' What values and principles lie behind management's approach to its task?

* The answers, as scored values, are:
(a)   −2.
(b)   −5 They will pay anything to stay alive, of course, right up to the limit of what they and their families can afford. But how can you live with yourself?
(c)   +5.
(d)   +1.

Marketing and ethics

Take 20 minutes to deeply consider your position in relation to each of the alternatives to the following scenario in the light of the examples given in this unit and those that you have collected.

You are a junior marketing manager and have been urgently sent to the home of a person who has phoned to complain that one of your company's vending machines came off the wall two hours ago and fell on to their foot. Your brief is to 'Settle the matter quickly and without publicity.'

You find that the injury is serious. The victim is a single parent with two young children to support and a part-time job that provides just enough to live on. The victim will be away from work, you think, for at least two weeks but will still have to run the home. She will suffer considerable pain.

A   What do you do if she:
   1   Says thanks for coming, but it was her fault really.
   2   Is not literate and has no idea of how to proceed.
   3   Is willing to settle for an immediate cash payment of £50.00.
   4   Will settle for a cash payment of £250.00.
   5   Asks you to make a settlement offer?
B   What do you do in exactly the same circumstances if she is from a cultural background which is alien to you?

Note: The morally correct thing is to call a doctor and/or arrange for her to go to hospital and/or put her in touch with a local help group or a solicitor but you are expected to settle the issue. Considering the pressures on you what would you actually do?

(**See:** Debriefing at the end of the unit.)

Obviously British Aerospace decided that they were no longer in the business of selling cars when they sold Rover to BMW. But they did not have the courtesy to mention the negotiations to Honda who were then shareholders in and partners with Rover. Honda was not even given the chance to comment, let alone to bid! What does this behaviour tell us of the ethical standpoint of the BAe directors? And what damage will it have done to Anglo-Japanese relations?

Remember that organizations do not have moral or ethical viewpoints. They have legal status but are not sentient beings. It is the staff in any organization who set the values of that organization, it is always one or more individuals that have to authorize an organization's actions. Would you feel secure if working for one of the BAe directors who was party to this decision?

Strategic considerations

Increasingly managements are accepting that their organizations have other responsibilities than the economic need to be profitable. That long-term profitability depends on long-term commitment to be a 'good citizen'.

The pyramid of corporate responsibility in Figure 3.3 shows the four levels of responsibilities that have to be provided for at corporate strategic level. Managements have a choice of three broad, overriding positions. They can be:

● *Passive* – and adopt an ostrich-like approach to changes in society and its expectations. Such organizations become, of course, prime targets for the consumer and environmentally friendly lobbies and cannot long continue as isolates.
● *Reactive* – where pressures are responded to, but to the minimum levels found to be necessary to meet society's requirements.
● *Proactive* – where the organization takes a leading role in the development of positive social policies and bases its continuance and profitability on an acceptance of philanthropic responsibilities.

Figure 3.3
The pyramid of corporate responsibility. (Source: Carroll (1991) The pyramid of corporate social responsibility: Towards the moral management of organizational stakeholders. Reprinted from *Business Horizons*, July/August 1991, pp. 39–48, by Indiana University Kelley School of Business with permission.)

PHILANTHROPIC
responsibilities

Be a good corporate citizen
Contribute resources to the community
Improve the quality of life

ETHICAL
responsibilities

Be ethical
Obligation to do what is right, just and fair
Avoid harm

LEGAL
responsibilities

Obey the law
Law is society's codification of right and wrong
Play by the rules of the game

ECONOMIC
responsibilities

Be profitable
The foundation upon which all others rest

An ethical policy has to have a firm foundation, and this must be established at the level of corporate strategy. Managements will, of course, be influenced by the ethics in the nation, culture and/or society where they were brought up, and where the organization has its base. They must also, of course, provide for the needs of the ethical and moral understandings within nations, cultures and societies with which they want to relate.

Fundamentally all cultures call for honesty and integrity; differences, however, occur in the interpretation of what is honesty and in how integrity is judged. Thus what is a bribe in one society is a perfectly acceptable commission in another.

Ethics and the law

Many ethical principles have been established as law within particular societies and, of course, all laws are based on an understanding – explicit or implicit – that they are good for society.

It follows that marketers have to take both laws and ethics into consideration, especially in areas where legislation does not yet exist. There are four possible alternatives for any possible action:

- Ethical and legal.
- Ethical and illegal.
- Unethical and legal.
- Unethical and illegal.

Many would argue that alcohol and cigarettes are unethical, and that they should be made illegal. There is a strong belief that government revenue is so dependent on duty from these products that they cannot be banned. Also, of course, making them illegal may even make them more attractive and open a profitable market for criminals, as did the prohibition of alcohol in the US in the 1920s.

There can be a very thin line distinguishing ethical from unethical behaviour and even the most rigidly held beliefs of one society can be totally reversed within the same society with the passage of time. Ethics, then, are temporary states which reflect the cultural values of a society at a moment in time. They have extraordinary power over individual actions but are in a constant state of flux.

In order to codify acceptable behaviour societies have developed a complex series of laws and codes of practice.

Environmental concern

The concept of ethical behaviour has extended to include an explicit concern for the environment in general rather than to business dealings in particular. There is a growing feeling that products must now be produced at acceptable cost to the environment, preferably to in some way benefit the environment or, at the very least, the producer should show that he has a replenishment policy.

Societal responsibility focuses on the responsibilities of the organization for ecological matters as well as to the general public. Not only is it necessary to produce environmentally friendly products, it is also becoming necessary to produce them in an environmentally friendly way.

Biodegradable and recyclable products produced in environmentally friendly factories are fast becoming the norm rather than the exception. A major issue, however, concerns how these new standards are to be financed. It is one thing for consumers to demand 'green' products but if 'greenness' adds cost will the consumer pay the extra price?

It would not be surprising to see some organizations reluctant to make improvements unless their competitors also made changes. Therefore, the pace of change is conditioned by the need for pioneers not to be forced out of business through the acceptance of higher costs which the public, who demand the changes, are unwilling to cover. Legislation, actual or threatened, is needed to ensure that industries move together and much behind the scenes discussion takes place through Trade Associations to result in agreements and codes of practice.

Legal and voluntary controls

The dictum *caveat emptor*, let the buyer beware, was for centuries the controlling factor in commercial exchange. The buyer was required to validate the truth of the seller's claims, and there was no obligation on the seller to reveal the truth about his offers.

Today's sellers are under both legal and voluntary controls to give the purchaser a considerable level of protection. Partly this is due to the ever more complex products being made about which the customer could not reasonably be expected to form an accurate judgement, partly it is because of a far greater ethical awareness in society.

The buyer has to trust the seller and the seller has to be trustworthy if normal commercial transactions are to be possible. *Caveat emptor* is giving way to *caveat vendor*.

Legal controls originate in the UK from both common and statute law. *Voluntary or self-regulatory controls* are established by the industry itself.

Legal controls

Legal controls protect the customer/consumer with the force of law and penalties can be extracted from offenders.

Common law covers civil wrongs and 'torts' which require the plaintiff to take legal proceedings against the defendant with a judge deciding the facts of the case and awarding remedies as appropriate. Common law is unwritten and relies upon precedents that have been established in courts since 1066.

The law of contract relies upon common law and is particularly important to marketing managers because of their need to enter into binding agreements with both suppliers of services and purchasers of their product offerings.

Statute law consists of written laws that have been entered upon the Statute Book having passed through Parliament and received the Royal Assent. Ministers of the Crown in some cases have the legal right and/or duty to issue Statutory Orders or Regulations or Statutory instruments and these have the full force of law even though they will not have passed through Parliament in their own right.

Statute law covers an exceedingly wide range of concern to the marketer but there is really no way that an active marketing manager can keep up to date with the detailed requirements of the law. The cardinal principle must be to ensure that you have any planned activity checked by your organization's lawyer before you commit to it. This is especially important when entering an area of activity in which you have no experience but it is good practice to regularly check that no new legislation has come on stream which affects your activities. Monitoring of the Trade Press usually provides sufficient advance warning of proposed changes, but the effects of the detailed legislation must be confirmed with a specialist lawyer.

Note that at least 200 laws and statutory regulations impact on promotion alone. Not all will apply to your product offering, but it is crucially important not to miss one that does. Similarly there is detailed and continually changing legislation affecting ingredients, labelling, packaging, etc. It follows that even when specialist agencies are used they should not be trusted to correctly interpret the law. *Always* run proposals across the desk of your lawyer. Always!

Voluntary controls

Voluntary controls are by definition without legal force and rely upon the integrity and self-interests of the individual members of an industry.

Until 1926 there was virtually no control over what advertisers chose to say in their advertisements. Most advertising was ethical but some was both unscrupulous and unethical. The purveyors of patent medicines were especially at fault in making outrageous claims for their products. It was decided that something had to be done.

To pre-empt legislation the advertising business set up the National Vigilance Committee in 1926. This was quickly followed by the creation of the Advertising Association (AA).

The AA campaigned against misleading advertising and established the ground rules which led to the British Code of Advertising Practice and the independent Advertising Standards Authority. Both were established in 1962. Together they form the basis from which many other codes of practice have been drafted.

There is a continuing balance to be achieved between the interests of consumers and of suppliers. By establishing and enforcing Codes of Practice industry and service providers can argue that there is no requirement for government action. Legal requirements tend to be inflexible and slow to change. Voluntary controls can flex with societal changes far more easily.

Ethical behaviour is thus forced on those who may prefer to trade unethically by a combined pressure from ethical traders, the consumers and the legislators. The result is a high standard of behaviour achieved from the traditional British desire to form committees, and coupled with a reluctance to submit to bureaucracy.

Relationships with customers and suppliers

In Unit 1 we established the need to distinguish customers from consumers. Once this concept is accepted it is obvious that all those in the channel of distribution have customer needs which must be identified and provided for.

We have already seen how the quality chain ensures that there is an on-going relationship between suppliers and customers that extends all the way from raw material production to consumption.

We shall return to this important topic in Unit 8.

Relationships with outside resources

Exactly the same principles apply to the need to use resources (suppliers) that are external to the organization as to those which are external to marketing but within the organization. The one key difference is in the issue of *transfer pricing* – see box below and also Unit 7.

Transfer pricing

Some managements make the mistake of treating internal funds as though they are real money. On the surface this is quite reasonable – but internal transfers simply move funds from one part of the organization to the other. Paying external suppliers forces money out of the organization.

Thus, whilst it may seem more expensive to use an internal supplier, the full, true cost-effectiveness of the decision must be evaluated.

The British Broadcasting Corporation (BBC), for example, required their service providers such as their record library to generate a 'profit'. This forced internal 'prices' up to the point where it was 'cheaper' for a producer to go and buy a CD in the high street rather than borrow it from the library! Thus real money was spent and the record library manager was forced into an impossible justification of his service in terms of cash and profit.

Any functional manager calls on others when:

- They have special skills.
- It is not appropriate to add those skills to the functional team.
- It is more cost-effective to use outside resources.

The need for some outside resources is obvious:

- Product manufacture requires a large capital investment, plus specialized management and technical skills needed.
- Legal and financial skills require a long investment in individual time, plus an ongoing awareness of current requirements.

Others are less obvious:

- Distribution was regarded as simply the delivery of goods, akin to the management of the sales team. Sales offices and distribution depots were often located together, under the control of one manager.

  It was only in the 1970s that the importance of distribution as a separate function became apparent. Unilever were one of the first major companies to form their own dedicated delivery subsidiary to specialize in the delivery of goods from all Unilever companies.

  The emergence of specialist distribution managers revealed the cost savings that distribution effectiveness and efficiency could bring (see Figure 3.4). The increasing safety requirements introduced by government forced fleet owners to designate managers to be licensed and take responsibility for compliance with commercial vehicle legislation. Cross-border traffic increased considerably, with components being switched from factory to factory as manufacture became more specialized and, at the same time, long-distance deliveries by road across Europe were requiring appropriate vehicles and specialist staff to cope with the complexity of cross-border documentation.

  Physical Distribution Management is now a recognized skill and the distribution function is commonly either run as a strategic business unit (SBU) or devolved to an outside provider.

The need for other outside resources is sometimes challenged:

- Why should marketing source any of their functional skills from outside? Marketers have the necessary communication and research skills, so why pay agencies to supply them?

73

Selling price – £100

10	Profit	15
90	Costs	85
old		new

Profit change = +£5
= +50 per cent on old

To achieve the same profit increase through sales it would be necessary to increase turnover by 50 per cent!

The cost reduction from £90 to £85, just £5 on £90, produced a 50 per cent profit involvement. This is called a 'gearing effect'.

Figure 3.4
Profit leverage through cost reduction

Activity 3.2

Why agencies?
Take a few minutes to identify why marketers use agencies, why they choose not to carry out the work in-house.

(**See:** Debriefing at the end of the unit.)

The same general principles that apply to the use of outside agencies also apply to the use of other support services. There are two strategic directions that any organization can take:

- To increase in size to encompass all the functions it needs to operate effectively and so have them within the organization's direct control.
- To concentrate on its core activities and draw upon other organizations to provide its non-core needs.

The trend to the core-centred approach has been dramatic. From a slow start it has escalated, fuelled by the success of those who have first taken the route and stimulated by the number and quality of the facilitating organizations that have sprung up to meet the demand.

Many of the new organizations have been founded by middle management displaced as organizations have cut back in the face of recession. They are hungry, in a way that few middle managers in large organizations ever can be, and they have to be cost-effective in what has become a very competitive marketplace.

This general approach has been mirrored even in the procurement of large quantities of physical supplies from huge organizations. The move to 'Just in Time' management is part of the overall move to core concentration with dependence on outside suppliers.

The end result is that organizations are still provided with the services they need, but have gained in:

- The ability to source through competitive tendering.
- Cuts in staff numbers and salaries.
- Reductions in the Human Resources budgets for recruitment and training.
- Reductions in the number of detailed problems that management have to tackle directly.

Outsourcing

Today the practice of outsourcing is as far removed from sub-contracting as the computer is from the adding machine.

Everything from security to plant maintenance and from secretarial services to management can be secured on a short- or long-term basis from outside the organization. Capital can be preserved through leasing, data can be processed off-site; it is theoretically possible for a small team, with minimal financial investment, to co-ordinate a complex manufacturing and sales operation from a tiny office using only computer interface to achieve their objectives.

We are beginning to see the grouping of outsource suppliers around a common focus. Research needs may well involve specialists in fast response quantitative research, on-going tracking studies, motivational studies and piggy-backed omnibus surveys. It is tempting for a client to rely upon a trusted researcher's judgment for the selection of supporting or little used service providers. It is valuable for individual research operations to be able to work with others that they know and trust.

Establishing a loose network of similar providers also increases the probability of the network securing work since any one member who secures a contract will be motivated to recommend others in the network for secondary work.

The client must recognize the danger implicit in this arrangement. Outsourcing depends to a great extent on competitive tendering. If services are grouped (or 'bundled') are the secondary suppliers as competitive? On the other hand, is it worth seeking an alternative? The casual marketer is likely to find that his costs are creeping slowly up because he may not be able to make a case for seeking an alternative in each instance but collectively the results are significant.

Outsourcing control

The major advantage of having control in-house, and within the budgetary control process is lost when outsourcing. It is vital, therefore, to ensure that suppliers have effective and efficient controls in place, and that they are used correctly and continuously.

One should not accept any statements made at time of tender on face value. The rule is to go and see for one's self if at all possible. If a personal visit cannot be made, for reasons of distance perhaps, then control has to be delegated but checked at the secondary level of receipt of the goods or service.

There is little point in ensuring that control exists at time of contract unless there is determination to monitor continuously to ensure that quality standards are maintained.

Remember that the quality of the goods or services you deliver to your clients will be attributed to you. So far as your clients are concerned they are buying your products, your brand. An outsourcer will be damaged by your collapse, but not destroyed if he has other clients.

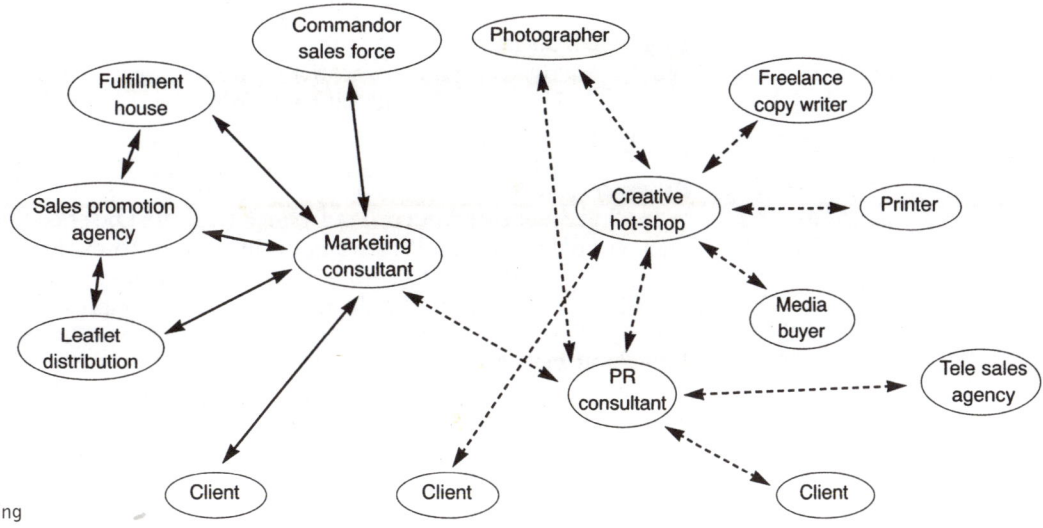

Figure 3.5
Outsourcers grouping

75

Outsource selection

The principles of selecting any external supplier are very similar. They depend on:

- *Clarity of purpose*   What do you want the supplier for?
- *Analysis of need*   What do you want the supplier to provide?
- *Selection criteria*   Specified in writing.
- *Fair selection*   Suppliers given equal opportunities in briefing, submission of tenders, decision process.

Note that this process closely resembles the one used in the recruitment and selection of individual members of staff.

Extending Your Knowledge

Marks & Spencer's were a pioneer in the use of outsourcers. They take nothing for granted. Their Head Office staff are recruited from high quality specialists who are paid well and enjoy excellent conditions. They are required, expected and motivated to at least keep up with developments in their area, and to use what they learn to benefit the outsourcers. In this way M & S ensure that their retail customers are always offered products and service of the highest quality.

Marks & Spencer's are afraid of no other organization. Every firm that wants to tender has to open their production and control operations to detailed study by Marks & Spencer's experts. Global companies who are fiercely proud of their quality control have been surprised to find that M & S have located areas for improvement and these improvements have been implemented to the overall benefit of the organization.

On-going control is rigorously maintained, with M & S having an open door to their suppliers, and an internal system of quality monitoring.

Marks & Spencer were the first major UK retailer to offer a no-questions-asked returns policy. This played a major part in their spectacular success since all the pressures associated with complaining in other stores tended to discourage shoppers. The freedom to exchange on demand (providing the garment was not soiled or damaged) liberated people from the fear of making the wrong decision. Even a change of mind over style or choice of colour – entirely down to the customer – was grounds for exchange or refund, no questions asked.

The exchange policy not only encouraged more sales, it provided M & S with key management information. They maintained careful control over the reasons for exchanges and put that information to use to inform their production control, new product design team, promotional specialists, and so on.

Clarity of purpose

What, exactly, do you want the supplier for? Why is an outsource necessary? How will the outsource improve your overall effectiveness and efficiency?

Analysis of need

What do you need from your supplier? This must be specified in human as well as process terms. It is crucially important to evaluate the chemistry between the individuals who will be working together and between the organizations in terms of culture, style and expectation.

Selection criteria

Identification of purpose and need will enable selection criteria to be produced in writing. These criteria must have the full approval and support of all concerned within the organization. They may be shared with those short-listed as outsources – they may even be improved by one or more of the potential outsourcers.

They are needed to ensure that a 'level playing field' exists and that all are 'playing with the same shaped ball'. In other words to ensure that each potential supplier has an equal opportunity to succeed.

Fair selection

The selection criteria will provide the framework against which each supplier is evaluated by the individual managers engaged in the selection process. It is important that this process be explained to, and thoroughly understood by, each manager. The evaluation of each tender or presentation must be recorded immediately, while the facts and impressions are fresh in the mind. Unless this is done, managers will find themselves trying to evaluate by memory and by confused and subjective opinion.

As an example of the process we can consider the selection of an advertising agency.

Exam Hint

Agency selection has been a regular question in both the Marketing Communications and Planning and Control papers in the Diploma stage of the CIM exams. It is therefore important to be totally confident in this area. It is useful to devise your own methodology – using a proven framework as the basis – because you will then be able to modify your own work to suit specific need. This ability will extend from the immediate examination need to become invaluable in your marketing career.

Agency selection

A checklist can help considerably in making the first broad decision whether an agency is needed, or not.

Checklist – do I need an agency?

- *Knowledge.* Do I know about advertising/SP/PR, etc.?
  If so I have the option to do it myself.
- *The task.* Is it simple or complex?
  Can I actually do it?
- *Resources.* Can I afford to hire an agency?
  Could an agency do it on my budget because of their contacts and experience?
- *Confidence.* Do I need a second opinion?
  Is one available in-house?
- *Workload.* Have I the time to do the task?
  How long will it take? Is there a mass of detail?
  Can I actually fit it in?
- *Staff.* Do I have staff who can do it for me?
  If so, are they experienced?
- *Back-up.* Is there a corporate department I can call on?
  If so, are they any good? How much priority will I get?

Figure 3.6
Checklist – do I need an agency?

Selection is a complex matter because so many subjective judgments are required. When contracting for the supply of raw materials the major part of the negotiation has to do with physical matters such as quality, quantity and availability. Integrity and personal chemistry must never be overlooked but the central issue is product.

People are the central issue with agencies. People, and the quality of their work. Thus the subjectivity quotient is extremely high.

The stages of agency recruitment and selection are:

- **Decide what you need**. List the key elements that must be present and any that must not:
  Agency size – to allow you to be an important client.
  Current clients – none who compete with you.
- **Market search.** Actively search for advertising that impresses. Track it back to the agency. Secure the agency's promotional videos and other background information. Locate perhaps as many as eight agencies who interest you. This is your long list.
- **Produce your short list of three or four by** cross-checking the materials sent to you against the competition and your selection criteria. Seek second opinions from existing clients of the agencies and from the advertising trade associations. Perhaps meet the Managing Director of each agency on an informal basis. Check out how you both feel about a potential association. Are there reasons why he cannot tender?
- **Produce an agency brief** (see later in the unit) as a basis for evaluation.
- **Make a check list of key characteristics.** This will include such as:
  - Track record.
  - Present clients.
  - Technical expertise.
  - Integrity.
  - Market experience: yours and others.
  - Creativity.
  - Range of services offered.
  - Chemistry between you.

Extend this basic list as you need, and itemize the key issues that are contained in each major point. It is a useful tip to list the inter-personal aspects that you would look for in a manager about to join your organization. Chemistry and the ability to work together – to effectively join your team – is all important.

- **Brief each of the short-list identically and in writing.**
- **Set up a panel of three or four key people** from your organization to receive the pitches.

Provide each with a copy of your checklist against which to write detailed comments immediately each pitch concludes and before you allow any discussion.

Hold back all but minimum discussion until all pitches are complete; this may mean up to a week in total.

- **Convene a meeting of your panel and analyse each pitch and each agency.**
- **Take a decision to either appoint one or none.**
- **If you don't appoint consider why, revise your thinking and start again.**
- **If you do decide to appoint do so wholeheartedly; an agency operates most effectively from inside your team.**
- **Negotiate and sign the contract before you announce the appointment.**
- **Be courteous and kind in your notifications of rejection.**

Extending Your Knowledge	When briefing an agency, or in asking a potential supplier of any sort to quote, many managers expect the supplier to carry all their costs. This is not fair, even though you can probably get away with it. A lot of work has to be done to prepare a quotation and you will benefit from this whether the supplier gets the contract or not. In a four-way pitch there must be three losers!
	As you are gaining benefit it is morally right to make a financial contribution. Offer a fair fee for the work that must be done.
	Quite apart from fairness the long-term relationship with the successful bidder must be considered. If you start off mean how will the relationship continue? What will be the impression on them?
	Some firms, when advertising a marketing post require all applicants to submit ideas for their marketing. Although a very clever way to secure a range of free suggestions from talented people it causes considerable resentment because potential applicants feel exploited.

A brief provides the essential information required to achieve the task. No more. The amount of information needed will vary with the agency (or product supplier). For example, a creative agency will need far more detailed information than a research agency. A product supplier may only require product specifications.

Creative agencies that are closely involved with marketing decision taking must become members of the client marketing team. They have to be trusted with strategic level information because they must work from the same facts as the client team if they are to be truly effective.

Research agencies obtain specific information to aid in a particular decision. Working outside of the decision process they only need briefing on the exact information required. Researchers are briefed on a need to know basis.

The principles of briefing hold across the range of outsource providers, both of products and services. The detailed contents will change but not the style and methodology. Use the following creative agency brief as a model.

Creative agency brief

A creative agency briefing may be oral but it must always be supported in writing. The key objectives must be stated and rationale given to help understanding. The briefing session should allow ample time for the agency to ask questions; basic communications theory shows that successful communication depends on the receiver understanding, not on the sender transmitting.

The agency should be encouraged to suggest improvements and should always repeat back the brief to show full understanding. Go firm on the brief only when both you and the agency are happy.

A creative agency brief has no set form since each brief will be unique to its purpose. Key points must be covered in every brief, however, they are:

- *Situation* A full background of your current market position, your strengths and weaknesses, policies that must be taken into account, competitive activity, etc. Often best in outline since the background can be provided later (see Activity 3.3 on the next page).
- *Objectives* The marketing communications objectives and, if appropriate, the supporting marketing objectives.
- *Strategy* How you broadly intend achieving the objectives.
- *Tactics* Possibly not yet decided. Or possibly not in detail since the agency contribution may be awaited. Ensure that the exact position is spelt out clearly.
- *Budget* State the budget, if known. The budget parameters if a detailed budget has not been determined. Specify if you want the agency to recommend a budget.
- *Product technical specification(s)* Details of the product (or service), how it works, what it does.
- *Customer satisfactions* The product benefits, what the user gains from it. The agency team will probably need to try the product for themselves. They should be encouraged to think of additional product benefits and customer satisfactions.
- *Organization profile* An agency will need background information and will research it unless you provide it. As you can give the details easily it is considerate and good practice to do so.
  A profile update is always needed since personnel change both in the client and agency.
- *Market analysis* Market information must be provided. The client, who knows the market, should provide hard information, not raw data.
- *Pricing and/or pricing policy* must be provided.

79

- *Distribution* The agency must know when, where and by whom the product or service will be sold.
- *Evaluation criteria to measure campaign effectiveness* Marketing communications objectives establish the control criteria. A methodology for measurement may be asked for; it is for the agency to provide.
- *Timescales* Specific deadlines for submission of proposals and by when the decision will be taken should be established.
- *Personnel* The names and contact numbers (if applicable) should be provided to show who will be assessing the pitch; who will take the final decision; who should be contacted if further information is needed. It is best to give this information since an agency will want to research the DMU just as you do when quoting for a job. As you have the actual information it is far better to give it than to force three or four agencies to attempt to find out for themselves.

Activity 3.3

Creative brief

You are the Marketing Manager of Home from Home, a new company that will provide a kennels and cattery at the English end of the Channel Tunnel. You have 10 qualified and permanent employees offering a round-the-clock service 365 days a year. These are supplemented by up to 20 part-time staff as demand fluctuates.

You are fully registered by the local authority and are a Kennel Club recognized establishment. You are not, however, a recognized quarantine establishment although you aim to apply for registration in the near future.

You intend to offer a 'Home from Home' service to the pets of British travellers going through the tunnel. (British quarantine regulations are strict. No dogs or cats can be imported without going into quarantine for six months. This applies even to animals who go abroad for a short time with their owners.) You have carried out a market assessment and know that sufficient pet owners will travel through the tunnel to justify your investment. Assume that this assessment is available and can be attached as an appendix.

You have short-listed three ad agencies and are about to invite them to pitch for the account. The focus of the pitch should be to create a house style for the company. You are willing to contribute £400 to the pitch, and your first year spend will be a maximum of £100 000.

Make any further assumptions you need and write an outline briefing document.

(**See:** Debriefing at the end of the unit.)

Extending Your Knowledge

We are living in the age of the Consultant. Many consultancies undoubtedly have great talent, and do a good job. But some are brought into an organization without careful planning and often with no specific brief. There is even a lack of understanding about consultancy types, of which there are three. The Expert consultant is called in to solve a specific problem where he has advanced skills. The Doctor is called in to diagnose the problem(s) in an area and prescribe remedies to restore or improve a specific situation. Process consultants are concerned with helping others to help themselves, not in solving their problems for them.

It is, of course, foolish to hire a process consultant for a quick-fix solution; equally bad to hire an expert when the need is management development.

Management, as we know, is the achieving of results through people. We also know that it is people – individuals – that determine organizational policy. The issue, then, is not how one organization should interface with another, it is how individuals should interface.

The keys to successful inter-organizational relations are:

- *Common purpose* Agreement is necessary on the central focus of the relationship, and there must be commonality in pursuing agreed objectives.
- *Team work* All need to see themselves as part of the same team, with mutual survival a common focus.
- *Long-term commitment* The best relationships mature over time as mutual trust develops and strengthens.
- *Integrity* A genuine commitment to what is negotiated and an openness in dealings.
- *On-going evaluation* Rigorous evaluation of achievement coupled to market needs, in a spirit of mutual support with the purpose of constant improvement.

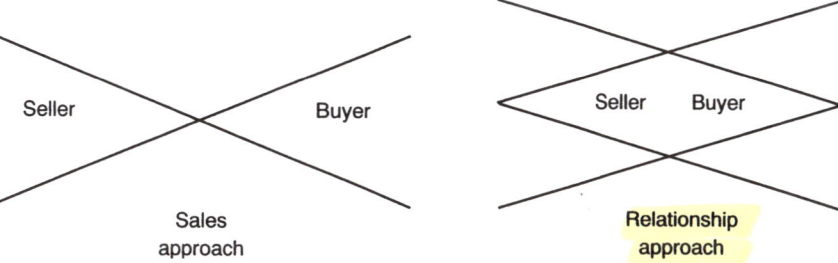

Figure 3.7
Sales and relationship management approaches

Negotiation

Negotiation is a fundamental skill in which we all have some ability. Consider this typical example:

Parent: Time for bed.

Child: Do I have to? Will you read me a story?

Parent: Just a short one.

Child: Can I have *Wind in the Willows*?

Parent: The first chapter, but only if you are in bed five minutes from now.

Note that both have achieved their objective, both are happy.

It is an error to see a meeting, any meeting, except in terms of a negotiation. It is asking for trouble not to prepare, and it is courting disaster not to go into a negotiation targeting a win:win result.

Often the axes on the negotiation matrix are labelled Buyer and Seller but this can lead to a serious misinterpretation. Those with a traditional understanding of 'negotiation' may believe that one party (the Seller) is attempting to win agreement from another (the Buyer). In fact, in any negotiation both parties have something to offer and something to secure. The roles of 'buyer' and 'seller' therefore switch so often that they are valueless as descriptors of the process. It is far better to conceive of both parties as negotiators.

Negotiation is only possible where the parties have a willingness to move. If one party forces agreement on another it is not negotiation, it is duress. If one reluctantly concedes points it is not negotiation it is resentful acceptance.

Negotiator Y

	Win	Lose
Win	Both are winners	X wins Y loses
Lose	X loses Y wins	Both are losers

Negotiator X

Figure 3.8
Negotiation matrix

Activity 3.4

Negotiation
Consider the likely outcomes of each of these forms of 'negotiation':

1 A monopoly supplier 'arranges' a price increase with its customers.
2 An employer, in times of high unemployment, 'negotiates' a wage increase below the level of inflation.
3 A sales person 'negotiates' a price deal based on quantities too high for the buyer to handle.
4 A buyer 'negotiates' an additional cash discount on top of an already satisfactory deal.
5 A home buyer, about to sign the contract, 'negotiates' a further price reduction.
6 A car salesman 'negotiates' a special price for a car that is available but in a horrid colour.

(**See:** Debriefing at the end of the unit.)

Win:win negotiation is at the heart of relationship marketing and the quality chain. Selfishness will prevail unless all parties actively promote the common good. It is imperative to understand that short-term selfishness precludes long-term security.

Before a negotiation it is essential to:

- Define your objectives, in terms of what you would 'like' to get through to what you 'must' get.
- Decide what concessions you might make and what you require in return.
- Decide what information you need and what you are going to disclose.*
- Prepare a simple – flexible – strategy to achieve your objectives.

Successful negotiation requires you to identify accurately at the preparation stage:

- The other's needs.
- Your needs.
- The point of balance.

* This need is lessened when working in a quality chain. It is vital when negotiating in a more adversarial context such as when a potential buyer is known to adopt self-centred strategies.

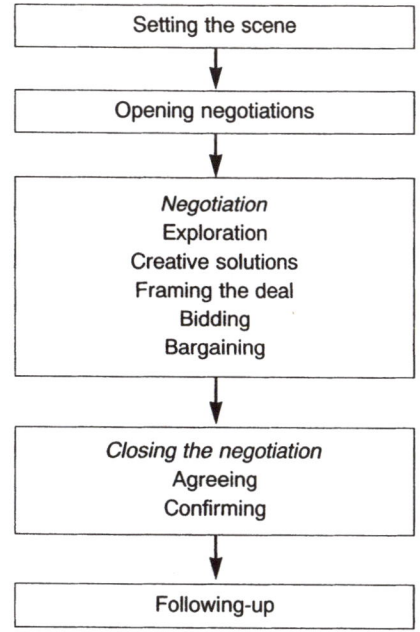

Figure 3.9
Negotiation stages. (Source: *Effective Management for Marketing*, Hatton and Worsam, Butterworth-Heinemann.)

- Value of your potential concessions to the other.
- Value of the other's potential concessions to you.
- How the 'cost' of the other's potential concessions can be minimized to him.
- The other's likely initial stance.
- How you can move him to the point of balance (i.e. your strategies).

Only when thoroughly prepared should you enter into the stages of actual negotiation. These are:

Setting the scene
Prepare carefully so that negotiators are relaxed and comfortable. Breaking the ice is essential before negotiations proper can begin.

Opening negotiations
There is need to secure agreement to the process, perhaps the agenda, perhaps to agree a timetable and an approach. It is essential to ensure that all work to the same ground rules.

Negotiation
- *Exploration* is the research stage. It ensures that everyone has a basic understanding of the situation. Clarity and brevity are important as every party states their position, interests, priorities and attitudes. This is not a time for argument. It is time to ask for clarification if necessary.

  Note: 'Argument' is used in its classic form of 'advancing reasoned propositions or courses of action'. It should lead to reasoned debate but not, in negotiation, to a heated debate.
- *Creative solutions* need to be generated to show ways forward. A flexible approach to the range of options will depend on the personalities and experience of the managers involved.
- *Framing the deal* consists of clarifying a solution from the broad approach identified and accepted. Individuals are able to know the 'value' of the contract (etc.) on which they are to bid. Within the overall deal there may be details which will require separate negotiation. It is important to keep a clear picture of progress, and of agreements as they are made.
- *Bidding* the notion that one party bids high, the other low, and then they 'split the difference' would greatly simplify all negotiations. Unfortunately it doesn't often happen that way. Instead there will be a process of Discussion and Signalling.

Whilst discussing and signalling the intention is to:
- Test assumptions.
- Explore interests and inhibitions.
- Recognize, confirm, enlarge and reward signals.
- Exchange information.
- Listen and watch for signals.
- *Bargaining* requires that each negotiator knows the limits of their authority, and the limits within which they can negotiate.

  The process is one of Proposal and Packaging. The key phrases are:
  - What if . . . ?
  - . . . consider . . .
  - Maybe . . .

  Proposals are suggestions that advance the negotiation. They are stronger than arguments, but they are not at this stage commitments. Packaging is the bundling together of several proposals and counters as in:
  - So if we can . . . then it would be possible for you to . . . ?
- *Closing* cements the deal. It is important to agree what has been agreed. One negotiator should go through the whole agreement in detail and secure the other's approval to the accuracy of the summary. Then the agreement should be put into writing, so that an action plan can be implemented.
- *Following up* is essential to ensure that there has been no misunderstandings and that the agreement is working as it should.

Negotiations are seldom 'once and never again' scenarios. Usually you, or a colleague, will have to return for further discussions. It is obviously counter-productive to swing a deal which will cause either party to regret the negotiation since long-term satisfaction is more important than short-term gain. Especially in relationship marketing.

Activity 3.5

Value

Value is judged from the perception of the individual. What are the cost-benefits to each party in these situations?

1. A wholesale buyer asks for an additional 5 per cent. The supplier offers one free with 20.
2. A neighbour asks for a lift to the station and offers to pay your petrol costs.
3. You have two big dogs and a friend going on holiday asks you to look after his dog to save the kennel's fee.
4. You are considering closing the Medical Centre in your head office. The Staff Association argue that it is cheaper to keep it open.

(**See:** Debriefing at the end of the unit.)

Competitive tenders

Major buyers, notably government agencies, take advantage of their buying power to enforce a system known as tendering. This has the added benefit of ensuring that the strictest honesty is seen to exist; that government servants do not enter into negotiations with potential suppliers.

In fact there is a considerable amount of negotiation to be done, but ahead of the tendering process as we shall see.

Under tendering the lowest bid to supply or the highest bid to buy is accepted.

Sealed bids are required to be submitted in sealed packages that are publicly opened at an appointed time in the presence of designated individuals (often a committee) and immediately processed through the decision phase.

In all tendering there is need to go directly to the 'best' price, since there is only one opportunity to submit a price. The additional security of the sealed bid is designed to prevent any leakage of the details of open bids submitted ahead of the deadline.

Negotiation

There is not intended to be any negotiation within the tendering activity but there are two recognized situations where negotiations may take place.

- Specifications have to be drawn up if tenders are to be called for. A wise purchaser allows negotiation on the specification so that it more accurately reflects actual need. Such negotiation will be with one, at the most two, potential suppliers and it can be of crucial importance to take part in that negotiation. Obviously the aim will be to influence the drafting of the specification so that it most closely matches the abilities of your organization to fulfil it. If you have a machine that produces 25 copies a minute and the competition have machines at either 20 or 30 copies it is a major disadvantage to them to have the specification call for 25 copies per minute. But of major benefit to you. Providing this is not important to the client then it is ethical behaviour.

  Equally the client may not realize that in calling for a machine to run at, say, 60 a minute when he actually only needs 25, he is forcing the costs up unnecessarily. It is, of course, good salesmanship as well as good ethics, to point this out if possible.

- The most successful tender may be subject to negotiation at the instance of the potential buyer even though it is supposed to be accepted at face value. This may be regarded as sharp practice – but might has right and there is often little option but to enter into negotiations that are intended to weaken your position. You are not, of course, obligated to change your tender – but neither is the buyer obligated to accept any tender. He can start the process again and ask for bids to be resubmitted.

Approved lists

Tenders are called for so that the most suitable (best price or cash offer) may be accepted. It is therefore necessary to know that all who tender are acceptable providing that their tender is the winner. Approved lists contain only those organizations who have met the criteria established by the buyer on such issues as: quality, equal-opportunity employment, credit worthiness, etc.

Securing a place on an approved list can be a complex and long involved process, but without a listing no tenders can be submitted no matter what the circumstances.

European Union

As part of the process of forming a Single European Market the EU are opening the borders to different forms of trade as quickly as they can secure harmonization across the member countries. From 1994 all member governments have been required to accept bids for public works contracts from companies in all member states. Technically it is no longer possible to favour a supplier from one's own country, but it seems that the regulation is largely ineffective. The legal requirement to advertise contracts is being followed but the home tenderers seem to be favoured in many instances.

Commercial practice

Tendering, as practised in government, is not common in commerce. A similar process operates for large contracts but with considerably more flexibility. Commercial managers are far more concerned to negotiate a fair fee for the exact job than to protect themselves from charges of misappropriating funds or manipulating a commercial process.

Internal relationships

The Marketing Manager is a co-ordinator of the activities of others through the planning process. But however good the plan, it is only as effective as the commitment of those responsible for its implementation. A clear plan, communicated and disseminated throughout the organization, means that everyone:

- Understands their contribution to customer and consumer satisfaction.
- Has a quantified and relevant objective(s).
- Has benchmarks against which to monitor work performance and quality.
- Is empowered with the authority necessary to be responsive to customer and consumer needs.
- Is motivated to care about customer satisfaction.
- Has the skills necessary to do their job.

A marketing plan has to involve the whole organization. It has to be understood. It has to be accepted wholeheartedly. Every communication leaving marketing is by definition a marketing communication. All should have the same level of care and concern for their effect on the recipients. Just as we want clients to respond favourably and we know we have to identify where they are on the Awareness–Attitude–Action continuum, so we need our internal audiences to respond favourably. The same skills used externally must be used internally.

Even so, there is a strong argument against the Marketing Manager being responsible for internal marketing overall.

Taking the wider concept of an organization's need to communicate internally as well as externally, it follows that each function has important messages to transmit. Senior management need to pull the organization together into a synergetic whole, and so need to use marketing skills. These are probably best supplied by a marketer appointed or seconded to corporate level.

He or she, perhaps supported by a team, can then be responsible for the internal marketing of corporate policies and decisions – within which the operational marketing plan is of key importance. This has the added benefit of removing any inter-functional bias or prejudice and allows the marketing operations to each concentrate on their specific tasks.

Note: There is a strong move by Public Relations professionals to adopt the internal marketing role as an extension of their control of corporate communications policy. Unless marketers actively seek corporate management positions they may find themselves operating in a purely functional role.

Internal marketing

Whoever is responsible for internal marketing, they need to adopt the same professional approach as is devoted to external marketing. A modified communications plan provides the frame:

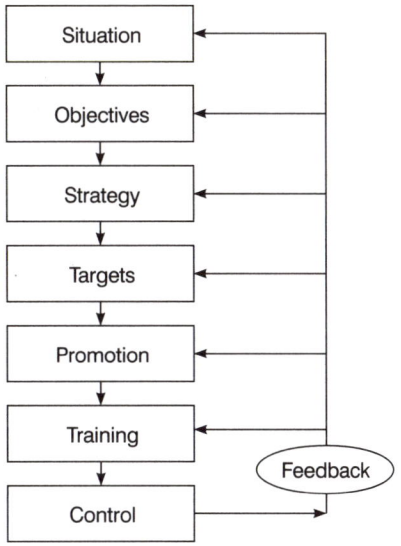

Figure 3.10
The internal marketing plan

Situation

Determine the target audiences with a modified marketing audit. Identify both formal and informal channels of communication. Identify the needs of those in each target audience. Note that there will be considerably more target groupings than in external marketing. Internal communications are complex!

Objectives

These should be SMART but couched in terms of changed behaviour instead of increases in market share, etc.

Strategy

If the objective is change, a long-term view will have to be taken. What is the long-term need, and what are the short-term issues?

Short-term strategic goal(s) will include such factors as new product introduction, procedural changes, and so on.

Targets

Target audiences will range from internal groupings such as individuals, sections, departments, etc. to include those 'exterior' stakeholders such as the organization's shareholders, bankers, lawyers, agencies, consultancies and so on. All must be identified, all must be provided for.

Promotion

Internal contact can be two-way in a direct and intimate way that is not available externally. Target audience members can and must contribute. This is an area not normally open to the external marketer, and is of major benefit when used to its maximum extent.

Opportunities such as recruitment and selection, training, cross-functional team-working and so on are available as 'tools' to the internal marketer. (See *Effective Management for Marketing*.)

Internal communication media include meetings, newsletters and noticeboards – used effectively to *communicate*, not simply as to announce decisions.

Training

All forms of training offer communication opportunities to the internal marketer. Available are such as on-the-job training, classroom instruction (short- and longer-term), distance learning, computer-based learning, secondments, transfers, etc.

Control

Control procedures must be established in order that achievement against objective can be measured. It is axiomatic that objectives must be set, and that evaluation procedures are devised and implemented. Only then can the budget be justified.

The 7Ps of internal marketing

Understanding each of the 7Ps as they apply internally helps the marketer to more clearly understand what has to be achieved.

Product

The product offering is a totality of benefits which must be packaged to make them attractive to each target audience. Change is normally resisted, yet it will usually be change that is being marketed. Why, therefore, should the change be accepted? What benefits will it bring?

Price

The price to an internal audience is measured in terms of inconvenience, extra work, coping with unfamiliarity, and so on. The question *Why bother?* must be answered, and answered well.

Place

The internal marketer sees place as when and where a change will be introduced and implemented. New systems will be resisted (even resented) if introduced at a busy time. Training will be ineffective unless planned and delivered well, and within a tightly scheduled package. Meetings also need to be carefully planned, and held when maximum results can be achieved (i.e. not on a Monday at 0830!).

Promotion

As has been said above, promote the benefits – the benefits to those in each target audience.

Process

Think through what has to happen, draft, pilot, evaluate, modify, re-pilot, supervise. Get it as right as possible to maximize the probability of ready acceptance.

Physical evidence

Change must be seen to be happening. The promised benefits must be delivered – and seen tangibly in some form. If the change must bring extra workload, then the amount should have been forecast, the rationale sold, and the actuality match the proposal.

People

All must accept a new situation, and implement it, especially those in prominent positions whose example will be followed by others. If senior management do not adopt a new policy there is little chance that others will.

Extending Your Knowledge

You can learn a lot from observing where things go wrong but only if you think through what has probably happened and how you can (hopefully) prevent it happening to any of your planning. Two examples to illustrate the point:

1 The Automobile Association introduced a new mobile telephone package in their members' magazine in the Autumn of 1994. But information had not reached their High Street branch staff even a week after members had been told. Bad marketing and worse internal marketing.

2   Mercury One-2-One mounted a high-profile drive for new subscribers in November and December of 1994. A major promise was that all new subscribers could phone anywhere in the world – free – on Christmas Day. This against the background of criticism in the trade press that Mercury connections were already hard to get.

The service was grossly over-subscribed and much consumer dissatisfaction was caused. Members of the public were being interviewed on the radio and television early morning programmes immediately after. Without fail they spoke of hassle, irritation and of 'the company getting away with it.' No spokesperson from Mercury was available and the interviewer on BBC's Radio 5 Live programme was typical in concluding his interview with the comment 'We'll try to talk to Mercury some time.' If they ever did it would have been too late. Bad marketing and even worse after-market and PR management.

Exam Hints

When writing a report, a letter, a memo or any form of note you are presumably doing so because you want to communicate something you regard as important to some other person or persons. The onus, therefore, is on you to ensure that what you write actually achieves your need.

Your correspondent has little idea of the contents of your communication and perhaps only a minimal interest in reading it. We all have far too much written material coming at us from all directions to be much concerned with any one document. Consider:

Much of direct mail is never opened. It has even acquired the sobriquet junk mail!

- A marketing communicator's tasks are to add interest, to get the envelope opened, the contents read, understood, accepted, acted upon. Each of these is a separate but sequential task.
- New forms of adding excitement and/or urgency, to communication quickly become routine. Faxes were at first treated with urgency, now they are as routine as letter post. Marketing reports are routinely word processed, if not fully desk-top published.

If you are not at least working to currently acceptable standards then your work is likely to be accorded the low priority that your presentation seems to indicate. Modern marketers routinely present professionally. Those at the forefront of communications development are exploring more powerful and user-friendly ways of getting their material accepted.

Activity 3.6

Examiner communication
A major key to examination success is to understand the communication needs of your examiner. Remembering that he or she is faced with a stack of around 500 examination answer books all identical in colour, shape and size. What are the communication problems that you have to overcome? And how will you do it?

(**See:** Debriefing at the end of the unit.)

This activity is a single question from the CIM's pilot question paper. It is therefore exactly the type of question you can expect to meet in the examination room.

Set yourself 60 minutes in total to answer the question. Time check your work at 30, 45 and 60 minutes (if you haven't finished by then). These checks will help you to assess how much you can reasonably expect to write in the time allowed, and give you valuable practice in time management.

When you have finished put your answer on one side. The next day read it through and make a judgement on how good it is in terms of content and presentation.

Then compare your work to the Debriefing at the end of the unit.

Question
The following is an extract from a letter sent by a management consultancy company to a UK industrial company. The consultancy company has undertaken a series of interviews with senior managers on the organization of marketing activities with a view to helping in the preparation of the current year's marketing strategy.

Mr G. A. Brown
Managing Director
Brown Industrial plc
Northington

Dear Mr Brown

Further to my recent visits and interviews with managerial personnel, please find a brief resume of our consultant's findings:

1 Poor communication of marketing information between and within departments.
2 Insufficient interaction between marketing and sales functions.
3 Limited understanding of customer needs.
4 Low awareness of the nature of competitive threats.

In view of these observations it is our recommendation that your company conducts a full marketing audit prior to the preparation of this year's marketing plan. This exercise should identify information gaps and help you appraise future marketing opportunities.

Yours sincerely,

J. A. Smith
Senior Consultant

Draft out the contents which Brown Industrial should cover in the marketing audit and explain why it is a useful technique for the company to use.

(**See:** Debriefing at the end of the unit.)

Summary

In this unit we have seen that:

- Relationships are a key part of any marketer's concern.
- Quality underpins today's successful organizations.
- The quality chain links raw material suppliers with consumers through a series of suppliers and customers.
- Total Quality Management (TQM) is a development of the marketing concept to include all those on the supply side of an organization.
- Just in time (JIT) management reacts speedily to the needs of the consumers.
- Ethical, moral and legal imperatives exist and must be dealt with at corporate level.
- Individuals must work within the limits of their own consciences.
- Common law is based on precedent, Statute on decisions taken in Parliament.
- Marketers should always seek good legal advice.
- Voluntary controls exist to establish codes of practice and to obviate the need for government action.
- Outside resources are called on because of their special skills and cost-effectiveness.
- It is essential to carefully determine the objectives for using outside suppliers, and to manage them effectively.
- Agency selection is a time-consuming process requiring much preparation and thoroughness throughout.
- Negotiation is a fundamental human skill that should try to achieve a win:win solution.
- Tendering is a once-only chance to secure a contract. It depends to a great extent on careful planning.
- Internal marketing is probably best achieved from corporate level.
- The internal marketing plan is a modified communications plan that takes each of the 7Ps fully into account.

Debriefing

Activity 3.1

A lot will depend upon the morality and ethical behaviour of your organization and your boss. They should be well insured for such eventualities and so the financial issue should be far less important than protecting the corporate image.

Obviously you could settle the matter in the first four scenarios but the potential insurance claim would net her a far higher payout, especially if she lost her job through non-attendance or because she could no longer stand to work. She could also have private hospital treatment with her children looked after professionally. This would have the added benefit of giving her a break, which as a single parent could be most welcome. Her long-term losses would be covered if the injury turned out to be more serious than it appears.

Settling for any of the first four scenarios would finalize the matter but you would need a written agreement that prevented her discussing the incident or the settlement with anybody.

Activity 3.2

Any argument for the use of agencies that is based on the size of the marketing team is false. The issue is budget and its use. Why spend on an agency when the alternative is to provide an in-house specialist, or department? Obviously where the organization is very small, and its needs modest, there may be no alternative to the use of agencies – but global organizations choose to use agencies rather than provide in-house specialists. Why?

The general arguments for using agencies are:

- *Expertise* — Specialized expertise, in depth. But the big organizations could provide this.
- *Cost-effectiveness* — Costs come out of the commission payable by the media. Used to be true, but not today when fees are becoming far more common and media independents are taking over the media buying function.
- *Time* — Marketers need to allocate their time to planning. Again the big organizations could provide additional staff.
- *Control* — Promotional control and co-ordination is in the hands of experts. Again, why not an internal department?
- *Independence* — Agency staff answer to agency management. Their career is not directly dependent on client organization's management. Nor are they personally affected by organizational internal politics. Agencies can challenge, often unconsciously, pre-conceived views and attitudes that have grown up within an organization. They can put forward ideas unencumbered by political considerations: a major benefit that any internal team could not replicate. Asking 'Why?' is a valuable agency contribution. Agencies can be used as whipping boys, somebody to carry the blame, an important consideration in some organizations.
- *Catalysts* — Agency staff work for different clients in different sectors. They are able to bring new thoughts, different approaches to the discussions.

Specialist agencies are now providing a range of services that previously had to be bought through one central organization. Marketers can therefore elect to manage the process, be it promotion, research or whatever, calling on specialists where they are needed. But this brings into question the very purpose of marketing. Is it a management function? Does it seek to secure the best by opening its thinking to the wider environment? Or is it a functional operation, with high functional expertise? Can it, perhaps, be both?

Activity 3.3

There is no 'correct' answer to this activity since much will depend on your personal interpretation of the brief. Your answer should, however, be close to the specimen brief that follows.

HOME FROM HOME

Home from Home has been set up with a prime focus which we summarize as 'Be sure your pet is happy and safe'. We shall operate close to the entrance of the Channel Tunnel, in Kent, so that clients can quickly and easily deliver and collect their pets with minimum disruption to their holiday.

We are anxious to establish a long-term relationship with an advertising agency and, as a first requirement, need a house style as a focus for our subsequent promotion.

The following provides the key information you will need.

1 Objectives year one
　1.1 To generate a revenue of £500 000.
　1.2 To generate a 20 per cent awareness amongst UK pet owners.
　1.3 To secure bookings from 500 persons (families) for two-week pet board.

---

2 Budget
Our maximum promotional spend must not exceed £100 000 in year one.

3 Strategy
3.1 To achieve fully paid bookings of 20 000 animals for two-week holidays in year five.
3.2 To concentrate our catchment area below a line from Chester to the river Humber.
3.3 Naturally our target market is composed solely of car owners who also have domestic cats and/or dogs.

4 Product
4.1 We are fully licensed by the local authority and are an establishment recognized by the Kennel Club.
4.2 The animal's accommodation is beautifully appointed. Each has an individual and self-contained area that provides for his every need. (See specifications in Appendix A*).
4.3 We employ only qualified staff.
4.4 We are located close to the entrance to the Channel Tunnel, in Kent, and can accept and return animals with the maximum efficiency.
4.5 Our unique benefits are:
- We shall welcome the animals as guests, and treat them as such.
- Home from Home comfort.
- Total safety.
- Plenty of exercise in secure areas.
- Guests' unique dietary requirements will be taken care of.
- Highly qualified and dedicated staff.
- Easy to find.
- Convenient to the tunnel.
- Open 24 hours, 365 days a year.
- Real value for money.

5 Customer satisfactions
Our typical customer will want to take a holiday in mainland Europe but be concerned that their pets should not be unhappy or unsafe. They will see the benefits of Home from Home as:

- They have their pet with them for the maximum of time.
- Our guests will be totally safe, secure and happy; therefore they can relax.
- They will be able to ring us at any time to enquire about our guest.
- All can go on holiday together; no bother with finding local kennels and catteries.
- Drop off and pick up when convenient to them.
- Minimal additional cost, justified by the pet's happiness.

6 Organization
6.1 Our full-time staff are all fully qualified and at least one will be on duty at all times. Kennel maids, etc., will work directly to their supervision.
6.2 Directors will be on duty at peak times in addition to regular staff schedules.

7 Market analysis
7.1 Our market research has been thorough and we believe that a clear market opportunity has been identified (see Appendix B*).
7.2 You will see that we intend to target by ACORN category to maximize the effectiveness of our promotional spend.

8 Pricing
- Our rates are, per dog: daily £10; three days £28.50; seven days £65.00; two weeks: £110.00. Small dogs have a 35 per cent discount and cats 50 per cent.
- A 50 per cent deposit is required at time of booking with the balance paid when the animal is delivered to us.

9   Distribution
     9.1 We intend to market direct.
     9.2 Our target customers are well defined and media is already
          targeted upon them.
     9.3 Specialist magazines exist, dedicated clubs provide access
          and direct mail is available through ACORN profiling and
          national institutions to whom we are affiliated.

10   Campaign effectiveness
     10.1 We shall measure effectiveness through response and then
          conversion.
     10.2 We shall welcome specific input upon this point.

11   Timescales
     We need to receive your proposals and presentation within four
     weeks from the date of this brief. A decision will be made no
     more than one week later.

12   Personnel
     12.1 Your proposals will be considered by our Managing
          Director, Joanna Kennedy; our Catering Director, Charles
          Michaels; and myself.
     12.2 If you require any further information please contact me.

13   Other
     • I shall be happy to add further details to this brief on
       request.
     • We positively welcome your creative input ahead of your
       presentation, if this will help to clarify points or improve the
       brief.
     • I confirm that we expect you to bill us for £400, plus VAT,
       after your pitch.

Signed

Marketing Manager

*Appendices not included in this example.

Activity 3.4

1   Customers will resent the price increase, but what can they do? They
    will actively seek an alternative supply and switch if they can. They
    will harbour long-term resentment, which may do damage to the
    monopolist's reputation for decades and which will, eventually, result
    in some action being possible against him.

2   The employees will resent the employer's power. Morale will suffer. In
    time they will hold the whip hand and force higher pay settlements
    than are reasonable. This cycle is, of course, the bane of wage
    negotiations in the UK.

3   The buyer will not order in sufficient quantity and the negotiation will
    have to begin again when he demands the agreed prices. The sales
    person should have found out the maximum that could reasonably be
    handled and priced on that basis.

4   The seller will be forced to reappraise the situation and a further
    negotiation will be necessary sooner rather than later.

5   He will probably get away with it if the seller is anxious to move or to
    clear an outstanding mortgage. But the action will be resented and will
    colour the seller's approach to future negotiations.

6   This should be a win:win situation provided that the buyer is fully
    committed to the deal and thoroughly appreciates the long-term effects
    of living with what to him is a horrid-coloured car. If this is not the case
    he is likely to create a false memory of the situation and become
    convinced that he was cheated by slick salesmanship. **Note:** It pays to
    put agreements into writing at the time and to exchange correspond-
    ence with the other parties to ensure that everyone has the same
    understandings and commitments.

Activity 3.5

1 The cost to the supplier is either 5 per cent in cash or the cost of the product which may be as little as 1 per cent. The wholesaler will not be happy since he has to buy in multiples of 20 and sell out before he sees the benefit.

2 You gain company and incur no extra costs. He saves his bus fare or petrol and parking fee or, perhaps, gets to the station dry. It is probably unlikely that you would accept money – but you may say: 'That's OK, buy me a drink this evening.' The point is that the benefit would be acknowledged and agreement reached on the need for, or amount of, payment.

3 He saves the kennel's fee, you have an extra dog for a week or so. A lot will depend on the dog's behaviour. The cost of keeping it will be marginal given you have two to feed and exercise anyway. Probably the cost of food, plus a small gift brought back would suffice. But you may never agree to have the dog again if it is badly behaved!

4 The Medical Centre incurs a substantial cost, which can be seen, as would be the savings achieved by closing it. The Staff Association's position is founded on the productivity argument that whilst staff can get advice and treatment on the premises they will not have to take time off to visit their local surgeries. Also that the emergency cover is a valued staff benefit. This could be difficult to settle since so many subjective and non-quantifiable factors are involved.

Activity 3.6

Here are some of the communication problems you have to take into account:

- *Boredom* Marking a succession of answers to the same questions starts as interesting, but as the answers become more predictable, through repetition, a boredom threshold is reached.

  Try to make your answers original. Present the facts in an interesting way. Use current – never textbook – examples. Avoid such cliché examples as Coca-Cola and McDonald's.

- *Habit* Examiners expect the lower numbered questions to be answered first. Thus an examiner can begin marking your Question 3 under the impression that it is actually Question 1!

  Number your questions very clearly so there can be no mistake. If possible, answer in question number sequence.

- *Time* Your examiner has only to grade your work firstly as pass or fail and then to determine how good (or bad) it is. He is working to broad bands and 50 to 59 is all the same grade. He is not concerned with fine marking except for papers which fall just below the magic 50.

  Make it easy for the examiner. You need him to be impressed with your work. The first impression should be 'This is good. I wonder how good?' Be certain to leave white space to set your work off and to allow the examiner to add his comments. Always underline and draw diagrams, etc. with a ruler. Aim for a style that is clear, well laid out, easy to understand and easy to read.

- *Pressure* Results have to be declared by a given date. The examiner has to work to deadlines.

  Again, make it easy for him to give you a pass. You are a marketing professional he will expect a professional communication standard from you.

Use the checklists in Figure 3.11 (page 96) to self-evaluate your work.

```
┌─────────────────────────────────────────────────────────────────────────┐
│ CHECKLIST ONE – Overall impression                                        │
│ Turn the pages on your work:                                              │
│                                                                           │
│   1  Is it well laid out?                                  Yes      No    │
│                                                                           │
│   2  Have you used report format?                          Yes      No    │
│                                                                           │
│   3  Have you used a ruler to underline headings, key points, etc.?       │
│                                                            Yes      No    │
│   4  Is there plenty of white space on the page making it easy to identify │
│      sections of your arguments?                           Yes      No    │
│                                                                           │
│   5  Does it look professionally credible?                 Yes      No    │
│                                                                           │
│   6  Can someone else read it easily?                      Yes      No    │
│                                                                           │
│   7  Would you accept this piece of work from one of your staff?          │
│                                                            Yes      No    │
│   8  How many person hours went into the assignment, both of analysis     │
│      and decision?                              ............. hours        │
│                                                                           │
│      Would you be prepared to show your work to your manager as the output │
│      of that amount of work and effort?                    Yes      No    │
│                                                                           │
│   9  Would you pay a consultant £60 times the hours in (8) if this was    │
│      submitted as the end result of a project?             Yes      No    │
│                                                                           │
│  10  Overall – is it a creditable piece of work?           Yes      No    │
└─────────────────────────────────────────────────────────────────────────┘
```

Any 'no' and you are throwing marks away. Commercial credibility is the acid test of a management report and that means professional standards. Make sure the same mistakes don't happen again!

```
┌─────────────────────────────────────────────────────────────────────────┐
│ CHECKLIST TWO – Content                                                   │
│  1   Does your answer DIRECTLY respond to the actual question as asked?    │
│                                                            Yes      No    │
│  2   Does your answer contain:                                            │
│      (a)  Clarification of assumptions?                     Yes      No    │
│      (b)  Clear decisions and recommendations for actions?  Yes      No    │
│      (c)  Quantified objectives?                            Yes      No    │
│      (d)  Time scales?                                      Yes      No    │
│  3   Are your decisions practical and realistic?           Yes      No    │
│  4   If you were an examiner or a line manager how would you evaluate      │
│      the competence demonstrated in this answer?                          │
│      And say why?                                                         │
│                                                                           │
│      Excellent _____          │
│                                                                           │
│      Good _____          │
│                                                                           │
│      Fair _____          │
│                                                                           │
│      Poor _____          │
│                                                                           │
│      Awful _____          │
│                                                                           │
│  5   Make lists of:                                                       │
│      (a)  Three things which you can improve in your style and/or technique. │
│      (b)  Three things you are pleased with about your style and/or exam technique. │
│  6   Reserve a time in your diary to produce a personal action plan which will build on your │
│      strengths and eradicate your weaknesses.                             │
│                                                                           │
│                            REMEMBER:                                      │
│                                                                           │
│                    Examiners have needs too . . .                         │
│                      . . . are you satisfying them?                       │
└─────────────────────────────────────────────────────────────────────────┘
```

Figure 3.11 Checklists to help you evaluate your answers. (Source: *Effective Management for Marketing*, Hatton and Worsam, Butterworth-Heinemann.)

Promotional operations – communications

Objectives

In this unit you will:

- ❑ Examine the importance of communication to a marketer.
- ❑ Discover the need to study customer and consumer behaviour.
- ❑ Investigate the stages of purchase behaviour.
- ❑ Consider the importance of each promotional tool.
- ❑ Develop an understanding of promotional budgeting and evaluation techniques.

By the end of this unit you will be able to:

- ❑ Create effective communications.
- ❑ Make use of an understanding of customer and consumer behaviour.
- ❑ Write promotional objectives.
- ❑ Set promotional budgets.

Study Guide

Marketing is more akin to an art than a science. Success often comes from initiatives that break new ground, explore new approaches, than from following a given 'truth'.

Certain basics do apply, however. If target customers and consumers do not know of a product offer they cannot buy it – so communication skills are a marketing necessity. How to communicate a given message to an identified audience at a specified time – that is where individual initiative and creative skill are at a premium.

Expect to take two hours in working through this unit, but also expect changes in your attitude to and understanding of what is happening in the marketplace. You should find that you begin to notice and evaluate marketing communications in a far more penetrating and critical way. You need to, because marketing communications is so vital to a marketer's career.

Communication

The need for marketers to be effective and efficient communicators should be self-evident. They are the people in any organization that have on-going and primary responsibility for contact with prospective, current and past customers and consumers. It follows that all marketers are expected to have developed communication skills.

Developing communication skills requires basic knowledge of the communications process, and then the acquisition of more in-depth understanding alongside the development of personal communication skills. Because the topic is so important it is covered in depth in the *Effective Management for Marketing* Workbook. What follows is a brief overview of the process to provide a basis for understanding promotion.

The communications process

It is easy to assume that one simply addresses another, as in Figure 4.1(a). But a moment's thought shows that we take note of the other's reaction. There is feedback, as in Figure 4.1(b). This feedback is reacted to automatically when one is in personal contact, but may be difficult to achieve when in non-personal communication (i.e. when writing a letter, or placing an advertisement).

A developed model of communication is shown in Figure 4.2. This shows the process to be complex:

- *Sender* Working from their own frame of reference, and guided by personal perceptions and understandings ... which probably are not shared by the intended receiver.
- *Encoding* A code is the translation of a thought into a transmittable form. Thus the alphabet is a code, one that is used differently in a range of languages. Codes must be selected in terms of the receiver's ability to decode them.
- *Message* Content must be constructed from the selected code(s). It must be possible to transmit the message along the selected channel.
- *Channel* The medium that carries the message. Consider the difference between a radio and television news broadcast of the same event. The radio commentator has to describe the scene that can be shown visually by television. Note also how television people go to extraordinary lengths to get movement into their pictures.
- *Decoding* A reversal of the procedure, so that what was encoded translates accurately to what was intended. Examine a typical multi-language instruction booklet to see examples of miscoded 'communication'.
- *Receiver* Hopefully will receive the message, decode it accurately, understand exactly what meaning it carries and will be motivated to take whatever action is needed. It takes great skill to achieve this result with any degree of reliability.
- *Feedback* The only way the sender has to judge the success of the communication attempt is to evaluate the actions taken by the intended receiver. What people do is far more informative than what they say they will do, or what they say they understand.
- *Noise* All messages are transmitted against a background of 'noise'. Anything and everything that can interfere with the communication attempt is classified as noise. The sender should endeavour to identify potential noise and provide suitable filters so that the message gets through.

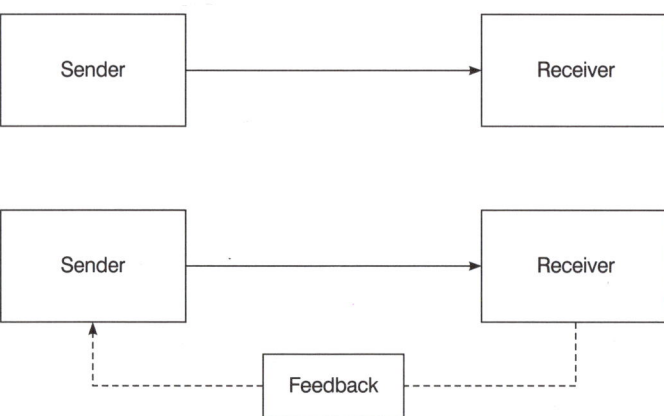

Figure 4.1(a)

Figure 4.1(b)

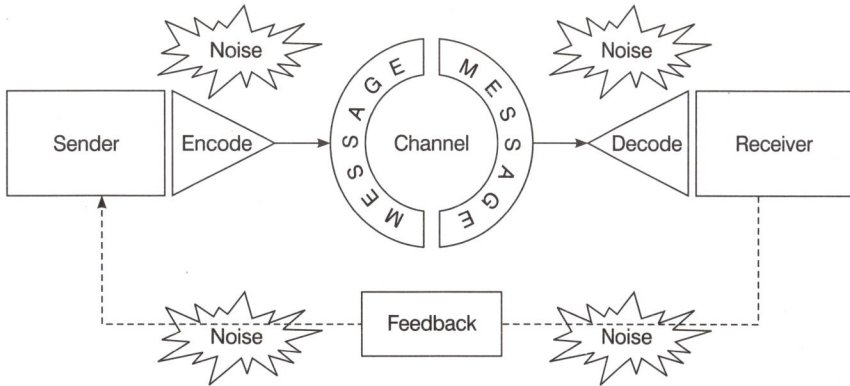

Figure 4.2

Activity 4.1

Begin the process of becoming aware of promotional messages by identifying three product offers that are of personal interest and which are currently being promoted.

Carry out a media analysis by noting the promotions in as wide a range of media as possible: everything from magazines, through newspapers to radio, TV, the cinema and, if appropriate, such media as billboards and taxi cabs.

Evaluate how targeted each promotion is, try to deduce upon whom it is focused, cross-evaluate the perceived effectiveness to you. Locate people from different cultural backgrounds and ask them for their opinions. Finally, ask somebody on whom the promotion was definitely not targeted and ask them for their opinion.

(**See:** Debriefing at the end of the unit.)

Promotion

Marketers use their communication knowledge to good effect in promotion. They know that to achieve success the promotion has to be:

- *Seen* It must be placed where members of the target audience can see it. It must be run when the target audience will be watching or listening.
- *Noticed* Seeing and noticing are different. Selective attention must be secured, otherwise a sweeping glance may be all the notice given. (Research shows that we each 'see' over 5,000 ads every day – how many do we notice?)
- *Interesting and relevant* In the opinion of members of the target audience. Thus the elderly company director is not likely to be a good judge of what is suitable content for an ad targeted at teenagers.
- *Appealing* To as many individuals in the target audience as possible.
- *Motivating* Promotional messages are used to induce specific behaviour change.

Customer and consumer behaviour

Marketers are intensely interested in how people behave. We have seen that behaviour is the one certain way to evaluate communication success. But the intended behaviour does not have to be a purchase. For most of promotional activity the sought behavioural changes are of attitude rather than direct action.

In promotional terms the ultimate desired behaviour change is in terms of a purchase – either a trial purchase or a repeat purchase. But the message has to be more subtle than 'Buy this' – 'OK'.

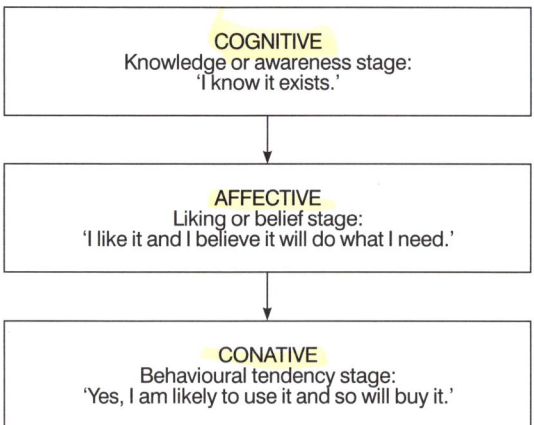

Figure 4.3
Psychological theory underlying
how promotion might work

The need is to help each individual progress through three stages. Only on rare occasions can this be done quickly. Usually a reasonable time has to be taken to achieve the progression. The stages are shown in Fig. 4.3.

This basic three-step model must be further developed if it is to be of help in producing detailed promotional plans. The continuum of behaviour model in Figure 4.4 is a development of the three-stage model for a FMCG product offer.

The continuum of behaviour (also called the 'hierarchy of effects') model shows that each of the three basic stages must be broken down into their specific sub-stages. What *exactly* has to be achieved? Only with this detailed understanding is it possible to produce promotional budgets that target the promotional spend in the most cost-effective and efficient way.

Note, also, that superimposed on the basic model are the promotional tools. Each has a function that should be used with care to achieve maximum return on investment.

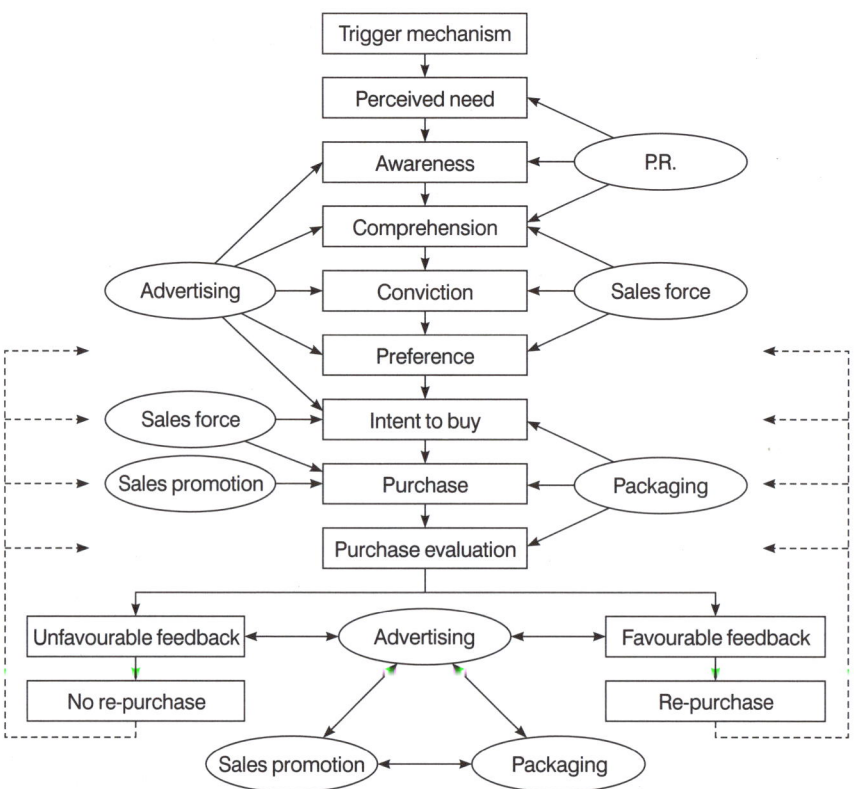

Figure 4.4
Continuum of behaviour (showing
likely target areas for promotional
tools)

Attention, awareness, action

It is possible to shorten the process to the 3As of awareness, attitude and action – but only after the importance of working with the sub-stages has been grasped. The 3As provide an acceptable shorthand to describe what has to be achieved by any given promotional campaign or action. They do not replace the need to achieve each of the sub-stages.

Working with the 3As allows promotional objectives to be stated in SMART terms: 'to increase awareness of Brand X in target market Y from 40 to 50% at latest by 1st July next'.

It follows that one has to know the level of awareness now, and to be able to monitor change. An effective research operation is necessary. (See Evaluation, later in this unit.)

AIDA

The acronym AIDA is in common usage, but is not as effective as the 3As. AIDA stands for Attention, Interest, Desire, Action – but does not identify what exactly must be achieved to attain each stage. Even when a stage of Comprehension is added to make AICDA, the model lacks the needed detail. It is, incidentally, derived from sales – where it is of value in guiding a sales interview.

Activity 4.2

Select two recent purchases that you have made personally, or which have been made by people close to you. Evaluate for yourself, and/or with the others, exactly how you passed through the purchase process.

At first you are likely to think 'saw it, wanted it, bought it'. But why? 'Why?' is the key question that you should learn to constantly ask of yourself and of others. Why did you do that? Why not take another action? Why be bothered?

It can be difficult at first to penetrate to the actual reasons for an action, but do persist. At the same time, ask yourself why it is so difficult to establish the truth.

(**See:** Debriefing at the end of the unit.)

Adoption process

Understanding the process of adopting a new product offer as a regular purchase is obviously of major importance. Academic studies began about 100 years ago with the 'black box' model (Figure 4.5).

This model shows that something is happening between the input of promotional stimuli and the output of customer action. But what? What exactly?

Fortunately the CIM does not require its candidates to have a detailed knowledge of the studies of buying behaviour, but you should be aware that detailed studies exist, and you will find it beneficial to examine them as part of your own self-development.

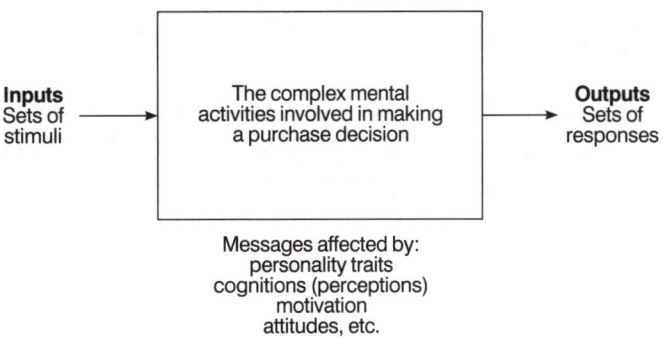

Figure 4.5
The black box model of buying behaviour

At this time it is only necessary to explain one key model, that developed by Howard and Sheth in the 1960s.

The Howard and Sheth model is in four parts because they were able to show that four issues are of key importance. Their studies show that buyer behaviour is affected by:

- *Inputs* Individuals receive inputs from three key sources:
  - *Significative* Including such factors as the promoted item's quality, price, distinctiveness, service and availability. But seen in functional terms.
  - *Symbolic* The same qualities, but taking into account the explicit and implicit messages such as are conveyed by branding, i.e. status, reward, confidence, etc.
  - *Social* Including such things as the influence of the family, of reference groups and of social class.
    - i.e. The inputs from the marketer are seen in the context of the function to be obtained and, more importantly, how the product offer fits within the psychological background and needs of the individual.
- *Perception* Whilst perhaps making an overt search for a product offer to meet their needs individuals are always working within an environment. Factors that impinge include: how to secure their attention, what perceptual bias they may already have created and any ambiguity in the messages that reach their conscious and unconscious minds.
  - i.e. The past and present experiences of each individual come together to affect current messages. Past experience works as a filter to exclude 'known' disliked or distrusted brands, etc.
- *Learning* Individuals learn through experience. They develop confidence in their decisive capability, and in individual brands. Their motivation to act is increased or decreased by a number of factors, among them the level of satisfaction attained from previous purchases. They develop an advanced brand comprehension and use this, together with motivation and attitude, to develop a set of 'choice criteria'.
  - i.e. Intention to purchase comes only after all the internally established choice criteria have been met. To a great extent these are learned, which goes most of the way to show why it is easier to make a repeat sale than a first sale.
- *Outputs* After the initial purchase the individual puts the product offer into use and feeds back the results into his learning, especially into the section labelled 'satisfaction'. The more positive the feedback, the more likely that repeat purchasing will occur. The more often a repeat purchase is made, the less likely that a competitor will be able to induce a brand switch.
  - i.e. It is far better, and far cheaper, to retain existing customers than to constantly seek new ones. (Obviously new customers are needed, but existing ones must be well serviced so that they remain loyal . . . and also tell others by example or by actual recommendation.)

Extending Your Knowledge

A brand almost attains a personality within the minds of members of its target audience(s). This can have a major effect on purchase behaviour because people learn to trust the products marketed under a particular brand.

Having bought and been pleased with a Bosch electric drill, say, it is far more likely that the next purchase will be a Bosch saw, and not one from Black & Decker. This belief in one brand can easily extend to a distrust of, even an aversion to, other brands. Dislike of, or bad service from, a branded product can cause an individual to avoid all other products carrying that brand. More positively, good service from one product can help build a preference for the brand, and therefore for other products that carry that brand.

Hence marketing managers must do everything possible to ensure that a consistent level of quality and service extends across a brand family.

If a lower or higher quality product is to be launched it should normally not carry the same brand. The only exception may be if the brand is qualified 'XYZ De Luxe' or 'XYZ Economy'.

We shall return to branding in Unit 6.

Decision making unit (DMU)

Remember that every purchase decision has a DMU behind it. You will have met the DMU in your previous studies, but may not have been introduced to the SPADE/F acronym. This shows that a DMU is made up of:

- *Starter* Somebody or something must begin the decision process. It may be as simple as an empty jar, or as overt as a TV commercial.
- *Purchaser* Somebody has to actually make the purchase. But the buyer may have no decisive capacity – as when a child is buying to a parent's instructions.
- *Advisor* Advice comes from many quarters: other users, past experience, advertising, etc.
- *Decider* The person who actually makes the decision to buy. There is always a person who makes this decision, but the salesperson may not be able to meet him or her.
- *End-User* The person who uses up the value of the purchase – sometimes with an influence on the purchase, often not.
- *Financier* Whoever provides the finance to allow the purchase to go ahead – a Building Society Manager, the Chief Accountant, a parent, etc.

Decision making process (DMP)

Again, you will have met the DMP. Remember that all purchase decisions follow a process. This will operate within the context of the adoption process described above. The DMP stages are:

- *Define the problem* What, exactly, is the situation that needs to be addressed?
- *Analyse the situation* Discover all the relevant facts.
- *Identify actions* Identify all the possible courses of action.
- *Establish criteria* Set out the criteria against which the possible actions can be evaluated.
- *Select a course of action* Having eliminated the impossible and unsuitable, select a specific course of action.
- *Implement* Go ahead and make the purchase.
- *Evaluate* Make a judgement on the degree of success of the *whole process* so that you can be more efficient and effective next time.

Note: The DMU and DMP are more complex in business-to-business purchase decisions. See Unit 11.

Marketing strategy

In Unit 2 it was said that marketing strategies are based on three key issues:

- Segmentation of profiled target markets.
- Positioning.
- Differential advantage.

Segmentation and profiling were covered in Unit 1. It is now time to put positioning and differential advantage into place.

Positioning

In promotion, and therefore in marketing strategy terms, positioning is the establishment of a concept, product, brand, etc., clearly and distinctly in the minds of individuals in the target audience(s).

Try Activity 4.3 to establish the importance of positioning.

Activity 4.3

Select six national or regional newspapers, or six glossy magazines. Take each in turn and place it in a context of who would read it – the *Daily Express* would be read by . . .; the *Daily Telegraph* by . . . and so on.

The easier you find this, the more firmly the title is positioned in your mind.

The more detailed the profile that you can create, the more clearly the publication and its promotion have been focused.

(**See:** Debriefing at the end of the unit.)

A Positioning Statement is marketing's equivalent of a corporate Mission Statement. For each brand a statement is prepared that encapsulates the inherent qualities of the brand in terms of what it means to the consumer. This statement is vitally important, such that it will usually take several months to write, polish and perfect. It will usually be approved at Board level, and remain the central guiding force against which all promotional planning is tested.

Some blue chip organizations mount their brand positioning statements in meeting rooms and read them aloud at the beginning of promotional planning meetings. They are that important!

Differential advantage

Product offers need to be distinctive if they are to stand apart from their competitors. Distinctiveness gives advantage, and advantage can be one of two kinds:

- *Distinct advantage* is an inherent advantage that is held by the product offer and by none of its competitors.
  Nescafé had a distinct advantage for the first 25 years of its life because it was a unique product that had the protection of a patent. As soon as competitors were able to replicate the product the Nescafé marketers were forced to create differential advantages.
- *Differential advantage* is created to provide a unique positioning for the product offer. A famous example is Avis, who created a differential advantage because they 'Tried Harder'.

Media

Fortunately no marketer needs to become a media expert. This is an extremely dynamic business, and specialist media agencies exist to maximize the impact obtained from any given promotional budget.

Basic facts regarding the different media must be known, of course, as must the best utilization. Figure 4.6 (pages 106 and 107) sets out the key facts for the major media types.

Targeted media

The number of media is constantly increasing, and with each increase the competition increases also. A media owner has as much need of marketing as any other business person and so researches non-targeted niches in the market for which specialist media can be developed. Provided there are enough marketers, with large enough budgets, who want to reach that niche the publisher has a viable product.

Media owners hold profiles of their readership, based in ACORN or MOSAIC, and so it is a relatively easy matter to match the profile of each target audience against the media and so discover which is most suited to a particular need.

New technology

Technological developments are opening up major opportunities to the alert marketer. An example:

When a retailer seeks approval for a credit card purchase from Visa a security validation is now also included. Individual purchase behaviour is monitored and if the proposed purchase is out of the normal pattern the transaction is flagged for a detailed identity check. This is a major step in the fight against credit card fraud but has not been used in Visa's promotion to the public. It is, however, a strong selling point to the trade.

Technological advances are so rapid that only current media can hope to keep abreast of them. For that reason you are advised to monitor the specialist press, and to keep alert to the possibilities that are opening up almost every day.

A major change that is sweeping through all forms of marketing is the new ability to interact directly with the customer and consumer. Sky Digital television, for example, offers a special deal to those subscribers who connect their TV to Sky through a modem. It allows them to interact with Sky – and, of course, with clients of Sky. It also allows Sky to interrogate each TV and so collect accurate research data.

In the management of marketing these are typical of today's key issues:

- The PC and the database are becoming essential parts of a marketer's personal equipment.
- Telemarketing, now supported by auto-dialling equipment, is becoming ever more efficient and is extending into ever wider areas.
- Electronic communications mean that paper-free memos, reports, copy, visuals, even design blueprints, can be passed between individuals in different continents, annotated, adapted, agreed and approved for action.
- Forecasters can use highly complex models that can be accessed easily and routinely.
- Video-conferencing – and video phones – can open up face-to-face contact.
- Fax, answer machines and e-mail mean that nobody need be inaccessible.
- Personal phones, and personal phone numbers, will soon liberate us from wired phone points.
- Database marketing is becoming available to even small organizations.
- Internal data can automatically be interrogated for management information.
- Real-time reporting is routinely available to the major retailer's internal and confidential systems.
- Cable and satellite systems are set to revolutionize targeting, with individuals in households – and neighbours of individuals in households – being 'narrowbanded'; i.e. if the next-door neighbour buys a new hi-fi you might be offered a soundproofing system.
- Multimedia through the computer, as well as the TV, will affect every link in the marketing chain: salespeople will run video demonstrations; video booths will open direct visual access to staff in organizations; product development groups will interact with research focus groups; digital assistance will prompt marketing research interviewers, who will record data electronically; market analysis software will allow data to be cut, compared, adapted, accessed in ways that are currently impossible.
- Touch-screen contact will extend into the home to allow fully interactive contact.
- Fibre-optic, laser and ever faster chip technology are the current foundations of the new communications 'superhighway' that is about to open for traffic.

These changes are happening gradually, and it is easy to miss the developments and to wake up one morning and suddenly discover that something new has happened. The analogy is with a parent and child. The child grows slowly, but the parent doesn't realize until – suddenly – the

		TV	Radio	Cinema	Press Daily, Evening and Sunday	Press Regional	Press Magazines	Posters	Direct mail
AUDIENCE	Audience size	Some wastage, large and national (some international)	National and tightly segmented local coverage	Small, no national coverage	Large and mostly national	Small, no national networks	Mostly national (and international)	National coverage is difficult	Large national and international
	Audience type	Few 15–24-year-olds	Many housewives, commuters	Many 15–24-year-olds	Socio-economic	Geographic segments	Lifestyle segments	Commuters, car drivers etc.	Any target available
	Audience state of mind	Relaxed and passive TV couch potato = visual wallpaper	Background/audio wallpaper	Captive audience – willing suspension of disbelief	Deliberately read		Relaxed and involved with magazine		
COSTS	Cost of production	High	Low	High	Low–Med.	Low	Low–Med.	Med.	Low
	Minimum cost of space	High	Low	Low	Med.	Low	Low–Med.	Low–Med.	High but can experiment in small quantities
	Average cost per thousand	Low less than £2	Very Low less than £1		Low–Med. £8	Med. £30	Med. £12–£70		High £500
	Extra advantages	Adds credibility to product or company	Transportable medium	High impact and captive audience					

	TV	Radio	Cinema	Press			Posters	Direct mail
				Daily, Evening and Sunday	Regional	Magazines		
MESSAGE								
Variable/senses	Sight, sound, colour, movement, time constraint	Sound and time constraint	Big impact enhanced sight and sound	Mostly black and white, some colour	Black and white	4-colour	4-colour big impact	4-colour and 3-D possibility
Serial ad sequence	Viewed serially – no competition from other ads or editorial but zap	Serially, less zapping	Serially and no zapping	Must compete with other ads and editorial on same page			Ad clutter	
Transitory	Highly transitory since you cannot refer back to ad once shown (unless taped)			Can keep clippings or refer back if desired			Can refer back, walk back or drive past	Can refer back/keep coupon
Demonstration	Ideal for usage and impulse purchases	Difficult	Yes	Benefits or results can be shown but not product usage demonstration			Only short image benefit	Yes
Detail/technical	Viewer cannot absorb detail	No urgency and topicality	No	Yes	Yes	Yes	No	Yes
Urgency/topicality rub-off	No	Unique immediacy urgency and topicality	No	Yes	No	Magazine image spills onto ad	Cult image?	
Flexible	Inflexible and pre-emptible	Flexibility		Flexible			Inflexible	Flexible
EASE OF MEDIA BUYING								
Lead times	Long	Short	Long	Short			Long	Short
Clearance	Script (1 week) finished film (1 week) ITC	Same day clearance ITC	One week clearance cinema ad and assoc.	Code of advertising practice (clearance is not compulsory)				
Audience research	BARB and TGI	RAJAR	CAVIAR	NRS	JICREG	NRS and ABC	OSCAR	
High frequency facility	Hourly and daily	Hourly and daily	No	Yes	Weekly	Weekly/monthly		
National coverage	Expert's job but network exists and international cable/satellite	No national network		Yes	No national network		Difficult	

Figure 4.6 Summary of media characteristics. (Source *Marketing Communications – an Integrated Approach*, P. R. Smith, Kogan Page, London 1993.)

child can reach something that was previously safe from sticky hands. Grandparents notice, because they see the child at intervals. Many a parent has said 'If only I had taken photos, recorded the changes . . .' As a student of marketing you need to 'take photos and record the changes' so that you are at least with, if not ahead of, the game and can benefit from the opportunities.

Direct marketing

As we shall see in Unit 8, direct marketing is a channel of distribution that allows a manufacturer or supplier to bypass the traditional wholesale – retail chain.

It has been argued – wrongly – that direct marketing is a form of promotion. A moment's thought shows that direct marketers use the tools of promotion, but that they act as sellers with the need to contact their clients with promotion and then ensure that their product offerings reach the purchasers.

Direct mail, of course, is still used. It is now regarded as part of direct marketing, along with the other forms of direct and interactive contact with customers and consumers.

The Internet and the World Wide Web are set to become major marketing vehicles. Already companies such as Dell and Apple Computers and the 'world's biggest book shop' are claiming turnovers in millions of dollars per month. A major block has been, and to some extent still is, the problem of security of credit card and personal data. Much attention is being focused on these issues and shortly they will be resolved. Then a trading revolution leading to an explosion in volume is forecast.

Marketing through the Internet is opening up new creative opportunities. At first standard press and TV visuals and approaches have been used. Gradually, however, we shall see specialized communication techniques being developed as this new medium's potentials are explored.

Extending Your Knowledge

Direct Line Insurance was formed by the Royal Bank of Scotland in the early 1980s on the initiative of one man who foresaw the opportunity to break into the motor insurance market using new technology. Traditionally Underwriters provided the product (the policy), and Brokers sold it to the customer, who is also often the consumer. Brokers work on a 15 per cent commission, and carry no risk. Underwriters had no sales operation.

Direct Line realized that IT made it possible for them to exclusively operate through direct selling. That the traditional 'push' methods of distribution could be replaced with a 'pull' strategy.

They invested in an Expert System database and started with a carefully targeted market segment – individuals aged 35–50 driving a limited number of car models. They used the freephone 0800 service as their only sales contact, and invested heavily in direct response promotion using all the main media – posters, press and television. They also actively sponsored popular but minority sports, particularly tennis.

Traditional insurers felt that products sold down the telephone could not be differentiated – some felt that insurance was a commodity market. Traditionalists felt it important to make the buying experience 'memorable', and that the brokers' closeness and personal service were vital factors.

It transpired that the traditional view was wrong. People responded extremely well to the Direct Line approach, and obviously were prepared to deal by telephone – to be their own brokers, as it were.

As Direct Line's experience grew, and as their database expanded, they widened the range of risks they were prepared to carry. Moving one step at a time they extended the range of models, and the ages of the drivers, until they could offer a wide range of cover. They do not – and will not – cover everybody. They carefully assess the risks they are prepared to underwrite, and the premium to be charged.

Experience has shown that the more detailed the information obtained from the clients, the more accurate the quotation. Different risk factors are associated with the same car model depending on issues such as colour, the number of doors and the fitting of a sunroof. Not factors which would have been thought significant a couple of decades ago.

Service is important in the motor insurance market. Direct Line, again through their Expert System, have built a reputation for the speed with which they process claims. It is commonplace for the Direct Line notification of a claim to arrive at a broker's in the same post as the initial contact from their client.

Direct Line's approach minimizes the costs of operation because they can site their telesales anywhere they choose – no need for a high street presence. They open longer hours – allowing sales to be made in the evenings and at weekends when their customers are free to get to the telephone. Their system allows them to assess the probability of fraud and so to determine which claims to investigate and which to accept. Their overall cost savings are passed on to the customer in reduced premiums and added benefits. In 1994, for example, they became the first insurer to offer a 70 per cent no-claims discount to older drivers.

Not everybody wants to use a direct writer, of course. But Direct Line, and its followers, have revolutionized the motor insurance market.

Expert system

An Expert System is a database which reacts in real-time.

The British Airways booking system is expert because all loading information on all aircraft is tracked. As one seat is booked or cargo is sold the aircraft status changes instantly. Thus a customer can be offered a seat, check his or her diary, and in that moment find that the seat has been sold elsewhere in the world.

The benefits are obvious: management has an accurate source of reliable information that is always current, and customers can be immediately satisfied. The high cost of design, installation and maintenance is more than offset by the benefits it brings to the organization.

Activity 4.4

This is question 7 from the December 1997 Promotional Practice examination. Take time to analyse it before preparing an outline answer. Then compare your thinking to the specimen answer provided at the end of the unit.

The question is: Assess the implications of the predicted growth in interactive technology for regulation within the promotional industry.

(**See:** Debriefing at the end of the unit.)

Evaluation

As you should be well aware by now, the most valid evaluation comes from the establishment of SMART objectives as a basis for the activity. For that reason we examine promotional objectives and promotional budgeting before coming to evaluation.

Promotional objectives

There is a danger, especially amongst non-marketers, of an assumption that there is a linear relationship between promotional spend and sales. Thus some try to use factual measures of success:

- How much business is generated for each unit of spend in advertising?
- How much from the overall spend on advertising and sales?
- Etc.

The problem with this approach is that whilst the end result will be counted in numbers – eventually in profit or loss terms – the individual achievements needed to ensure overall success are often non-numeric. The move through the 3As, as we know, has to be achieved in sub-stages each of which affects behaviour. And behaviour is difficult to measure.

Thus awareness and attitude objectives can only be non-numeric. Even the Action stage requires some non-numeric evaluation since a purchase may be prevented by circumstances such as an out-of-stock position.

Promotional objectives can quite easily be written:

- To generate by 31st July an awareness of Product A in 20% of Target Market 3.
- To create by 31st July a favourable attitude towards Product B in 45% of Target Market 1.
- To stimulate by 31st July purchase intention for Product C in 15% of Target Market 2.
- To achieve sales in the week of 1st August of 2000 cases of Product D by members of Target Market 5.

Easy to write – but fiendishly difficult to evaluate!

- *Awareness* – what, exactly, is meant? What response will indicate that a person is sufficiently aware of the product? Simple recognition of the label, or of the branding overall?
- *Attitude* is extremely difficult to define, let alone to measure. But unless there is a clear definition *in writing* a researcher cannot measure attitude. It is *not* sufficient to say 'Well, we all know what we mean'.
- *Purchase intention* is a form of attitude. It is easy to build desire – many have an intention to buy a house in the country, to run two or three cars, to send their kids to good schools and on to university. But is this a dream or a serious intention?
  If an intention is thwarted, how will this be known?
- *Sales achievement* should be easy to measure . . . but how does one know who has made the purchase? It could easily be that the sales were made to another segment altogether, as with the Yorkie bar. Targeted at youngsters, it was bought in quantity by young women.

The major promotional objectives must be set in terms of desired behaviour, and effective action can only be taken when this has been done. Thus there is need to measure the number of prospective customers at each stage of the hierarchy, and to decide how many must be helped to move further down, and how many must be held in the repurchase loop.

When desired behaviour has been established and quantified it is possible to consider which promotional tools are appropriate, and how much budget to allow.

It is now time to examine promotional budgeting.

Promotional budgeting

Setting a promotional budget is difficult because one is dealing with qualitative rather than quantitative issues. Massive budget campaigns fail, whilst low budget campaigns succeed beyond anyone's wildest expectations. The difference is in the *quality* of the spend, never in the *quantity* of money invested.

The problem is to judge how members of designated target audiences will respond to any proposed campaign. As always when one is forecasting it is impossible to take environmental changes into account. Therefore what appears from research and pre-testing to be a winning campaign may be negated by events prior to, or coincident with, the campaign actually running.

The cost of a campaign, or of a particular medium, cannot be directly relevant. 'Expensive' and 'cheap' are value-loaded terms – i.e. it may seem expensive to use £1 m in one medium against £100 K in another. But what response is pulled? If the one brings in business worth £5 m and the other only £50 K, which, then, seems the best value? If one produces 10 000 responses and the other only 400, where is the money best spent?

This is a trick question because 10 000 responses from a £1 m spend works out at £100 per response. 'Only' 4000 from £100 000 come out at £25 each. Further complexity is added by the value and volume of the potential sales. If it is a big ticket operation, such as a worldwide timeshare scheme, a lot of responses at £100 each may be acceptable. But what of the quality of the response? The 4000 responses are more welcome if there is an 80 per cent chance of conversion, compared to only 10 per cent of the 10 000.

The marketer must establish the objectives clearly, unambiguously and in writing. Only then can a budget be established, and an evaluation plan put into place.

Establishing the budget

There are essentially four methods of setting a promotional budget.

1. *Percentage of sales*
   Where the forecast sales revenue determines the amount to be spent on promotion.
2. *All you can afford*
   Where the budget is set at the maximum possible.
3. *Competitive parity*
   The aim is to match what competitors are spending.
4. *Objective and task*
   Where the budget is set to achieve specified tasks.

Activity 4.5

Examine each of these methods of setting a promotional budget. Make detailed critical notes about each method and determine which you think is the most effective. Why?

(**See:** Debriefing at the end of the unit.)

Promotional evaluation

Objective factors to consider include:

- *Media selection* — Was the spend wisely split between the media?
- *Content* — How did content affect sales?
- *Market* — What did the customers and consumers actually need and want?
- *Competitors* — What were the competitors offering? What advertising were they doing? What special offers were they making?
- *Environment* — What factors, such as unemployment, inflation, social changes, acts of God, etc., need to be taken into account?

Factual information is the first to gather – data such as: advertising spend, media circulation, coupon redemption, sales calls made, orders taken, etc.

Primary research must be targeted on specific information need. In promotion the requirement is to attempt to either predict how a new launch or campaign will be accepted, or how well a campaign met its objectives. Primary research is therefore mostly concentrated on obtaining objective rather than subjective data.

Subjective research is used to discover levels of awareness and attitude. It is necessary to probe in depth to identify the subjective rationale that underpins buying behaviour. It was this need that caused the invention of Depth Research (also known as Motivation Research).

Promotional research

The basic principles of advertising research spill over into other promotional areas and so this one area is concentrated upon as it is key to the approach to the others.

- *Copy testing* Respondents are asked to look through a collection of alternative advertisements and are then questioned as to what they can remember. The aim is to hone the copy to optimum effectiveness.
- *Content research* This is concerned with the ability of an ad to achieve impact and to project the desired message to the target audience. An ad must be judged only from the perspective of its target. The purpose is to confirm that the copy platform, the general theme and presentation of the advert, achieves the desired results.
- *Pre- and post-testing* The one takes place ahead of publication to confirm that the ad will work as intended. The other monitors the actual results. See below.
- *Tracking study* A continuous research that allows trends to be identified and tracked. Persil is reputed to have kept a tracking study running for nearly 90 years.
- *Focus groups* Discussion groups are formed around experienced researchers so that a proposal for an ad, a new product, a below-the-line scheme, can be addressed by typical members of the target audience. They can be very powerful, but must be in the hands of highly experienced researchers.
- *Effectiveness research*
  - *Post-testing* takes place after publication to test the actual achievement. Post-testing techniques are of Recall and Recognition. Tests may be oral and/or pictorial.
  - *Recall* is 'Unaided' (spontaneous). Respondents are asked if they have seen a particular advert, and if so, what they remember about it.
  - *Recognition* is 'Aided' (prompted). Respondents will be shown a series of adverts and asked how much of each of the advertising messages, brands, etc., they can remember. Recall and Recognition may be 'same day' or 'day after'.
- *Split-run* A technique that allows two different ads to run in alternate copies of the same publication. Post-testing can then determine which was the most effective.

- British Airways claim to be the 'World's Favourite Airline'.
  Thought: On what criteria? Who carried out the research? When? What does 'Favourite' mean? How big is their 'world' – does it include areas to which they don't fly? Who was questioned? Airline passengers, a cross-section of the public? Many opportunities to use critically in a question dealing with marketing research, promotion (truthful?) or, possibly, management information.
- Cats prefer Kit-E-Kat.
  Thought: Really? Who asked them? How? When? Do they actually mean that cat owners think that the product does the cat no harm and so prefer to buy it? Or what? Again, a good example for a research or information or promotional question.

Unit Activity

This activity is in two parts:

1 To thoroughly convince yourself that people's behaviour is more important than any other aspect of marketing communications, consider why:

   1.1 Reported circulation for quality press exceeds the print run by 1000 per cent, yet popular papers printing in millions reportedly sell very few.

   1.2 When asked for an opinion on the Metallic Metal Act the respondents answered: A good thing if dealt with by government – 21 per cent. A good thing if at local government level – 59 per cent. OK for foreigners, but not here – 16 per cent. It is of no value – 4 per cent. (The Act did not exist.)

2 Actively monitor behaviour around you. Note how many people say things such as 'Oh, I've only got a xxx, I know you have a yyy.' What does that tell you about xxx, yyy, and the person? What would it mean to you if you were marketing xxx or yyy?

(**See:** Debriefing at the end of the unit.)

Summary

In this unit we have seen:

- The importance of communication to a marketer.
- That messages have to be constructed and targeted with great care.
- That feedback is vital.
- How customer and consumer behaviour must be understood and provided for.
- That a purchase decision is dependent on a range of psychological stages being passed.
- That the DMU and DMP behind each purchase needs to be understood by the seller.
- Distinct advantage is intrinsic, differential advantage has to be created.
- New technology is opening up many possibilities to the alert marketer.
- Direct marketing is a channel of distribution.
- Budgets and evaluation depend on objectives put into writing.
- The best, but most difficult, promotional budget is Objective and task.
- Promotional research must, of necessity, be heavily biased towards subjective evaluation.

Activity 4.1

This is a self-development activity intended to widen your perception of the promotional techniques in common use. You will probably have found that people's perceptions of the promotional messages varied. But why? Was it a lack of interest in the product offer? Something about the brand itself? Did the message(s) reinforce or contradict existing attitudes and beliefs?

An example of a person with little interest in a promotion is a man asked about a depilatory cream. It is likely that the promotion will have gone entirely unnoticed since it will have been targeted only at people who have a definite interest in what the cream might do for them.

Activity 4.2

If you found this activity easy it follows that you have not been rigorous enough in your analysis. Even if the purchase was of a routine, repeat nature, you need to discover why you continue with the same product offer. Do you believe it is the best? How do you know? When did you last try an alternative? Are you fooling yourself? What are the promoters working to reinforce? How are they doing it? How effective is it?

It will be especially difficult to determine the rationale if the purchase was a luxury product, or if a diet was being broken. The psychological rationales that we unconsciously establish, and the psychological half-truths that we create (and believe in), have to be identified, analysed and put into context.

Activity 4.3

For well positioned product offers you should be able to say 'She's a Corn Flakes breakfaster' or 'She doesn't eat Weetabix'.

If this shorthand description conveys your meaning to others it indicates that the product offers are similarly positioned in their minds. Note that the underlying profile will extend to other behaviour. What is typical of a 'Corn Flakes breakfaster' will also likely apply across the range of behaviour of the young woman in question. (Not infallibly, of course, but with a strong probability of holding true.)

If you are unable to identify a typical reader it means that either the promoters do not include you in their target audience, or that their promotion has failed to break through your perceptual filters.

Activity 4.4

The following is a specimen of an answer that would be awarded good marks. Note that this is but one of the alternative ways to approach this question. Provided your answer is of about this length, is well structured, and establishes key points, it also would score well. There is never one perfect answer to a question in a marketing examination.

Answer – Question 7

Implications of the growth in interactive technology for regulation within the promotions industry

The promotions industry in part derives its success from an understanding of the dynamics of the market place and the impact of change on human attitudes and behaviour. As an industry, promotional practice now faces substantial change which may have significant implications for its own future development and control. Many factors contribute to the changing environment in which promotional practice finds itself, but none more so than the impact of new technology. New technology has facilitated new ways of communicating with customers and stakeholders; witness the increase in the use of the marketing database within promotional strategies. The development of interactive technology offers further opportunities and challenges to the promotions industry.

Interactive technology provides the opportunity to establish dialogue between stakeholders, but in particular between producer and consumer. Such dialogue in turn facilitates enhanced targeting of messages. Interactive television is on trial within the UK, but the area of interactive technology which has attracted most attention during the late 1990s is that provided by the internet.

The internet has provided access to an audience on a global scale for many companies which could not previously dream of mounting such a communication strategy. It is the scale of the communication opportunities and the increased access which presents problems for the control of communication using such technology.

The credibility of the promotions industry relies on the conduct of its members and the protection of the consumer from inappropriate messages. The development of the industry has seen parallel development of structures of regulation and control, legal and voluntary. These controls are essentially underpinned by the concepts of legality, decency, honesty, truthfulness which are evident within codes of practice prepared by the ITC and BCAP to regulate communication within traditional media. These codes of practice can be extended to interactive technology, although many of the controls stipulated within the 1990 Broadcasting Act do not apply to cable and satellite broadcasters.

The internet seems to present a problem on a far greater scale. The freedom of the internet, one of its main attractions, makes control very difficult indeed. It may be the case that the current period of growth is one which presents particular problems, and that once the internet as a medium matures, so will structures and controls emerge which allow it to be suitably and effectively policed. Arguably consumers themselves will have to take on the role of policeman, investing in equipment which allows appropriate messages to be selected. Nevertheless, whilst such systems would prevent the exposure to messages from certain types of companies, they may find control of the content of the messages more difficult to monitor. Controlling influences which emerge within media such as the internet will have to take on the mantle of control in order for the credibility of the medium and indeed interactive technology as a whole, to be preserved.

Interactive technology can learn much from the successes and failures of regulation within traditional media. The benefits of speed and flexibility offered by voluntary control, should be reflected within any emerging system of control which applies to interactive technology. The successful growth of interactive media such as the internet will ultimately be dependent on the audience's perception of the quality of information available, and this quality will in part be determined by the effectiveness of controls exerted upon and within the media.

Activity 4.5

Only one method establishes the budget against the objectives that are to be achieved – against the actual task that has to be accomplished has to be the most effective. Clearly Objective and task is the best method to use.

1 Percentage of sales can only be a crude method since it relies on past precedent. We know that advertising and sales are not directly related and, in any case, sales should surely result from promotion and not dictate the amount to be spent?

  Under this system the successful products will have more spent on them than those which are newly introduced and others that are struggling to attain or hold market share.

2 All you can afford can be a formula to waste money. If all you can afford is not sufficient to reach the objectives, then it is money thrown away. The good manager budgets sufficient funds to do the job. Too high a spend is wasteful, too low is ineffective and therefore also a waste.

3 Competitive parity allows the competition to set your budget! Do they have the same promotional strategy? Do they have the same costings, the same short-, medium- and long-term objectives?

4 Objective and task is the most difficult to introduce, but is by far the most valuable. Depending on clear objectives, specific planning and detailed controls it enables the effectiveness of the spend to be measured. Promotional objectives in SMART terms should underpin all promotion, but for Objective and task are mandatory.

Unit activity

1.1 Obviously status is important to individuals, and the press is clearly positioned as a medium that reflects status. Newspaper buying habits are felt to reflect something of an individual's status, and so people tend to claim to read what they perceive will add to their status.

1.2 The readiness to give an opinion, regardless of knowledge, allows researchers to secure answers to what they want to know. The above answers show much about attitude to government, even though the question was superficially invalid.

2 Issues that impinge on behaviour tend to be complex and have to be approached indirectly. One way to discover biscuit preferences, for example, is to set up a discussion about anything that will interest the group. Then serve tea and a range of biscuits. Observe the biscuit behaviour, ignore the discussion findings – and *don't* ever tell the group what has been done.

In the same way, monitor the way people select items in a store, how many buy a quality paper but do not read it, where people choose to shop (is a Harrods bag for the shopping really worth the higher prices?). Note how people choose to keep some shops' bags (e.g. Harrods) and to spurn others. Also ask yourself why a sports brand on a T-shirt allows about £20 extra to be charged (and paid) for it?

Always check what it would mean to you if you were working in that market.

Promotional operations – tools

In this unit you will:

- ❏ Identify the significance of personal and non-personal promotion.
- ❏ Understand the importance of synergy in promotion.
- ❏ Examine the use of the key promotional tools.
- ❏ Identify the importance of crisis management planning.
- ❏ Develop an understanding of how to develop creative and media briefs.

By the end of this unit you will be able to:

- ❏ Create synergetic promotional campaigns.
- ❏ Brief an agency.
- ❏ Manage the key promotional tools.

Study Guide

If a marketer has one core area of expertise, it must be in the management of the promotional tools. Whatever else may fall into the job description, it will certainly include effective communication. Indeed a marketer should be able to communicate more effectively than any other manager. Even than a public relations practitioner – because the marketer's range of communication tools is wider than those with which a public relations person normally operates.

It follows that a CIM examiner will expect to see evidence of an ability to communicate. Not only in your descriptions of how marketing communication and promotion work – but also in the way that your answer book is presented.

In an examination you will be required to write for just under three hours. For those who normally work on a keyboard this can be tiring. Guard against over-tiredness and its effects on your presentation by practice. In effect, put yourself into training for the exam.

Allow about two hours to work through this unit, but continue to concentrate on the outside environment to help develop your abilities to critically evaluate the promotional work to which you are exposed.

Promotional synergy

The continuum of behaviour that we met in Unit 4 shows the promotional tools in use at different stages of the purchase process. It follows, therefore, that each can have more than one role. Advertising, for example, can help to create awareness, develop attitudes and reinforce belief.

Unfortunately it is not possible to segregate those who will see each advertisement (nor be exposed to any of the promotional tools) and so the core message must be suitable for people at different levels of the continuum. Thus whilst an ad may be designed to attract new interest it must also reassure those who are regular users.

When all the possible exposures are taken into account it will be seen that there is need for extremely careful management, and that the creative input is far more complex than most people would imagine.

Additionally, of course, each of the promotional tools must work closely with the others. Mixed messages confuse and must not be allowed to happen. Marketers mounting promotions must ensure that everybody concerned is aware of the positioning statement since this provides the central focus, as we saw in the last unit.

Usually a range of skills will be needed, and this may mean that several agencies are engaged on the one campaign (public relations, advertising, media, sales promotion, etc.). The marketer's role is strategic, not tactical.

Personal and non-personal promotion

Selling is the only personal promotional tool available to the marketer. The others are all non-personal because they work through media to achieve contact with their targets.

Traditionally it was a major promotional task to get salespeople into contact with potential customers. Whilst this is still true in big budget selling, where sales teams are often used, it no longer applies to the majority of purchase situations.

Beginning with FMCG, marketers have learned how to assist the package to communicate, and the importance of merchandising techniques at point of sale (PoS) and point of purchase (PoP).

Technology is opening up the possibility for increased use of personal techniques through, in particular, telemarketing. Although not face-to-face, telesales people can address potential customers directly, and modify their conversation in the light of the feedback.

Video and film can show a product in use, but it is far more effective to get the product offer in the hands of a potential customer.

Campaign planning

There is no mystery to the planning of an advertising (or any other promotional) campaign.

Determine strategy
In terms of each target audience: where are we now, where do we want to be, by when?

Set objectives
Establish SMART objectives, in writing, that are couched in terms of quantity and/or quality against time. Take into account the needs of people at different stages of the purchase process.

Write brief
A brief is a key statement of intention that can be initiated by either the client or the agency, but which is finalized after discussions. Budget limitations must be made clear at this stage.

Establish tactics
Usually the agency will recommend the tactical plan. As specialists they will have far more experience in the creation of promotional campaigns, and will have been hired for that expertise. The agency should recommend a detailed plan that must include control methodologies.

Note the vital need to gain distribution before the public campaign starts. In many cases the plan should include a trade promotion to achieve support at PoS.

Secure and give approval

Client management approves the plan and authorizes the budget. The agency can then proceed.

Monitor and evaluate

Agency and client keep in close touch, with the client 'signing off' promotional materials before they are put into use. Control procedures should operate smoothly, as planned.

Progress check

Maintain a check on progress as the campaign develops. In particular, note the impact on sales – there may be need to step up production or to ask distribution to move stocks to areas where sales are doing particularly well.

Review results

As a guide to future planning it is essential that the client and agency together review achievement.

Creative briefs

Campaign strategy should contain, as a minimum:

- Statement of overall purpose or intention.
- Positioning.
- Objectives.
- Key Unique Selling Points (USPs) expressed as consumer benefits.
- Secondary USPs, again expressed as consumer benefits.
- Requirement for control mechanisms.

A detailed creative brief can be developed only from a clear strategy. The strategy provides the direction and the focus for the creative people to work to and within. It is much easier to work up creative ideas from a focus than from a blank sheet of paper. Brainstorming will probably be used, but maximum tactical benefit comes from a sense of direction, of purpose.

Agencies have their own preferred way of presenting their creative briefs. As they are internal documents the actual format is not important to the marketer. What matters is that the creative team – copywriters, artists, visualizers, etc. – know what is required. This brief should be contained to a single page so that it is crisp and clear. Creatives need information which shows them exactly what has to be achieved. Never even suggest a way to achieve the aim. You are hiring people for their creativity. If the work is not up to standard, then, perhaps, suggestions can be made. Or the agency can be changed.

The creative brief is an important document which has to be signed off by the agency creative director and, usually, also by the client.

Activity 5.1

Put yourself in the position of a copy writer in an agency. You are about to be asked to produce copy for an advert to create awareness for a new product. What information would you require in order to do your job effectively?

Extending Your Knowledge

There is a careful line to be drawn between managing and over-managing the process. The need is for involvement – for a proactive approach that is supportive of the agency staff.

Unfortunately the marketer has to be actively involved – it is his or her product, his or her reputation that is ultimately at stake . . . and mistakes do happen:

A reputable printer delivered colour proofs of a 12 page newsletter to be checked and signed off. They then went ahead to print 40 000 copies. Twenty copies were sent to the marketer, the balance to the mail house.

The colour on the finished job differed from that in the proofs! But 5000 copies had already gone in the post.

It transpired that a print operative had pulled the proofs on paper he had to hand as they were temporarily out of the proper stock. The paper was almost the same, but did not accept ink in the same way. Thus the paper change affected the density of the ink and therefore the resultant shade.

Quality control identified the problem – but did not prevent its occurrence!

Moral: always sign off proofs *and final versions*, even from sources that have been reliable in the past.

Advertising

There are two key issues to do with advertising that have not yet been covered. They are copy and scheduling.

Copy

The words in an advertisement are crucial to success. Copywriters are highly skilled at creating copy that precisely meets the specified need. This is what two of the greatest had to say on the subject.

David Ogilvy, arguably the greatest modern advertising man, said:

> 'I believe that all copy should be signed by the agency. This is never done in the United States on the ground that manufacturers buy space to advertise their products, not their agencies. Short-sighted. My experience suggests that when agencies sign their ads, they produce better ones. When *Reader's Digest* asked me to write an advertisement for their magazine they specified that I *had* to sign it. Golly, did I work hard on that ad, everyone was going to know who wrote it. The FCB – Imact agency in Paris even gives its copywriters a by-line. Jolly good.'

Master copywriter *Nick van Rijn* is quoted:

> 'Of ad copywriters there are three kinds: apprentices, journeymen and masters. The first attend award dinners, the second go to receive the awards. But master copysmiths send their regrets, from the Bahamas. They're far too busy to attend.'

A basic principle that all agree on is:

If it needs to be simple, never make it clever. If it will work in black and white, never pay for colour. If it can communicate effectively in ten words, never use eleven.

Scheduling

Schedules are designed to achieve the optimum number of viewings by members of the target audience. The measure is of Opportunities To See (OTS).

It can be shown that the incremental OTS decreases with the frequency, but this does not deal with the central issue of how often an individual should be exposed to an ad.

Learning theory suggests that the best learning is *cognitive* – that individuals restructure their cognitions with regard to given problems and/or situations, and that this restructuring leads to greater insight. The Double U principle of Learning – the need to Understand and to Use – is cognitive in nature.

A simplistic view is that advertising works best on the level of stimulus-response plus reinforcement – a form of parrot-fashion learning. For some product offers this approach may be suitable, but for the majority a more developed approach is needed. It is crucial for the advertiser and his agency to determine how the minds of those in the target audience best operate, then to produce advertising that penetrates to the active perception of those in the target segments.

Again, there is debate over the length of an advertising campaign. Broadly speaking, there are two alternatives. *Burst* scheduling concentrates advertising into a short time period. *Drip* scheduling spreads advertising more steadily over a longer period.

Neither is right, neither wrong. It is important to decide which is most likely to be effective for a situation and then to evaluate response to determine if the decision was correct.

Multi-use

Learning theory also shows that advertisements can be planned to achieve multi-use at economic rates. The planning takes time, and costs more, but the benefits can be substantial.

- There is no requirement for the full ad once the target audience has been exposed sufficiently. The principle of *completion* ensures that individuals recall and fill in the missing part. An original 28-second TV ad can therefore be cut to an 8-second reinforcement ad.
- A cinema ad can be longer than a TV ad because the audience is more receptive, having little 'noise' to distract them.
- Radio ads can come from the visual's sound track, suitably modified and re-recorded, but still clearly identifiable.
- Stills from the ad can be used in press, sales promotion, merchandising, etc.

Public relations

The role of Public Relations is to create and maintain goodwill and mutual understanding between an organization (or person) and its publics. It therefore has a wider remit than advertising, which is more focused on obtaining behaviour change within the context of purchase behaviour. Both Public Relations and advertising, however, exist to create awareness. Both have major effects on attitude. Neither sells directly, but both are major influencers of behaviour.

A further, major, difference is that Public Relations does not pay for media coverage. Advertising buys space for its messages. Thus Public Relations practitioners cannot control what appears whereas advertisers can. (Within the limits of the law and voluntary codes of course.)

Public Relations is not free to the organization, however. A substantial budget is needed to set up and run the department (or to hire the consultant). It is a skilled art to ensure that the right copy reaches the right influential people – not only journalists – at the right time to achieve the specified objectives.

Target publics and target audiences

Public Relations practitioners talk of publics. Marketers and Advertising people refer to target audiences. Both terms refer to exactly the same thing – an identified group of people with whom it is necessary to make contact.

There are eight prime Public Relations publics. Each, of course, sub-divides so that there can be several hundreds of individual publics. Fortunately every one does not have to have a separate message on each occasion. The target publics are shown in Figure 5.1.

Within Public Relations there is a detectable move towards audience and away from public, and so the term audience will be used in this book for the sake of continuity. Remember, however, that it is technically correct to use 'public' when defining a Public Relations target group.

Public relation or PR?

Public Relations practitioners never use the abbreviation PR to refer to Public Relations. This is because it can also mean Press Release and Press

Figure 5.1
The eight publics of public relations

Relations, both of which are common terms in the profession. In this unit we shall follow convention and use the terms without abbreviation. Throughout the remainder of the book we shall use PR as marketers normally do – to refer to Public Relations itself.

Publicity

Do not confuse publicity and Public Relations.

Publicity is either generated by Public Relations, or it is generated from natural causes or associated events. A health official finds fault with a product and suddenly the manufacturer has major and unfavourable publicity to deal with. Not only has the product to be withdrawn and replaced – a routine matter – the public confidence in the product has to be restored. Thus Public Relations is used either to generate good publicity or to counter bad publicity.

Attitude change

Public Relations practitioners are concerned to ensure that members of target audiences hold attitudes that are favourable to the organization – or, at the very least, are neutral. Figure 5.2 shows the transfer process of attitude change.

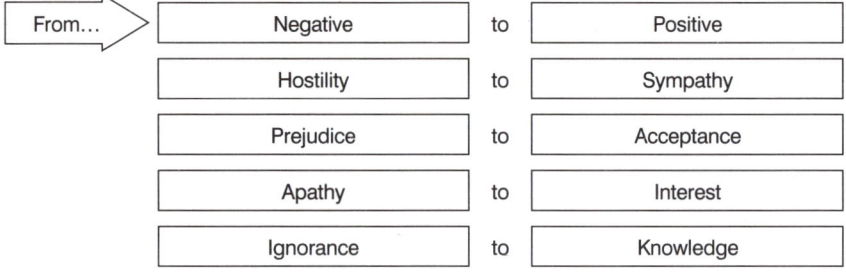

Figure 5.2

Media relations

The process of maintaining positive contact with journalists used to be called 'press relations', and that term is still in everyday use to describe what is correctly termed 'media relations'. The same principles apply, of course.

Control of the media is in the hands of journalists and their editors and proprietors. What is printed or broadcast is determined by them, not by the public relations person. Working journalists are busy people and so they welcome a story that is written in their style. It is far easier to lift copy from a press release than to re-write material that is not targeted on their needs. Standardized, blanket releases will not attract much journalistic attention.

Jim Dunn, an eminent British Public Relations consultant, has established his golden rules for dealing with the media. They include:

- Get to know reporters as individuals. Discover their preferences and their dislikes in terms of personal contact – a hundred and one small things can make a difference.
- Return journalists' calls promptly.
- Be thoroughly prepared before you meet.
- Never say anything 'off the record'.
- Brief everyone who is to meet a journalist of the likely areas that may be explored.
- Have a comprehensive library of photos – in black and white – of all key personnel.
- Don't chase journalists to know when the story will be published – it isn't their decision.
- Don't expect to influence by generous entertaining.
- Only use professionally produced visuals and audio-visuals.
- Don't expect a visit by a famous celebrity to be newsworthy of itself.
- Never use 'lined-up' photos. Ensure there is action in the shots you offer to the media.
- Target your press releases. Blanketing the market is ineffective.

Activity 5.2

The medium most suitable to convey exactly the right message to exactly the right audience(s) at exactly the right time must be selected. The same message must then be tailored for different audiences.

Select an event from your own life (current or past) and outline how you would present it as a story for use by a:

1 Local weekly newspaper.
2 Local radio chat show host.
3 School or trade or other specialist magazine.
4 Feature writer.

(**See:** Debriefing at the end of the unit.)

Lobbying

In the Houses of Parliament at Westminster is a large ante-room, or lobby. One of its uses is for interviews between MPs and members of the public. Lobbying, therefore, is seeking to influence people in authority in order to secure their support to achieve a desired action. It is used worldwide, and not only within a political context.

Specialist Public Relations practitioners have developed lobby skills and have built long-term relationships within the lobby. Some are private consultants, but all of the major consultancies have established lobby specialists.

Lobbying, and especially political lobbying, tends to be a long-term process because Parliaments and large organizations move slowly. New ideas and proposed changes must be gradually fed into the system in a planned and sustained way. A lobbyist is promoting an idea, persuading others to take a certain course of action. Therefore a DMP is operating, and there is a DMU to be identified.

The principles of lobbying, adapted as needed, are used wherever there is need to persuade a person in authority to take a certain line of action. There are, of course, usually pro- and anti-lobbyists. Some of the best known lobbies are: the American gun lobby; the pro- and anti-smoking lobbies; the gay movement's lobby.

Costing and budgetary control

The costs of Public Relations include:

- Executive and support time, office space and equipment, overheads, etc.
  These will be incurred in-house, or paid for within a consultant's fee.
- Costs of production and organization.
  Included are such issues as: Public Relations materials, organizing and paying for exhibitions, hotel costs, entertainment on visits to production facilities, etc.

A Public Relations budget, overall and for each campaign, must be set up and managed as for any other management activity.

Activity 5.3

Take the role of a Public Relations consultant and select a story in an early morning news broadcast. Pretend that you originated it on behalf of a client. Follow the story through the day in all the media you can access. Note:

- How it is treated by each. Who runs it major, and who uses it as a filler. Why?
- How it changes through the day. Does it grow in importance? Why?
- Is it dropped, or followed through? Why?

You are to meet your client tomorrow. Make notes that critically evaluate the coverage.

Crisis management

It is normal to cover crisis management under the heading of Public Relations because the skills of Public Relations are much needed in crisis management. It is, however, a major responsibility of senior management.

It is inevitable that every organization will at some time suffer an event that could be a major threat to its continuing existence or, at least, to its image and reputation. An airline, for example, must expect some form of aircraft emergency. A car manufacturer must expect a vehicle to be involved in a major accident.

An alert management thinks ahead, and plans for each eventuality that may occur. *Contingency planning* is the identification of eventualities that could occur, and the preparation of detailed plans ahead of need. To be successful managers must:

- Identify what could happen.
- Quantify and evaluate each alternative.
- Make plans to deal with each contingency.

They must also ensure that the plans are kept up-to-date and that key staff have regular opportunities to rehearse. Contingency planning is so effective at London's Gatwick airport, for example, that when the airport was closed by a security alert a newly appointed airport manager was able to travel from his home to an alternative control centre and manage the crisis from there.

Sales promotion (SP)

It was only in the 1960s that sales promotion was created to fill the vacuum left at PoS by the arrival of self-service in retail shops. With counter service there was a sales:customer interface, but this no longer existed. A way had to be found to move the products from the shelf. A sales inducement was needed. Hence, sales promotion.

The concept has now spread into every market. Wherever a short-term inducement to purchase is offered, a sales promotional opportunity has been created. In all instances the marketer who can add incentive at point of decision is better equipped to succeed.

Naturally SP has to be appropriate. A £1 m hire car fleet purchaser is not likely to be influenced by the kind of offer seen in a supermarket. More appropriate may be a personal invitation to the Grand Prix where the manufacturer has a car racing.

A problem is to define where the cost of short-term inducements falls – in the P of price, or the P of promotion. Frankly, it doesn't matter to the negotiator. At the crucial interface the need to add an inducement has been met. It is for the administrators to sort out which budget supports the cost.

Sales promotions must be legal, decent, honest and truthful; they must be fair and follow the spirit as well as the letter of the Code of Sales Promotion Practice and the law. Consumer interests must be protected. Responsibility rests with the promoter, and evidence of compliance with the Code must be provided if called for.

To avoid transgressing the Code, always check the legal and moral position. Take special care over the clause concerning the 'spirit of the Code' because this is open to subjective interpretation.

Sales promotional objectives

Although the prime rationale for SP is to induce a purchase, the reason why the purchase is needed by the supplier will vary. Thus there are different objectives within the overall SP concept. Figure 5.3 shows how objectives are linked to the mechanics of an offer.

Objectives / Mechanics	Immediate free offers	Delayed free offers	Immediate price offers	Delayed price offers	Finance offers	Competitions	Games and draws	Charitable offers	Self-liquidators	Profit-making promotions
Increasing volume	9	7	9	7	5	1	3	5	2	1
Increasing trial	9	7	9	2	9	2	7	7	2	1
Increasing repeat purchase	2	9	2	9	5	3	2	7	3	3
Increasing loyalty	1	9	0	7	3	3	1	7	3	3
Widening usage	9	5	5	2	3	1	5	5	1	1
Creating interest	3	3	3	2	2	5	9	8	8	8
Creating awareness	3	3	3	1	1	5	9	8	8	8
Deflecting attention from price	9	7	0	7	7	3	5	5	2	2
Gaining intermediary support	9	5	9	5	9	3	7	5	1	1
Gaining display	9	5	9	5	9	3	7	5	1	1

Each square is filled with a rating from 0 (not well matched) to 10 (very well matched). Use it as a ready reckoner for linking your objective to the mechanics available.

Figure 5.3

(Source: Cummins, J. 1990)

The five most popular uses for SP are:

Free mail-in

An item of interest to the target audience is offered either free, or for the costs of postage and packing. Usually tokens or labels, etc., must first be collected.

Volume discounts allow the promoter to offer substantial value, but administration costs can be high, and uptake can be hard to predict.

Price reduction

Technically, a price reduction is only SP if the reduction is both temporary and financed by the promotional budget. See above.

Claims of relative value must be fully substantiated. Thus the practice of inflating a retail price to allow an apparently massive discount is no longer legal. Manufacturer's Recommended Prices are also illegal, even as a so-called basis for a special price offer.

Examples of legal price SP offers are:

- 20 per cent extra at the same price.
- Three for the price of two.
- Coupons offering reductions on the next purchase.
- Cashback – as when a manufacturer pays a cheque direct to a purchaser in addition to the deal done with the retailer.

Competitions

Always very popular and widely used. Care must be taken to comply with the law, since what constitutes terms such as 'chance' and 'lottery' is clearly defined. Again, legal clearance is needed.

Competitions need to be easy to enter and to answer or play. Entry usually cannot be conditional on purchase. An additional benefit can be the personal details supplied by the respondent. Unless he or she opts out (and a clause must be provided for this) these details can be added to the database and provide valuable marketing information.

Coupons

Around six million coupons are issued in the United Kingdom each year, with a redemption rate of about 10 per cent. The average value of each coupon is increasing, partly due to inflation and partly to add extra value to the offer.

There is a danger of artificial redemption if a retailer decides to accept any coupons no matter what the purchase. Manufacturers have greatly tightened their controls, and the major retailers now will only accept coupons that match purchases.

Couponing has many advantages: they can encourage trial and retrial; trigger a sale; secure a repeat purchase. Coupons can give a short-term price benefit; be set up quickly through the press to respond to competitive activity. Costing can be controlled with some accuracy because redemption rates can be predicted; the retailers and a clearing house cost-effectively handle all the administration.

Tailor-mades

Any type of 'purchase' can be aided by SP. A creative imagination can devise inducements that will encourage people to donate to a charity, stock up ahead of a promotional campaign, take a test drive in a new car. It is hard to think of any sales opportunity where an SP opportunity cannot be devised.

Targeting employees

Because the targeting of individuals with SP offers has led to abuse, the Code now features the requirement to make the offers to the employing organizations. Thus company car drivers can buy fuel on an organization's credit card, with any bonus points, coupons, etc. being credited to the organization. Airlines have similar arrangements within their frequent flyer programmes.

Fulfilment and coupon redemption

Fulfilment refers to the supply of whatever goods have been offered. Specialist agencies exist to take all the responsibility from the client – but only within the terms of the agreement, which must be established as objectives are set.

Fulfilment should be rapid, and effective. Respondents must be satisfied, and a long delay can harm overall attitudes. Packaging is also important. The offer is significant to the respondent, and so the package should look neat, and fully protect the contents.

Retailers who handle the coupons take them in place of cash. They expect, therefore, that redemption will be quick, and that they will be paid a handling allowance.

Activity 5.4

Take 15 minutes and consider how you could use SP to achieve each of the 'tailor-made' examples given above.

(**See**: Debriefing at the end of the unit)

Extending Your Knowledge

Competitive sales promotion
Tesco announced the Grand Opening of a new hypermarket in south London. As part of their SP they promised to redeem any other local retailer's coupons.

The local ASDA flooded the area with £20 coupons valid only at their nearby store over the weekend that Tesco opened. ASDA redeemed very few. Tesco redeemed an awful lot!

Time bombs
Nescafé printed an 'unnecessary' and unnoticed red cup and saucer on the back of their labels for some time before it was needed. When they learned through the trade press that Maxwell House were about to ship new Special Offer packs into stores, they activated their 'time bomb'. The cup and saucer labels became SP labels. Press and radio advertising are quick to mount, and so Nescafé had their competing offer up and running, *with product on the shelf*, as Maxwell House were selling theirs in.

Personal selling

The sales team is the only personal element in the promotional toolbox. Salespeople are the only members of an organization who are in constant contact with buyers. Good sales management is essential to maximize their effectiveness.

Good salespeople build a relationship with their contacts. The more complex the buying decision, the greater and more penetrative this relationship needs to be. For a multi-million pound contract, a salesperson may well lead a team of specialists from all functions so that all the buyer's needs can be handled quickly.

In these cases the salesperson manages the process of selecting, briefing and supporting specialists so that all have a united and focused set of objectives.

The relatively new term of Relationship Marketing describes what good sales teams have been doing for centuries:

- Putting the customer's interests first.
- Supplying to customer needs.
- Maintaining a positive and involved interest in the customer and their markets.
- Involving the customer in product development processes.
- Building long-term profit for both organizations through the development of mutual concern.

Personality

Salespeople constantly put themselves into positions of psychological danger. Most of us avoid situations where rejection is possible, but a salesperson must face rejection in every call. And be resilient enough to go in fresh to the next.

Some salespeople make around 20 calls a day. If weather conditions are bad, and it is a grey day at the end of a bad month, it can be difficult to keep going – especially as salespeople work alone. They do not have the support of office colleagues.

It follows that Sales Managers operate a specialized form of management. They must know how to motivate salespeople, how to get the best from them. Unfortunately, on some occasions marketing managers can unwittingly damage a salesperson's confidence. A badly phrased letter received at the beginning of a tough day can affect attitude, and thus sales. All salespeople believe that marketers should spend time in the field, and theirs is a compelling argument.

Types of sales force

Sales forces should be designed to meet the needs of the buyers in the market(s) in which the salespeople will be working. Each should be composed of the right mix of personalities, and organized to meet the needs of the market.

The Nestlé organization in the UK, for example, had over 650 salespeople who were divided into three sales forces: grocery, confectionery and catering. Some people were surprised at this decision. Could there be such a difference between three markets handling substantially the same products? The answer was, and is, yes. The markets differ, and so the people within them also differ. Selling to each requires matching personalities. So successful people selling in one market do not find it easy to transfer to another.

In addition to personal selling skills, individuals may need to have specialist knowledge. A medical training, perhaps, or engineering skills.

Structure

Four structures are in common use.

Geographical

Simple to design because there are natural and man-made boundaries to be followed. Whatever boundary system is chosen, it should match up with the key statistical sources used in budgetary control – for many this means the ITV regions.

Salespeople will be close to their customers, and travel time and expenses are likely to be lower than for other structures.

A potential weakness is that salespeople have to sell all the organization's products, and are likely to be less skilled in some areas than others. It is unreasonable to expect any one person to be an in-depth expert across a wide range of products.

Product

Where the product range is complex and/or technical or specialized, it can be beneficial to have specialist salespeople.

Problems that can arise have to do with:

- High travel and accommodation expenses.
- Morale issues, as people are away from home for extended periods.
- Possibility of call duplication, as different specialists target the same customers.
- Co-ordination difficulties, e.g. If Specialist A encounters a customer perfect for Specialist B's products.

Customer – market

Industry type is the determinant. Thus the same computer hardware may be sold by different sales teams into different industries. If the salesperson is an industry specialist, the computer is sold in context to industrial needs.

Cost and time of travel, linked with fewer sales calls, are the downside, but sales are often made more expediently. There is need to balance effective costs against results, not to take costs as a stand-alone issue. This, of course, applies to some degree in all sales assessment.

Customer – account

Account-size structure is appropriate where there are many outlets but few big buyers. The grocery retail industry is the prime example because of the volume of business controlled by the buyers for the top retail chains.

Some organizations adopt a three-tier system, with senior 'Key Account' salespeople negotiating with the biggest accounts, salespeople selling to medium-sized accounts and telesales handling the smaller businesses.

Sales force size

The best way to determine optimum sales force size is from workload coupled with sales response. An example, using notional figures, will make the method clear:

Market size   – £3647 m
Number of outlets   – 100 000
If visited 10 times each year = 1 m calls
Salesperson calls 20 per day = 100 per week. 5200 per year

Thus number of salespersons apparently needed = 1 m ÷ 5200 = 192.3. Say 193.

But:

80% of £ share is controlled by 50 buyers each to be visited every week:
   = 50 calls per year = 50 × 50 = 2500 calls per year

Say:

A senior salesperson calls 2 per day = 10 per week = 520 calls per year
Number of senior salespeople needed = 2500 ÷ 520 = 4.8. Say 5.

Then:

50 buyers control 60% of 100 000 outlets   = 60 000 outlets
5000 buyers control 40% of 100 000 outlets = 40 000 outlets
At 10 calls a year   = 50 000 calls
Salespeople needed = 50 000 ÷ 5200   = 9.61. Say 10.

But:

Average total turnover of each of the 5000 smaller buyers = 20% of £3647 m ÷ 5000 = £145 880. So trade must be via middlemen in the main, since average *total* revenue does not support full sales cover.

Conclusion:

A maximum of eight, perhaps ten, senior salespeople should concentrate on the big retailers and wholesalers, and, if possible, visit the bigger of the independents.

Effective use of time

A salesperson's time is one of the most expensive resources that are deployed by an organization. Unfortunately there is a massive body of evidence to show that a salesperson's time is seldom used to optimum effect.

When a Field Sales Trainer conducts a detailed survey of the use of time, the results are always going to be informative. Some will use their time to better advantage, and the information gained can be used as the basis for on-going training. The following example is typical of the results of such research.

Wholesale drugs plc

Element	10 most efficient		10 least efficient	
	Minutes	%	Minutes	%
Selling	28.9	55.8	21.5	41.0
Assistance	.9	1.8	.6	1.1
Collections	4.6	8.9	1.9	3.5
Sales promotion	2.2	4.2	2.0	3.6
Miscellaneous	1.5	2.9	.8	1.5
Total essential time	38.1	73.6	27.8	50.7
Waiting	3.9	7.5	11.2	20.5
Broken interview	5.2	10.0	8.4	15.3
Conversation	4.4	8.5	6.4	11.7
Idle time	.2	.4	1.0	1.8
Non-essential time	13.7	26.4	27.0	49.3
Total call	51.8	100.0	54.8	100.0

It can be seen that the more effective calls are shorter, but devote more time to the productive elements of the contact. Selling time is a full 7 minutes longer. More collections are made, implying more concern. More assistance is offered, although SP time is the same.

The less efficient are either kept waiting or, more likely, have not planned their calls as effectively. More time is spent in conversation rather than in selling, and idle time is higher.

A sales manager would want to discover just what the more efficient were doing that the least efficient were not, then to spread the better practices amongst the whole team.

Sales force effectiveness

It is essential to base judgements of effectiveness on *objective* facts. Commonly used bases for evaluation include these subjective 'facts':

Evaluation method	Problems
Number of calls made	Open to manipulation. What is a 'call'? Who confirms that a 'call' has actually been made? What value is there in knowing how many calls are made?
Order:Call ratio	Purports to show effectiveness. But if calls can be manipulated it has no value. Further, it gives no indication of the *size* of order taken. Should orders sent in the post or secured by telephone be credited to the salesperson?
Number of orders taken	Open to manipulation. One order can be split into two or, far worse, the sales force can sell small regular deliveries without regard for overall costs.
Number of new accounts	Any new account? Or just the profitable ones?

It is essential to evaluate on objective facts such as:

- *Achievement against budget.*
  If budgets are fairly set, taking into account the different opportunities open to individuals, they can be a very effective measure of evaluation.
    Note: Budgets should be achievable, as against targets that are commonly set deliberately high – and often demotivate.
- *Achievement against quota.*
  In some markets, e.g. Christmas boxes of chocolates and Easter Eggs, there is a maximum quantity of each type to be sold. Anyone can sell what turn out to be the more popular designs. The requirement is to sell the production – i.e. to sell the quota *and no more*.
- *Profitability.*
  The one true yardstick – but detailed records have to be maintained. The 'profit' figure must be calculated using the factors within the control of the salesperson, i.e. the negotiated price, discounts agreed, credit period, size and frequency of order, etc. It is unfair to charge costs that are outside the control of the salesperson.

Commission is charged directly to sales and is a variable expense. Management should be pleased, therefore, when they approve large commission payments.

Sales force objectives

Typical strategic objectives may be:

- *Primary*
  Within the period to 31.12.20xx to achieve:
    - A composite gross profit figure of 20%.
    - Industrial customer gross profit return of 30%.
    - Retail customer gross profit return of 17%.
    - An industrial customer base of 1000 accounts.
    - A retail customer base of 3500 accounts.
    - The transfer of all designated Small Accounts to telesales contact.
- *Secondary*
  Within the period to 31.12.20xx to:
    - Reduce controllable expenses from 24 to 20% of sales.
    - Reduce the proportion of industrial orders under £500 by 5%.
    - Reduce the number of retail orders under £200 by 15%.

Sales support

Sales support takes two forms: support of the salespeople and support of the sale.

Salespeople support

When active in the field, the salesperson is dependent upon the Sales Office for support. In some cases this support is highly detailed, and comes through the computer.

- Routing is planned.
- Prompts remind what to say, what to feature.
- Customer history and potential are set out clearly.

Computer support can involve multimedia presentations directly over the client's desk; technical and price estimates; accurate and binding quotations via modem link to head office. Customer records can be fully computerized with on-line transmission for processing in the Sales Office.

Whether support is paper-bound or computer-free, there is still need for an empathic understanding of need from those who supply quotations, make contact on behalf of salespeople, and generally ensure that the front line is kept supplied and motivated.

Sales support

No sale is complete until the goods have been delivered, paid for, and used satisfactorily. It is important to be prepared to follow through every sale – even the routine re-orders. For some products there is, of course, the need for a full after-sales service.

Customers who *feel* they have a problem actually *do have* a problem! It is just as important to deal with a perceived problem as a 'real' problem. Remember that to us our perceptions are very real indeed.

Sales Engineers

Vital to the continued operation of a product, the Sales Engineers are sometimes treated as menials instead of the valuable ambassadors that they actually are.

Sales Engineers spend more time with clients than the salespeople, and they meet different members of the DMU. Often they get to know Operatives and Supervisors very well indeed. They often know where there are problems that could be fixed, and how to fix them.

Marketing/Sales operations that regard Sales Engineers as full members and reward them accordingly find that their number of leads increases and product usage improves as well.

Sales literature

The 'presenters' with which salespeople are equipped must be designed with care, and with the active assistance of experienced and successful salespeople who are currently earning their living in the field. It is a very different thing to carry a stocked briefcase around an office for a while, and to carry the same thing eight hours a day, every day, in all conditions. A successful presenter can always be identified – the sales force uses it!

Salespeople are not silly:

- They won't carry things that don't work, that they can't use.
- They welcome anything which improves the probability of securing orders.

Sales literature must conform to the positioning statement, of course, and be targeted upon current need. It must translate any consumer promotions into trade benefits. It is essential that it be fresh, crisp, and up-to-date.

Sales management

A Sales Manager's place is in the field, not in the office. A National Sales Manager is probably forced to spend a lot of time in the office, but operational management should be out with the salespeople and meeting the customers.

An old anecdote sums up a perspective on Sales Managers:

> Golfer is offered 'Salesman', a dog, as a caddie. With reluctance, accepts. Is most impressed. Dog runs everywhere, is always cheerful and anxious to do more, even pre-thinks the golfer's requirements.

> Next month the golfer returns. Asks for Salesman. Is told he has done so well is now 'Senior Salesman' and costs 50 per cent more. Golfer hires him and is a little less impressed. Still knowledgeable, the dog doesn't run quite so far nor so fast. But they have a good round.

> Next month the golfer asks for Senior Salesman. Is told he is available at 25 per cent of the original fee! Asks why. Is told the dog has been promoted again. To 'Sales Manager'. But now will only sit in his kennel and bark!

The role of the Sales Manager is:

- To recruit, select, train.
- To motivate.
- To supervise record keeping.
- To transfer best practice around the team.

- To discipline.
- To represent the team to senior management and to marketing.

The better Sales Managers also have their own accounts to manage so that they keep their hands in as salespeople. In Sales Management one is on the front line and needs to be able to sell effectively.

Sponsorship

Essentially a business deal, sponsorship is intended to be of advantage to both the sponsor and the sponsored. It is the provision of resources to build a relationship of mutual benefit.

The true value of sponsorship is expressed in the phrase 'enlightened self-interest'. A cause is supported with cash or consideration in return for satisfying specific corporate or marketing objectives.

Almost anything can be sponsored – provided that the proposal is legal, practical, cost-efficient and controllable. Marketers need communication channels to identified target audiences. Provided a cost-effective channel can be made available it is in the marketer's interests to provide sponsorship.

The importance of the communication channel cannot be over-stated. In late 1998 the organizers of Britain's entry into the Admirals Cup sailing challenge said that the necessary cash was readily available. Unfortunately the event was so badly managed that commercial sponsors preferred to support the round-the-world races where media coverage was guaranteed.

These days everybody must be familiar with sponsorship deals. These are typical of the range of opportunities that are being exploited:

Type	Example
Personality	Individual sports people are sponsored by kit manufacturers.
Bodies	Sports teams play with a sponsor's name on their kit.
Titles	The Nationwide Football League is England's old First Division.
Events	Cadbury's sponsor Christmas shows in UK theatres.
Tournaments	The ATP tennis tour is sponsored by Mercedes.
Happenings	Budweiser sponsor the kick-off in American Football.
Creations	Pizza Hut promised every spectator at a Pittsburgh Pirates baseball game a free soda and/or pizza if a spectator chosen at random could catch one, two or three 'pop-up' balls. Three were caught and 33 789 people shared pizza to the value of £150 000. Pizza Hut made international headlines, which more than justified the cost.

Budget

Sponsorship is paid from the promotional budget, but it can be difficult to cost precisely because far more is involved than the simple provision of resources in the form of cash or kind. To be successful, sponsorship must be supported with a range of promotional tools.

Target audiences must be researched in detail; clear management objectives established; appropriate sponsorship vehicles researched, defined and chosen; contracts have to be negotiated; and a programme of integrated communication budgeted, created, implemented, evaluated and reviewed.

Coca-Cola, for example, sponsored the 1999 one-day cricket tournament in Sharjah. The pitch carried painted Coke logos, the sight screens behind the batsmen carried Coke advertising, as did boards around the ground. Each stump was emblazoned with the Coca-Cola identity.

TV, radio and press advertising featured the event, players took part in SP activity and – of course – Coke was prominently on sale at the event. Catchment was local – but far more important was the opportunity to communicate with the team's supporters in India, Pakistan and England.

The advantages of sponsorship include cost-effectiveness, integrated and targeted activities, and thorough evaluation. Disadvantages are hard to find, but possibly include the alienation of those who support a competitive activity. There is also a danger that sponsorship will be entered into for the wrong reasons – perhaps to support the Chief Executive's favourite team!

Properly organized sponsorship offers major benefits to brand advertisers, including:

- Prominent exposure.
- Precision targeting.
- Editorial context, if programmes selected accordingly.
- Control over the promotional environment.
- Associative value.
- Brand visibility.
- Cost-effectiveness.
- High exploitability.

The advantages far outweigh the disadvantages – possibly even to the point where the sharp edge of sponsorship is blunted by familiarity. If this is so, it makes it all the more important to conceive and manage sponsorship that has an edge, a measurable value. Anything less is a waste, is potentially an indulgence.

Extending Your Knowledge	Ambush marketing occurs when a third party overrides the main sponsor. In 1991, for example, the Rugby World Cup sponsorship was attributed by most people to Sony. Yet all they sponsored was the ITV television coverage. Use ambush marketing when possible, and guard against it always!

Exam Hints	Questions normally have several sub-sections that may or may not be immediately obvious. Even those with numbered parts may contain more than one query in each part. It is imperative to thoroughly analyse each question to identify everything that the examiner expects to see addressed in your answer, then to provide thorough answers that flag each sub-section so that the examiner can easily find it. It is amazing how many marks are lost because candidates do not analyse questions.

Unit Activity	This is question 4 from the December 1997 Promotional Practice question paper. Allow yourself 40 minutes to answer it as though you are in an examination room. You work for a sponsorship agency and have been approached by a potential client who manufactures healthy 'crunch' bars aimed at an active 25–45-year-old ABC1 target audience. The client has requested that you come to the first meeting prepared to discuss the advantages and drawbacks of sports sponsorship as a promotional tool for the client's market. Prepare your thoughts for this meeting using examples of sports sponsorship to illustrate your points.

Summary

In this unit we have seen:

- The importance of synergy throughout all the promotional tools.
- That personal selling is the only personal promotional tool.
- That campaign planning requires the same management discipline as for other activities.
- Agencies should handle tactics under the strategic guidance of the client.
- Copy is crucial to success.
- Multi-use of material is made possible by a knowledge of learning theory.
- Publicity happens. Public Relations creates or counters good or bad publicity.
- Publics and audiences are identical.
- Journalists and editors control the media.
- Lobbying requires specialist knowledge and contacts, and considerable time.
- Public Relations are not free, although non-paid-for space is used.
- Contingency planning is needed ahead of potential crises.
- Sales promotion is possible in every market.
- SP offers should match the needs of the target and help achieve a specific objective.
- Fulfilment must be both effective and efficient.
- Good selling depends on good relationships.
- Sales force structure and size must be developed to meet market needs.
- Sales force evaluation should be on objective facts.
- Commission is a semi-variable expense.
- Salespeople need good support.
- Sponsorship is 'enlightened self-interest'.
- Opportunities for sponsorship must be carefully evaluated.
- Ambush marketing should be guarded against.

Debriefing

Activity 5.1

It is likely that your list will contain at least these points:

- Product details — Actual products to taste, play with, use.
- Strategy
- Positioning
- Target audience — And its perceptions.
- USPs — In consumer benefit terms.
- Proposition — The focus message to be put to the target audience.
- Tone/style — Especially if anything is precluded by policy.
- Audience reaction — How should they feel? What should they do?
- Probable media — By type, if not by title.
- Evaluation methodology — How will success be judged?

Activity 5.2

The story is about my winning of a sponsored half marathon. These are approaches that would work, but you have probably thought of other, better ones. The key thing is to tailor the same story to suit the needs of the journalist. Remember that journalists are marketing their stories as product offers to defined target audiences. They also need to meet consumer needs.

1 *A local weekly newspaper.*
   Knowing they would be covering the event in depth in their sports pages, I would provide a basic fact sheet giving the key information the journalist would need to flesh out the story. This would include, but not feature, the name of my charity and the amount donated.

   I would also send a story, with photo, to the news desk. This as a press release, constructed much the same as for the chat show.

2   *Local radio chat show host.*
    Focus on the benefits brought to the charity. Minimum background on the charity itself (even if nationally known). Key notes on my background, and on my role in the community.
3   *School or trade or other specialist magazine.*
    Provide action photo from local paper and studio shot from my own archives. Reasonably lengthy story focused on the key interest of the publication: e.g. school runner earns £XXX for Oxfam.
4   *A feature writer.*
    Work with Oxfam to provide in-depth facts on the ways to secure interest in supporting the charity. Use the current news as a lever to a more in-depth piece on the charity overall.

Activity 5.3

You should find that the quality of the story is dictated by the editorial slant of the media, and by the pressure of news on the day in question. A thin story will be ignored on a busy day, but may receive extensive coverage on a slack day.

Targeting of content and timing are two crucial issues in Public Relations.

Activity 5.4

Possibilities include:

- Charity donation
  - lapel badge to indicate status as a giver.
  - entry to a competition.
  - free trip to exciting destination to take part in a sponsored event.
  - opportunity to try something new, e.g. sponsored parachute jump.
- Stocking up
  - sale or return.
  - additional merchandise (13 for 12).
  - stocking allowance.
  - co-operative advertising budget.
- Test drive
  - national competition to win a car outright.
  - dealer competition to win the use of the car for a weekend.
  - special deal on trade-in, insurance, roadside recovery, etc.

Unit activity

Preparation for meeting with 'Crunch' brand team:
Thoughts on sponsorship

Key issues to remember during the meeting
- Target audience for product is active 25–45 ABC1. Can we discover more about this audience. How active are they? What involvement do they have in sport? Are there regional biases? Is the audience equally divided between males and females?
- What other promotional activity is the brand engaged within? What is the core communication proposition of the brand?
- What are the underlying reasons for the client's interest in sports sponsorship? Has the team had any previous experience (good or bad) of sports sponsorship within the context of other brands? (assuming that there is no evidence of past involvement in sports sponsorship with 'Crunch').

Advantages of sports sponsorship
- Building brand awareness with a series of stakeholders. The audience for the sport may not necessarily be the consumer, e.g. in the case of Hewlett Packard's sponsorship of Tottenham Hotspur.
- Developing associations for the brand, e.g. Coca-Cola with football, national sport and community in its involvement with the Coca-Cola Cup. In this way aiming to enhance the likeability and integrity of the brand with the target audience.

- Extend or reinforce brand values, e.g. Stella Artois' sponsorship of the Queen's tennis tournament reinforcing the values of exclusivity and maintaining salience.
- Media exposure critical to the success of sponsorship. Aim to get involved with an event or activity which will command media interest and thus coverage. This will be of particular value in building awareness of the brand and its involvement.
- Seek opportunities to leverage sponsorship effects by integrating activity with other forms of marketing communication, in particular public relations, but also potentially sales promotion and advertising activity.

Disadvantages of sports sponsorship
- A long term communication tool. The brand must be prepared to invest and reap the benefits over the long term.
- Competition with broadcast sponsor for events televised on Channels 3, 4, 5 or Sky. Research has shown that broadcast sponsors may take a higher share of mind than event sponsors (e.g. Sony's successful sponsorship of the broadcast of the 1991 World Cup).
- Increasingly competitive environment in which 'ambush marketing' is more prevalent, where other brands compete for the audience's share of mind and steal the uniqueness of the sponsorship association.
- Sports are dynamic but unpredictable. The sponsor may find themselves embroiled in the effects of this unpredictability. E.g. Martell's sponsorship of the Grand National which has had to bear the consequences of a non-starting race, and one year's postponement due to a bomb scare.
- Taking over a sponsorship from an established sponsor may result in carry-over effects to their benefit. For example many people still associate the London Marathon with Mars even though their sponsorship was nearly a decade ago.
- Leverage requires substantial investment, often doubling the budget requirement.
- Isolating sponsorship effects can be difficult, thus evaluation may be problematic.

Intended action from meeting
- Generate answers to first questions about the brand and its target audience.
- Try to book in another appointment to present recommended sponsorship activity.

Unit 6 Product operations

Objectives

In this unit you will:

❑ Examine the nature of products and product offers.
❑ Identify the product life cycle.
❑ Consider the significance of product portfolio planning.
❑ Develop an understanding of brands and branding.
❑ Understand the key stages of new product development.

By the end of this unit you will be able to:

❑ Create packages of benefits that meet customer and consumer needs.
❑ Manage a product offer at each stage of its life cycle.
❑ Achieve optimum results through portfolio planning.
❑ Create effective brand policy.
❑ Manage the process of new product development.

Study Guide

From Advanced Certificate onwards, and especially in the Diploma, examiners expect candidates to have a marketplace awareness. Not only of promotional campaigns, take-overs and mergers, but also of the more fundamental issues.

When answering a mini-case scenario, for example, you may have to produce an outline budget. You can't do this without some idea of actual costings. It is reported that candidates tend to automatically recommend that TV is used in promotion – no matter what the product offer, size of company or market!

Your plans should be as realistic as possible, which means that you need to gain a feeling for real-world marketing. A Marketing Facts Book is a good idea. Open one, and in it keep notes of actual costings, etc. that you can secure from trade press, etc. It will also be of value in your own marketing career.

Allow about 90 minutes to work through this unit.

Products and product offers

The traditional view has been that 'products' and 'services' can be distinguished by the fact that a product is tangible whereas a service is not. This is classic P centred thinking. When we adopt the consumer's viewpoint we find that it is solutions to problems that are bought.

One buys a toothbrush and toothpaste because one wants healthy teeth, and to clear away that 'night before' taste. (Research shows that more toothpaste is bought for clearing the palate than for reasons of hygiene.)

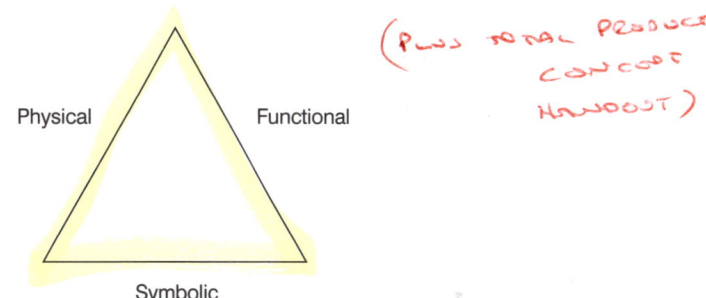

Figure 6.1
Physical, functional and symbolic attributes combine to make a whole product offer

One buys a motor car for its function as transport, but also for its style, attractiveness and contribution to status.

There are, in fact, three components in a product offer. Figure 6.1 shows them to be:

- *Physical*   Any tangible aspect of the offer.

- *Function*   What the offer will do for the consumer. What use benefits it brings.

- *Symbolic*   What the offer in use will mean within the consumer's psychological profile.

Consider one of your recent purchases. How important was the function as compared to the symbolic value? If it was a wristwatch, how far were you influenced by style and brand? How much did you take its timekeeping function into account? Were you bothered at all about its physical make-up? Were you concerned about its components?

For most purchases it is the symbolic element that is the most important to the buyer. You will have noticed how powerfully symbolism is used in promotion. Walk through a supermarket and see how fast branded goods sell by comparison to the plain labelled 'value' goods. Convince yourself of the importance of symbolism over function by observing what people do, what they respond to.

Extending Your Knowledge	Every so often the media features a survey reporting that people buy on price . . . so the quality of food served in our homes is falling! The fallacy that the media fails to notice, in the interests of a good story, is that people do not use language precisely. When they respond 'price', they actually mean 'price-in-use', or value. Value is different from price. A low-priced product may seem attractive, but how long will it last? A higher priced product may give many years of service. Thus the best value purchase may well cost more initially.

It has always been difficult to support the tangible–intangible distinction. Is a hairdresser offering a product or a service? The hairstyle is intangible, but there is need for products in the form of scissors, shampoos, property and so on.

When the C approach is taken we can ignore artificial distinctions and concentrate on supplying the benefits the customers and consumers will value. We can market product offers as *packages of benefits*.

Components are normally assembled by a manufacturer, and so it may appear that the symbolic aspect is missing. Not so! Buyers are individuals who are affected by the same emotions and drives at work as they are when shopping for themselves. They prefer to buy whole packages that make their life easier. They prefer to deal with people they like, who put themselves out. They buy on overall value terms.

139

One component above all others has taken on a life of its own through brilliant marketing – the Pentium chip. *Pentium inside* has been developed into a guarantee of speed and efficiency. Never mind that the computer may be tacky, it has a Pentium chip. Never mind that Apple's Power chip is faster. Apple do not sell through to the consumer, and so only specialists know of the power chip's benefits.

Portfolio management

Product life cycle

The product life cycle (PLC) is a valuable concept to help understand the stages through which a product offer will pass. That is its sole value. It cannot be used for forecasting or evaluation, because there is no way to quantify the curve. It is not a tool of management.

The PLC, however, is probably the best known model in all marketing education and training. It is simple to understand and use. It puts obvious common sense into graphical form. It provides a shorthand way to describe the overall position of a product offer. It is an essential concept, but it is not a management tool.

The PLC was developed into a management tool by the Boston Consulting Group. The original BCG matrix was a major breakthrough in management thinking. It has formed the basis from which today's sophisticated product portfolio and strategy models have been developed.

A product offer has a life span. It will be developed and launched. If successful it will grow, and settle into a period of maturity. Eventually it will decline. This can be plotted as a curve as in Figure 6.2.

The classic shape of a PLC curve is an S on its side, but the shape of the S will vary with the longevity of the product offer. A short-lived fashion product's curve, for example, may look more like a U than an S. Some PLCs are a succession of S shapes, as succeeding models lengthen the life of the original concept.

Figure 6.2 also contains the seven decision points:

- Go/no go decisions have to be made as the concept passes through the new product development (NPD) process.
- A test market may be run, which will provide valuable management information but may also alert competitors to the new product offer.
- Many decisions have to be made concerning the launch, and the growth period must be fully supported. (See below.)

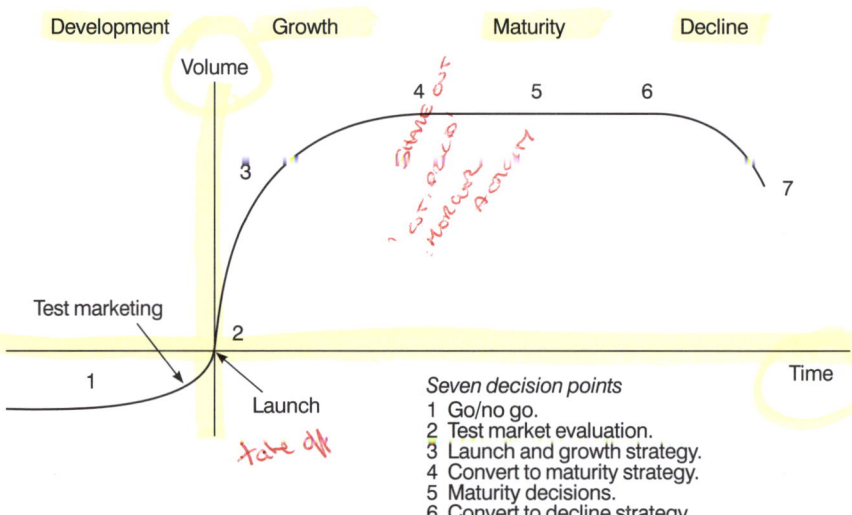

Figure 6.2
Produce life cycle

- Once maturity is reached the aim must be to maintain market share and enhance profitability.
- Decline is inevitable, but many products have been rejuvenated by a combination of skilful management and an on-going demand. (Persil has been a leading brand for nearly a hundred years, but was badly shaken as a result of management misjudgement at the beginning of the 1990s.)
- Death is also inevitable, but management at least has the option of closing down a product offer rather than waiting for sales to cease.

We shall return to these decision needs as we cover portfolio management and NPD.

The PLC's value
Marketers make much of the PLC because it:

- Helps managers to understand the stages through which product offers must pass.
- Identifies the key decision points where strategies and/or tactics must change.
- Allows strategies and/or tactics to be developed that are best suited to each stage.

There is no way that any of the decision points can be predicted with accuracy – it is for each manager to use his best judgement. The PLC warns that a decision will have to be made, but is of no help in showing when, nor what type of decision it should be. For strategic planning we need portfolio analysis.

Planning
Operational planning is concerned with the tactical matters of achieving strategic objectives. In times of fast growth organizations can get away with operational planning alone simply because there are so many opportunities. This is not to say that the best choices are made – but when an organization is making a healthy profit many managers feel no need to plan strategically to achieve more.

The need for strategic planning is emphasized when market conditions tighten, when there are fewer opportunities and competition increases.

Strategic planning can be based on a 'portfolio' approach. An organization's businesses can be managed in much the same way as one manages a portfolio of shares on a stock exchange. Which opportunities ought to be supported, which maintained, which abandoned?

Organizational focus
The concept of organization or business is too wide for effective planning ... especially as organizations become larger through acquisition and merger. The adoption of the marketing concept changed the focus from a business-centred to a market- or customer-centred approach. Levitt made it clear in the 1950s that a business must be seen as a customer-satisfying process and not a goods-producing process.

When this major conceptual step has been taken it is possible to re-define the purpose of an organization. It is selling benefit, not product.

Product orientation	*Market (Benefit) orientation*
We run an airline.	We help people to travel.
We sell groceries.	We help housewives to nourish their families.
We supply telephones.	We help people to communicate.

Ford, in April 1999, announced a major shift in emphasis. Their new chairman, William Clay Ford, announced:

Our 21st century vision is to become the world's leading consumer company that supplies automotive products and services.

This major change of focus occasioned a revolutionary reappraisal of what Ford should be offering. Their first actions were to:

- Launch a joint insurance venture with a major British insurance group.
- Take over Kwik-Fit, Europe's leading car-repair chain.
- Make a bid for the RAC's roadside service and recovery arm.
- Strengthen Hertz, their car rental chain.
- Refocus their product ranges into strategic business units (SBUs) that best meet the needs of the new markets.

Mr Ford is also quoted as saying: 'In five years from now we will be a different company, and five years from then we'll be another different company.'

Portfolio planning at strategic level is a key tool in such strategic decisions whether the organization be global, such as Ford, or simply a small independent operator.

Strategic business units

The process of business identification shows that within organizations there are units that can operate alone, but within the main organization. From the market's viewpoint they are separate businesses. They are termed *Strategic Business Units*. An SBU has three characteristics:

- It can be planned separately from the remainder of the organization because it is a single business, or a collection of related businesses.
- It has its own competitors.
- It is run by a manager who is responsible for strategic planning and profit performance and has control over most of the factors affecting profit.

A manager of an SBU can take strategic decisions without interference from corporate planners. Yet he is supported by a corporate planning team who want to ensure that his return on investment is at an acceptable level. It is a very effective way to run a business.

Product portfolio

Most organizations have more than one product and each will be positioned on its own PLC. Management therefore has the problem of managing the portfolio of products as well as each product itself. Judgements have to be made about which products to support, which to capitalize upon, which to run down and terminate. In particular there must be decisions about the areas of research and development (R&D) from which new products should come.

None of these decisions is helped, except in a general way, by the standard PLC.

The Boston Matrix

The Boston Consulting Group, a leading management consultancy, transformed the classic PLC into a quantified form in the 1970s. The Boston Matrix has the major advantages that it is both visual and dynamic. It can be used to map an organization's products, or the product's market-place(s). It is particularly useful to indicate strategic strengths and weaknesses. It is helpful to cash flow management. It is therefore extremely useful at strategic level. Figure 6.3 shows the basic BCG growth/share matrix.

The two axes represent market growth rate and market share. New products would only be entered into markets with growth potential, and would, of course, start with a zero share. Thus they would appear in the upper right quadrant – named as either wildcat or question mark.

In time they would either gain share and so move across into the star box, or fail and decline into the dog quadrant.

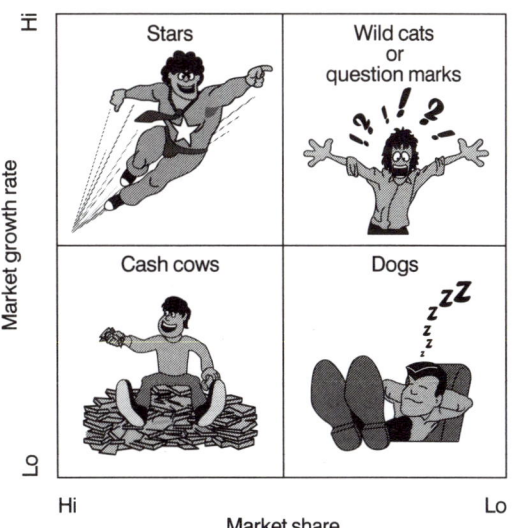

Figure 6.3
Boston Consulting Group, growth/
share matrix

From the star box, as they gained a maturity status they would become cash cows. In the course of time their share would decline as new products entered, and so they would shift across into the dog kennel.

Each product is represented on the matrix by a circle that is proportional to volume sales. All data is quantified and so the BCG concept is an ideal basis for computer modelling to facilitate forecasting and contingency planning.

Market growth rate

The matrix is designed to be of major benefit in growing markets, and it is for management to decide on the rate of growth which they feel is needed if they are to invest in new product development. In many markets the growth rate is negligible – in FMCG it is around 1 per cent – and for these the Boston Matrix is not an appropriate tool.

Relative market share

The strength of a product has much to do with market share (i.e. size), and with market dominance. If product A has 60 per cent of the market and B has 20 per cent the relative market share is 3:1. If A had 40 per cent it would be 2:1, and if both were equal the ratio would be 1:1.

Relative market share indicates the power held by each product in the market relative to the major competitor. This power usually translates into profits and cash flow.

Cash flow

There are only three sources of cash available to an organization: from the shareholders, reserves and profits. Shareholders require a return on their investment, which can only be paid from profits, and reserves have been generated from profits. Therefore the only valid source of long-term cash is profit.

Management are concerned with cash flow above all other considerations. Without cash a business must fold. Even a business that is trading profitably will close if customers do not settle their accounts. This is quite hard for young managers to understand, but it is extremely important. 'Paper profits' have to be turned into cash flow if they are to have meaning. The importance of efficient and effective control on cash cannot be stressed highly enough.

Quadrant strategies

- *Question marks* (Low market share, high market growth rate) Products entering the market need full support. They cannot generate enough to

143

pay their own way and so risk capital is invested in them until they succeed, or are forced out of the market. A common error is to expect success to come too quickly, and to underfund products in this quadrant.

- *Stars* (High market share, high growth rate) Star products are successes. They are gaining in volume, by acquiring market share in an expanding market. Market share is now built most easily because the market is new and growing. Once the market stabilizes it is far more difficult – and expensive – to acquire market share.

  It follows that investment is needed until maturity is reached. This short-term investment pays back over the long term and so investment decisions have to be concerned with volume achievement and market/product life.

- *Cash cows* (High market share, low growth rate) Established products in stable markets need sufficient support to maintain their position, but are substantial generators of revenue and profits. It is from this quadrant that the bulk of an organization's profits will come.

  A major error is to assume that because the product and market are established there is little cause for concern. Managers who expect every market to be under challenge will be taking positive action to replace their products before a competitor does so.

  It follows that a proportion of profit should be devoted to R & D as well as to the support of products that in time will become cash generators.

  There are two forms of cash cow product: the 'cash cow', which is expected to generate funds over a substantial period, and the 'milch cow'.

  The cash cow will normally be of major importance, and hold a substantial market share. It follows that it will have to continually fight off competition, and that funds must be allocated to its long-term healthy survival. It is a major error to drain away too much of the profits earned to support projects that have yet to prove themselves.

  Milch cow products are those which are in the process of replacement, but which are still generating substantial funds. Cross-ply tyres were not replaced by radials overnight – but once their demise was certain they ceased to have long-term value and so could be milked heavily with no investment to sustain their life. Milch cow products are on their way into the dog quadrant.

- *Dogs* (Low market share, low growth rate) In the 'dog kennel' are all the products that have either passed through the cash cow stage or fallen straight into the kennel from the quadrant above. They need not be making a loss, but they are not of long-term value in themselves.

  Dog products can supply limited funds for quite a time before being eliminated. They can be useful in support of established products. Finally, it is possible that competitors have similar products and it may be possible to either sell the product to a competitor or to buy from a competitor. Thus two or three 'dogs' may be brought together and between them make up a sufficient force in the market to survive profitably for longer than any one could do alone.

  When used in support of an established product they can act as 'loss-leaders' and be sold below a competitor's price; they can be promoted heavily in areas of competitive strength; they can be used in sales promotion activity. They can even be used to distract a competitor by aggressive marketing in a market where he is vulnerable.

Relative market share

The basic matrix is easily adapted to one of relative market share. Figure 6.4 shows a relative share matrix for RTJ Engineering (which was a company that appeared in a CIM mini-case).

Note that the market growth rate axis relates to the markets in which RTJ had a presence. Thus it includes two quadrants of negative growth, and because we know they exist we omit the line of distinction between the upper quadrants.

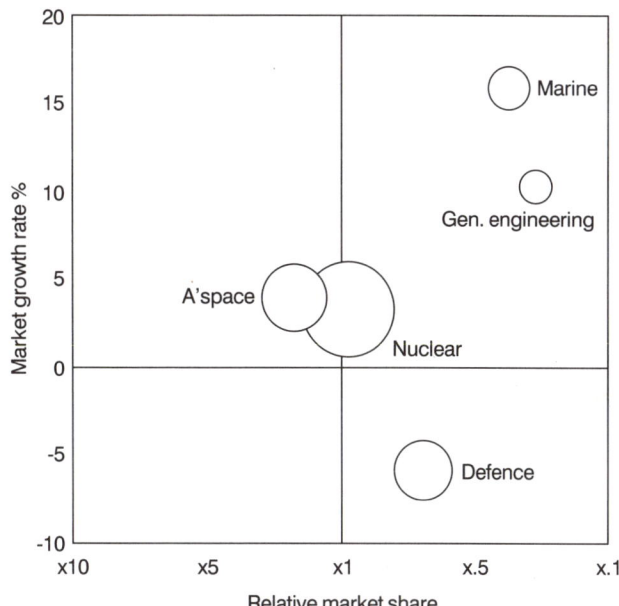

Figure 6.4
RTJ Engineering Ltd, relative
share portfolio matrix

The market share axis now is logarithmic, and so each SBU can be shown as relative to the major competitor in each market.

Figure 6.5 shows the data from which the relative market shares were calculated.

Two examples to show how the calculations are made:

- *Nuclear* RTJ's sales are £13 m, as are those of the major competitor. The ratio is therefore 13:13 or 1:1.
- *Aerospace* RTJ's sales are £12 m. The nearest competitor's sales are £9 m. Ratio is 12:9 or 4:3. Therefore the relative share of RTJ to the competitor is 1.33.

This matrix would be only one of a series, a snapshot in time, and so tells us very little. As one of an on-going series, however, the dynamics of the market would be revealed.

	RTJ's sales 1994 (£m)	Number of direct competitors	Sales of the 3 largest firms in the sector (£m)	Forecast annual growth rate (%)
Nuclear	13	5	13* - 13 - 8	3
Aerospace	12	8	12* - 9 - 6	4
Defence	9	12	15 - 12 - 11	(6)
Marine	6	7	18 - 12 - 6*	15
General engineering	4	16	15 - 14 - 10	8
Total	44 (Forecast)			
Note: Figures asterisked represent RTJ's sales within the sector				

Figure 6.5
RTJ data

BCG

Take 10 minutes and calculate relative market share for each of our products. Then add them to the BCG matrix. Remember that you plot with circles, each of which indicates the volume sales of the product. Note that the X axis is logarithmic, not linear.

We have five products, each in a separate market:

Product	Sales £m	Sales of the top three competitors			Market growth rate (per cent)	Relative share
A	0.7	0.7	0.7	0.6	15	
B	1.8	1.8	1.6	0.5	18	
C	2.0	5.2	2.5	2.4	7	
D	10.8	10.8	6.6	5.3	4	
E	0.5	0.5	0.2	0.1	2	

(**See:** Debriefing at the end of the unit.)

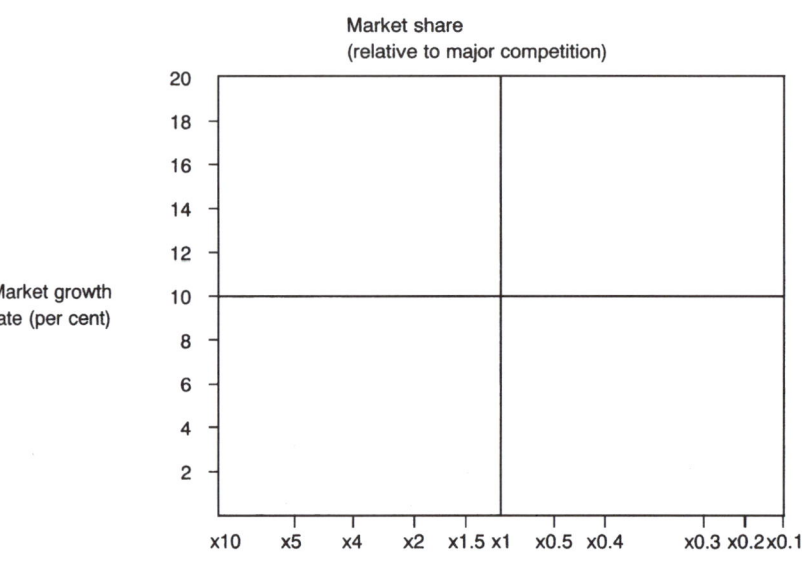

Figure 6.6
BCG matrix

Product mix

Most organizations will prefer to have a mix of product offerings, often within a range of markets. By so doing they cover the risk of collapse of any one market or product – but they also take on the responsibilities of managing different product/market conditions

On the one hand they risk having their eggs in one basket. On the other they risk over-extension.

There is no right answer – individual managements' judgement and style will determine the route. There are, however, two main ways of extending a product mix: by width and by depth.

- *Product-mix width* refers to an extended line of different product offers.
- *Product-mix depth* refers to a range of types of the same product offer.

Figure 6.7 illustrates a typical FMCG manufacturer's use of both width and depth.

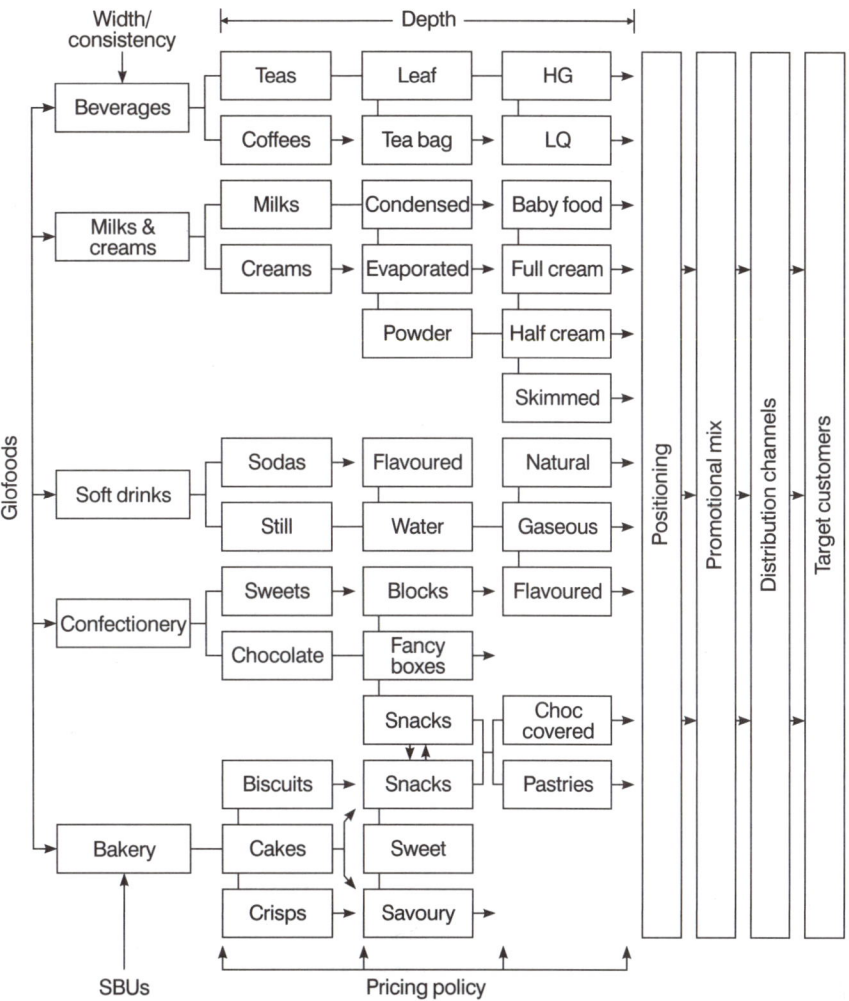

Figure 6.7
Marketing mix strategy. Source: *Marketing in Management*, Worsam and Wright (1995), Pitman, page 323.

Branding

Marketing's role, as should be clear, is to focus the efforts of the organization so that corporate objectives are met. It doesn't matter if the marketer works in industry, commerce, the social services or for a charity, the basic principles remain the same. Marketing is an exchange of value for mutual satisfaction. It is only necessary to determine 'value' and establish a way to effect mutual exchange.

For many organizations the concept of value is encapsulated in Brand Identity. With the development of self-service in retail came the realization that products have to sell themselves from the shelf. The advent of mass communications has allowed marketers to develop and refine this process and international brands are now commonplace. This is because communications are transcending national boundaries and people are far more mobile than ever before. Consumer expectation has been developed by marketing to the point where they expect to find their favourite brand wherever they are. They do not expect to have to hunt for it under a different name or in a different package.

The big brand

A major argument raged throughout the late 1980s and into the 1990s. Is the day of the big brand over? Can any manufacturer now afford the major investment needed to establish a big brand? Many answered 'No' to the latter and went on to show that there would be no more KitKats, no more Coca-Cola.

147

But they reckoned without the major changes that are taking place within the channels of distribution. Power has shifted in the grocery market from the manufacturers to the big retailers. It is the Tesco's, Sainsbury's and Safeway's who determine what will be stocked and what promoted. It is the retailers who are the new big brand owners.

Whereas Tesco and Sainsbury are still predominantly British brands, Safeway is international, as is Marks & Spencer. Continent, Auchan and Carrefour are big brands in France. Such is the power of an established brand, and so prohibitive the cost of establishing a new one, that new big brands are likely to grow steadily as the supermarkets have or be extensions such as Virgin.

It must also be remembered that branding is not an exclusively retail-centred activity. The big motor brands seem totally secure. Ford are keeping the Jaguar brand rather than merging it into the Ford family. BMW are doing the same with Range Rover. Banks are trying to brand themselves and each has an exclusive logo.

In the non-commercial sectors the idea that they can benefit from branding is only just beginning to be appreciated, but who has not heard of such brands as Oxfam, the Red Cross and BUPA?

Nestlé concluded a joint marketing agreement with the French hyper-market, Casino and grocery chain, Auchan, in October 1994. This initiative includes the placement of corporate representatives in store in order to secure the future of Nestlé brands in the face of determined moves to create pan-European 'own-label' brands.

Yves Barbieux, Nestlé France's president is quoted as saying:

It is a question of survival. If we cannot find a way for retailers to earn money with our products we're doomed in the long term. No brand today is irreplaceable. Not even Coke.

Extending Your Knowledge	The British Producers and Brand Owners Group was formed in March 1994 by Unilever, Mars, Proctor and Gamble, Nestlé and Guinness to defend their brands against what they regard as 'passing off' by retailers of own-label products.
	There has been a long-term policy of stocking only the top two brands plus the store's own-label. Now that own-label is established as a brand there is a tendency to cut back to top brand and store brand only. Billions of pounds have been invested in the established brands yet retailers can cut them from their shelves as soon as they feel strong enough. Nestlé and Unilever between them account for 11 of the UK's 50 top selling brands and if they are worried you can see that the situation in the marketplace has already changed.
	Will they be too late to protect their key brands? Only time can tell – but if you were a betting person, where would you put your money?

Brand values

To be successful a brand must sustain a differential advantage in the minds of the target audiences. Purchasers of a brand are confident that the product will perform as specified, and that any problem will be dealt with promptly, efficiently, and without hassle.

The value of the brand lies in its long-term delivery of satisfactions. In its reputation. These intangible values have long been understood, but only recently has it been possible to assign a cash value to a brand.

In the 1980s a series of hostile take-overs of major brand owners revealed that the book value did not reflect the real trading value of the brands. Nestlé created a major precedent when they paid £2.5bn for Rowntree. This was six times asset value, but Nestlé acquired the Rowntree brands: KitKat and Smarties, in particular.

The Accounting Standards Committee in the UK became unhappy about organizations capitalizing their brands' value when Ranks Hovis McDougall added a brands value of £678m to their balance sheet. There is ongoing debate about the rights and wrongs of quantifying brand values, but there is no doubt that brands have considerable value as long as they are well managed.

Brand management

Many marketers begin their career as assistant brand managers, and progress to brand managers and group brand managers. Occasionally, even today, the term 'product manager' may be used – but as branding becomes ever more important it is no longer a credible title.

The brand manager's job was to take full responsibility for the brand. To operate as 'managing director' of the brand company. With the increasing importance of brands to organizations, however, top management take a close interest, and so many brand managers now recommend actions that a short time ago they would have initiated on their own authority.

There are two major benefits to the brand manager approach:

- *Cross-functional co-ordination and management*
  All activities centre on the one individual (or team). All decisions concerning the brand pass over the one desk.
- *Consumer orientation*
  At the focus of all information the brand manager must be aware of customer and consumer reaction and needs. With a direct line to any and all concerned the brand manager can make quick and effective contact with internal functions such as costing and production, and with externals such as individual salespeople and customers.

  Consumer complaints should also flow through the brand management office, and are possibly the most important source of data on consumer satisfaction. (We shall return to the subject of complaints in Unit 8.)

Brand promotion

Branding has traditionally been of product offers, but it is now recognized that corporate branding can add value to the organization itself, and be supportive of individual brands.

The big supermarket chains now each have powerful brands, and sell a range of their own-label products under these 'umbrella' brands. Figure 6.8 shows how Nestlé is used as an umbrella corporate brand, within which exist individual family and product brands.

Brand extension

This occurs when a new product offer is added within an existing brand, i.e. the addition of Nescafé Cappuchino within the established Nescafé brand.

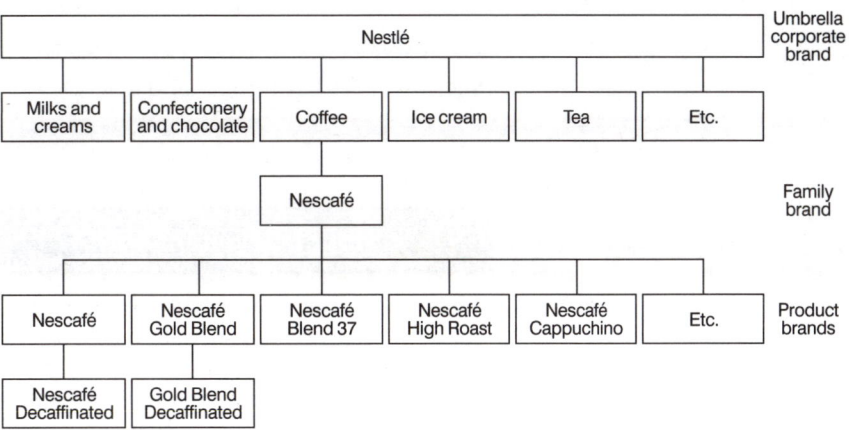

Figure 6.8
Brand family

There is a danger that a brand can over-extend. This danger was pointed out earlier in regard to Virgin's apparent proliferation of product offers with no discernible common focus.

Threats

There are two major threats to any brand:

- Those from competitors – which are the same as any product offer must face.
- Those from branding itself – which come from the very successful promotion and performance of existing brands. As consumers learn that heavily promoted brands can be trusted to deliver satisfactions it becomes ever harder to differentiate. In the electronic industry, for example, how much perceived difference is there in the delivery of product offers from Sony, JVC, Panasonic, etc? How much perceived difference is there in the small cars from Honda and Nissan?

There are national pride and status considerations when comparing Honda, Fiat and Renault – but how far do the brands actually differ in the satisfactions that they deliver? How long will image, based in part on nationalism, be a differentiating factor?

Activity 6.2

Branding
Using a simple matrix identify the key advantages and disadvantages of branding to the manufacturer/supplier and the customer/consumer.

	Advantages	Disadvantages
Manufacturer/supplier		
Customer/consumer		

(**See:** Debriefing at the end of the unit.)

New product development

There is common agreement that the majority of new products fail, that the rate of failure does not seem to be changing over time, and that many firms see failure as one of the prices to be paid for on-going success. An NPD policy is certainly needed – even such a product as a Mars bar has a limited potential (and life).

The new product development process is designed to act as a catchment for the maximum number of new ideas and developments on a theme; for these to be screened for suitability and practicality; for those that pass initial screening to be evaluated for their marketing potential; and only then for the survivors to go through to market testing and commercialization. There will typically be a high dropout rate at each stage, for each has specific criteria that the developing idea/concept/product must meet. Figure 6.9 shows a typical NPD progression.

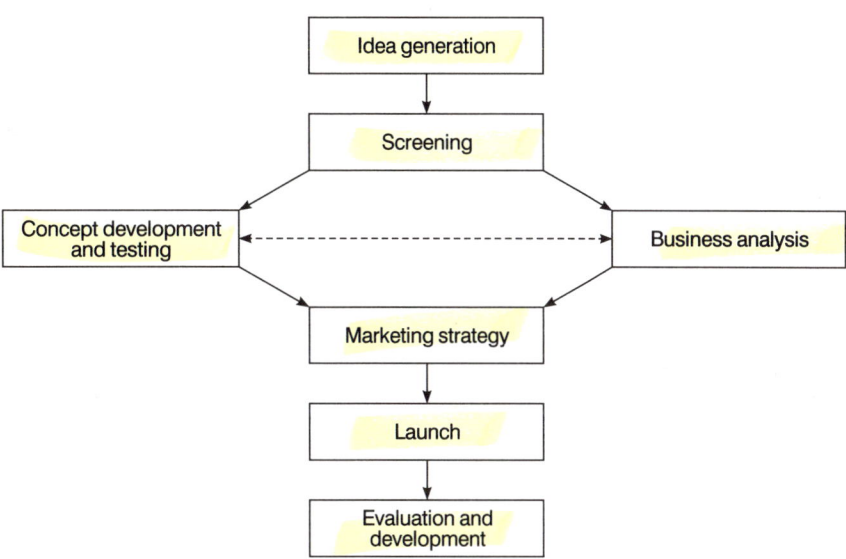

Figure 6.9
New product development

The stages of the NPD process are as follows.

Idea generation
The maximum number of new ideas must be generated, from whatever source, and on an on-going basis. This necessitates an active search of the environment, and for no suggestion to be rejected out of hand. Ideas may be saleable even if they do not fit within organizational strategy.

Customers and consumers are excellent sources of ideas. Observing what people do often indicates ways to facilitate a process. Complaints are also a fruitful source since they contain the problems that people are experiencing and to which solutions may be found.

Screening
Rough-sort ideas for similarity, and then for compatibility with organizational policies, strategies, resource constraints, etc. Note that there is opportunity here for a well organized screening process to sift out ideas that may have potential in another SBU, or even in another organization to which they can be sold.

Concept development and testing
This must be focused on consumer need. Can we find a concept that wraps the idea up into a package that will be welcomed by sufficient consumers? (See below.)

Business analysis
Running along at much the same time as concept development, the business analysis stage begins the process of determining whether the concept would be profitable if brought to the market. There are four 'screens' of evaluation:

- *Screen One: Policy and strategy fit.*
  Does the idea fit within the declared policy and strategies? Is it going to add strength, or disperse and dilute effort? Will it be of a quality to fit with the other product offers/brands?

- *Screen Two: Market audit.*
  Is the potential target market suitable in terms of size, access, etc.? Is it one in which the organization has experience? Are the channels of distribution known, and open?
- *Screen Three: Product technology.*
  Does the needed technology exist within the organization? If not, what would be the investment needed? Would this investment be justified within overall capital planning?
- *Screen Four: Financial.*
  If the concept went to the market, could it command sufficient volume/price/profit to justify the necessary allocation of resources and effort?

Marketing strategy

The development of an affordable marketing strategy that will support the concept. The resultant marketing plan must include all aspects of the marketing mix, including such issues as production scheduling and distribution.

Launch

There may be one or two stages to the launch, depending on market conditions and competitive alertness. If there is time, and security is not an issue, there may well be one or more market tests. Otherwise the risk factor may necessitate an immediate launch.

Findus, for example, were the first to put the frozen savoury pancake onto the British market. They tested it, found it was successful, and went into production. Bird's Eye moved faster. They noted the test, liked the concept, pressed urgently into production, and launched first. They are now regarded as the inventors of the product, and Findus lost their market opportunity.

Evaluation and development

A time for steady nerves, because a new product offer requires support as it moves up its growth curve. Under-finance it and it cannot succeed. Over-finance it and waste money.

A major problem is when to move from a growth to a maturity strategy. Pull resources too soon and all the potential market share may not be gained. Remain in a growth strategy too long and waste resources.

The key thing to remember is that market share obtained early can be protected. If a competitor secures share it is unlikely that it will be relinquished.

Concept testing

All selling is 'concept selling'. Individuals must be sure that the product will deliver a value that they need, at the time needed; and the judgement will be in symbolic terms, i.e. the value of a washing machine will be judged on the pride and satisfaction derived from the clean clothes it facilitates – not on the functional use of the equipment.

Panels of potential consumers are gathered and the concept is presented to them in some appropriate form. There is no requirement for a physical product at this stage, although the addition of specific examples adds reliability to the research. The consumers are presented with a clear description of each concept under test and are then asked for their responses.

Qualitative research of this nature is of key importance in the development of every new product offer, and requires very skilled and experienced researchers.

Task forces

It is a bad mistake to approach the NPD process as a linear exercise. If each stage is taken in turn, then it tends to be handled by specialists who focus on the needs of that stage. Later, however, other specialists may find a problem that they are not equipped to handle. So back up the line comes the whole project.

152

Given the number of departments that have to work on the project, and remembering how internal politics always intervenes, it is surprising that so many projects ever make it through to the market. It is not known how many might have made it ahead of competition if the process was not taken stage by stage.

Today's practice, introduced by such as Ford, sees a task force appointed to manage each new concept that appears to have a chance of viability. This group is made up of representatives from all the key departments. Thus even while one aspect is under focus the other parties are actively present. Potential future problems can be identified and be immediately put under investigation.

No stage is cleared until all identified problems have been solved. All in the task force bear equal responsibility, and share equally in the rewards. The focus is to make the idea prove itself. There is no kudos in simply completing the process. Kudos actually comes from a successful report that justifies a decision to progress or abandon.

Activity 6.3

You have the capability to produce and market a fold-up support that facilitates the reading of newspapers on crowded public transport. You need to test the concept before progressing. Outline your thinking before initiating marketing research.

(**See:** Debriefing at the end of the unit.)

Exam Hints

Management, as we know, is more of an art than a science and there is no one best way of being a manager. Your approach to a situation will be conditioned by your personality, skills, experience and management style. It is unlikely that different managers will take identical approaches, nor come up with identical solutions. Yet each individual manager can achieve the objectives set.

Marketing is not like accounting where there is a legal form to follow and basic numbers always add, subtract, multiply and divide to give the same results. Marketers work with people and it is never possible to totally predict behaviour.

It follows that you should be pleased when you arrive at unique solutions to given situations. Initiative and creativity, coupled with clarity, brevity and determination, are key elements of a successful marketer's make up.

Unit Activity

Use the following matrix to compare the strengths and weaknesses of the product life cycle and portfolio planning.

	PLC	Portfolio planning
Planning strengths		
Planning weaknesses		
Control strengths		
Control weaknesses		

(**See:** Debriefing at the end of the unit.)

Summary

In this unit we have seen:

- That people buy benefits packaged as product offers.
- A product offer is made up of physical, functional and symbolic attributes.
- The PLC is a valuable concept, but not a management tool.
- Strategic planning is based on a portfolio approach.
- The BCG matrix allows the PLC to be quantified.
- Cash flow is the most important management concern.
- Relative market share allows the comparative strengths of products to be evaluated.
- A product mix should have width and depth.
- Brand values add considerably to an organization's worth.
- Brand management focuses on the brand as though it is a business in itself.
- Brand managers co-ordinate from a consumer viewpoint.
- New product development is an essential on-going activity.
- The process should be carefully planned and well managed.
- A task force approach is more effective and efficient than a linear process.

Debriefing

Activity 6.1
The relative market shares are:

Product	Sales £m	Sales of the top three competitors			Market growth rate (per cent)	Relative share
A	0.7	0.7	0.7	0.6	15	1.0
B	1.8	1.8	1.6	0.5	18	1.13
C	2.0	5.2	2.5	2.4	7	0.38
D	10.8	10.8	6.6	5.3	4	1.64
E	0.5	0.5	0.2	0.1	2	2.5

Note: The top three in the market includes our product, if applicable. Ratio is taken against the major competitor. Sometimes this will be larger, sometimes smaller.

When plotted the portfolio is shown to be:

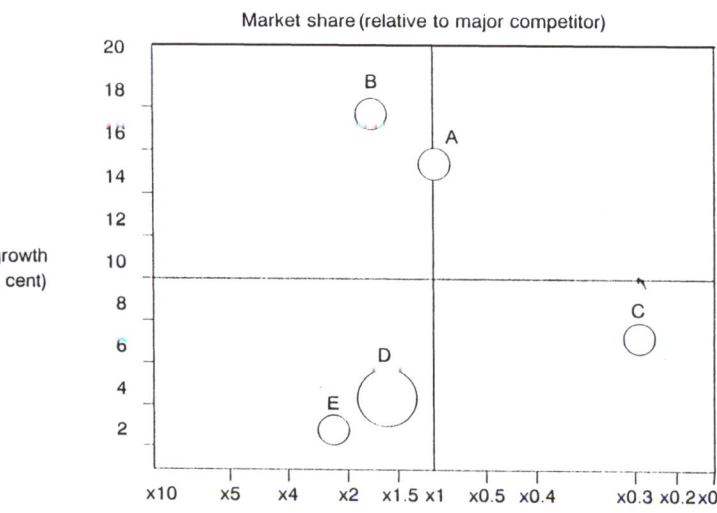

Figure 6.10
BCG Matrix, complete

154

Activity 6.2

Compare your thoughts with this completed matrix.

	Advantages	Disadvantages
Manufacturer/supplier	• Differentiates the product. • Creates customer loyalty. • Acceptance by middlemen. • Sells product off shelf. • Transfers positive values to sister products. • Gives manufacturer more control over marketing through the channel. • Helps new products achieve reputation quickly. • Brands can be targeted to segments. • Selling a branded product is easier. • Ability to sell through direct marketing.	• Consumers beginning to believe that all branded products are equally good. • Middlemen beginning to create their own brands. • Transfers any negative values to sister products. • Retailers becoming more powerful and competing with manufacturer brands. • Retailers piggy-backing on brand concepts. • Suitable mainly for national and international brands. • Large capital involvement in establishing brand identity.
Customer/consumer	• Assurance of known quality/value. • Security of after-market support. • Confidence to buy untried products that carry a trusted brand. • Easy to find in stores, or through direct-marketing channels. • International availability. • Status attached to certain brands.	• Perception that one 'is paying for the name'. • Caution that the product may not live up to the name. • Status attached to certain brands does not match desired lifestyle image.

Activity 6.3

You need to get feedback from potential consumers, and so you need to profile your potential consumer. Then you will be interested in discovering factors such as:

- How welcome is the product offer?
- Would it add value in the consumer's opinion?
- What changes are needed to make it marketable?
- What is the likely price that would be paid?
- How can the consumer be accessed with promotion and with product?

Your research objectives, therefore, would be something like this:

Within ten weeks, research typical consumers to:

- Identify their perceived needs for the stand.
- Identify modifications/improvements.
- Determine market segmentation.
- Gain an indication of price.
- Determine the point(s) of purchase.
- Discover the media that targets the potential consumers.

Unit activity

This is an important activity since examiners tend to ask questions that require the ability to discuss and cross-relate these topics. Be certain you can handle this area. These are some of the points that you should have identified:

	PLC	Portfolio planning
Planning strengths	Five-stage view Easy to understand	Focus on SBU or products Allows variety of planning approaches Can be quantified Allows prediction
Planning weaknesses	Historical only No predictive capability Not quantifiable	Circle sizes may not reflect true benefits Likely to distort true picture as visuals are simplistic Quadrant position dependent on management decision, not objective data
Control strengths	Can suggest possibility of need for action Provides a useful visual shorthand	Relative market share shown Accurately reflects position Can be current or future based Encourages forward planning
Control weaknesses	Totally useless Imprecise and inaccurate Not quantifiable	Little value in stable markets, but has been developed into models which are useful

Unit 7 Pricing operations

Objectives

In this unit you will:

❑ Examine the importance of price to a marketer.
❑ Discover the relevance of value in the purchase decision.
❑ Investigate methods of determining price.
❑ Consider the importance of psychology in pricing.
❑ Develop an understanding of transfer pricing.

By the end of this unit you will be able to:

❑ Establish pricing strategies.
❑ Calculate prices that fit anticipated market conditions.
❑ Conduct a break-even analysis.
❑ Adapt prices to achieve short-term tactical objectives.

Study Guide

If you are working through this book in sequence it is now time to review your study techniques. For many of us, unfortunately, the good intentions that we begin with fall away with time. At the mid-point of the study year the exams can seem too far away to be significant. Yet in only a few short months you will need to revise.

At revision time you do not want to have to re-learn material you have already covered. But that is what will happen if your notes are not memorable . . . and if you do not review them regularly.

Exam success comes from methodical progress, not from flashes of inspiration. The golfer, Gary Player, stated a philosophy that holds good in all walks of life. 'The more I practise', he said, 'the luckier I get.'

You need both theoretical and current market knowledge that is accessible and fresh in your mind. And you need to be skilled in examination technique. Get these all together and you will have no troubles on 'the day'.

Expect to take about two hours to work through this unit and its activities.

Price

Price is a constant feature of life, and goes by a variety of names. Fares, premiums, rates, interest and retainers are all alternative names for price. Wages and salaries are part of the price of employing staff. A Road Fund Licence is part of the price of taking a vehicle onto state-owned roads. Tolls are charged by motorway companies.

There are two sides to price, however. What is price to the supplier is cost to the buyer. The P of price is matched by the C of cost.

If the cost is judged too high it will be resisted. It may have to be paid if there is no alternative, but there will be continuing discontent, and a rapid switch to a competitor when the opportunity occurs.

157

Differential

A commodity has no unique features to distinguish it from its competitors, and so its price is determined simply from the relationship between supply and demand.

Differential provides a value to which potential customers will be attracted, and so enable an enhanced price to be charged.

It is of major importance to prevent the loss of identity and, worse, the loss of product status. Hoover found its brand name being used to describe all vacuum cleaners – 'I'd like to buy an Electrolux hoover, please'. A major promotional strategy for Nescafé in the 1960s was to protect the brand. To prevent: 'I'd like a Maxwell House nescafé, please'.

Importance

Price is the only element in the marketing mix that produces revenue: all the others incur costs. It is the most flexible element in the mix: it can quickly be changed. It also creates the number-one problem for marketers:

- *Prices tend to be fixed from supplier's cost, not from the customer's perspective.*
  Adding a percentage to costs is a simple way to set a price, but that price is unlikely to relate to the value put on the product offer by the purchasers. If it is too high there will be few sales, if too low there may be excessive sales at lower profits – or no sales if the low price is seen to indicate poor quality.
- *Prices are not revised often enough.*
  Marketers should be aware of market conditions and set prices accordingly. There are often opportunities to capitalize on market changes.
- *Price is set independent of marketing strategy.*
  The integrated nature of the marketing mix means that the same message must be transmitted by each element. When prices are set from a financial viewpoint they can convey a perceived message that is out of line with the strategies of the other six Ps.
- *Prices tend to be static.*
  Opportunities exist to vary prices with market segments and purchase occasions. Yet there is a tendency to charge the same price for what seems to be the same item. This functional viewpoint disregards the customer's perception of value. The same ice cream is valued higher on a hot day at the seaside than when bought in bulk from a supermarket for the home freezer.

Figure 7.1 shows why price is a unique element within the marketing mix.

Figure 7.1
The uniqueness of price

When the Mini was launched into the UK car market it was a revolutionary product that was far ahead of its competitors. It could easily have commanded a price premium. Instead it was priced at economy level. This forced the competitors to also price low. The result was a negative impact on car manufacturers' profits for a decade. Not a bad thing for the consumer? Perhaps – but the R&D budgets were hard hit. What effect did this have on the overall quality of motoring?

It is felt that the Mini pricing decision was made in finance, not marketing, and based on the original concept of a 'car for the people'. Nobody appreciated that the Mini offered a unique and exciting motoring experience that should not be priced low.

Incidentally, it was reported 20 years later that costs were never fully calculated and that the huge sales over the two decades had achieved break-even at best.

Value

The concept of value was mentioned in Unit 3. It is vital to always remember that buyers make their value judgements on factors that include price, never on price alone. These are typical of the factors that can affect value:

- *Benefit package offered.*
  What the product offer will do for the buyer.
- *After-sales service.*
  How long the product offer will work, and how quickly it will be put back into service if it fails.
- *Status.*
  Certain brands carry high status, and carry a high value because of it. Rolex watches are excellent, but are they that much better functional timekeepers than their immediate competitors?
- *Ease of installation and/or use.*
  Setting up a PC is complex. Setting up a Mac is easy. The Macintosh carries high value from its simplicity in use. (But the PC carries high value because of the range of products available, and because it has become the standard in use.)
- *Useful lifetime of the product offer.*
  A long life often commands a higher value since the average cost over time is lower. Not for fashion products, however, where purchases are discarded whilst still holding functional value.
- *Reputation.*
  Supplier's reputation can be crucially important. A low price is only attractive if there will not be long and difficult arguments about delivery, after-sales service, and so on.
- *Guarantee/warranty period.*
  Generally a longer guarantee period is highly valued. Not, of course, if the supplier is suspect, or if the product is required only for short term use.
- *Price asked, gross and net.*
  In some markets the practice is to haggle. If so, there must be price flexibility built into the asking price. Where taxes have to be changed, a decision must be made – price net or gross?

Remember: Marketing always aims for an exchange of value. Price is simply a convenient method for indicating an important part of the value package.

Consider the way that prices change for what would seem to be an identical facility. Why:

- Do seat prices in a sport's stadium change when the league champions are due to visit?
- Does the same seat in an auditorium command a different price for a cinema, concert and a theatrical performance? Does the price change by day and/or time of day?
- Do season ticket holders receive a discount?
- Do airlines have such a wide variety of seat prices?

(**See:** Debriefing at the end of the unit.)

Profit

The difference between revenue and costs is profit – but there are many levels of profit that can be taken into account. These will be calculated in great detail by our financial colleagues. Marketers' main concern is to generate a *return* that is consistent with the agreed financial objectives. To achieve this requires an understanding of return.

The aim should be to turn over the same capital investment as often as possible and the profit per unit should be set so as to maximize the overall return. Fast-selling goods can yield an excellent return with only a small profit margin. Slower-selling goods must have a higher margin to yield the same return.

Let us assume that we have £1 000 to invest. Is it better to put it into goods that yield 5% or 25%? The answer comes from the number of times the investment is turned:

£1 000 invested at 5% yields £50 each time the stock is sold out.

If it sells out daily, then the return is $365 \times £50 = £18\,250$ per annum.

To achieve the same return on goods with a 25% margin they must turn over 73 times. (18 250/250)

If the stock-turn is only 12 (monthly), then the profit margin on revenue must be 152%.

Thus slow-selling goods such as Rolex watches have to be expensive because they have a relatively small target market and relatively few repeat sales within it.

The situation is complicated because normally not every unit in stock will be sold each period, and seasonal goods may not sell out completely. Thus capital can be tied up in stock, and generate no income. In many cases it is better to clear slow-moving stocks at a low profit, even at a loss, providing that the capital thus released is reinvested in stock that will move.

Objectives

Selection of price strategies and tactics can be related to:

- *Resources*
  A dominant organization can subsidize a low price if necessary.
- *Cash flow*
  When cash is urgently needed a price reduction can sometimes offer a short-term solution.
- *Promotion*
  Price tactics must match the promotional objective. If market share is the aim, then prices must encourage additional sales.

- *Distribution*
  Securing distribution may require bonuses in stock, or a contribution to the retailer's advertising.
- *Market segments*
  In a fully segmented policy every element of the marketing mix, including price, is tailored to the segment's perceived needs.

Pricing strategies

Six major objectives are available to the commercial organization:

- *Survival*
  When under pressure from competitors, changing market conditions and so on the need may be to generate enough cash to keep the plant operating and to retain key staff. It may be necessary in the short term to trade at the margin (see below) even though this will mean that revenue does not cover all the costs. Cash is always the most important management consideration, for profits on paper may never turn into actual cash.
- *Maximum current profit*
  The emphasis is on current, short-term financial performance. Management must know the demand and cost implications and estimate accurately. As market conditions and competitor response can never be accurately forecasted the long-term effects of this strategy are likely to be damaging.
- *Maximum current revenue*
  Aiming for long-term sales revenue growth may lead to increases in market share, increased production and economies of scale that reduce costs.
- *Maximum sales growth*
  The aim is to increase unit sales, reduce unit costs and so increase long-term profits. By setting the lowest price consistent with an acceptable return management puts pressure on the competition and focuses on *penetrating* the market.
- *Maximum market skimming*
  High prices are set for new product offers to *skim* the purchases from the early adopters. As the adoption curve rises, so prices are brought steadily down to maintain interest, hold market share and generate long-term profits.
- *Product-quality leadership*
  To emphasize the quality of the product offer a management may price it sufficiently above the competition to differentiate it. When establishing Nescafé as the market leader the price policy was to always be 7.5 per cent higher at retail than the other instant coffees. Individual salespeople were authorized to immediately change prices to maintain the differential no matter what competitors did.

Other pricing objectives include *partial cost recovery* and *social pricing*. The first is typified by a university making up the shortfall in grant income. The second by a charity providing for the needs of the elderly.

Psychology in pricing

An understanding of consumer behaviour is essential if prices are to meet the agreed objectives. Experience over thousands of years has established what has only recently been proven – that people's perceptions rule their decisions. Prices are read optimistically. Thus £4.99 is seen as *far cheaper* than £5.00.

For the same reason it is better to display higher prices as £999, £1999, even £99 999.

When taxes have to be added at PoS, as is sales tax in America, it is normal to price at, say, $1.99, knowing that the customer will expect to pay the tax on top.

Price points are psychologically significant prices. These vary by the market and product, but the principle is consistent. If the £1.99 price can no longer be maintained, for instance, the best increase will be to £2.09, even

161

£2.19. Even if a price of £2.03 were possible it is best to go to the next psychological point. Customers perceive no difference between intervening prices, and the larger increase allows the new price to be held for longer.

Pricing tactics

Within an overall strategy it is, of course, possible to modify tactics. These forms of pricing tactics can each be an overall strategy, depending on the organization's market and needs.

- *Skimming*
  Setting a deliberately high price as a product offer enters the market to maximize revenue from early adopters. Often used in conjunction with (or forced by) limited production capacity.
- *Penetration*
  Setting the price low enough to thoroughly penetrate the market, to ensure that as many as possible buy and use the product offer. Often used to build market share so that on-going sales levels are maximized.
- *Imitative*
  Simply following competitors and matching their tactics. This need not be, but usually is, a tactic for a weaker competitor to adopt. Stronger competitors may use it for a specific purpose, as in the Nescafé brand protection example given above.
- *Competitor-based*
  Similar to imitative, but used in a more determined way, as between equals.
- *Buyer-based*
  Prices are set at the level that the 'market will bear'. If the buyer's price can be met, well and good. If not, there is need for a reappraisal.
- *Cost-plus*
  Prices are directly related to cost. Retailers traditionally have used this form of pricing by determining the *mark-up* needed on each category of goods to achieve the target return.
- *Target*
  Also known as *price lining*, this is the leveling out of a range of items bought at different prices so they can be sold on recognized price points.
- *Going-rate*
  Where demand is elastic the prices follow demand. Stock markets are governed by going-rate pricing since share prices vary with demand.
- *Sealed-bid*
  After full negotiations each potential supplier submits his price in a sealed envelope by a given date and time. Much used in government tendering, and in large civil engineering contracts, etc.
- *Marginal*
  Based on the marginal cost of producing one extra unit. No contribution is made to fixed costs, and so marginal pricing is available for special offers only. We shall return to costings when we come to break-even analysis.

Price wars

These occur when a supplier cuts a price, a competitor cuts deeper and the first retaliates. In exceptional conditions prices can tumble to silly levels. Rival filling stations have been reported as selling petrol for coppers in a bid to outdo a rival.

The only (short-term) winners are the customers. The traders each lose profits, and one or both may be forced out of business. Eventually prices must return to economic levels, but may not return to the levels of before the price war. If this happens, then all the suppliers have been forced into a price reduction. All have lost profits. And no commercial advantage has been gained.

Competition through price is foolish. Competitors can match price changes, and so only a short-term gain is made. The best policy, seen every day in the fuel stations' pricing policies, is to make short-term *promotional* reductions. In turn each supplier makes his offer, but always from the base price. Thus promotional campaigns can be based on short-term price differential, without damage to the overall market.

Strategic determinants

Prices are asked by a supplier, but are set by what the buyers will pay. The skilled marketer is led by the market, and sets prices at a level where they will achieve the strategic objectives. Key factors that must be taken into account include the following.

Demand

Goods must be produced, and be available, at the time when the customers want to buy them. This can be within a narrow window of opportunity, such as during the run-in to a period of celebration. It can be a need to have a constant supply of essential products permanently available, such as electricity, gas and water. It may be a need to keep regular customers supplied to maintain loyalty and shut out competitors. Whatever the need, demand can be extremely difficult to forecast.

Demand is said to be *inelastic* when a price change does not significantly affect demand. Figure 7.2 shows that a 25 per cent price fall only increased sales by 5 per cent. Demand is inelastic.

An *elastic* demand responds to price change. Figure 7.3 shows that the same 25 per cent price fall has generated an additional 40 per cent in sales. This product offer has an elastic demand.

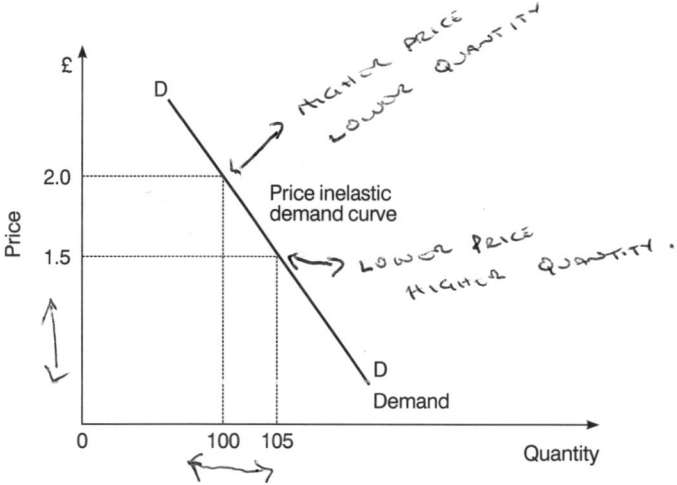

Figure 7.2
Price inelasticity

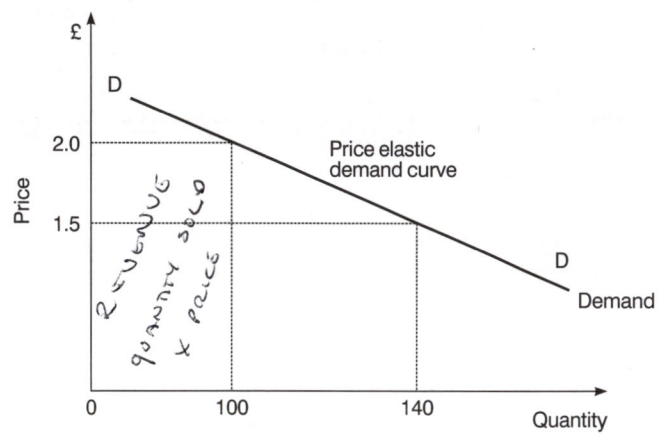

Figure 7.3
Price elasticity

For each of these product offers, determine whether the demand is likely to be elastic or inelastic. Then consider the actions that are open to a marketer in each case.

1 A non-prescription medication such as a cough syrup.
2 A prescription medication such as a strong analgesic to relieve muscular pain.

(**See:** Debriefing at the end of the unit.)

Competitors

Obtaining the *response profile* of each competitor is a major research objective, since with a foreknowledge of likely reaction management is better equipped to make the key strategic decisions.

Positioning and life cycle

Pricing affects demand and therefore impacts on positioning decisions. Likely pricing changes are:

- *Introduction* High promotional costs.
  High prices.
- *Growth* High promotional costs.
  High sales growth.
  Prices begin to come down, to become competitive.
- *Maturity* Lower promotional costs.
  Sales growth slows down, profit is taken.
  Prices stabilize at a level determined by market share/volume/cost/demand relationships.
- *Decline* Minimal promotional costs.
  Sales volume declines.
  Prices remain stable – aggressive price tactics possible within a portfolio approach.

Debtors and creditors

Price negotiation must include provision for prompt payment. There is a danger, especially with large customers, that an agreed payment period may be exceeded. Thus the calculated profit will not be achieved, since interest charges will have to be paid on the capital tied up in unpaid invoices.

There is also a danger that managements may pay bills on time, but not receive payment themselves. Thus a negative cash flow position can be created.

There is a move in the UK to allow suppliers to add a penalty for late payment, but it is also felt that many suppliers will not be able to enforce this against the power of a large customer.

Price floor and ceiling

Hatton and Oldroyd show that there is a price floor and ceiling within which the marketer has to establish price. (See Figure 7.4.)

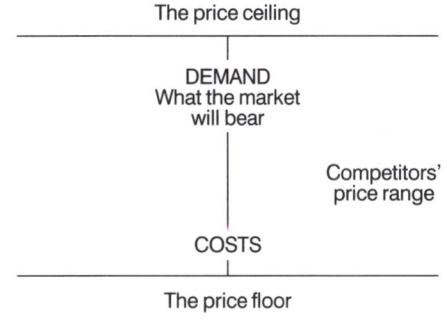

Figure 7.4
Price floor and price ceiling.
(*Source:* Hatton and Oldroyd (1992), *Economic Theory and Marketing Practice.*)

In between the floor and the ceiling are a range of price point options that are available.

Break-even analysis

In all pricing decisions it is necessary to calculate the expected profitability at various levels of sales and price. In all the calculations a point of balance will be observed. This point, where return on sales equals costs incurred, is known as the *break-even* point.

To calculate break-even, costs and expected volume sales at a given price must be estimated. When the two are plotted on a graph (or calculated mathematically) the minimum sales volume for those costs and price is indicated. Management can then determine if this is a realistic sales figure to achieve – if it meets their strategic objectives.

Costs

Costing is a specialized form of financial management and most marketers will be able to call upon a cost accountant for assistance. Remember that he or she is there to advise. In a marketing-oriented firm it is the marketers and management who make price decisions, not the accountants!

Broadly speaking, there are three kinds of cost of concern to marketers:

- *Fixed costs*
  These include all the costs that have to be borne whether the organization trades or not. The costs of servicing capital debt, rent, rates, key staff salaries, etc., are all fixed. They do not vary with activity.
- *Variable costs*
  These vary directly with production volume. Thus the number of glass jars, labels and lids to contain a product offer must be directly related to production volume.
- *Semi-variable costs*
  These contain a mixture of fixed and variable costs. The standing charge for electricity is fixed, while electrical usage may be related to activity, i.e. to production volume.

For marketers' needs a break-even calculated from fixed and variable costs is sufficient. The accountants will happily identify all costs for you and discuss ways of allocating them to fixed and variable.

Constructing a break-even graph

1 Construct a graph with the X and Y axes representing volume and price/cost. Then draw in the fixed cost curve. This will be horizontal because it remains unchanged no matter what volume is produced (Figure 7.5).

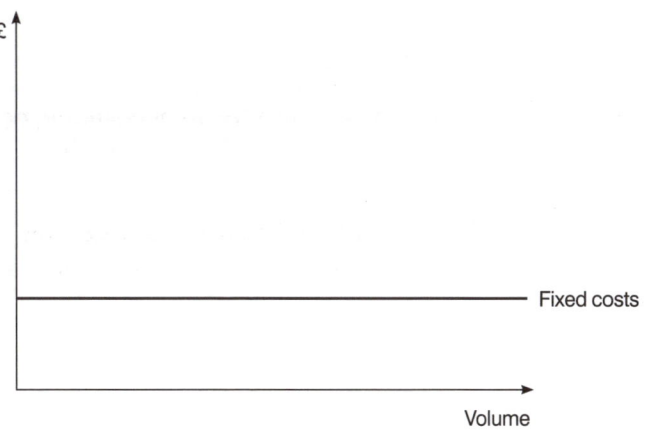

Figure 7.5
Constructing a break-even graph – fixed costs

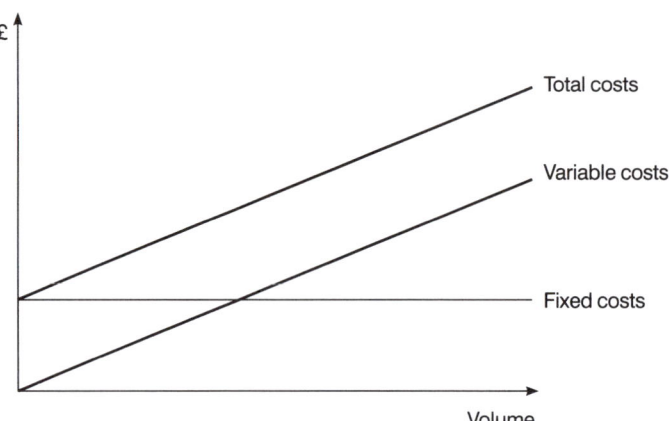

Figure 7.6
Constructing a break-even graph –
variable costs and total costs

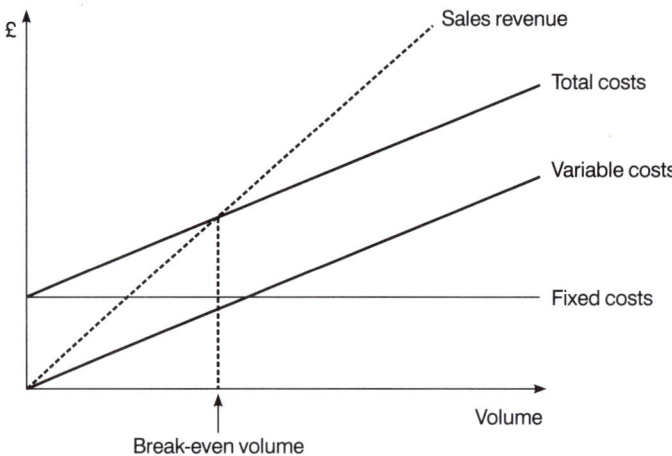

Figure 7.7
Break-even volume

2 Draw in the curve that represents variable costs. This must start from zero when there is no production and extend in a straight line because variable costs are directly proportional to production volume.

Note that in Figure 7.6 the variable cost curve appears twice, for illustration. In practice only the upper curve is needed.

3 Draw in the sales revenue curve. Again, this must be a straight line since it is calculated from price related to volume.

Drop a vertical from the meeting of the revenue and total costs curve – this indicates the sales volume, in units, needed to achieve break-even. (See Figure 7.7.)

Accurate costing is fundamental to accurate pricing, yet it is extremely difficult to allocate costs to individual units of production. How may fixed costs be allocated across departments? To individual production departments? To specific plant? How are semi-variable costs identified and allocated?

Fortunately it is only for tactical marketers to achieve the financial targets established at strategic level. Strategic marketers, however, must have a detailed understanding of costing since the way in which costs are allocated can have major effects within tactical marketing.

Marginal costing and pricing

Given that there are two forms of cost it follows that sales revenue must first cover these if a gross profit is to be made. Revenue must cover the variable costs of production, distribution and marketing, etc., and make a *contribution* to overall fixed costs.

If a price is set to recover only variable costs, then the recovery is at the margin, and the practice is called *marginal pricing*.

166

When considering price it is helpful to know the marginal cost of producing one more unit. If a photographer knows that an extra ten sets of copies will add £200 to costs for chemicals, paper, etc., then he can do the job without a direct loss for that price. It may be that he wants to sweeten a deal, and so would offer a price of £200 or above for the extra work.

Note that anything over the marginal price makes a contribution to fixed costs. Profit is not earned until both fixed and variable costs have been recovered.

Activity 7.3

Consider the circumstances where it would be helpful to understand marginal costing and pricing, and what dangers there are to the organization in allowing uncontrolled pricing at the margin or just above.

(**See:** Debriefing at the end of the unit.)

Price tactics

It is important, as we have seen, to establish and maintain a pricing level within a market. It is easy to drop prices – but very hard to increase them again. Thus tactical tools have been created to allow price variation without damage to overall strategy.

Bonus

A bonus is paid as a reward for some action – to secure the first purchase, perhaps to obtain a 'hot spot' display site.

Bonuses are used in trade and retail promotions (13 for the price of 12, an extra 20 per cent, a special price on a frame when a photographic enlargement is ordered).

Discount

Discounts are sums allowed off a price in consideration for some action. Always expressed as a percentage, they are commonly expressed as *list less five*. In traditional trades such as wholesaling there can be as many as four levels of discount: 20 less 15 less 5 less 2.5 – 20 as the retailer's discount, 15 to cover the wholesaler's margin, 5 as an incentive and 2.5 for cash within 30 days of invoice.

Be careful when negotiating discounts. It is easy to mix real numbers and percentages. If the buyer asks for one free with ten and you want to offer one with twelve, do not offer a 12 per cent discount. That is one with eight (almost). Don't laugh – it is terribly easy to do.

Sale or return

Buyers will sometimes only agree to stock an item if there is no risk to themselves. If no property in the goods passes, then they remain the supplier's property, although in the buyer's premises. Payment is made when the goods are sold. If they do not sell, then they must be collected and returned to stock.

Thus not only is the seller subsidizing the buyer by carrying the costs of the goods, he is allowing the products to go into stock. That is not the same as having them actively promoted. With no inducement to sell it is most likely that sales efforts will be directed to those products where the buyer has accepted the risk of placing a firm order.

Sale or return is not a wise policy for a supplier, but it is extremely popular with buyers. A solution is often to offer a percentage on sale or return – perhaps up to 50 per cent. Both sides, of course, will want the split loaded in their favour.

Promotions

When pricing is used as a form of promotion it is normal for the promotions budget to carry the cost. A Special Offer, for example, is a discount that is limited by time and therefore is categorized as a sales promotion and budgeted accordingly.

Goods or cash?

Inducements paid in goods cost the supplier less than those made in cash because marginal costing applies. Buyers are alert to this, however, and negotiate additional quantities to share in the cost savings. If a bonus offer is accepted, say at 10 per cent, the buyer will be aware that this will actually cost the supplier about 5 per cent. Stress the generosity of the offer, but don't press the 10 per cent.

Transfer pricing

The same term is used in two contexts: internal and export.

Internal

In Unit 3 we met transfer pricing when used internally. The example quoted was of the British Broadcasting Commission's requirement for internal managers to make a 'profit'. Thus managers were forced to quote for their work that other managers would pay for.

Unfortunately the BBC found, as have many managements before them, that they had not distinguished between internal transfers, where resources in notional money are transferred between profit centres, and external contracts, where real money leaves the organization.

Costing is usually at the base of the problem. Large organizations tend to have high fixed costs, which are allocated to individual managers. Small external suppliers tend to have low fixed costs but the same variable costs, i.e. photocopying uses the same amount of paper, toner and electricity. Therefore the external quote tends to be lower, and is accepted. The fallacy, as has been indicated, is that actual money then leaves the organization. Real profitability is made more difficult to achieve.

Export

When an organization's goods are shipped between countries, it must be decided where to take the profits. There are three options: in the producing country, in the marketing country, in a tax-friendly country.

Many considerations must be taken into account, including the generation of sufficient profits in each trading company to keep the shareholders and tax authorities happy.

It obviously makes sense to maximize profits where tax liability can be minimized, and so multinationals adopt an invoicing structure as shown in Figure 7.8.

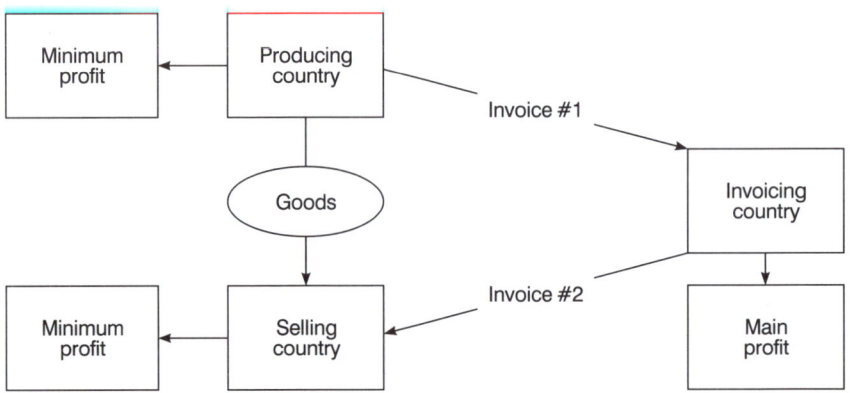

Figure 7.8
Transfer pricing

It will be seen that by invoicing through a tax-friendly country the goods actually travel direct, but become the property of a third party for a period whilst in transit. The minimum price is charged by the producing company and the maximum price is charged to the marketing company. The difference between the two is profit, made where costs are low and taxes non-existent.

Governments naturally seek to see that transfer prices are fair in order to levy taxes on normal rather than artificial profit levels. They are also anxious to collect VAT (sales tax) on normal rather than artificially low prices. They also find difficulty with *barter deals*, where goods are exchanged but little or no money changes hands.

Exam Hints

How to fail your exams – 11 Golden Rules:

1 **Play it by ear**. No need to plan for an examination.
2 **Don't revise**. If you don't know it, revision is a waste of time. If you do know it, why bother with revision?
3 **Aim to just pass**. No wasted effort.
4 **Don't learn exam technique**. Exams are bad enough without learning technique as well!
5 **Do not anticipate questions**. You may be wrong and have just wasted time.
6 **Don't read previous papers or examiners' reports**. It is just not cool.
7 **Just do the first five questions**. They're all as bad anyway.
8 **Don't worry about the actual question**. It's more interesting to write what you want, and showing the examiner you know the subject is what it is all about.
9 **Ignore the instructions**. They only put you off.
10 **Don't check the time**. You could write a few more words instead.
11 **Never check answers**. There will only be a few minor errors.

Acknowledgements to David Pearson
Source: Issue 2, *Marketing Success*, Hints & Tips/2

Another 11 rules will be found in Unit 8.

Unit Activity

As a marketing manager you have been asked to make a 20-minute presentation to undergraduates in their final year on the subject of opportunity cost. You have decided to use an example to which they can all relate – should they take a year off work to take a master's degree? What would be the financial cost and opportunity cost?

Prepare your notes.

(**See:** Debriefing at the end of the unit.)

Summary

In this unit we have seen that:

- Price goes under a number of names but is always a cost that a buyer has to bear.
- Differential distinguishes products with price control from commodities.
- Price generates revenue. The other Ps incur costs.
- Prices should be set from the customers' viewpoint.
- Prices should be consistent with marketing strategy and be adapted as market conditions change.
- Value is the criterion used by customers in choice. Price is a part of value.

- Profit is the difference between total costs and revenue.
- Actual profit is a function of yield and stock-turn.
- An overall pricing strategy is essential.
- Cash is more important than profit.
- Price points are psychologically significant prices.
- Price tactics should vary, within strategy.
- Price wars are to be avoided.
- An elastic demand responds to price change.
- Debt collection is a key part of pricing management.
- Costs, for marketing purposes, are fixed or variable.
- Contribution is made to fixed costs until they are covered. Then profit is earned.
- Marginal costing and pricing depends on a knowledge of the cost of a single additional unit.
- Transfer pricing internally can confuse internal resource transfers with external cash payments.
- Export transfer pricing ensures that profits are taken in a tax-free economy.

Debriefing

Activity 7.1

Prices tend to reflect demand, and are set in the light of anticipated demand.

- More people will want to see the league champions, and so all seats can be sold at a high price. For a reserve team game, in mid-season, prices are lowered to encourage attendance.
- Pricing is not of the seat (the function) but of the symbolic elements to do with the performance. Films are best seen from the back, theatre from the front. Concert seating will depend on the acoustics. Seats where the sound is better will command higher prices. In Starlight Express, for example, the performers race around the auditorium on roller skates. The best views come from the centre of row Q. The higher priced seats are therefore in the centre of the stalls.

  Some days and/or times are more popular than others. Mid-week matinées, for example, are usually priced lower than evening performances.
- Season ticket holders are loyal supporters who will commit themselves to regular attendance, and will pay for a whole season in advance.
- Airlines extend their product offer to create extra comfort and levels of status for their First and Business Class offers. The additional costs are well below the enhanced prices, and so it must be a factor of convenience, comfort and status that provide a value package to some travellers.

President Lyndon B Johnson refused to allow White House staffers to fly in exclusive cabins. As he said, 'the rear of the aircraft gets there at the same time as the front'.

Activity 7.2

Hopefully you remembered that these examples are taken from an ethical market, where both formal laws and cultural practices restrict the marketer's freedom of action.

1 A cough syrup is needed at certain times of the year. Demand is not likely to be elastic since price is not a strong determining factor where health is concerned. It is most likely that the marketing drive will be to build confidence in the brand, to ensure that it is on the retail shelves in time for the bad weather, and to encourage the retailer to feature and to recommend it.

2   Prescription medications require qualified people to prescribe and dispense them. Thus the target markets are within the relevant professions. The consumers will accept in trust what the doctor or pharmacist recommends. Price may be subsidized by a Health Service; alternatively, people will pay the price charged since (a) the professional prescribes it and (b) health care takes priority over other expenditure. (**Note:** Ethical and moral considerations apply to pricing in a health market, as we saw in Unit 3.)

Demand is conditional upon securing the confidence and support of the medical professionals and, in many cases, a listing from the Government Health Ministry.

Activity 7.3

Knowing the marginal cost allows a negotiator to work from a firm price floor. Agreeing a price below the marginal cost will not even recover the essential costs in manufacture and supply. It follows that a competitor who has allocated costs differently, with more shown as fixed, may have a lower marginal cost and so be able to offer a lower marginal price. Thus marketers, and salespeople especially, tend to argue for a high proportion of costs to be fixed – an argument designed to assist the sales effort without strategic regard.

Marginal pricing should be used as a tactical marketing tool: hotels let rooms at marginal rates in slack times, car hire firms offer weekend rates, theatres price midweek matinées near the margin.

The concept of *opportunity cost* runs in parallel to marginal costing. If you didn't take the opportunity for business, how else could the resources be used, and what would they earn?

Dangers include: low prices today may be a precedent for low prices in the future; other clients may demand the same special deal; competitors may price down to the same level and a new price platform be formed; costing is not an exact science.

Unit Activity

The financial costs would be calculated by adding up the money paid out during the year for fees, books, living and travel expenses. See table below.

Financial costs of a year at college

Items of expense	£
Fees	2 500
Books and materials	500
Living expenses and travel	3 250
Miscellaneous	750
Total	7 000

£7 000 is clearly not the true cost. The opportunity cost of your year at college includes the income foregone from your year off work, plus lost opportunities for promotion at work. Also there is need to consider what the next best alternative would have been for your expenditure exclusively related to attending college, in this case fees and books + £1 000 worth of travel and miscellaneous expenses (£2 500 + 500 + £1 000 = £4 000). What else could have been done with this money? Invest for a year in a building society account? Achieve benefits from a nearly new car? Travel across America? See table below.

Opportunity costs of a year at college

Losses	£
Financial costs	4 000
Lost year's income	15 000
Lost interest on £7 000 invested	400
Total	19 400

Looking at it this way, the costs of a year at college seem to be substantial, but we must not mislead ourselves in such decisions. A year at college may be the best use of resources, both time and money, if it leads to a better job and higher future income.

You may have used the technique of opportunity costing when listing the advantages and disadvantages of buying a new car. The higher price of the hatchback is offset by the benefits of more luggage space and improved rear view visibility.

In the everyday process of filling your shopping basket you make comparisons between the utility of your chosen product divided by its price and the utility of other options divided by their prices. The one you perceive to offer the best value for money ratio is the one that will maximize your satisfaction. This will remain true while your income is unchanged and all other factors stay constant.

(Source: *Economic Theory and Marketing Practice* (1992), Hatton and Oldroyd, Butterworth-Heinemann.)

Place operations

In this unit you will:

❏ Examine the importance of distribution to a marketer.
❏ Discover the importance of the physical distribution function.
❏ Confirm the vital differences between customers and consumers.
❏ Consider the importance of managing customer and consumer relations.
❏ Develop an understanding of the after market.

By the end of this unit you will be able to:

❏ Select appropriate channels of distribution.
❏ Operate within a relationship marketing environment.
❏ Manage customer and consumer relations.
❏ Control the after market.

There have been, and are, many marketing and management authors, and a considerable number of books in print. This allows a student to select from a range of approaches, and to quote from a range of sources and source material.

Because of the wealth of material available it is not reasonable to expect anybody – even an examiner – to be *au fait* with them all. Communication theory tells us that it is for the sender to communicate in a way that the receiver can understand – therefore it is for you, the candidate, to make your work understandable by the examiner.

Obviously your answers should be well planned and logically structured. They should be clearly written, using the style called for in the question. Finally, *always quote your sources*.

Examiners will accept definitions, etc., from named sources. Never assume that the examiner will recognize a source. In any case, by quoting the source you are proving that you have done the study and not made up a quote from simple common sense – or desperation!

Expect to take about two hours to work through this unit and its activities.

Channels of distribution (CoD)

A product offer has no value unless and until it reaches the consumer. It follows that ways have to be devised to either take the offer to the consumer, or bring the consumer to the offer.

Product offers from FMCG to Capital Goods have to be physically moved to where they are needed. Entertainment venues normally have to bring the consumers to them (with a vital secondary market through media such as television and radio). Those that are predominantly services can do both: operate from fixed premises, and/or visit clients in their own homes.

New channel opportunities are constantly becoming available – and competition is forcing suppliers to adopt them to add value to their offers. Thus the major UK supermarket chains are opening home delivery services, with orders placed by phone, fax and Internet. Dentists are now visiting homes, especially of the elderly, and window cleaners obviously have to be mobile.

Physical distribution management (PDM)

In Unit 3 we met PDM and established how profits can be levered through cost reduction. It is the realization that cost savings have so much leverage that has caused so many organizations to sub-contract their deliveries to specialists, and which accounts for the phenomenal rise of international carriers such as Federal Express and UPS.

Kotler suggests there are eight areas that must be taken into consideration:

- The speed of filling orders.
- The supplier's willingness to meet emergency merchandise needs of the customers.
- The care with which merchandise is delivered.
- The supplier's readiness to take back defective goods and re-supply quickly.
- The installation, repair services and availability of parts from the supplier.
- The number of options on shipment loads and carriers.
- The supplier's willingness to carry inventory for the customer.
- The service charges – are services included in the cost or separately priced?

The major benefits of using a PDM specialist are:

- No capital costs.
- No property to maintain.
- No need for specialist management or equipment.
- No responsibility for ensuring that the operation meets legal requirements.
- Revenue costs can be directly attributed to sales.
- No long-term commitment.
- Benefit from shared costs with others to whom the distributor is contracted.

Minimum total transactions (MTT)

Middlemen can only justify their continuing existence if their presence reduces the total cost of the channel. Grocery wholesalers in the UK were forced out of business as the large supermarket groups found they could operate their own internal distribution networks. Direct marketing has become so successful, and is set to grow, as communication channels have opened, credit cards have become ubiquitous, and specialist PDM contractors have become established.

Figure 8.1(a) and (b) illustrate the logic supporting the middleman. By accepting deliveries from several suppliers (A and B, plus others) the middleman can *break bulk* and make up mixed orders for each of the separate, smaller customers. In Figure 8.1(a) there is need for 20 small deliveries. In Figure 8.1(b) only 12 large ones are required.

PDM strategy

Contracted out or in-house, there is need to establish distribution objectives:

- How intensive the distributive cover should be.
- How fast a response is required.
- How inventory should be controlled.
- How the returns procedure should operate.
- How legal requirements should be met.

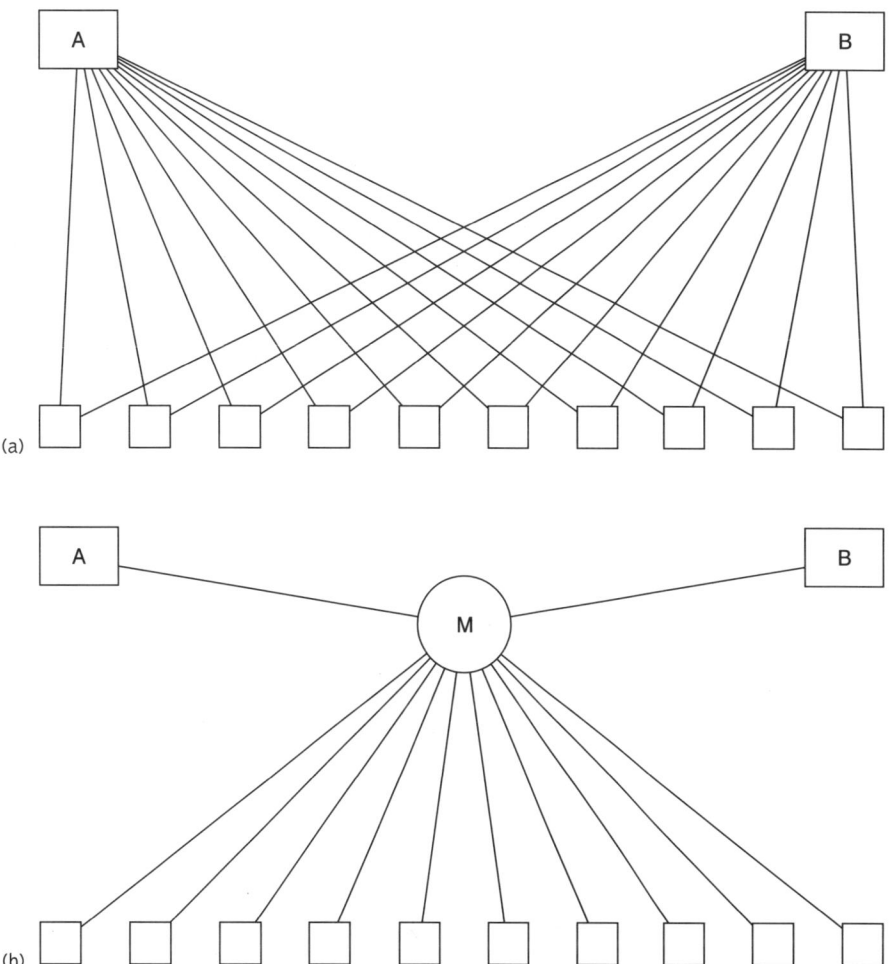

Figure 8.1(a) and (b)
Principle of minimum total transactions

From these strategic objectives the specialist PDM manager can establish the number of depots, the type of equipment, stockholding in each depot, control systems, staffing, etc.

Figure 8.2 shows the process of determining whether or not to subcontract the PDM function.

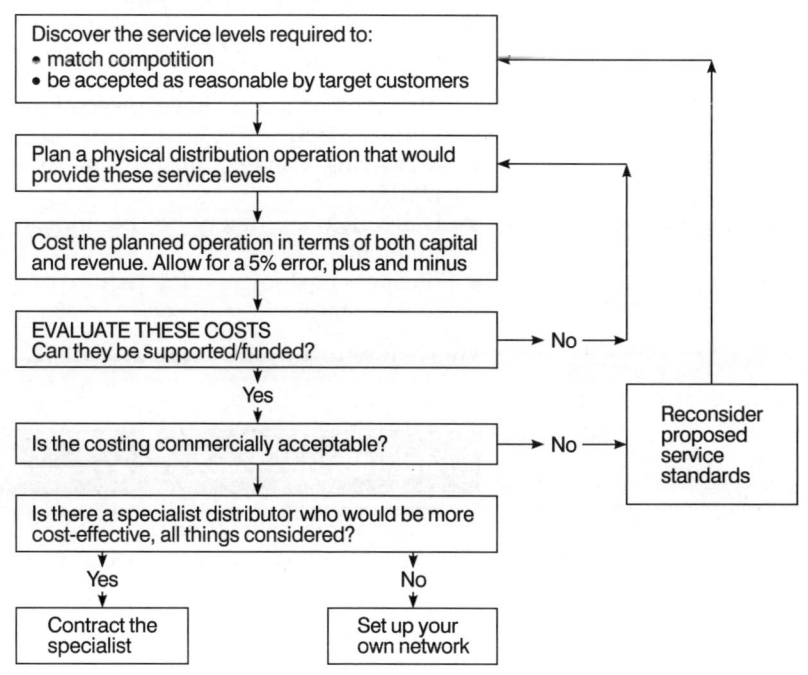

Figure 8.2
Determining the form of distribution

Channel options

The channel alternatives available in a consumer market are shown in Figure 8.3. It will be seen how the direct marketing concept (to the left of the model) has extended from simple mail order.

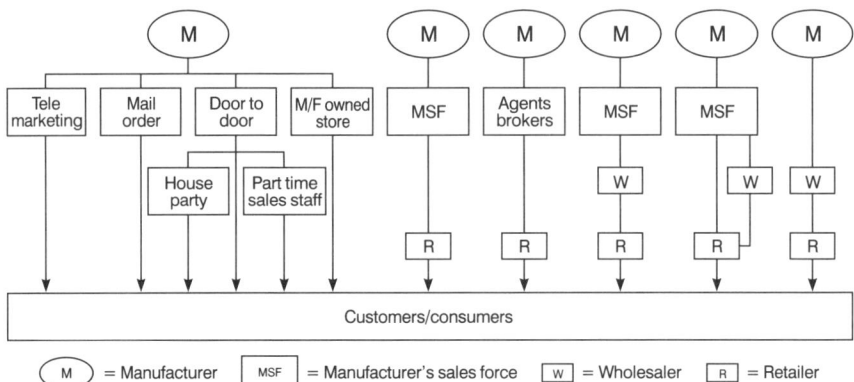

Figure 8.3
Marketing channel alternatives (consumer products)

Direct marketing, it should be noted, is a channel of distribution, *not* a promotional tool. This is because direct marketers have identified ways to make direct contact with customers and consumers and so have cut out the middlemen (following the MTT principle).

Customers and consumers

It is important to distinguish between customers and consumers:

- Consumers are those who use up the value in what is purchased or made available.
- Customers buy to resell, or on behalf of another person or party. They can, of course, also be consumers if they use up the value of what is bought.

Thus, all those in the supply chain are customers, whose main motivation will be some form of profit gained through satisfying the next person – customer or consumer – in the chain.

Business-to-business channels

The same principles apply within business-to-business markets as within consumer markets. The differences are that:

- Businesses tend to have professional buyers, who control the prime sales contact.
- Marketing contact must reach to individual members of extended DMUs.
- Deliveries are likely to be far larger, and will be needed more frequently.
- Business customers often require on-going supplies, often on a routine re-buy status.

We shall return to this topic in Unit 11.

Packaging

The days of plain, functional packages are over. It is now realized that the packaging itself can act as a medium, and reinforce the brand message as the protected goods move through the CoD.

Figure 8.4 shows that packaging has five roles, and must meet legal requirements:

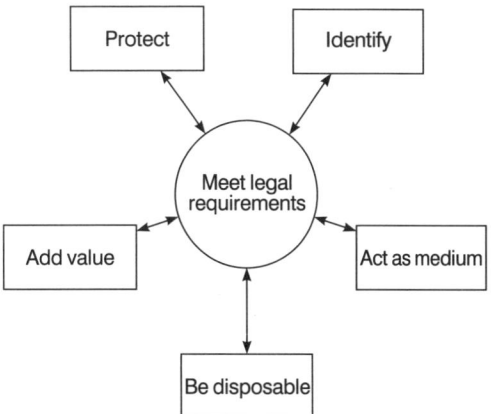

Figure 8.4
Packaging's roles. (Source: *Marketing in Management*, Worsam and Wright (1995), Pitman.)

- *Protection*
  A balance has to be struck between the minimum packaging needed to ensure that the product offer reaches the consumer in good condition and over-packaging to provide a promotional vehicle. Legal requirements must be met; i.e. in the UK only 32 aspirin tablets can be sold at one time without a doctor's prescription, petrol must be dispensed into clearly labelled metal containers, and so on.
- *Identification*
  Labels, etc., must carry such things as weight, size, ingredients, etc., in the correct size of font, and with the required emphasis. Additionally the supplier will want to use the label to carry the branding message, and to provide instructions, helpline numbers, and so on.
- *Add value*
  In many cases value can be added to what would otherwise be a boring container:

  - Secondary uses   - tea packed in a tea caddy.
  - Attractiveness   - colour and interest added through good design.
  - User-friendliness   - easy-to-open cans, salad cream bottles that stand upside down.

  It is important to not simply add value but to feature it so that customers and consumers are aware of the benefits.
- *Act as a medium*
  The package itself is a valuable medium that can be incorporated within the promotional campaign. Manufacturers such as Kellogg's make extremely good use of their packages to communicate the values they have added. Trade suppliers such as Black & Decker now routinely use their retail brand names on commercial weight products because of the spin-off effects in both markets: professional buyers recognize the brand, amateurs are impressed to see professionals using a brand they can buy in the DIY store.
- *Be disposable*
  Empty packaging has to be safely disposed of. Environmentally friendly packaging should be biodegradable. Clear instructions for disposal should be given where the container has toxic qualities or presents some other disposal problem.

Services packaging

Packaging is obviously necessary for physical goods, but services must also consider a form of packaging – that is closely associated with their promotional planning. The ambience of a hairdressing salon or restaurant is part of the value package and must be designed *and maintained* with care. Service Engineers carrying out on-site maintenance and repair need to be well turned out, clean and smart. They, in particular, have influence on future purchase decisions.

Take a little time to check through the contents of your kitchen, office and bathroom. Critically appraise the packaging of everyday products from a consumer's viewpoint. Then reappraise the contents from the viewpoint of a 75-year-old lady with bad arthritis in her hands. List the products where the consumer's needs have not been taken into account, and analyse why this may be.

(**See:** Debriefing at the end of the unit.)

Customer relations

We have examined the quality chain in Unit 3, and established the need to secure attitudes of mutual trust and support that extend from supplier(s) right through a chain of manufacture and supply that extends to the consumer.

These attitudes will not simply form, they have to be achieved through careful planning and long-term commitment. Here we again meet the concept of value. To achieve a value package to which customers will respond it is necessary to make the delivery of quality a key part of the Mission. Unless all of the *core business processes* are committed to the delivery of value the package will not be entire, and customer satisfaction will not be delivered. Kotler emphasizes that four key processes are especially crucial:

- *New product realization process* – all the activities involved in identifying, researching, developing and successfully launching new products with speed, high quality and target cost attainment.
- *Inventory management process* – all the activities involved in developing and managing the right inventory locations of raw materials, semi-finished materials and finished goods so that adequate supplies are available while avoiding the costs of high over-stocks.
- *Order-to-remittance process* – all the activities involved in receiving orders, approving them, shipping goods on time and collecting payment.
- *Customer service process* – all the activities involved in making it easy for customers to reach the right parties within the organization and receive quick and satisfactory service, answers and resolutions of problems.

Activity 8.2

Power in the grocery distribution channels used to lie with the manufacturers, who could dictate terms and conditions to retailers. That power swung to the retailers as supermarket groups formed and grew large.

Consider the power actually held by buyers in:

(a)   a domestic household.
(b)   a supermarket group.
(c)   a large manufacturing company.

Retaining customers

It is possible, in some markets and at some times, to easily acquire new customers. If this is so it may not matter that customers are being lost as quickly as new ones are located. A condition of high *customer churn* is normally unacceptable for three reasons:

- The cost of acquiring new customers is higher than that of retaining existing ones.
- Acquiring new customers, and retaining old ones, increases the customer base and adds to sales volume.

- Existing customers who are satisfied speak well of the organization. Word-of-mouth testimonials are worth far more than any media advertising. Non-satisfied customers will speak badly of the organization, and a word-of-mouth condemnation is extremely damaging.

The cost of lost customers
To evaluate this cost:

- Define and measure the customer retention rate (memberships renewed, continuance of regular orders, etc.).
- Identify the possible customer actions, and identify those where better management would have an effect. (Customers growing out of an age-related product or leaving a town are lost and no management action can retain them. They can still promote through word-of-mouth, of course, so ensure they leave happy.)
- Estimate the profit lost from customers who leave unnecessarily. A typical calculation would be:

Number of accounts	300 000
Lost through poor service	3% = 9 000 accounts
Average revenue per account	£15 000
Revenue lost in year therefore	£135 m (15 000 × 9 000)
Profit margin	10%
Unnecessary profit loss	£13.5 m

Cost of retention
It is ridiculous to suggest that anything up to the profit loss should be invested in promotion to keep customers loyal. Instead the investment should be in a programme of *retention*. The problems are real and need to be dealt with by internal behaviour change, not by external puff.

Extending Your Knowledge

Viking, the direct mail stationery and office equipment supplier, closely monitors customer behaviour. Their catalogues, sent in the post, are personalized to each customer, with special offers relating to previous buying behaviour. Catalogues also contain reminders of when products were last ordered, and personalized order forms are already pre-completed. Phone contact is made if an order is not received when past experience suggests that one is due.

All of this is supportive of a most efficient ordering and delivery service. Order before 10 for same-day delivery. Pay by credit card or by invoice . . . and achieve a substantial discount on high street prices.

Relationship marketing
The ladder of customer loyalty (see Figure 8.5) shows how relationships should develop, from the first contact with a prospective customer until he or she has developed into an advocate for the supplier.

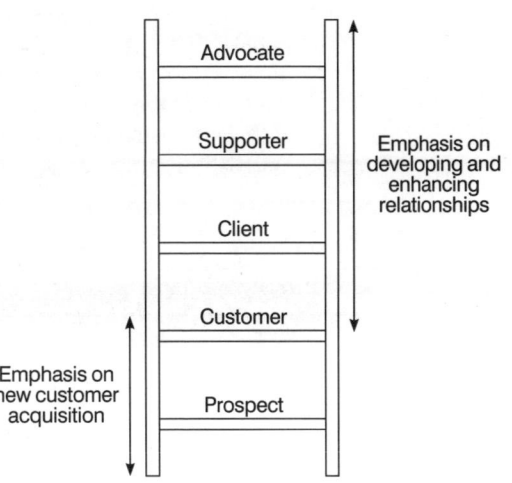

Figure 8.5
(Source: *Essence of Services Marketing*, p. 33, Adrian Payne (1993).)

- *Prospect*

  Not everybody is a prospective customer. Giving a sales force carte blanche to seek out new business can be a recipe for disaster. If a profitable customer is first defined it helps to target both marketing and sales efforts. A typical target prospect definition is:

  > a business that will yield a revenue over time that will exceed by an acceptable amount the investment in attracting, selling to, and servicing that customer.

- *Customer*

  A customer is one who buys to resell, or for a consumer's use. Buy, in this sense, means to place an order, accept delivery and pay the agreed sum, to time. A good customer is one who repeats the process and so becomes a regular purchaser.

- *Client*

  Turning a customer into a client means personalizing that contact so that the customer ceases to be just one among a mass of others. Clients are served on an individual basis as part of an on-going relationship that is valued by both sides. Clients are individuals, served by individuals.

- *Supporter*

  A client who becomes a supporter has associated with the supplier and the product offer(s). They are a part of the preferred lifestyle. A supporter will advance arguments on behalf of the supplier and the product offers because they are believed in and trusted.

- *Advocate*

  The final stage, that of advocacy, is reached when the client actively recommends the product offer(s) to others. In big ticket marketing where the purchase risk is high it is beneficial to have influential clients who will willingly act as advocates by giving testimonials, allowing potential customers to view the product offer in use, etc.

It is sometimes argued that relationship marketing should be established with privileged customers who in some way 'merit special treatment' – usually because they are (a) large and (b) profitable.

Good salespeople have always known that *every* customer can and should be given special treatment. Good marketing people would do well to adopt the long-standing good sales practice.

Extending Your Knowledge

Advertising in March 1999, the Royal Mail said:

In business, 67% of customers go elsewhere because no-one keeps in touch. Sadly, breaking up isn't that hard to do. When someone stops communicating in a relationship, the easiest thing to do is walk out. Why should a customer stick around if you're not showing any interest in them? A simple thank you note or newsletter lets them know their business is important to you, and puts your company's name at the front of their minds. Think about it. If your customers go, you could end up following them out of the door. To find out how Royal Mail can improve relationships with your customers, visit our website at www.royalmail.co.uk. DO WHAT WORKS

After market

The importance of the after market can hardly be over-stressed. Making a sale is relatively easy. Creating and keeping a customer is far more difficult. It is in the after market that loyalty is generated, where long-term commitment is secured.

Consider what happens in many cases: an attractive deal is offered through a promotional campaign. Stocks are available, payment is facilitated. The product offer, a computer, say, is delivered. The prospect, nowhere near customer status yet, opens the box and takes out the goodies. This is what he finds:

- A power cable for the wrong country.
- An on-line manual only accessible once the computer is up and running.
- A complimentary SCSI device, but no terminator so that it won't boot.
- A registration card promising information on upgrades, new products, etc., and giving a phone contact for technical help.

He rings the technical number, and is greeted with a recorded announcement telling him how good the products are and offering a choice from a menu to be selected via the key pad. If he is unlucky, there may be three sub-menus to work through. Then the packing reference number and perhaps the customer reference must be keyed in. If all these hurdles are surmounted there will be an announcement that the technicians are busy; connection will be made as soon as possible. After a time (probably with music and adverts) he will be asked to hold on . . . and then again. Finally, he will be offered the chance to leave a message for immediate attention. He does so. And never hears anything from anybody. Frustrating? Likely to build a positive relationship with the company and its products? Of course not. But it is common practice today.

After market rationale

The after market makes good marketing sense because profits:

- Come from repeat business.
- Customer satisfaction is the base of repeat business.

The importance of the after market is shown in Figure 8.6.

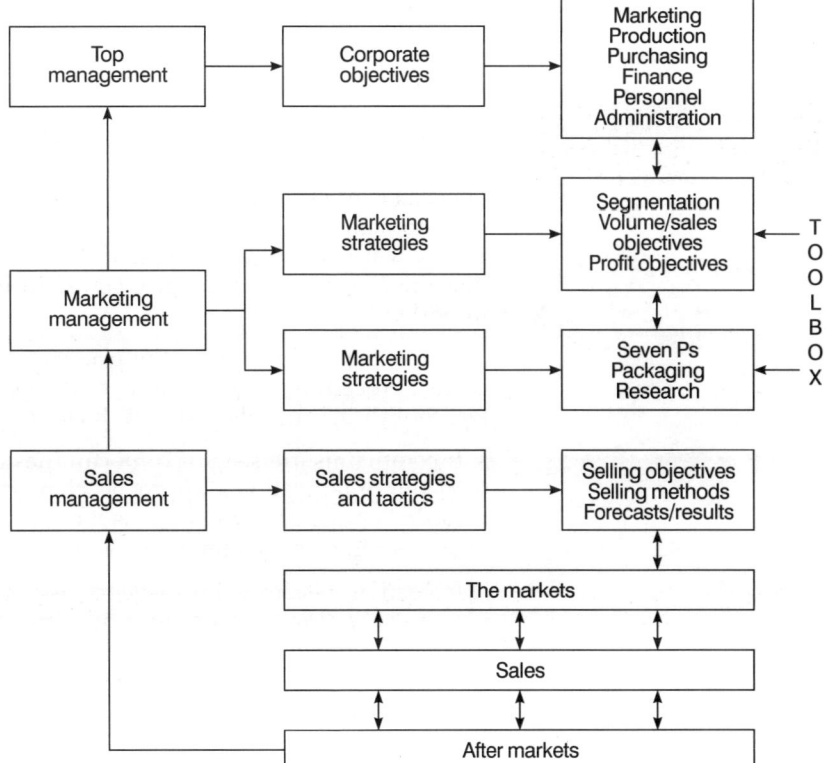

Figure 8.6
The importance of the after market

181

After market strategies

The aim must be to reassure and support customers so that they are able to derive the satisfactions that were promised as part of the marketing programme. The product offer should:

- Arrive complete, and easy to set up.
- Be easy and safe to use.
- Do exactly what it is claimed to do.
- Deliver value for money.
- Be supported by people who demonstrate their concern for the customer and his needs.

It can be argued that management of the after market is more important than the promotional aspects of marketing. If one accepts that the sale is just the beginning of a long-term relationship it is easy to see why effort must be directed to building that relationship. Such building is done after purchase, never before.

Complaints

The *Concise Oxford Dictionary* tells us that 'a complaint is an utterance of a grievance'. Therefore, for a complaint to be effective a person has to both have a grievance *and* express it.

It is of major importance that marketing make it possible for consumers to express any grievances they may have.

Activity 8.3

Complaints
Spend some time over the next few days actively seeking evidence of grievances and how they have been handled.

Start with yourself. Have you any grievances about products or services that you have bought, or have to use? If so, have you expressed them? To whom? How? With what result?

Then carry through the same research with people you know, people that you meet. You will find it an excellent way to start up a conversation since most (if not all) have grievance experiences. Aim to interview 10 people, drawn from a range of activities and life-styles.

Finally see what general issues emerge as important to the individuals who have (had) the grievances.

(**See:** Debriefing at the end of the unit.)

Complaints or opportunities?

If customers or consumers have grievances with your product it doesn't matter if it is genuine or false. If it is real or imaginary. What matters is that the client perceives a grievance. To him it is genuine, it is real, it is important.

It does not help to have the grievance identified and to be shown the correct procedure if, at the same time, the client is made – or allowed – to feel foolish because they should have understood the instructions.

If complaints are seen as opportunities to improve the product offering then the organization's approach changes radically. No longer are they regarded as a chore. No longer is it a low-level job for someone new to the organization or someone not good enough to do other things.

Instead it becomes an issue of major importance requiring quality personnel and an effective and efficient system with immediate feedback to the responsible marketer. Nothing should be more urgent than a complaint where a real fault is exposed.

Relationship Marketing, of course, has issues such as complaints at its very heart since no lasting relationship can exist without client satisfaction.

Customer reaction

The Customer Reaction Continuum provides a basis for understanding client behaviour.

Most of the time most clients are probably to be found in the centre three sections. They are neutral, just using the product or they have a degree of satisfaction or grievance which they don't express.

People are naturally reluctant to express satisfaction but are usually quick to find fault. So why may they not articulate a complaint? Perhaps it is:

- Not sufficiently important to complain about.
- Too much trouble.
- Because they 'don't want to cause a fuss' (a typical British attitude).
- Because they don't think anything will be done.

Articulated satisfaction
Unarticulated satisfaction (Won't say)
Unarticulated satisfaction (Can't say)
Neutral
Unarticulated complaint (Can't say)
Unarticulated complaint (Won't say)
Articulated complaint

Figure 8.7
Customer reaction continuum. (Source: *Inspired Customer Service*, Clutterbuck, Clark and Armistead, Kogan Page, 1993.)

It can take a quite serious problem to occasion a move into the lower box of the continuum. For many, articulating a complaint is an occasion that takes considerable courage. We know that even experienced sales people have clients that they are reluctant to face, yet they are temperamentally suited to face-to-face contact, and have many years experience. How much more stressing, therefore, for a person without a sales personality and without training or experience.

Those who complain face-to-face are generally stressed and concerned that the person they contact will react badly, that the interview will degenerate into an acrimonious dispute. Attack being the best form of defence it follows that many complaints will be expressed forcibly. A major concern for the marketer is therefore to de-fuse the situation, to get the discussion on to a rational level. To gain the confidence of the person with the complaint.

Above all the marketer wants to hear the complaint. Wants to do something positive about it.

It is a maxim, built from experience that an unsatisfied complainant is likely to tell at least eight others and so spread bad word-of-mouth. A satisfied client will also tell others and be far more loyal to the product, the brand and the organization than before.

British Gas, for whom complaints are vital since many refer directly to potentially life-threatening situations, have made a special study of the topic. Their results confirm that satisfaction increases if complaints are handled well. However they also show that the additional cost of attracting more complaints outweighs the benefits. It is far more important to use complaints to eradicate the causes for complaint.

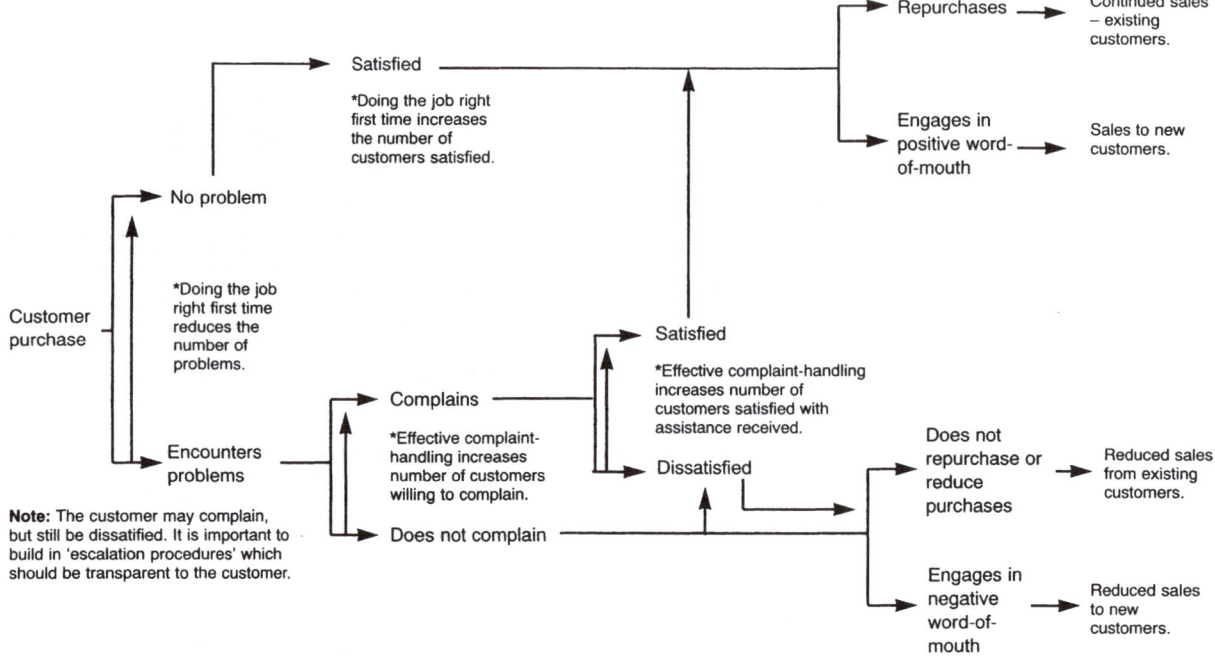

Figure 8.8 The TARP model. (Source: British Gas, *Marketing Business*, Sept. 1994.)

Complaints handling

Organizational culture must be (or become) non-threatening if complaints are to be handled effectively. Employees must be encouraged to resolve and analyse complaints so that benefit accrues to those who complain, the organization and future customers.

In the UK the Citizen's Charter Complaints Task Force has produced a set of principles and a checklist covering effective complaint systems in an effort to encourage organizations of all types to react favourably to their customers. This is in response to an identified need for public sector organizations to become less bureaucratic and to treat their users as commercial organizations routinely do. Cultural change is necessary for this to succeed. British Rail began switching from carrying passengers to serving customers. Some hospitals are trying to switch from a 'patient' to a 'client' culture.

When complaints are received they must be individually processed to endeavour to secure client satisfaction. They must also systematically be recorded as data and that data processed into management information that reaches the appropriate managers in order that action can be taken.

British Gas see the procedure as:

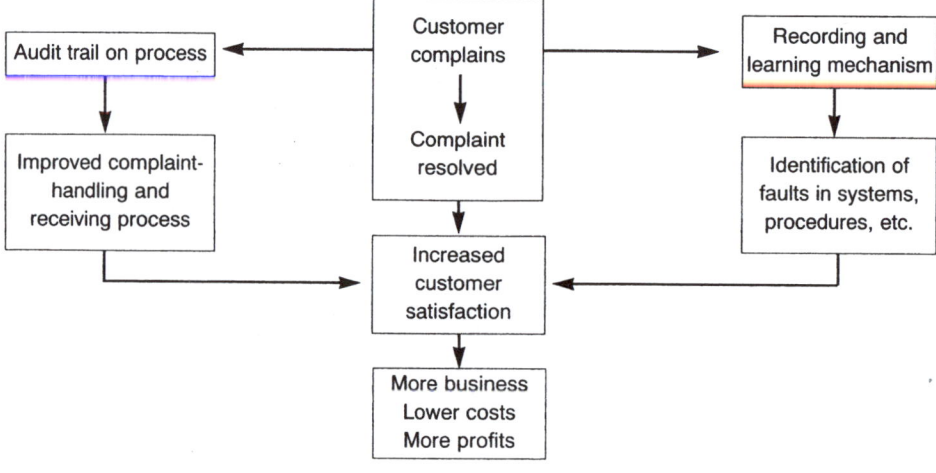

Figure 8.9 Measuring complaints. (Source: Peter Barley, British Gas, *Marketing Business*, Sept. 1994.)

184

Complaints system
Select an organization that you know well and plan – in outline – the stages of handling a complaint from receipt to successful conclusion. i.e. Concentrate upon the middle box of Figure 8.9.

(**See:** Debriefing at the end of the unit.)

Extending Your Knowledge

It always pays to treat customers, and potential customers, well. Individuals deserve fair and respectful treatment as a matter of course – and certainly if the firm wants to remain in business. Bad treatment can sometimes lead to unforeseen and serious publicity:

1   When the author was teaching marketing at a large college a local electrical supplier refused to exchange a defective £3.99 light switch. It had to be authorized by the manufacturer, they said. Not true, of course – the law holds the retailer responsible. In any case no manufacturer is going to quibble about a single, low-priced item.
    The result was that the retailer was used, by name, as an example of bad customer service in all teaching from then on. At a conservative estimate some 3500 students heard about the store, and its unfriendly and unhelpful approach.
2   A reporter writing in the *Sunday Times* in May 1999 reported a tea-rooms in Rye by name for refusing to allow her two children to enter the premises.
    Exactly the kind of publicity that marketers should be striving to prevent!

Extending Your Knowledge

The *Daily Mirror,* in spring 1999, decided to see what would happen if companies received letters of praise. So two of their reporters wrote letters to well known companies. One such was addressed to Vimto, and read in part: 'Growing up in Manchester there was always a bottle of Vimto in the cupboard. Even today, the rich fruity smell takes me right back to picnics on the beach in Morecambe.'

They also wrote in praise of the Mars Bar, Ribena, Batchelors Tasty Soups, Cadbury's Dairy Milk, Kellogg's Corn Flakes, Hovis, Tetley Tea Bags, and several other products.

Not only replies – free gifts flooded in. Cadbury sent a history of the company, *The Story of Cocoa and Chocolate*. Colgate sent £3 worth of vouchers to spend on toothpaste. Kellogg's sent three booklets about the dietary advantages of a high-fibre diet.

Thirty-five letters were sent out. Postage cost £9.10. Tokens and goods worth £41.50 were received. And, of course, booklets about the value of a high-fibre diet.

Even Batchelors, who no longer make canned soups, sent vouchers to the value of £1.50.

McDonald's, unfortunately, sent out the letter they use to answer complaints; they were sorry to learn about the 'disappointing visit'.

Moral: Don't miss a chance to cement good relationships. And do read the letters that are received.

How to fail your exams – 11 more golden rules:

12 **Always start with an introduction and end with a summary**. That way you can forget about the middle.
13 **Never write a report**. That will only prevent you following rule 14.
14 **If in doubt, waffle.** The examiner will probably think you know what you're talking about.
15 **Write illegibly, especially the words that really matter.** The examiner will give you the benefit of the doubt.
16 **Do not structure multi-part answers.** Let the examiner guess which part belongs where. It's his job, after all.
17 **Do the second part of a two-part paper first.** It shows initiative, makes you stand out from the crowd.
18 **Arrive late and leave early.** It impresses one's friends, and what's a few minutes anyway?
19 **Be disorganized.** You can always get a pen from the invigilator.
20 **Have a little drink just before the exam.** It helps you relax, and one must not be over-stressed.
21 **Don't bother with question numbers.** It will be obvious which question you are answering.
22 **Include a note to the examiner wishing him or her a Happy Christmas and to explain how pressured you have been.** Examiners are human, and a bit of flattery never goes amiss.

(Acknowledgements to David Pearson. Source: Issue 2, *Marketing Success*, Hints and Tips/2.)

Background

In the UK newspapers are distributed through wholesalers to established newsagents, some large, but many very small independent traders. The smaller newsagents are spread throughout the community and carry a wide range of other goods of immediate use to their near-at-hand customers. Often known as confectioners, tobacconists and newsagents (CTNs), they have widened their ranges to include groceries, soft drinks, greetings cards. Some are sub-post offices, some have a small video hire section. Many in the UK regard them as essential to community welfare.

Large supermarkets, often in out-of-town locations, are insisting on a strategy of intensive distribution. Some are already selling newspapers and magazines.

Questions

1 As a newsagent:
   (a) Analyse the main reason(s) why newsagents are against intensive distribution.
   (b) Itemize the arguments they can use to support their case.

2 As an assistant marketing manager for a major newspaper:
   (a) Determine the issues facing your organization.
   (b) Itemize the arguments for and against moving to a policy of intensive distribution.

(Source: *Marketing in Management* (1995), Worsam and Wright, Pitman.)

Summary

In this unit we have seen:

- That a product offer has no value until it reaches the consumer.
- Physical Distribution Management is a specialism that can be in-house or sub-contracted.
- Packaging has five roles in support of the marketing mix.
- Services must also be packaged.
- Careful evaluation and selection of the channel(s) of distribution are needed.
- Customer relations management is a key part of the P of Place.
- Retaining customers is far more cost-effective and beneficial in the long term than allowing a high churn.
- Relationship marketing should be applied to all customers.
- The importance of the after market can hardly be over-stated.
- Complaints should be well managed, monitored, and taken notice of.
- All customers should always be well treated.

Debriefing

Activity 8.1

These are the kinds of problems that you will probably have encountered:

- Barcode labels with adhesive that is difficult (impossible) to remove without damage to the product.
- Inner seals on salad cream, etc., that must be cut with a sharp knife.
- Boil-in-the-bag products that have to be cut open while scalding hot.
- Ointment tubes that have 'easy open' caps that need to be reversed to pierce the seal.
- 'Child-proof' lids.
- Boxes with two or more layers, but the lower layers mostly shaped plastic.
- Small items packed in twos or fours when only one is needed.

Were you surprised by the difficulty that some of the packs would present to an elderly person? Why do these annoyances happen?

- Many designers fail to work from the typical consumer's viewpoint.
- Product security takes precedence over simplicity in use.
- Availability of such items as sharp, pointed knives is taken for granted when they may not be present in a typical consumer's location (salad cream at a picnic spot, face cream in a bathroom).
- The excitement of creation of a new concept masks the consumer's problem (boil-in-the-bag products tested by Home Economists in laboratory conditions).
- Lack of understanding of consumer's level of awareness or concern (markers that damage whiteboards in classrooms).

The only solution is to pilot new packages with typical consumers, and to maintain a careful watch on complaints so that unforeseen problems can quickly be dealt with.

Activity 8.2

(a) Domestic buyers work from a DMU in which they may or may not be the decision maker. Their actual power may be over the decision itself, or it may be limited to choice of product or brand. They certainly will have the power to complain about retailers to the decision maker, and strongly influence future purchases. They will also be able to 'spread

187

the word' amongst their friends and colleagues and so make recommendations about retailers. Their power with the actual suppliers will be very limited, just one small user among millions.

(b) A supermarket group buyer is a very powerful person. He or she and the team take the actual decisions about which products will be purchased, and which featured. Access to the stores in the group is available only through buyers in head office. It follows that key account salespeople must be senior and able to negotiate at the highest level. Supermarket group power is now so strong, and they are so confident within it, that famous brands such as Black Magic have been excluded from stores until the makers met the supermarket buyer's terms. Through 1998 and 1999 Tesco, in particular, have been demanding that British and European law be changed to allow them to source branded goods such as Levi's from countries where they are cheaper than offered in the UK. At the time of writing it seems most likely that they will succeed. The laws are likely to change. Manufacturers, and *governments*, seem about to give way.

(c) Buyers in large manufacturing companies are working in a DMU that is similar to the consumer DMU. (See Unit 11.) They act on behalf of the DMU, but have considerable powers of selection of those who will be invited to tender, and over the tender document itself.

Activity 8.3

You will have found that most people have grievances but for one reason or another take no action to have them rectified. They will, however, be very happy to talk about it with their contemporaries, with anyone who will listen whilst the grievance is fresh.

This can degenerate into a mutual commiseration session with grievances from long ago brought forth and given a new lease of life. Significantly the organizations which deal with grievances quickly and fairly are not reported. Only the non-settled grievances are remembered.

You may have found that consumers are willing to ignore a grievance from an organization of high repute: 'That's not like them at all.' But in response to a sequence of grievances there will be an attitude change.

It follows that a high reputation has to be earned, and continually justified.

Activity 8.4

A typical procedure is shown opposite. Remember the need to ensure that each complaint is diagnosed and logged in detail so that management information becomes available to improve the organization's service. (See Figure 8.10)

Unit activity

1(a) The main reason is survival. It is more than simply a fall in profits. Without a near monopoly on newspapers and magazines the regular flow of customers each day would fall, and with it would go the additional business they transact whilst buying their newspaper. Falling revenues would mean reduced staff and lower levels of service. Opening extra hours to make up the shortfall would incur additional costs – and add severe strain to the proprietors.

1(b) Arguments are likely to be:
- We provide a valuable service because we are close to our (and your) customers.
- We are efficient, proven, established, in place.
- Many customers are too far from a supermarket to switch purchases there – but we shall not be able to survive if even a percentage of our trade is taken away. Margins are already very slim!
- If we go out of business your overall sales will fall.
- Your costs will rise, and so will your cover prices ... therefore your sales will fall still further.

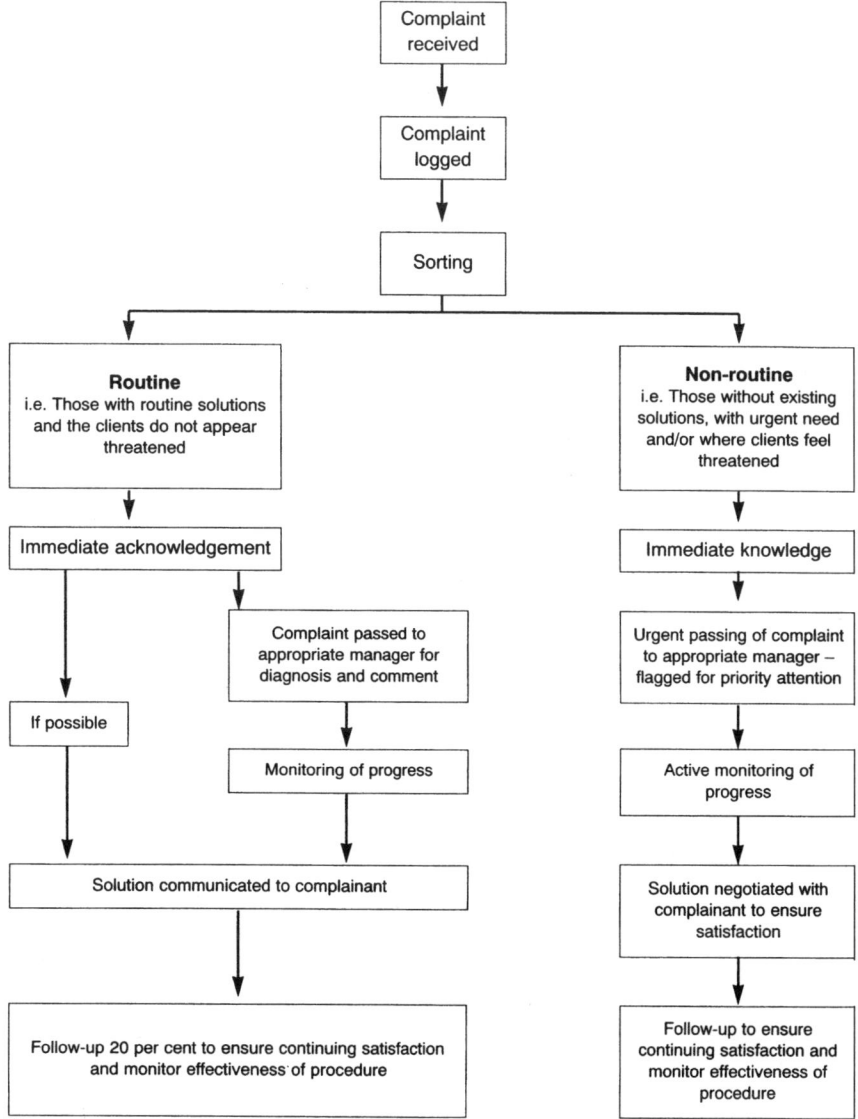

Figure 8.10
Complaints handling

- With lower sales your advertising revenue will fall, and your profits will suffer.
- In summary – you need us, we need you.

Note: Note that the argument turns to the effect that change will have *on the supplier*. Organizations are self-motivated!

2(a) The issues facing the newspaper are:

- An established channel of distribution is in place and working well. *General principle:* don't touch something that is working fine.
- The supermarkets are huge, and very powerful.
- Supermarkets advertise in our paper, and have strong influence with their suppliers, who are major advertisers. It would be possible for them to reduce their advertising, even switch all funds for a time to other media. How long could we hold up in profit terms if that happened?
- Other newspapers may be tempted to switch to intensive distribution. If they do, we shall be left behind while they sign the special deals.
- How powerful is the consumer lobby in comparison to the supermarkets?

- Will our sales fall as badly as the newsagents predict? If so, will our profits fall even if circulation is reduced – costs may come down too with fewer delivery points?
- Can we find a compromise position?

2(b) The arguments for staying with selective distribution are:

- It is established, in place.
- It is costed and budgeted.
- It is close to our customers.
- Channel members individually are weak, we are in control.
- If we change, the supermarkets may secure power over the channel.

For moving to intensive distribution:

- Much larger volume to fewer delivery points.
- More powerful PoS tactics.
- Guaranteed payment of our accounts.
- Larger advertising revenue through higher volume.
- Lower costs through fewer accounts, larger and fewer deliveries, etc.
- The CTNs have a range to rely on; the newspaper element is not as crucial as they say.

Unit 9 Services marketing

Units 9 and 10 are closely related because Services and Not-for-profit Marketing share so many characteristics. The major part of each unit will therefore apply across both – it will be easy to identify issues of specific reference to each topic.

Objectives

In these units you will:

❑ Understand the key factors that distinguish services and not-for-profit marketing.
❑ Examine the strategic needs for each sector.
❑ Identify the importance of personal contact in each sector.
❑ Appreciate the difficulties of effective control.

By the end of these units you will be able to:

❑ Apply marketing methodologies in services and not-for-profit marketing.
❑ Select appropriate organizational structures.
❑ Initiate effective marketing research techniques.
❑ Apply appropriate marketing mixes.

Study Guide

The two areas covered in Units 9 and 10 are so closely interrelated, have so much in common, that it is far easier to take them as one integrated subject than to try partly to cover each main topic only to have to return to it within a slightly different context. You should therefore keep your focus on the common issues throughout both units.

This is an area where you will have considerable personal experience but it is important that you do not rely upon anecdotal evidence coming from word-of-mouth (gossip). Even your own experiences will be coloured by your personal biases, prejudices and attitudes. They should be carefully and objectively analysed to ensure that you get as close as possible to the underlying truths, and remember that the others involved in transactions – the service providers – will have their own perceptions of the provision. Try to approach a situation from both sides.

This is not to say that the service provider can be right whilst the customer is wrong: without doubt the task is to satisfy the customer. This is not always achieved, however, and you will find it instructive to analyse why. What went wrong? Was it an actual failure or a perceived failure? Were expectations on either side too high? Were assumptions made where they should not have been?

Before you begin to work these units, identify incidents (perhaps three or four) where you have knowledge of service or not-for-profit transactions that have not been satisfactory. Write them down in brief summary form so that you can re-visit them as you work through the activities in these units.

You should allow three hours to work through this unit and its activities.

The Unit Activity is one question from the CIM pilot paper to be taken under exam conditions within a strict 36-minute time period.

Preparing for the examination is rather like preparing for a job interview. You need make yourself aware of the examiner's requirements and you need to prepare yourself in order to demonstrate the attitude, skills and knowledge which are expected of a successful candidate. Unlike a job interview you can very easily find out what you need to know. You can reduce the areas of uncertainty to a minimum. Furthermore you are not in competition – there are as many vacancies as there are acceptable candidates. Any pressure is therefore self-generated!

Examiners make their requirements very clear through the syllabus, tutor guidance notes and a report on each examination. These are supplemented by articles in *Marketing Success*. It is your responsibility to identify the areas which you need to develop more fully in order to do well in your examination.

What is a service?

We know that a product is tangible, with a physical presence, a function to perform and a symbolic value. We also know that the physical presence is far less important than the function and that is often less important than the symbolic (or psychological) value attributed to the product by the purchaser and/or user.

Bosch and Hotpoint dishwashers are made in the same factory, perform to the same specification and are serviced by the same team of Service Engineers. The Bosch name is exemplified by only a badge change, not a major cabinet re-design, yet allows a substantially higher retail price to be willingly paid by some purchasers. Many still choose to pay extra even when a source that they trust tells them that performance is identical. Why? It can only be explained in behavioural terms.

Presumably those who select Bosch over Hotpoint do so because it makes them feel better to have hard evidence of their taste or their ability to pay more. It must be to do with the satisfaction they derive from the intangible aspects of their purchase since their crockery and cutlery will be no cleaner than their neighbour's who bought a Hotpoint dishwasher and an electric kettle and a coffee percolator for the same price. The neighbour will, of course, derive satisfaction from the way he spent his money.

The two are unlikely to understand each other's rationale.

Not tangible

A service is not tangible. It has no physical presence. Function, yes: a service helps you achieve something. Symbolic, yes: a service helps you on a behavioural level. Physically, no . . . but . . . wait a minute . . . surely there has to be some physical input to some services?

Haircutting is a typical service, as is health care, as is motor insurance. In all of these there is an element of physical presence. Not in the personal skills of those who perform the service but in the support they need in order to perform. (Health care is, in the UK, dominated by the National Health Service and is not intended to make a profit. To manage its budget, yes. To make a commercial profit, no. So it is Not-for-Profit (NFP) marketing which is offering a service.)

Your choice of a café or restaurant is conditioned not only by your functional need for food. You are also concerned with the ambience, the cleanliness, the service quality, as well as with the type of food, price, speed of service, and so on.

It quickly becomes obvious that we cannot simply define services as intangible products.

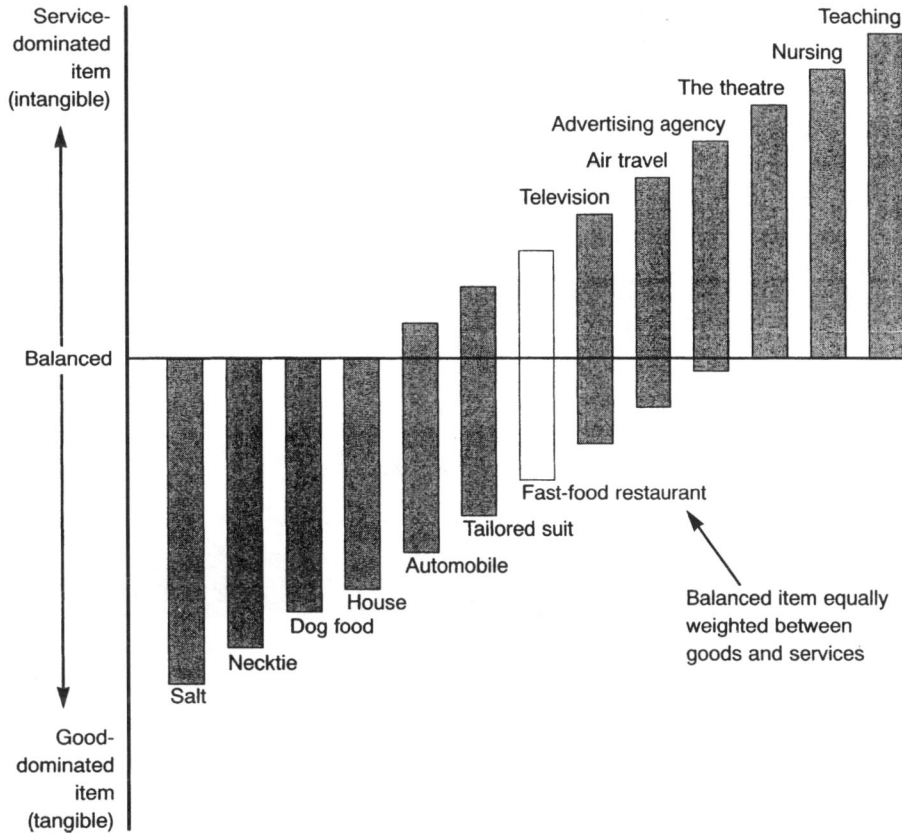

Figure 9.1
A scale of elemental dominance.
(Source: *European Journal of Marketing*, Shostack.)

It is because physical presence is so unimportant in behaviour terms that we can promote products and services as 'packages'. Customers and consumers have needs they want fulfilled. They do not care if they buy a service or a product. We do not sell services or products, we sell benefits. We sell solutions.

If we need to package user benefits and communicate them effectively to individuals in our target markets we have to forget the nature of what we sell and work in terms of what customers will buy and consumers will use. There are, in fact, very few pure products and very few pure services. Most of what we buy and sell lies on a continuum between these two extremes.

Our so-called service sector is therefore only a convenient label to distinguish a type of marketing. One where there is no (or almost no) requirement for physical distribution, but a higher emphasis on the mix areas where intangibility rules.

Hence the full 7Ps and 7Cs are vital in services and NFP marketing.

Services defined

Kotler defines a service as:

> Any activity of benefit that one party can offer to another that is essentially intangible and does not result in the ownership of anything. Its production may or may not be tied to a physical product.

A key phrase that encapsulates the essence of a service is that a service does not result in the ownership of anything . . . *any thing*. You will receive a certificate of motor insurance, which is tangible, but you have bought intangible protection. You have been helped to feel really good by the chef but you don't own the ingredients he bought at the same market you visited that morning. The nurse dresses your wound but any ownership of the bandages is only loosely peripheral to the service provided.

193

Scripting a service

In order to understand the complexity of the processes involved in service provision it is helpful to identify what actually has to happen for a service to be judged satisfactory. It is very difficult to identify all the stages – those visible and invisible – and in this a 'scripting' approach can be helpful.

In 1979 three academics, Bower, Black and Turner researched the scripts for a variety of service occasions. The following is the result of their research into 'Going to a restaurant'.

Items in upper case were mentioned by most subjects, items in italics by fewer subjects and those in lower case by the fewest subjects.

Going to a restaurant:

Open door	*Talk*
Enter	Drink water
Give reservation name	*Eat salad or soup*
Wait to be seated	Meal arrives
Go to table	EAT FOOD
BE SEATED	*Order dessert*
Order drinks	Ask for bill
Put napkin on lap	Bill arrives
LOOK AT MENU	PAY BILL
Discuss menu	Leave tip
ORDER MEAL	Get coats
	LEAVE

In scripting a service the provider is, of course, auditing his offering. Auditing the totality of his package. Without this audit there can be no efficient and effective way of controlling the operation.

Activity 9.1

Scripting
Select one of your service examples, or choose 'Visiting a doctor' and work out a detailed script. **Hint:** You will be unlikely to complete it fully at first attempt and your results will benefit from discussion with others who have similar experience(s).

(**See:** Debriefing at the end of the unit.)

Tangible and intangible actions

Mercer has categorized services into four broad types. See Figure 9.2.

Clearly there is need to understand segmentation in services marketing, but those coming new to the topic often do not realize the need to provide packages that tangibly and intangibly target both people and things. Obviously people are always involved – in all marketing, as has been emphasized, our prime role is to deal with people.

Distinctive features

Services can be compared by their degree of labour intensity and of interaction and customization. See Figure 9.3b. Within this broad categorization we need to appreciate that services have four distinctive features in addition to their absence of a 'thing' to sell:

Intangibility Purchases have to be made 'on trust' as it were because the actual service that a customer is going to receive will be uniquely created for him. There is no way to see what the service will actually do for the purchaser. He can see what it has done for others and buy because he expects the same result, but the result cannot be guaranteed in quite the same way that a physical product's performance can be guaranteed.

The nature of the service act	Who or what is the direct recipient of the service?	
	People	*Things*
Tangible actions	Services directed at people's bodies: ● Health care ● Passenger transportation ● Beauty salons ● Exercise clinics ● Restaurants ● Haircutting	Services directed at goods and other physical possessions: ● Freight transportation ● Industrial equipment repair, etc. ● Janitorial services ● Laundry and dry cleaning ● Landscaping/lawn care ● Veterinary care
Intangible actions	Services directed at people's minds: ● Education ● Broadcasting ● Information services ● Theatres ● Museums	Services directed at intangible assets: ● Banking ● Legal services ● Accounting ● Securities ● Insurance

Figure 9.2 Understanding the nature of the service act. (Source: *Marketing*, Mercer, Blackwell Business.)

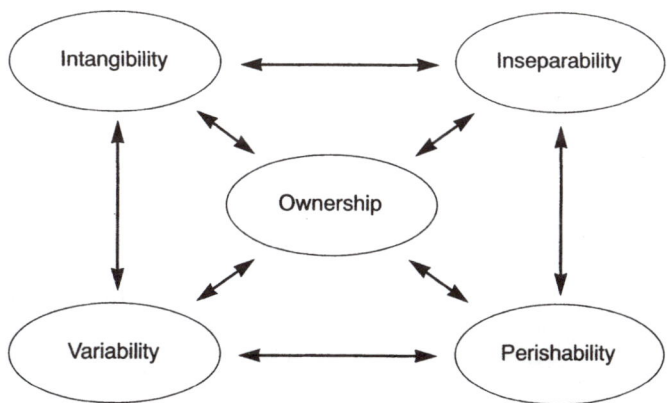

Figure 9.3a Service features

Degree of labour intensity	Degree of interaction and customization	
	Low	*High*
Low	Service factory: ● Airlines ● Trucking ● Hotels ● Resorts and recreation	Service shop: ● Hospitals ● Auto repair ● Other repair services
High	Mass service: ● Retailing ● Wholesaling ● Schools ● Retail aspects of commercial banking	Professional Service: ● Doctors ● Lawyers ● Accountants ● Architects

Figure 9.3b The service process matrix

- *People* are often the most tangible aspect of quality since service marketing is heavily reliant upon personal contact. We know that as soon as a human element becomes involved the service can only be as good and consistent as the persons who administer and/or offer it.

  Disney found this out the hard way when they tried to run EuroDisney on the same lines as the American Disney World. Young Europeans will not tolerate the same levels of discipline and certainly not the uniformity that Disney expected. As a result the female staff in EuroDisney wear stockings and light make-up, something unheard of in Disney's American parks.
- *Place* presents special opportunities. Obviously the customer can usually be brought to the service but a service is usually far easier to take to a customer than a product. When the service is totally intangible – such as auto insurance – then the whole transaction can be completed by electronic means, except for the documentation which must still travel by conventional means.
- *Promotion* is responsible for packaging the service. It is usually the major ingredient, after people. Certainly it is the main shop window for service providers.
- *Branding* is a very powerful tool in the service marketer's kit. All the elements of trust, reliance, expectation, etc. that branding creates, develops and extends are highly relevant to concept selling.

Note: We shall return to the 7Ps later in the unit.

Inseparability It is almost always impossible to separate the production and consumption of services. Generally the sale occurs shortly before the production and often consumption is immediate.

'Ownership' of a service provision can be very short-lived. The direct benefits of auto insurance should last a year but be totally unseen and probably unappreciated unless there is need to activate the policy. A hairstyle may last some time as an indirect benefit of the service.

Thus the customer and/or consumer has to rely on memory to aid in his next purchase decision. Memory fades over time, and we tend to remember selectively, so it can be seen that unless the service provider is really memorable (very good or extremely bad) the purchase decision process is less likely to develop into a routine re-buy in the same way as jars of instant coffee are replaced with the same brand from the same shop.

The need to produce in line with demand causes major problems for many service providers. We have all suffered as bank tellers sit behind their 'closed' signs. They are obviously doing something important – but is it more important than serving me? Of course not! Tesco began to advertise in January 1995 that they would 'do all they could' to open new check-outs when queues began to form. Note that they couldn't promise to open check-outs, only to do 'all they could'. Nice try, perhaps, but not very convincing, nor reassuring.

Perishability Many services are instant, or at least extremely time constrained. We don't want seats in a cinema after the programme has finished; airlines can't hold back a scheduled service if the seats are not taken. Being in the right spot at the right time is important to a customer. Having the right service, in sufficient quantity, in the right place at the right time is important to the service provider.

Walls Ice Cream, when servicing major events such as the Surrey Agricultural Show, are concerned to evaluate demand and so are keenly interested in previous years' figures and this year's weather forecast. They ensure that they have a three-ton freezer truck on site, filled with replenishment stock, and others running shuttle services to and from their nearest depot. Ice cream not sold is never sold. The moment has passed.

Demand also fluctuates over time and with season. It is vital for a service provider to identify the demand peaks and troughs, and to provide for them.

Activity 9.2

Demand
In some areas peak demand regularly exceeds supply. In others supply regularly exceeds demand. Identify three areas within each category and comment on the marketing implications.

(**See:** Debriefing at the end of the unit.)

Variability It may be yet another cup of coffee – one of hundreds served in a morning – but it cannot be guaranteed to be identical in all respects to those that have gone before, and to those that will follow.

Services require a very high focus on the interface between customer and front line staff, with a high level of managers to employees. Training is vitally important but this must be based upon a detailed performance manual which itemizes the standards that must be achieved.

Philip Kotler commented in a seminar that he re-dialled Federal Express because they didn't answer on the second ring, as they always do. Because they didn't, he assumed he was in error and had mis-dialled! When this standard of service is established and maintained a service provider is adding a differential that will be noticed, appreciated and generate business.

Organization

Seven structural variables need to be taken into account. These are shown in Figure 9.4.

Strategy and structure These variables can be taken as determinants of organizational culture. They have a marked influence upon everything which happens within the organization and begin the process of

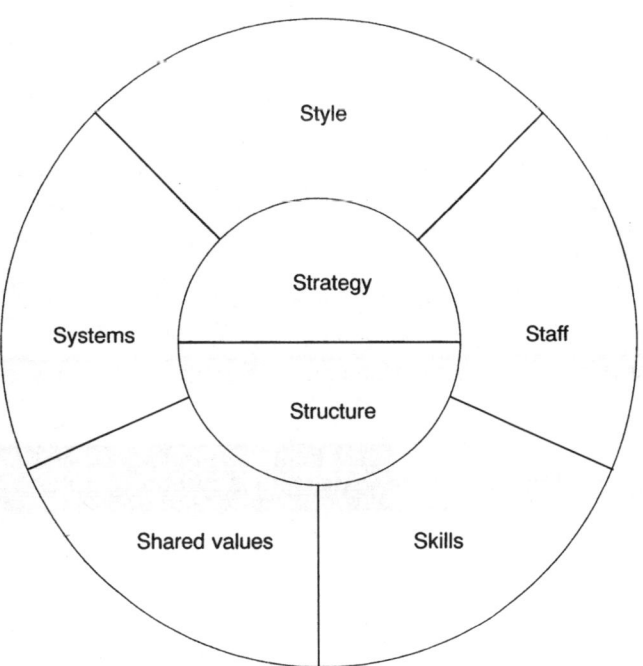

Figure 9.4
Organizational variables

197

establishing a culture of shared values into which the other four variables will fit and from where they must be generated.

Individual roles are established by the organizational culture. The amount of freedom that each has to act, what they are expected to achieve, how much knowledge they have, all are key determinants to the success of a service organization.

Upside-down organization

Service organization requires an 'upside-down' approach. Flat structures are needed since service speed is essential and many operational decisions must be made in real-time when actually with the customer. Conceptually a service organization can be seen as:

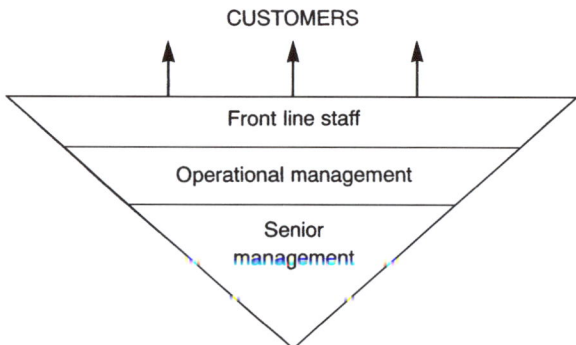

CUSTOMERS

Front line staff

Operational management

Senior management

Figure 9.5
Service organization

Strategic considerations

Service management and service marketing are so closely interrelated as to be virtually indistinguishable. We know that there is a major move to absorb strategic marketing into top management, without necessarily having a marketer on the board. That marketing is having to fight for a place at the top table.

In service organizations there has always been a recognition that marketing is the key to their success. Without a marketing/quality orientation a service organization will not survive very long. Therefore services are permeated by the marketing philosophy and operate to the marketing concept.

The strategic issues, then, revolve around the issues which generate and retain satisfied customers; there cannot be a production focus but there can be an over-emphasis on finance and/or sales. In all cases procurement is very important but it can never be as dominant in a service industry as it, and especially production, can be in a supplier of products.

Strategic issues are therefore very closely linked with operational necessities. Remember that the much flatter structures and the preponderance of front-line staff ensure that service management are far closer to their markets than in most product organizations.

Key issues are:

- *Service* The marketer must be alert to changing market needs, and be flexible in keeping up with them. Competitors can relatively easily enter, and just as easily add differential advantages. Unless there is a high level of competitive research, and fast decision processes, even the most successful services can be eclipsed remarkably quickly.
- *Supply and demand* Price can be used to help smooth out demand fluctuations but some demand shifts cannot be affected by price changes. Promotional efforts can also be used to attract and change demand; 'Happy Hours' in bars and 'Early Bird' menus in restaurants attract customers into slacker time periods. Air fares and package holiday prices vary with the low-, shoulder- and high-seasons.

  Note, however, that it is often not the same service that is offered. Low-season holidays are not the same as those in high season. Usually it is the climate which is different and the same island is very different when experienced in tropical sunshine rather than in the rainy season.

  Where holidays such as Easter cause demand to rise, the service is again different. Getting through London Gatwick airport is a very much more pleasant experience in mid-week than at a holiday weekend. There is likely to be space to spread out on the aircraft – three seats occupied by two people – and the resort is not likely to be over-crowded.

  Strategies to cope with the various reasons for demand variation must be developed and implemented.
- *Demand cycles* Services demand is often cyclic in nature. Detailed records can show unexpected demand variation by hour of day, day of week, and of month, week of year and month of year. Ice cream demand in the UK switches, for example, from ice cream to ice lollies when the temperature hits 65° Fahrenheit (18° Centigrade).

  Strategic awareness of demand allows major competitive advantage providing that operational plans are in place.
- *Competitive edge* Distinctive competence is the way into a market, but differential advantage is the way to sustain market presence. Of major strategic concern is the need constantly to refine, upgrade and improve the service whilst at the same time holding if not reducing price.

  The services sector tends to be extremely competitive and short-, medium- and long-term planning all tend to be within very proximate time horizons.

  It is often argued that differential advantage is difficult to achieve because services tend to be:

– Intangible	– Without patent protection
– Easy to enter	– Hard to control
– Difficult to staff	– Productivity inelastic
– Easily imitated	– Restricted by regulation (especially in the professions).

In fact the successful service providers prove how easy it is to establish and maintain a differential advantage. They tend to be:

– Clearly focused	– Market aware
– Fast on their feet	– Constantly seeking to improve
– People oriented	– Promotional heavyweights.

They are aware of their market segmentation and never try to offer too many things to too wide a market. Above all they invest heavily in Human Resource Management, especially in on-going training. Managers are encouraged to motivate and to build a sense of camaraderie to which their customers respond.

In short, differential advantage comes from a value package that is sustained. Not from a short-term campaign which secures market entry but runs out of drive and cannot sustain the long-haul.

Activity 9.4

Strategic possibilities

Actions are needed at both Strategic and Operational levels. Consider the kinds of things that can be done in each of the industries shown in the matrix, below. An example is provided to get you started.

Industry	Outcome sought by buyer	Strategic possibilities	Operational possibilities
Higher education	Educational attainment	• Select only highly qualified applicants. • Offer foundation courses for those with potential. • Target medium- or low-qualified applicants.	• Train lecturers to make them better tutors. • Offer distance learning, perhaps computer based. • Modularize courses over time and/or by form of teaching.
Doctor's surgery			
Bank			
High-street butcher			
Insurance			

(**See:** Debriefing at the end of the unit.)

Franchising

Franchises have become so much a part of our life that we do not – cannot – distinguish them from operations that are centrally owned and operated by a single management. Renting a Hertz car, photocopying at Prontaprint, buying a wedding gown at Pronuptia de Paris, all involve trading with a franchise.

Franchising is big business. In the United States in 1992 franchising accounted for sales of over $1 trillion or 25 per cent of GNP. This from a sales figure of over $175 billion in 1988! The growth of US franchise business outstrips the growth in the economy, which signals a significant shift from centrally owned firms.

The benefits of franchising are considerable:

Franchisors:
- Get into the market much faster and for much less cost.
- Secure the use of the franchisee's capital.

Franchisees:
- Gain the use of a proven package and a protected location in which to operate.
- Secure the back-up of the franchisor's expertise and buying power.

It is in the interests of both parties for a good contract to be established and for its terms to be honoured fully. Cheating on a franchise is bad business policy.

Franchising success

Franchising reverses the position on start-up with a 90 per cent success rate compared to a 90 per cent *failure* rate for non-franchises. The major high street banks have set up special franchise units – Barclays has its own hot line – to offer tailored finance to would-be franchisees.

About 370 business format franchise systems were on offer in the UK in 1992 (down from 430 in 1991). The average number of units per franchisor is 36, with some 18 000 outlets in total. Franchising employed some 184 000 people in 1992.

How franchising has grown

Year	Annual sales £bn	Number of units	Jobs created
1986	1.9	10 900	126 000
1987	3.1	15 000	169 000
1988	3.8	16 000	181 500
1989	4.7	16 600	185 000
1990	5.2	18 260	184 000
1991	4.8	18 600	189 500
1992	4.5	18 100	184 000
1993	5.0	24 900	188 500
1994	5.5	26 400	192 300
1995	5.9	25 700	212 200

Figure 9.6
How franchising has grown.
(Source: *Taking up a Franchise*, 12th edition, Daily Telegraph Guide, Kogan Page, London.)

Franchising offers the independence of self-employment with the security of a business format. The relatively few business failures coupled with the large percentage who sign-up again when their contract expires proves that the format is an on-going success.

Franchising ethics The British Franchise Association (BFA) published their Ethics of Franchising in 1987. Their ethical standards apply to BFA members (who are all franchisors) and establishes the BFA as arbiters in any dispute between members and their franchisees. Without full evidence of compliance with the BFA Code it is unlikely that a financial house will offer support.

Branding Franchises are branded packages that are shared by a range of franchisees who are each independent business people. It follows that brand identity must not be compromised by a bad franchisee and that franchisors must monitor performance and take prompt action to ensure that standards are maintained and contractual agreements on such as promotion in a locality are honoured.

Each franchisee benefits personally from getting it right as do the other franchisees, the franchisor and the public. Franchisors need to hammer this message home, not simply in the franchise agreement, but in everyday contacts. Unless there is an effective central marketing team that operates with the franchise as with any other branded product, it is unlikely that any cohesion will survive for long.

Franchising and the EU The European Commission recognize franchising as an employer of considerable significance. The EU anti-cartel laws might have prevented franchising but in 1987 the Commission released the distribution of goods and services from those constraints.

Attempts have been made to regularize franchising. Franchisees can be restricted to specified locations; franchisors can legally pursue and restrain former franchisees who attempt to launch look-alike operations; to encourage the standardization of pricing across national frontiers franchisees have been given flexibility in pricing and allowed to buy from each other. It should not, of course, be in a franchisor's interests to allow price differential by geographic area. Market forces, it is felt, will take care of any tendency to increase prices rather than cut them.

Common factors

A licence to franchise is a contractual agreement which should include:

- The franchisor's rights to a name, idea, manufacturing process, piece of equipment or service.
- The granting of a licence by the franchisor to the franchisee which permits the use of the name, idea, equipment or service.
- Conditions relating to the operation of the business through which the franchisee exploits commercial opportunities.
- The fees payable by the franchisee to the franchisor for the rights obtained in the franchise agreement.
- The means of settling disputes, probably by the use of the BFA as arbiters.

The franchise agreement is a legal document which must be drawn up meticulously, with the help of a lawyer experienced in franchising.

Activity 9.5

Franchising

If you were marketing a franchise, what would you see as the key benefits and disadvantages to both the franchisee and franchisor?

(**See:** Debriefing at the end of the unit.)

	Franchisee (per cent)			Franchisor (per cent)		
	Very Important	Important	Not important	Very important	Important	Not important
Previous management experience in same industry	0	20	80	2	14	84
Previous own business experience	12	46	42	16	47	37
Management ability	84	15	1	66	31	3
Desire to succeed	90	10	0	93	7	0
Willingness to work hard	92	8	0	93	6	1
Creativity	26	56	18	12	44	44
Strong people skills	63	32	5	64	34	2
Financial backing	71	27	2	67	27	6
Support from family	52	28	20	46	32	22

Figure 9.7 Personal franchisee characteristics required for success. (Source: *Taking up a Franchise*, 12th edition, Daily Telegraph Guide, Kogan Page, London.)

Synergy

Synergy is needed if long-term success is to be ensured. All are mutually interdependent and if one franchisee is below standard it will reflect on the trade, and profits, of others. The franchisor must insist on standards being maintained and take firm action if they are not. Franchisees depend on the franchisor to set and maintain standards so that the whole operation continues as a profit-making venture. The franchisor must have an efficient and effective system of management and control which is targeted on the actual needs to the entire operation.

Franchisee personal characteristics

Professor Russell M. Knight of the University of Western Ontario researched the qualities needed for success as a franchisee. He reports that franchisors and franchisees disagreed only in their ratings of management ability and creativity – a point that may provide some clues as to what franchisors are really looking for in a franchisee.

The 7Ps and the 11 elements

Mudie and Cottam recognize 11 design elements that underpin service marketing. These, to some extent, parallel the 7Ps, but remember that they refer to the service design whereas the 7Ps relate to the service overall.

It is possible to evaluate the design elements against each of the 7Ps as an indication of their relative importance in a given situation. The example generalizes about services, but the matrix can easily be adapted to the specific needs of a particular services marketer.

Remember that there is almost always an element of product in every service and of service in every product.

	Product	Place	Price	Promotion	People	Physical evidence	Process
Customer contact	X	XXX	XX	XXXX	XXX	XXX	XXX
Service mix	X	XXX	XX	XX	XXXX	XX	X
Consumed where?	XXX	XXX	X	X	XXXX	XXX	X
Design	XX	XXX	X	XXXX	XX	XXXX	XX
Technology	XXXX	XXXX	XX	XXXX	X	XX	XXX
Employees	X	X	X	XXXX	XXXX	XX	XX
Structure	X	X	X	XX	XXXX	X	XX
Information	XXXX	XXXX	XXXX	XXXX	XXXX	XXXX	XXXX
Demand	XX	XX	XX	XX	XXXX	XX	XX
Procedures	XX	XX	XXXX	XXXX	XXXX	XX	XXXX
Control	X	X	X	X	X	X	X

Figure 9.8 The 7Ps and 11Es matrix

Design issues are:

- *Customer contact* How much contact will a customer have and what form will it take? Is it a short visit once a year (insurance) or a daily visit (banks)? Is it for a take away or a sit down meal?
- *Service mix* Width and depth are the key questions. How many items in a line, how many lines?

  How far should the product range be extended for, say, a quick tyre service? To jacks and safety triangles? To first aid kits? To wheel spanners? To tool kits? To pressure gauges? To pumps? To . . . ?
- *Location* Should the service go to the customer or the customer be attracted to the service? Or should both be offered, as in pizza bars that offer a home delivery? How many outlets will be needed, and where should they be sited?
- *Design* Physical design extends from basic logos and letterheads through staff uniforms to the physical structures from which the service operates.

  Consider the impression made by a five-star hotel. Everything from deep pile carpet to shining buttons on the doorman's uniform are designed to signal quality and a readiness to provide a high level of comfort. (But pass through the green baize doors to the staff areas and the design becomes highly functional and often very shabby, even dilapidated in some cases.)
- *Technology* These days the staff will definitely be supported by technology. It needs to be reliable, i.e. computer systems should not crash (often!). When they do they must be brought back on-line very quickly. This requires forethought, careful planning and resource allocation.

  How will technology impact on the customers? Will it simply be a convenience as in just giving name and postcode to display all relevant details. Will it be more significant as in joining the 'quick start' programmes of Hertz or Avis so that a phone call and reference results in a car ready, all documents completed, and a special immediate service desk is provided? Will it be exclusively used by the customer, as in an ATM (automated teller machine, a cash point)?

What information will the technology provide to management and how quickly?

- *Employees* The P of People depends on the double P of Personnel Policy. Success will hinge on the quality and quantity of the staff and the front-line people must have back-room support. What flexibility is needed and how much initiative is required and/or can be allowed? The ratio of full- to part-time staff, and of management to employees, must be determined.
- *Structure* The structure will go a long way towards determining the organizational culture. It will also establish the roles of line and staff. Without a clear understanding of structure any organization will founder.
- *Information* Management information is needed for decisions and this must come through in sufficient detail and in adequate time (see Technology above). There is also a need for information to flow to the contact staff. The database must be constantly updated – preferably it should be real-time – since without hard and reliable information the customer cannot be satisfied on the spot.
- *Demand* Management of demand and supply depends on staff reporting accurately, and on relating practical experience on the ground to the data that flows through the MIS. It is an error to work only from the technologically generated material since there is always an underlying reason for variations and only the staff on the spot can say what it is. A sales drop may be no more than a temporary problem as a new water main is installed outside. It may be more serious as when a nearby office block is vacated.
- *Procedures* Relating directly to the P of Process, the design of procedures is crucial to the smooth processing of customers. Bad design can take months to correct. In the meantime customers are not served as efficiently as they should be, unnecessary cost is incurred and management's information flow is unreliable.
- *Control* One of the most difficult areas to manage because service marketers are dealing not only with the intangible nature of their service, but also with behavioural aspects of their customers and staff. We shall be examining marketing research and aspects of control in Unit 10.

Concepts

The marketing of concepts is the most intangible of all. It is even difficult to define 'concept' in simple terms. Here are two definitions:

The *Concise Oxford Dictionary* gives:

Idea of a class of objects; general notion (the concept of evolution); *invention* (a new concept in caravans).

The *Dictionary of Psychology* refers the reader to *conception*:

That type or level of cognitive process which is characterized by the thinking qualities, aspects, and relations of objects, at which therefore comparison, generalization, abstraction, and reasoning become possible, of which language is the great instrument, and the product of the concept – normally represented by a word.

Thus we have the notion of a generalized understanding which can be transmitted through language from one person to another.

Unfortunately language requires the receiver to share the conceptual understanding of the sender. Often assumptions are made about conceptual awareness, and shared conceptual understanding, with the result that the communication attempt is doomed to failure: *'Why did you do that!? I asked you to . . .'*

Evaluate conceptual understanding

Try this proven, simple and fun-to-do test. First on yourself, now. Later on several different people. You may be surprised at the results.

Prepare your subject by saying 'I am going to ask you to name something when I snap my fingers. Don't think, just give me the first thing that comes to mind. Ready?

'Name me something *large*.'
– Listen to the response and say, 'let's do it again. Ready?'
'Name me something *huge*.'
– Listen to the response and say, 'let's do it again. Ready?'
'Name me something *gigantic*.'
– Listen to the response.

Did you do the test? If so you should be aware of part of the problem. The assumption is that large, huge and gigantic are in ascending order of magnitude. When they come in a series, as in this test, people accept that they are. But ask people without the test and there can be strong arguments about the order of huge and gigantic. (Large is always the smallest.)

Equally importantly what do people say is large? And then huge? And then gigantic?

Common results are:

Large	*Huge*	*Gigantic*
Elephant	Department store	The Moon
London	England	The World
The world	The galaxy	The universe

Some start with the universe, however, and boy are they in trouble with questions two and three!

Interestingly, in the UK almost everybody mentions an elephant somewhere in the sequence and a department store is commonly used as well.

Compare the results you get and you will begin to understand how difficult it is to communicate concepts. If your promotion says 'huge sale', what will it be taken to mean? Will a 'large' event be understood to be really quite small?

Our concept of 'value loaded' words comes from exactly this difficulty of achieving a common conceptual understanding even for basic aspects of communication need. That is why marketing managers (and examiners) are constantly demanding quantified objectives. We know exactly what we have to do when our objective is to sell 75 packs at £1.00 each before five o'clock today. We don't know what is expected if asked to quickly get rid of as many as possible at a good price.

Activity 9.6

Conceptual awareness
Take time to go through carefully the examples you prepared before starting this Unit. To some degree you were not satisfied. What was (were) the cause(s) of your problem(s). How many were objective and how many subjective? How many were, or could have been, due to simple misunderstanding? Remember that conceptual misunderstanding is not deliberate, and need only be minor to throw a communication wildly off track.

Marketing concepts

Many service and NFP marketers have to market concepts. Health marketing is about prevention, and who wants to conceive of themselves as being at risk? It is a short step away from marketing life assurance which only pays out on the death of the person covered. Can you conceive of your own death? Not many can in hard-nosed practical terms. Thus life insurance is easier to sell than life assurance; we can conceive of injury, and welcome the idea of the policy paying out in 10 or 15 years, or when the mortgage runs out. We expect to be there to take the cash!

Puppies are not just for Christmas is an attempt to get people to ignore the appeal of a little puppy and the short-term pleasure it will give to a child at Christmas.

Keep your town tidy. Use the bin attempts to link to an emotional need for tidiness which seems absent in many people today.

Don't drink and drive campaigns try to get people to conceptualize that they are not safe drivers when under the influence of drugs or alcohol and that others have a right to expect responsible behaviour.

We shall return to conceptual marketing in Unit 10.

Extending Your Knowledge

WHEN THE GOVERNMENT KILLED THE DOG LICENCE THEY LEFT US TO KILL THE DOGS

This emotive headline ran alongside a dramatic picture of a mound of dog's bodies. The advert, from the RSPCA, was an attempt to communicate the need for a dog registration scheme.

About two-thirds of respondents to the RSPCA's promotional research had seen the advert. Most felt that it was shocking but effective, with a minority objecting strongly. 'It's horrible, but I think that people would contribute through shock' was a typical response.

The ad worked on the level of shocking people into comment and created some awareness of the problem. But it failed to communicate the dog registration scheme. The RSPCA were left wondering if this was because there was no concern for dogs, hardly likely in a country where appeals to help animals are always better subscribed than appeals to help children! It is probably more likely that the advertising campaign did its job of raising awareness, but the RSPCA did not have the rest of the mix in place.

The people factor

All services depend upon personal contact for their success. Whilst many are selling something tangible, many are selling 'only' their professional expertise. This can be so far removed from any layman's ability to understand that it has to be bought on trust.

- There is no point a brain surgeon attempting to explain what he is going to do, very few are equipped to understand let alone judge competence.
- Accountants can translate the same figures into a variety of forms in order to satisfy different needs. They sell their detailed knowledge of fiscal law coupled to their numeracy.
- Designers and composers visualize and innovate to add magic to situations. Have you ever seen a rough cut film without the musical soundtrack? Have you seen the same piece of film but with different sound tracks added to create changed moods?

All specialist and professional people sell their talents but all require the support of people to handle the routine interface with their customers and potential clients. Consider how many non-medical people surround your doctor. Are you as satisfied with the way they treat you as you are with the professional consultations? How difficult will you allow a receptionist to become before you change to another doctor?

207

Contact people
Return to your scripting example or use the doctor's surgery example. This time itemize the number of personal contacts that you have to make and consider how important each is within the totality of the service being offered.

Assuming that your personal views were supported by a substantial number of customers what changes would you expect a marketer to make?

(**See:** Debriefing at the end of the unit.)

Operational issues

The effective service and NFP organization has a very clear focus on the details of the operational issues that affect the degree of success achieved. Strategy has to be guided by the needs of the customers and their interaction with the front-line staff upon whom so much depends. It is not practical to establish strategy from a remote viewpoint: the strategic bridge between corporate mission, corporate objectives and operational planning has to be built mainly from the operational end.

Product

Customer value is evaluated by a complex system of internal judgement criteria. There is virtually always some element of physical product features associated with service and NFP marketing. Even in 'pure' services such as nursing and teaching, the customer finds it hard to distinguish 'product' from 'physical evidence'.

It is wise to regard the environment as part of the product offering because that is how it will be perceived by the customers.

The product-related elements will have a major effect on the overall perception of the service and this perception will vary by market segment.

Consider the ways in which a soda can be served to meet the expectations of different market segments. As a starting point we will generalize around broad age groupings.

Soda can be served to:

- *Kids* – in cartons with straws.
- *Teenagers* – in bottles and cans to drink from; in styrofoam cups; in lidded cups with straws to drink on the move or in cinemas, etc.
- *Young adults* – as for teenagers but with more of a tendency to want to sit whilst drinking.
- *Middle-aged* – a definite need for a glass (preferably) to drink from. A reluctance to drink from the bottle or can, or even through a straw.
- *Elderly* – glass expected but far less likely to drink sodas.

This very broad generalization can only be a first step but it does show how the product-related elements of even a basic service must be tailored to customer preference. Naturally these will vary with environment and time; standards expected from a fast-food outlet and a bar differ considerably from those acceptable in a sports arena or a restaurant.

The perceived quality of the soda will vary with the way it is served and this aspect of service extends from the focus of the product itself to everything that is associated with it.

In NFP marketing, especially, customer values are related to product elements that reflect expectation:

- Dress code is important as a product feature. Professionals are expected to dress appropriately, yet what is considered appropriate varies from culture to culture.

- Service engineers should clean up after them, for which they need the necessary equipment.
- Charities need to be high profile, but must achieve this without the hype and gloss associated with commercial ventures.

Price

Cost to the customer is what counts. Prices must be regulated by customer cost considerations. Remember, however, that a customer judges cost within an overall appreciation of value.

Many charities have successfully used psychological pricing techniques to increase their income. Instead of blanket appeals for funds they have learned how to link their appeals to worthwhile results: *Your £15.00 will feed this child for a month.*

They have also learned to suggest how much should be donated instead of leaving it to the judgement of the potential donors: *You are asked to donate £5, or more.*

They now make it easy to pay: *Use the reply paid envelope to send your donation, or ring us now on 0800 123123 with your credit card ready.*

Place

Convenience is all important. Services must be located where they are needed.

It is not by chance that similar services group together: books in Charing Cross Road; electronics in Tottenham Court Road; theatres in London's West End; and financial services in the City of London.

There is an old saying in the catering trade: 'Never build an hotel where there isn't one already'. It is, of course, far easier to attract extra business to an area than to generate demand from scratch.

Service providers are ideally placed to take their service to their customers. In many cases there is no need for a fixed base incurring commercial rents and rates since the provider can work from home and a car or van. Often the service is offered by an ex-employee of a service, as in the case of hairdressers, but providers can just as easily be part of a commercial or social organization.

Mobile shops offering most of everything obtainable on the high street have been touring the streets of towns and villages since time immemorial – today's technology allows speedier and easier access – a development of what has long been practised, not an innovative new service.

Information Technology and Telemarketing have opened access to a whole range of providers and, as we saw in Unit 4, new ventures such as Direct Line Insurance have exploited the new opportunities.

Interactive technology, coupled with the information superhighway and the Internet, promises a radical shift in purchase patterns, especially as ever more branded products and services become available.

Promotion

Communication is crucial to service and NFP marketing. The promotional mix emphasis alters radically in favour of personal selling, with the salespeople actually part of the service they provide. We shall return to the personnel aspects shortly.

Customer expectations are developed from a range of sources, of which external communications is only one.

- Past experience, made up of the quality of the sales effort and the results, is a major influence. We share a behavioural drive to repeat pleasant experiences (or less unpleasant in the case of medical services).
- Appearance is a combination of the physical environment, of the service premises and its surroundings, and any sales promotional offers which may encourage a waverer to 'give it a try'.

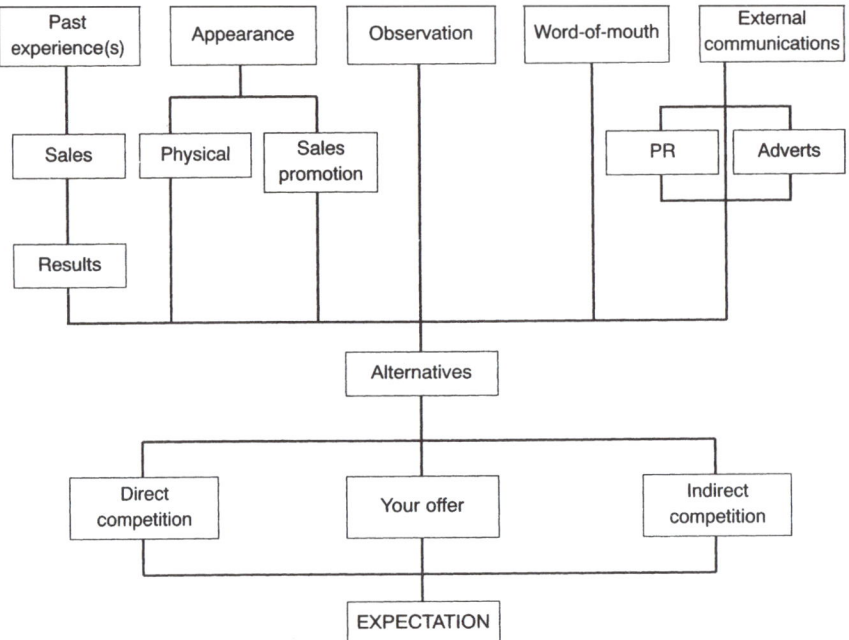

Figure 9.9
Developing customer expectations. (Source: *The Management and Marketing of Services*, Moodie and Cottam.)

- **Observation** relates to the investigation stage where a customer attempts to judge the quality and reliability of the service by the physical evidence that he can secure. This ranges from the physical senses – is the oil fresh in the deep fryer? – to the intuitive feel conveyed by a brochure sent in the post.
- **Word-of-mouth** is always related to the value that one puts in the judgement of those expressing an opinion and is tempered by one's own experiences with the service and/or provider concerned.
- **External communications,** especially PR and advertising, are powerful. They build awareness and develop confidence just as in other forms of marketing. There is a big danger in service marketing that the advertising promise will be too big to sustain. Actors look sharp and service bays are clean. The reality is that operatives who must wear the uniforms are not as trim as the actors, their uniforms quickly show signs of wear and tear, and service bays cannot always be clean and fresh.
- Beware not to create too high an expectation of service. 'Puff' is expected in advertising but it is less sustainable in the areas of instant and personal gratification than where a complex product is involved.
- **Alternatives are always evaluated.** Direct competitors may offer a look-alike service; McDonald's and Burger King are very similar in many respects, yet Wimpey have failed to achieve the same level of sharpness. Indirect competitors are possibly the most dangerous since they cannot be tackled directly. Your offer has to be differentiated today, and tomorrow, and every day after that for as long as you want to stay in business.

Customer expectation evolves over time. It is partly fuelled by your own service, and especially by your own promotion, but mainly by the changes in the social environment of which your organization is but a part.

Extending Your Knowledge

OSSIE's FISH BAR

Situated in south London Ossie's is a typical fish and chip shop of the sort that can be found all over England. It has half a dozen tables for those who want to eat in, but their main business was across the counter. On their window they claimed to provide 'The Best Fish In Town'.

People came from miles around, because their food was superb. Every evening from 6.30 until after 8.00 there was a queue of at least 20 waiting to be served by the team of five who worked at speed and without stopping.

On Fridays and Saturdays the queue was 40 or 50 deep, and a 20-minute wait was inevitable at any time up to 9.00. Parking was anything up to 50 yards away.

Ossie sold out. New management took over. Working with exactly the same equipment, and with all the goodwill established over a decade they were surely on to a winner! But they got it wrong.

Within a week queues were much shorter. In the second week there was hardly any wait in mid-week and only a short queue at weekends. Inside three weeks there were no queues at all!

The business still exists but only the husband and wife are behind the counter, there is never anybody eating at the tables and never any queues.

The lesson? Service businesses are about far more than simply putting fish into batter and then frying it. The overall personality of the team, the quality of the provision and the general approval of the customers must come together into one composite whole. Let one element slip and the whole comes unravelled.

Physical evidence

Confirmation is always sought. If the physical evidence does not match expectation then the customer will withdraw.

The elements of product and physical evidence are closely related as the only tangible features of the service are likely to be at point of purchase. This may be across the counter or by telephone supplemented by confirming documentation. The counter must match expectation and the documents must be presented so that they reflect the relative significance of the transaction.

It is a matter of nice judgement to create an ambience that completely expresses the core values of the service in a way that meets customer expectation. Again we are faced with a need to know how customers react to given stimuli. We do not want them saying of a charity 'look how they are wasting their money. There is no need for such high-quality stationery'.

Customers expect to be able to park close to a service provider, they will not stop if the neighbourhood looks threatening, nor if the customers already being served look 'the wrong type'.

People

Consideration is the key word in service and NFP marketing. Without an empathy with the customers and clients the marketing cannot work at the human level, where it has to be effective. It takes just one bad-tempered front line employee to undo months of good work and put a relationship at risk. If the problem is noticed by management, or brought to a manager's attention, the follow-through must be speedy and efficient if it is to be effective.

We all have stories to tell of incidents where things went wrong and in many cases we know of managers who rectified the situation. Unfortunately we all know of intransigent staff who defy customers and defend the indefensible.

There was a great deal of concern with Customer Care through the late 1980s and lots of Customer Care packages were run for the larger organizations. Unfortunately customer care is not something that can be picked up in a day's seminar. It has to be designed in along with quality, for it is intrinsic to the quality provision.

We shall return to the question of people a little later in this unit.

Process

Co-ordination of activities and concern that customers be fully satisfied must underpin the systems and procedures. Again this is a design issue since unless the needed processes are identified and designed in they will be incomplete and/or unsatisfactory.

Both sides of an organization must show genuine concern for the customer but unfortunately they often do not. The sales side is usually sweetness and light. It is the credit control and claims people who can destroy a relationship.

Obviously an organization wants to be paid and does not want to pay out if it doesn't have to. But it is unwise in the extreme to treat all debtors alike and to regard all claimants as fraudulent. It is always better to begin any potentially confrontational contact in a reasonable manner. One can always step up to a firmer, more aggressive stance but it is very hard to come down from aggression to reasonableness.

Customer interface

Interface occurs at three levels:

- *Remote* – impersonal contact through the post, ATM, etc.
- *Indirect* – personal contact by telephone or, just beginning, by computer.
- *Direct* – face-to-face contact.

In addition there are a host of other encounter points, as we saw when looking at the visit to the doctor's. Particularly important contact points are the receptionist and telephonist; both are the advance guard, ahead of the front line, yet both are commonly not appreciated, badly briefed and badly accommodated.

In particular note the potential problems inherent is having individuals from other organizations in contact with your customers. The security guard at the car park, your building's main reception area if you have a suite in an office block, the maintenance crew from the cleaning agency.

Service interface is often described in theatrical terms, with a set designed to achieve a given effect, staff wardrobed to convey meaning, and lines scripted and gestures rehearsed. There is a level of truth in this approach, and many organizations find that standardizing the approach is most effective. It can be in routine transactions such as buying a hamburger. It is less effective when discussion is needed, such as when negotiating as a house sales agent.

Power and commitment are important factors in relationships, and it is helpful to understand the role which is required of individuals when meeting with customers.

When seen from the customer's perspective, power relates to the strength of his position relative to the service provider. Commitment relates to the intention of continuing or maintaining a relationship. The perceived role that the customer adopts – whether consciously or not – requires an appropriate response from the service provider.

A power approach calls for a reasonable acquiescence, not for a stand-up fight!

A commitment is fundamental to marketing and requires to be nurtured.

Off you go to the Customer Service counter. Same problem. One is locked into conflicting systems. Bar coded three packs have to be replaced or refunded as three packs but worn garments cannot be exchanged. No matter that the identical garments are on the counter in single, double and treble packs. They are not the same because the bar code is different.

Eventually, if you are insistent and lucky, an accommodation is reached and you leave with two replacement pairs. But should this not be provided for in advance? And should not the Customer Service staff have the initiative and authority to cut through obviously silly policies?

Scripts

It is when analysing the interface – in its widest sense – that the importance of scripting becomes clear. Without a detailed understanding of the contact points there is no chance of providing for the maximum of positive contact.

Complaints

The Pareto Principle (80:20 rule) applies. The majority of problems will come from the minority of contacts. So far as possible these need to be identified, analysed and provided for. The aim is to cut back from 80:20 to 90:10, or even further. Problems can never be eradicated – we are dealing with human contact (!) – but the number of incidents can be reduced. With training the nature of incidents can be changed from potentially violent to mutually reasonable.

Human resource management (HRM)

The management of the human resource is crucially important in all organizations, but especially so in service marketing where every employee is (or potentially is) in direct contact with customers.

HRM is covered in the Effective Management for Marketing syllabus, and the Butterworth-Heinemann Workbook has major sections on all the key issues. It is not appropriate to go into detail about such a detailed and key subject in this book, but it is important that you take the time to cover at least the major HRM issues even if you are not taking that exam at the same sitting as Marketing Operations.

You need to have at least a working knowledge of:

- *Recruitment and selection* – job definitions, personnel specifications, interviewing techniques.
- *Training* – training programmes and training plans.
- *Motivation and incentives.*
- *The Manager as a leader.*

Exam Hint

Marketing is now a Chartered Profession and the title Chartered Marketer has already been conferred on those Full Members and Fellows who have completed the requirements for Continuing Professional Development (CPD). This is a major achievement in the on-going campaign to ensure that marketing's corporate value is fully appreciated. At corporate level, especially, marketers must possess effective management skills. You as a student, soon to become a candidate, must show management as well as marketing skills to your examiners.

Remember that managers achieve through others, that they need to persuade not dictate, that marketers are expected to communicate well. You will need all abilities at a high level in these areas to make a success of your marketing exams and career.

This question is taken from CIM's pilot paper. Allow yourself an exact 36 minutes and complete your answer in that time. This must include time for reading and understanding the question, planning your answer, writing your answer and checking through.

Leave the answer overnight and then review it harshly. Pick up every good point, and any bad ones. Then set a date in a few days time to take the question again, from scratch.

Finally, review your second attempt and compare it to your first effort. It should show marked improvement.

Question
Services marketing is often said to involve extending the marketing mix to include the three additional elements of people, process and physical evidence.

Assume you are a marketing analyst acting for the board of a company in a service industry of your choice. Prepare a report which explains why the marketing mix is extended in this way. You should pay particular attention to the role of the people in delivering service and maintaining service quality.

(**See**: Debriefing at the end of the unit.)

Summary

In this unit we have seen that:

- Services and not-for-profit marketing share many characteristics.
- Services are rarely 'pure'. Instead there is almost an element of tangibility associated either directly or indirectly with the service offer.
- The full 7Ps/7Cs are required for success.
- Scripting a service is essential to full understanding and therefore to meaningful management actions.
- Services tend towards intangibility, inseparability, perishability and variability; thus the issues of demand and supply are very hard to manage.
- Strategy, structure and shared values are determinants of organizational culture. These must build around the needs of staff, skills, style and systems.
- Considerable planning is required to design in the elements necessary to secure and maintain differential advantage.
- Meticulous records are needed in order to manage effectively.
- Franchising is big business, with major advantages for both the franchisors and franchisees. It must be carefully managed and synergy must be created, fostered, maintained.
- Concept marketing is the most difficult of all, with the problems of communicating by concept extending across all areas of management communication.
- Value loaded terms allow no sharing of understanding. Worse, they can be responsible for actual misunderstandings.
- Customer expectation (s) are in a constant state of change. Differential must be continuously monitored, reviewed and restored.
- The importance of the people factor is almost impossible to over-state.

Debriefing

Activity 9.1
Personal experience is of much more value than working with an academic example so do try to generate at least one personal script in the near future. The following is taken from research. The uppercase elements show how superficially most patients think about what is actually happening.

From their point of view the process is straightforward, but from the service provider's viewpoint there are many intermediate stages to identify and provide for. How often have you, for example, been bored (or annoyed) at the quality, quantity, age and type of magazine provided in a doctor's waiting room? This, apparently insignificant element of the service can have a major effect on how the service is judged overall, especially if other areas of service provision fail to meet acceptable standards.

Visiting a doctor:

> *Enter office*
> CHECK IN WITH RECEPTIONIST
> SIT DOWN
> Wait
> Look at other people
> READ MAGAZINE
> *Name called*
> Follow nurse
> *Enter exam room*
> Undress
> *Sit on table*
> Talk to nurse
> NURSE TESTS
> Wait
> Doctor enters
> Doctor greets
> Talk to doctor about problem
> Doctor asks questions
> DOCTOR EXAMINES
> Get dressed
> Get medicine
> Make another appointment
> LEAVE

Activity 9.2

Compare your examples and the marketing implications with the following typical examples.

Demand regularly exceeds supply:

1 *Restaurants* – popular restaurants are in such demand that they are reserved weeks ahead. Marketers should not change the winning formula but will certainly move prices up gradually (not too far though because no demand is totally elastic). Adding extra tables – upstairs, perhaps – may remove the waiting list but also lose the restaurant's major distinct advantage, that of exclusivity, the place to be seen.

2 *Tax accountants* – income tax year-ends bring a spate of work, enough to double, even treble, the work-load. But could additional staff be gainfully employed through the slack season? Unlikely. Therefore the accountant either must encourage a staged work-load by fixing target dates with his clients and/or call on short-term assistance to get through the peak period.

3 *Banking* – customers want to bank in their lunch hours but bank staff also need to go to lunch. Therefore peak demand flow occurs at the time of lowest staff coverage. Automated teller machines and quick-service counters help but do not fully alleviate the problem.

Supply regularly exceeds demand:

1 *Sports team in a lower division* – the stadium may accommodate a crowd of 30 000, but attendance may be only 5000. Most of the association football teams in the UK find themselves in this position since the competing availability of other leisure activities has reduced demand. Achieving Premier League status (and bigger crowds) is a dream for many but a possibility for only a few. The forecast is that many less successful clubs will have to close despite their long and cherished heritage.

215

2   *British seaside hotels and guest houses* – suffer from surplus capacity. They were opened to meet the demand for seaside holidays in the 1920s and 1930s; even into the 1950s and 1960s they were viable. But the jet aircraft and guaranteed sunshine at modest prices has taken their trade away. Again the forecast can only be that many will have to close.

3   *Services – water, electricity and natural gas* – are usually available at the turn of a switch or a tap. Only in rare instances does demand exceed supply. In the UK it is taken for granted that service provision will be immediate and of high quality. This means that even minor deviation from high standards results in violent reaction. Marketing's need is to encourage 'off peak' demand but, more importantly, to provide for the after-market needs of communication access, empathic response and efficient and effective service.

Activity 9.3

Ringing the central reservations numbers of three major airlines in the UK at 07.00 on a weekend produced the following results:

1   Answered on the third ring and the sales clerk was knowledgeable and helpful, attempted to close the sale, tried to secure an option rather than a firm booking, then accepted cheerfully that I was 'thinking about it and would come back'.

2   Didn't open until 08.00 but a line wasn't free until 08.20. The sales clerk was rushed and the computer was playing-up. After a long delay the detailed information was given and an attempt made to sell a flight. No transfer to an option, no encouragement to call back.

3   An answerphone directed callers to an alternative number at Heathrow. Calling Heathrow resulted in an answerphone that directed callers to the central number! Twelve attempts were made throughout the day. The phone was never answered. **Note:** This was the only state-run airline of the three.

Out of 10 the airline sales operations could be rated:

	1	2	3
Style	9	4	0
Staff	10	5	0
Skills	9	5	0
Systems	10	2	–10

Given that all three flew on the required route it is obvious which would be chosen, even if there were a small price premium. Only if the route was exclusively flown by airline 3 would increasingly desperate attempts be made to reserve a seat.

Activity 9.4

The potentials can be identified quite easily but that is nowhere near enough. Careful selection from the range of possibilities is needed so that a clear focus is achieved. Then imagination, determination and flair are needed to achieve market penetration.

A quick glance at the service market shows that the originators of a concept tend to dominate a market even though their operation can easily be copied. **Note:** Copied not replicated.

Activity 9.5

Key benefits to the franchisee:

- *Training* – in business and in the needs of the specific franchise.
- *Independence* – yet backed up by an established brand name and proven operation.
- *Brand* – the franchisor's name, reputation, logo, and decor.
- *Time* – the established brand and format save the time (and investment) otherwise required to build a business from start-up.
- *Capital* – less needed than for independent operation.

Industry	Outcome sought by buyer	Strategic possibilities	Operational possibilities
Higher education	Educational attainment	• Select only highly qualified applicants. • Offer foundation courses for those with potential. • Target medium- or low-qualified applicants.	• Train lecturers to make them better tutors. • Offer distance learning, perhaps computer based. • Modularize courses over time and/or by form of teaching.
Doctor's surgery	Health and reassurance	• 24-hour emergency service cover. • Staff to cover a wide range of specialisms. • Offer preventative clinics and well-woman, well-man checks.	• Train all staff, doctors, nurses, reception secretaries, in customer care. • Routinize repeat work such as prescription issue. • Actively promote preventative services.
Bank	Security and simplicity of money management	• Automate with cash machines and telemarketing. • Extend the range of 'money' services. • Demystify the process.	• Routinize most common procedures. • Bring cash machines into premises in addition to being on the street. • Train staff to proactively offer help.
High street butcher	Domestic fulfilment and easy shopping	• High quality meats, with personal service. • High quality, self-service. • Adequate quality, self-service. • Range of associated products.	• Train staff to personally advise customers. • Make the shopping experience easy and enjoyable. • Add a personal touch through identification of segment response.
Insurance	Security	• Locate on high street for personal service. • Telemarket for economy, speed, simplicity. • Price competitively. • After-sales support of high quality.	• Train staff for cheerful effectiveness as well as for efficiency. • Add-on sales of other forms of insurance. • Monitor quality of the after-sales providers.

Completed matrix for Activity 9.4

- *Business planning* – from site location to stock control.
- *Promotion* – benefits from franchisor's campaigns.
- *Risk reduction* – and the support of a head office organization to give confidence.
- *Purchasing* – bulk buying advantages.
- *Unique selling points (USPs)* – based on the use of patents, trade marks, secret processes and logos.
- *Regular progress checks* – with practical help available as needed from the franchisor.

Disadvantages to the franchisee:

- *Cost* – need to pay an initial fee and also a percentage of sales, or an annual fee, or both, to the franchisor.
- *Capital* – the initial fee has to be paid as capital from £5000 to over £250 000 depending on the franchise.

- *Royalties* – and/or regular payments, are a drain on the franchisee's profits.
- *Independence* – freedom of action is curtailed.
- *Resentment* – potential to feel resentful of the constant need to pay a royalty after the business is a success.

Key benefits to the franchisor:

- *Focus* – the franchisor can concentrate on operating a small core business. The day-to-day problems are delegated to the franchisees.
- *Specialism* – a specialist management team can control a sizeable empire of small businesses.
- *Finance* – investment capital is provided by the fees paid by franchisees.
- *Growth* – lots of small operators each anxious to expand rapidly ensure the growth rates of the franchisors.
- *International expansion* – eased through contracting to local franchisees who have no language nor cultural problems in their own market.
- *Motivation* – franchising attracts motivated people. Organizational conflict is reduced because of the type of staff and of the organizational structure.

Disadvantages for the franchisor:

- *Ownership* – franchisors manage a network of small businesses but do not enjoy the advantages of full ownership.
- *Criticism* – of the marketing back-up operation by the franchisees.
- *Complexity* – control procedures, training courses and monitoring can easily take more resources than planned.
- *Fraud* – franchisees can falsely declare their takings and/or buy local stocks so that they pay less to the franchisor.

Activity 9.6

The staff supporting a doctor have an established reputation for a certain type of self-importance which can almost reach the heights of arrogance. 'We control your destiny', they seem to say, 'so behave properly and do as I say'. Also there is always the sneaky knowledge that they have access to our secret medical data. They know things about us that not even our closest relatives know – this gives them power of which some are obviously well aware.

Thus a wise doctor takes steps to ensure that his staff are trained to behave professionally, and also ensures that their performance is monitored.

Overriding all, incidentally, is the use of the terms 'patient' and 'practice'. The behavioural implications of these terms are considerable:

- As a patient we are expected to be patient. It is for us to wait for the doctor. Yet he is being paid by us, we are his source of income!
- A doctor practises on his customers. The only professional able to openly admit that he is not perfect, in fact he is still learning. This is certainly true of many people. The more experience we gain the better we become – but would you willingly put your car in for repair to someone who said he was practising at coach building and paint spraying?

The typical points of contact are:

Contact	Customer reaction
Enter office	Disorientation, looking for directions.
Check in with receptionist	Am I known? Am I expected? Am I valued?
Sit down	Hope I don't catch anything.
Wait	Why can't they keep the place tidy?

Look at other people	Am I as ill as they look?
Read magazine	Why can't these be current?
Name called	Didn't hear . . . was that for me? Nobody else is moving. I'll get up.
Follow nurse	Why won't she wait for me?
Enter exam room	Disorientation.
Undress	Loss of individuality, loss of dignity. Embarrassment perhaps.
Sit on table	Discomfort.
Talk to nurse	Need for reassurance, for friendly interaction.
Nurse tests	Oh gosh . . . I hope it will be all right.
Wait	What did she find?
Doctor enters	Hopeful.
Doctor greets	Relief. He knows me, remembers my problems.
Talk to doctor about problem	Release, the problem is being shared.
Doctor asks questions	Concern if can't answer.
Doctor examines	Hope it is simple, routine.
Get dressed	Trying not to hurry, but anxious to hear result.
Get medicine	Only medicine, thank goodness.
Make another appointment	Oh dear, is it essential?
Leave	If the situation has been fraught the natural sense of relief will be tempered with a desire/determination not to visit there again.

The actions that a marketer would take should be self-evident. There is bound to be a sense of unease, at least, in every person visiting a doctor for examination. All concerned should be actively aware of the need for positive if unobtrusive support and the whole practice should be designed and managed to ensure maximum client consideration and reassurance.

Unit activity
Check your work against these answer guidelines provided by the Senior Examiner.

Approach
This question requires that the special characteristics of services marketing are considered and explained. Showing an understanding of these characteristics will help explain why it is necessary to include additional marketing mix elements. It is necessary to link this explanation into a discussion about a named service industry. The choice of industry is unimportant, what matters is that the example chosen helps demonstrate an understanding of how the extended marketing mix works in practice. The role of people in services marketing and in maintaining service quality is especially important and should therefore receive particular attention.

Introduction
Services marketing is playing an increasingly important role in the world economy. All products, whether goods, services or ideas, have a certain degree of intangibility. A service is defined as an intangible product which involves a deed, performance or effort which cannot be physically possessed. Although it is not always simple to classify an item as either a pure good or pure service, services as a category have certain characteristics which affect the way they are marketed.

These characteristics are taken into consideration in the extended marketing mix, which comprises three new elements people, process and physical evidence in addition to the well-known four of product, price,

219

promotion and distribution. The personal nature of services means that people play an especially important role in the delivery and maintenance of the service product and quality.

The characteristics of services marketing

Services are said to have a number of characteristics which distinguish them from goods and which impact on the way in which they are marketed:

Intangibility – although services do sometimes have tangible aspects, in general they cannot be seen, touched, smelled, tasted or physically possessed. This can make it difficult for customers to judge the quality of services or even understand them properly. For example, a significant proportion of customers for insurance schemes do not really fully understand what they are buying.

Inseparability – the production and consumption of the service usually take place at the same time. Visiting the doctor or hairdresser cannot be done remotely.

Perishability – because the service consumer must be present and involved in consuming the service when it is produced, services cannot be stockpiled for future use. A hotel room left empty for a particular night is a lost sale.

Heterogeneity – most services involve people and are labour intensive. Because absolute consistency is difficult to achieve (different individuals perform to varying standards at different times), there will be variation in the service delivered.

Extending the marketing mix

The characteristics of services marketing make it necessary for the traditional marketing mix of product, promotion, price and distribution to be extended to include three new elements: people, process and physical evidence. This explanation focuses on these last three elements:

People – the delivery of most services involves a customer interacting with a service provider. In some cases customers also interact with each other. For many service organizations the personnel are the most important asset. The importance of individuals in the provision of services places particular importance on employee satisfaction, motivation and training. For example, a restaurant is only as good as the chef cooking the food.

Process – because buying and consuming services directly involves the customer, the transaction and process of delivering the service are particularly important. This can cover a host of issues including appointment or queuing systems (doctors, solicitors, hairdressers), efficient payment systems (processing of bills in hotels and restaurants), appropriate information and documentation (details about bank accounts and insurance policies) and so on.

Physical evidence – the environment in which a service is delivered is central to the customer's perception of satisfaction with that service. In banks, hairdressing salons, hotels, hospitals, concert halls and sports centres the appearance and physical ambience (feel) of the environment is crucial. Decor, noise levels, standards of upkeep even smell are all important.

Delivering service quality

Services marketing has similarities as well as differences to the marketing of goods. Here, too, the marketer must start with a clear understanding of the benefits required by customers, appreciate how the service provider is perceived relative to competitors, as well as understanding the wider marketing environment in which he/she is operating. Ultimately, the marketer must be able to deliver the right service, to the right people at the right price, in the right place and be able to communicate all this with the customer.

The service provider is the representative of the service organization and thus has a major impact on how the company is perceived. The personnel are the main asset of many service companies because the quality of the job they do directly impacts on customer perceptions of the quality of service provided. Employee training and motivation must remain at the centre of service company philosophy.

Operational process issues significantly affect the consumer's perception of the quality of a particular service. For example, some restaurant chains expend considerable resources ensuring that dealings with customers are quick, efficient and friendly.

When the surroundings in which a service is delivered are poorly cared for and uncomfortable, the customer will tend to leave with a poor impression of service quality. Attention to the physical evidence details helps ensure that perceptions are as favourable as possible.

Useful tips
For this question, good answers require that the theoretical explanation is carefully integrated into the industry example chosen. The characteristics of services should also be linked with the need to develop the extended marketing mix.

Charity and not-for-profit marketing

Unit 10 is closely related to Unit 9 because services and not-for-profit marketing share so many characteristics. The major part of each unit will therefore apply across both; it will be easy to identify issues of specific reference to each topic.

Objectives

In these units you will:

- ❏ Understand the key factors that distinguish services and not-for-profit marketing.
- ❏ Examine the strategic needs of each sector.
- ❏ Identify the importance of personal contact in each sector.
- ❏ Appreciate the difficulties of effective control.

By the end of these units you will be able to:

- ❏ Apply marketing methodologies in services and not-for-profit marketing.
- ❏ Select an appropriate organizational structure.
- ❏ Initiate effective marketing research techniques.
- ❏ Apply appropriate marketing mixes.

Study Guide

You should now appreciate how difficult – and unnecessary – it is to distinguish services and NFP marketing since both rely upon the same extended marketing mix and both are concerned with marketing intangibilities.

Charity may not be an area where you will have considerable personal experience, but you should be aware of at least the major charities and their activities no matter where in the world you live. NFP marketing, of course, is universal.

Your work in Unit 9 should have stimulated further examples of services and NFP marketing which you can use as a basis for understanding as you work through this unit. Again try to approach a situation from both sides. What went right, what wrong? Was it deliberate or accidental action(s) that were responsible? Were expectations on either side too high? Were assumptions made where they should not have been?

Allow three hours to work through this unit and its activities. One activity is based on a mini-case to give you a final chance to practise your technique. The Unit Activity is your last chance before the mock examination in Unit 13 to work a question in exam conditions within a strict time period.

The end of your work through this subject is approaching and now is a good time to review your progress and to identify areas which need further attention.

Before starting on this unit take the time to check out the following. Set yourself SMART objectives for the achievement of each issue that you identify as needing attention.

- Study notes
  - Are they revision friendly?
  - Have you added your own ideas and illustrations?
  - Have you added current examples?
- Activities
  - Have you completed the activities and extending exercises for each unit?
  - Is it worthwhile to go over any you found difficult or confusing? (You won't want to but is it worthwhile? Should you?)
- Cuttings file
  - Have you some easy way of accessing material secured from outside this workbook?
- Presentation
  - Are your presentation skills up to standard?
  - Are you (when will you start?) practising your skills of report writing against the clock?

Non-business marketing

Non-business marketing can be divided into two categories: not-for-profit marketing and social marketing.

- *Not-for-profit marketing* This sector is not so simple to recognize as it may at first seem. This is partly because of the ambiguity in the use of the term 'profit', and partly because many NFP organizations are anxious to achieve a cash profit on trading activities.

  Marketing is all about exchange relationships and we know that exchange need not be of cash for satisfaction. We learn very early in our studies that the marketing philosophy extends across all of life and that it is for each individual and organization to conceptualize profit for himself. Now we are asked to accept that there are not-for-profit marketing organizations!

  Strictly speaking NFP organizations should be termed 'not-for-cash-profit' organizations because they are interested in cash profits only as a means to achieve their overall ends. Thus the major charity Oxfam has more retail shops than any commercial organization in Britain, but uses the trading surpluses (profits) as income to the charity. Similarly other charities generate income by identifying opportunities to sell greetings cards and diaries, opening their premises to the public for a fee, etc.

  It will help considerably if we recognize NFP organizations by their major objective, which is not to make loss. They need to generate sufficient income to cover their costs and allow them to fulfil their prime objective, whether that be the marketing of a charity, a hospital, a concept or some other non-commercial objective.
- *Social marketing* The application of marketing techniques to influence the acceptability of certain ideas which bring benefit to individuals and society. The societal marketing concept, as expressed by Kotler, illustrates the breadth and depth of social marketing's concerns:

  The societal marketing concept holds that the organization's task is to determine the needs, wants and interests of target markets and to deliver the desired satisfactions more effectively and efficiently than competitors in a way that preserves or enhances the consumer's and the society's well-being.

Thus societal marketing encompasses all organizations no matter in which sector they are working, and no matter what their field of activity. The societal marketing requirement is that well-being is preserved or enhanced.

The societal marketing concept requires marketers to balance three considerations in setting their marketing policies:

● Profits   ● Consumer wants satisfaction   ● Public interest.

Activity 10.1

Social marketing
Identify three examples of excellence in social marketing, and three where the organizations are ignoring the social marketing concept. Think through the implications – you will probably find the examples useful in your examination.

(**See:** Debriefing at the end of the unit.)

Environmentalism

Do not confuse environmentalism with consumerism. The one is concerned with the ecology, with maximizing life quality. The other with ensuring that the consumer is treated fairly and that the consumer's rights are respected.

Environmentalists are concerned with issues that affect the global environment upon which we all depend. Probably the issue that has caused the widest concern is the so-called hole in the ozone layer and the greenhouse effect which is forecast to make major changes to our climate. CFCs are banned in some manufacturing but replacements have yet to be introduced throughout. In the meantime the damage continues.

Of concern are such issues as strip mining, forest depletion, the effluent from factories, smoke, nuclear waste and the destruction of wildlife habitat to build new motorways. Quality of life issues such as loss of recreational areas, excessive outdoor advertising and litter also fall within the remit.

Environmentalists are not opposed to marketing – their desire is to ensure that organizations, and individuals, operate on good ecological principles. That decisions are evaluated for their impact on the environment with only those that have positive value being progressed. Thus environmentalism is at first a concern of top management since its principles must be adopted at corporate level, as policy, before an organization can properly adopt them throughout.

Marketers who are environmentally aware need to check into the environmental results of their potential actions. All the potential consequences of product decisions have to be identified and taken into account. This includes everything from the damage arising from extraction and transport of raw materials to the production process and its wastes, and on into package design and disposal. Environmentalists are concerned about the excessive packaging which, even at a minimum, wastes precious natural resources and they are concerned about promotion that encourages conspicuous and unnecessary consumption.

Environmental protection naturally incurs cost, which raises prices, and so many organizations are reluctant to take the long-term decisions for fear of doing short-term harm. As the 'Green Movement' gathers pace, however, it is becoming obvious that consumers are pressing for environmentally sound products and services and as this shift becomes established as a consumer need it is to be hoped that managements will respond, not least because it will be in their short- as well as long-term interests.

NFP marketing

Organizations without a commercial profit motive have only recently begun to appreciate their need for both management and marketing to be integrated into their operating principles.

Traditionally an organization's control has been the responsibility of senior people with skills in the core activities of the organization. Thus hospitals were run by doctors, the RAF promoted pilots to their senior ranks, accountants managed their practices. Some professionals were forbidden to advertise their services.

Marketing for many in the NFP sector was seen as exploitive. Marketers were considered to be high-pressure salespeople concerned only with maximizing their income with no concern for those with whom they came into contact. Management was not identified as a need since it was taken as intrinsic within life.

Throughout the 1980s competitive pressure increased across all sectors. There was greater rivalry in the marketplace (charities), a surplus of provision (higher education) and a reduction in Government funding (local authorities). In addition, the British Government wanted the commercial principles of management to a budget to be adopted. Vigorous steps were taken to encourage/oblige major changes – notably in the health service which has had to adopt a tiered system of management and to manage commercial style budgets.

The rights and wrongs of these governmental decisions are for political discussion. Their results are of concern to managers and marketers.

Marketing opportunities

With the value of marketing beginning to be appreciated there was opportunity for marketers to become active in non-commercial sectors. Obviously some marketing had always taken place, some formal marketing posts had long existed, but in general marketing in the NFP sector was seen as 'advertising', a necessary evil.

Unfortunately for marketers the profession is superficially easy to understand and practise. It can appear to be only applied common sense. It is certainly easy for intelligent people to pick up the rudiments quite quickly. Thus senior professionals began to add marketing to their skills base.

225

Accountants and lawyers began to understand and use marketing in their corporate planning. The professions relaxed their restrictions to allow some forms of non-aggressive marketing. Non-marketing graduates began to add the CIM Diploma to their base qualification.

As a result marketers may find themselves relegated to a functional role, with marketing strategy the responsibility of specialist managers who have added the needed marketing skills. This issue is peripheral to the development of marketing in the NFP sector but it has major significance for the career planning of marketing specialists.

Marketing's adoption

- Colleges and universities
  - The product range is under constant review, the physical environment is of concern and more efficient methods of teaching are being devised.
  - Promotion has sharpened and the importance of internal marketing is being recognized.
  - Staff needs, both teaching and support, are identified using HRM techniques; recruitment ads are more professionally produced and placed; selection is more concerned with effectiveness than qualifications. Training is budgeted and encouraged.
  - Funding sources are targeted and marketing plans developed to maximize the probability of achievement. Trans-EU funding requires a long-term commitment. Commercial sponsorship needs activities targeted to meet the sponsor's needs.
- Hospitals
  - Excess demand and budgetary constraints are causing hospitals to allocate their resources very carefully.
  - Funds are now transferred between health service organizations as services are 'bought and sold'. Thus there is need to attract patients from general practitioners who hold funds – yet there is a crucial social need to ensure that those who need medical aid are not denied on monetary grounds.
  - Sponsorship and the aid of voluntary groups such as 'Friends of the Hospital' has to be solicited and the benefits be seen to be valued.
- Doctors
  - Excess demand and budgetary constraints are causing doctors to consider which patients they can afford to accept on to their lists.
  - There is a growing resentment in the population because the tradition of open access is now restricted. This presents a serious need for doctors to use marketing to show that they are not responsible for Government actions.
- Charities
  - Funds must be solicited from a variety of sources.
  - Beneficiaries of the charity must be located and encouraged to apply and/or accept support.
  - Internal marketing must co-ordinate and motivate the individuals who work for the charity either in an employed or voluntary capacity.
- Social organizations
  Many long-standing organizations such as the YMCA, the Scouts and the Churches are losing members and suffering from lack of income. Marketers face the twin problems of redefining mission and corporate policies to provide what people require today and securing the necessary funds to generate an upturn in membership.

The spiral of cause and effect

Nothing is static – nature abhors inactivity. Thus organizations are either growing or shrinking. The spiral of cause and effect is either positive or negative. Unfortunately positive spirals are easier to break than negative ones.

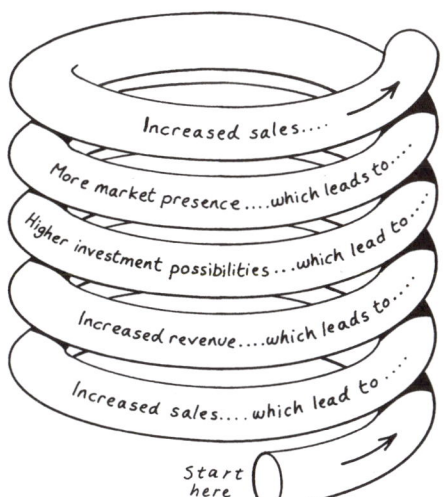
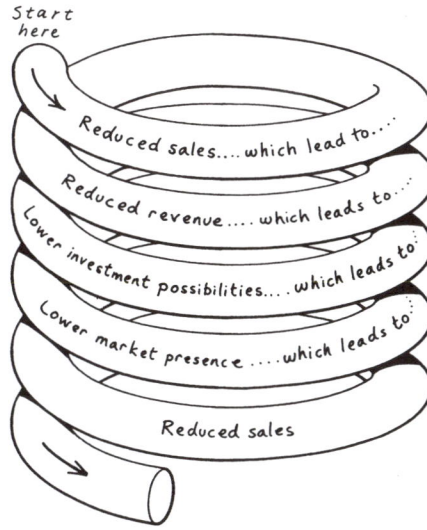

Figure 10.1

Citizen's charter

A British government initiative has resulted in the emergence of citizen's charters. As of 1994 there were 32 in place. They are intended to protect the quality and levels of public service that a consumer might expect and are expressed in statements of time, quality and service.

The intention is that public service organizations should be leaner, fitter and more competitive, with a focus on consumer need. The term was chosen to describe the basic and fundamental levels to be provided by each service.

Information is given on what should be expected, and what actions the consumer can take if the terms of a particular charter are not met. For example, Virgin Rail will pay a sum to compensate for lateness of a service on which the passenger is travelling, providing it is outside their charter conditions. They will not compensate those who are waiting to board a late-running service.

Charity marketing

Anne Frazer-Simpson, joint managing director of Will for Charity, expresses the current state of the charity market when she says: 'The days of the "lady bountiful syndrome" are long over'. What she means is that charities are now businesses in all but name. The dictionary definition of charity is something that charity managers are consciously keeping in the background.

The *Concise Oxford Dictionary* defines charity as '... beneficence, liberality to those in need or distress (alms giving)'. This underlying concept is still of vital importance, but it is rather passive in nature and charities have found the need – and the tools – to be proactive.

Charities are organizations registered with the Charity Commission that enjoy certain privileges regarding taxation and the regulation of their financial affairs. They are recognized by the state as important contributors to the environment and, as such, are enabled to recover the income tax paid on covenanted donations, benefit from legacies and can elect to be excluded from value added tax.

The fact that charity marketing is big business marketing is emphasized by the revenue involved; see Figure 10.2.

227

Income		1998	1997	1996	1995	1994
Legacies	£m	905	737	628	666	600
Sale of donated goods (gross)	£m	252	227	196	153	107
Other voluntary income	£m	3149	2804	2736	2569	2273
National Lottery income	£m	118	74.9	24.7	11.5	–
Public grants, fees	£m	3376	3362	3248	3224	3064
Fees and charges	£m	4928	4628	4224	3939	3595
Non-charity trading (net)	£m	164	146	123	94.7	87.3
Interest, dividends, rent	£m	1896	1847	1793	1663	1519
Total	£m	14788	13826	12973	12320	11244
Expenditure						
Grants awards made	£m	2614	2539	2278	2314	2239
Other direct charitable expenditure	£m	9126	5604	8026	7243	6566
Management, admin costs	£m	1088	977	1046	1153	1184
Fundraising	£m	514	456	396	341	292
Sale of donated goods	£m	157	141	124	108	72.6
Capital unusual	£m	242	286	368	339	296
Total	£m	13741	13003	12238	11498	10649

Figure 10.2
Top 3000 British charities –
Aggregate income and expenditure.
(Source: Top 3,000 Charities,
Barings Asset Management, 1998.)

It is big business indeed when aggregated income for one year totals some £m 14 788. Voluntary income accounts for only 21 per cent of takings – which emphasizes the need for marketers to concentrate on more than one target market area. The steady growth in total income – well ahead of inflation – perhaps indicates how effective the marketing efforts have been.

Aggregate expenditure runs at about 93 per cent of income. The ratio of charitable expenditure to income is always of concern, but perhaps slightly less now than in the recent past.

There used to be a strong feeling that resources should only be used to further the prime objectives of the charity. All costs were scrutinized with meticulous care and the larger the percentage of funds that could be passed on, the better the charity was performing. Thus a charity with an income of £1 m and costs of 4 per cent was judged to perform better than one with an income of £5 m and costs of 6 per cent.

It was not until the mid-1970s that marketers began to make serious impact in the charity market. At first these were retired people who had the necessary skills and could afford to donate their time, perhaps in return for an honorarium and expenses. They began to argue for a return on investment approach and gradually began to secure funds for marketing. They were a long way from having a marketing budget!

Evaluation of results began to prove their case. Marie Curie Cancer Care were one of the first into active marketing and by 1981 they were achieving a return of at least five times their marketing investment. Today the expectation, according to the Institute of Fund-raising Managers, is closer to 10 per cent of a charity's income: a return of 10:1.

Rank	Charity	Period	Fund-raising costs as % of total income	Management, administration costs — as % of total expenditure	Management, administration costs — as % of total income	Direct charitable expenditure — as % of total expenditure	Direct charitable expenditure — as % of total income
1	Charities Aid Foundation	April 1998	1	1	1	98	88
2	National Trust	Feb. 1998	2	1	1	69	55
3	Oxfam	April 1998	20	2	1	95	71
4	Salvation Army Trust	March 1998	3	2	1	99	71
5	Church of Scotland Unincorporated Boards	Dec. 1997	1	3	3	97	99
6	Ludwig Institute for Cancer Research	Dec. 1997	N/A	16	19	84	77
7	PPP Healthcare Medical Trust	Dec. 1997	N/A	17	N/A	83	1
8	ACTIONAID	Dec. 1997	21	3	3	80	77
9	NSPCC	March 1998	20	N/A	N/A	83	77
10	Macmillan Cancer Relief	Dec. 1997	33	1	1	66	56

Figure 10.3 Top ten British charities by voluntary income. (Source: Top 3,000 Charities, Barings Asset Management, 1998.)

Figure 10.3 shows the relevant statistics for the top ten charities in 1996. It will be seen that some of the charities with the largest incomes devote substantial funds to support their fund-raising efforts. Most also manage to keep their management and administration costs very low. Thus they can pass a substantial portion of income along to those in need.

Target markets

Charities have three target market areas: Funding sources, Beneficiaries and Internal. The major external targets are shown for a typical charity (see Figure 10.4).

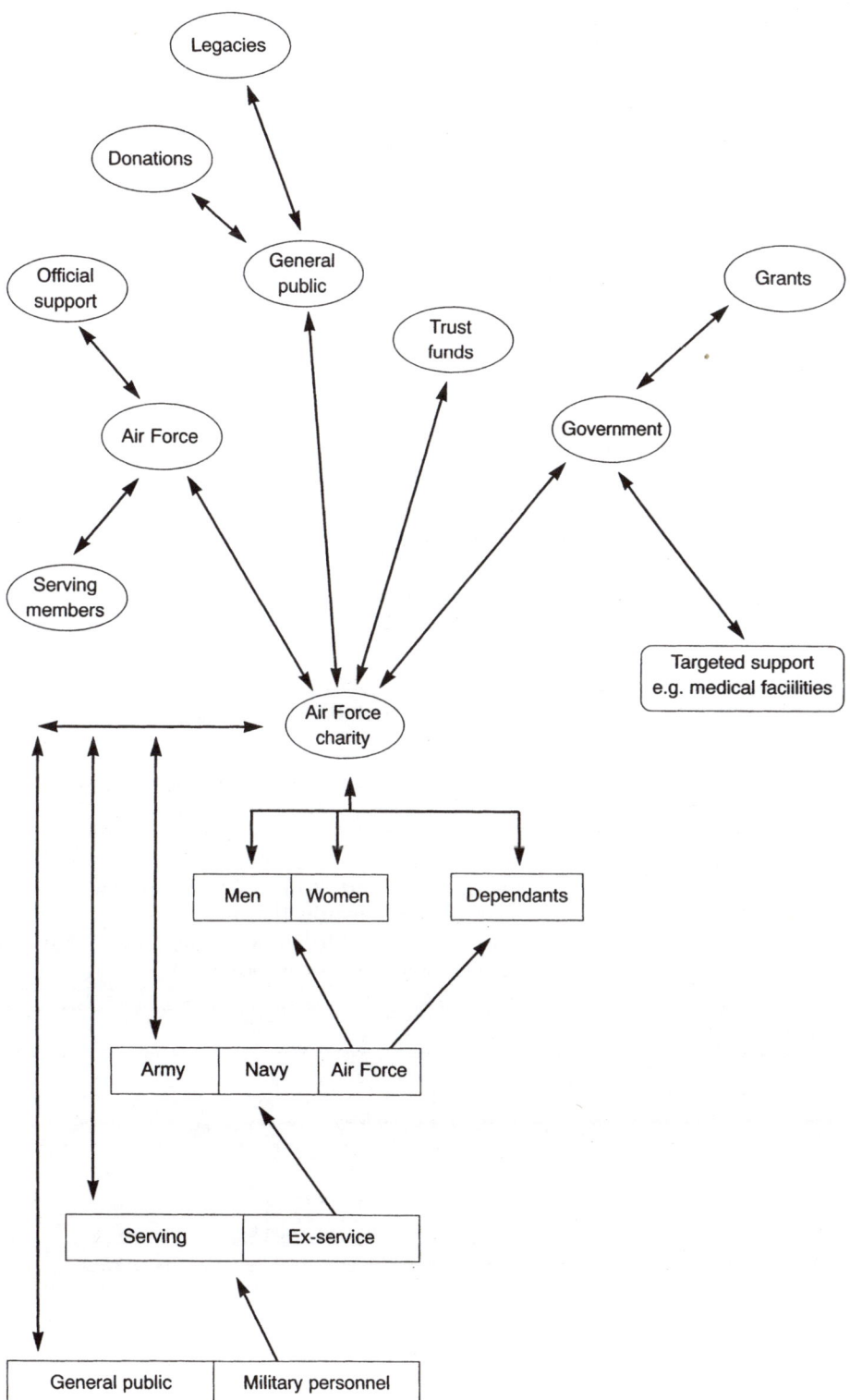

Figure 10.4
Major marketing targets for an Air Force charity. (Source: *Marketing in Management*, Worsam and Wright, Pitman, 1995.)

229

Rank	Charity	Period	Legacy income (£m)	Growth %*
1	Lankelly Foundation	April 1998	67.0	–
2	Royal National Lifeboat Institution	Dec. 1997	49.6	6
3	Imperial Cancer Research Fund	Sep. 1997	42.4	6
4	Cancer Research Campaign	March 1998	39.2	7
5	RSPCA	Dec. 1997	31.8	13
6	National Trust	Feb. 1998	30.7	7
7	Guide Dogs for the Blind Association	Dec 1997	25.0	7
8	Royal National Institute for the Blind	March 1998	24.6	8
9	British Heart Foundation	March 1998	22.7	8
10	Barnado's	March 1998	22.3	9

*Legacy growth is based on a four-year average.

Rank	Charity	Period	Voluntary income (£m)	Growth %*
1	Charities Aid Foundation	April 1998	134	14
2	National Trust	Feb. 1998	58.8	6
3	Oxfam	April 1998	46.6	4
4	Salvation Army Trust	March 1998	43.7	66
5	Church of Scotland Unincorporated Boards	Dec. 1997	40.3	1
6	Ludwig Institute for Cancer Research	Dec. 1997	37.0	11
7	PPP Healthcare Medical Trust	Dec 1997	34.6	(33)
8	ACTIONAID	Dec 1997	33.1	7
9	NSPCC	March 1998	31.7	8
10	Macmillan Cancer Relief	Dec 1997	31.5	8

*Voluntary income growth is based on a three-year average.

Figure 10.5 Top ten British charities by legacy and voluntary income. (Source: Top 3,000 Charities, Barings Asset Management, 1998.)

Funding sources

Whilst legacies and voluntary sources such as donations are very important it has been shown in Figure 10.2 that these accounted for only some 27 per cent of charity income in 1998. It is immediately apparent that some charity marketers target specific areas, where they develop contacts and special skills, i.e. charities such as Oxfam have highly developed retail skills and run a chain of retail shops using empty property donated by the owners and staffed by local volunteers.

Figure 10.5 shows that the top ten charities by legacy and voluntary income are not the same. Should this be a matter of concern to their marketers? How would it be best to attract legacies?

Legacies are a very important source of income for many charities. Many people are left without next-of-kin and need a home for their bequests; others want to help do some good by supporting a particular charity with which they have a special affinity, perhaps through the good it did for a relative or friend. Will to Charity provides a regularly updated guide to charities and ensures that every solicitor and accountant receives a copy since it is often to these professionals that a person contemplating a bequest will turn for information.

Figure 10.6
The top ten corporate donors.
(Source: Top 3,000 Charities,
Barings Asset Management, 1998.)

Rank	Company	Period	Worldwide community involvement (£m)	
			This year	Last year
1	Glaxo Wellcome	Dec. 1997	24.0	18.0
2	Diageo	June 1998	21.7	11.9
3	Lloyds TSB Group	Dec. 1997	21.5	13.9
4	British Petroleum Co	Dec. 1997	19.5	18.4
5	Barclays	Dec. 1997	15.1	11.5
6	British Telecommunications	March 1998	15.0	15.0
7	B.A.T. Industries	Dec. 1997	10.5	8.8
8	Marks and Spencer	March 1998	10.1	9.8
9	Smith Klein Beecham	Dec. 1997	8.4	7.4
10	Reuters Holdings	Dec. 1997	8.4	6.6

Major organizations are becoming an ever more important source of funds as they adopt good neighbour policies. The top ten corporate donors (see Figure 10.6) between them gave over £154 m in 1997/98, an increase of some 27 per cent on the previous year. Again, ahead of inflation.

Remember, also, that large donors are also moving into sponsorship. This has many features in common with charitable giving in the sense that it provides a platform on which organizations can be seen to be doing good. Thus a 'giving budget' may now extend beyond the traditional charity concept.

Funds disbursement

Charities have to work at dispersing their income. Whilst most are inundated with requests for help, not all of those who most need the help know of the charity, nor will they apply for help even when they do.

Many older folk were brought up not to accept charity, and the need to stand on their own feet and 'be beholden to nobody' is a very strong cultural heritage. This may well alter as the generations change and people used to support from Social Services come to need charitable help but there will always be a need to inform those qualified for aid that it is available.

Charities face a problem in making themselves known to potential beneficiaries. The high costs of a full-blown marketing campaign absorb funds that ought to go to those in need. Obviously there will be a spin-off from the fund-raising activities but this is not a targeted effort.

Often the route is indirect, through a social worker, community nurse or social group. But reaching the person who is in need is not enough. They have to accept their need, and also the help that is being offered. The task of persuasion requires special skills and long-term patience since the individual has to be helped to appreciate that accepting help today is no stigma.

Internal marketing

Charities face a unique need for internal marketing because they are so dependent on voluntary workers.

- There is need for careful selection, yet a charity cannot afford to be too choosy.
- There is need for management, yet a charity cannot be too prescriptive.
- There is need for control, but a charity is not working with professionals, nor with the same equipment as commercial organizations.

Generally charity workers are highly motivated, getting a tremendous kick from their work. As a highly people-centred organization a charity can only ask so much of its staff: generally staff put in longer hours, more willingly, if they are encouraged to respond to need and their own efforts are noticed and rewarded in non-tangible ways.

Note: See the units on motivation, incentive and the manager as a leader in the *Effective Management of Marketing* workbook.

Cash or kind?

Much assistance will be willingly provided by individuals and organizations if they know what is required and believe that it will be used effectively. The effective marketer prepares a shopping list of needed items and sets about securing as many as he can without parting with cash.

Those fresh into charity work from the commercial sector tend to bring their commercial values with them. Thus they expect state-of-the-art computers, when the charity can work perfectly well with recently outdated equipment. They expect modern offices, with all conveniences, when a charity can function very well using wooden desks without matching chairs. This is not to say that charities are not efficient, far from it. The key difference is that charity employees evaluate their need against that of those they exist to help rather than against a commercial profit.

Low budget social marketing

This activity is based on 'A case of contra-communication' which was set as a CIM Marketing Communications examination. It requires a public service of considerable importance to be marketed on a low budget.

The budget to promote non-smoking is tiny when compared to the tobacco industry's spend. A routine marketing approach is therefore contra-indicated.

Consider how you might create an imaginative solution to harness power that is more equal to the task. Remember that the Examiner will be impressed by imaginative answer(s) to the question(s) set.

Select one of the alternatives that could be open to you and *outline* a recommended plan of action to submit to Harold King.

Remember that a mind map is an excellent way to generate alternatives.

The salient facts are:

1 Harold King, Research Officer of the Public Health Advisory Group, must persuade a target audience not to consume.
2 The product is 'anti-smoking'.
3 His budget is £185 000 for a twelve-month marketing communications 'initiative'.
4 Competitors spend multi-millions on 'seductive messages'.
5 The theme has been hard-hitting, negative and focused on health damage from smoking.
6 96 per cent of the population now accept, to some extent, that smoking is dangerous.
7 70 per cent have tried to give up the habit at least once.
8 A threatening message is now felt to be counter-productive.
9 The negative, probabilistic, intangible, long-term ill-effects of smoking can be compared with its immediate, tangible, positive and definite perceived benefits.
10 Middle-class males are now only half as likely to smoke as 20 years ago – but there has been no significant behaviour change among working-class males.
11 If point 10 is true the present message is inappropriate.

Harold King has to present his thinking to the Public Health Advisory Group's Publicity Committee. He is primarily concerned to maximize the effect of his budget given that pound for pound he will be overwhelmed if he attempts a mass-media campaign.

(**See:** Debriefing at the end of the unit.)

THE DILEMMA OF THE ARTS

Theatres, opera, ballet, museums, etc., find themselves in a major dilemma. They cannot support themselves through income since they are appreciated and supported by only a minority of the population. They cannot make significant cost reductions since their appeal depends upon the quality of their service.

Traditionally they have been supported – some would argue they have been featherbedded – by grants and donations to supplement their income, but grants have been cut back and commercial organizations have been struggling with recessionary problems of their own.

There is a general feeling that the arts are a 'good thing' and that they should be maintained – but comparatively few are prepared to donate, especially when there are life-saving causes desperate for funding.

Arguments that without the arts the cultural heritage of the country will suffer grievous harm fall on stony ground with the majority, for whom the concept is too esoteric to be of short-term importance.

Thus the arts are being forced to turn to more commercially attractive activities and to bow to the demands of the pragmatic environment. What damage this will do long term has yet to be seen but it may mean that the British entertainments industry will contribute far less to the UK balance of payments through its invisible earnings. If this is so it will not only be the cultural heritage that is damaged.

Marketers in the artistic world face the tremendous challenges not only of securing attendance and support but also of convincing individuals of the necessity to invest in what can easily be seen as a self-indulgent sector that is of no great importance.

Extending Your Knowledge

THE SOCIAL WORKER'S DILEMMA

'I say' said a social worker in the refectory of a teachers' training college, 'Can you help us, please?' 'I'll try' said the marketer, 'What's the problem?'

The social worker took the marketer over to a group of 18 of his colleagues and explained. 'We've been combing the media for job advertisements and then sharing our results. We have worked out an ideal application letter and put a CV up on the computer. But none of us is getting any interviews. We don't understand. We are targeting the market. We have identified market need. We have researched and tested our promotional material. Why isn't our marketing working as it should?'

It was a difficult task to explain what was happening because the social workers just did not understand — and neither could they accept — the concept of open competition.

Extending Your Knowledge

THE LECTURERS' DILEMMA

Manpower, the international recruitment agency, devised a poster campaign to run in colleges where there was a sizeable population of office worker students. They intended that their posters should go in refectories, students' union offices, cloakrooms, etc. They were also budgeted to take space in college and student magazines. They saw their actions as mutually beneficial. They would attract staff; the students would get work; the college would get their students into paid employment.

Unfortunately they ran into two major problems:

- Some staff saw it as unfair to other recruitment agencies. They had to be given the same prominence.
- The more extreme feminists refused to have anything to do with an organization called Manpower.

It was very frustrating for College Marketing Officers!

Extending Your Knowledge

MY OLD DUTCH

Those of you who know this lovely old song from the turn of the century music halls will know that it is about a sad old man singing about his wife and their lifetime together. What is not often appreciated is that the sentimentality of the song is based on the fact that the two are about to be split apart. After 50 years together they have to go into the 'Workhouse' to finish their days. And the workhouses divided the sexes.

'As cold as charity' is an expression that has real meaning to those born in the UK before 1930.

Shopping list

Imagine that you are an appeals director and have a shopping list of needed items that runs from a colour laser printer, through a fast running photocopier, to mobile phones for staff on outside locations and on to notepaper and internal memo pads. There is always need for consumables, of course.

Consider how you might set about securing items without parting with any cash.

(**See:** Debriefing at the end of the unit.)

Service quality

There is as much need to design quality into a service offering as into physical products. The major problems are in defining the needed quality and in monitoring the service to ensure that quality standards are consistently met.

Objectives

In commercial organizations the formal planning process follows business lines, and the mission, corporate objectives and strategies can be set through a managed process of proposal and negotiation. Budgets follow and budgetary control is usually possible.

In NFP organizations, however, the structure of the organization is likely to be far more loosely based and individuals at relatively junior levels in commercial terms are likely to expect and be expected to input their views. Decisions are far more likely to be by consensus, with personal judgement and internal politics playing major roles.

Many NFP organizations are administered by full-time employees but controlled by an elected committee, often with an annual change of chairman. Continuity is attempted by ensuring a high profile for the immediate past chairman but the actuality is that while focus is unlikely to change the policies are likely to vary.

NFP management committees are commonly made up of volunteers who devote part of their time to the organization but who cannot be required to attend, nor be held fully responsible for their actions.

Titles vary widely but there will always be a senior full-time employee – the director general, chief executive – who reports to the management committee. This is a key role since organizational effectiveness depends on this individual being strong, having the trust of the committee and being hard working to sustain that trust. Thus there is considerable need for personal political skills as in addition to the individual's professional skills. This is, of course, necessary in any top manager but in NFP marketing the need for political and persuasive skills tends to be higher than in commercial organizations.

Quality

Always a subjective issue, the quality of a service rests almost entirely within the perception of the customer/consumer. There is no physical product to test, no way to confirm that the product offering is working correctly. With a physical product the old saying 'When all else fails, read the instructions' often opens the way for consumer education. But there are no instructions in most service marketing.

How do you cope with value loaded comments? For example:

- The coffee is too bitter.
- The bed is too hard.
- The room is too cold.
- The delivery came too late.

Scripting offers a key to a quality approach (see Unit 9). When a service is scripted in detail it identifies every issue that needs to be taken into account, that is a potential problem.

Targeting, segmentation and positioning are important tools in providing for the needs of particular segments. Without a clear focus a holiday centre may find itself having to cope with the conflicting needs of parents with young families, teenagers, the middle-aged getting away without their children and the elderly. Not a mix likely to share values on what makes for quality!

A service quality model provides a management focus to be used alongside scripting.

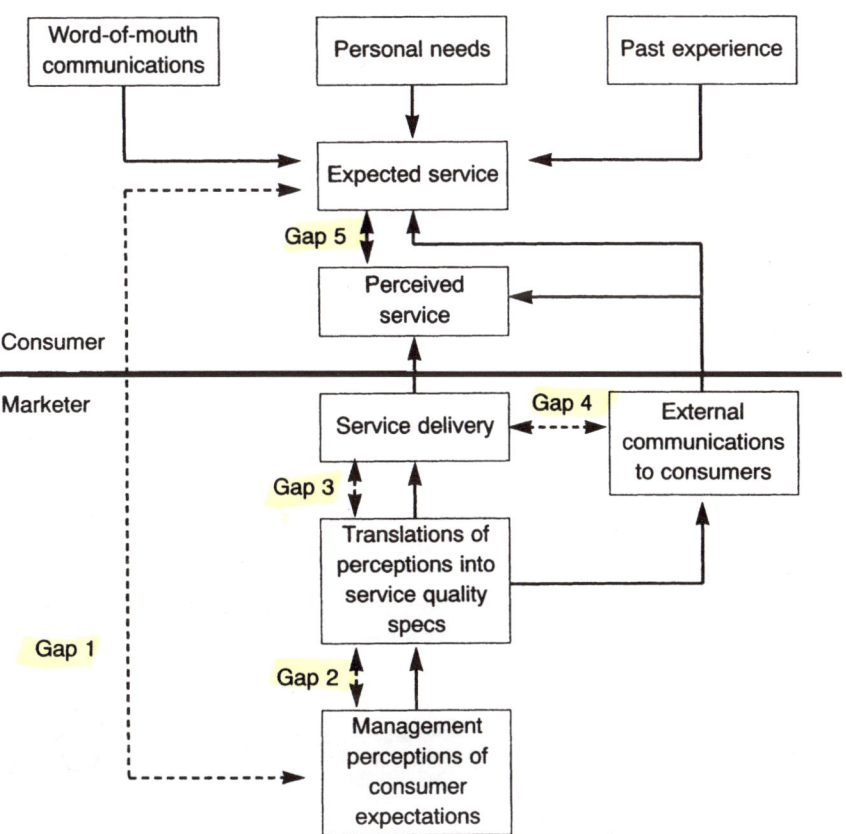

Figure 10.7
Service quality model.
(Source: Parasuraman, Zeithanil and Berry, 1995.)

Management attention is required throughout, but in particular in the gaps shown in the model.

Gap 1   Management must identify and provide the service that is expected. There may be need for consumer education since there may be a lack of knowledge of how to use the service, and/or the consumer expectations may be totally unreasonable.

Gap 2   Producing even the specifications for service quality can be difficult because the wide variation in customer type and need, by a range of variables such as sex, age, time of day, etc. may require too wide a range of options for the organization to resource.
     Demand is often hard to predict so, where the service is especially perishable and takes time to prepare, it is inevitable that there will be times of surplus and times of shortfall.

Gap 3   Front-line staff must deliver the service and, as we saw in Unit 9, it is impossible totally to control the variables that make up human performance.
     Additionally, as we also have noted, the physical environment – including uniforms and personal hygiene – will deteriorate over time and the costs of refurbishment can be substantial.

Front-line management have to be totally committed to service delivery and constantly alert to the need for proactive contact with their teams.

Gap 4   Promotions can be conceived in the cosy comfort of the ad agency and result in an offer that exceeds what the provider wants to communicate. This communication can, most dangerously, be on the unconscious level where what is taken as implied may not at all be what the provider thinks he is communicating.

Gap 5   Perceived service quality is the comparison of expected service with what consumers perceive to have been delivered.

Quality culture

Without exception the top service providers have a quality culture. This was developed in the marketing of services long before it was adopted by production industries and is so well established in many organizations that it is routinized. This is not to say that it doesn't have any attention! Far from it. Simply that it is accepted as a key issue and resources allocated to it in the first cut of the budget allocations.

A quality culture depends on an on-going concern with the fundamentals:

- *Human elements* – job descriptions, etc., that have real meaning. Selection that fits people to jobs; training that equips people to deliver quality; motivation to reward good performance and encourage those who are slipping.
- *Structure and systems* – that are designed to support the front line staff.
- *Management* – that is trained, alert, active, motivational.
- *Measurement* – evaluation of delivery reported to management in time for action as needed.
- *Communications* – that are effective in the perception of the target audiences. Both internal and external communications need to reflect the personal nature of the service delivery. Remember that the communications must work on both conscious and unconscious levels.

Monitoring service delivery

> When you can measure what you are speaking about and express it in numbers, you know something about it; or when you cannot measure it, when you cannot express it in numbers, your knowledge is of a meagre and unsatisfactory kind (Lord Kelvin).

For service marketers a key need is to turn subjective opinions into objective measurements.

Turnover figures, for example, are objective, but the reasons for their achievement will often be subjective. Some factors will be within control, others – such as the weather – outside. Marketers, of course, must work to improve the controllable factors and to minimize/maximize the bad/good effects of those that are uncontrollable.

What to measure?

The actual needs will vary with the provision, but the key issues will be in areas such as:

- Environment within which the service is delivered.
- Consistency of service quality compared to specification.
- Customer satisfaction with the service provision.
- Competence of staff members, to include all areas such as skills, courtesy and efficiency.
- Effects of both internal and external communications.

Objective measures

Typical objective measures will be such as:

- Turnover by time of day/of week, etc.
- Service in demand, by time (for those where a range is offered).
- Number of responses by individual.
- Punctuality.
- Length of time taken to respond/fix/complete, etc.
- Number of call-backs.

These are relatively easy to identify, if less easy to ensure accurate reporting.

A problem is often experienced in defining terms. For example, is a sales call where the salesperson:

- Secures an interview with the buyer?
- Makes contact with a gatekeeper?
- Attempts to make physical contact by visiting the location?
- Attempts contact by telephone?

If it is defined as an interview with a buyer – what form of interview, against which objectives, taking what time? Why is a gatekeeper interview less important given that one has to sell one's self past the gatekeeper? Who determines the type of call – the salesman? How do we know he is reporting accurately? If inaccurate, is it deliberate or accidental or the result of a misunderstanding?

Productivity is a measure of a relationship between an input and an output. Thus productivity measures can be used as monitors of overall performance, and also used (with care) to compare individuals, units, branches, etc. Examples of productivity ratios are:

- Sales/cubic space.
- Sales/number of employees.
- Telephone connect time/number of calls.
- Mileage/clients seen.

Extending Your Knowledge

EXPERIENCE COUNTS
Ring a long-established plumber as spring is approaching and report a minor leak. The odds are he will say 'Oh yes, we get lots of these at this time of the year.' Apparently the pipes, in recovering from the winter frosts, expand and contract differently and tiny leaks appear in joints, typically under the sink. 'It is often denied by the experts', your plumber might say 'but I know it happens. Been at this game too long not to know and be ready.'

Activity 10.4

Productivity
Select a service organization with which you are familiar, perhaps as a regular customer.

Identify the key productivity ratios which would enable you to monitor performance.

(**See:** Debriefing at the end of the unit.)

Subjective measures

The need is to measure not only activities, but also the quality of the activities. There will be a minimum of three perceptions on service quality.

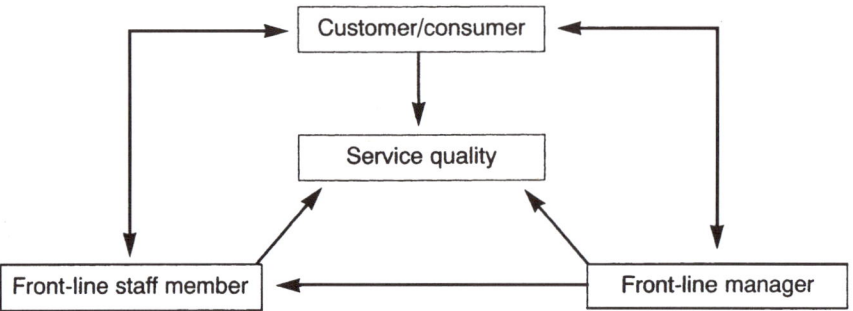

Figure 10.8
Perceptions on service quality

To evaluate subjectively we need to use qualitative research techniques. The results will be non-scalar and therefore can only be used to evaluate trends. For example, a tutor can use the same research instrument on a series of classes, each taking the same course, and put a considerable degree of trust in the trend that develops over time.

If the same instrument is used to evaluate different courses taught by the same tutor, the results are only comparable in the broadest sense. The trend that develops for each course will be separate and it does not follow that actions taken in response to one trend will have the same effect if used in the other class.

Standard qualitative research techniques may be adapted to help evaluate service marketing. In particular, service marketers are concerned to identify areas of strengths and weaknesses so that specific actions can be targeted and the results reviewed. Remember that changing questions in a non-scalar test such as semantic differential affects the response. It is important, therefore, to pilot thoroughly before commitment.

The questionnaire in Figure 10.9 was used for over five years to evaluate student response to a range of short courses. Every course was evaluated and the results tabulated using semantic differential. The major values were:

- Students were actively canvassed for their opinions.
- Particular problems were voiced on the day itself so they could be dealt with promptly
- Individual tutors typically began with a score of 4.6, and over time increased this to over 6. Those who did not reach at least 5.5 in reasonable time were dropped from the programme.
- Open questions allowed students to express their views and it was easy to pick out the key issues.
- The consistency of the research was a powerful tool in the internal negotiations for improved accommodation and support equipment.

Constraints on marketing research

The constraints in service and NFP research are the same as throughout marketing. They can be remembered as CATS: Cost, Accuracy, Time and Security.

- *Cost* Research has to be cost-effective. Management is concerned to evaluate risk and the cost of research must never exceed (or come close to) the potential benefit it can bring.

  Thus it is important to ask enough – but never too much. The cost of adding a single questions to a major piece of research such as the Census of Population is measured in seven figures! A similar sum, in proportion, is added to all research when unnecessary questions are added. The argument 'While we are there we may as well also . . .' is non-valid. The better approach is 'Prove to me why we have to do it at all'.
- *Accuracy* Inaccurate research cannot be relied upon, so what is the point? Bias must be removed through careful piloting; interviewers must be well trained and disciplined; results must be audited in the field, data input and manipulation must be precise, and correct.

SHORT COURSE EVALUATION

Course: Date:

Please help us to improve our Courses by giving your opinion of the Course you have just completed. Your answers will be treated in the strictest confidence and you need not give your name.

For each question please place a ring around the number that most indicates your opinion ...... i.e.

DO YOU KNOW YOUR NAME? Yes   7 6 5 4 3 2 1   No

THE COURSE AS A WHOLE:

Overall Impression	Excellent	7	6	5	4	3	2	1	Poor
Content — Theory	Very advanced	7	6	5	4	3	2	1	Elementary
— Theory	Too much	7	6	5	4	3	2	1	Too little
— Practical	Very advanced	7	6	5	4	3	2	1	Elementary
— Practical	Too much	7	6	5	4	3	2	1	Too little
Overall length	Too long	7	6	5	4	3	2	1	Too short

RELEVANCE:

To present job?	Very relevant	7	6	5	4	3	2	1	Not at all relevant
To future job/career	Very relevant	7	6	5	4	3	2	1	Not at all relevant

YOUR TUTORS:

Mr. _____

Easy to learn from?	Very easy	7	6	5	4	3	2	1	Very hard
Command of subject?	Excellent	7	6	5	4	3	2	1	Poor
Overall impression?	Excellent	7	6	5	4	3	2	1	Poor

Mr. _____

Easy to learn from?	Very easy	7	6	5	4	3	2	1	Very hard
Command of subject?	Excellent	7	6	5	4	3	2	1	Poor
Overall impression	Excellent	7	6	5	4	3	2	1	Poor

PLANNING AND ORGANIZATION:

Course planning	Excellent	7	6	5	4	3	2	1	Poor
Course organization	Excellent	7	6	5	4	3	2	1	Poor
Visual aids	Excellent	7	6	5	4	3	2	1	Poor
Handouts	Excellent	7	6	5	4	3	2	1	Poor
Room	Excellent	7	6	5	4	3	2	1	Poor
Meals	Excellent	7	6	5	4	3	2	1	Poor

Did learning take place?   Yes   No
Would you return for another different or more advanced course?   Yes   No
Would you recommend this Course to your Company?   Yes   No
Would you recommend this College to your Company?   Yes   No

SPECIFIC COMMENTS AND SUGGESTIONS WOULD BE WELCOME

Should any topics be omitted from this Course? _____

Should any topics be included in this Course?_____

Should the time devoted to topics be re-allocated? _____

Do you have any further comments? _____

Thank you for completing this evaluation

Figure 10.9

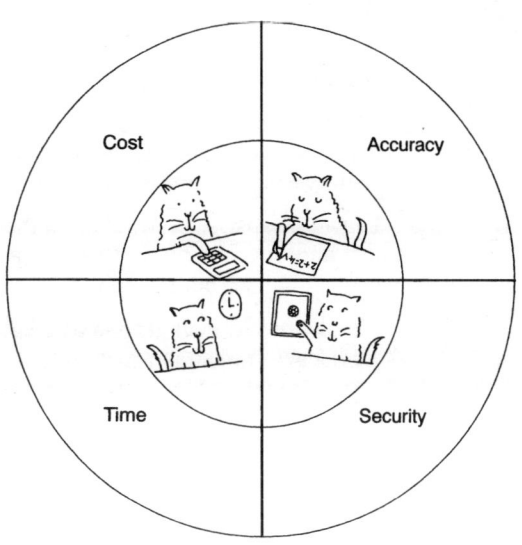

Figure 10.10
Research constraints

- *Time* Results are needed in time to assist in decision making. Excellent research – late – is useless! At the same time research needs to be as current as possible. The lead time that a manager can give is crucial to the quality of the research findings.
- *Security* Confidentiality is always a factor in research. Respondents should be given the opportunity to withhold their names and addresses in all but isolated circumstances.

  Security refers to the need for secrecy: in new product development the need to prevent competitors becoming aware will restrict the researcher in the methodologies he can use.

A guiding principle for all research is: Never do more than you need to.

Exam Hints

Think carefully about exactly what you are required to do before answering any question. What role are you given? If none is prescribed do you write as yourself? Or establish a suitable role and communicate this to the examiner?

Remember that the same knowledge must be packaged (presented) differently in the light of the needs of the target audience. A managing director is motivated differently from a marketing director. A sales manager has needs that differ from those of a marketing research manager. Equally, the form of your answer must be suitable.

An answer covering the same facts would be different in content and in style if presented as a:

- Report to a senior manager.
- Brief to an ad agency.
- Operational plan for action by your team.
- Presentation for the next sales meeting.

Always answer in the context of each question. Take care when reading it to establish:

- Who you are and what is your role?
- What are your objectives?
- Who is your audience and what are their needs?
- What format/approach has been specified?

These questions should be the starting point, the way into every exam question.

Unit Activity

This is your final chance before the mock examination to get your exam technique squared away. Answer, review and repeat this question exactly as you did the one in Unit 9.

Allow yourself an exact 36 minutes and complete your answer in that time. This must include time for reading and understanding the question, planning your answer, writing your answer and checking through.

Leave the answer overnight and then review it harshly. Pick up every good point, and any bad ones. Then set a date in a few days' time to take the question again, from scratch.

Finally, review your second attempt and compare it to your first effort. It should show marked improvement.

Question
You have recently taken up a new position with a well-known national charity. Your job is to oversee and organize marketing activities for the charity. Your previous work experience has been entirely in the commercial sector so not-for-profit marketing is new to you.

Your new boss, the charity's director, has asked you to make some notes on the similarities and differences you expect to find between your new and old positions. Prepare a document which does this and explains how these contrasts will affect the marketing activities which you carry out.

(**See:** Debriefing at the end of the unit.)

Summary

In this unit we have seen that:

- Service and NFP marketing rely upon the same extended marketing mix and both are concerned with marketing intangibilities.
- Non-business marketing divides into NFP and social areas, with the societal marketing concept extending out from non-business marketing to cover all organizations.
- Environmentalism is to do with ecology and the maximization of life quality. Consumerism is focused on consumer rights.
- Marketing has been seen as exploitive by many in the NFP and social sectors but this view is changing as the benefits of the marketing concept are being appreciated.
- The positive spiral of cause and effect is far easier to break than the negative spiral into which it can quickly turn.
- Low budget marketing requires initiative and creativity.
- Charities have long ceased to operate through the 'lady bountiful' approach. Instead they are becoming very businesslike, albeit without commercial structures and management.
- There is need for charities to manage three target markets: fund raising, beneficiaries and internal.
- Service quality is very dependent upon subjective views of the consumer, front-line staff and front-line management. The consumer's view is paramount.
- Objective and subjective measures must be used to evaluate and manage quality. The normal tools of marketing research can easily be adapted to meet the need.
- A quality culture is intrinsic to the better service providers. It is not taken for granted but worked at consciously to maintain the sharpness.
- Research must be commissioned and judged within the CATS areas of Cost, Accuracy, Time and Security.

Debriefing

Activity 10.1

Typical examples follow but remember that you need examples of your own, preferably from your home market, rather than using those quoted in workbooks and texts.

Excellent:

1 Shell ran a famous series of adverts showing, for example, a beautiful country valley. The copy read 'Would you let an oil company put a pipeline through here?' The ad went on to say that the picture was taken *after* the pipeline had been run through. The picture showed the valley as Shell left it.
2 All the motor car manufacturers offered free conversion of existing vehicles (that had suitable engines) to use unleaded petrol.
3 Local councils actively encourage traders to sponsor litter bins so that their town is well provided for. The better ones add extra litter collections and supplement their team of road sweepers and maintenance staff.

Awful:

1 The British government is deciding whether the Solent should be classified as open sea. If it is, the water authority will be required to upgrade their sewage treatment plant. It seems open sea beyond a doubt to anyone who has been to the Solent (the channel between the Isle of Wight and the mainland). Even a glance at a chart shows that it opens directly into the English Channel at both ends. In any case, should not sewage treatment be of the highest quality wherever it outflows?

2 A major builder tried to buy a tennis club in an affluent suburb in the 'stockbroker belt' just south of London. They wanted the land for building and attempted to secure planning permission for the 'sports facility' to move into Green Belt (protected) land. Their plans were rejected by the Local Authority and the members of the tennis club.

3 Cod stocks in the North Sea are reduced to levels where, unless fishing stops for a decade, the fisheries are likely to be destroyed. There is much concern that action should be taken, but the individual fishermen are motivated by the short-term demands of an ignorant and/or uncaring marketplace and the nations who have to introduce and enforce a ban are unco-ordinated in their reactions to the crisis. It is likely that by the time an effective ban is imposed it will be too late.

Note: Each year 45 tons of old engine oil are poured down the open drains by DIY motorists. Each probably thinks his 7 or 8 pints is insignificant and is not motivated to take the oil to the nearby disposal point. Is this a failure in social marketing by the government, a failure to educate people about environmental damage or a break-down in social responsibility within the community? Perhaps a combination of all three?

Activity 10.2

This is a classic situation where many candidates will call for TV advertising despite the clear warnings that Harold King's budget is inadequate for mass media usage. (A national TV campaign must cost over £5 000 000 without the press campaign that would need to run alongside!)

It is tempting to make an assumption that obtains additional funding from a charity, or government but the set task is the management of a limited budget. An assumption that secured a large budget would negate the examiner's purpose and result in a loss of marks.

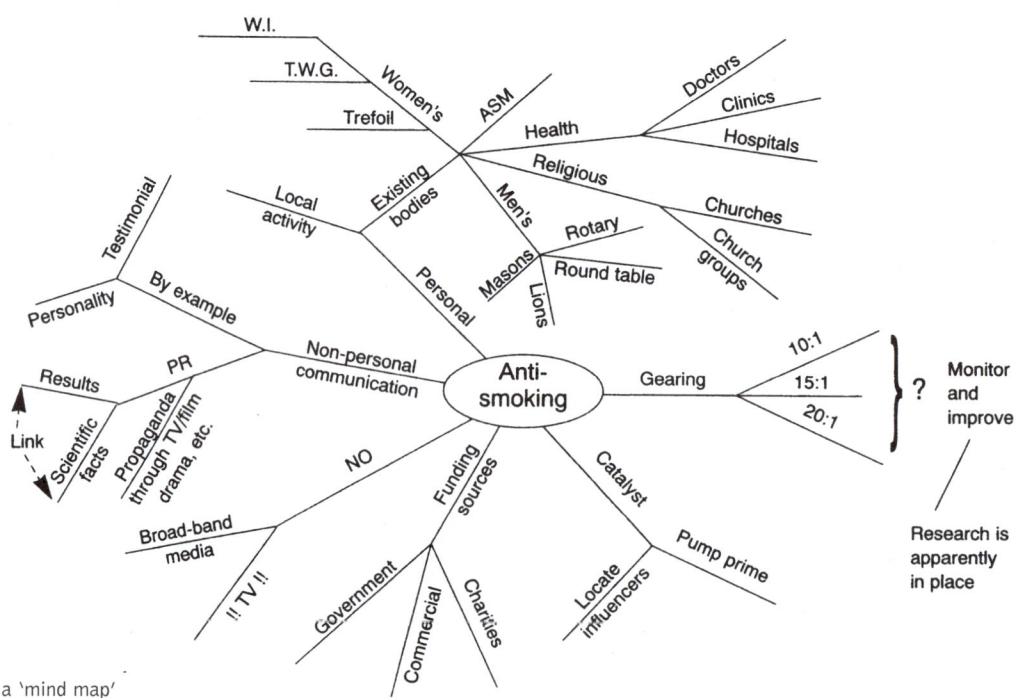

Figure 10.11
Brainstorm shown as a 'mind map'

No role is provided for us and so we have the flexibility to establish ourselves where and how it will be of most benefit to our answer. Providing we are reasonable there is no role that we cannot adopt.

It should be obvious that if a head-to-head communications battle is contra-indicated we have to find a way to gear up the budget. We have to get far more than £185 000 worth of communications but we have only the £185 000 to do it with.

The mind map clearly shows that we have to gear up the budget. But by how much? We need to set an objective – 10:1? – and then monitor it as a base for improvement in subsequent periods.

We are in a market where there is already considerable pressure working for us and where many people and organizations already devote time and effort to our cause. We can therefore suggest some catalyst-type activities and have some funds with which to 'prime the pump'.

PR is obviously called for. This can extend from encouraging TV and film directors to portray smoking as evil or bad for you, to featuring role models who have given up (perhaps in preference to those who have never smoked).

Suggested solution:

Let us be employed by ASH – Action on Smoking and Health – the charity that exists to discourage smoking. We have to tell the examiner of our assumed role and so would answer as follows:

Note to the Examiner
This mini case is answered upon the assumption that I am Marketing Officer to Action on Smoking and Health (ASH). In this capacity I would know and work with Harold King and be both willing and authorized to donate my services.

Proposal

1 Summary
It is impossible to match the spend of even one of the tobacco giants, and it is questionable if this tactic would, in fact, work effectively.

There is no quick solution to the problem. Basic awareness has been achieved but it is necessary to take a long-term view and establish a consistency of approach that maintains the public's awareness of the damage done by smoking whilst at the same time targeting on those most at long-term risk, the down-market youngsters.

We must:

- Gear up the effects of the budget by a factor of 10:1.
- Monitor results to evaluate success and aid in future planning.
- Use the marketing communication tools which can be afforded: public relations, lobbying, and a support role for ASH and other Charities who share the same concern.

The overall objective should be to bring together, focus and support all those groups and individuals who share a concern about smoking and to generate considerable activity at grass roots level.

2 Objectives
Within the 12 months from April, 20xx to:

2.1 Maintain awareness of the health danger at above 90 per cent of the population older than 12 years.
2.2 Generate a desire not to smoke in:
60 per cent of young people aged 12–16, and in 80 per cent of those aged 8–11.
2.3 Generate non-smoking as an acceptable form of behaviour in young adults below 21 years of age.

2.4 Form an influential grouping that will work in concerted fashion at grass-roots level.
2.5 Form a parliamentary lobby to achieve a legal requirement for all schools to actively campaign against smoking.

3 Targets

The most cost-effective budget use is to encourage and support others who have access to funds and are working to achieve the same ends. Therefore targeting is indirect, in the main. The main targets are:

3.1 Journalists, across appropriate media.
3.2 Identified individuals with influence within concerned charitable bodies, for example Marie Curie Foundation (cancer).
3.3 Popular sports and music personalities from the background of our prime targets.
3.4 Life assurance companies – discounts to proven non-smokers.
3.5 Owners of venues – to extend the non-smoking areas.
3.6 Local schools, the National Union of Students, the Scouts and other similar organizations.

4 Copy platform

Stress the positive side of life:

- Active, fun people need energy and stamina.
- The more stamina, the more fun. Build stamina, build fun.

5 Creative platform

Healthy fit youngsters enjoying themselves. Wit, humour and topicality are essential. Instant identification at grass-roots level is essential, for such things as pop concerts for non-smokers.

6 PR and advertising

Major on PR. Minimal use of press advertising.

7 Conference

One major conference during the year. All associated bodies to share experiences and agree a common policy. Maximize the PR benefit.

8 Staff

Appoint one Field Officer whose task will be liaison, motivation and to act as a two-way channel of communication. Anticipated age: 25.

9 Timing

January:	Agreement of proposals and production of agreed plan.
February:	Agency brief, start recruitment of Field Officer. Designate senior staff for spokesperson role.
March:	Creative proposal agreed, production process initiated. Train spokespersons in handling the media.
April:	Field officer takes post. Press conference to launch new creative plans.
May:	Mail shot to all identified bodies/charities, etc., likely to join a concerted initiative. Field staff active in making contacts.
June/July:	Continuing grass-roots activity. Securing of TV documentary/Anneka Rice Challenge, etc. (for the autumn). Securing invitations to comment on current affairs programmes and chat shows.
September:	Press campaign, supported with PR, in targeted media.
October:	Conference (see 7, above).
December:	Pre-Christmas burst of concentrated activities co-ordinated by the Field Officer and Head Office.
January/March:	Plan activity for next year. Continue intensive work at grass-roots level.

10 Budget

One Field Officer: salary, insurance, car, expenses	30 000
Ad agency fee and production costs of basic materials	40 000
Staff training	10 000
PR budget	25 000
Press advertising: highly targeted	50 000
Field Officer's grass-roots budget	20 000
Contingency	10 000
	£185 000

11 Evaluation

Evaluation of achievement against objectives, established in 2 on the previous page, should be added to the existing research operation.

There should be little difficulty in obtaining the data needed to inform the decisions for future action but it is recommended that the information be presented in a more detailed and segmented fashion.

Signed: XXXX XXXX

Note: This is a rather more detailed plan than the outline called for in the answer. It is provided to illustrate the depth of thinking necessary. All that the examiner would actually want is the summary and objectives, plus the other headings supported by brief explanations.

Activity 10.3

Your creativity and initiative come into full play when operating in a low budget organization. The major benefit that charity (and some social) marketers have is the latent goodwill that exists within individuals and the organizations they work for.

Jane Tewson, director of Charity Projects which runs Comic Relief, was interviewed by the *Daily Telegraph* just as she returned from a trip to Tanzania. British Airways had provided the tickets, Hilton the hotel room, Boots developed her films free.

The key is never to refuse any offer, however small, and always to be grateful. It is a useful technique to ask those you approach if they have thoughts on where you might turn for help. Far better to make an approach on the recommendation of a friend!

An outline of possibilities is shown in the mind map. They will vary, of course, by organization and need.

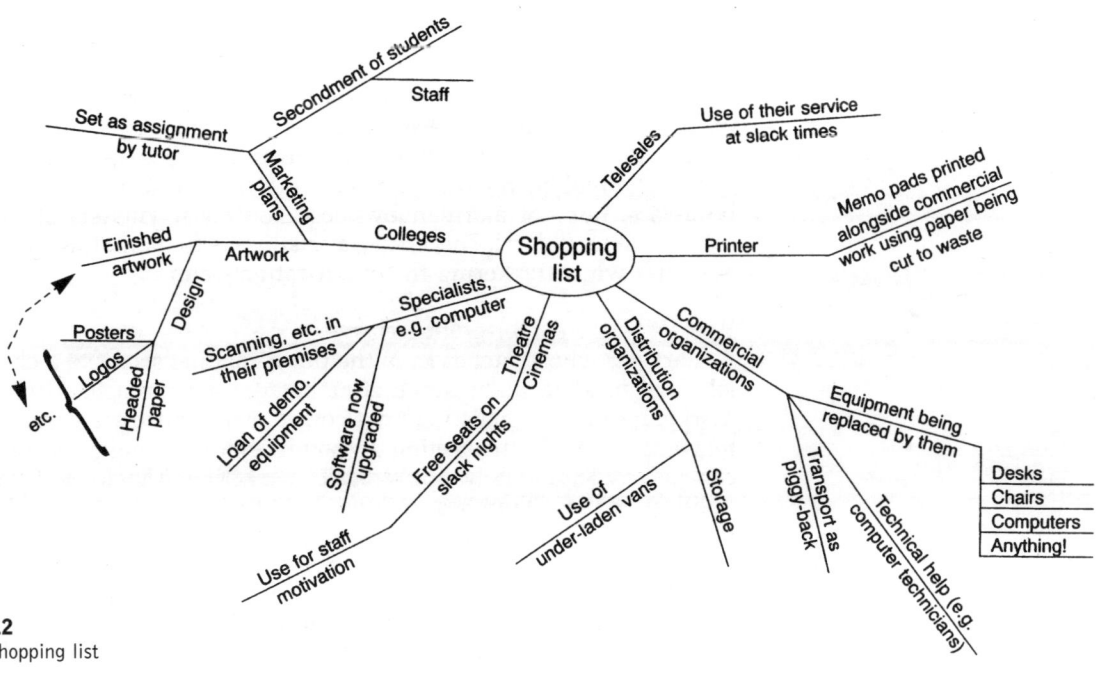

Figure 10.12
Mind map shopping list

Activity 10.4

If we take a college as a typical service with which most students are familiar we need to think about such productivity ratios as those shown below. Remember that we must be concerned both with effectiveness and efficiency.

Typical ratios are:

- Students on register before exam/students enrolled.
- Students taking exam/students enrolled.
- Students qualifying/students enrolled.
- Students passing exam/students taking exam.
- Cost of promotion/student enquiries.
- Cost of promotion/students enrolling.
- Employers making first enrolments/employers enrolling students.
- Employers making subsequent enrolments/employers enrolling students.
- Room-hours used/room-hours available.
- Car park demand, by time period/car park capacity.
- Satisfied students/enrolled students.
- Satisfied students/number responding.
- Number responding/enrolled students.

Note: Satisfaction needs to be defined very carefully, as an overall measure that is made up of subsidiary points, each of which can be separately evaluated.

Unit activity

Check your work against these answer guidelines.

Approach

Answers to this question need to show that marketing can be equally applicable in a range of different applications. Just because marketing activities are usually linked with profit-making businesses does not mean that the principles are not relevant elsewhere. While there are certain contrasts in terms of marketing objectives, target publics, marketing mix elements and monitoring and control, non-business organizations are just as legitimate users of marketing as companies seeking profits. After all, marketing aims to provide a body of knowledge and concepts to help further different types of organizational goals.

Introduction

For not-for-profit organizations such as charities, marketing activities can be just as important in ensuring that objectives are satisfied as those consumer and industrial concerns which are profit seeking.

Although certain differences exist in organizational objectives, marketing programmes and control activities between profit and not-for-profit sectors, many of the underlying marketing principles remain the same. For a marketer making the transition between the two sectors, it is necessary to be aware, but not alarmed by these contrasts. This should enable the individual to make the necessary adjustments to marketing objectives and activities while furthering the organization's aims.

Working in the not-for-profit sector

A marketer who switches from the profit-making sector to a charity based job, will need to make some adjustments in approach. Although many marketing professionals may not consider non-business exchange to be a relevant forum for marketing activities, evidence suggests that this area can just as legitimately apply basic marketing principles. Charities like political parties, churches, unions and student bodies may all find that these concepts can help in the achievement of objectives. Indeed, some would argue that non-profit sectors have more flexibility for using marketing principles in a creative way. Other differences lie in the difficulties sometimes experienced in judging performance in non-profit areas and in the sometimes controversial goals of such organizations. For example, some charities must aim to allocate resources for powerful lobbying activities with which not all members of the public may be in agreement.

Similarities and differences

The particular characteristics of marketing for charities can be reviewed by considering the nature of the marketing objectives set, target markets, marketing mixes and control activities.

Objectives: Charities, like other non-business organizations, aim to achieve a particular response, perhaps a donation of finance or services or a change in values, from a target market. The objectives set and the target aimed at will depend on the charity chosen. Some common aims include raising funds, appealing on behalf of disadvantaged groups, informing the public and generating support.

Target markets: The concept of target marketing is slightly different in non-business situations. These are not buyers, but often a range of different audiences. A target public is defined as a group of individuals who have an interest or concern about an organization, a product or a social cause. Those benefiting from the charity's activities are known as the client public, while those taking part in the organization's activities might be referred to as the general publics.

Marketing mixes: Marketing mixes are used to achieve an organization's goals. Charities often deal more with ideas and services than with goods. This means that it may be relevant to consider the additional service marketing mix elements of people, process and physical evidence. In general, the marketing mix for non-business organizations has particular characteristics. As already stated, the non-business product may well be a service or idea. Developing distribution which maintains the flow of non-business products to clients is important, but often occurs through shorter channels and with fewer intermediaries than in profit-making sectors.

Promotion is important with both advertising, for example, Public Service Announcements (PSAs) and publicity used. Many large charities, such as Oxfam, also use direct mail and have membership schemes. However, the high costs of many media means there may be a particularly large people element, with personal selling used to recruit new supporters and request donations. Competitions, entertainment and special events are widely used.

Pricing is probably the most different of the mix elements in not-for-profit sectors. Quite a broad definition is required as financial price may not be a relevant issue here. The concept of opportunity cost, where an individual is persuaded of the value of donating time or funds to a cause may be relevant. For example, individuals donating time to counselling activities presumably regard this as a suitable way to invest their time. Strategies for the charity may involve seeking funds and donations to cover costs and stress the importance of public and client welfare over costs.

Controlling marketing activities:

For charities, control activities aim to ensure goals are achieved, spot any problem areas and revise marketing strategies accordingly. Many charities are increasingly monitoring their own effectiveness and performance by measuring the proportion of income which is spent directly for charitable purposes. Such monitoring is complicated by the difficulty in judging whether objectives have really been met. Techniques used to control marketing activities must be compatible with the charities' aims. For example, the control of budgets is not linked to profit and loss considerations as it would be in profit-making organizations.

Useful tips

The style of answers will depend on and should reflect the choice of charity example. For instance, the objectives and target publics described should be consistent with the particular choice made.

Unit 11 Industrial/ business-to-business marketing

Objectives

In this unit you will:

- ❑ Identify the principles of organizational buying behaviour in a range of markets.
- ❑ Examine the necessary variations to the basic marketing concepts that apply in business-to-business marketing.
- ❑ Appreciate the importance of personal selling in business-to-business marketing.

By the end of this unit you will be able to:

- ❑ Identify the purchase decision process and the decision making unit.
- ❑ Recognize the importance of covert behaviour.
- ❑ Plan effective business-to-business marketing.

Study Guide

Many managers fall into the trap of supposing that they are marketing to organizations whereas the salespeople have long known that they are selling to individuals. The need to market to individuals within organizations is crucial to success. Consider for a moment how a body with legal identity but no physical presence can possibly take decisions; obviously it cannot.

Decisions are taken by the individuals who are responsible for any organization at any moment in time. Thus organizational policy will change to reflect the value judgements of the individuals holding the top posts.

It is for marketing to determine the DMU and DMP which, in business-to-business marketing is a far more complex and individualized process than for consumer marketing.

You should allow four hours to complete this unit and its Activities. The Unit Activity is a full scenario which you should aim to complete in 90 minutes. Arrange to set yourself up in exam conditions and complete your answer against the clock.

Study Tips

When the examination becomes a tangible presence, looming upon your perceptual horizon, you need to be prepared to shift from student into candidate mode.

Hopefully you have kept your notes in memorable fashion, and have kept up a 'drip feed' of revision to keep what you have covered fresh in your mind.

If so, you are in good shape. If not, there is still time to go back through your notes and ensure that they are set out so that they help you to remember.

In the final run-in to the exam you should be able to check through Key Notes, or Key Headings, without having to struggle to find the central issues from pages of notes that all look the same.

Industrial or business-to-business?

The terms industrial and business-to-business marketing today are synonymous. In the past they were separate, with industrial referring to the marketing *of* industry and business-to-business referring to marketing *between* industrial and 'business' concerns.

It is obviously incorrect to use 'marketing' to refer to an internally focused concept and, in any case, the marketing *of* industry was targeted both upon other industrial and business concerns *and* the domestic and private customers and consumers.

Thus the term business-to-business marketing more accurately describes the process of marketing by 'business' to 'business' as distinct from the marketing of 'business' to 'non-business'.

Note: Business-to-business marketing has been extended to describe the marketing of organizations to organizations. Strictly speaking all that is needed is 'marketing-to-business' or – better – 'marketing-to-organizations', but the terminology in common use is business-to-business and we shall follow convention in this workbook.

Remember, however, that business-to-business in practical terms actually means: 'Marketing (of anything by organizations) to organizations (of any type).'

Industrial products

The classification of industrial products has, of itself, no intrinsic bearing on the business-to-business marketing process. Obviously industrial products have their own characteristics, and user benefits can and must be determined, but a marketer is concerned with customer and consumer need. In principle, therefore, a marketer can work in any industry. The fact that some are more suited to one industry and/or sector than another is a personality characteristic that does not detract from the argument that marketing is able to operate on the same basic principles whatever the market, whatever the product or service.

For the record, industrial products are classified into seven categories:

- Raw materials.
- Accessory equipment.
- Process materials.
- Major equipment.
- Component parts.
- Consumable supplies.
- Industrial services.

Industrial classification

The Standard Industrial Classification (SIC) system has been developed to classify selected economic characteristics of industrial, commercial, financial and service organizations. In the UK this system is administered by the Central Statistical Office.

THE STANDARD INDUSTRIAL CLASSIFICATION	
A000	Agriculture, Forestry and Fishing.
1000	Energy and Water Supply Industries.
2000	Extraction of Minerals and Ores other than Fuels; Manufacture of Metals, Mineral products and Chemicals.
3000	Metal Goods, Engineering and Vehicle Industries.
4000	Other Manufacturing Industries.
5000	Construction – General construction and Demolition Work.
6000	Distribution, Hotels and Catering: repairs.
7000	Transport and Communication.
8000	Banking, Finance, Insurance, Business Services and Leasing.
9000	Other Services.

Figure 11.1

The 10 broad divisions (see Figure 11.1) are divided into classes, then into groups and finally into activity headings. The numbering system follows that of NACE, the classification system of the European Union.

The Census of Distribution runs in parallel with the SIC and categorizes manufacturers in further detail.

Government sources alone provide a considerable amount of detail such as:

- Number of industry shipments.
- Number of employees.
- Compound average rate of growth.
- Number of establishments.
- Exports as a percentage of shipments.
- Major producing areas.

Commercial sources such as Dun and Bradstreet, Kompass and Kelly's Directory provide data on SIC sectors and on individual organizations within them. There is a wealth of lists available which target named individuals by areas of responsibility within given types of organizations.

It is therefore very easy to segment by type of potential customer. Because of the nature of the marketplace it is usually possible to identify each potential purchaser and to target individually. This is in total contrast to the consumer market, of course, and results in a different blend of the marketing mix.

Market auditing

Auditing of the business-to-business market is greatly simplified by the ability to identify by customer and potential customer. McDonald and Leppard, in *The Marketing Audit*, suggest a methodology.

Step 1 In column 1 list all those industries that are consumers of your goods or services. Please note that there is no need to structure this list, just write them down as they occur to you.

Step 2 In column 2 write the actual turnover figure.

Step 3 In column 3 write down the percentage value of turnover that results from each of the industries.

Step 4 In column 4 indicate whether or not this, when considered from the point of view of profitability, is high or low, by scoring 10 for high, 5 for good, and 1 for low. (Here 'profitability' means whatever your company considers it to mean.)

Step 5 Using column 5, consider what capacity and skills you have at your disposal to continue supplying each industry. A score of 10 would show you have considerable capacity, with minimal interference to other products or services: 1 would indicate severe limitations.

Step 6 Using a similar scoring procedure, complete column 6. Ask yourself how confident is your company that it can supply each industry with the right quality and design of goods/services, delivered on time. Are you more confident about some than others?

Step 7 Now consider the market potential (demand) for your output in each of the listed industries. Using column 7, score 10 for high potential and 1 for low.

Step 8 Add the scores you have allocated in columns 4, 5, 6, 7, and enter them in column 8.

Step 9 Using the information you have put together, identify your key market segments. They ought to be those industries which collected the highest aggregate scores, but for your type of business you might identify other factors that would influence your choice of market. Make a note of these in column 9. In addition, use column 9 to record any particular opportunities or threats presented in each market.

Step 10 Balancing the notes you made in column 9 against the arithmetic calculations (column 8), study the information you have assembled, and select what you regard as the best industrial market. Enter 1 against this in column 10. Continue ranking each industry, using 2 for the next best, 3 for the third, etc., until column 10 is filled.

We shall cover segmentation later in the unit. It is first necessary to determine what distinguishes the business-to-business market area, and then examine organizational buying behaviour.

1	2	3	4	5	6	7	8	9	10
Industry	Actual T/O	% T/O	Profitability LI 10H	Capacity LI 10H	Confidence LI 10H	Potential LI 10H	Total (Cols 4, 5, 6, 7)	Additional factors, opportunities/threats	Rank

Extending Your Knowledge

Consider why we need to look at buying behaviour before moving on to segmentation.

(**See:** 'Buying behaviour' later on this page.)

Business

Business, as we have seen, must be taken to include organizations of all types – even down to sole traders who find a place in the channels of distribution within some business sectors.

Thus profit and non-profit organizations are included, as are private and public sector concerns.

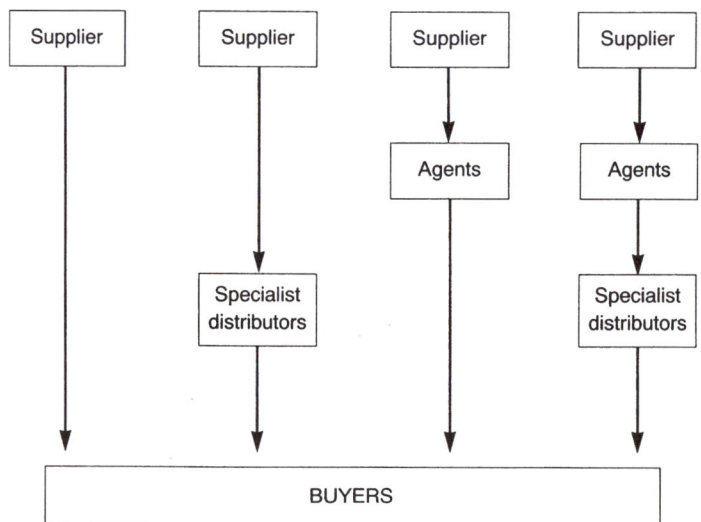

Figure 11.2
Channels of distribution in business-to-business marketing

Buying behaviour

We need to understand buying behaviour because segments should be based on human factors as well as upon physical data. Just because a large organization exists it does not follow that the individuals within it can or will trade with you or your organization.

The common elements which differentiate business-to-business marketing are:

- Potential customers can be individually identified.
- Decision processes will be institutionalized.
- The buying (procurement) process is likely to be handled professionally.
- Volumes and/or values are likely to be high and/or the repeat purchase pattern is likely to be extensive.

Activity 11.1

The approach
Use the 7 P/Cs framework and note the major features that you will probably need to take into account when marketing to the business-to-business market.

(**See:** Debriefing at the end of the unit.)

Organizational buying behaviour

Virtually no organizational purchase is the sole responsibility of a single individual. Certainly every significant buying decision is subject to a DMU which is more complex than the typical consumer market DMU.

In marketing to organizations we should think in terms of buying centres rather than of individual buyers and remember that buying centres are aggregates of individuals. We know that individuals are driven by personal motivations and even in a professional environment these personal factors will affect each individual within their organizational role.

Individuals within what we conceive of as a buying centre may not be consciously aware that such a relationship exists. In many organizations the 'decision web' is complex and far reaching. When marketing to an organization it is important to identify the DMP, and the buying centre concept provides a useful framework into which to slot individuals.

The elements making up a buying centre have been identified by Hill and Hillyer as:

- *Control unit* – the source of finance, as well as of controls on the purchase decision and, possibly, the performance of the purchase in use.
- *User unit* – the individuals who actually consume the product or service. In many cases these will be junior employees with very little influence on the purchase decision.
- *Information unit* – the individuals who provide information on external matters such as whether the economic climate is favourable to further investment and internal factors such as decisions on the length of working life expected from a piece of capital equipment.
- *Buyer unit* – organizational buyers are usually professionally trained. They are as experienced and skilled as the salespeople they meet, and work to SMART objectives. Their task is to secure the best deal. Often they work to specifications prepared elsewhere in the organization. Concentrating only on the buyers may therefore be ineffective. It is necessary to penetrate to the other units within the buying centre if at all possible.

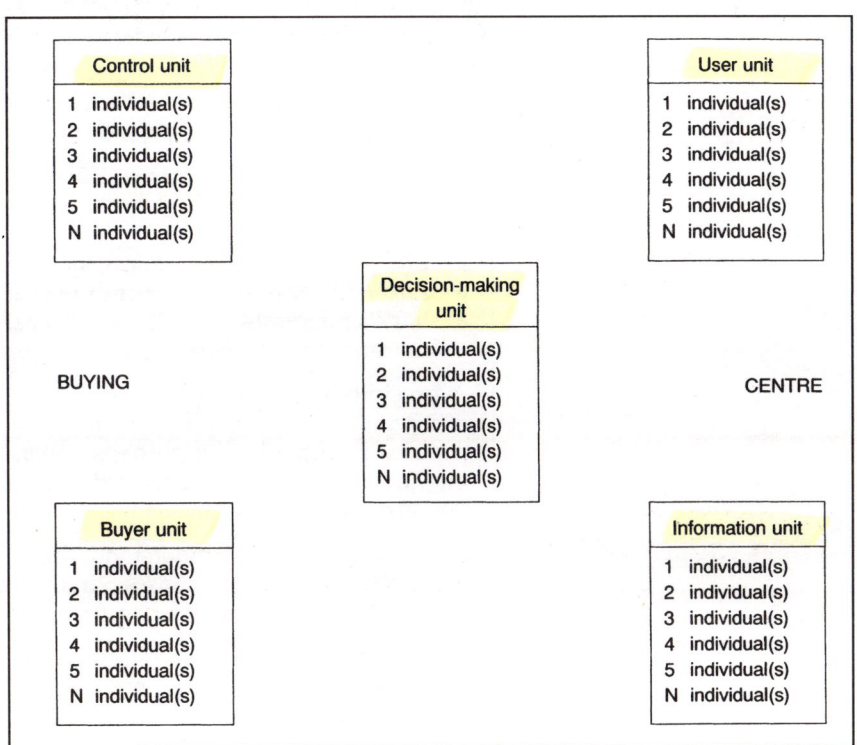

Figure 11.3
Buying Centre. (Source:
Organizational Buying Behaviour,
Hill and Hillyer.)

253

- *Decision Making Unit* – the buying centre we may regard as an extended DMU. At its heart is the actual DMU. Organizations often have a team who make the final decisions but remember that within the team there will always be one who will tend to lead (or dominate) for each particular decision. This leadership may vary with the type of purchase under discussion.

The decision making unit

The DMU roles are similar in industrial and consumer marketing – but the industrial process is usually more complex. The acronym BADGIES gives you the seven roles:

- Buyers
- Approvers
- Deciders
- Gatekeepers
- Influencers
- End-Users
- Starter

Buyers
Those with formal authority to seek out suppliers and arrange the terms of purchase.

Approvers
Those who authorize decisions. Obviously if a decision is subject to higher approval there is doubt as to where the definitive authority lies. It may be necessary to secure a decision to recommend before there is any chance of getting a decision to purchase. It can be extremely frustrating to have one's arguments put by another without your depth of knowledge or commitment.

This hierarchy of decision levels is typical of organizational buying, however, and partly explains why personal contact and so much time are required.

Deciders
The people who actually take the purchase decision. We know that in every group there will always be those who carry more clout, whose views the others respect. There are four levels of decision within a typical purchase.

Organizational decisions

The four levels of decision are:

- *Precipitating decisions*   Form the basis for product decisions.
- *Product decisions*   Form the basis for supplier decisions.
- *Supplier decisions*   Form the basis for commitment decisions.
- *Commitment decisions*   Allow the contract to be signed.

A precipitating decision enables the purchase to go ahead. Decisions can be taken in principle, but then deferred because they have a low priority. Eventually, but perhaps never, the priority switches and the intention to purchase is activated. Only then can product and supplier decisions be taken and a final commitment made.

It is important to understand this process in relation to specific organizations and purchases so that incentives can be found to transform an intention into a purchase.

Note: Incentives do not automatically equate with discounts, etc. They should lock on to the motivations of the individuals concerned in the process.

Gatekeepers

Persons with the power to prevent sellers or information from reaching members of the buying centre. Receptionists, telephonists and secretaries can make formidable gatekeepers. Many salespeople batter their heads against a wall of people dedicated to protecting their managers without ever penetrating to the corridors of power. It is essential to devise a way to secure an interview with a person of significance, which explains why sales research is such an important factor in organizational marketing.

Influencers

Can be categorized as:

- *Primary* Members of the control unit with executive authority.
- *Secondary* Members of the information unit.
- *Tertiary* External to the organization.

End-Users

May initiate the buying process. Where re-buying is routine, a low stock position will be identified automatically and a purchase triggered. In many cases the necessary order will be automatically raised.

Starter

Just as in the consumer market, something has to start the process. It may be a simple matter of a re-buy, a new product may be at concept stage, a promotional campaign may trigger interest. Many people and factors are likely to influence a buying decision (see Figure 11.4).

TWO MAJOR AREAS OF INFLUENCE

Economic	*Emotional*
(Task)	(Non-task)
Source searching	Ego enhancement
Supplier appraisal and evaluation	Office politics
Purchase research	Personal-risk reduction
Value engineering and analysis	Tactics of lateral relationships
Product-cost analysis	Previous experience
Purchase-price analysis	Other emotional activities
Other objective techniques	

Figure 11.4
Major areas of influence

Extending Your Knowledge

The direct approach often fails to get one past a gatekeeper. Typical is the receptionist who picks up the phone and says: 'It's the rep from XYZ Company. You don't want to see him, do you?' Try as one might it is almost impossible to get this rephrased to: 'It's the rep from XYZ Company. Have you time to see him?'

Professional buyers will often allow a salesperson one visit, both as a courtesy and because it is their job to know what is available in the marketplace. Make a success of that visit and you are at least on the way to regular calls. But the buyer is himself a gatekeeper. There is need to research and penetrate further but without causing annoyance that will get you barred!

In organizational marketing the importance of exhibitions, conferences, seminars, etc., is partly in demonstrating product, but mostly in securing leads and contacts.

Organizational buying

Organizational buying will be found wherever structured entities exist. Notably in the:

- Industrial
- Reseller
- Not-for-profit markets
- Government agencies

The major differences will be in the:

- Objectives that underpin the purchase need.
- Level of competition between organizations.
- Levels of autonomy and/or degree of control.
- Influences on the buyers.
- The decision making process.

Mechanistic buying

Organizations, where possible, adopt a mechanistic approach to buying decisions. There are two main reasons for this:

- They are routinely buying.
- They have to make far more buying decisions than any individual.

Many people routinely buy – the motorist who uses the same brand of petrol, the housewife in the supermarket – but whereas an individual can switch brand very easily it is not as simple to move from one organizational supplier to another.

Purchase decision process

The Buygrid, originally established by Robinson, Faris and Wind in 1967, shows a typical eight-stage Purchase Decision Process. It also shows that the buyer's task varies with the 'buy class'. It will be clear that the repurchasing-buying process can be routinized in many cases. Certainly it should not occupy a senior buyer's attention other than in a general supervisory way.

Note: The Buygrid shows the eight stages of the PDP. As can be seen, the number of stages required varies with the type of decision. A straight re-buy requires the minimum of management attention.

		Buy classes	
	New task	Modified re-buy	Straight re-buy
1 Problem recognition	Yes	Maybe	No
2 General need description	Yes	Maybe	No
3 Product specification	Yes	Yes	Yes
4 Suppliers' search	Yes	Maybe	No
5 Proposal solicitation	Yes	Maybe	No
6 Supplier selection	Yes	Maybe	No
7 Order-routine specification	Yes	Maybe	No
8 Performance review	Yes	Yes	Yes

Figure 11.5
Buygrid. (Source: Robinson, Faris and Wind, 1967.)

deBono has said that the 'object of thinking is to remove the need to think', in other words that we try to routinize our lives and remove the need for decisions as far as possible. A professional buyer follows exactly this principle. He wants to remove the need to go through all the stages of the DMP for every purchase decision. The more routine and trouble free he can make the process the better. Understanding this need, and providing for it, are essential if the business-to-business marketer is to succeed.

Figure 11.6 shows the decision making process. It is not possible, or desirable, for managers to go through every stage for re-buys. They want, and should be helped, to accelerate the process.

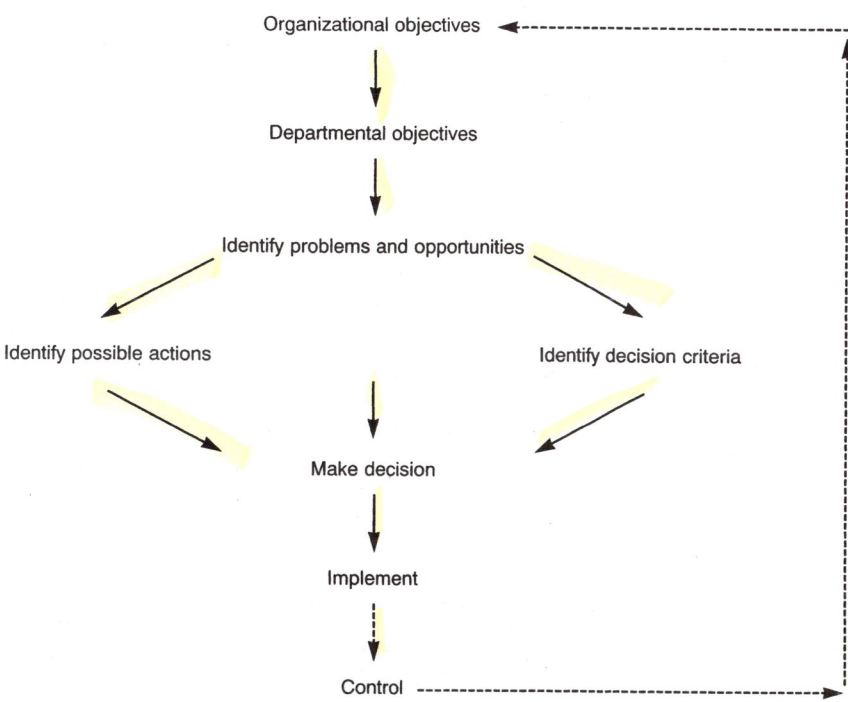

Figure 11.6
DMP

Organizational environment

Everybody concerned with organizational marketing operates within an environment which empowers them even as it restricts their freedom of action. Organizational environment, structure, climate and group structure are key influencers that effect both overt and covert behaviour. The effective salesperson endeavours, through sales research, to secure as much information as possible about the buyer's environment and, in particular, his or her constraints and freedoms. (See Figure 11.7.)

Activity 11.2	*Objectives* Itemize the key factors that are likely to underpin buying decisions in the four organizational buying areas (industry, reselling, not-for-profit, government agencies). (**See:** Debriefing at the end of the unit.)

Overt and covert behaviour

Always when marketing it is necessary to identify and deal with the overt and covert behaviour of the target audience. We all know the old adage 'believe the actions not the words' and many sales people have experience of broken promises such as, 'I'll have the order for you next visit.'

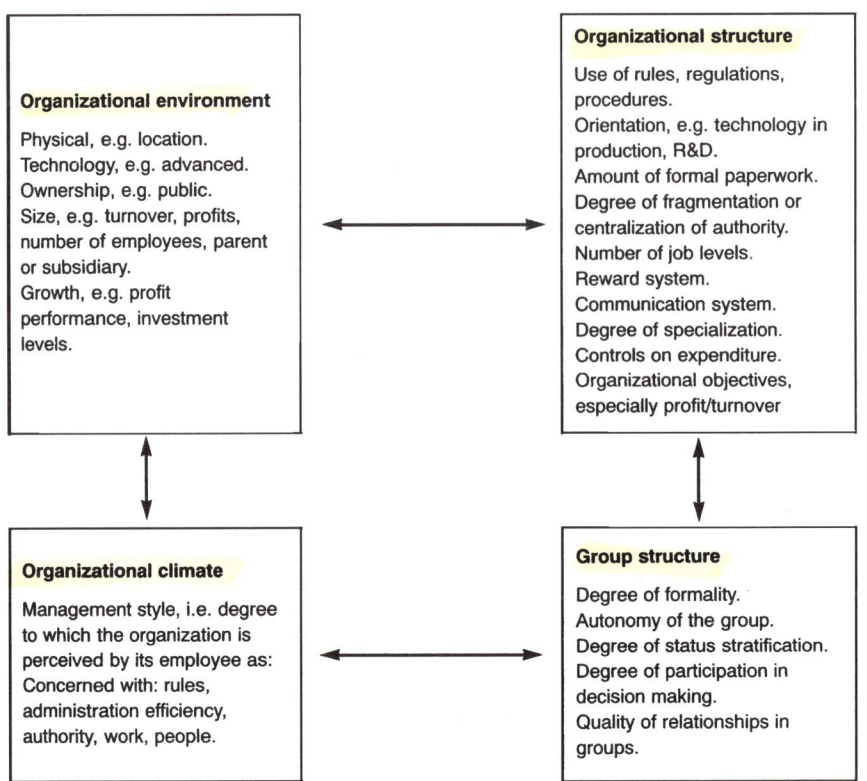

Organizational environment

Physical, e.g. location.
Technology, e.g. advanced.
Ownership, e.g. public.
Size, e.g. turnover, profits,
number of employees, parent
or subsidiary.
Growth, e.g. profit
performance, investment
levels.

Organizational structure

Use of rules, regulations,
procedures.
Orientation, e.g. technology in
production, R&D.
Amount of formal paperwork.
Degree of fragmentation or
centralization of authority.
Number of job levels.
Reward system.
Communication system.
Degree of specialization.
Controls on expenditure.
Organizational objectives,
especially profit/turnover

Organizational climate

Management style, i.e. degree
to which the organization is
perceived by its employee as:
Concerned with: rules,
administration efficiency,
authority, work, people.

Group structure

Degree of formality.
Autonomy of the group.
Degree of status stratification.
Degree of participation in
decision making.
Quality of relationships in
groups.

Figure 11.7
Relationships

Overt behaviour can be seen and monitored relatively easily. A buyer who is actively searching the environment is radiating a signal that a good sales team should pick up and home in on. In negotiation the overt behaviour is again obvious and procedures are most often committed to writing.

But proceeding overtly does not always secure the business. In fact it often does not even come close!

The emotions of individuals concerned with any purchase will be covert as will their motivations. There is a bank of evidence which clearly shows that all being equal an order will be given to the individual who is liked the best. People like to deal with others who are pleasant.

The obvious covert need is in the area loosely covered by the term bribery. British and American firms have generally coped badly in this area, at least we overtly believe that to be the case. Organizations trading across cultures are put into an impossible position when one culture expects that a gift shall be donated to facilitate a response and the other believes that this is wrong.

Extending Your Knowledge

The physical chemistry between buyer and seller is very important. In many cases relief salespeople who take over a territory for a short time succeed in accounts where the regular salesperson cannot even get an interview. But the situation reverts when the regular salesperson returns. Equally there are accounts where only the regular salesperson can do business.

Logic says that territories should be divided by chemistry and not geography, with salespeople calling where they get on well with the people in the organization.

Unfortunately logic does not often hold – overtly it should, but there are many covert reasons why it cannot be allowed.

Similarly there are covert reasons why, when an important buyer changes jobs (or posts), the salesperson covering the area to which he has moved is not informed and so cannot greet him with the benefit of a full briefing. Some call this behaviour 'human nature' others 'pure selfishness'. Perhaps both are right?

This is a fascinating and frustrating topic, but perhaps one with which organizations and their cultures are beginning to come to terms.

Covert needs can be far more straightforward, however. An individual may:

- Want to achieve status through making a good decision.
- To build a reputation as a sharp negotiator.
- To please the Managing Director, irrespective of the commercial considerations.

Covert needs are significant in every purchase decision. Individuals may be unaware of them, or perhaps be aware but keep them suppressed. Seldom will they surface and be expressed openly. Usually it is better if they are identified and satisfied covertly and therefore it becomes even more important to attempt to discover:

- Exactly who is involved with any purchase decision.
- The behavioural set of each individual.
- The overt and covert needs associated with the decision.

Selling to organizations

It is always necessary to discover the key facts about a buyer, in particular what their particular motivations are and what they desire to achieve from the purchase.

When selling FMCG through a channel of distribution it is only cost-effective to determine the key facts about target groups of customers and consumers. As one moves through consumer goods into white and brown goods, however, the situation changes. These 'high ticket' goods are higher-risk purchases from the customer's viewpoint and greater care will be taken in their selection.

Perhaps three or four visits will be made to the high street in order to gather sufficient information to choose between brands, models and vendors. In between such visits the decision process will be progressing towards the point where the DMU feels that a decision can and should be made. With this achieved the purchaser(s) visit the store of their choice and make their purchase. (At least this is how it should work.)

The salesperson in each outlet has opportunities to both impart and secure information. At each visit the sale is progressing further and the experienced salesperson knows there is need to establish progressive objectives to mark each step along the way to the sale. On first contact he won't know, of course, how far the purchase decision has progressed and so should use open questions to secure the information that he must have.

Extending Your Knowledge

The lengthy progression through stages can often be shortened by an experienced salesperson. A Granada television rental manager expressed it thus:

I know that there is nothing to choose between the major rental chains. We match each other so very closely. People come into the shop regularly 'just to make an enquiry.' And I used to give them brochures and expect them back. Most didn't return. So I decided I needed to be more direct. Now I ask open questions and if I am reasonably sure they are actually in the market I go straight in to get the contract signed. My success rate, on first meeting, is now consistently over 70 per cent and I'm the highest achieving salesman in the country.

Organizational selling

A key factor of organizational selling is that it is extremely 'high ticket'. Sales are made individually, but the business can extend for months, years, decades. The after market is incredibly important in industrial selling since a sale will involve a long-term commitment.

This may be for after-sales service, spare parts, etc; it may be for an ongoing supply of components in conditions of derived demand; it may be for consumables such as stationery. Whatever the product or service the expectation is that the main sale is only the key to future business. Obviously the proportionate value of the first to subsequent sales will vary with the product, but the principle holds: organizational selling has a long-term expectation.

It was, of course, in organizational marketing that Relationship Marketing was born.

A sales team is often necessary

We have seen how complex the buying centre can be. Consider the implications of selling to a multi-national concern. It may very well be that the buying decision is taken by a group of individuals scattered across three continents and working to policies and guidelines established in production units and head offices far removed from the buyer-salesperson contact point.

If we assume that an important purchase decision for a major company involves only 20 departments across two continents we can deduce the complexity of the task:

If each department has five individuals we have 100 involved. Not all will be actively involved but which ones are not? Where do the elements of the DMU exist? Who is the decision maker and where is he located? Similarly we have to know where all the other elements are and who comprises them. Probably we shall find that some individuals take different roles at different times and the internal relationships must also be determined.

Quite probably we shall have to deal with two or more languages and certainly with two or more national cultures (plus the organization's culture).

It is apparent that this is a job for a sales team, not for a single salesperson. It is necessary to get a suitably qualified person alongside everybody in the buying centre so that individual needs can be taken into account within an orchestrated sales plan.

Selling early means long-term profits

If a component can be sold at design stage then business will continue as long as the product is on the market. Thus it pays to establish relationships which allow contracts to be secured long before a new product is even tested. This requires excellent relationships to be established over time.

Even in areas where change is possible it can take a long time to become established. Once a competitive product is in place the individuals in the organization become accustomed to it and to the ordering process. Unless (and until) something goes wrong it is very hard to sell a competitive product. Soup mixes for the catering trade, for example, were packed in 5 and 7lb tins by different manufacturers. Each made the same quantity of soup since the mix was more concentrated in the smaller tin. The result was that if a caterer bought the competitor, perhaps out of desperation or as a trial, it was likely that the kitchen staff would use the same amount of powder as they were used to. Thus the one alternative would be too strong, the other too weak!

Not surprisingly catering buyers preferred not to confuse the kitchen staff and kept to the one make or the other. The sale to dislodge the competitor was long and protracted and depended not on product quality but on keeping in touch so that in an emergency one could help out and so get the product into use. The good news is that in such circumstances it takes a long time to get in but it takes a competitor a long time to get you out!

Sales research sources

Salespeople should always maintain meticulous records of their customers. These must extend far beyond the simple recording of orders to include the vital personal information that helps one to understand the buyer's motivations. It is not reasonable to expect to keep all this information in one's head and, in any case, the organization requires the information to be available should the salesperson be transferred or leave. Salespeople, of course, are inclined to keep their customer information to themselves: it can help secure a new job, or prevent them being made redundant.

Sources are many and varied. They range from the open and easily accessible – Annual Reports, trade and local press – to the secret which is often obtainable without breaking the law. Some of the key sources are:

- The buyer himself — Both formally and informally. About the organization. About himself and other individuals.

- Secretaries, receptionists, etc. — Often these know more of what is going on than their managers and are surprisingly often willing to talk about it providing they like the salesperson.

- Assistants — Often flattered by attention and not appreciative of the value of the information they have.

- Others, specific — It is often possible to arrange to meet appropriate individuals, either formally through channels or at a social event or a Round Table or Rotary lunch. Exhibitions, etc., provide excellent opportunities to secure all kinds of vital information.

- Others, general — Having a coffee or a lunch in the staff restaurant can provide a wealth of background information simply from listening to the general conversations going on.

- Knowledgeable outsiders — Those who deliver to an organization have privileged access and often have considerable information. Delivery men, for example, know when fork-lift trucks are breaking down too often and not being dealt with under the service contract.

- Own staff — Often it is not appreciated how much knowledge is already held in an organization. See the following activity.

Activity 11.3

Industrial sales teams

The Sales Manager of a firm selling computer-controlled paint-spraying equipment to industry has two teams. One of six salespeople who locate new business, secure contracts and maintain on-going contact. The other of 18 sales engineers who carry out regular maintenance and provide an emergency call-out service.

Why is it wrong to keep the teams separate? What would be the benefits of establishing new teams, each of one salesperson and three sales engineers?

(**See:** Debriefing at the end of the unit.)

Industrial buyer behaviour

The Sheth model of industrial buyer behaviour (see Figure 11.8) shows how little importance the actual product has within the buying process. It is, of course, important, but other issues are of considerably more significance given that the product will perform to specification.

261

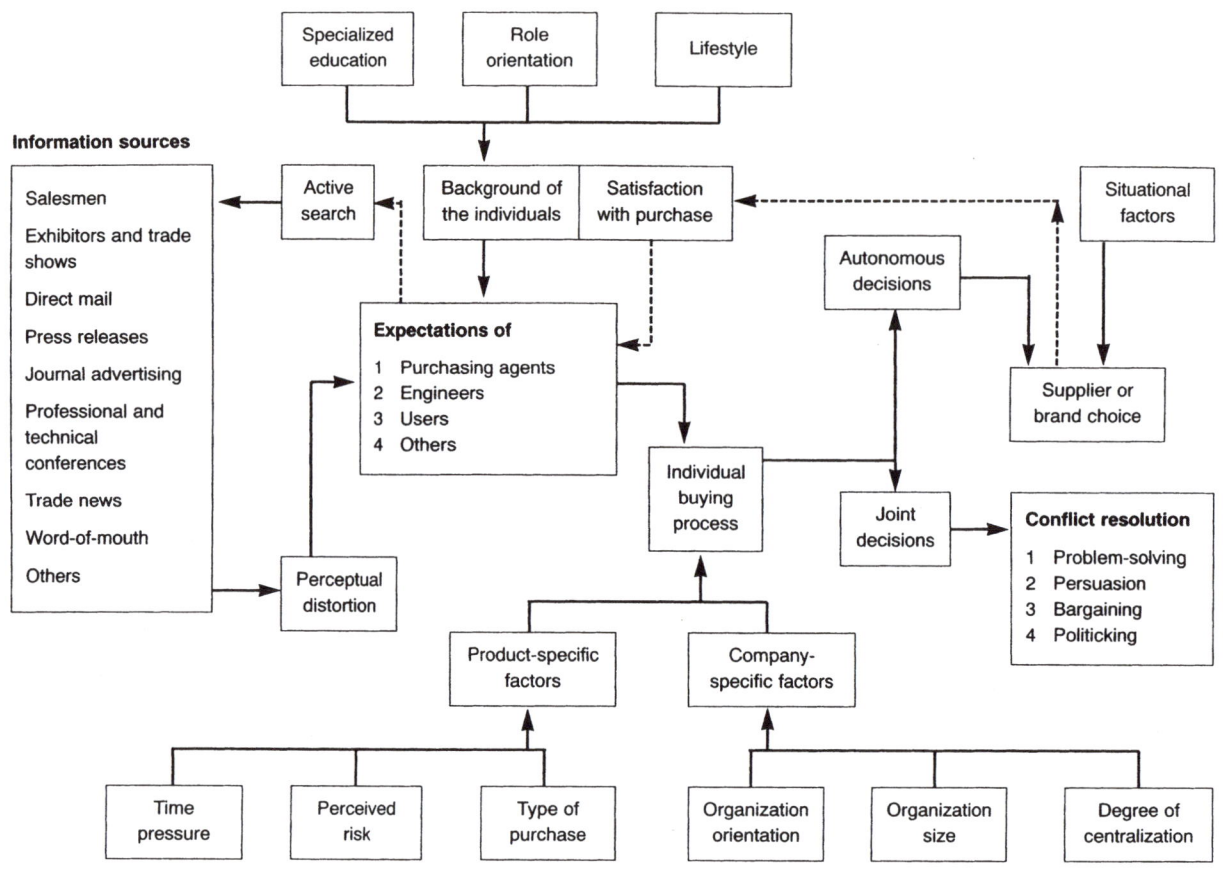

Figure 11.8 The Sheth model of industrial buying behaviour

The key issues of industrial buyer behaviour identified in the Sheth model can be summarized as:

- *Information sources* – which are subject to perceptual distortion exactly as one would expect.
- *Product factors* – simply one element. Note the issue of *perceived* risk. It is perceived risk that can be the most difficult to deal with since it is usually ill informed but deeply felt.
- *Company specific factors* – some of the issues that must be researched.
- *Expectations* – note the need to determine these by category of individual.
- *Background of individuals* – these are probably the most important to research and understand.
- *The buying process* – a small box in the model, but potentially a complex process that will require to be precisely met.
- *Conflict resolution* – this is an internal issue where even seemingly the most secure prospects can be lost in a concession to achieve a compromise that doesn't even involve your product directly.
- *Decision* – can a decision ever be truly joint? No, but it can be heavily influenced by consensus feelings.
- *Situational factors* – these are external and can range from competitive action forcing your buyer off the market through government legislation to a new market area opening and sales quadrupling.

Differentiation

The traditional approach to marketing between organizations has been based on a functional concept of demand. A typical argument has been: 'Buyers want a product to do a job, they won't pay for anything fancy'. Thus there has been (and still is in some organizations) a focus on the physical and functional aspects of the product offering.

The value of the symbolic area has been shown by many suppliers in the success they have enjoyed when adopting a three-aspect approach in business-to-business marketing:

- Maggi catering soups adopted four-colour labels for their professional range of soup mixes and secured market domination. Why shouldn't kitchen workers have a bright and cheerful environment?
- Black & Decker branded their professional range of hand tools. Dulux branded their professional paints. Both gained both retail and industrial benefits since the brand name boosted industrial sales and the professional's use of the tools boosted DIY buyers' confidence in the product.
- JCB is the best known back-hoe loader. Dexion wrapped up the steel shelving market.
- Viking use efficient direct marketing to sell stationery and sustain a price differential that is justified by the quality of their service.

Derived demand

Much of industry finds itself in conditions of derived demand, where sales are dependent on the sales of those ahead of them in the chain. As product moves through the chain the opportunities to add differentiation to the product increase – but note carefully that there is always opportunity to differentiate on non-product factors.

	Iron ore	Pig iron	Steel billet	Steel rod	Nuts and bolts	Gearbox	Machine tool
Raw material				$\longrightarrow$			Finished product
Low added value				$\longrightarrow$			High added value
Low level of superficial design				$\longrightarrow$		High level of superficial design
High price sensitivity				$\longrightarrow$			Low price sensitivity
Low brand loyalty				$\longrightarrow$			High brand loyalty
Regular purchase				$\longrightarrow$			Irregular purchase

Figure 11.9
Non-differentiated products in the chain of derived demand. (Source: *The Industrial Market Research Handbook*, Hague.)

Non-product features

In many cases the role of the product is extremely small within the decision process. The deciders do not share the priorities of the everyday users and the concerns of the organization overall must be taken into account. Most products are perfectly functional and are known to be so. If they are not then the marketer is wasting his and everybody else's time.

With functionality taken care of the issues of service and symbolism have a major role to play. Issues such as these add real value:

- Regularity of supply.
- Deliveries in buyer-specified quantities to dispersed sites.
- Packaging that reduces handling cost, is of an appropriate size, is clearly labelled.
- User-friendly ordering and invoicing procedures that are efficient and effective.
- Taking responsibility for buyer's stock holding.

Increasing the quality from acceptable through excellent to superb is less likely to achieve additional business than the application of psychological understanding to the decision processes.

Investment in targeted market, sales and competitive research is more likely to show a payback than if the resources are put into improvement of current successful products. Development funding of new products to secure/keep a leading position is also of key importance, ranking above improvement of existing models.

263

Segmentation

Marketing principles remain constant across different marketplaces. Therefore the key questions when deciding business-to-business strategy are the same as when marketing to individual customers:

- With which market segments could we do business?
- With which do we want to do business?
- What product/service package should we offer?

The detail of the promotional task varies considerably, however:

- For which individuals – or groups of individuals – do we design the offer?
- When and how should we communicate with which individuals?
- What message(s) are required?

Organizational demographics

Demographic factors are only of limited value in business-to-business marketing. They do, however, allow for a first broad cut which excludes the unsuitable. Demographic factors include:

- Standard Industrial Classifications (SICs).
- Census of Production.
- Industrial technology, e.g. chemical or electrical, etc.; extractive, processing or manufacturing.
- Size of organization.
- Seasonal purchasing trends.
- Geographic location.
- Type of product needed.

This approach relies on a potentially false assumption that organizations operating in similar demographic segments have similar needs, and will exhibit the same kind of buying behaviour. Thus, although of value as an excluder it is not a tool of positive selection.

More useful bases for segmentation include:

- Benefits sought.
- Title/position of key decision makers.
- The degree of formality in the buying organization.
- The type of people involved in the buying decision.

The type of product need is a great help in segmentation, the more so when expressed in terms of user benefits. Business buyers need to satisfy need, not to buy products or services. Show them how they can satisfy a need, and they will respond just as housewives do in the supermarket. It can be more difficult to get the message through – certainly different channels of communication and forms of promotion are needed – but the principle remains constant.

Activity 11.4

User benefits
Itemize the potential user benefits which could be offered by suppliers of these products and services:

1 Mild steel rods.
2 Heavy goods vehicles.
3 Drain cleaning services.
4 Photocopiers.

(**See:** Debriefing at the end of the unit.)

You will have noticed how difficult it is to come up with a unique benefit. This is because as a benefit is identified it is quickly copied on the 'me too' basis. The key issue to understand and provide for is the need to provide the benefit in a unique way. To present it as part of a complete package that is matched to individual buyers' needs and desires.

In business-to-business marketing the requirement is to identify target opportunities, research them thoroughly, and then devise a suitable package that is presented in an individual way. In other words, to mix and match to suit the needs of the buyer.

Segmentation criteria are relatively weak in business-to-business marketing. There is need for shoe leather research to provide the raw data and for a MkIS that produces target customers. These can then be grouped into segments, not with the sophistication of consumer marketing, but sufficiently to enable the business-to-business marketer to operate effectively. He will know that organizations:

- Tend to be more stable in their requirements than individuals, especially those which are highly capitalized and those which engage in long production runs.
- Are more visible than individuals and can thus be individually researched.
- Are fewer in number and thus individual sales research is cost-effective.
- Tend to congregate around trade associations, exhibitions, conferences, etc., and can thus be identified and accessed.
- Tend to concentrate because of a key need. Sheffield became famous for its steel because it had large quantities of suitable coal for the furnaces within easy reach.
- Develop long-term relationships because organizations transcend individuals and on the whole have longer life spans.

He will also be aware of the disadvantages of trading with organizations:

- It usually requires a long-term involvement to secure the first order.
- There is greater insecurity through having few, large customers.
- There are potential cash flow problems unless credit control is extremely effective.

The business-to-business marketing mix

Each element of the business-to-business marketing mix has potential to add differentiation. The potential of each of the 7Ps is shown in Figure 11.10.

Product The product must be functionally up to standard. It must perform at least adequately. This will almost be taken for granted by the buyer (but positively confirmed as a matter of routine). Whether the organization is an innovator or follows a 'me too' strategy the basic offering has to offer what the target customers need to buy. **Note:** Not need – need to buy – there is a difference because what they actually need (and what the buyer would like to buy) may not be what he needs to buy to comply with policy.

Place This will, again, almost be taken for granted by the buyer. It is an expected service that will only be noticed if there is a failure.

Price Not the most important area of the mix, but one that is significant nevertheless. For 'price' it is always better to automatically read 'value' because that is what the buyer looks for and what should be sold. A value package allows a reasonable amount of differentiation in most cases.

Process This can be a disaster area unless positive steps are taken to make it user-friendly. Buyers must be able to access the supplier when

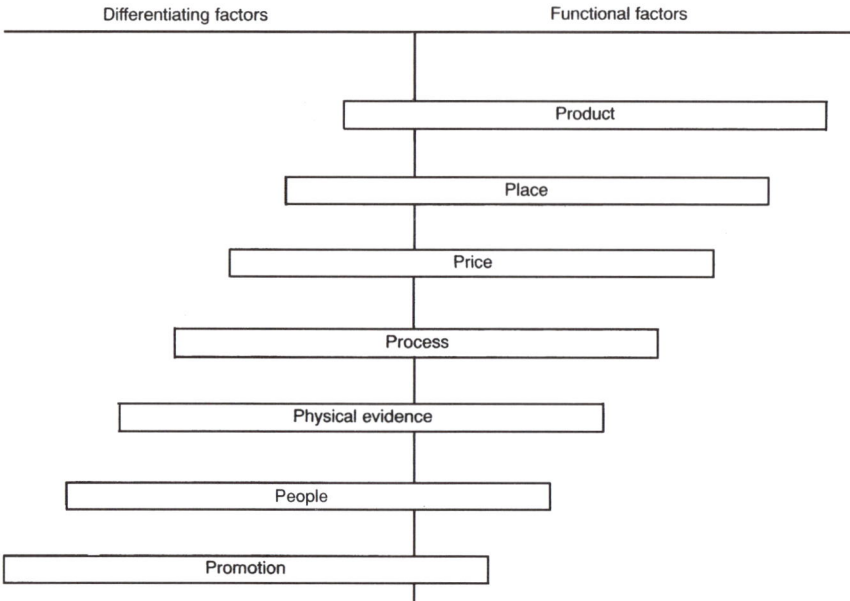

Figure 11.10
Differentiating factors in business-to-business marketing

and how they want to. The more that can be taken from them, the more cost-effective the deal becomes. But any commitment entered into must be fulfilled to the letter, or better.

Physical evidence Considerable opportunity for differentiation since this area is totally in the marketer's control. To an extent it overlaps with Promotion since sales-support materials are probably the first tangible experience that a buyer will have of the supplier. In seeking confirmation of the depth of support and commitment, a buyer will research the organizational culture of the potential supplier. It had better match the ambience projected by the salesperson.

People The second most important area for differentiation. Marketing and Procurement are both highly people-centred activities since both marketers and buyers know that organizations are made up of people. It is people who will facilitate, who will fulfil. No system can operate unless it is properly – enthusiastically – supported. A healthy budget for Human Resource Development is necessary.

Promotion The promotional mix offers the greatest opportunities for differentiation. As marketing is the communications centre of the organization, it is for the marketer to focus and communicate the unique benefits in terms that individual and targeted buyers will respond to. Unless this is done the responsibility for translation of product to user benefits is passed to the buyer, and why should he bother? Even if he does, how can the marketer be sure he has translated accurately and understood fully?

The promotional mix

The role of the promotional mix in business-to-business marketing is shown in Figure 11.11. At strategic level it closely parallels the promotional role across all of marketing. A major difference in this market, however, is that the buyers are carrying out purchasing research which is far more professional than experienced in other markets. They also have considerable experience in cutting through flim-flam to get to the nub of issues.

That does not mean that materials should not be attractively presented. They should. But the requirement for the contents is that it should give facts to support the imagery. A professional buyer does not want to have to hunt for evidence, he will turn to the supplier with the clearest presentation and use that as a yardstick.

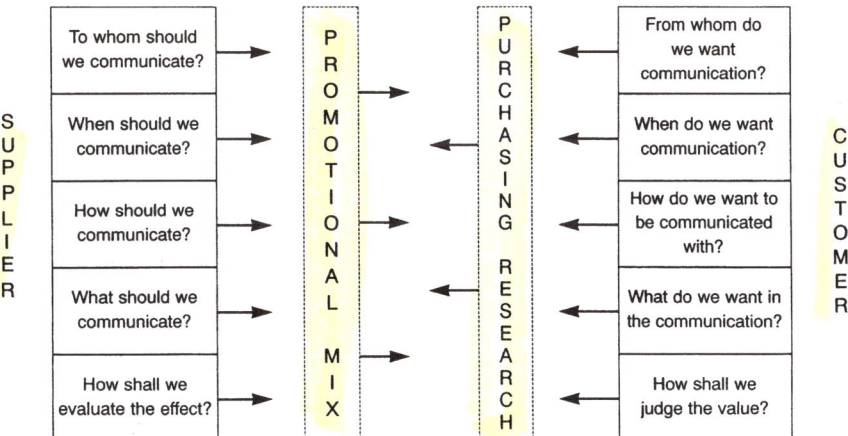

Figure 11.11
Role of the promotional mix.
(Adapted from *Organizational Buying Behaviour*, Hill and Hillyer.)

Budgets

Usually these are smaller than in consumer marketing but this is a measure of quantity which has no direct bearing on the task. Unfortunately they are often controlled by a Sales focused manager who, perhaps, has added Marketing to his title. The result can be messy, unco-ordinated and wasteful.

Materials can become stale and repeating last year's spend can be the basis of media selection. Exhibitions can be seen as important but not the need for properly trained salespeople to manage and staff the stand.

There is no excuse for sloppy promotion, and too high a dependence on salespeople and their personal contacts can be a road to disaster when faced with a competitor who is deploying the promotional mix effectively.

Budget allocation across the four elements of the promotional mix will vary by industry and sector but it is likely that sales will require around 50 per cent of the available spend. Possibly more.

Tactics

Tactically the need is to secure leads; to qualify them; to ensure they are followed-up effectively; to monitor the on-going contact with potential customers all the way through until they become established users or it is determined that no further resources should be expended on them.

The promotional mix therefore has two broad objectives:

- To secure leads.
- To follow them through to a decision.

Securing leads

Targeted media exists in profusion. Everything from trade press through to direct mail. Providing there is clarity of purpose (i.e. clear objectives) there need not be any problem securing leads. How good these leads will be is another matter!

Qualifying leads involves sorting and evaluating them against established criteria so that they are sorted into types and levels of urgency.

It is essential to have an effective records system in place since it is only through meticulous records that the quality of the leads can be increased by modifications and improvements to the initial promotion.

Salespeople must report back accurately and quickly on the quality of the leads, and marketers must act to improve promotional effectiveness.

Following through

Sales contact is essential in business-to-business marketing. Sometimes this can be by telephone but usually it is face to face. Given the relatively small number of buyers and the relative importance of each it is easy to see that a sales force is not just affordable, it is essential.

Salespeople must be properly supported. They need proper training which is updated regularly, they need field support that is proactive and routine (not simply a 'day out to motivate the lads'). Above all they need hard information as a basis for their first contact.

Qualified leads should brief the salesperson with key details. He should not go in on a virtually cold call basis. The buyer should not have to repeat information he already has given or which could easily have been researched.

Types	Use
Public Relations	As in all forms of marketing, to secure favourable mention and restrict and/or counter unfavourable. With trade press and industry specific features in the major newspapers there is ample opportunity to create PR opportunities.
Press advertising	National press is broadband and not often cost-effective, with the obvious exceptions of those organizations who operate in the consumer markets and thus allow the industrial marketer to ride along if brand extension has been achieved.
Trade press	Highly targeted. Most effective for awareness and to stimulate a first response perhaps via a reader's enquiry service. Major opportunity for linked advertising and PR. Quality of trade journals varies widely.
Direct marketing	Mainly direct mail because many lists exist. Need to be careful to select with care and shorten where possible. Can be very important to develop one's own list and protect it rigorously.
Directories	Very valuable for services in particular. *Yellow Pages* and *Talking Pages* are extremely effective for certain businesses. Beware not to subscribe to an unknown directory and never pay for space without having ordered it first.
Exhibitions	Most valuable in many areas. An opportunity to display product, to meet with existing customers, to develop and qualify leads and to sell (many forget that they can sell from a stand!). Also a valuable opportunity for competitive contact and research. Should be used positively, never simply to 'show the flag'.
Brochures, sales literature	Educational and informative, they should supplement, not be expected to carry the whole message. A range of mix and match, targeted literature will be needed in most areas.
Audio-visual	Can be simply educational and ephemeral but can also be used to positive effect if designed to achieve something that is otherwise difficult, such as a visit to a remote location. Can be mounted in the buyer's office using easily portable equipment as part of a sales pitch.
Computer	Few salespeople are today properly equipped without the ability to interrogate a database whilst with the buyer. Quotations can be printed on the spot, as can contracts. Via a modem a link to a senior manager can be established and a deal struck. Computers will also support audio-visual presentations that can easily be tailored to need ahead of each visit.
Sales promotion	It is possible in some markets to add a 'temporary inducement at point-of-sale'. Not to be confused with discounts, however. Unless SP gifts are of low value they may be perceived as bribes. It is better to target them on benefits to the organization or the department, not on to the buyer.
Give-aways	Can be useful as reminders of phone numbers, etc. They also provide an opportunity to make contact. Probably the best are the long-lasting ones such as desk pads and diaries – but these benefit from tailoring to need rather than simply being bought off the shelf with the buyer's initials added (i.e. It is better to invest quite heavily and do a proper job because the give-away says a lot about you and your organization).

Figure 11.12   Major uses of the promotional mix

Above all the salespeople should not see themselves as individuals. They are part of a team and should be trained to call in other people as support, to extend the drive for business or even to take over if the chemistry isn't working. Salary and bonus conditions should be tied to what is needed and never to a traditional package that was created no one knows why, nor when.

Major uses of the promotional mix are shown in Figure 11.12.

Exam Hint

Students know full well that presentation is important, yet when they become candidates many totally forget and submit answer books that can best be described as disgraceful! This applies at all examination levels – there appears to be an unexpressed view that it is the examiner's job to decipher handwriting and to give the benefit of the doubt where he has problems!

This could not be further from the truth – especially in CIM examinations. The Senior Examiner for Strategic Marketing – Case Study has clearly set out the position. The major criterion he uses to evaluate candidate's submissions is: 'Would I give this person a job?'

Your examiners want you to answer as a credible marketer; you are expected to have subject knowledge, current examples to quote, and to present your work crisply. If you imagine that you are in line for promotion, that there is one other hot candidate for the job, and that your managing director is to choose between you on the basis of your exam answer book you will set your self-motivation to the level needed for success.

Activity 11.5

Presentation
These are typical of approaches taken by failing candidates. What do you feel is the impression given to the examiner?

- Lack of examples and/or illustrations.
- Not decisive and specific.
- No underpinning theory or knowledge.
- Inappropriate tone or style.
- Many liquid paper corrections.
- Axes of graphs and diagrams not labelled.
- Freehand used for underlining and diagrams.
- Part of question not attempted.
- Last question unfinished.
- Unstructured.

(**See:** Debriefing at the end of the unit.)

Summary

In this unit we have seen that:

- Industrial and business-to-business marketing are synonymous and refer to marketing of organizations to organizations.
- Segmentation is demographically difficult but depends more on individual location of opportunity.
- Customers and potential customers are relatively few but each has a relatively high potential. It is thus cost-effective to target individually and necessary to heavily rely upon face-to-face contact.
- Individuals operate within organizational cultures and within buying centres. The DMU and DMP may be very widespread geographically and include a considerable number of individuals. A sales team approach is therefore mandatory in many cases.
- Decisions are often made in sequential stages, with the supplier unable to access the top levels of the decision process.
- Buyers try to mechanize the on-going buying process and welcome the positive assistance and support of the supplier.

- Covert behaviour must be looked for but is usually best dealt with in a covert fashion.
- Making an early sale is essential in many markets where conditions of derived demand exist.
- Product differentiation can prove difficult but there are many other opportunities to differentiate within the marketing mix.
- As in all marketing it is necessary to identify and feature user benefits.

Unit Activity

This scenario is taken from the pilot paper issued by the CIM. It should be answered in 72 minutes.

Time management is important. If you overrun, record the point where your 72 minutes are up, but finish your answer.

Part A – compulsory

IKEA: Furniture retailer

Swedish furniture manufacturer and retailer IKEA was formed in 1943 by Ingvar Kamprad. Between 1954, when the first store opened, and 1990 the company underwent massive expansion from a single Swedish outlet to more than 80 spread through 21 different countries, with over 70 per cent of revenue generated outside Scandinavia. The IKEA concept comprises large retail outlets (around 80 000 square metres) situated on the edge of sizeable towns and cities, selling a full range of furniture and furnishings. From beds to lounge suites, kitchen utensils to carpets, curtains, pictures and lighting everything the customer needs to set up and update the home. The stores also offer in-store restaurant and child care facilities to make the shopping experience a pleasant one. To help in the selling effort, the company produces an extensive catalogue, giving details of the items for sale, prices, colours, measurements and availability. In 1990 alone, around 35 million US dollars were spent producing 40 million copies in 12 different languages.

IKEA operates with an up-market brand image, linked to stylish and sophisticated Swedish taste, but its products are aimed clearly at the mass market. The company is not a market nicher and to maintain its growth must attract large numbers of customers of low as well as high incomes. To keep its prices low, IKEA must keep costs down. This is achieved by a clever combination of buying in bulk, making buying centres compete for orders, having large stores with self-service facilities and products which are flat packed, for self assembly at home.

The IKEA company mission is clearly stated 'We shall offer a wide range of furnishing items of good design and function, at prices so low that the majority of people can afford to buy them'. This philosophy is backed up by the following aims:

- IKEA should keep costs low and assist customers.
- Products should combine good quality, durability and be functional.
- Profit should be used to build and expand.
- A keen understanding of the company's cost base must be maintained and good results achieved with careful investment.
- Energy must be concentrated carefully and time used efficiently.
- Simple solutions should be found to product and company problems.
- IKEA should take responsibility and put things right.
- IKEA should find alternative solutions to problems by experimenting.

Currently IKEA seems to appeal particularly to customers aged in their 20s and 30s who are furnishing a home for the first time. These customers want their homes to look stylish and smart, but with relatively low disposable incomes must carefully consider price. The company is also keen to attract other customer types, from many different countries and of all ages and lifestyle stages. Although IKEA does not formally use demographics and psychographics to segment its market, it divides its markets into different geographical areas, each with a standard product range but having the flexibility to include products which match local, cultural requirements.

Questions
Answer the following questions with reference to the IKEA case:
(i)   Briefly define marketing planning and say why it is important for IKEA to use it.   (10 marks)
(ii)   How should the marketing planning process relate to IKEA's corporate planning?   (10 marks)
(iii) Describe the elements of a detailed marketing plan and show within this framework what types of information might be included in a marketing plan for IKEA.   (25 marks)

5 Marks will be allocated for presentation.

(**See:** Debriefing at the end of the unit.)

Debriefing

Activity 11.1
These are only some of the key features. The actual needs of your target markets must be identified in considerable detail. We shall be covering these points as we progress through the unit.

Consumer value – organizations mainly will want 'professional' quality (i.e. heavy duty). The individuals buying and using the products still respond to value issues such as style, colour, packaging, etc.
Cost – in use should be the yardstick. It will normally be calculated very precisely because a professional buyer will be involved. Cost elements such as occasioned by late delivery, low quality, etc. may have to be indemnified against.
Convenience – JIT deliveries in many cases. Certainly the supplier has to get the goods or services where they are needed, when they must be there. After-sales service must be exemplary.
Communication – can be targeted direct but expect a long process between first contact and establishment as a regular customer. The promotions mix will typically require a large proportion of face-to-face contact.
Confirmation – the product or service in use has to justify itself, not simply to a customer/consumer but to professionals such as the workers who use the product, the foremen, the factory manager and the production director. Unless these are happy the professional status of the buyer who did the deal will suffer.
Consideration – the after-market is particularly important since one plans for a long-term relationship in most business-to-business situations. Contact has to be easy, and contact staff need to be knowledgeable and helpful.
Co-ordination and concern – the process is all important, especially when ordering is routinized and the more so when the supplier takes responsibility for ensuring that stock holdings are adequate. Invoices must be submitted to time and correctly referenced. Credits, when necessary, must go through smoothly.

Activity 11.2
The key factors are likely to differ widely, partly because the goods and services differ and partly because of organizational matters.

Industrial buyers – purchase mainly to facilitate manufacture. They will buy to specification. They are in competition with other buyers for goods which are perhaps in limited supply, for the best prices and best delivery. They will be interested in how a product performs elsewhere but are unlikely to share their knowledge with other buyers. They will be judged on their ability to secure good terms in line with specifications produced by specialists in the organization. They will be influenced by the culture of the organization and their behaviour will be geared towards compliance with organizational norms.

Resellers – are concerned with adding value to existing products. They will evaluate sales volume against mark-up to achieve a price that is competitive and will generate an acceptable profit. They are, within limits, not over-concerned with the contents of any 'boxes' they buy to resell. Their main concern is: 'Will our customers like it and buy at our price?' They will be in the fiercest competition and will guard their information jealously. Their ability will be judged on sales of what they buy, and on how fast they unload goods that do not prove popular.

Not-for-profit buyers – must justify purchases on cost as well as on value grounds. Cost is likely to be the more important if the organization is not run by professional managers. They will be intensely interested in how to be more effective and will want to share their experiences with others for mutual benefit. Buying is not likely to be a professional activity and may not be considered a very important role. The decision-making process is likely to be muddled and unclear. The buying function, therefore, is likely either to be spread across managers in a disjointed fashion or to be delegated to middle management. Perhaps even junior management for all but major decisions.

Government agencies – have strictly formal procurement procedures which have to be followed to the letter. This formality is designed both to prevent employees from gaining personal benefit from transactions and to help ensure that the best possible terms are obtained. Buyers are concerned with procedure, with ensuring that regulations are followed and are seen to be followed. They have little, if any, responsibility for the product in use since they are following procedures which allocate responsibility on to the specifier. Motivations will be to do with personal survival which means strict compliance with regulations.

Activity 11.3

It is wrong to keep the teams separate because this supposes that sales and service are separate functions. In fact the long-term sale depends on the after-sales service. The buying organization see far more of the sales engineers than they do of the salesperson and the engineers penetrate to the shop floor where the salesperson cannot easily go.

The engineers see the product in actual use and talk with the users. They are uniquely able, if encouraged, to feed back vital information to guide redesign and/or modifications, etc. It was a sales engineer, for instance, that eventually told a major maker of X-ray equipment for hospitals that the unit was badly balanced and the female staff operating it were suffering strain injuries that nobody was doing anything about.

The benefits of linking the two activities closely are considerable. Deduce what can be done with intelligence from the following:

- The salesperson is put in touch with what is actually going on.
- He can penetrate to the shop floor if he visits with an engineer.
- The engineers become trusted friends within the buying organization and, as with all friends, share information. This means two-way exchange at the operational level. Your information will be going into the buyer (if he is wired in) and his information will be coming out. This can become a managed exchange if the engineers are sufficiently motivated. Then the information flow will be outward from the buying organization and the seller's confidentiality will be protected.

It is not uncommon for sales engineers' status and salaries to change markedly where an organization suddenly appreciates their value. Until then they tend to be regarded simply as mechanics doing a technical and not very interesting job.

Activity 11.4

The user benefits are limited only by the marketer's imagination. They do not, of course, have to be tangible providing that they are perceived to be of value. Thus such issues as brand values are more widely applicable than many appreciate. Typical user benefits (omitting the obvious functional features) include:

1	*Mild steel rods*	Consistent quality. Cut to size. Delivery to requirement. Note: These are far easier to promise than to provide.
2	*Heavy goods vehicles*	Compliance with legal regulations across whole area where they may be used, e.g. Britain and the EU, Europe, the Middle East. Service network across the same area. Speed of service/mechanical repair. Standard costings of service/mechanical repair. Easy replacement of body parts – bolt off, bolt on. Design of livery and supplied fully painted. Added safety features: anti-skid, driver comfort, etc.
3	*Drain cleaning*	Ease of contact (0800 number). Speed of response supported by indemnity. Health and Safety checks additional to preventative maintenance. Proactive suggestions for improvements.
4	*Photocopiers*	Unbiased advice from concerned staff. Compatibility with other equipment. Security coded to control usage. Add-on facility, e.g. fax, scanner. Exchangeable for upgrade or sidegrade at any time. Lease or buy.

Activity 11.5

These typical characteristics all result in diminished marks. Many candidates who achieve a D (marginal fail) would have passed if their technique had been up to standard.

Characteristic	*Impression given to the examiner*
Lack of examples and/or illustrations.	No practical experience; no interest in real-life marketing.
Not decisive and specific.	Not credible as a manager and/or didn't read the question. In other words, not credible as a candidate.
No underpinning theory or knowledge.	Didn't read the question and/or did no serious study.
Inappropriate tone or style.	Inability to tailor communication to needs of target audience.
Many liquid paper corrections.	Grossly unprepared. No consideration of the effect on the reader.
Axes of graphs and diagrams not labelled.	Careless. Assuming that the reader will understand what is meant.
Freehand used for underlining and diagrams.	Sloppy, unconcerned with need to impress the reader.
Part of question not attempted.	Weak candidate lacking in knowledge and poor manager for not at least making an attempt.
Last question unfinished.	Poor time manager, i.e. poor manager.
Unstructured.	Careless – didn't plan – not concerned with the reader.

Unit activity

Your time management should be under control by now. If you are not using time effectively your marks will suffer!

Leave your debriefing until you can come fresh to your work but be sure to establish and then practise what you need to do to correct your problem.

Part A

Approach

The first two questions play an important role in scene-setting for the marketing plan which follows. Answers should address the definition for marketing planning, consider the role which the process plays for a company like IKEA and show the relationship with corporate planning.

The third question provides the opportunity to demonstrate that the different elements of a marketing plan are understood. It also allows students to suggest some details which might be included in a marketing plan for IKEA. Obviously, the level of information provided in the case makes it impossible to provide much detail, but answers should be able to show that the types of information to be included in the different sections are understood.

Defining marketing planning

Marketing planning is the systematic process of assessing marketing opportunities and resources, determining marketing objectives, and developing a plan for implementation and control. Marketing planning involves the creation of a marketing plan, which may be short range (one year or less), medium range (two to five years) or long range (over five years).

The need for marketing planning

Many of the benefits of marketing planning are self-evident and not particularly industry specific. Applying marketing planning will help IKEA to do the following:

- Stay in touch with trends in the marketplace. Marketing planning hinges on analysing key trends and environmental changes so companies which use it tend to maintain awareness of what is going on.
- Ensure an understanding of customer needs. Marketing planning will require IKEA to regularly appraise and review key customer needs and how well they are being satisfied.
- Keep competitors under scrutiny. Competitor analysis is an important part of the process which IKEA will go through and should help the company understand the strategies and likely future actions of key international and local players.
- Develop strategies which target appropriate customer groups. The background analyses which have been carried out help identify the most suitable customer targets and segments where the greatest potential exists. By understanding its own strengths and weaknesses IKEA will also be able to understand the feasibility of particular actions.
- Put together appropriate marketing programmes (mixes) for targeted customers. The understanding of customer needs, competition and marketplace which IKEA has developed will help the company fine-tune its marketing mixes.
- Ensure the appropriate level of resourcing which has been developed with the particular strategies and programmes in mind.

The relationship with corporate planning

Corporate planning is important in determining an organization's overall mission. It helps set goals which relate to all departments of the company, including R&D, Engineering, Production, Finance, Personnel and Sales, as

274

well as to Marketing. Corporate planning is therefore a plan of all aspects of an organization's strategy in the marketplace whereas a marketing plan deals with implementing the marketing strategy as it relates to the target markets and the marketing mix.

Detailed marketing plans

Company mission – to offer a wide range of furnishing items of good design and function, at prices so low that the majority of people can afford to buy them.

Product/market background information – here IKEA could review the nature of segmentation and sales within the market in which it operates. This could include an understanding of customer needs by segment as well as an appreciation of key operators within relevant target markets.

SWOT analysis – this is a review of IKEA's key strengths and weaknesses as well as the available opportunities and challenges which the company may be facing. While the strengths and weaknesses will be concerned with internal organization issues, the opportunities and threats will relate to conditions in the external environment. The details included will vary but may include some of the following issues:

Strengths
- Low cost base.
- Up-market brand.
- Stylish Swedish image.
- Full range of furniture and furnishings under one roof.
- Good customer facilities.
- Self-service stores.
- Mass-market appeal.
- Provision of full colour catalogue.

Weaknesses
- Out of town.
- Flat packed items.
- Reliance on mass market.
- Need to keep prices low.
- Need to follow/set fashions.

Opportunities
- Move into new geographic markets.
- Attract new demographic/psychographic groups.

Threats
- Price competition from other multinationals.
- Local, more culturally tuned in competition.
- World recession and low consumer spending power.

Statement of objectives – these objectives will relate to what IKEA aims to achieve with its marketing programmes. These will combine general objectives, such as keeping costs low, maintaining service quality, finding simple solutions to problems with specific sales targets and expected results by target segments.

Strategies – which target segments are under review, what the basis for competing (competitive edge) will be and how the offerings are to be positioned. For IKEA these strategies could be specified in terms of the customer targets such as couples in their 20s and 30s setting up home for the first time and what is being offered to them such as the stylish, sophisticated, Swedish, keenly priced product range.

Programmes – these concern the tactics in terms of products, price, promotion and distribution. For example, this will involve specifying the core global product range, as well as suggesting local additions to the portfolio. Given IKEA falls roughly within the service sector, it may also be appropriate to consider people, process and physical evidence. For example, standard staffing levels, store layout, order processing systems etc. are all part of the offering to be determined.

Allocation of resources/tasks/responsibilities – making programmes happen involves the allocation of resources to a range of activities as well as determining the tasks and responsibilities which individuals, both centrally and locally, must carry out. For example, the global nature of the IKEA offering means that much promotional activity must be co-ordinated centrally.

Financial implications/budgets – these include a breakdown of costs, estimates of sales and revenues and discussion of the expected return on investment of implementing the marketing plan.

Operational implications and implementation – here any operational considerations associated with implementing the plan are reviewed. Measures of performance and ways of evaluating whether goals and objectives have been achieved are put in place. IKEA is likely to set these performance measures centrally and on a store-by-store basis. This will help identify under performing areas.

Appendices – these provide any supplementary information which may support the arguments presented in the plan and help those preparing, reading and using it. For example, IKEA might include detailed sales figures for the last few years, which help marketers determine likely trends and make forecasts.

Useful tips

It is not possible to outline a definitive answer for case questions of this type. Different answers will tend to place greater emphasis on certain areas. However, the answer should be carefully organized around the relevant marketing plan sections and must apply some of the case material.

Unit 12 International marketing

Objectives

In this unit you will:

- ❑ Understand the key factors that distinguish international marketing.
- ❑ Identify the international marketer's task.
- ❑ Examine the effect of the emergence of major trading blocks and the moves towards the expansion of international trade.
- ❑ Appreciate that international marketing is fast becoming intercultural marketing.

By the end of this unit you will be able to:

- ❑ Apply marketing methodologies internationally.
- ❑ Appreciate and cope with the limitations on international marketing research.
- ❑ Use key international terminology.
- ❑ Adapt the marketing mix to international requirements.

Study Guide

Throughout this workbook you have constantly been reminded of the need to read widely so as to keep up with the current marketplace, and provide yourself with individual examples to illustrate your examination answers.

This need is even more important where, by definition, you must know about markets other than your own. You must use your experiences of foreign travel, share experiences with others from around the world, watch foreign television, listen to foreign radio stations.

It is of major importance actively to seek an understanding of other cultures since much of international marketing is actually intercultural marketing, as we shall see.

Most countries now have a substantial number of immigrants and these tend to hold on to their home culture at least for a few generations. Visit ethnic events, shop in ethnic markets and retail shops and open your perceptions to the fact that others manage perfectly well without necessarily conforming to your traditional expectations and preferred ways. In short, try to identify and understand how other lifestyles operate. In time, perhaps, you will also understand why they are different.

You should allow three hours to work through this unit but note that you will need a lifetime of interactive exposure to other cultures to begin to understand them. The activities in this unit can be taken superficially, or you can begin on a road that has no end but is a fascinating journey.

The Unit Activity is a scenario which you should tackle under strict examination conditions. It is your last chance to practise before you tackle Unit 13's full mock examination.

It is probably now time for you to begin the run-in to the examination. Your time as a student is very nearly over, and your active revision and exam preparation will soon begin in earnest.

Obviously revision is extremely important and it needs to be managed very carefully. But there are other things which need your attention. You have to make certain that you are enrolled for the examination, for instance, and that you will be directed to the exam centre that you will prefer.

You need actively to manage every stage of the process. In marketing one must never assume: always check. Always be positive. If something is not right, or you are not sure then check it out. Always be courteous, of course. But know what you need before you aim to achieve it and you will most often succeed.

It would be a good idea to now turn to Unit 13 and confirm that you are organizationally and intellectually prepared.

International or intercultural?

An underpinning concept of international marketing is that organizations trade between nation states. Would that it was so simple!

Nation states are themselves each composed of a variety of potentially disparate elements: some willingly within the nation; others forced for one reason or another to remain a part of the nation; others using peaceful and/or violent means to obtain their independence.

We must regard the nature of international marketing as having at least two key levels:

- Trading across frontiers established by national governments.
- Trading across boundaries established by cultural heritage.

It is far easier to trade across national frontiers where laws are established than across cultural boundaries where human expectation and behaviour establishes the parameters that must be identified and satisfied. Today almost every organization is trading multiculturally, even if not internationally.

Some, of course, elect to trade within their own cultures, making no provision for the needs of others; the major supermarket chains in the UK do not cater for the needs of the Chinese, Indian, Pakistani and West Indian cultures, nor for such as the orthodox Jews whose culture is based on religion. These segments exist, have special needs, and are targeted by specialist retailers.

At the same time we must recognize that cultures are changing under the influence of modern communications and the ability of individuals to travel more freely and easily than ever before.

Communications know nothing of nation state boundaries and the accidental over-spill of previous years is fast turning into a deliberate marketing communications strategy to address a range of national and cultural areas at the same time.

- Shell have introduced the first European motor oil, Helix. This is marketed throughout the European Union under the same positioning statement and in the same packaging (with only minor variations allowed if there is a proven local need).
- Major brands such as Ariel and Mars now promote across the EU, following Coca-Cola's lead. With the established soap powder message of two housewives comparing laundry, with one changing brands to achieve better results, the spoken language is not important. Thus Ariel's German language TV advertising works just as effectively in Holland, France, the UK, Spain, Greece, etc.

- The widespread use of domestic appliances as seen on imported TV programmes and in pan-European advertising has accelerated their acceptance in France where electric kettles are beginning to replace the traditional use of saucepans to boil water.

Activity 12.1

Regionalization

The trend to regionalization is occurring at the same time as national governments are establishing multinational trading blocks such as the European Union. Global corporations are growing bigger and more powerful, with many having larger budgets than the smaller nations.

Establish an on-going programme of critical review so that you are actively aware of what is happening at the three levels of region/nation; nation/trading block; global organization/nation/region.

(**See:** Debriefing at the end of the unit.)

Theodore Levitt, marketing guru from Harvard Business School, says that different cultural preferences, national tastes and standards, and business institutions are vestiges of the past. Some die gradually, others prosper and expand into mainstream global preferences – Chinese food, pitta bread, pizza, Country and Western music are good examples.

Levitt goes on to show that many of today's differences among nations are because multinational corporations believe that there are fixed local preferences and so accommodate them. Marketing should not, Levitt argues, give the customer what he says he wants. They should find out and deliver what the customer would like.

He does not argue that national preferences should be ignored, simply that ways of doing it better should not be ignored.

Extending Your Knowledge

Coca-Cola is often quoted as the archetypal global company. Probably it is. But it started out by making sure that it built up a local infrastructure and understood local demand. In Japan, for example, the long-established preference was for *saida*, a carbonated lemon drink. Coke, to become the market leader, had to push as well as pull its product through the channels of distribution.

Its standard policy is to become an 'insider'; to work from within a market rather than to predetermined policies established outside. It also takes the long view and doesn't push for early returns.

Coke is now a universally desired brand that can be found anywhere in the world. It is a truly global organization, but it didn't start out that way.

Regional trading groups

Powerful moves towards regional trading groups have resulted in the world dividing into associations of nation states that have come together for mutual support. The major regional groupings are:

Europe

EU

The European Union (EU) was formed from the countries of the European Community on 1 January 1994 following the ratification of the Maastricht Treaty by the EU's twelve member governments. On 1 January 1995 three other countries joined, with the people of Norway rejecting membership in a closely fought referendum.

With some 350 million inhabitants in 15 advancing economies the EU is a powerful force in world trade and rivals the US market for size if not homogeneity. It is expected that membership will remain at 15 until agreement is reached that selected Eastern European and Mediterranean countries can join. Iceland seems determined to stay independent because she has only the one export – fish – and that is in secure demand.

The 15 member states are:

Austria	Germany	Netherlands
Belgium	Greece	Portugal
Denmark	Ireland	Spain
Finland	Italy	Sweden
France	Luxembourg	United Kingdom

EFTA

The European Free Trade Association (EFTA) was established in 1960. It now comprises Iceland, Liechtenstein, Norway and Switzerland. Six other countries were members, but have left to join the EU. They are: Austria, Denmark, Finland, Portugal, Sweden and the United Kingdom.

Asia

ASEAN

The Association of South East countries (ASEAN) was formed in 1967. Founding members were Indonesia, Malaysia, the Philippines, Singapore and Thailand. Brunei and Vietnam joined in 1984 and 1995 respectively. Laos and Myanmar joined in 1997. Cambodia has observer status.

The Asian Free Trade Area (AFTA) is to be implemented by 2003, with Vietnam to join by 2006. A common preferential tariff was introduced in 1993.

APEC

Asia Pacific Economic Co-operation (APEC) currently comprises 18 nations and will cover the area 'from New York to Bangkok and Chile to China'. Developed nations plan to have the free trade area open by 2000, with the developing countries joining by 2010.

The Americas

There are many initiatives in this area of the world and it seems likely that a pan-American trading block will emerge in due course. The major entities are:

ALADI

The Association Latinamericana de Integracion (ALADI) is an association of 11 Mid- and South-American countries.

ANDEAN

The Andean Group has membership from Venezuala, Colombia, Ecuador, Paraguay and Uruguay.

CACM

The Central American Common Market comprises the five countries of Guatemala, Honduras, El Salvador, Nicaragua and Costa Rica.

CARICOM

The Caribbean Community has 14 member nations, with others associated.

FTAA

The Free Trade Association of the Americas is planned to form in 2005. The intention to proceed was anounced by the US President, Bill Clinton, at a summit of leaders of the area's countries (except Cuba) on 10 December 1994.

MERCOSUR

A collaboration between Brazil, Argentina, Paraguay and Uruguay.

USFTA

The United States Free Trade Association (USFTA) is an association of Canada, the USA and Mexico to form a trading block larger than Europe. Mainly English speaking, it is a vast market: rich in raw materials to the north; production- and marketing-oriented in the centre; and with a population surplus, and therefore cheap labour, in the south. Canada and the US have the largest and most successful trading relationship in the world. Canada is worried that firms may be tempted to leave their northern climate and head off to Mexico where it is far warmer and labour is cheap. Chile hopes to join.

Africa

COMESA

The Common Market for Eastern and South Africa is in the process of development. Twenty-two nations are in membership.

OAU

The Organization of African Unity has 52 members and aims for Afric-wide economic unity by the year 2000.

The Middle East

Gulf Co-operation Council

Comprises the six countries of the Persian Gulf.

International institutions and agreements

The two conflicting pressures of the need to protect and develop the home market and home suppliers whilst trading overseas results in a dilemma which it has taken consistent and long-term effort to begin to resolve. Whilst statesmen have long seen the need for global trade, politicians have found it difficult to secure the necessary short-term support of their electorates to bring about the necessary changes.

GATT

The General Agreement of Tariffs and Trade (GATT) is a multinational initiative to reduce national tariff barriers and expand the volume of international trade. It was formed in 1947 to 'reduce discrimination, settle disputes and simplify procedures' in international trade. There are now 115 trading nations in membership.

A series of international conferences, called 'rounds' has been held and tariff reductions that range from 5 to 40 per cent agreed. The volume of international trade has increased twenty-fold since GATT was formed.

The 'Kennedy' round (1972) reduced tariffs, by an average of 35 per cent, on 60 000 commodities valued at $40 billion.

The 'Tokyo' rounds (1973 and 1978) were targeted on the liberalization of world trade. Some liberalization did take place but overall the outcome was disappointing since it proved difficult to reconcile different styles of government and types of economy.

The 'Uruguay' round (1986 to 1994) saw major achievements within the concept of freeing trade. The major stumbling blocks were between the US and the EU. The Americans wanted a reduction in European farm subsidies. The French wanted to protect the 5 per cent of their population who are small farmers. There was also concern to protect the

European film and video industry. Eventually aircraft, films and videos and financial services were put aside for further negotiation and a compromise reached. The GATT protocol was ratified, crucially, by the US Senate only days before the end of 1994.

It is expected that an increase in world trade of some $150 billion will result in an extra 400 000 jobs created in the EU.

GATT principles are summarized by Chee and Harris:

- Member nations adhere to the Most Favoured Nation (MFN) rule, trusting others without discrimination or trade restrictions.
- Members must eliminate tariffs and quotas between nations.
- Preferential treatment must be given to developing nations.
- When disagreements arise, member nations must negotiate a settlement.

OECD

The Organization for Economic Co-operation and Development (OECD) has the 24 leading industrial nations as members. It is a consultative organization which also provides significant statistical information and economic reports to member nations.

The World Bank

The International Bank for Reconstruction and Development has become known as the World Bank. It exists as an intermediary to advise and influence governments. Through its member countries it provides capital on favourable terms to assist in economic reconstruction. If assistance is required its advice tends to become mandatory, especially if the economic failure is a result of internal mismanagement.

IMF

The International Monetary Fund (IMF) is a forum for international negotiation with a focus on currency stabilization. The ability of today's money markets to influence national governments, as evidenced by the attack on the weaker EU currencies in the autumn of 1992, has somewhat eroded the influence of the IMF. Within the EU there is fierce debate about the need for a single currency and a Central Bank is established in Frankfurt to take on the role of currency stabilization.

Time – not distance

The introduction of the jet aircraft has changed the concept of distance. Places that were 'far away' are now in cost-effective reach and the six-week journey from the UK to Australia is now possible in under 24 hours. With supersonic passenger aircraft it could be done in half that time.

It is practical to cross the Atlantic, have a meeting and return the same day. Airports and railway stations are opening conference suites and providing for the needs of the business person on the move: showers, lounges, fax, phone and office back-up. Airlines are beginning to install workstations into aircraft seats. Soon it will be possible to be in close contact wherever one is and whenever one wants.

The benefits have reached ordinary people as well. Holidays are regularly offered in the Spanish islands or Greece for less than £100 for a week from London and that includes the return flight, a hotel and breakfast each day!

People are beginning to establish new routines. Working at home is made possible by communication links to the office; living further away from work is possible because of easier commuting and open frontiers.

Nothing need now be out of season; it always can be available, at a price.

Overseas experiences

This is another activity which you will need to complete over time but you can make an immediate start.

We are born and brought up in a society, exposed to certain cultural values, and come to rely upon what we know we can expect, what we know will work, what we must avoid. This is perfectly natural and is well expressed by the Jesuits who are quoted as saying 'Give us a child until he is seven and he will be ours for life'.

Given that culture has such a major part to play in the formation of our attitudes and that governments have a vested interest in encouraging national pride, it is not surprising that the great majority of people look with some distrust at new things and new ideas, especially those from outside the culture they know and in which they feel safe.

You need to discover how much of this national pride you have and whether it is helping or handicapping you.

The first step is to take an audit of your belongings, especially of things you have bought personally. For each major item identify your buying process. How influenced were you by cultural and national factors. Don't say that you were not affected because you will have been at some level.

The next and on-going stages are to identify your overall and specific attitudes by monitoring your reactions to events, news items, sports results, products, etc. Only after identification will you be able to decide whether you want (or need) to start a process of change.

This activity will, importantly, provide you with useful examples to quote in both the Marketing Operations and Strategic International Marketing examinations as well as helping you to develop a more rounded approach to this ever more international of worlds.

Air freight costs are affordable, especially as the weight of products is declining through miniaturization and the use of plastics. This is opening up more opportunities for the fast supply of goods thereby reducing the logistical problems of ships and shipping, and reducing the amount of stock (capital) tied up for weeks on ship.

Products are becoming standardized (and branded), with localized specialist manufacture for components that are then shipped to central assembly points. Ford claim to have introduced the first 'World Car': the Ford Escort which was essentially the same wherever it was marketed. All major manufacturers now routinely market their models globally.

A problem, likely to be with us for a long time, is that whilst people can physically journey to foreign parts they are less able to make the cultural changes necessary to accept and be accepted by the natives. This can be as minor as a need for unsalted butter at breakfast or as major as a need for clinical level efficiency.

Note: It is very easy and very dangerous to stereotype – not all of one nation are efficient, not all demand a certain diet. Be very careful if using examples to either prove or qualify them. It is a short step from stereotyping to racism and unconscious racism is the worst form.

Domestic to global

The classic stages through which many organizations pass are shown in Figure 12.1.

Overseas selling

An introduction to international marketing can come from occasional and unsolicited orders that are received from overseas. These can be filled and

Figure 12.1
Domestic to global

forgotten, or provide the trigger to initiate a more active interest in trading outside the domestic economy.

Exporting

Active exporting requires an understanding that foreign markets exist and that they can and should be targeted. Sales are attempted across national boundaries but exporting is secondary to the domestic strategies.

In time, as the potential becomes apparent, an organization can become a committed exporter, and export strategies are seen to be as important as domestic ones.

International marketing

Markets are identified at home and overseas and international marketing is an integral part of marketing strategy. Divisions and/or subsidiaries may be established to serve markets more effectively.

Multinational marketing

Multinational generally denotes an organization with significant operations and market interests outside its home country. At strategic level there are two types of multinationals: Multidomestic and Global.

Multidomestic organizations pursue separate strategies in each of their foreign markets while viewing the competitive challenge independently from market to market. Each overseas subsidiary is strategically independent leaving the multinational headquarters to co-ordinate financial controls and marketing policies worldwide. R&D may be centralized but strategy and operations are decentralized with each subsidiary a profit centre. Proctor & Gamble is a typical example of a multinational.

Global marketing. The true global marketing organization is stateless. It exists to serve a range of markets and will establish itself and its subsidiaries in the most efficient and effective locations. It will make decisions primarily with regard to global ambitions without taking national interests into account.

Individual country subsidiaries are highly interdependent in terms both of strategy and operations. Country profit targets vary with the individual impact on the cost position or the effectiveness of the worldwide system. An organization may establish policy in one country to have an effect on the market position in another country. General Electric and Siemens are examples of global companies.

Note: that as an organization becomes more international so the role of marketing changes from a centrally controlled to a decentralized activity. Whilst corporate marketing strategy will be set centrally it is inevitable that local needs will dictate local marketing strategies and operations. Professor

Michael Porter refers to marketing as a *Downstream* activity, along with service and outbound logistics. Inbound logistics and Operations he sees as *Upstream* activities.

Downstream activities are usually inherently tied to the country in which the buyer is located. Upstream activities may be carried out anywhere in the world.

Legal and organizational formats

Participation in international markets, once an organization has passed beyond the overseas selling stage, can be by a variety of routes. The most important are:

- *Exporting*

  Sales are through distributors or importers probably under a form of agency agreement. (See page 286.)

  Investment is minimized, as is fixed-cost commitment.

  Agency agreements must be carefully drawn up to ensure they are fair to both, that there are escape clauses, and that the agent is motivated to work hard on behalf of the exporter.

  Exporting is often the route to international expansion, which makes it doubly important to secure agency contracts that allow the organization to take control of the overseas market when the time is right.

- *Licensing and franchising*

  Patents and technical expertise can be exploited by licensing their use to others. In some markets it may be the only way to participate, in others it may be the chosen way, especially if heavy capital investment is needed.

  Commitment is limited but so is control.

- *Joint ventures*

  Co-ownership with a local partner can be highly advantageous. Your technical expertise is matched by his local knowledge and contacts. This is the only possible route into some countries and in many will reduce political risks.

  The local partner will realize the power he has and may attempt to exert it unfairly. There is little that can be done in these circumstances and it is therefore crucial to select partners with care. The more so if confidential and/or patented information has to be made available.

- *Strategic alliances*

  Organizations can agree to co-operate on a specific project for mutual benefit. Risks and costs are shared but the objectives of the partners may differ. If specialized knowledge has to be shared the short-term benefit may be outweighed by the long-term damage caused by loss of trade secrets.

- *Wholly owned subsidiary*

  This is the stage of maximum commitment to the market. Maximum control is held by the parent – but there is a danger that the local Chief Executive may be second-guessed by corporate management who do not know the market.

  Market entry may be by establishing a new venture, or by acquisition.

Note that it is possible to export from any market in which you have a presence. Thus it may be possible to access a market from a subsidiary when it is not accessible from the home country.

Agents

Specialist agencies will be found across the world. Some are traders, others provide support services such as research, advertising, etc. The principles of agency selection are identical to those adopted in the home market, with the proviso that it is necessary to visit and thoroughly understand the market in which your agency will operate. It is dangerous in the extreme to appoint overseas agents without the most rigorous checking and double-checking; actively seek out personal recommendations in addition to checking credit rating, legal status, etc.

The main types of trading agents are:

- *Commission agents*

  They do not hold stock but actively sell for you and pass the orders on for fulfilment.

- *Stocking agents*

  Stocks are carried and deliveries made to fulfil the orders they take.

- *Spares and servicing*

  Hold stocks of spares and provide manufacturer approved repair and after-sales service.

Agency agreements should be formalized in writing and contain, as a minimum:

- The legal code that applies.
- The detail of the agreement: purpose, products, territories, responsibilities.
- Exclusivity (within any legal requirement that may be in force regarding restraint of trade).
- Responsibilities and payment: stock holdings, commission rates, terms of trade and of delivery.
- Duration of contract and termination terms.

Organizing for international marketing

We examined organization in Unit 3 and the key principles covered there can easily be extended to the needs of the international organization. Key terms used to describe international organization will be useful, however. They are:

- *Ethnocentric* – this describes an organization where the emphasis is on the domestic country. Where international marketing is secondary to home marketing.

- *Geocentric* – a geocentric organization applies 'single market' mix strategies worldwide.
- *Polycentric* – when an organization adopts an orientation which is specific to each host country and market.
- *Regiocentric* – similar to geocentric but the organization applies 'single market' mix strategies to specific regions rather than across the board.

Trading overseas

A key requirement that is sometimes taken for granted is the need to secure payment and/or to extract profits from the overseas country. Unless this can be guaranteed there is no point in going forward.

On occasion it proves necessary to barter rather than sell and the practice of countertrade became established in the dark days of the cold war when it was almost the only way to trade with Warsaw Pact countries. Some countertrade deals became complex, with grain from one country bartered for wine from another so that electrical goods could be shipped from the third.

The *Export Credits Guarantee Department (ECGD)* is a Government department which will provide guarantees to banks on behalf of exporters so that banks will be prepared to lend money to exporters or their overseas customers. It also provides guarantees to banks that provide bonds on behalf of exporters.

Until 1991 it sold 'credit insurance' to exporters to cover them against the risk of non-payment by overseas buyers. This activity has now transferred to a private insurance house although the government has said it will continue to act as insurer of last resort for short-term political risk.

Factoring is a method of releasing working capital quickly by selling trade debts for immediate cash to a factor who charges commission. Most factors offer three services from which one can choose:

- An accounting, credit-checking and debt collection service.
- Credit insurance against bad debts.
- Immediate cash against invoices. Usually of 75 to 85 per cent immediately with the balance, less the commission, which follows later. This service normally requires the organization to take out credit insurance.

Exchange rates
Often holding the key to profit or loss, the management of foreign exchange is crucial to success in overseas trading. In price negotiations it is important not only to agree a price for the contract, but also to agree the currency in which settlement is to be made.

All rates of exchange move as dictated by the money markets of the world, which are operating 24 hours a day, every day of the year. Businessmen are subject to the variations in money rates and yet can do nothing to control them. To some extent, therefore, one is gambling when negotiating a contract which will be paid for at some time in the future. The buyer and seller both hope that his currency will appreciate in value against the other.

Large organizations maintain a Treasury Department specifically to work in the money market. Primarily this is so that their foreign exchange risk becomes as much of a managed risk as possible but it is also to ensure that their working capital, especially cash flow, is put to good use earning maximum interest rather than being allowed to sit in a low yielding account.

Exchange rates

Complete the following matrix to determine the difference it makes to both parties to a contract worth £100 000, or FFr 850 000, when the exchange rate changes.

Rate of exchange	Contract £	Paid in francs FFr	Contract FFr	Paid in sterling £
8.50	100 000.00	850 000.00	85 000.00	100 000.00
8.45		845 000.00		100 591.72
8.40		840 000.00		101 190.48
8.35		835 000.00		101 796.41
8.30		830 000.00		102 409.64
8.25		825 000.00		103 030.30
8.20		820 000.00		103 658.54
8.15		815 000.00		104 294.48
8.10		810 000.00		104 938.27
8.05		805 000.00		105 590.06
8.00		800 000.00		106 250.00
7.95		795 000.00		106 918.24
7.90		790 000.00		107 594.94
7.85		785 000.00		107 280.25
7.80		780 000.00		107 974.36
7.75		775 000.00		109 677.42

(**See:** Debriefing at the end of the unit.)

Multinational organizations probably make as much profit from the money markets as they do from their trading operations.

Treasury Managers (or Finance Directors in the absence of a specialized Treasury section) have to determine the best way to provide for the foreign exchange needs of their organization. The straightforward way to handle foreign exchange is to buy sufficient funds in advance (buying forward) to meet the contracted needs. Thus the French buyer may purchase £100 000 in sterling at the time of contract. He will pay FFr 850 000 but not risk the exchange rate moving against him. In our example the rate moved in his favour and so he can be said to have lost FFr 75 000 on the deal. (Actually he will have paid FFr 75 000 more than he needed to.)

An alternative policy is to buy the foreign currency needed at the time the payment falls due. If this 'swings and roundabouts' policy is followed whilst the currencies are moving around a comparatively fixed point it may well be a viable option. But if one currency is weaker than the other it may be an unwise policy for the manager working in the weaker currency to follow.

Finally it is, of course, possible to evaluate the money market and attempt to manage the risk by taking currency decisions in the light of the best information available. Unfortunately money market fluctuations are impossible to predict with any degree of certainty and even the best informed and most experienced managers cannot guarantee success.

Using a third currency as the price determinant is a common option in international trade. The contract is then agreed in a currency selected for its stability. Each party to the contract then is concerned only with changes in the rate of their currency against the contracted currency. The same need to determine whether to buy forward applies but this policy does, to some extent, moderate the exchange rate volatility that is experienced by some of the weaker currencies.

Transfer pricing

In multinational and global organizations where goods are shipped around the world it is possible to invoice through a third country.

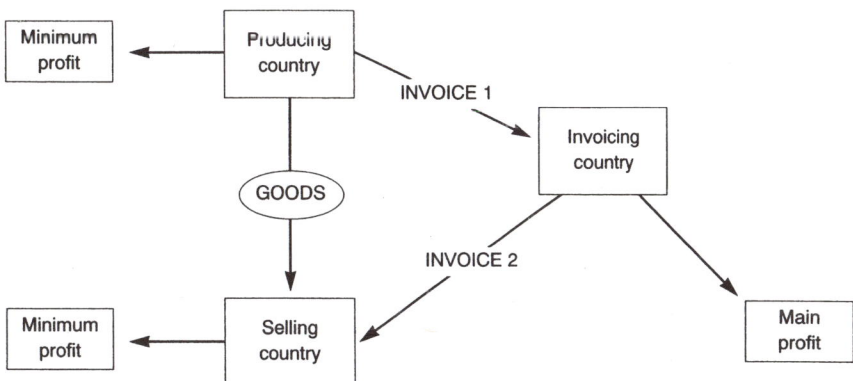

Figure 12.2
Transfer pricing

The goods can be shipped direct but the producing country invoices a trading company established in a tax haven. The trading company never sees the goods but invoices them to the buying organization. Thus maximum profits can be extracted where taxation is lowest.

Governments naturally frown on this practice and so it is necessary to set transfer prices at the minimum profits acceptable to the governments in the producing and buying country.

Marketing internationally

It is very helpful to treat international marketing as simply another form of marketing. As a development of the overall marketing concept. International marketing simply requires the tools from the marketer's toolbox to be used in an international context.

In the same way that a carpenter can use a saw to cut wood for a table top, door frame or garden fence, so a marketer can use his tools in an industrial, services, consumer, not-for-profit or international context. At base there is no difference in the tools used, nor in their purpose.

Understanding this basic truth greatly simplifies the marketer's task because it demystifies what is often treated as an esoteric subject that requires unique and highly expert treatment.

The marketer's toolbox contains, as we know, nine key divisions: nine classifications of tool. They are the 7P/Cs held together by Planning and supported by Marketing Research.

International marketing mixes differ from the mixes used in other forms of marketing – but in detail, not purpose. It is thus relatively simple to understand the needs of the international marketer, even though the factors involved – such as language, distance, market and buyer sophistication – present specialized problems and opportunities.

A major problem for many organizations is to cope with the need for actual market presence and for detailed market understanding. Inter-

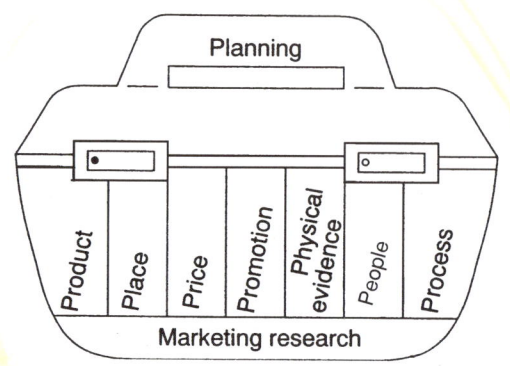

Figure 12.3
Marketing toolbox

national marketing requires hands-on contact; it cannot be done from a distance. And it is necessary to understand thoroughly foreign customs and laws before taking any decisions. It does not follow that custom should be followed but 'doing it better' must be perceived from the perspective of the foreign market.

Those from overseas fall into the common trap of superficial judgement. In hot countries a very early start and a late finish are almost mandatory, yet a person from a cooler climate often sees only the long midday siesta. It can comes as a major culture shock to have a service engineer call at 7.30 pm and work through until the job is finished. But he will have had a long break over the heat of the day.

But it is the more subtle cultural habits and expectations which can be the undoing of the marketer from elsewhere. These take time to identify, yet can be crucial to success.

Activity 12.4

Cultural habits and expectations
Imagine that you have to meet with a marketer from another country who wants you to be his agent. Note some of the key factors that are different in your country which it is important for him to appreciate.

(**See:** Debriefing at the end of the unit.)

Planning

The need for marketing to be a part of strategic management and to contribute to corporate planning is never more evident than in an international context. Management decisions are of major importance to market success and marketing should be heavily involved with this process.

Unfortunately in many organizations, especially those just starting on the export/international route, marketing planning – if carried out at all – is tactical and operational, very seldom strategic.

To be a successful international organization requires full commitment from top management. The mission has to change and with it corporate policies and strategies. Trying to operate in an international area with a set of domestic priorities is a recipe for disaster.

International marketing planning is no different in principle from any other form of planning. Exactly the same needs must be satisfied, exactly the same ground must be covered. The differences lie in the specialist skills needed (especially of language and cultural understanding) and the problems associated with management at a distance. The differences in domestic and international planning are shown in Figure 12.4.

	Domestic planning	International planning
Language	Single language and nationality. Trend to more than one culture.	Multilingual/multinational/multicultural.
Market	Relatively homogeneous.	Fragmented and diverse.
Data availability	Usually available, accurate and easily collected.	Often difficult to secure, and with doubtful accuracy and reliability.
Political factors	Relatively unimportant.	Frequently vital.
Government interference	Governments usually relatively passive.	Governments often actively seek to influence business decisions.
Environmental effect	Individual corporation usually has little effect.	Large corporations can have major effect(s).
Chauvinism	Often helps.	Usually hinders.
Business environment	Relatively stable.	Multiple environments, many of which are unstable (but may be highly profitable).
Financial climate	Uniform.	Various – and many unstable.
Currency	Single currency.	Currencies differ in stability and real value.
Business 'rules'	Mature, understood and usually complied with.	Diverse. Often changeable and unclear.
Management	Generally shares responsibilities and uses financial controls	Frequently autonomous and not familiar with budget and controls.

Figure 12.4
Domestic and international planning. (Source: Paliwoda. *International Marketing*. Taken by him from Cain, *International Planning, Mission Impossible?*)

Marketing research

Research is needed exactly as for the home market. Exactly the same information needs exist and an environmental audit using STEEPLE is mandatory.

The procedure for researching overseas is identical to that for the home market. What is actually researched, and the research priorities, will change but no more than if a consumer durable firm considers entering an industrial marketplace.

Market opportunities must be assessed so that priorities can be established; again this is no different in principle to any other form of segmentation prioritization.

The major differences occur in operational areas.

Information sources
- *People*
  As in all marketing a major source is the organization's people in contact with the market and the environment. Properly encouraged and briefed the personnel in the market can provide a flow of key information and – most importantly – help to indicate the degree of relevance.
  Those in the channel(s) of distribution, potential target consumers and competitors are all valuable sources.
- *Published*
  A considerable amount of information is likely to be available but for the less developed markets this is likely to be generalized rather than

specific. Its relevance and reliability must be questioned far more rigorously than similar data originating in a Western country.

Government statistics will probably be available – but how reliable they are for each country must be a matter of judgement. In many cases it is simply impossible for a government to conduct a complete census, and trade figures – if available – are likely to be only as reliable as the firms submitting them want them to be, given their overriding need to cope with taxation and other financial regulations.

International sources include the:

- UN, EU, IMF and the OECD.
- Department of Trade and Industry.
- Embassies and Consulates in the target market.
- Bank of England and the major UK banks' information services.
- Economist Intelligence Unit.
- Major Trade Associations and Chambers of Commerce in the home and target countries.
- Trade Directories such as Kompass and Dunn & Bradstreet.
- Confederation of British Industries.
- Syndicated research and abstract services such as Mintel and ANBAR.
- Broadsheet and trade press when they run specialist reports on countries and/or regions.

● *Personal*

Personal research requires direct observation and specialist knowledge. It may be carried through by the marketer himself or, more usually, by a range of trusted individuals.

It is essential that the research objectives are clearly defined and that as much secondary research is carried through prior to undertaking primary research in the market. The dangers of duplication and omission must be guarded against since it is unlikely that one can easily revisit the market in the short term.

Activity 12.5	*Personal research*

In conjunction with your on-going personal investigation you will find it valuable to discover how others react to 'overseas'. What is their level of understanding?

Devise a questionnaire – you will find that you will have to be very basic in your expectations – and pilot it with a couple of close friends.

Hint: You will discover what you need to enquire about from introducing 'overseas' topics into conversations. Prejudice and stereotyping will show up and you can then structure your research around areas where you know you will get a useful response.

If you decide to extend this activity you will have a firm basis from which to develop into more sophisticated levels of understanding – but it is anticipated that most of those you question will have limited understanding, at best. Imagine the problems this causes to the international marketer!

(**See:** Debriefing at the end of the unit.)

Research agencies exist in most countries but it is an error to expect them to be as efficient and effective as in developed countries. Partly this will be because of the limited number of trained personnel, which affects research through planning to sampling to analysis. Partly it will be because of the difficulty in accessing respondents.

The cultural factors will also play their part. Some questions just cannot be asked in some countries, in others key consumers cannot be reached. Language usage varies, as does the purpose and importance. For example, bicycles are transportation in many countries, recreational in others. Safety regulations are welcomed and abided by in some countries, resisted and avoided in others.

Therefore even if an agency can produce data, it may not generate information that is usable, especially where an intention is to use the information as part of a cross-market comparison exercise. Trying to measure like against like can be virtually impossible.

Key questions that must be asked of international research include:

- Who collected the data?
- Were the facts within the data misrepresented? Deliberately? Accidentally?
- Why was the data collected? (In other words, is it reliable for my purpose?)
- When was the data collected? (In other words, is it current?)
- How was the data collected? (In other words, was the survey method statistically valid?)
- How was the data processed? (In other words, can it be relied upon as being accurate?)
- Is the data consistent? (In other words, can it be validated from other sources? Does it provide what I expected and need?)

Agencies that are resident in the country should know their market and the better ones will know and admit their strengths and limitations. A foreign agency with a domestic subsidiary or associate will attempt to apply home office standards, whether they will succeed depends upon a variety of factors and their claims should be thoroughly checked. Foreign agencies sending staff into a market will only be effective if the staff are thoroughly conversant with the market to the level of colloquial language and cultural understanding.

Research is possibly the major problem area for the organization wanting to trade overseas but it is vital to secure the needed facts before taking decisions that will involve the organization in a major long-term commitment. Far better to take the time and devote the effort to get it right, than to rush ahead over-enthusiastically.

Extending Your Knowledge

Fraud risks

ORGANISED criminal gangs and ex-KGB operatives play a major role in the econo- mies of eastern Europe, according to John Conyng- ham, of Control Risks Group, yet half of British businessmen are not aware of the problems.

According to Opinion Research Bureau, the big- gest problem in eastern Europe was perceived as government regulations, specified by 54pc of com- panies in the survey. After that came integrity of part- ners with 51pc, closely fol- lowed by legal issues at 49pc.

It may be the lower level of alarm about getting involved with someone unsavoury in eastern Europe that prompted 62pc of the businessmen to say the problems are unlikely to deter them from doing busi- ness in the area.

The most important pre- caution before going in is to carry out business and mar- ket research, said a third of the businesses questioned. Mr Conyngham thought the business-men underrated the problems of fraud and extortion in eastern Europe. But opportunities probably outweigh the risks.

From the *Daily Telegraph* of 23 January, 1995. © The Telegraph plc, London, 1995.

Product

When simply selling – not attempting to market overseas – the same home market product will usually suffice. There will probably be need for minor changes, such as to an electrical plug, and there will be need for instructions to be translated. When dumping products (at below cost to clear, or for strategic reasons) there is no long-term interest and so little need for product planning.

It is when an organization begins to take international marketing seriously that careful planning of each of the 7Ps becomes mandatory.

As with the domestic market a product has to comply with the legal requirements of the market into which it is to be sold. Nothing unusual in that, but there is a definite need to find out and keep on top of the requirements in each market. If it needs after-sales service that must be provided; it is surprising that many EU wide firms still confine their guarantees to the country of purchase even though the EU is one – big – domestic market and they sell and have after-market support in place throughout.

There are three broad strategies that can be adopted:

- Sell unmodified/standardized products throughout.
- Modify and/or adapt products where necessary.
- Develop products specifically for markets or groups of markets.

The first strategy is unlikely to be successful for many organizations. It allows for little if any differentiation to meet actual market needs. If the P of Promotion is expected to create all the differentiation it is asking too much of even this powerful marketing tool.

Modification and/or adaption can be a viable strategy, providing that it does not become too unwieldy and/or too costly as the number of product adaptions multiplies and the logistical problems of stock control and distribution increase.

Developing products especially for overseas markets is the only long-term strategy that is viable for most organizations. Providing that there is clear purpose, based on the best research evidence, the market requirements can be designed into the product just as quality must be designed in from the first concept.

Universal product: can there be one?

Is it possible to produce a universal product? One that will sell, unmodified, across the world? The evidence of Pepsi and Coke seems to show that it is possible, but remember that these are essentially simple products.

Every product has physical presence, function and symbolic value; it is a combination of these features that customers buy and consumers use. We know that cultural values are still very localized and more complex and important products have to meet the needs of the target segments.

Nissan is typical of a company that has developed a successful global product strategy. Instead of producing a 'global car' it has identified the key needs of the three major markets: the USA, Europe and Japan. It then produces carefully engineered 'lead-country' models which are carefully tailored to their target market segments. Only then do they ask their top managers elsewhere whether minor changes can make any lead model suitable for local sales.

This form of thinking halved the number of basic models they needed and, at the same time, allowed them to cover 80 per cent of their sales with cars designed for specific national markets. The balance of their sales is made up from additional model types adapted to the needs of local segments.

Brands across borders

There is a marketing truism which insists that if there is one product sector where cultural and national differences are more deeply ingrained than any other in terms of a single European market, it is what we eat and drink. To take a few examples:

- Breakfast in Mediterranean countries is typically coffee, while in northern Europe people are more likely to eat meat, cheese and/or cereals.
- Europeans in northern countries want confectionery fattier and sweeter than their counterparts in the south.
- Consumers in different countries view the description 'natural' in quite different ways – in the UK it means 'fresh' compared to 'eco-logically-sound' in Germany and Holland.

The supposed strength of these differences would seem to make it unlikely that food and drink companies would find it as easy to exploit pan-European branding economics of scale as, perhaps, their counterparts in cars or computers. And yet, within the past year or so, many food and drink companies operating in the European market have begun to focus more on finding what is common across borders than on being immobilised by what is not. The result has been a slow but steady increase in the number of brands travelling across borders – in some cases, with few changes to product formulation and/or packaging.

There are several key reasons for this. Firstly, the fact that the Single Market has officially arrived in name – despite being less than truly single in reality – has begun to focus corporate minds looking for lower costs through harmonisation of R&D, production and, where possible, marketing. This process has been accelerated by the trend to fewer but bigger food and drink groups on a Europe-wide scale. For example, the food market is becoming increasingly dominated by companies like Swiss-based Nestlé, French group BSN, Grand Metropolitan and Uni-lever, all of which have spent the last few years snapping up smaller and medium sized national businesses to get hold of their brands. Those acquisitions have given these large groups the incentive to audit their portfolios to see which brands can travel, which can be pruned and which can be developed and extended.

McVitie's, part of United Biscuits, is also making large inroads into harmonising its brand portfolio in Europe. With sales approaching £800 million, it is the second largest biscuit business in Europe, with a market share of about 11 per cent. Having operated traditionally in the Anglo-Saxon world and developing countries like China and Brazil, it decided to turn its attention to Europe. Since 1989, the group has become market leader in Denmark, Finland, Hungary and the Netherlands as well as the UK. It also has a partnership with market leaders Barilla in Italy and a strong position in France, Spain, Sweden and Norway.

McVitie's has had to analyse which of the brands in its diverse portfolio can cross borders, and which reflect local tastes. As managing director Hartwig Conzelmann explains, different countries show quite different eating habits of biscuits even when sharing borders. In Spain, for example, certain types of biscuits are eaten as a bread substitute for breakfast, a pattern which does not exist in northern Europe, while Portuguese habits are far closer to those of the UK. In France, children are given biscuits for school.

Nevertheless, McVitie's research has shown there are similarities, mainly fuelled by converging consumer trends such as a more cosmopolitan approach, demand for convenience food and a willingness to spend money on indulgence products. As Conzelmann points out, 'All over Europe, with very few exceptions, chocolate biscuits are growing faster than dry ones. Now this category might be only 10 per cent in one country and 80 per cent in another but it will be growing faster than other sectors. The same is true for snacking which has less to do with produce type than format and packaging. So our market is a hybrid one, with strong local habits but also unexploited similarities.'

Understanding the way the retail system works in the various countries is considered crucial to success. But the challenge facing food and drink makers, and an incentive to get into stronger European positions, is that there are signs that retailers in other European markets are beginning to emulate the UK and are establishing larger, more concentrated retail groupings. This is being further extended across borders: most notable has been the joint venture set up in 1990 by the UK's Argyll group (owners of Safeway), Ahold of Holland and Casino of France.

The advent of more powerful suppliers and distributors who operate across Europe thus makes the rise of the Eurobrand seem inevitable. AC Nielsen, the major market researcher, estimates there are about 50 'Europroducts', defined as one for sale in eight different European countries. It might not seem a lot, but as recently as 1983, no one product, not even Coca-Cola, was on the top 10 list in the four major European countries. Nielsen predicts there will be demand for strictly local products for a few years yet. But there is also a strong indication that, over time, our shopping baskets will begin to look a lot more alike wherever we are in Europe.

Laura Mazur is a freelance journalist and director of The Conference Board European Marketing Council.

Condensed from *Marketing Business* of October, 1993

Kenichi Ohmae, writing in the *Harvard Business Review* of May/June 1989, says that in high-school physics he learned about a phenomenon called diminishing primaries: 'Mix the primary colours (red, blue and yellow) and you get black. If Europe says its consumers want a car in green, let them have it. If Japan says red, let them have red. No one wants the average.

'When it comes to product strategy, managing in a borderless world doesn't mean managing by averages. It doesn't mean that all tastes run together into one amorphous mass of universal appeal. And it doesn't mean the appeal of managing globally removes the obligation to localize products. The lure of a universal product is a false allure. The truth is a bit more subtle.'

Place

Once again it is clear that decisions on distribution are identical in principle to those applying elsewhere in marketing. Again it is a difference of degree. But in this case, the degree of difference is quite substantial. We have established, earlier, that distribution is a specialized management activity. If this is so within a domestic market, it is obvious that the needs for specialist knowledge are more acute in an international marketplace.

Quite apart from the additional range of transportation opportunities to evaluate, there is the question of securing the necessary paperwork. Fortunately, as a marketer, you do not have to understand the complex paperwork needed to ensure safe passage of your goods, but you do have to understand the need for the correct documentation to be accurate down to the last comma and full stop.

You also have to understand the need to get the goods through the port of entry and into the country's distribution network. This is partly a matter of having the correct paperwork but it is also a question of having the goodwill of those who control the docks. If your container of frozen foods is to stay connected to the electricity an accommodation has to be reached with those who have physical control. You need a local person on the spot to take care of both official and unofficial procedures.

Paliwoda compares the alternatives open to an exporter and matches corporate objectives with the needs of channel members (see Figure 12.5).

The key issues of channel design, channel structure and the choice of exclusive, selective or intensive distribution are, as in all marketing, a matter

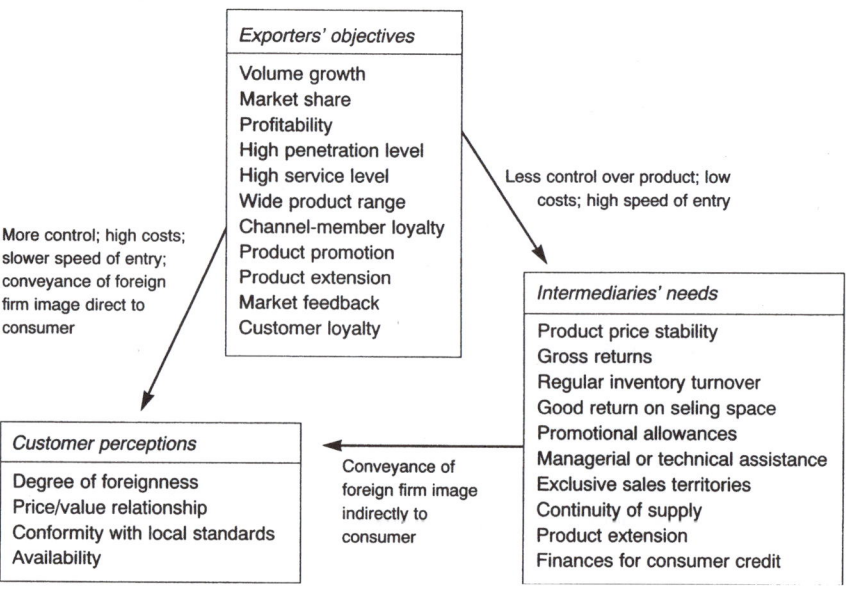

Figure 12.5
Foreign market distribution.
(Source: Paliwoda, *International Marketing*, Butterworth-Heinemann.)

for decisions based on marketing strategic objectives as determined by the market infrastructure, customer and consumer expectation and preference, and the needs of the after market. Whether to attempt to break new ground with a different form of distribution is a strategic decision that will have long-term effects.

The opportunity to do things differently should always be considered. It can take courage and determination to succeed, but new channels are constantly being invented and old ones modified. It is unwise to blindly follow established practice. The decision should be an informed one, made after all alternatives have been evaluated. Levitt reports that the SmithKline Corporation broke with tradition when introducing Contac 600 into Japan. They used only 35 of the 1000 plus wholesalers traditionally used and established daily contacts with wholesalers and retailers, also in violation of established practice.

Logistics

International logistics are almost always more complex than domestic logistics. Certainly they are until manufacture is established within the overseas market. Not only is there need to ship goods over longer distances, there is the cost effectiveness of shipment to take into account. What method of transport is most suitable? Is speed of the essence and are the goods light enough to be flown? Is cost the major factor with time relatively unimportant? Can shipments be merged, within containers perhaps, to minimize cost and also the paperwork?

Orders have to flow in the other direction and be filled efficiently. Goods in transit tie up working capital. How should this cost be entered into the equation? What is the lead time between supply and sale? What is the shelf-life of the goods? How many spare parts need to be shipped, and when?

The choice of transport – by road, rail, water or air – can only be made when logistical equations have been worked through.

It is the marketer's task to liaise with the international logistics manager to ensure that the correct decisions are made in each of his five key areas:

- Traffic management.
- Inventory control.
- Order processing.
- Materials handling and warehousing.
- Fixed facilities location management.

Shipping terms

The physical movement of goods from factory to customer must be staged. Typically the stages will be:

- Factory to docks.
- Loading aboard ship.
- Transportation.
- Unloading to docks.
- Clearance: customs, duties, etc.
- Transport to customer or agent.

Prices may be quoted for the goods at factory gate or for any of the stages along the way. The terms of delivery are covered in the following section (and are also in the explanations and definitions at the beginning of this unit).

Price

Price is always a complex matter; it is the only part of the marketing mix which produces income instead of incurring cost but depends on accurate costings if it is to be both competitive and profitable.

In international marketing the usual issues of price determination, discounts, credit terms, etc. are present. But the process is made far more complex because of the additional factors unique to the international situation.

Decisions have to be made, as in all pricing, at strategic level on such as:

- Mark-up, target-return, perceived value, going-rate?
- Skimming, penetration, premium, psychological?
- Discounts, allowances, special offers?
- Credit terms?

Should prices be set on geographic criteria where those furthest away (in cost terms) pay more? How should price policy discriminate between customer-segments, product types, location, time of day or season of the year?

How should promotional pricing be used – if at all? Is there a case for loss-leader or special-event pricing?

Should pricing be by product line? Feature optional benefits? Is there a captive-product (film for a camera, blades for a razor)? Are there fixed and variable elements (phone lines and phone usage)?

How important is price within the entirety of the perceived purchase? Remember that customers buy value and value is a totality, a bundle of user benefits.

International considerations

If exporting is seen as a peripheral activity it is possible to price from marginal costs. This will (should) provide a competitive price but not form a basis for long-term market exploitation. Unless, perhaps, it is used as a penetration policy in which case a long-term view is being taken.

What are the true incremental costs of selling overseas? It is difficult enough to apportion costs in a domestic market. It is very much more difficult to assess accurately all the additional costs incurred when selling overseas. Many of the costs have to be estimated since they are not within the control of the organization.

If freight charges change is there provision for an increase in price? Can there be? Will the market be able to sustain it? If not, has provision been made? This, and other key questions, have to be taken as contingencies and provided for in advance. Answers will be needed ahead of sales negotiations because terms have to go into the contract whether it be with an agent, or one's own subsidiary.

Costing, and pricing, have to be provided at the stages of delivery which are in common use. The delivery terms are explained at the beginning of the unit. Figure 12.6 shows how a price increases as it passes down the logistical channel.

Stage	Cost (£)	Accumulated cost (£)	Quotation
Price ex-works	10 000	10 000	Ex-works, unpacked.
Cost of packing	300	10 300	Ex-works, packed
Transport to docks	750	11 050	Free alongside ship
Port dues/loading	100	11 150	Free on board
Freight by sea	1400	12 550	
Insurance	120	12 670	Cost, insurance, freight
Landing charges	110	12 780	
Duty payable	2500	15 280	
Transport to buyer	850	16 130	
Insurance all risks	200	16 330	Franco domicile

Figure 12.6
Quotation stages in international marketing

Tariffs

Tariffs are financial barriers to trade. They are, in effect, taxes imposed by governments on goods coming in to their countries. They take several forms:

- Ad valorem – a percentage of the value as at port of entry.
- Specific – levied by weight, length, volume, etc.
- Import duties to raise prices to the level of the domestic market.
- Import surcharges to raise prices and protect the domestic producers in the short term.
- Anti-dumping duties to prevent below-cost clearance and unfair trading.

The intention of governments when they impose tariffs is either to secure tax revenue through raised prices in their country or to handicap or prevent imports. They cannot be circumvented but both black and grey markets flourish where artificial price barriers are raised.

Extending Your Knowledge

OFFSHORE ENGLISH

Offshore English is defined by Guy and Mattock as the English language as spoken by people with other first languages, who have learnt it as adults for practical rather than academic purposes. It is important to the international marketer because Standard English is a very difficult language to speak well. It has the ability to make a meaning absolutely plain – as in the difference between 'by next Friday' and 'until next Friday' – but requires a student to labour long and hard to reach this level of fluency.

Consequently what Guy and Mattock call Offshore English has developed as a form of communication that is shared across people from a range of nationalities and languages. Oddly it is the native English speakers who have the most difficulty with it.

Two examples will suffice to indicate the differences:

Standard English:	Can I get a word in before you get rolling?
Offshore English:	Can I say something before you begin?
Standard English:	You took your time! What kept you?
Offshore English:	At last! Where were you?

It is worth taking the time to learn Offshore English because it goes much deeper than sentence construction. In Offshore English many common words have taken on new meanings and these, put into simple sentences, will allow you to be understood far wider than if you acquire fluency in one foreign language. Some Offshore English follows to give you a flavour for the differences:

Offshore/Standard English	Example
Achieve/Finish	We have achieved the project.
Actual/Current	Our actual Personnel Director.
Actually/At the moment	They are reviewing the situation actually.
Charge/Load	I didn't know the ship was charged.
Compensate/Compensate for	Big sales at Christmas compensated the bad summer.
Control/Check	I control his expense claims.
Figures/Diagrams	The figures in this report tell us little about the numbers involved.
Issue/Outcome	What was the issue of the meeting?
A lot of/Much/many	He made a lot of money and a lot of enemies.
Politics/Policies	We have strict politics on this matter.

'Yes' covers a range of meanings from 'You are absolutely right and I agree to do what you suggest,' to 'I am listening to what you are saying but reserving judgement until I work out what you really mean'.

Payment

The most common methods of payment, in order of increasing risk to the supplier are:

- *Payment in advance*
  Payment in full – and cleared through the supplier's bank – is of major benefit to the supplier. It is commonly used when beginning to trade with an unknown customer but cannot be expected to remain a long-term method. It is more common for a cash deposit of about 20 per cent to be paid with order.
  Note: Ensure that payment is to a home bank, not to an account in the overseas market unless you are certain that the funds can be and will be remitted.

Activity 12.6

Use of language
With the needs for clear communication in mind, review and redraft the following international communications:

1 It can hardly have escaped your attention that our competitors have been stealing a march on us recently. That being the case I need your considered recommendations as to actions that you deem appropriate and which are supported with detailed costings.
2 Short of taking him out and shooting him, I don't see how we'll ever get shot of him.
3 You should be very pleased because the last quarter's figures were not at all bad. Let us hope that you can keep up the good work and not let the side down in the current period.
4 It is never correct to not submit your reports! Please note that in future you are expected and required to conform to regulations.
5 Much midnight oil has been burned in the achievement of this quotation. Hopefully it gives you what you need to tie the customer down.

(**See:** Debriefing at the end of the unit.)

- *Letters of credit*
  The buyer asks his bank to issue a letter of credit in favour of the buyer. The bank is then guaranteeing payment providing that the specific terms and conditions of the contract have been met.
  The overseas bank contacts the supplier's domestic bank to advise the credit. The home bank may or may not add its own guarantee to 'confirm' the letter of credit.
  After shipping the supplier presents the documentation and, if they are in order, the funds are transferred.
  A revocable letter of credit allows the buyer to amend or cancel without notification to the supplier. An irrevocable letter of credit can be amended only with agreement from all parties.
  Naturally banks charge handsomely for this service.
- *Payment on shipment*
  Payment is made whilst the goods are in transit. If it is not received the supplier still holds title to the goods because he has the documents of title. The buyer has the security of the goods being in transit and the unlikelihood that the supplier will have another buyer or want to pay the costs of recovering them.
- *Open account trading*
  This accounts for about 70 per cent of UK's overseas trade, if one includes the EU countries as 'overseas'. It works exactly as trade accounts operate in the UK and relies upon the commercial integrity of the parties to the agreement.
  It is very important to specify under which legal system the contract is drawn since terms of trade, including periods of debt and penalties for late payment vary from country to country.

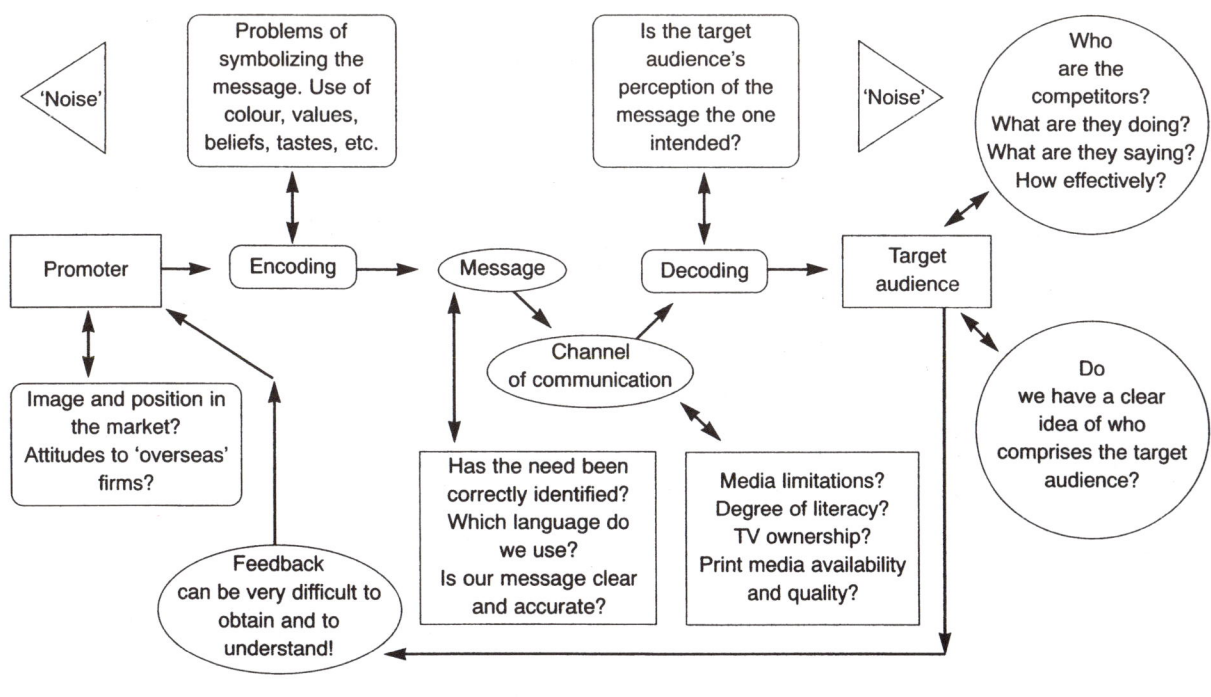

Figure 12.7
International communications

Promotion

The communications model will help us to identify the major problems that face the international marketing communicator.

- *Attitude* In the beginning there will probably not be an attitude to the supplier but there will certainly be one to the supplier's country and/or region and/or culture. Japanese car manufacturers, for example, entered the UK market under western names such as Colt instead of Mitsubishi because of the long-lasting cultural resistance to anything Japanese following the Second World War.

    As time passes, of course, each supplier (and/or brand) will generate a presence in the market and an attitude in the population.
- *Encoding* There can be major problems in symbolizing the message. Even the apparently straightforward use of colour is a potential minefield. For example, the symbolism of white reverses from marriage to death in the West and the East; it is illegal to use the colours of the Zimbabwe flag on products; green used to be an unlucky colour, now it represents good health and products are sold as 'Green' (environmentally friendly).
- *Message* Even marketers within a society can make grievous mistakes. A building society in Zimbabwe screened commercials with a white man saying: 'A year ago I could have bought one house but now I own a house and a car since I invested with X . . .' and a black man saying: 'A year ago I could have bought a bicycle but now I own a bicycle and a tricycle since I invested with X . . .'

    Even in avoiding such major errors it is hard for a non-native to understand the subtlety of a foreign language and a foreign symbolism. A local input is essential if a promotional campaign is to be effective.

    Pepsi, in a well documented attempt to create a pan-European commercial, brought in a top British director and took over an Italian hill village for a week. The commercial was supposed to be an exuberant tribute to the fun of Pepsi but by the time that the Pepsi marketer had removed everything that was unsuitable to one or another culture the result was little more than a pack shot in an unidentifiable village square. As has been said before, the average is bland.

301

- *Channel* Communication channels can be very limiting. For example, in India, radio coverage is extensive, there is little TV but cinemas are a powerful channel. National press is non-existent in most countries but powerful where it has a presence. Satellite communication transcends national borders, with TV and radio but can the messages they transmit yet be appropriate for anything other than standardized products, notably FMCG and consumer durables?

  Literacy standards are falling in developed countries even as they are rising elsewhere, but a huge number of illiterates will continue to exist for decades to come. In any case, in which language(s) will they become literate? And what level of literacy is accepted as the norm?

Extending Your Knowledge

ZIMBABWE AND ZAMBIA

The following quotes are taken from a marketer's report following an assessment visit.

- In a multi-cultural society, beliefs and taboos are a prominent feature. This would hinder our market research since, for example, it is taboo to count children.
- In multi-cultural societies, such as in Zimbabwe, the Apostolic Sector do not allow children to go to school. They have to learn handicraft at an early age. So the working class people who can afford to buy are limited in number.
- Zambia is a multi-cultural society with about seventy-two ethnic groups speaking different languages. It does not have a local language that is widely spoken throughout. English has not been widely assimilated.

  Complex messages are hard to transmit because of the literacy level and the attention span of many potential customers and consumers.

- *Decoding* Do members of the target audience share the cultural values that enable messages to be translated accurately? Can the message be translated into their value system? If it can't be translated is it the message or the product function that needs to change?

  Speed of understanding is a major factor. Compare films from only 20 years ago with those made today – you will see that Western audiences have been educated to respond far more quickly and this media understanding spills over into their reaction to promotion. In countries where visual and aural media is not yet as widespread it is understandable that the messages have to be transmitted more slowly.

- *Target audience* Segmentation is not now a problem in developed countries. Audiences can be identified and targeted. But in many countries the techniques have not developed, and will not for some time to come. As one student put it in an examination answer: 'I don't believe that ACORN will be useful in my country because we do not have numbers on our homes in the village'.

  Segmentation is essential, of course but it will often necessarily be broad rather than specific, with all the wastage through over-spill that this implies.

- *Research* It can be very difficult to identify what the competitors are saying, let alone how effective they are. Where market research is difficult, promotional research is a virtual impossibility.

Objectives

Promotional objectives are required, exactly for the home market – but they must be written from the perspective of the target market. Simply running a campaign across borders is unlikely to succeed. There are notable exceptions, of course. The Esso Tiger in the Tank campaign ran globally with minor modification to meet cultural expectations concerning tigers. The campaign became so powerful that it was in danger of eclipsing the product message and so was abandoned. It is, however, an exception that proves the rule.

Awareness, Attitude and Action are the keys to effective promotion and the specific tools of the promotional mix must be targeted on identifying prospects and then moving them through to the role of committed and regular user.

Legal requirements vary considerably, as does what is culturally acceptable. It is essential to have local expertise that can be relied upon.

Planning

Promotional planning follows exactly the same stages and has exactly the same needs whatever the market.

Trade fairs and missions

These are an important part of international marketing for many organizations especially in the business-to-business sector. They provide the opportunity for producers, distributors and customers to meet and for products to be demonstrated and compared.

The organizers will usually provide a range of support services, including translation, and fair attendance is of value to those established in the market as well as to potential new entrants. As with all exhibitions there is a wealth of opportunity to secure information – including marketing research – for the well prepared delegate.

Trade fairs are frequently sponsored, and home government agencies will often provide financial support to an organization that is seeking to sell overseas.

Packaging

As we know, packaging is often regarded as a fifth P because its importance extends far beyond a simple protection role.

In an international context it has to comply with legal requirements and, if the product is standardized, it will have to comply with the protection and labelling requirements of every country into which it will be sold. Philips shavers now have instructions printed in 16 languages.

Packaging is vitally important as a promotional tool since in almost all cases how a product looks will affect how it is received – how it sells. Even industrial products need to look good – and be easy to open. The key need is for user-friendliness. Everything must be provided: from 'buy me please' through 'this is why I'm so good' to 'now you know the benefit you get'.

Again this is standard packaging practice. The need is to recognize the specific needs of non-domestic markets.

Exam Hints

Any published media cannot be current no matter how many new editions are issued. Some media has a short lag but even daily newspapers commonly are unable to carry news that radio and TV can report almost instantly.

Students are best advised, therefore, to use text and workbooks as background. They are essential to ensure that adequate cover of the syllabus areas is achieved. But a candidate is unwise to rely upon textbook examples in the examination. Partly this is because so many other candidates will quote them – not good because the examiner knows them back to front. Also it shows a serious lack of initiative, especially in marketing where so many compelling examples can be found in a single week's coverage of the trade and daily media.

The most alert candidates include current examples to illustrate their answers – those gleaned from the papers on the day before, even the day of the examination are especially impressive. But it is useless simply to include an example.

Examples must be used to illustrate a point, or points. They must show how something was achieved (in line with or contrary to basic theories); or perhaps they can show how you would set about a given task. There really is no substitute for illustration to prove that you are in command of the subject.

Allow yourself exactly 72 minutes to complete your answer. As before this must include time for reading and understanding the questions, planning your answer, writing your answer and checking through.

Leave the answer overnight and then review it harshly. Pick up every good point and any bad ones. Then set a date in a few days time to take the scenario again, from scratch.

Finally, review your second attempt and compare it to your first effort. It should show marked improvement.

Yourtown centre

Yourtown stands on Yourtown river. It was for centuries a town of strategic importance and was fortified by the Romans. It controlled the major east-west route from the capital city and they built a deep water port where ocean-going ships could dock and transfer cargo to and from canal barges, in time replaced by the railway.

The main route continued through the centre of the town until a road bridge was built alongside the railway bridge just to the south of the town. A bypass relieved town centre congestion and this has been further supplemented by a motorway which sweeps across the river some five miles north of the town.

Yourtown has always been a thriving market town and its architecture extends from well preserved Roman remains, including an arena and a unique aqueduct, to the present time. The old town, clustered around the market square and along the riverside, is still surrounded by city walls, some of which are open to the public.

Many of Yourtown buildings have been listed as of historical interest, and the sixteenth-century market cross and butterwalk are particularly fine examples of their period. The port has long since ceased to carry commercial traffic, but is now a thriving marina since the sheltered harbour provides close access to some fine sailing water.

Yourtown has been moved into the sidestream of history and its major income now comes from a healthy tourist trade. Yourtown Tourist Office is very active and successful. Several major hotel groups have been encouraged to build modern hotels on the outskirts of the town. They promote the town actively both in the UK and overseas. In particular they target the US market from which a constant stream of visitors descend on the town every spring and summer.

The major tourist season runs from early May to late September. In the winter a range of activities attract visitors. The Classical Music Festival, each January in the medieval town hall, is the major attraction drawing conductors and soloists from across the world. Of slightly lesser importance is the Shire Horse Show in October, the Antiques Fayre in February and the Agricultural Exhibition in March. Additionally there are many weekend and specialist events organized by the hotels and by independent entrepreneurs.

Unfortunately, many ancient buildings are in serious need of renovation, which must be carried out to the high standards required by English Heritage for listed buildings. Their owners are unable to afford the high cost, yet cannot sell for the same reason. The result elsewhere has been continual disintegration until buildings either fell down or became unsafe and could be demolished.

Yourtown Charity has been formed, and properly registered, by a group of interested citizens led by a well-to-do landowner. Start-up capital has been provided by grants from the local council, donations from prominent local citizens and local fund-raising events. Funds are strictly limited, however, and a major effort is needed to establish the charity.

Question

The charity has asked for assistance from the marketing tutor at Yourtown College, where you are studying. You have also agreed to help. You are due to meet your tutor in a couple of days to compare notes on what should be done. Prepare your notes with particular regard to:

1 Marketing planning recommendations. (20 marks)
2 Identifying and reaching the charity's target markets. (10 marks)
3 Creative thoughts on the location of short-term funding. (10 marks)

(**See:** Debriefing at the end of the unit.)

Summary

In this unit you have seen that:

- International marketing uses exactly the same tools and techniques as domestic marketing.
- There is need for top management commitment and determination if an organization is to move from occasional overseas selling to a fully integrated international marketing force.
- Intercultural marketing affects virtually every organization as they trade across cultural boundaries, even if not across national frontiers.
- Truly global companies are stateless. They have clear vision and focus tightly on what they do best.
- There is much pressure to open world trade at statesman level. It is hampered by political resistance but the trend appears strongly established.
- Time, not miles, now dictates distance.
- Locals in overseas markets are essential, not least to evaluate accurately the true situation in the light of colloquial understanding and cultural awareness.
- Agents and overseas distributors must be secured with a contract that is carefully constructed to be understood by and fair to both sides. Relationships tend to be long-term.
- Managing the exchange risk is difficult but essential.
- Information from overseas markets can be patchy and unreliable. Partly because of the nature of the markets, partly because the research firms are not as experienced as in Western society.
- Offshore English differs from Standard English but is a most useful tool of international communication.
- Marketing mixes must be developed from the perspective of the market (s).
- The logistics of international trade must be understood and provided for. International distribution requires very specialized management.
- Always be certain that revenue and/or profits can be extracted from overseas markets.

Debriefing

Activity 12.1

You need to be aware not only of what is occurring now, but what this potentially means for marketers over the medium- and long-term. Concentrate on the issues of most direct relevance to you and your markets. For example: what is the likelihood, and what would be the effect if the Basques secure independence from Spain, if Ireland becomes one nation, if Scotland secures its own parliament?

What do you see as the future of the global corporation? The clear trend is towards centralization – only partly because the costs of R&D are too high for individual companies to bear. A classic cultural description has been the 'IBM person' where the IBM culture was more important than national culture, and IBM personnel moved around the world in an IBM existence that was little affected by the country they happened to be working in. Can you see a future where there will be individual global corporations for energy, transport, communications, food, health?

Awareness and understanding of the international and multicultural environments are very important to marketers today and particularly to CIM Diploma students because one quarter of the Diploma syllabus is devoted to International Marketing Strategy.

Activity 12.3

The prices actually to be paid and received vary quite substantially in real terms, as can be seen. Exchange rate fluctuations can easily wipe out the profit from a deal and exchange management is crucial to success.

Rate of exchange	Contract £	Paid in francs FFr	Contract FFr	Paid in sterling £
8.50	100 000.00	850 000.00	85 000.00	100 000.00
8.45		845 000.00		100 591.72
8.40		840 000.00		101 190.48
8.35		835 000.00		101 796.41
8.30		830 000.00		102 409.64
8.25		825 000.00		103 030.30
8.20		820 000.00		103 658.54
8.15		815 000.00		104 294.48
8.10		810 000.00		104 938.27
8.05		805 000.00		105 590.06
8.00		800 000.00		106 250.00
7.95		795 000.00		106 918.24
7.90		790 000.00		107 594.94
7.85		785 000.00		107 280.25
7.80		780 000.00		107 974.36
7.75		775 000.00		109 677.42

Activity 12.4

All countries are different, and there are also regional differences within countries. An Arab businessman may appreciate guidance on points such as these about the UK.

- *Contact*   Considered polite to shake hands but keep at a distance when negotiating. Appointments should be kept punctually.
  Good manners to accept offer of tea or coffee on arrival. But not mandatory.
- *Tipping*   Waiters, taxi drivers, etc. about 10 per cent.
  Do not tip usherettes in cinemas and theatres.
- *Payment*   Correct to pay accounts when due but common practice to delay.
  No penalty for delayed payment.
  Queried amounts should be paid to the level believed correct and the balance disputed.

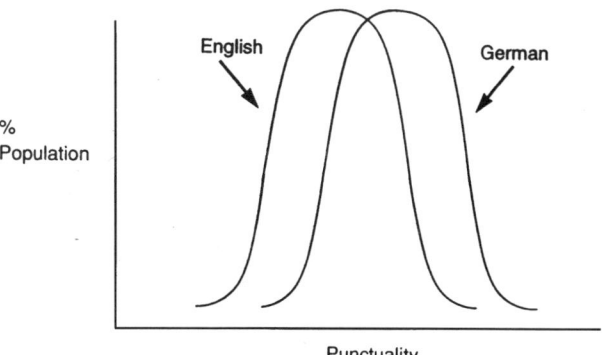

Figure 12.8
Bell curves to illustrate cultural expectations

A useful way to compare cultural expectations is given by Guy and Mattock in *The New International Manager*. They suggest that you draw a bell curve to indicate normal for your home market. Then the centre indicates normal and the areas to left and right are 'less than you' and 'more than you'. Then determine the curve for your target market. In the example in Figure 12.8 the Germans are shown as tending to a higher expectation of punctuality than the English.

The variable on the lower axis can be changed to meet your needs, for example, helpfulness, loyalty, thoroughness, etc., and the technique is a useful and quick way to achieve an overall understanding.

Activity 12.5

As some guidance to the level of understanding you may expect, here are some actual quotes from British people on holiday in France in 1994. They are taken from the diary of an English lady who has been resident in France for some years.

- No I don't have a green card. You don't need motor insurance in France do you?
- Why do they have fireworks on July 14 instead of on Guy Fawkes Day?
- I never leave a tip: 10 per cent is exorbitant and I want to choose how much to leave.
- The girl in the cinema expected a tip just for showing me to my seat. The nerve!
- What's that funny blue flag with the gold stars?
- How can they drive on the wrong side of the road?
- Drivers never stop at zebra crossings and the police do nothing!

Just in case you don't know:
Motor insurance is definitely needed! Guy Fawkes Day (November 5) is a British celebration. July 14 is the French National Day. Waiters and cinema usherettes are paid on the expectation that customers will tip and restaurant and cinema ticket prices are adjusted accordingly. The flag is of the European Union – it is seen everywhere in France. Britain and Ireland are the only European countries to be 'right' in driving on the left! Zebra crossings are British and it is mandatory to stop. In France they have pedestrian crossings and nobody has right of way.

Activity 12.6

Simple language is never wrong but is vital when communicating with a non-native speaker. Your answers may differ in degree, but not simplicity, from the following:

1 You will have seen that our competitors have been quicker in their response than us.
   Please tell me what you propose and how it can be afforded.
2 I think it will be very difficult to remove him. Do you have a gun?
3 Last quarter's figures were good! Keep them at the same standard!

4 Reports must *always* be sent in. Please follow the rules in future.
5 We have worked late to prepare this quotation. I hope it helps you to get the business.

Unit activity

Note that your presentation should be in note form. This means crisp, short, numbered sentences which carry the key points only. There is no need for justification because the notes are *aide-memoires* for your own use but they should, of course, be of sufficient length that you will understand them clearly in a few days time (and so that the examiner will understand your points).

Your answer should be headed with something suitable like:

Yourtown Charity Recommendations,
or
Yourtown Charity Thoughts.

It should be clearly structured into three sections, with the amount of time devoted to each proportionate to the marks available.

These comments, addressed to you, show an acceptable style which you could use in answering these questions. The details of each part of the answer are, of course, in your head and in your notes.

1 Marketing planning recommendations

- A charity needs corporate planning just as much as any other organization. Have you remembered to indicate the need to start with a Mission and work down? Or have you tried to make notes about marketing planning in isolation?
- Advanced business skills are not likely to be present in those who have started the charity. The more reason to spell out what needs to be done to complete a thorough corporate and marketing planning process. Use diagrams to ensure clarity.
- Show how all parts of the charity (however it is divided functionally) must be part of the overall plan. How all must pull together. Show the value of synergy.
- Take the stages of the planning process and relate them to a small charity that is just starting up. Use the 7Cs structure as a framework.
- Persuade them of the need to take time to get the planning right. Not to expend their limited capital on fund raising too soon.
- Persuade them, also, not to fund any restoration out of start-up capital. A need to be hard-hearted perhaps but necessary to long-term success.
- Show the need not to go public until plans are made: target something like six months to get the plans in place and be ready to go active.
- Prove the need to involve professionals to handle promotion in particular. This need not be expensive if creative thought is used (see question 3, below).
- Stress the after-market. Collecting and distributing funds requires efficient processing of donations and effective and efficient internal management. Amateur labour needs motivating and training even more than professional.

2 Identifying and reaching the charity's target markets

- Broadly any charity has two target markets. Those who donate and those who are the purpose of the charity's existence.
- Both of these must be broadly identified; detailed identification can come only as part of the detail of the planning process when corporate objectives have been finalized. At this time only a broad view can be taken. It is necessary since further funding is likely to be needed and the potential targets need to be classified:

  Major potential targets such as the hotel chains should be targeted with the full plan and signed up over a long-term period. Substantial revenue should be derived from these. We don't want to take small sums now and risk the long-term potential.

Official agencies can safely be targeted for small sums. They are used to on-going grant requests and will not be deterred by short-term requests. Note especially that at the end of the financial year departments often have small sums left which they need to dispose of.

Minor funds, such as local events, can safely be fostered because there is already goodwill which needs to be kept alive; they require little management from the charity, they will form a base for on-going drives whatever the corporate strategies.

- Guidance as to how to position, segment and target will be invaluable at this stage. It can be given as part of the target market rationale and will inform the planning process. It is also a highly professional approach which newcomers to marketing can find disconcerting and so may be more readily accepted if included with other material which can be seen to be relevant.

Remember that the Americans can be very generous when approached to save genuine olde worlde sites. It would not be difficult to identify and then profile the visitors in order to segment and then target the tighter.

3 Creative thoughts on the location of short-term funding

- Marketing is about exchange. Short-term funding should therefore not be begged. Even the offering of a lapel flag is a valued exchange.
- Founder membership of the charity can be sold: at gold, silver and bronze levels.

    Note: Need for value package, from free pass to the Music Festival to a newsletter to justify the membership differences.

- Corporate membership should be available later but, in the meantime, local professionals such as the bank manager, can be signed up as individuals.
- Secure gifts in kind, for example, free passes to the Music Festival for gold members. This would include free (or heavily subsidized) services from a local ad agency, printer, PR consultant and the like. Also such items as redundant computer systems that local industry is disposing of: perfectly good for the charity's needs.
- Solicit support from local groups: Round Table, Lions, Rotary, Women's Institutes, etc.
- Local and national government agencies (as mentioned above).
- Local events such as raffles, bingo, sales of work, etc.
- A stall could be placed at the motorway service station through weekends in the summer. Jointly with the Tourist Office perhaps?
- Similarly the railway station could be targeted, and also the marina.

Focus on the examination

In this unit you will:

- ❏ Examine the tools and techniques for improving your learning and thinking skills.
- ❏ Identify the examiner's requirements.
- ❏ Discover the techniques needed to ensure a pass in your examination.

By the end of this unit you will be able to:

- ❏ Understand the importance of meeting the examiner's requirements.
- ❏ Manage your time before and during the examination.
- ❏ Select questions and plan your answers.
- ❏ Present your answers effectively.

Study Guide

When approaching your examination you need to make a major behavioural change. As a student you have been studying, learning, absorbing. Now you must become a candidate, and make practical use of what you know.

In the Marketing Operations examination you must show that you are a credible manager who has an understanding of, and interest in, corporate matters as a foundation for organizational success. Marketing is a vitally important function in helping to ensure success, but it cannot achieve success without integration of organizational effort.

You have to make decisions regarding the examiner's requirements, be able to select the appropriate response in terms both of content and style of presentation and manage your time so that you fully answer all the questions asked.

Examiners continually report two key candidate failures:

- To present their material in the style called for.
- To answer the questions asked.

It is vital that you:

- Acknowledge the importance of good presentation (in all its aspects).
- Practise answering so that you are experienced in the process.
- Take time in the exam to read and thoroughly understand the questions.
- Plan your answers before starting to write them.

Passing any examination is not difficult providing you have a minimum of basic knowledge and have developed your exam technique. This unit is devoted to helping you build the needed competence to handle yourself well in the examination itself.

Note: If you also have the *Effective Management for Marketing* Workbook you will find that the key details of this unit are the same in both books.

You should allow two hours to complete this unit and a further four hours to undertake the activities which include a full mock examination as the Unit Activity.

Study Tips

CIM examiners want to see that you have taken the time to plan your answers. This indicates a professional approach, and, by implication, indicates that you can be trusted to work effectively with professional marketers.

The traditional approach to examinations – last minute cramming of academic facts – will not get you a pass. You must:

- Show through your skills of analysis, planning and presentation . . .
- That you can apply theory appropriately . . .
- In support of management decisions . . .
- That are concisely conveyed in correct style.

You will find a full CIM Examination paper and answer scheme at the end of this unit. Do not be tempted to read ahead – not the questions and certainly not the answers!

Explanations and definitions

Examiners are precise in their use of the English language. They say what they mean, and you must take it that they mean *exactly* what they say, e.g. market and marketing research are often interchanged in everyday speech. To a marketer, however, they have special and precise meanings. The one is, as we know, contained within the other. Take the examiner's wording literally – be extra careful to read and fully understand each question.

Be quite clear about the exact meaning of the following terms:

Briefly: short, concise.
Compare: look for similarities and differences – perhaps reach a conclusion about which is preferable.
Contrast: set in opposition in order to bring out differences.
Compare and contrast: do both of the above.
Criticize: give your judgement about the merits of the subject. Back your views with evidence and/or reasoning.
Define: write the precise meaning of a word or phrase. Quote a source if possible. Show that the distinctions contained or implied in the definition are necessary or desirable.
Discuss: investigate or examine by argument, sift and debate, give reasons for and against. Examine implications.
Describe: give a detailed or graphic account of.
Evaluate: make an appraisal of the worth of something, in the light of its truth or usefulness.
Explain: make plain, interpret (see below), and account for. Give reasons for.
Identify: recognize, establish; select the key issues.
Interpret: expound the meaning (or possible meaning) of; make clear and explicit.
Illustrate: give examples to make clear and explicit. Demonstrate understanding.
List: number of names, items, things set out clearly in order.
Outline: give main features, or general principles. Omit minor detail. Emphasize structure and arrangement.

Relate: show how things are connected to each other, and to what extent they are alike, or affect each other.
Specify: name expressly, mention definitely.
State: present in clear, brief form. (**Note:** Brief!)
Summarize: give a concise account of the chief points; omit details and examples.
Trace: describe development or history of a topic from some point of origin.

You must also be able to write in *report* and *memo* styles, and to produce *notes* for your manager and *presentation* notes for yourself.

Activity 13.1

Lateral thinking
It is often best to write the answer to an examination question before writing the question itself. Take 15 minutes and test the validity of this statement. Consider its importance to you as a student about to become a candidate.

(**See:** Debriefing at the end of this unit.)

Learning

Much work has been done on learning theory, but you don't need to delve deeply unless you get hooked on the subject. What you need to understand fully is that what most people call 'learning' is actually only memory. Revision, for example, is of little use to many people because they treat it as a passive activity and read and re-read their notes. Learning is actually understanding and use:

The double U principle:

- To truly learn anything you have to *understand* it.
- To remember you have to *use* it.

There should never be any shame in not understanding something. Everybody has a different make up and all find some topics easier than others. Share your particular skills of understanding with others, and benefit from their abilities in return. You will find that this mutually supportive activity greatly enhances your own understanding because you will be using your knowledge. So it is worth helping others even if they can't help you back.

If you are in a job where you can use your learning then you have the ideal situation. If you are not, then you have to create opportunities so that you can put your learning to use.

Note: If you don't use learning you are extremely unlikely to remember what you have 'learnt'. How many times have you gone back to your notes at revision time, and found that material covered in the first part of a course is coming at you almost as new? What a waste!

Extending Your Knowledge

Does this situation ring true to you? One of the computer technicians in a large college wanted to improve her memory, so she got a book on how to do it from the library. She discovered that her memory could be improved but that it would take effort. Her comment was 'It'll take so much time to learn the system that it's better not to bother'. Recognize the situation?

It is the same when a boss does the work himself because 'it takes too much time to show anyone else'. The argument is not sound for the boss (he cannot do everything) and it is not sound for the technician — just think how much time she would save over the next 40 years if she invested three months work now.

Be very clear about your needs both short- and long-term.

Exercise is important

It is necessary to schedule both physical and mental activity into your learning. The mind needs time to assimilate and process new data and the body needs to rid itself of the physical and mental tension that builds up during concentrated periods of study.

Research indicates quite clearly that more learning takes place if the periods of study are brief and interspersed with physical activity. An effective break can be as little as five minutes but it must be taken outside the study area, preferably in the fresh air. It must certainly involve physical stretching – perhaps a short walk.

Review

Tony Buzan's research shows that if you don't review your work regularly you will forget most of it very quickly. You have to impress your subconscious mind with the importance of the material and of keeping it both stored and accessible.

It may seem like hard work, but you really only have to glance over your notes. If they are set up with good triggers and you understand the material you will get to know the notes very quickly. You will also be able to recall them in the exam room.

Studies show that properly spaced review, as part of planned learning, can keep recall constantly high.

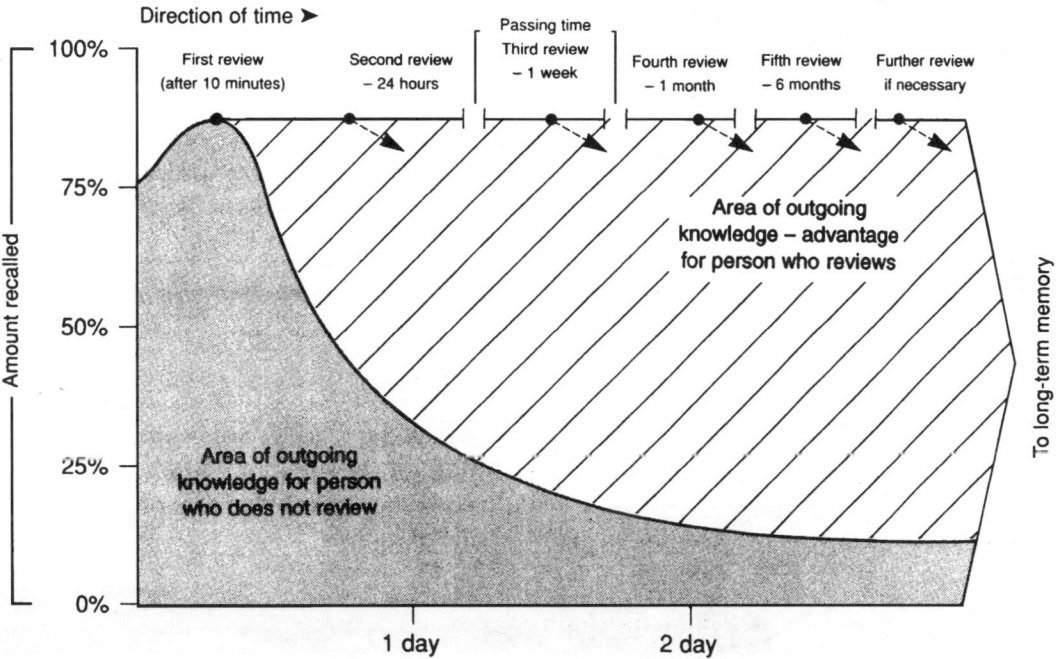

Figure 13.1 How properly spaced review can keep recall constantly high (from *Use Your Head* by Tony Buzan, reproduced by permission)

Revision notes

Notes made whilst learning form the basis of your revision notes. They should be full of triggers – key points that stand out and stimulate a mental response. Triggers should be memorable, unique and link into your preferred learning style. They can be humorous, dramatic, stylish – anything that makes them stand out to stimulate a recollection when you come across them in review.

You should actively seek to build triggers into your notes so that they are there as associative links which your subconscious mind can identify and index. Your aim should be to establish key issues as triggers and links so that a flow of association is stimulated whenever any one of the triggers in an associative chain is activated. Mind maps, of course, work on exactly this principle.

Trust your memory

Your learning notes are too long for effective revision. They must be reduced to the key points – the triggers and associative links. But you cannot really go in one bound from lengthy notes to abbreviated Flash Cards. Reduce your notes in stages over time. As you pass through each stage you will be moving from passive student to active candidate. The aim is to have a set of postcard-size notes, each with a key area of learning on the front as a trigger, with the key points briefly extended on the back.

Revise actively

Whatever you do, *avoid* the standard form of 'Revision' used by almost all candidates. Do not sit for hours on end with textbooks trying to cram knowledge into your head. It is not subject knowledge that is most important. You need skill in pulling out and presenting the right knowledge at the right time.

Extending Your Knowledge	Pat Cash, the Australian tennis star, was being interviewed about his ability to win. 'You can't win', he said, 'until you have time to read the game and get to where the ball is going to be before it gets there. Then, if your shots are in the groove, you can pass the other player.' Having time is what distinguishes the professional from the amateur. You have to become professional at passing examinations. That can only mean practice, rehearsal, to get your skills 'in the groove'. Skill comes only from practice. So revision has got to be active – you trying, failing; trying again, getting better; trying again, getting confident; trying again, getting it right; trying again, getting it perfected; trying again, getting it to a routine. Take a little time to learn how to learn. Learn how to make notes so that they will help your revision. The work of both Tony Buzan and Edward de Bono is very helpful (and fun).

Preparing to pass

Preparing to pass begins at the second you decide 'I'm going to pass', not before. Not at the moment you sign on for a course, not when you enter for the exam, not when you hope to pass, not if you expect to pass, not if you think it would be a good idea to pass. Only when you decide to pass. When you set passing as a specific objective.

Activity 13.2	*Why do you want to pass?* Take 15 minutes and clarify why you want (need?) to pass this examination. (**See:** Debriefing at the end of this unit.)

Physical presentation

The examiner must be impressed by your paper. The first response is critical. It is likely to be 'This is good, how good?' or 'This is bad, how bad?' The successful candidate gives the examiner every opportunity to award marks. The actual layout, crispness and overall impression are powerful influencers for good, or ill. The basic rules are:

1 Write your personal details clearly and neatly on the front of the answer book. Enter the numbers of the questions you have answered in the order you have answered them.
2 Do all your rough work in the *back* or *centre* of the answer book. (No matter how professional the examiner it is better to keep the rough work out of the way.)
3 Start your first answer on the right-hand page. Use white space, do not crowd your work!
4 Never use red or green ink! (These are the examiner's colours.)
5 Do not use liquid paper – neatly cross through any work that has been replaced.
6 Always underline, draw diagrams, cross through with a ruler. Never freehand!
7 Label the axes of graphs and matrices.

Activity 13.3

What does the examiner require?
Take 10 minutes and jot down the things that the examiner requires of you. What should you do to make a good impression?

(**See:** Debriefing at the end of this unit.)

First impressions count

The whole aim and purpose of your overall presentation must be to communicate marketing credibility to the examiner. The reaction you are seeking is – 'This is a good paper – I wonder how good?' From that beginning it is very difficult for an examiner to give a fail grade. On the other hand, a start of 'Oh dear, wonder how bad this will be?' is very difficult to turn into a pass!

Therefore, the cover should be pristine – you have ample time to get that right. And your first three pages should be written with special care. It is probably best to write your second best answer first. This allows you to relax into the paper, yet presents a good first impression to the examiner.

The best answers are planned answers. The best planned answers are those where a candidate's knowledge is displayed so that it will gain most marks. It is too easy to throw all one's best material into the first two questions and then be short when it comes to the third answer. Play the percentages – it is much harder to increase a 14-mark answer to Question 2 than to secure 6 or 8 marks from Question 3.

Use the Checklists to self-evaluate your work between now and the exam.

Eight months ahead of the examination

When it is eight months ahead, the exam is a very long way off. It will either seem very frightening, or so unreal as to be of little concern. Either way you will be tempted to blot it out of your conscious mind. Unfortunately, your subconscious isn't going to forget. It'll worry away, nag at the problem, and throw up all kinds of mental blockages at the most unexpected times.

You have to be clear in your thinking, and be sure your subconscious is clear too. Then, if you set your objectives and make an action plan, your whole mind will be working in the same way, on the same things, at the same time. Your action plan must provide for these issues:

1 *Get the routine out of the way*:

- Check you are a registered student.
- Note the date for exam entry – and make a note in your diary of the need to enter three weeks before.
- Obtain past exam papers, Examiners' Reports, Guidance Notes, etc.

2 *Learn to learn* Plan time into your studies so that you are able to learn easier and to retain what you have learned. Try to learn something just before you have a real-life need for it. Or organize a real-life usage immediately after a topic has been covered on your course.

3 *Learn the subject* Your study of learning will show you how to set out your notes so they are memorable. It will also show you ways to keep your learning fresh.

There is no question that review plus use ensures little forgetting. One effective way to review is:

- Whilst learning make notes (linear or mind map), work on the activities, note the explanations, relate to your practical experience. Let the material flow into and around you. *Ensure that you understand*. If necessary, ask questions of anyone who can help. Most people are flattered to be asked for their assistance.
- The next day rewrite your notes into an organized format. One that works for you. It is now that you are setting up your revision for months ahead. You do not want page after page of notes that all look alike, there have to be associative hooks and triggers, and you must build them in – now.
- The next week flip through your notes before you start to study; and again before you write up that week's work.
- Always do the activities. Do more as voluntary work; and get a second opinion on it from somebody that you trust.*
- Always put your learning into the context of your main motivation – work, or whatever it is for you.
- Don't worry about exam question technique too soon. If you know your subject, and you know how to learn, you will pick up exam technique quickly.
- Once a month quickly review all your notes on each subject. Take time to rework examples, and/or to check understanding.

It is good to have someone with whom you can share part of your learning. So make it your business to find one or more.

One month ahead of the examination

Assuming you are working, and that your exam is in four subjects, taken in the same week, here is what you do:

1 Clear your social calendar, except for Saturday and Sunday evenings.
2 Secure a quiet area in which to work undisturbed. If necessary, get down to the local college library (you don't have to be registered as a student).
3 Programme two hours and ten minutes into each weekday evening and the same into either Saturday or Sunday morning.

- In each session work 35 minutes on one subject. Then take ten minutes out of your study area. In the open air if possible. (You need to blend academic and physical activity.)

*If you are learning alone, with no tutor, you will still find that there are people near to you who will help. (Sometimes they may not know your subject, but if they are intelligent and look at the Examiners' Reports and Guidance Notes they will be able to comment on your style; and on whether they have learned something from your work.)

- Then 35 minutes on subject two, 15 minutes for coffee. (No television!)
- Back for one more 35-minute session, and stop. Roll the subjects around day-by-day. (This gives 13 hours work, per week, for four subjects.)

4   Ensure that your support team are on your side – your spouse, parents, and close friends, must know that it is only temporary, but that it is definite. No exceptions. You only have just over two hours blocked out each evening for only a month – there is still time available for priority things (you can get out socially). And there are video recorders so you don't miss important television programmes.

5   Plan answers to all the past questions you can get hold of. Refer back to this workbook after your first plan – then improve the plan. Refer back to your first plan as an aid to your second attempt to plan the question – then use the workbook to improve your plan. Always work from your mind and your notes first and from the workbook only if needed.

6   Reduce your learning notes to key points. Put these onto A4 sheets first. Then reduce to A5, and finally to postcards. It is a good idea to have a question on the front, and an outline of the answer on the back. Carry these cards everywhere and use them as flash cards, as self-testers, when on the bus, the Underground, waiting to see a client.

7   Do not *read* a textbook – refer to texts by all means, extract what you need, but don't read chunks of text. To pass you have to understand. To understand you have to use.

8   You are practising when you work on exam questions but you also need to practise under exam conditions. Plan, in your third week, to spend two full, three-hour evenings, in a library. Set yourself up exactly as for an exam with a paper you haven't worked on before (one is provided at the end of this unit). Self-evaluate, as described later.

9   Check your exam answer plans against your flash cards. Go back to the book(s) at this stage only if absolutely necessary.

10   Keep your flash cards going up until the evening of two days before the exam.

11   Do no exam work at all on the day before the exam. Your mind needs the time to absorb and categorize the material, and to begin unconsciously to prepare for the exam itself. It has things to do which are beneficial, and you can use a break! So remind yourself that the world is still there. Relax in your favourite way (don't overdo it). Get a good night's sleep.

The day of the exam

The most important thing to develop is self-control. Do not get flustered! This is, of course, very easy to say, but very hard to do. Yet it is vital. The best way to control your nerves is to understand what is happening to you.

- You are putting yourself into risk, into danger.
- You are going into the unknown.
- You are going into an atmosphere of stress and tension.
- You badly want to do well – whatever you might say to friends to keep up appearances.

It will be the same for everyone else, one cannot avoid it but you can control it if you understand what is happening, and why.

Why does it happen?

We possess very old-fashioned bodies, and very old-fashioned mental systems. They were not designed for this century, nor have they adapted to it. So far as our autonomic (subconscious) systems are concerned, nerves are just a form of physical fear. There are only two responses to fear. One is to run away, the other is to stand and fight.

Both responses call for the same protective measures – which are completely automatic. The blood supply is taken back into the main body cavity, leaving just sufficient for function in the parts most at physical danger. The blood-carrying vessels tighten down, to make them both smaller and tougher. A surge of adrenaline is automatically released. This substance (a hormone) is a very powerful stimulant. The whole body goes into a state of alert. Secondary systems such as digestion are shut down – the body is ready to run, or to fight. Unfortunately, the exam candidate can do neither. There is need for calm; for confident relaxation.

It is very important to recognize this and to take action to control the nervous energy that the body will provide for you.

Activity 13.4

The advantages of nervousness
Take 15 minutes to work through the advantages that controlled 'nerves' offer. What are the implications to you – personally?

(**See:** Debriefing at the end of this unit.)

Preparing for the exam

The basic rules are:

1 Find out the location of the exam centre a week ahead. Check travel details (bus and train timetables, parking, etc.). If possible, visit the centre; use the route you intend to use on the day. Buy the ticket the day before if you can, and ensure that you have enough small change on the day to cope with tickets you have to buy and any emergencies. If the exam is in your college be sure to visit the exam room days ahead. Walk around it, get the feel for it. Be sure *not* to decide where you want to sit! (This can be a great let down if you are told that you have to sit in another place on the day.) In everything you must have one aim – to know what is about to happen and to be prepared for as many eventualities as possible.

2 You may have to sit near a radiator, or in a cold room, so you will need to be able to vary your clothing. A shirt or blouse, with sweater and jacket gives you a range of options on the day. You have to be comfortable in yourself.

3 You know what equipment you will need, but make a list well ahead of time, and prepare two easy to carry bags at least 24 hours before. (One can fit inside the other.) You will need to pack under two headings:

   (a) What you need on the day – basic day-to-day materials, packed lunch (can only go in on the morning), revision notes for the exam and perhaps for a second exam after lunch. This bag will have to be placed at the front of the exam room, out of your reach throughout the exam.

   (b) What you need in the exam – special materials, e.g. pens, pencils, rulers, and calculator; study notes and/or reference book(s) (if allowed). This bag you can keep with you on your desk or table, so you should also include some sweets, a small and carefully sealed drink – whatever is going to help you through the length of the exam. The guideline here is *not* to include anything that may upset other candidates (apples are noisy, oranges are messy and smelly).

   If you need to add anything on the morning of the day make a note of it the night before when you make your final check. In the morning you do not want to be harassed with detail – so get as much behind you as possible.

4 Good-luck mascots – be very careful about mascots. The good candidate makes sure of doing well with careful planning. Candidates' confidence can be shattered by simply forgetting a mascot!

5 The day starts early for most candidates; their nerves see to that! Fine – expect it. Be sure to have something to eat and to drink, whatever your

normal breakfast habit. An exam day is a different day – give your system something light to work on.

Avoid any tranquillizers, anti-sickness tablets, and so on. They may quell your tummy but they slow down your mental processes. Is it better to be sick? Probably, but if you have planned carefully you should be in charge of the situation and should not be so nervous as to need medical aid. (Don't say, 'But it always happens to me, I can't help it'. You can help yourself to overcome the problem, if you think and plan ahead.)

Often parents are the worst problem. They are so anxious that they can infect you with their nervousness. You should have dealt with this problem much earlier – by getting your support team on your side. If not, you must be prepared to cope with it now. (Probably by forcing yourself not to argue, it will do no good – it will only set your adrenaline flowing in a negative, tightening, frustrating way.)

6　Leave home in good time, you will know how long each part of the journey takes, so you should be able to be reasonably relaxed about the travel.

7　On the journey you will probably feel better if you go through your flash cards one last time. Or glance through your notes. But by now it is too late to affect your true knowledge. You are filling in your time and reinforcing the knowledge you already have.

8　At journey's end you should have some time in hand, so plan to use it well. Don't go into the Centre and stand around with the other candidates. Don't stand around outside. Go to a coffee shop or for a walk in the park. You must *not* become infected with the nerves of the other candidates. You cannot expect them to be as well prepared as you. There will be nervous ones, troubled ones, upset ones. The organized ones will be off, like you, securing their own peace of mind.

9　Take possession – this is important. The space around you, your desk and chair should become yours, psychologically. Your seat may have been allocated but you can still take charge. All you have to do is move the desk very slightly, to a different position. A position you have chosen. Move the chair too. Again, a very slight movement is all you need. By taking charge and creating your own space you will exert a very strong psychological boost to your ego. It is a small technique – but a most valuable one – remember you are playing a psychological game, and you have to play to win.

10　Fill your time by carefully entering your name/number on every piece of exam stationery that is waiting for you.

Your examination paper

You are sitting in the exam room. All is quiet now that the candidates are settled. Any time now and the invigilators will bring round the exam paper. It can get very tense. Fine. No problem. Why shouldn't you get tense? It is natural and you are prepared for it.

Then they make it worse, they give out the paper, face down and you can't touch it. Then they look at the clock and wait for the second hand to sweep around. It's agony, can time ever move so slowly? Be prepared for this anguish. Wait it out. It will all go in a rush when you can get to the paper, you just have to sweat through.

At last: 'Turn the paper over, begin'. This is when many candidates lose control. They rush, all their good intentions are forgotten in the excitement of the moment. It is a very powerful psychological release! This will not happen to you, because you will have thought ahead and planned exactly what you are going to do.

The Marketing Operations paper is in two parts. A mini-case worth 40 marks and a requirement to answer three 20-mark questions from a choice of six. It is necessary to know in advance exactly how you are going to tackle the paper. That is the only way to move smoothly and effectively when under exam pressure. Go into the exam knowing exactly what you are going to do.

Two exams

Effectively you have two exams to sit. For the mini-case you must allocate 40 per cent of your time, i.e. 72 minutes. When you allow a time for preliminary reading through and for question selection you actually have 65 minutes for the mini-case and 32 minutes for each question.

Remember that there are effectively two exams in the one paper because the technique for answering the mini-case is different from the technique needed for the three questions. Thus you need to put your mind into gear for the first half of the paper, take a short break midway and then gear up slightly differently for the second half. You may therefore plan your time like this:

Minutes
0–5	Quick skim through the whole paper.
5–70	Mini-case.
70–75	Break – stretch, clear the mind.
75–171	Three questions.
171–180	Read through and correct.

Alternatively you may prefer to take the questions first – the choice is yours. Do not, however, mix questions and the mini-case. Keep the two parts separate. Ensure that you know which you are going to take first before you go into the exam room and don't change your mind!

A compelling reason to separate the two parts is the benefit to be gained from a single planning session within each section of the exam.

Planning your answer to the mini-case requires a lengthy period of analysis and synthesis as you determine the interrelationships within the case and structure a planned answer that will meet your examiner's requirements. It makes complete sense to then write your answer, whilst the plan is fresh in your mind. You have 65 minutes for the mini-case which you may divide:

Minutes
0–2	Quick read through.
2–10	Detailed penetration.
10–25	Answer planning (all questions).
25–55	Answer writing.
55–62	Check through.
63–65	Break – clear the mind.

It also makes good sense to plan all three answers before beginning to write answers. Thus Part B may be timed:

Minutes
0–5	Read through and select questions (see below).
5–20	Answer planning (all three questions).
20–45	Write one answer.
45–70	Write second answer.
70–73	Break – clear the mind.
73–98	Write third answer.
98–110	Check through whole paper.

Taking part-way breaks will result in better answers since you will be able to stretch the cramped shoulder muscles, relax the fingers, take a drink and clear the mind before getting down to the next part of the exam.

Choosing three from six questions to answer can take a long time and can cause anguish as you find that there are questions that you prefer to avoid. (There always are questions you'd prefer to avoid!) The tick, cross and question-mark technique prevents the anguish and gets you into answer planning very quickly and confidently.

Tick, cross or question-mark

The technique relies upon your intuitive sense of knowing which questions are OK, which are possibles and which are best avoided. It works like this:

1 With a pencil in hand read down the questions very quickly. Don't try to analyse them, don't ponder over them.
2 Against each put either a tick, a cross, or a question-mark. (A tick means you can do the question; a cross 'no way'; a question-mark 'possibly'.)
3 Count the ticks. If you have two or more you are on your way to a good pass.
4 Count the question-marks; if you have a further two you have a paper with which you can do well.
5 Ignore *totally* the crosses. For you they *don't exist*. They are no problem, they do not get in your way.

So you are, within 45 seconds, in a position to know how good a pass you can get. And you have eliminated the difficult questions and don't need to worry over them. There is no agonizing over an early question that you hate when an easier one is waiting further down the page!

The maths work out like this:

Each question = 20 marks. Pass = 30 marks (50 per cent).

	Marks achieved		Safety margin
Ticked questions	14	$3 \times 14 = 42$	12
Question-mark questions	9	$3 \times 9 = 27$	–3
Two ticks + one question-mark		$28 + 9 = 37$	7
One tick + two question-marks		$14 + 18 = 32$	2

But you should do better on question-mark questions than 9 out of 20 – and probably better on at least one ticked question!

You should be able to guarantee a minimum of 20 from the mini-case because of the time you have to devote to it and the fact that it asks for your recommendations. *Your* personal recommendations that come from your understanding, background and experience. Providing that you have practised and write a report you shouldn't have any trouble.

Plan your answers

Plan all your answers in each section before starting to write. Ignore the many other candidates who will start straight in to answer without planning first. In the mini-case, if there is a sectioned question, plan the answers to each section first. In the questions part, plan your answers to both questions at one time. Why?

Because you must have your mind doing one thing at a time. When it is switched into planning mode it is actively searching for pertinent information. Mind maps provide an excellent stimulus to this process. When in active search mode you will find that thinking about one question will trigger ideas for another. Getting these ideas out before you switch to writing mode enables you to make better plans, quicker, and you will not find excellent ideas for the first question popping up whilst you are writing the second or third answer.

So plan your answers on a double-page spread of your answer book, and remember to neatly cross through the rough work before you hand the answer book in at the end of the exam.

It is worth repeating that first impressions are vital. An examiner is likely to have a strong first impression: 'This is a pass paper, how good?' *or* 'This is a fail paper, how bad?'

How, then, to discover what the examiner requires?

There are *key words* that you must first look for in a question. (These were listed earlier in this unit.) Key words are about *style* – they tell you what type of answer is needed. They are also about *content* – they tell you on what subject knowledge to focus the answer.

Always look for style words first because they tell you what has to be done. They indicate much of the context of your answer. Turn back and check on 'Discuss', 'Outline' and 'Evaluate'. Do you agree that each requires a different approach?

An examiner will give you a variety of questions to choose from. You can see that some will be easier in style for you; they will require less work. Always choose the ones with the minimum of work (provided you know the subject, of course). Let us take three similar questions, using the key words you have checked.

1   It has been said that general management is a skill that must be learned by any manager who intends to attain and secure a position on the Board of Directors. Discuss.
2   Outline the skills of general management that are necessary for a director of a company to possess.
3   Evaluate the general management skills that are needed if a company director is to be successful in his post.

Many candidates would target on 'general management' only. Some would write all they knew on the topic. Some would present an essay, very few would give a report. Some would write about 'general management skills' – again in a standard essay. Yet the examiner is asking the candidate to put his or her knowledge of general management into a context. To show three things:

1   Knowledge of management and of the skills a general manager needs.
2   Skill is using the correct style so that the set task is carried out – a discussion is very different from an evaluation; an outline is again a different requirement. An essay would be correct for the discussion answer, an essay or report for the evaluation, a report better for the outline.
3   Presentation of the knowledge, skilfully used, so that it is comprehensible. The candidate's command of language, both in comprehension and use, is being tested. This is a necessary skill for anyone who wishes to become a manager.

Note: The examples show how the same knowledge could be tested in different ways. Obviously the same topic will not appear three times on a paper. (If you think it has, then you are misunderstanding the examiner.) These questions are not typical of the Marketing Operations paper; they have been used as examples because they are simply presented and easy to understand.

Presenting your answer

It is crucially important to present your answer in the form that the examiner requires. To do this requires careful analysis of the question, followed by careful planning of the answer. There is also a need for good physical presentation of your answer. A shorter answer that directly responds to the examiner's need and which is presented in a clear style will impress – and attract high marks.

As we explained earlier in this unit, there is need to look for key words for style and for content. Look at these three typical questions and decide two things:

1 What presentation style is called for?
2 What subject knowledge is required?

A Orders from overseas have now reached what you consider to be a sufficient volume to justify the creation of an Export Sales Manager's post. In a report to your Marketing Manager set out the rationale that supports your recommendation(s).
B 'Charities face a double marketing challenge.' You have been asked to explain this statement at a meeting of the local Chamber of Commerce. Provide the outline of your contribution. Include the draft of up to three visual aids.
C You are the sales manager of a components manufacturer. A customer has complained of marginal deliveries under your JIT contract. You have discovered that several others are worried that deliveries are only just scraping in ahead of need.
   Briefly identify what the problem may be. What actions might you take?

Presentation-style	Subject-knowledge (content)
Key words:	*Key words:*
A Report.	Overseas orders; Export Sales Manager; recommendation(s).
B Outline; draft of visual aids.	Charities; double marketing.
C Briefly; identify; actions.	JIT; marginal; several customers.

Once the key words have been identified it is possible to plan an answer that meets the requirements of the examiner. The key words help you firstly to identify style, secondly to target relevant theory and practical examples. Remember it is *never* acceptable to write all you know about a subject! It is *essential* that you give just enough knowledge, demonstrate the required skills and use the correct style. A short answer that does this will always beat a rambling unstructured response.

In these questions you would need to bring in specific content – which the key words would trigger. To illustrate:

A There is hint (recommendation(s)) that more than just a new post is needed. Export must be a top management commitment that affects the firm from mission statement downwards. The new post must be supported by the appropriate team. Outline costings/budget would attract bonus marks.
B Charities must market themselves to those who should benefit from them, and they also have to raise funds and attract personnel. This double aspect is not appreciated by most lay people who see only the outward face of charities. Speaker's notes are required, with 'up to three' (which actually means 'do three') visual aids. Bonus marks come from creative aids rather than from routine 'Welcome, my name is . . .' material.
C The problem is not isolated; delivery times are too close for comfort. Is this from a bad internal briefing to distribution? Or perhaps from optimistic or unclear understanding/agreement at contract stage? There is need for internal contact with distribution to revise delivery instructions for existing customers; also for revision to negotiation techniques so new customers' deliveries are scheduled with a sufficient margin of safety.

Summary

- Learn about learning.
- Set up your learning notes so they have triggers and associative links.
- Review regularly.
- Understand and use.
- You have to decide to pass – nothing less will do.
- A plan is essential, a plan in writing which you will follow.
- Clear your diary for the run up to the exam, schedule practice sessions, work up to exam speed.
- Get your support team on your side. Don't try to do it alone.
- Work from your notes, not from text or workbooks.
- Reduce your notes, gradually, to flash cards. Trust your mind.
- Work on the skills of communicating what you know, impressively.
- Examine your own work. Would it impress? Would you pass it?
- No exam work on the day before – if you don't know it by then an extra day won't help and your brain needs a break.
- Use 'nerves' to your advantage. Channel them into heightened perception, and an ability to concentrate and work for a longer stretch than is usual.
- Rehearse the day. Plan it ahead.
- Don't mix with ill-prepared candidates before the exam.
- Take possession of your exam-room space and equipment.
- Take charge of the question paper. Use ticks, crosses and question-marks to quickly select the questions you are going to answer.
- Do not worry about crossed questions, they do not apply to you, they are not your problem.
- Plan your time. Maximize your marks by planning all answers at the beginning, despite what the other candidates do.
- Key words clearly identify the examiner's requirements.
- Length is *not* needed, nor is volume.
- Share your knowledge around the questions.
- The best answers are well planned and well presented.
- Make certain that the first three pages are impressive. You must catch the examiner's attention, early and positively.
- Plan a 5-minute break at about half way.
- Be sure to read through and catch as many errors as you can.
- Make certain you have named everything you are handing in and that all loose papers are tied into the main answer book.
- If in doubt, always write in report style. In a marketing exam this is never wrong.

Debriefing

Activity 13.1

Writing the answer outline first enables an examiner precisely to target the area(s) of the syllabus that are to be tested. With this objective established it is possible to draft a question that guides candidates to the anticipated answer.

If the question is written first it will almost inevitably be open to several interpretations and have to go through many more redrafts than a targeted question will need. Even a question written to elicit an answer can be ambiguous in the perception of some candidates, in which case the examiner will take the answers that are genuinely based on a logical interpretation of the question.

The implications for students and candidates are that the questions contain clear and specific clues to the expected answer and that a logical interpretation will be accepted even if it is unexpected. The need is to read, understand and interpret each question carefully.

Activity 13.2

Only you will ever know the full reasoning behind your need to pass this examination. As this is the case you can be completely honest with yourself. If status and/or pride are the motivators well and good. If you are only entered because of somebody else's expectations (perhaps your boss has insisted) you need to consider that if it is inevitable perhaps you ought to gain from it and not resist? Only when you know your motivations can you locate and tie in incentives that will work for you. Given clear objectives your task becomes so very much easier.

Activity 13.3

A survey of Examiner's Reports from a whole range of examinations shows a consistency in requirement. The key factors an examiner requires are:

- Prepare before the examination – subject and exam skills.
- Read and understand the questions.
- Do as instructed in the questions.
- Answer the questions set.
- Do not force your knowledge into your answers, despite the questions set.
- Attempt an answer to the full number of questions.
- Allocate time and effort to the available marks.
- Write answers that are long enough to cover the question.
- Show command of subject through practical examples.
- Read through and eliminate careless mistakes.

We are constantly told that many candidates are ignoring the examiners' advice. It must therefore follow that an examiner is going to be so pleased to receive a well presented script that answers the questions asked, that the natural inclination is to pass it! The only question is 'How good a pass to award'.

Activity 13.4

The advantages are likely to be:

- You will be alert, perceptive, full of energy, ready to accept the challenge of the examination.
- Your alertness will sharpen your mental skills and strengthen the associative links.
- Your subconscious will know that it needs to become fully active.
- Your whole system will be poised to 'fight', not run away from the exam paper.
- Above all you will be in control of your destiny.

You, if you think about it, will form your own best solution to the problem of control over your own destiny. But you have to learn to harness this major strength – learn to use it to your advantage.

Unit Activity

Practice examination

These are the most recent examination papers, and are supported by the CIM's Specimen Answers, that are produced by the Senior Examiner. You, therefore, have the opportunity to practise under simulated exam conditions, with real papers, and to check your work against the Senior Examiner's expectations.

Do not attempt to answer any questions until you have set up as close an approximation to exam conditions as you are able. You need:

- Three hours uninterrupted time for each paper.
- A clear workspace.
- A supply of A4 paper – wide lined if possible.
- A clock.
- Other materials you would normally take with you into an examination.

When you are ready, note the time of start, and the time that you must finish. Then take a paper and work it as in a real examination.

When your three hours are up note the fact in your paper – but continue to finish the question on which you are working.

Note: As there is no specimen paper set from the new syllabus both the December 1998 Marketing Operations and Promotional Practice examinations are provided.

Use the Marketing Operations paper for your examination practice. Then select questions from the Promotional Practice paper to increase your probability of passing.

You should attempt the mini-case in Part A, and three questions from Part B. Later, as part of your revision, you should attempt answers to the other questions in Part B.

Review

Immediate:
Review in writing how you believe you have done in answering each question. Do you feel that you would have passed in each? If not, where are your shortcomings?

Next day:
- Read through your paper as if an examiner. Grade it using the materials in this unit.
- Check through the suggested answers, and then re-grade your paper.
- Compare your initial feelings with the two gradings. What have you learnt? What changes will you make before the real examination?

Note
There is seldom a single correct answer to a marketing question. Check your work against the checklists (page 96), and evaluate it against the specimen answers for style and completeness.

Action plan
Produce a detailed action plan to consolidate your strengths and repair your weaknesses.

Assignment checklists

Use the checklists on page 96 to help you self-assess your own work. It is important to work hard to improve your presentation so that the key points are routine when you reach the examination room.

Advanced Certificate in Marketing

Marketing Operations

PART A

Cafédirect

Cafédirect holds approximately three per cent of the UK fresh ground and freeze-dried coffee markets despite very little marketing spend. The company began trading in 1991 as a non-profit joint venture involving the following ethical trading organisations; Equal Exchange, Oxfam Trading, Traidcraft and Twin Trade.

Cutting out the middlemen is key to the organisation's success. The company buys coffee beans directly from small co-operatives in Latin and Central America and Africa. Cafédirect guarantees an agreed trade price for the coffee beans which means they have occasionally paid suppliers more than twice the normal market rate. If the international coffee price rises above the agreed trade price, they pay the international price plus a ten per cent 'social premium' which the co-operatives distribute as they see fit. Cafédirect also provide an upfront subsidy of up to sixty per cent of the value of one contract. It also provides regular updates on world coffee prices. This is important because the fourteen co-operatives who supply the company only sell a quarter to one half of their beans to Cafédirect.

What does all this ethical trading mean for the consumer? The recommended retail price for a 227 gram jar of roast or ground Cafédirect is £2.09. A jar of the leading brand Kenco costs £1.99. Cafédirect's 100 gram freeze-dried product retails at £2.39; Nestlé Gold Blend sells for £2.19. The UK supermarkets have maintained their profit margins and have passed on the cost of ethical business practices to the consumer, a number of whom are clearly willing to pay a slight premium if they believe the company behind the brand is operating ethically.

The issue of ethical trading has been driven by publicity about poor working conditions in factories and plantations in some developing countries. A recent documentary focused on the relationship between a major supermarket chain, and one of its larger suppliers of peas in Zimbabwe where it revealed that out of the retail price of a 99 pence pack of peas, the pickers got less than 1 pence. Supermarkets have been prompted to initiate audits of their supply and production lines and make public statements about their commitment to ethical trading. For example Tesco recently set up a team of ethical advisors to help monitor the goods it sells in its stores and develop an ethical trading policy. Other major chains, such as the Co-operative, have signed up to participate in a project with the Fair Trade Foundation to investigate the mechanics of implementing independent auditing procedures to meet international ethical trading standards. These include agreements to negotiate with independent worker organisations and to honour or better any locally agreed minimum wage.

As the profile of ethical trading increases, the retailers' position that consumers will have to pay a premium may become untenable – especially if one of the supermarket chains takes a more definite ethical stance to distinguish itself from the other companies.

Question 1.
In the role of an independent Ethical Advisor working for a large supermarket chain in a country of your choice, prepare a report which:

a Defines and explains the strategic approach taken by Cafédirect, the Co-operative and Tesco to the social responsibility issues raised by ethical trading.   **(10 marks)**
b Outlines the marketing operations issues that should be included in the development of a code of ethical trading.   **(10 marks)**
c Make recommendations on how the chosen supermarket chain could take a definite ethical stance to differentiate itself from competitors. This should include details on the marketing strategy and mix to be adopted.   **(20 marks)**

(40 marks in total)

PART B – Answer THREE questions only

Question 2.
As a Marketing Consultant who specialises in the car industry, you have decided to undertake a review of how the industry segments its markets. In order to conduct this review you want to attract sponsorship from car manufacturers. Prepare a proposal aimed at attracting funds from car manufacturers which explains what market segmentation is, its benefits and describes some of the base variables which would be appropriate in the car market.

(20 marks)

Question 3.
You are applying for a position as Marketing Planning Manager and have been asked to provide an outline of a marketing plan that you have previously been involved in writing. Select an industry and company of your choice and provide an outline plan in report format.

(20 marks)

Question 4.
You are the Sales Director for a company which manufactures domestic and industrial heaters. The domestic variety is a range of standard items and the industrial heaters are made specifically to meet customer requirements. You manage two different sales forces, one for each activity. You have been asked to make a presentation at the next board meeting outlining the principles of the marketing control process and how you evaluate the performance of each of your sales forces.

(20 marks)

Question 5.
You have recently taken a position as Senior Product Manager for a major computer manufacturer. As part of your role you brief and work with a number of outside suppliers including advertising agencies. Prepare a short briefing paper recommending how your company should select a new advertising agency and identifying the criteria by which agencies pitching for the account should be short-listed.

(20 marks)

Question 6.
A publishing company specialising in marketing texts wants to publish a book made up of cases illustrating excellence in marketing operations. You have been approached to write a case history which illustrates excellence in the practice of business-to-business marketing. Select an example of your choice and provide an outline case history for the attention of the

editor. You should include a justification of why you think the case illustrates excellent practice in this context.

(20 marks)

Question 7.

Your Managing Director has recently been to a conference where the topic of internal marketing was raised. As the Marketing Manager, you have been asked to prepare a report which explains the concept of 'internal marketing', why it has been the subject of increased attention over the past few years and what factors should be taken into account when developing a programme of internal marketing for your organisation? Base your report on a company example of your choice.

(20 marks)

Specimen answers follow.

Turn to them only when you have completed your review.

1a.

To: The CEO, Co-operative Supermarket
From: The Ethical Advisor
Date: 11th December 1998
Subject: Possible strategic approaches to ethical trading

Introduction

Social responsibility refers to a company's obligations to maximise its positive impact and minimise its negative impact on society. Closely related is the issue of marketing ethics, which can be defined as moral principles that define right and wrong behaviour in marketing (Dibb et al. 1997). Ethical trading is both a moral issue to guarantee decent employment and environmental conditions for suppliers, and a question of good business practice, driven by consumer pressure for choice, and City pressure in deciding whether to invest. Ethical and socially responsible practices represent an opportunity for favourably distinguishing the Co-operative Supermarket from its competitors, resulting in increased profit. It can also represent a threat if we ignore the issue. A recent television documentary highlighted the vulnerability of major supermarket chains to allegations of unethical trading practices by the media. The case in point concerned a Zimbabwe supplier of peas to a United Kingdom supermarket chain whose pickers received less than 1 p for the contents of a pack of mangetout retailing at 99 p. We have now reached the stage when ethical auditing by consumer representatives, the media and indeed the City, is increasingly likely to identify and publicise unethical practices by the major chains. Strategies are therefore needed to address this situation.

Strategic approaches being adopted

Dibb et al. (1997) suggest there are 4 basic strategies for systematically dealing with social responsibility issues:

- Reaction strategy.
- Defence strategy.
- Accommodation strategy.
- Proactive strategy.

1 **Reaction strategy**

This is where you do nothing until exposed and are then forced into action. Tesco followed this strategy in the case of mangetout referred to above. This strategy can work but is highly risky. It also spurs the media on to find more instances, as well as to check on the efficacy of the action taken. Worse still, you are seen to act only when forced, a stigma that tends to linger in the customers' minds.

2 **Defence strategy**

This is where a company attempts to justify its position and guard against possible future legislation or consumer pressure. Tesco have recently set up a team of ethical advisors, to assist in the monitoring of the goods it sells in its stores and to help to develop an ethical trading policy. Not only will this help to avoid further incidences of the mangetout variety, but also in any future circumstance, Tesco can, in defence, point to its preventative mechanisms.

3 **Accommodation strategy**

This goes a step further and assumes responsibility for this issue; in recognition of the growing pressure from consumer groups and indeed the environmental auditing already being undertaken by some financial investors. The Co-op and some other major chains have signed up to participate in a project with the Fair Trade Foundation to investigate the mechanics of implementing independent auditing procedures which meet *international* trading standards.

4 **Proactive strategy**

Fairly obviously, this is where you assume responsibility without any outside pressure or threat of Government intervention. Whilst to date no major UK supermarkets have gone wholly along this route, other chains like Marks & Spencer, B&Q and The Body Shop are seen to have adopted this strategy and been rewarded by images of consumer champions and trustworthiness, resulting in a high degree of customer loyalty.

In contrast, Cafédirect have become a major force in ethical trading and consumerism by guaranteeing minimum trade prices, which can occasionally be twice the going market level. Supermarkets have passed on the costs of these ethical business practices to consumers, who are clearly willing to pay a small premium if they feel the brand is operating more responsibly.

Conclusions

Social responsibility issues include ethical trading practices for which a number of strategies are possible, some of which are being adopted by competitors, as described above. The Co-operative Supermarket chain need a clear strategy to avoid adverse publicity and to benefit from the favourable differentiation that would result.

1b. Marketing issues to be included in a code of ethical trading

Introduction

Many companies have Codes of Ethics, of which a code of ethical trading would form a part. Ethical purchasing should guarantee decent employment and environmental conditions for suppliers worldwide. There are a number of marketing issues associated with the development of an ethical trading policy, in addition to the strategies described above. These extend up to the Co-op's Mission Statement and down through the marketing operations.

Marketing operations issues

Mission statement

In order to demonstrate commitment at the highest level, the Co-op's mission statement should contain the message that the company intends to fully accept its social responsibilities by trading both ethically and profitably. This could be extended and given greater substance by the addition of a Code of Ethics, which many companies now have.

Objectives

In addition to the normal sales and profit objectives, qualitative objectives can be set which reflect the ethical trading intent voiced in the mission statement.

Strategy

As indicated in the first part of this report, the Co-op should adopt a proactive strategy in this area. In addition, supplier/partner selection and operating relationship should be considered. Criteria should be established to ensure suppliers meet employment, production and product quality standards with which we are satisfied. Dealing with suppliers in an open and honest way, respecting confidentiality, avoiding manipulation and having a fair payment policy would all form a part.

Adopting a stakeholder perspective, customer and employee relationships should also be included in a code of ethical trading. Dealing with customer enquiries/complaints in an open and honest way is important. So too is ensuring ethical employment policies, working hours and conditions, and pay for employees.

The marketing mix (expounded on in section 1c.)
1 **Products and services**

    The Co-op should scrutinise all new product development from an ethical standpoint, particularly the sourcing and packaging aspects.

2 **Price**

Trading terms should be developed to generate commitment and trust, and to allow a fair profit to be made to invest in improved product yield and quality. Agreed minimum trade prices, pre-finance and commercial information services are all considerations.

3 **Promotion**

How far this ethical stance should be incorporated into the company's brand positioning should be carefully considered, before setting a promotional policy. Given the development of an ethical trading policy, all the elements of the promotional mix can be deployed in communicating this to the Co-op's target audiences.

4 **Place**

Marketing ethical issues also arise in this element of the marketing mix. In particular there are the questions of where to build new stores, where to lay down stocks and the even more contentious issues of transportation – noise, pollution, road congestion, etc.

Control and evaluation

Ethical, green and social audits must be made regularly, to establish the extent to which our ethical code of practice is being adhered to and also to ascertain the level of our ethical trading image.

Conclusions

Other supermarket chains are already implementing *independent* auditing procedures. The Co-op should follow through developing a code of ethical trading, with full attention to the above marketing issues, if it is to avoid being accused of paying only lip service to its societal responsibilities.

1c. Ethical positioning

Introduction

Since no UK supermarket chain has yet established itself positively on the ethical spectrum, the Co-operative Supermarket chain clearly has an opportunity to do this in a way which differentiates it from the others, and hopefully gains a *sustainable* competitive advantage (Porter 1980, 1985).

Benchmarks could be established with reference to best practices by other chains both in the UK and abroad. Marks & Spencer, B&Q and The Body Shop have already been instanced in this respect.

Since another business unit in the Co-operative movement has already developed a very successful niche position on this basis, The Co-operative Bank, we can work with our colleagues and their agencies to take best practice into the supermarket business. In addition, their excellent work has already inferred ethical brand values onto the 'Co-operative' name, so the budget we will require should be reduced.

We should develop a marketing plan to achieve a co-ordinated approach to achieving a definitive ethical stance, in order to distinguish ourselves from competitors.

Current situation

This should include a detailed macro, micro and internal analysis, summarised into a SWOT analysis and key issues (McDonald, 1995). A PEST analysis would highlight such factors as the Labour party's charter for ethics, and the socio-cultural trend towards increased ethical awareness. The UK supermarket situation shows that no other supermarket has taken this position, so a clear opportunity exists.

The Co-op would need to know more about the extent of public feeling on ethical issues and which issues were the most important and/or growing. Research would then be able to establish how we rate on these crucial issues in the public eye. It should also be possible to estimate how many customers would be likely to switch from competitors to the Co-op, given substantially higher ratings. Again case studies with regard to non-supermarket chains performances could help. Some pre-testing and post-testing of the ethical communications programme would also be necessary.

Mission and objectives

Taking from the mission and code of ethical trading outlined earlier, we should have a clear vision of what we want to achieve. The sales and market share objectives would be increased commensurate with the investments needed and the results of marketing research. Targets would also be set with regard to unprompted awareness and acceptance of the re-positioning.

Marketing strategy

This involves determining target markets and brand position. Target markets would include current supermarket customers, banking custom-ers and green/dark green consumers who shop with competitors. We should position ourselves as the ethically and socially responsible supermarket retailer, with the widest range of ethically sourced products – thus incorporating both image and functional values into the brand.

Positioning Map

Ethical/Socially Responsible

Tactics

These would be very much in-line with those stated under section 1b) above, modified as necessary by marketing research findings.

Price: should, where possible within profit objectives, be comparative to 'normal' products and not passed onto the customer, even though there is some lee-way as current research indicates consumers are not very price sensitive in this area.

Product: issues such as product types, quality, quantity, packaging, own label-policy, joint new product development, waste minimisation for product design, all need to be considered. New products and services would also be introduced to meet the needs of these new customers, and also in response to demand from existing customers following the repositioning campaign.

Promotion: guidelines on PR, in-store POS and sales promotions, direct mail to ethically responsive customers, wider promotional and advertising activity, sponsorship and internet communication should be developed. PR can be used to gain favourable publicity in the media; sales staff can emphasise the ethical aspects; advertising, mailshots, etc. can be targeted at the more ethical market segments. Needless to say, any misleading promotional messages, however clever or tempting, should be avoided.

Place: store location for prominent ranges such as Cafédirect and Kellogg's breakfast cereals – which are currently featuring their pledge of £1 m in working with the Cancer Research Campaign, to help raise public awareness about how this disease can be prevented, should be planned.

Control and evaluation
This should be based on the annual ethics/green/social audit results, consumer awareness and brand preference ratings on ethical trading measures, media coverage, employee satisfaction measures and bottom line performance measures.

Conclusions
It would seem that the Co-operative Supermarket chain have a window of opportunity in which to exploit the relative absence of ethical market leadership in the supermarket sector.

Failure to grasp this opportunity would mean that we would be likely to gravitate towards a reactive strategy, losing considerable face in the eyes of the general public, especially if competitors adopt a more aggressive approach to their social responsibilities, as our competitors appear to be doing.

Answer – Question 2.

To: Marketing Directors Of Car Manufacturers
From: Ann Student, Marketing Consultant
Date: 11th December 1998
Proposal: Sponsorship of a segmentation study in the car industry

Introduction
In the 1990s marketers have to come to terms with the accelerating fragmentation of many markets. A few years ago, Henry Ford's statement that, 'You can have any colour you want as long as it's black', was true. Now consumers and fleet buyers have a vast array of car colour choices such as Audi's 'Lifestyle Blue' and fleet ranges tailored to specific corporate needs.

The purpose of this brief proposal is to attract sponsorship for a detailed market segmentation study, in order to identify new and commercially valuable segments. The proposal will cover the definition of the segmentation process, the benefits to car manufacturers and examples of base variables that would be appropriate for this market sector.

What is market segmentation?
Market segmentation has been defined as the process by which customers in markets with some heterogeneity can be grouped into smaller, alike or homogenous segments (Kotler, 1997). What good marketers have realised for years is that customers' needs vary, and companies have limited resources. In order to make the two parties meet it is necessary to aggregate customers with similar needs into groups.

The process of segmentation, as detailed by Dibb et al. (1997), involves a series of stages:

Market segmentation
1   Identify segmentation variables and segment market.
2   Develop profiles of resulting segments.

Market targeting
3   Evaluate the attractiveness of each segment.
4   Select the target segment(s).

Product positioning
5   Identify positioning concepts for each target segment.
6   Select, develop and signal the chosen positioning concept.

Benefits of market segmentation

The process of market segmentation, targeting and positioning has a number of benefits which can be viewed at a number of different levels. At the customer level marketing managers have a better understanding of customer characteristics and therefore should be able to match their needs and wants better. At the competitor level a clearer picture of the competitive environment, who competes where, and where opportunities lie should emerge. At the resource allocation level the process offers more effective allocation of personnel, budgets and material resources. At the strategic marketing planning level segmentation allows gaps to be identified, in mature or declining markets it promotes a focus on those segments that are still in growth, and it guides marketing actions and mix development in each target segment.

The dangers of not segmenting when competitors do so are great. A company practising a mass marketing strategy in a segmented market against competitors operating a focused strategy can find itself being the jack of all trades but master of none.

Segmentation variables appropriate for the car market

Car buyers are both consumers and fleet buyers, thus we should segment using consumer and business-to-business bases. The variables used for segmenting consumer markets can be broadly grouped into two main classes. Firstly descriptive customer characteristics; which include demographics, socio-economics, geographic location, personality and lifestyle. So, at a simple level car consumers could be grouped by income, thus identifying used car buyers and new car buyers. In addition, a variety of small cars such as the Fiesta and Corsa are aimed at younger adults with a need for economy. This can be combined with psychographic variables; the Renault Clio comes to mind with its cosmopolitan and chic brand values. With recent advances in segmentation techniques we see cars being developed for various lifestyles, such as the Fiat Cinquecento for city dwellers and the Range Rover for country dwellers. The second class is product related behavioural characteristics, such as purchase behaviour, purchase occasion, benefits sought and attitude to the product. Part of Daewoo's brand strategy was based on an understanding of certain consumers' annoyance at 'pushy' car salespeople in dealerships. Volvo position on the benefit of safety, and have a mid to high priced range of cars, thus they target richer, safety conscious consumers.

Bonoma & Shapiro suggest business buyers can be segmented by purchasing approaches, situational factors, personal characteristics, demographic and operating variables. Thus buyers can be segmented into local, national, and international fleet buyers, by type of industry, turnover, and record of past fleet purchase – such as straight re-buy, modified or new task. For example, if dissatisfied Ford buyers could be identified, they could be heavily targeted by other car manufacturers in a likely modified/re-buy situation.

Conclusions

After segmenting the market and developing profiles it becomes necessary to decide target market strategy. First the attractiveness of each segment has to be assessed. The company can then decide whether to follow a concentration strategy; this is where all marketing efforts are directed towards one segment, as is the case with Ferrari who concentrate on high income consumers who want exclusivity and the ultimate in functionality and image. The alternative to this is to adopt a multi-segment strategy where effort is directed at two or more segments by developing a marketing mix for each. The larger car manufacturers such as Vauxhall and Ford do this with a number of cars, prices and advertising campaigns.

The final stage of the process is to develop a defendable position for the product. Positioning is the perception or image that the target market holds of the product. It describes to customers how the company differs from the current or potential competitors. Therefore Volvo positions on its safety attributes at a corporate level, and BMW as the ultimate driving machine.

As a marketing consultant who specialises in the car industry I hope this proposal indicates that I can help you achieve greater profitability by conducting a detailed review of how the car market segments. I would very much like to set up a meeting to discuss this proposal further and agree sponsorship terms.

Answer – Question 3.

To: The Recruitment Manager
From: A. Candidate
Subject: Example marketing plan

Introduction

In support of my application for Marketing Planning Manager with your organisation I attach an example marketing plan which I wrote when working for Ben & Jerry's Ice Cream. Whilst this is not the current plan I would ask that the information enclosed is treated with confidence.

The structure of the plan follows the accepted approach as offered by various academic authors (Dibb, Simkin and Bradley, 1997; McDonald, 1995; Brooksbank, 1994).

- Company vision/mission.
- Product/market background information.
- SWOT analysis.
- Statement of objectives.
- Strategies (target markets, competitive edge, brand positioning).
- Marketing programmes (detailed marketing mixes).
- Allocation of resources, tasks, responsibilities.
- Financial implications/budgets.
- Control implications.
- Operational and internal marketing implications.
- Appendices.

Example marketing plan

Company vision/mission
Ben & Jerry's company vision is to be the world leader in ethically and socially responsible ice cream and related product manufacturer.

Situation analysis – where are we now?
Ben & Jerry's needs to establish its strengths and weaknesses through an internal audit of the effectiveness of the following operations:

- Marketing strategy.
- Marketing programmes.
- Structure and reporting relationships.
- Systems, information and planning.
- Marketing efficiency.

An external audit of the micro- and macro-environment will highlight any threats or opportunities that the company needs to be aware of when entering the UK market:

- Political, legal and regulatory forces; for example consumer protection laws.
- State of the economy, consumer confidence, disposable income, unemployment and inflation.
- Social trends; in terms of how consumer lifestyles and attitudes are changing.
- Technological innovations in production, procurement, distribution and storage.
- Competition; in terms of their strengths and weaknesses, strategy, objectives and response profiles.

- Customers; in terms of likely buying behaviour and segmentation profiles.
- Substitute product demand.
- Likely market growth rate and new entrants.

SWOT analysis

From this marketing audit the SWOT analysis can be developed and the key factors for success in the market identified. It is likely that Ben & Jerry's differentiated brand image will be a strength in the UK market, their lack of an established market share a weakness, the growth in consumerism and environmental concerns an opportunity, and competition, especially in the form of Häagen-Dazs and supermarket own label premium ice cream, a threat. The key factors for success in this premium market are likely to include credible brand position, strong communications, access to distribution and product quality.

Marketing objectives – where do we want to be?

The next step is to develop clear marketing objectives. This lays the foundation for the creation of strategies and more detailed operation plans. Appropriate objectives for Ben & Jerry's would be:

- To achieve sales in the first year of £1.5m, representing 10% market share.
- To establish distribution in the top four supermarkets and top four leisure parks in the first year.
- To create positive awareness, interest and trial of the brand in 30% of the target market in the first year.

Marketing strategies

Competitive advantage: differentiation focus based on luxury ice cream product attributes and promotional uniqueness.

Target markets: the market for luxury ice cream should be segmented using the following bases:

- Consumer characteristics, i.e. demographic, geographic, geodemographic and psychographic.
- Product related buyer behaviour, i.e. purchase occasion, usage, benefits sought.

It is likely that multivariate segmentation will be used and that target markets are likely to have higher disposable incomes, be reasonably well educated, have strong social and environmental attitudes and seek luxury ice cream for special occasions and treats for the kids.

Brand position: position distinctly from Häagen-Dazs which is based on indulgence for adults and the sensual experience of luxury ice cream. Ben & Jerry's brand position could be based on responsible indulgence for the family and the symbol of an ethical consumer choice.

Marketing programmes

Taking on board the strategic guidelines of differentiation based on social and environmental positioning for responsible, family orientated adults, the marketing mix of product, promotion, pricing and distribution can be developed accordingly.

The product packaging and names need to be distinctive and consistent with brand position and offer interesting flavours. Heavy public relations activity should focus on social and environmental campaigning, with part of the purchase price being donated to charity. Pricing should be premium to reinforce the luxury product category and charitable contributions. Distribution should be in quality supermarkets, smaller retail outlets and family orientated leisure parks.

Allocation of resources, tasks, responsibilities

A Gantt chart should be developed which clearly outlines research and tactical activities, sectioned into pre-launch, launch and post launch activities. It should be clear which personnel, both internal and external, are responsible for these activities.

Financial implications and budgets
A projected sales forecast and profit and loss statement should be produced. The necessary marketing budget should be allocated based on an objective/task approach.

Implementation
The appropriate organisational structure needs to be established with clear reporting relationships and responsibilities for profit and market share. Control measures should be established related to monitoring key financial and non-financial targets, i.e. turnover and attitude tracking. Internal marketing is important in terms of our own employees and key external relationships with distributors and agencies.

The marketing plan should be developed in detail for the first year of operation for Ben & Jerry's in the UK, and developed more broadly to cover years two and three, to ensure the necessary strategic focus for marketing operations.

Answer – Question 4.

To: The Board
From: Sales Director
Date: 11th December 1998
Presentation: Evaluation and control of the sales force
Equipment: PC projector and screen, handout – summary of main points

Introduction
Good morning ladies and gentlemen of the Board, welcome and thank you for coming. Perhaps contrary to your impressions, we do try to control marketing here, and within this the control of our sales force is particularly important.

I intend to briefly outline the principles of marketing control before proceeding to sales force control, and the different approaches needed for our two sales forces. I shall use the PC projector throughout the presentation, which will take approximately 30 minutes, leaving 15 minutes for questions and discussion before lunch. A summary of the main points is in your folders for convenience.

Principles of marketing control
Marketing controls are very much the same as the financial controls you are familiar with in the form of balance sheets and profit and loss accounts. That is to say they include figures for sales and market shares and costs, which compare current performance against previous performance, and against targets set by your executives, including myself. However, there is a great more to it than this.

The purpose of these controls is, of course, to detect variances and to take corrective action, so as to ensure the company performs according to plan insofar as possible. Again perhaps contrary to impressions, not all variances are adverse, and I am delighted to inform you this morning that industrial sales have recently surged well above target, due to a major competitor going into liquidation. Not that this does not have its problems as we shall see.

Perhaps these diagrams taken from Kotler (1997) will clarify the marketing control process:

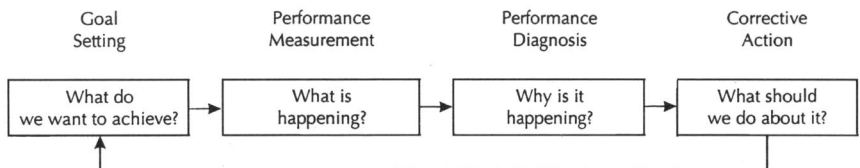

Goal Setting	Performance Measurement	Performance Diagnosis	Corrective Action
What do we want to achieve?	What is happening?	Why is it happening?	What should we do about it?

Control can be defined as the continuous comparison of actual results with those planned, and taking management action to correct adverse variances or to exploit favourable variances. To be able to do this targets and standards need to be set, and measurement and evaluation of performance needs to be undertaken. Evaluation and control is a natural part of the marketing planning process, ensuring that planned strategy really happens, and that results of such actions are properly monitored. Successful companies rely on the effective implementation and monitoring of strategy.

Sales force evaluation and control

Coming now to our own sales force, the following data is useful in monitoring individual representatives' performance:

- Sales against target.
- Sales across the product range.
- Number of new customers.
- % sales new versus existing customers.
- Call rates achieved.
- Selling expenses incurred.
- Contribution (sales less expenses, less overheads).
- Coverage of territory.
- Territory sales as a moving annual total.

In addition to the above *quantitative* control measures a number of *qualitative* assessments are desirable as follows:

- Complaint handling.
- Feedback on competitors and market intelligence.
- Contribution to team effort.
- Customer assessments.
- Training and development.

Differences between the two sales forces

We have two sales forces here because of our two distinct product ranges. Each range is sold to different types of buyers with different buying motives. For example the domestic heaters are bought by retailers for resale. Retail buyers are mainly interested in how quickly these will sell and at what margin. Industrial heaters made to order are by contrast bought either for own use, or for incorporation in the company's own equipment, and the buyers are mainly interested in performance.

For these reasons different types of people are needed for each of the two sales forces. The domestic heater representative tends to be younger, less qualified, and more extrovert, than the relatively patient, older and qualified sales engineers needed to sell industrial equipment made to specification.

Controls reflect these differences. For example, the number of calls made is less important for the sales engineers, where the emphasis tends to be on the number of enquiries generated, the number of conversions and the average size of order. We also have to allow for a much greater seasonality on the domestic front compared to the industrial segment. For the domestic representative, a cold winter can make a big difference to sales.

Conclusions

In conclusion, I hope I have been able to demonstrate to you that whereas all functional controls have a certain commonality, in the case of marketing and sales there are some specifics and complexities which need to be taken into account.

Overall sales volume/value/target achievement is vital, but also situational factors and qualitative performance measures should be used, with different evaluation suitable to our two markets.

Please raise questions or make comments as you think fit – we have about 15 minutes left before lunch. Thank you.

Answer – Question 5.

Briefing paper

From:	**Senior Product Manager**
To:	**Marketing Colleagues**
Date:	**11th December 1998**
Subject:	**Selection of a new advertising agency**

Introduction

It would appear from my enquiries that most of you share my concerns regarding our current advertising agency's performance, and agree that it is time for a change. It is towards this end that this briefing paper is presented.

In order to ensure the change represents a considerable improvement over the status quo, the following principles and procedures, based on best practice, should be followed.

Principles and procedures

- A Selection Committee should be appointed, consisting of the Marketing Director (Chair), and those members of the marketing team who will be using the agency's services. We should, I feel, also invite the CEO to sit in at appropriate times to ensure a more corporate and objective approach.
- Three agencies should be asked to make a competitive pitch for our account, which is not only substantial, but growing. The selection of these 3 agencies is of course critical, and should be made against the sort of criteria identified below.
- It is suggested that our current marketing consultant is asked to develop a ranked shortlist of not more than 6 candidate agencies, based on desk research and trade enquiries, against the broad criteria given below and our brief. It would however be the committee's decision to select the final 3 to be invited to pitch, and of course to decide on the winner. This procedure provides for the possibility that an invitee may decline to pitch.
- The 3 agencies invited to pitch should be given the fullest possible brief. This should include our mission statement, broad objectives and strategies, competitive positioning, market trends, previous advertising and an indication of the budget.
- Agencies should be made to pitch on the same day, on our premises, each being allocated one hour for the pitch, and a half hour for questioning by the committee.
- Committee members should score each agency individually against the agreed criteria before any general discussion takes place. However, moderation should then be allowed before the scores and comments are passed for collating.
- It is normal practice to let the competing agencies know the decision soon after it has been taken, ideally on the day following their pitches.

Criteria for shortlisting

Items which should be considered for inclusion as criteria on the checklist are:

1. PRESENT WORK	Efficient and effective? Proof?
2. PRESENT CLIENTS	Any clashes that will worry Computer Co., the agency or their other clients? Are the agency/client relationships long or short lived?
3. STAFFING	Will the people presenting today work on the account? How stable will the account team be? What depth of experience is in the team?
4. EVIDENCE	Of account management, creative and media planning ability? Delivery on time, within budget?
5. THE COMPANY	Its size, age, structure? International capability? Workload? Financial stability?
6. SPECIALIST KNOWLEDGE	Has the agency demonstrated realistic and satisfactory understanding of Computer Co.'s needs?
7. THE PRESENTATION	Is it tailored specifically? Does it cover all the points set out in the brief? Is it professional and creative?
8. PRICED	Do the fees represent value-for-money?
9. CHEMISTRY	Is the chemistry between you good? Would you trust this agency? Will this trust be reciprocated?
10. JUDGEMENT	Is this the agency for you? Reservations?

All criteria should be scored high, medium or low, and explanatory comments made. Discretion within grades to be quantified i.e. 0–3 for low, 4–6 for medium and 7–10 for high.

It is strongly recommended that the committee agree upon criterion weightings, on the basis that not all criteria are equal. For example, we should consider giving a weighting of 2 to criterion 5, and perhaps 3 to criterion 6.

Conclusion

The selection of a new advertising agency is an important decision, one that could critically affect the future success of our company. It is only fitting therefore that we take a highly professional approach to this issue of selecting outside suppliers.

To: The Editor, Marketing Texts
Date: 11th December 1998
From: A. N. Author
Subject: Case history – business-to-business marketing

Introduction

The following case history illustrates excellence in business-to-business marketing. For reasons of confidence the name of the company and some of the data have been altered.

The needs and wants of business-to-business markets differ quite radically from those of consumer markets. Most consumer goods/services are aimed at the personal gratification of the buyer or his/her family, i.e. food/drink pleasures, comfort (furnishings), entertainment (TV, hi-fi), leisure (holidays), etc. However, in business-to-business markets, products are usually bought for use in manufacturing other products, and for the profit or other motives of the purchasing organisation.

Kotler (1997), defines the business market as consisting of 'all the organisations that acquire goods and services used in the production or services that are sold, rented, or supplied to others'.

Case history – DLC computing

Background

DLC is essentially a distributor of computer hardware, consumables and spares. DLC was founded in the early 80s as a division of its parent company, demerging 5 years later to build a company turnover today exceeding £50 m and employing over 200 staff. This transformation of size and status is compelling evidence of its excellence in marketing. Although originally sales and product orientated, the company has developed into what could now be termed as a fully marketing orientated organisation with winning strategies.

Mission statement

'To involve every member of staff in meeting the needs of our business customers better than any other player in this market'.

Objectives

Consistent with the above, the broad objectives are:

- To focus on service, productivity and efficiency in all aspects of operations.
- To build lasting customer relationships, so as to utilise our personal resources in continuing to expand profitably.

Strategies

The company's dramatic growth has been achieved through 3 major strategies:

- *Segmentation.* DLC was observably the first company in this market to recognise the different needs of segments, such as retail, local government, the Health Service – with regard to distributor services.
- *Positioning.* By listening to customers and acting on identified segmental needs, also by imbuing all staff with the marketing concept, DLC has been able to establish itself as 'the most reliable and responsive supplier with the widest range of products and services, at competitive prices'.
- *Relationship Marketing.* Thanks to a Sales Director who took an early interest in this development of an old concept, DLC moved from key account management to a system of relationship management, which involves customers in the selection and training of their Customer Relationship Managers, and adopts a partnership approach. This strategy paid huge dividends as the market developed.

The marketing mix

Products and services

Consistent with segmental needs, distinct ranges have been developed which fall into the following groups:

- Hardware.
- Consumables.
- Spares.

Each of these is analysed for its contribution to turnover and profit, which currently stands at:

- Hardware = 52% of turnover, gross margin 11%.
- Consumbales = 34% of turnover, gross margin 15%.
- Spares = 14% of turnover, gross margin 44%.

This attention to contribution extends to lines within groups wherever possible, and also to individual customers.

Distribution and promotion

Perhaps unusually, DLC link these together in following through the principles of market segmentation.

For example, the local government and National Health segments need little promotional support, apart from reminder advertising in specialist journals. However, the provision of easy-to-use catalogues (some direct-on-line) is important, and speed of response can be vital. In the case of the National Health Service, back-up stocks are maintained by DLC on NHS premises for maximum availability where necessary.

On the other hand, retailers require more promotional support in the form of point-of-sale display material, which DLC acquire from the manufacturers. They usually wish to minimise stocks, and will not usually demand instant delivery.

Marketing research

DLC's excellence in business-to-business marketing is due in no small way to the constant monitoring of segmental needs, allied to feedback to its suppliers, i.e. an input into manufacturers' product development. In addition, a constant check is kept on manufacturers' offerings on a global basis, increasingly on the internet.

Justification for excellence

The principles for excellence in marketing operations are the same in any market, the serving of customer needs better than the competition.

However, in business-to-business markets where the buyers are professional and demanding, a great deal more tailoring of marketing operations is required.

DLC have exhibited a willingness to learn from its customers and to act on that knowledge. It is this facet above all others which results in the achievement of excellence in this difficult market.

Answer – Question 7.

To: **The Managing Director**
From: **The Marketing Manager**
Date: **11th December 1998**
Report: **Internal marketing**

Introduction

Bonoma and Clark's (1994) implementation model for a marketing plan includes: allocating, monitoring, organising and interacting skills. Interacting skills focus on how managers deal with employees, in order to win their co-operation and support for the changes needed as a result of a new marketing plan. The flip side of external marketing is internal marketing, which involves selling your marketing plan to your internal customers i.e. employees.

Marketing only works well when *all* employees appreciate they have an impact on customer satisfaction *and* fulfil their part in maximising this. For example, the work of the British Airways ticket issuer, the aircraft engineer and the flight steward, in getting a satisfied customer from London to New York, is all lost if disgruntled baggage staff handle the cases so carelessly that the contents are then damaged on arrival. For the marketing concept to be implemented effectively, all employees from top to bottom must feel part of the marketing process. In turn this requires the specific training and motivation of all staff to serve customers well.

For any marketing plan to work, it has to be sold to all its internal customers i.e. our employees, in order to win their support and co-operation and lessen the risk of an expensive failure.

The increasing importance of internal marketing

Since the publishing of 'In Search of Excellence' by Peters and Waterman, Boards have come to accept that service in all its aspects is at least as important as good products. Increasing global competition has added to the pressure to augment products with service benefits, in order to differentiate the offering and add value. Internal marketing plays a vital role in service quality. Service is the means to achieving a sustainable competitive advantage, in a world where products have tended to become 'commoditised'.

In the more recent book 'Market-Led Strategic Change', Piercy makes the point that a good strategy incorrectly implemented will not result in any advantages in the market place.

The example of British Airways internal marketing programme highlights many of the benefits of focusing on this issue. BA was privatised in 1987. At this time the business was variously described by analysts as 'a state owned shambles', and 'Bloody Awful'. The airline was showing some of the highest losses in the business and it had a worldwide reputation for poor customer service. Currently BA is the world's most profitable airline, having dislodged Singapore Airlines from that position in 1996.

There are a variety of factors underlying this excellent turnaround, one of which is their famous internal marketing programme, the details of which will be outlined in the next section.

Factors to be taken into account

- Getting the support of key decision-makers for our marketing plans, in order to gain the financial and personnel resources needed for success.
- Changing the attitudes and behaviour of all staff working at the key interfaces with customers and distributors, to those required to make marketing plans work profitably. This entails identifying the key influencers and decision-makers, and targeting them for appropriate action.
- Plans need packaging and promotion in order to win the support of, commitment to, and ownership of key problem-solving tasks associated with implementation of the marketing plan.
- Managers must make use of informal as well as formal networks of communication.
- Staff needs with regard to customer care training must be recognised and actioned.
- Incremental changes in the culture, from the way things have always been done, to the way they will have to be done in future in order to remain successful, must be planned and managed.

Piercy & Morgan (1989) offer an internal marketing model around the mix:

Product is the marketing plan which management wish to implement.

Price highlights that the costs and benefits to staff need to be assessed, and with any situation there may need to be negotiation.

Place internally is the timing and build-up to the announcement of the new plan, for example, the positive impact at a company-wide conference where all senior management are present.

Promotion in terms of poor communication is probably the biggest area for failure when evaluating internal company problems. Involvement of staff is key, therefore it is essential that meetings and discussion should take account of and utilise the skills of the workforce.

British Airways have had a succession of highly effective company-wide programmes for staff training and development to build customer focus: Customer First, Putting People First, A Day in the Life, To Be The Best and Winning For Customers. These involved measuring current levels of service quality and customer satisfaction, benchmarking against the competition, training and developing front-line employees and managers, and measuring and rewarding results. In 1996 the Break-through programme was initiated by BA's customer service training to address customer views that flight attendants were humourless and distant. This programme was part of a £500 m customer relations investment! Customer retention of complaining customers has doubled to 80%. The importance of employee commitment in the strategy of service driven profit is shown in the quarterly employee opinion polls, and the reward system for employees who uncover hidden problems.

Conclusion
Internal marketing is an essential part of a modern business operation.

I would be pleased to enlarge upon any aspect of this concept as required, or indeed to be involved in the drawing up of a formal internal marketing plan.

Specimen exam paper 2   December 1998

Advanced Certificate in Marketing
Advanced Certificate in Sales Management

Promotional Practice

PART A

Should you choose to make assumptions in your response to Question 1, please state these at the beginning of the answer.

Johnson Matthey fuel cell

In this case you are asked to take the role of a Public Relations Consultant hired by Johnson Matthey to aid the initial promotional activity for its newly developed fuel cell **within a country of your choice.**

Air quality, congestion and the need for sustainable transport are problems which increasingly occupy the minds of policy makers and the public. Complementary approaches are thought to offer the most hope, based on the use of technology to make cars operate in a cleaner and more efficient way, or on initiatives that aim to change behaviour in a way which will result in a reduction of car use.

Johnson Matthey, a company specialising in metal technology, has already had an impact on the former approach, with its development and enhancement of the catalytic converter, which when integrated within the design of a vehicle achieves a dramatic reduction in the level of emissions that vehicle makes.

Despite this advance in vehicle technology, the continued increase in the number of cars on the road, and the number of miles those cars cover, means that there is continued pressure to find more ways in which cars can operate in a cleaner way, with less harm to pedestrians and the environment.

Johnson Matthey believes that the solution is to dispense with burning fuel altogether, and to move to electrically powered vehicles. Battery-powered vehicles are the obvious solution. However range limitations and the need for equipment to recharge the battery, continue to hold this technology back. Johnson Matthey hopes that fuel cells may provide the answer.

Whereas a battery stores its own fuel and thus carries lot of weight, a fuel cell operates like an engine, converting fuel from chemical to electrical energy at a very efficient rate. The products of the fuel cell are electricity, heat and pure water (therefore no pollution). Cars that run on the fuel cell would look the same as any other, but would produce virtually no emissions and would run at approximately 90 miles per gallon of fuel. The technology has already been demonstrated by German manufacturer Daimler-Benz in one of its people carriers.

Johnson Matthey sees city centre buses as an initial prime market for fuel cells. Buses are one of the best ways of getting people out of their cars, but at the same time are a form of transport which currently suffers from concern about the level of engine smoke emitted and the impact this is having on city centre pollution and the health of city inhabitants. Electric buses make sense but big buses laden with passengers are too heavy for battery power, hence the opportunity for the fuel cell.

In the longer-term, the company hopes to penetrate the private vehicle market, believing that competitively priced fuel cell cars, that offer the performance and range of a normal car, but with two or three times the fuel economy, should certainly sell. Johnson Matthey believes that such a development is unlikely to happen within a timescale shorter than five years.

(Adapted from an article in Green Futures June/July 1997).

346

PART A

Question 1.

Your response may be based on a country of your choice.

As a Public Relations Consultant hired by Johnson Matthey to help promote its fuel cell over the next twelve months, prepare a report recommending the following:

a The promotional objectives Johnson Matthey should work towards with its public relations activity. **(10 marks)**

b The target audiences Johnson Matthey should address within its public relations. **(15 marks)**

c Public relations activity to be directed at priority target audiences over the next twelve months in order to achieve the objectives outlined in Question 1a. **(15 marks)**

(40 marks in total)

PART B – Answer THREE questions only

Question 2.

As Media Planner/Buyer on a large financial services account, you have recently recruited an assistant to work with you, who has not previously worked within the media department. Write a memo to your new recruit outlining the importance of media objectives within the media planning process. **(20 mark)**

Question 3.

Demonstrate the potential contribution of a marketing database to an advertising agency's promotional activity for the pursuit of new business.

(20 marks)

Question 4.

You are a Media Executive working for a large media independent. One of your key clients, a charity of your choice, has asked you to provide an evaluation of the opportunity outdoor media provide for its promotional activity, now and over the next five years. Write a short report detailing your analysis and recommendations. **(20 marks)**

Question 5.

As the Marketing Manager of a national magazine publisher, you have decided to appoint a sales promotions agency to work alongside your advertising agency. Write a memo to your Marketing Director detailing your recommendations for the process of selecting and appointing a suitable sales promotions agency to work on your account. **(20 marks)**

Question 6.

The hierarchy of effects model (awareness, knowledge, liking, preference, conviction, purchase) was developed as an approach to understanding how advertising works. To what extent can this model be used as an explanation of how sports sponsorship works? Illustrate your answer with reference to two examples. **(20 marks)**

Question 7.

Assess the current and potential impact of e-mail on the internal and external communication of an organisation of your choice. **(20 marks)**

Specimen answers follow.

Turn to them only when you have completed your review.

Johnson Matthey Fuel Cell: Public Relations Campaign (UK)

To: John Smith – Marketing Director, Johnson Matthey UK
From: Paul Ferguson – Public Relations Consultant, ABC Public Relations
Date: 7th December 1998

Contents

Section
Introduction   1.
Objectives   2.
Target Audience   3.
Public Relations Activity 4.
Summary   5.

1. Introduction

This report has been prepared for Johnson Matthey regarding the Public Relations campaign for the new fuel cell technology. The report will make recommendations on the following:

- Promotional objectives Johnson Matthey should work towards with Public Relations activity.
- Target audiences to be addressed with Public Relations.
- Public Relations activities should be targeted to achieve outlined objectives.

2. Promotional objectives

These objectives have been developed to be specific, measurable, achievable, realistic and timed.

2.1   Raise 85% awareness of the Johnson Matthey fuel cell within the city centre bus design and manufacturing industry within 12 months.

2.2   Generate agreement with the statement 'Fuel cell technology is kinder to the environment than traditional engines' within at least 70% of public and private sector city centre bus decision-makers. This objective will help ensure that fuel cell technology is at the forefront of the minds of those who purchase city centre buses in both public and private sectors.

2.3   The promotional objectives will have to be carefully measured. Both objectives will be measured using a combination of quantitative and qualitative research, such as questionnaires using a Lickert scale to measure objective 2.2, and focus groups to measure objective 2.1.

3. Target audience

Public Relations is the planned and sustained effort to promote goodwill and mutual understanding between an organisation and its publics. Johnson Matthey has many important publics who should be addressed with Public Relations activity. These publics are detailed below:

3.1   **Customers**
      Customers are obviously an extremely important public. To assist with the swift adoption of this technology two different groups of customer can be identified.
      3.1.1   **Designers and manufacturers of city centre buses**
              It is important to target this group of customers, to encourage them to design the fuel cell technology into their buses from the drawing board stage.
      3.1.2   **Public and private sector city centre bus purchasers**
              It is essential that these indirect customers of Johnson Matthey are aware of the technology and its environmental benefits so they can put pressure on manufacturers to use it.

3.2 Government: department of transport
The Government also needs to be targeted to make them aware of the environmental advantages of this technology, and encourage its use in the public sector, and indeed the private sector. The private sector could perhaps be encouraged to adopt the technology in return for tax incentives, which could be awarded for reducing emissions in city centres.

3.3 Employees
Internal Public Relations are vital to ensure all employees are aware of fuel cell technology and its advantages. Internal seminars and mini-exhibitions may be an effective method of communication.

3.4 Environmental groups
It is very worthwhile communicating with groups such as Greenpeace and Friends of the Earth, as they continuously lobby the government to adopt more environmentally friendly methods of transport. These groups could prove to be of great assistance in communicating the benefits of fuel cell technology.

3.5 Local authorities
Local authorities represent their local community. Local communities, particularly in city centres, are very concerned about levels of pollution. Public Relations should be directed at local authorities, so they are aware of the fuel cell technology, and can then put pressure on their bus purchasers and private bus companies operating in their towns/cities.

4. Public relations activity to be directed at priority audiences
The following two publics have been identified as priority target audiences over the next 12 months, in order to achieve the objectives detailed in Section 2.1 and 2.2 of this report:

- Public and Private Sector city centre bus purchasers.
- Designers and Manufacturers of city centre buses.

4.1 Activity directed at city centre bus designers and manufacturers
The first task will be to identify the organisations and individuals within them that fall into this category. The recommended activities are as follows:

4.1.1 Seminars
It is recommended that a series of seminars be held either at Johnson Matthey UK or conference locations abroad. This is because many city centre bus manufacturers are based outside the UK in European countries such as Spain and Holland. These seminars will be put on separately for each organisation so that they can feel free to ask all the questions they would like, without the fear of competitors making assumptions. The seminars could introduce the technology or give delegates the opportunity to discuss the technology with key employees from Johnson Matthey.

4.1.2 Exhibitions
Johnson Matthey should exhibit at all appropriate trade fairs. This target audience will attend in order to raise awareness of relevant developments, such as the fuel cell, which will allow the delivery of higher levels of value to their customers.

4.1.3 Multimedia CD-ROM
A computer presentation could be prepared introducing Johnson Matthey and fuel cell technology. This would allow detailed information to be presented at a pace tailored to the audience.

4.1.4 Press activity
Publications targeting these individuals should be sent press packs, including special articles written by Johnson Matthey on fuel cell technology. Individual journalists will also be targeted, and Johnson Matthey employees should make themselves available for press interviews with those publica-

tions which particularly target city bus manufacturers and designers.

4.1.5 Literature

Literature explaining the benefits of the technology should be distributed to all actual and potential designers/manufacturers of city centre buses. A suitable list may be available from a list broker.

4.2 Public and private sector city centre bus purchasers

Again all organisations forming part of this group need to be identified, as do the individuals amongst them forming the decision-making unit.

4.2.1 Demonstrations

In conjunction with a bus manufacturer, a prototype model could be built in order to demonstrate its capabilities to the purchasers of buses.

4.2.2 Environmental data

The objective relating to this specific group was directly linked to the fact that fuel cell technology is kinder to the environment. This claim must be backed up by environmental test results. The tests should be carried out by an independent body and presented to purchasers of city centre buses in an information pack.

4.2.3 Press activity

Again the press targeting this audience needs to be approached with news releases and interviews which specifically pertain to the environmental benefits of fuel cell technology.

5. Summary

The activities detailed in Section 4. of this report directly relate to the objectives laid out in Sections 2.1 and 2.2. Activities described to target bus designers and manufacturers will undoubtedly create a great deal of awareness.

Activities described to target bus purchasers specifically deal with environmental benefits, and should also ensure we achieve the objective listed in Section 2.2 of this report.

If you would like to discuss any aspect of this report please do not hesitate to contact me.

Examiner's comments on this response

A clear, well-structured response which lays out objectives and provides appropriate recommendations for activity targeted at priority publics. Although generally justified, there is opportunity for further commentary on objectives and activity in particular. It has a good range of publics, reflecting the business-to-business nature of the case.

General comments on all December 1998 exam responses

Similar problems to those in previous exam papers continue to be evident in the responses to the case study. The following general points are highlighted:

- Read questions carefully and engage directly with the case study scenario.
- Identify salient points from the case, but do not waste time regurgitating the case material – it should be used to justify proposals.
- There was a need for a stronger link between objectives, target audiences and activity.
- A clear report format is required of the answer.
- Avoid trying to shoe-horn answers into inappropriate formats e.g. SOSTAC, focus on answering the particular questions posed
- Many students did not recognise the business-to-business emphasis of the case.

1a.

This section of the question was answered adequately by many candidates, but well by very few. Issues which answers to Question 1a. highlighted were:

- Many responses sought to set objectives way beyond the realm of Johnson Matthey. For example, changing the general public's attitude towards pollution.
- A large proportion of answers confused marketing and promotional objectives.
- Some answers parrot the AIDA model as a structure for objectives, without sufficient consideration of the demands of the case.
- Surprisingly few answers included objectives within the realm of public relations – informing, gaining understanding and sympathy.
- There was a continued tendency for candidates to quote the need for SMART objectives, and then fail to apply this approach.
- Some candidates continue to apply SMART by providing five objectives, one specific, one measurable, one achievable, one realistic and one timed, rather than ensuring that all objectives are SMART.
- The use of adjectives in objective setting needs some care, e.g. to achieve 'bigger awareness' is not a clear description of an objective.
- Equally there must be clarity of what objectives are being focused upon, e.g. raising awareness – of the fuel cell or Johnson Matthey?
- A lack of specificity about which target audiences the objectives were targeted at – there is a great difference between achieving 80% awareness of the fuel cell amongst bus manufacturers and amongst all car users.
- Many answers provided little rationale or justification for objectives.
- There was little consideration of the implications of the prescribed timetable, and how short-term objectives might support longer-term objectives.

1b.

Many answers to this section of the question were rather brief, listing a few target audiences, but without any justification for their inclusion or attempt to prioritise their importance. Rather too many responses ignored the business-to-business publics, which would be paramount within the 12-month time period. Additional issues were:

- Some answers usefully categorised their publics into active, aware and latent states.
- The bus sector and associated publics (bus manufacturers; bus company purchasers; bus company employees) were generally given less attention than they deserved.
- The role of government, green pressure groups and the media was recognised.
- Some students identified those audiences which would be opposed to the fuel cell's development, but which would require inclusion within the PR plan.

1c.

Whilst this section of the question was allocated the same number of marks as 1b, generally students spent considerably more time discussing this part of their response. Links with the previous parts of the answer could have been stronger – comparatively few candidates clearly linked activity to target audience and objective. Some students seemed to include within their answer to earlier sections of the case, information which sensibly belonged in this section. Many responses focused on essentially achievable activity. Additional issues were:

- Fewer candidates than might be hoped identified the priority publics their activity would be targeted at.
- Many students focused largely on media relations, but provided insufficient insight to the range of opportunities they could tap into within this area.

351

- Whilst many candidates identified government as a target audience, few then discussed the role of lobbying as part of their PR activity.
- Many students picked up on opportunities presented by exhibitions and conferences.
- Sponsorship could have been legitimately included within proposed activity, but despite the majority of responses seeking to increase awareness of the fuel cell, few recommended it.

Answer – Question 2.

Memo

To: J. Smith
From: B. Anon, Media Planner/Buyer
Date: 7th December 1998

Welcome to CR Agency, I hope you will enjoy working with the team. I understand that you have worked briefly in account planning but wish to understand more about media planning and buying.

As a marketing graduate you will, I am sure, be aware of the importance of planning. However, for ease of reference, I have set out the main planning process so you can see the role and importance of media objectives in planning the scheduling and purchase of media for PP Building Society, (henceforth 'PP').

1. Planning process

1.1 Situation/background

The 'where are we now question'. PP. is a society that has recently become a limited company and floated. It wants to establish itself in the market place. It is based in the North-East and has 41 branches in total, and wants to expand southwards.

1.2 Objectives

As with all objectives, media objectives should be specific, measurable, achievable, relevant and timed.

I would like you to think about some objectives for PP – the following may help.

   1.2.1 To raise prompted awareness in the South of England from 5% to 35% within 2 years.

   1.2.2 To remain within the agreed media budget of £2 m.

   1.2.3 To position PP as one of the top three building societies in England within 6 years.

1.3 Strategy

Once the objectives are set out and agreed, the media strategy and target markets follow easily. The media planning is long-term and has geographical parameters.

1.4 Tactics

This is where we decide how to implement the strategy – the detailed plans:

- Advertisements in national and major regional press.
- TV/radio national and regional advertising, to achieve the objective of raising awareness.
- Direct mail to potential customers in the South of England, backed up with advertising that we need to plan in.
- The budget is known and must be adhered to.

1.5 Measurement

The success of our planning can be judged as to whether the objectives are achieved. Objectives may need to be revised if unrealistic, e.g. the budget for media raised.

I hope you have some idea of the importance of objectives, and I look forward to receiving your suggested objectives.

General comments on all December 1998 exam papers

This was not a popular question, and those who answered it rarely did so well. There seemed to be a lack of understanding of what media objectives were. Insights into the media planning process were better. Many responses included sensible, but generic, comments about objectives, unapplied to the media context. The format and tone of the memo was usually appropriate, but very few responses incorporated the financial services context provided. Additional issues include:

- There was very little understanding of the role of quantitative media objectives, such as coverage, frequency, and OTS/H, and qualitative objectives seeking to address the media environment.
- There was little recognition that media objectives might reflect the creative execution and impact.
- Evaluation of the media plan against media objectives was rarely mentioned.
- There was an opportunity for more examples to be included.

Answer – Question 3.

Memo
To: John Doe, C.E.O.
From: E. Shire, Marketing Director
Ref: Marketing database on promotional activity aimed at new business
Date: 7th December 1998

1. Background
Our business is creative, fast flowing and increasingly competitive. A marketing database can be used in the pursuit of new business by targeting our promotional activity.

2. Marketing database
A marketing database allows the planned recording analysis and tracking of customer behaviour to develop relationship marketing techniques.

The database shows the analysis of past, present and potential customers.

3. New business
Through the use of segmentation techniques we can see who our customers are and where we should be looking for new business.

Type of business: we can analyse which type of business we do most profitably.

Size of business: analysis will reveal the size of business we work with most successfully.

Geography: where are the businesses we work with; local, national, international?

Which of our services are most successful? Do we make more money out of research or production? Do we have more skill in one area over another?

How many leads turn into business? Are we poor at following-up and converting leads into business?

By segmenting our market base in the different ways above, we can work out our best areas and target those areas with specific promotional activities.

Promotional activity

The marketing database has provided the tools to segment our business. We are now in a position to analyse potential new customers in each segment and target those customers with our promotional activities. These promotions will/can be customised, personalised and tightly targeted. We can now use such tactics as:

- Direct Mail.
- Specific trade magazines.
- Promotional offers linked to specific customer needs.

Conclusion

The marketing database allows us to build up a profile of our customers. Through segmentation we can analyse the market and identify our strengths and opportunities for new business. We can then target our promotional activity towards those customers with the best potential for our success.

Examiner's comments on this response

A structured response which was correctly applied to the search of new agency business, recognising the basic opportunities the database provides of segment action and targeting for promotional activity. More detail could have been usefully provided, and limitations of the database should have been highlighted.

Comments on all December 1998 exam responses

This was a popular question. Many responses failed to recognise the business-to-business context, and instead discussed the role of the database within consumer marketing. Most responses clearly demonstrated an understanding of the marketing database, what it can do, and the essential concepts underpinning direct marketing. Too often this information was presented in an unapplied fashion. Additional issues were:

- There was very little discussion of the limitations of a marketing database, and the need to integrate with other new business activity.
- Similarly the extent of and validity of information added was rarely questioned.
- Many responses did give some thought as to where they would obtain information for the database, but often this was unrealistic.
- Very few students considered the ultimate aim of relationship building and the limit of the database within this context.

Report
To: Sarah Smith – Marketing Director, Help The Aged
From: Paul Ferguson – Media Executive, ABC Independent Media
Date: 7th December 1998
Ref: 12/AB

Evaluation of outdoor media for help the aged

1. Introduction
This report has been prepared at the request of Help the Aged to provide an evaluation of the opportunity outdoor media can provide for its promotional activity, now and over the next five years.

2. Outdoor media
Most of us are familiar with the forms of outdoor media in the UK but I have detailed a short list below.

Transport
This includes advertising space inside and outside buses, taxis, ferries, lorries, trains and tubes.

Posters
We are all familiar with posters. The most important issue with posters is location. Poster research details locations of all poster sites, including how many people pass them and how many people see them.

Other
Outdoor advertising is only limited by imagination. For example, the outside of buildings can be used, such as the lighting displays in Piccadilly Circus, London. Ambient media is increasingly available in a wide variety of places from golf holes to petrol pumps.

3. Analysis
Outdoor media could be extremely effective for Help the Aged for the following reasons:

3.1 **Awareness**
Poster advertising can be extremely effective so a campaign using this medium could create high levels of awareness.
3.2 **Low cost**
Outdoor media is significantly less expensive to use as an advertising medium than advertising, for example, in a national paper. This would allow the campaign to run for longer on a limited budget.
3.3 **Strategic positions**
By strategically using the location of the outdoor media it could aid Help the Aged target its audience more effectively, whether that audience be donors or beneficiaries.
3.4 **Recognition**
An outdoor media campaign could greatly increase the recognition of the Help the Aged logo. As has been said earlier in this report, outdoor advertising can be extremely effective and memorable. For example, who has not noticed the Compaq plastic lettering as you enter Heathrow Airport?

4. Recommendations
It is recommended that Help the Aged incorporate outside media advertising into their integrated marketing communications campaign. Using outdoor media to advertise will create an effective, memorable and high impact campaign at a lower cost than for other media.

I will contact you early next week to propose various possible sites, and to discuss your promotional objectives in more detail.

General comments on all December 1998 exam responses

This was another popular question, and generally handled better. Many responses gained a marginal pass, but few were excellent. The charity context was rarely used in any detail – most students introduced the charity at the outset, but rarely returned to discuss how outdoor media might fulfil its specific promotional needs. Students often focused on the advantages of outdoor media and disregarded any disadvantages. Few students reflected on potential changes over time (as required by the question), and some inappropriately proposed a five year schedule. Additional issues this question generated were:

- A wide range of outdoor media were incorporated within many responses, and some students picked up on ambient media.
- Few students included examples of contemporary usage of outdoor media by charities to support their debate, (or indeed recognised the comparative lack of activity from the charity sector within this medium).
- Recommendations were generally satisfactory, but were often left unjustified.
- Very few students took the opportunity to define promotional objectives which the charity might be seeking to satisfy – clearly if they had, their analysis could have been related back to these objectives.
- A good number of responses recognised the need to integrate activity with other advertising or marketing communications.
- Few responses recognised the limitations of the availability of good poster sites, and the fact that over the ensuing five years such availability (within the UK) might increase if tobacco advertising is withdrawn.

Answer – Question 5.

Memo

To:	A. Anderson, Marketing Director
From:	B. Breslaw, Marketing Manager
Re:	Recommendations for selection and appointment of sales promotion agency
Date:	7th December 1998

1. Background

Thank you for asking me to co-ordinate the selection and appointment of a new sales promotion agency to work with Gardens Today.

Our present advertising agency is not a full service agency and is not able to offer these services. The new agency will therefore have to achieve a close, trusting relationship with our existing agency (Ad Ltd.). I have therefore consulted our account manager at Ad Ltd. to gain his views on the choice of agency and how the agency is appointed.

2. Process

2.1 **Search**

For a list of possible sales promotion specialists I have looked in Campaign and Marketing Weekly Portfolios and selected five or six from the videos and brochures. These accompany this memo.

Ad Ltd. has recommended Lots of Sales Ltd., a niche agency with whom they have previously worked and enjoy a good relationship.

2.2 Credentials

We need to choose about 6 agencies and ask them to present brief details about themselves, clients, history and philosophy.

From these we should select 2 to brief on a pitch. Most agencies do not charge for such pitch work.

Ad Ltd. needs to be involved in this decision. They are going to have to work closely with the selected agency.

2.3 Pitch and afterwards

I recommend that you yourself and Ad Ltd. attend the pitches. We can select an agency after discussion and then advise both the chosen one, and the one who failed.

I have identified our selection criteria below.

A contract should be entered into with the new agency, setting out remuneration, expectations, termination, confidentiality, etc.

3. Selection

Selection criteria are numerous and I recommend we concentrate on the following:

3.1 Skills and resources

We are looking for new ideas and creativity for our magazine. We are newly established and need to gain more readers. We should look at past projects completed by the agency and focus on promotions targeted at customer acquisition.

We should ensure the selected agency has the necessary in-house skills to carry out projects and promotions.

The agency should be suitably qualified and a member of the Sales Promotion Society. It should be totally familiar with the Sales Promotion Code and other statutory restrictions.

3.2 Client base

We should check that there are no other garden magazines on their books; we do not want a conflict of interest. We should also ask Ad Ltd. to ensure there are no conflicts of interest with other publishers, as this would cause friction.

On the other hand we do want them to have magazine experience, especially in the consumer sector.

3.3 Communication

Gardens Today has a small team and we cannot afford the resources to co-ordinate the two agencies. We need an account manager appointed at the selected sales promotion agency with whom Ad Ltd. and ourselves can get on. Chemistry is very important to maintain the triangle of relationships.

3.4 Costs

We need to resolve the fees from the outset. Fee by project is more usual in the sales promotion sector. This should be agreed in the written contract.

3.5 Size

Our account is not large, and we do not want to be a small fish in a large pool. Ad Ltd. will not, as a small agency themselves, feel comfortable working with a large international agency.

4. Summary

The introduction of a third party could upset the balance with the Ad Ltd. relationship. It is vital that they, as well as ourselves, are satisfied with the choice of agency, and that we have their commitment to the on-going relationship.

If you would like to arrange a meeting once you have read my recommendations, to discuss how best to proceed, I would be pleased to arrange one to suit you.

General comments on all December 1998 exam responses

Again this was a popular question and was generally answered satisfactorily. Most responses addressed the selection process and could identify relevant selection criteria. Fewer candidates addressed the nuances of the question sufficiently. Thus there was an opportunity to further contextualise the answer to the publishing industry, and to reflect more clearly upon the particular characteristics of the sales promotions agency (rather than the advertising agency). Additionally the relationship between the existing agency and the prospective sales promotions agency was rarely sufficiently addressed – the better answers identified the role the advertising agency could play within the selection process.

Answer – Question 6.

The Lavidge and Steiner hierarchy of effects model lists:

- Awareness
- Knowledge
- Liking
- Preference
- Conviction
- Purchase

as the key stages a buyer goes through prior to purchase.

The key role of advertising is to take a person from unawareness to the purchase of a product.

For models to be effective they must be:

- Simple.
- Logical.
- Valid.
- Provide explanation (of behaviour).
- Provide method of evaluation.
- Provide for further research.

They provide a simple description of a system, to aid prediction, calculation and forecasting.

This model does not always meet all these criteria when it is used as a framework for sports sponsorship. Two examples will be used to assess the applicability of the Lavidge and Steiner model to this context.

Example 1.

Del Monte formerly sponsored Lazio Football Club to the tune of £2 m, and the club had the Del Monte name on its shirts.

Awareness

The use of Lazio created awareness of the Del Monte brand both in Italy and the rest of Europe. It reached a very large target audience, especially men and young boys.

Knowledge

This sponsor did very little to increase the purchaser's knowledge of the product. It did help develop the brand values as a healthy product (the perception being that it is used by footballers), and brand image.

Liking

As there is no opportunity to taste the product, the customer has little opportunity to develop liking. Any liking expressed is likely to be as a result of association – in the fan's eyes if the Lazio team drink it I must like it too.

The same argument applies for preference, conviction, and purchase.

As the greatest proportion of shopping is done by women, and the target audience is predominantly male, purchase is unlikely to result.

Example 2.

Tim Henman – Fyffes Bananas

This sponsorship covers supplying bananas to Tim Henman at all events, and uses him as a celebrity to endorse health benefits.

Awareness

This sponsorship is very good at raising awareness of bananas, but because of the small size of the product and inability to distinguish between a Fyffes banana and a Chiquita one, awareness of the brand is not greatly increased solely by usage. The PR events to promote the sponsorship allowed for greater association with Fyffes, and generated a great deal of awareness in the Trade Press, e.g. Get Fresh and Fresh Produce Magazine, as well as amongst the target audience. Tim Henman has a huge personal fan base and by sponsoring him Fyffes have been able, by association, to get across messages of health, fitness and goodness.

Again, as in the previous example, the model does not adequately reflect how sports sponsorship works; there are other models such as:

- AIDA – Awareness, Interest, Desire and Action.
- ADOPTION – Awareness, Interest, Evaluation, Trial and Adoption.
- DAGMAR – Unawareness, awareness, comprehension, conviction and purchase.

While these do provide a framework to develop advertising around, they are of limited use in the evaluation of sponsorship. This is because advertising is only one outcome of sponsorship.

Sponsorship objectives

Sponsorship, which is the giving of money or goods usually in return for advertising space, is not done solely for the advertising. It helps to:

- Build the prestige and image of the company.
- Creates goodwill within the company.
- Can be used to help build brands.
- Can benefit by association, as in the case of Beamish's sponsorship of Inspector Morse.

The use of the Lavidge and Steiner model as an explanation of how sports sponsorship works is limited.

Examiner's comments on this response

A satisfactory response which does two things well: it uses the required two examples to illustrate points made, and is critical of the model in this context, highlighting its limitations. There is the opportunity for this answer to be further enhanced. Towards the end it becomes less focused on the question, and does not link its final comments on sponsorship objectives to the central thrust of the discussion.

General comments on December 1998 exam responses

Those who chose this question seemed to find it difficult. Too many answers displayed a general understanding of sports sponsorship, but did not try to address the specific question posed. The answers which did focus on the demands of the question were often insufficiently critical of the applicability of the model. Whilst the lower stages of awareness, knowledge and liking were usually adequately addressed, far fewer responses considered the applicability of the preference, conviction and purchase stages. Answers generally included reference to examples as requested, but often the examples were not selected to make different points, but to reinforce the same point (e.g. the potency of sports sponsorship in raising awareness). Additional issues were:

- There was little reference to the impact of broadcast sponsorship and ambush marketing on the way that sports sponsorship works.
- There was the opportunity for further discussion of the need for integration/leverage to reach the higher levels of the model.

Answer – Question 7.

Report

Current and potential impact of e-mail on Microsoft

1. Introduction
Microsoft are a multimillion dollar international company who employ thousands of people at numerous locations worldwide. E-mail has many current and potential impacts on the internal and external communications at Microsoft.

2. Internal impacts
E-mail has radically changed the way large organisations communicate.

2.1 **Breaking through hierarchical constraints**
Internal e-mail makes it possible for any employee within the organisation to communicate with any other. This has tended to break down hierarchical barriers.

2.2 **Ease of communication**
E-mail has impacted a great deal on internal communication, because of its ease of use and its ability to communicate with many other individuals at any one time.

2.3 **Danger of casualness**
E-mail has recently had a large impact on Microsoft when a judge required copies of internal mail to be submitted to the Court. These e-mails contained inappropriate business language and caused negative publicity for Microsoft. This shows that care must be taken when using any channel of communication.

2.4 **Speed of communication**
E-mail is currently impacting Microsoft in that the speed of communication is much faster. Documents can be e-mailed to foreign subsidiaries much faster than using courier or postal methods.

3. External impacts
3.1 **Legislation**
OCTEL are currently introducing a law which will stop 'junk' faxes being sent without the receiver's permission. This is likely to also happen with e-mail if the current trend of junk e-mail continues.

3.2 **Lack of control**
Customers are using e-mail to communicate their requirements more and more. Internal procedures will have to be implemented to ensure that his does not impact on quality assurance procedures. Important e-mails must be filed where they can be accessed by all individuals, either on a computer network or in a filing cabinet.

This structured answer addresses internal and external issues, and in the main links analysis to discussion of impacts upon communication, rather than straying too far from the focus of the question. There is the potential for a fuller discussion of e-mail, which would have been rewarded with more marks.

General comments on December 1998 exam responses

Many interesting responses were provided to this question, and the majority related their discussion to an organisation as requested. Most answers did address the communication issues, but some departed on a tangent to discuss far more general issues, losing the required communication focus. Answers tended to focus upon current rather than potential impacts, but did usually reflect upon the advantages and disadvantages of e-mail, internally and externally. Few students attempted to apply diffusion theory to their response.

Marketing Operations

Aims and objectives
- To build on the knowledge of marketing fundamentals which the student is already expected to have gained
- To encourage students to test and apply modern marketing theory to the understanding and solution of practical marketing problems and situations. This will enable them to perform effectively in any single functional area of marketing at junior management level
- To provide students with a sound understanding of the process of marketing planning (analysis, strategy and implementation) and underpinning knowledge for the Diploma subject Planning and Control
- To provide students with a sound understanding of the marketing mix tools that contribute towards the effective implementation of marketing strategy
- To be able to evaluate the relative effectiveness and costs of elements of the promotional mix providing underpinning operational knowledge for the Integrated Marketing Communications module at Diploma level
- To encourage students to explore the multiple relationships which need to be formed and maintained to enable successful and ongoing marketing exchange
- To examine the need to adapt marketing operations in a variety of contexts; business-to-business, services, not-for-profit and international

Learning outcomes
Students will be able to:
- Conduct a basic marketing audit considering internal and external factors
- Understand the process of marketing planning at an operational level
- Develop marketing objectives and plans at an operational level
- Understand the need to integrate marketing mix tools to achieve effective implementation of plans
- Select an appropriate integrated mix (4 Ps or 7 Ps) for a particular marketing context
- Select and justify the use of one or more promotional techniques for a particular marketing context
- Demonstrate the adaptation of marketing operations principles in a variety of contexts
- Understand and appreciate the marketing operations process and how it can be delivered through multiple relationships
- Communicate ideas effectively in a variety of formats; report, article, presentation

Indicative content and weighting

1.1 The marketing planning process: an overview (15%)

1.1.1 *Conducting a marketing audit*
- Analysis of an organisation's marketing environment
  Macro: political, legal, economic, socio-cultural, technological
  Micro: market size/trends, customers, competitors, suppliers, distributors, publics
- Analysis of organisation's internal capabilities
  Financial resources, human resources, manufacturing, operations, R&D and marketing (strategy, mix, organisation, systems, productivity)
- SWOT analysis and key issues

1.1.2 *Developing marketing objectives and strategies*
- Marketing objectives as simple goal statements, links to mission statement
- How marketing strategy defines target markets (from segmentation bases and profiles), differential advantage and desired brand positioning
- Gap analysis and Ansoff matrix

1.1.3 Implementing the marketing plan
- Implementation barriers
- Allocation of budgets, tasks, responsibilities
- Control implications
- Alternative ways of organising marketing activities; by function, product, region, type of customer, matrix
- Internal marketing implications; gaining commitment for the plan

1.2 The marketing mix (50%)

1.2.1 *Promotional operations (20%)*
- Theories of communication: single step, two step and multi-step communication models, adoption models
- Advertising techniques: campaign planning, developing creative and media briefs, message content, evaluation
- Sales promotion techniques: objectives, mechanics (sampling, price-offs, in-pack, etc.), evaluation
- Public relations techniques: establishing publics, press relations, lobbying, crisis management, evaluation
- Direct and interactive communications: objectives, database marketing, direct mail, telemarketing, internet, evaluation
- Sponsorship: objectives, types (sport, arts, community, etc.), evaluation
- Personal selling techniques (sales force, sales support and sales literature)

1.2.2 *Pricing operations (10%)*
- The importance of price and its determinants
- Pricing models for decisions based on cost competition and demand (including basic break-even analysis, marginal costing and price elasticity)
- Pricing objectives and methods (cost-plus, perceived-value, competitive parity, etc.)
- Adapting the price (discounts, promotions, product-mix, etc.)

1.2.3 *Product operations (10%)*
- The nature of products, components and life cycles
- Brand management; brand values, brand planning and threats to the brand
- Product portfolio, product mix (product line breadth and depth)
- New product development (idea generation, screening, concept development and testing, marketing strategy, business analysis, launch, evaluation and development)

1.2.4 *Place operations (10%)*
- Distribution channels; consumer and business-to-business, new direct channels of distribution such as the internet
- Criteria to select and evaluate alternative channels for distribution

1.3 Managing marketing relationships (15%)

1.3.1 *Relationships with customers*
- Defining the concept, types of relationships; degree of importance

363

- The recognition of distributors, intermediaries, agents and franchisees as customers
- Customer retention planning; relationship marketing mix
- Managing customer relationships
- Key account management techniques

1.3.2 *Relationships with outside suppliers*
- Briefing, working, control and review of agencies and consultancies (specifying needs/time span/budgets)
- Working with distributors, franchisees and agents; building relationships and controlling performance

1.3.3 *Internal marketing relationships*
- The concept, organizational structures and cultures
- Effective internal marketing techniques (recruitment, training, communication, cross-functional team working, etc.)

1.3.4 *Relationships with the wider public and society*
- The importance of marketing ethics and social responsibility
- Ethics for marketing executives and within the marketing mix
- Codes of ethics
- Social responsibility issues: consumer, community, green
- Proactive, reactive or passive strategies to social responsibility

1.4 Marketing operations in context (20%)

1.4.1 *Industrial/business to business marketing applications*
- Distinguishing characteristics of business versus consumer markets
- Business buyer behaviour, factors affecting buying decisions and buying process
- Marketing mix differences (service component, bid and negotiated pricing, role of personal selling, use of distributors and agents)

1.4.2 *Services marketing*
- Basic characteristics (intangibility, inseparability, perishability, heterogeneity)
- Extended marketing mix (people, process, physical evidence)
- Importance of service quality

1.4.3 *Charity and not-for-profit marketing*
- Objectives differ from consumer/industrial markets
- Target markets (donors, volunteers, clients)
- Marketing mix differences (product usually ideas and services rather than goods, short distribution channels, approach to pricing, promotion emphasis on PR and face-to-face fund raising)
- Performance hard to measure

1.4.4 *International marketing*
- Identifying marketing information needs
- Marketing environment, managing the differences
- Structure choices: exporting, licensing, joint ventures, trading companies, direct ownership
- Necessary adaptations to the marketing mix

Glossary

Advertising: Any paid-for non-personal presentation and promotion of ideas, goods or services by an identified person.

After market: All post-sales efforts to satisfy customers and consumers and, if possible, to secure regular or repeat purchases (Jefkins).

Aims: General statements of intention that help to focus thinking but have no direct validity within the corporate planning framework.

Approved lists: A place on an approved list is necessary in order to be eligible to tender for a contract. Approved lists are established by buyers to ensure that all tenders are from acceptable organizations.

Barter: The exchange of one economic good or service for another (see Countertrade).

Bonus: A sum of money, or a quantity of goods, offered as a reward for some action from the customer.

Brand: A name, term, sign, symbol or design, or a combination of them, intended to identify the goods or services of one seller or a group of sellers and to differentiate them from those of their competitors.

Brand extension: The addition of new sizes, new flavours, etc., to extend the number of product offerings distinguished by an established brand.

Brand image: The perception of the brand in the mind of those exposed to the branding messages.

Brand mark: That part of a brand which can be recognized but not vocalized (e.g. the cockerel on the Kellogg's Corn Flakes packet).

Brand name: That part of a brand which can be vocalized (e.g. Kellogg's).

Budget: A formal document that sets out in objective terms what an organization, by its planned actions, believes is achievable and intends to achieve. Resources will be allocated to enable planned results to be achieved.

Business-to-business marketing: Marketing by organizations to organizations.

Certainty: a very rare decision-making condition in which managers have accurate, measurable and reliable information about the outcome of various alternatives under consideration.

Channels of distribution: The routes through which products flow to reach customers and consumers.

Charity marketing: Securing of funds and/or resources in order to fulfil the organization's beneficial objectives of helping people, animals and organizations in need.

Concept: A general notion which is held and which is expressed in short form through language.

Consultant: An advisor from outside the department or organization.
Expert Consultants deal with specific problems, for example, a plumber fixes a leaking washer.
Doctor Consultants diagnose problems and suggest remedies which they may or may not carry out personally.
Process Consultants assist individuals to diagnose problems and to develop the skills, confidence, etc., to fix them.

Consumer: The person who uses up the value of a product or service. **Note**: Customer and consumer are sometimes wrongly used as interchangeable terms. The term 'final consumer' is unnecessary if customer and consumer are used correctly.

Consumerism: An organized movement to protect the interests of consumers.

Control: The term given to active evaluation. (Evaluation, of itself, is passive.)

Controls: Used to indicate measurement, specific information. An objective, to be SMART, must be capable of evaluation against a control. Each single control can be identified and thus the terminology has the potential to confuse. Only within context will the usage be clear, for example, to assist control we have to put controls in place.

Corporate culture: The feeling or climate that is conveyed in an organization by the physical layout and the behavioural 'regulations' and expectations that are evidenced when people interact. Often overtly displayed in dress code and specialized language and covertly expressed by norms of behaviour such as timekeeping and mutual support.

Corporate objective: A statement of intention expressed in clear, specific, unambiguous terms which are quantified against time and relate to the overall performance of an organization. (**See:** *Goals.*)

Countertrade: A commercial transaction in which provisions are made, in one or a series of related contracts, for payment by deliveries of goods and/or services in addition to, or in place of financial settlement (United Nations). (See Barter.)

- *Cost, Insurance and Freight (CIF)* The exporter is responsible for goods until delivered at the overseas port, airport or entry point. Charges include insurance to this point, at which the title to goods passes to the importer.
- *Ex-works* The exporter delivers goods at the factory gate and title passes immediately to the importer, who is responsible for all shipment, insurance, etc.
- *Franco domicile* The exporter pays all charges to the importer's place of business.
- *Free Alongside Ship (FAS)* The exporter delivers the goods to the quay alongside the ship, when title passes to the importer. All loading charges, shipping and insurance from that point passes to the importer.
- *Free On Board (FOB)* The exporter pays dock charges and places goods aboard the ship with the export documentation correctly processed to show that the goods have been either received on board – i.e. 'shipped', or have a 'bill of loading' signifying that the goods are 'received for shipping'.
- *Free On Rail (FOR)* The exporter delivers the goods to the railhead, where the title passes to the importer.

Crisis management: The identification of potential dangers or threats to an organization and the provision of contingency plans to deal with them.

Critical Success factors: Issues of concern which are perceived to be of critical importance to those targeted by marketing both internally and externally.

Customer: Person or organization that buys a product or service, either for use by a consumer or for re-sale. **Note**: A customer can also be a consumer.

Data: Facts and information, especially as a basis for inference.

Database marketing: The use of computers and information technology (IT) to create and maintain detailed records of members of target audiences to provide marketing management information about them.

Demand: A factor of customer desire and willingness to buy coupled with the ability to make the purchase at a specific time.

Derived demand: Where the supplier is unable to directly influence demand because it is generated from more than one stage forward in the chain of production.

Differentiation: The design of different marketing plans and mixes for individual sectors, industries, customers, etc.

Direct response marketing: A channel of communication and distribution that allows providers of goods and services to interactively and directly access any person in the channel.

Discount: A sum allowed off a list price in consideration for some action from the customer.

Distribution: To transport goods and services in the most cost-effective and efficient way from where they are to where they need to be.

Dumping: The export of goods at a price below the full cost of producing them.

Effective and efficient: These terms are usually used together because being effective means doing the right things. Efficient means doing them right, and to time. If an organization is not both effective and efficient it may do the right things badly – effective but not efficient – or the wrong things superbly – efficient but not effective.

Empathy: Feeling oneself into, and losing one's identity in, a work of art; a characteristic of the essentially *aesthetic* attitude or emotion; used sometimes by psychoanalysts of the phenomena of *identification*; possibly more generally characteristic of perceptual experience of a situation than has generally been held (*Dictionary of Psychology*). Often confused with Sympathy. (See below.)

Environmentalism: Concern with issues that affect the global environment.

Ethics: Rules of conduct covering the whole field of moral science. Ethical concern is to be morally correct and honourable in one's behaviour. (**See:** *Morals*.)

Ethnocentric: A domestic country orientation where international marketing is secondary to home marketing.

Exception reporting: A system whereby control criteria are established in advance and only those results which fall outside one or more criteria are reported: everything is within control unless reported otherwise.

Exports: Goods, services and capital assets that are sold to foreign countries.

Franchise: A franchise is a contractual relationship between the franchisor and the franchisee, in which the franchisor offers, or is obligated to maintain, a continuing interest in the business of the franchisee in such areas as know-how and training. Wherein the franchisee operates under a common trade name, format or procedure owned or controlled by the franchisor, and in which the franchisee had, or will make, a substantial capital investment in business from his own resources (The International Franchise Association (IFA)).

Franchising: A particular form of licensing in which the franchisor makes a total marketing programme available, including brand name, product, method of operation and management advice (Chee and Harris).

Gamble: To act in the hope of some desired occurrence. To rely on luck to achieve results.

Gap analysis: Explores the variance between corporate objectives and what can be achieved by various strategies.

Geocentric: The organization applies 'single market' mix strategies worldwide.

Goals: Unquantified objectives. Often the term is used as a synonym for Corporate Objective.

Industrial marketing: This term has been replaced by business-to-business marketing (see above).

Information: Items of knowledge, news, facts concerning specific subject(s). Specific information is often contained within generalized data.

Intensive distribution: Maximum market coverage is sought.

Intercultural marketing: Trading across boundaries established by cultural heritage.

International marketing: The management process responsible for identifying, anticipating and satisfying customer requirements profitability across national frontiers.

Just in Time: A stock control method responsive to market pull to reduce stockholdings and the costs of their administration.

Knowledge: Theoretical and/or practical understanding of a subject gained through study and experience.

Law: *Common law* covers civil wrongs and 'torts'. It is unwritten and relies upon precedent which extends back to 1066. *Statute law* consists of written laws which have been voted on by Parliament, received the Royal Assent, and been entered in the Statute Book.

Licence: The grant by one firm to another firm (exclusive licence) or to others (non-exclusive licence) of the right(s) to manufacture its product, to use its technology or distribution facilities. Similarly the grant by the government to an authority or firm of the rights to supply a particular good or provide a particular service (*Dictionary of Economics*).

List price: The recommended retail price.

Logistics: Originally the art of moving, lodging and supplying troops. Now adopted by business to refer to the movement and housing of goods.

Management: The achievement of results through people.

Management Information System (MIS): A formal method of making available to management the accurate and timely information necessary to facilitate the decision-making process and enable an organization's planning, control and operational functions to be carried out effectively (Stoner & Freeman).

Marketing Information System (MkIS): Consists of people, equipment and procedures to gather, sort, analyse, evaluate and distribute needed, timely, and accurate information to marketing decision makers (Kotler).

Marketing planning: A systematic process that involves assessing marketing opportunities and resources, determining marketing objectives and developing a plan for implementation and control (Dibb, Simkin, Pride and Ferrell).

Marketing planning cycle: A systematized and timed series of activities designed to develop and implement a marketing plan. It is cyclic because implementation automatically leads to appraisal and the recommencement of the cycle.

Market share: The proportion of actual sales held by organizations (by volume or value) within a defined market.

Mission: A broad but definitive statement which covers an organization's purpose, values, distinctive competencies and its place in the world.

Morals: Concerned with the goodness or badness of character or disposition; or with the distinction between right and wrong.

Multinational enterprise: A corporation which owns (in whole or in part), controls and manages income-generating assets in more than one country. In so doing it engages in international production, sales and distribution of goods and services across national boundaries financed by foreign direct investments (Paliwoda).

Negotiation: Confer with another to bring about desired results through mutual agreement.

Non-business marketing: Marketing activities conducted to achieve some goal other than the ordinary business goals of profit, market share or return on investment.

Non-for-profit organizations: Those whose attainment of their prime goals are not assessed by economic measures.

Organizational buying: The decision-making process by which formal organizations establish the need for purchased products and services and identify, evaluate and choose among alternative brands and suppliers (Webster and Wind).

Outsourcing: Drawing on specialist services outside the organization to allow concentration on core values.

Package:

1 The physical protection that protects a product all the way to consumption.

2 Promotional 'packaging' is of user benefits. From the consumer's viewpoint there is no distinction between products and services since customers buy solutions to problems. Therefore a 'solutions package' is sought with no interest whether it is delivered by a 'product' or a 'service'.

Except when being specific we shall use 'Package' to describe offerings. 'Product' will be used to replace 'product or service'.

Performance gap: The difference between the objectives established in the goal formulation process and the results likely to be achieved if existing strategy is continued.

Personal selling: An oral presentation in a conversation with one or more prospective purchasers for the purpose of making a sale.

Plan: Formulated or organized method by which a thing is to be done.

Policies: The basic objectives of an organization. They define the fundamental long-term purpose and are therefore broad in nature. Policies serve as broad constraints which guide all management action.

Polycentric: The organization adopts an orientation which is specific to each host country and market.

Price: Money or other consideration for which a thing is bought or sold.

Process: A course of action or a series of operations which, taken in sequence, produce a desired result.

Product: A product has physical presence, function and symbolic value. (**see:** *Package*.)

Productivity: A relationship between an input and an output expressed as a ratio.

Profiling: Preparing a detailed description of a typical individual within a segment in order to facilitate understanding and action.

Promotions mix: The set of promotional tools that are used to communicate with customers and consumers.

Public Relations: The planned and sustained effort to establish and maintain goodwill and mutual understanding between an organization and its publics.

Quality: What attracts, delights and holds our loyalty.
It is a factor which can only be judged from the perception of the recipient since quality is a combination of both tangible and intangible factors. The quality of the internal operations of an organization is judged only in terms of the quality of the products and services it generates and the satisfactions these provide for its customers.

Quality chain: A supply line extending backwards from the consumer through a series of customers, who are also suppliers, bound together by a mutual focus of providing a quality offering.

Quality circles: A management technique for helping to ensure the positive motivation of those employed in the production of a good or service.

Quota: Commonly used in place of target, especially when setting sales force objectives. The term is more properly used in the sense of rationing, as when stocks are limited and a quota system allocates available stock to individual salespeople.

Regiocentric: The organization applies 'single market' mix strategies to specific regions.

Regular purchase: Refers to small unit FMCG items which are bought frequently.

Relationship marketing: A relationship marketing oriented organization brings together customer service, quality and marketing. See *Relationship Marketing*, Christopher, Payne and Ballantyne, Butterworth-Heinemann.

Repeat purchase: Refers to less often purchased items, such as consumer durables.

Risk: Decision-making condition in which managers know the probability that a given alternative will lead to a desired goal or outcome.

Sale or return: An agreement that allows a stockist to have goods on account and to return any for credit in the event of non-sale.

Sales promotion: Short-term incentives to encourage purchase or sale of a product offer.

Segmentation: The process of breaking down a total market into smaller groupings which are sufficiently similar to allow the use of a distinct marketing mix for each.

Selective/exclusive distribution: Using only exclusive and/or specialist dealers who are equipped and/or located to add value at PoS.

Service: Any activity of benefit that one party can offer to another that is essentially intangible and does not result in the ownership of anything. Its production may or may not be tied to a physical product (Kotler).

Skills: Expertise, practised ability, facility in an action or in doing something.

Societal marketing: The societal marketing concept holds that the organization's task is to determine the needs, wants and interests of target markets and to deliver the desired satisfactions more effectively and efficiently than competitors in a way that preserves or enhances the consumer's and the society's well being (Kotler).

Special offer: A sales promotional tool that adds value through a time-limited period.

Sponsorship: The provision of resources to build a relationship of mutual benefit to the sponsor and sponsored.

Strategic Business Unit (SBU): A single business or collection of businesses with its own competitors and under the control of a manager who has strategic planning and profit responsibilities and controls most of the factors affecting profit.

Strategies: Objective statements that identify a chosen set of actions by which an overall position is sought and maintained.

SWOT: Strengths, Weaknesses, Opportunities and Threats. A SWOT analysis is a vital management tool of analysis.

Symbiosis: Association of two living organisms attached to each other or one within the other to their mutual advantage (*Concise Oxford Dictionary*).

Sympathy: The tendency to experience the feelings and emotions expressed or manifested around one; contagion of feelings called by McDougall *primitive passive sympathy* to distinguish it from *active sympathy* which he regarded as the tendency to seek actively the sharing by others of one's own feelings and emotions (*Dictionary of Psychology*). Often confused with Empathy. (See above.)

Synergy: Combined effects that exceed the sum of individual efforts (*Concise Oxford Dictionary*). Explanation: While a single page can be torn by a baby, only a very few adults can tear the combined pages of a telephone book in half. Synergy is often expressed as 2 + 2 = 5. Good management is constantly seeking synergy because the gearing effect is usually considerably more than in the 2 + 2 = 5 example.

Tactics: Tactical management is concerned with achievement in the short term.

Target: A focus, something to be aimed for, but with no commitment to achievement.

Targeting: The development of products, promotional programmes, etc., specifically for an identified market segment.

Tariff: A duty (a tax) that is levied on imports. Non-tariff restrictions are such as import quotas, restrictive trade agreements, 'buy national polices', requirements to comply with national standards and restrictions on technical services.

Tendering: Offer, usually in writing, to supply goods or services, or to purchase goods, etc. A tender is a once-only opportunity to submit a quotation.

Total Quality Management (TOM): A deeply embedded strategic commitment to quality.

Transfer pricing: A policy of internal pricing which determines at which prices goods are charged between branches or subsidiaries of an integrated firm.

Value: The intangible package of benefits that the decision-making unit believe attaches to the product offer.

Variance: A deviation – plus or minus – from a control factor. Those that fall outside predetermined criteria will be reported to the appropriate management.

Wholesale or trade price: A price discounted from list price either as a straight acknowledgement of a wholesaler's status or, more likely, on the basis of sales volume.

Further reading

Principles of Marketing, second European edition, Kotler, P., Armstrong, G., Saunders, J. and Wong, V. 1999, Prentice Hall

Additional reading

Marketing Operations Study Text, BPP
Marketing Operations, Practice and Revision Kit, BPP
Marketing: Concepts and Strategies, third European edition, Dibb, S., Simkin, L., Pride, W. and Ferrell, O.C. 1997, Houghton Mifflin
Relationship Marketing for Competitive Advantage: winning and keeping customers, Payne, A., Christopher, M., Clark, M and Peck, H. 1998, Butterworth-Heinemann

Optional reading

Principles and Practice of Marketing, Jobber, D. 1995, McGraw Hill
Marketing Plans, McDonald, M. 1995, Butterworth-Heinemann
Marketing Communications, Fill, C. 1993, Houghton Mifflin
Business Marketing, Gross, A., Banting, P., Meredith, L. and Ford, D. 1993, Houghton Mifflin
Services Marketing, Woodruffe, H. 1995, Pitman
Marketing in the Not-for-profit sector, Kinnell, M. and MacDougall, J. 1997, Butterworth-Heinemann
International Marketing Strategy: Analysis, Development and Implementation, Doole, I., Lowe, R. and Phillips, C. 1997, Routledge

Index

ACORN, *See* Segmentation
Action, *see* Communication
Adoption process, *see* Communication
Advertising, 120–2
Affective, *See* Behaviour
After market, 180–2
Agency:
  briefing, 79–80
  selection, 77–8
Agents, international, 286
AIDA, *See* Communication
Aims, *See* Corporate
Ansoff matrix, 16–17
Attitude, *See* Communication (3As)
Audit, marketing, 54
Auditing, market, 250–2
Awareness, *See* Communication (3As)

BADGIES, 253–4
Behaviour:
  attitude change, 122
  black box, 101
  business-to-business
    buying, 252–7
  continuum/hierarchy of effects, 100
  customer and consumer, 99–103
  decisions, 248
  demand, 163
  DMP/DMU
    business-to-business, 253
    consumer, 103
  Howard and Sheth, 102
  industrial buying, 261–2
  overt and covert, 257–9
  price, 161–2
Benefits, 4
  package, 139–40, 159
Black box, *See* Communication
Bonus, *See* Price
Boston Consulting Group, 142–6
Branding, 147–50
  big brand, 147–8
  differential, 148
  extension, 149–50
  franchising, 202
  international, 295
  management, 149
  threats, 150
  values, 148–9

Break-even, 165–6
Brief:
  agency, 79
  creative, 119
Budget, 39–42
  budgetary control, 39
  control, 5, 41
  corrective action, 42
  documentation, 41
  flexible, 43
  organization, 42–3
  promotional, 110–11
  public relations, 124
  sponsorship, 133
  variance analysis, 41–2
Business-to-business marketing,
  249–69
Buygrid, 256–7
Buying, organizational, 256–7

Campaign planning, *See* Promotion
Cash flow, *See* Finance, 143–4
CATS, 238–40
Cause and effect, 226–7
Channels of distribution, 173–4
  business-to-business, 175, 252
  minimum total transactions, 174
  options, 175
  power, 178
Charities, 227–34
  funding, 230
  marketing, 227
  segmentation, 229
Citizen's charter, 227
Codes of practice, *See* Controls
Cognitive, *See* Behaviour
Communication:
  adoption, 101
  AIDA, 101
  black box, 101
  conceptual understanding, 206
  international, 278–9, 301
  offshore English, 299
  process, 98–9
  promotion, 99
  promotional synergy, 117–18
  skills, 97–8
  3As, 101
Competitions, 126

Competitive edge, 198
Competitors response profile, 164
Complaints, 182–5, 213
Conative, *See* Behaviour
Concept:
   marketing, 206–7
   testing, 152
Consultants, 80
Consumer
   behaviour, 99–103
   defined, 176
Consumerism, 224
Content research, *See* Marketing
   research
Contingency planning, 124
Contribution, *See* Costing
Control, 7
   codes of practice, 72
   legal, 71–2
   public relations, 124
   voluntary, 72
Copy, 120
Copy testing, 112, *See also* Marketing
   Research
Corporate:
   aims, 7
   ethics, 69–70
   goals, 7
   mission, 6
   objectives, 5, 7
   plan, 5, 10–11
   policies, 7
   responsibility, 70
   strategies, 7
Costing:
   contribution, 166–7
   fixed, variable, semi-variable, 165
   marginal, 166–7
   public relations, 124
Coupons, 126
Creative brief, 79–80
Crisis management, 124
Critical Success Factors, 51
Culture:
   habits and expectations, 290
   intercultural, 278
   quality, 236
   service, 198
Customer:
   behaviour, 99–103
   benefits, 4
   care, 211
   defined, 176
   interface, 212
   internal, 65
   reaction, 183
   relations, 178
   relationships, 64
   retention, 178
   7Ps and 7Cs, 4
   values, 208

Debtors and creditors, 164
Demand, 163, 199
Derived demand, 263

Differential, 159
   advantage, 104, 148, 198
Differentiation, 262–3
Direct marketing, 108–9
Discount, 194, *See also* Price, discount
Distribution, 73–4
Diversification, 16
DMP, *See* Behaviour
DMU, *See* Behaviour

Effectiveness research, *See* Marketing
   research
Elasticity, *See* Price
Environment:
   analysis, 34
   audit, 34
   concern, 71
   macro, 13–15
   micro, 15
   organizational, 257–9
Environmentalism, 224–5, 227
Ethics, 68–70
   franchising, 202
   law, 70–1
   policy, 70
   strategic, 69–70
Evaluation:
   promotion, 111–12
   sales, 130–1
Examinations, 310–24
   assignment checklists, 96
   examiner's requirements, 2-4
   examples, 303
   how to fail, 169, 186
   preparation, 192
   process questions, 56
   questions, 134
   role, 240
   specimen papers, 327–61
   What and how, 112
Expert system, 109
Exporting, 284

Finance:
   cash flow, 143–4
   international payment, 300
   trading overseas, 287
Focus groups, *See* Marketing research
Franchising, 200–3
Fulfillment, *See* Sales promotion

Gap analysis, *See* Planning
GATT, 282–3
Geodemographics, *See* segmentation
Goals, *See* Corporate

Hierarchy of effects, *See* Behaviour

IMF, 283
Industrial marketing, 249–69

Information:
    need, 34
    systems, 43–5
Inseparability, 196
Intangibility, 196
Internal marketing, *See* Marketing
International:
    institutions, etc., 281–2
    marketing, 278–303

JIT, *See* Quality

Learning, 312–14
Legal:
    controls, 71–2
    organizational formats, 285–6
Life cycle, *See* Products
Lobbying, *See* Public relations

Mail-in, 126
Management:
    brand, 149
    crisis, 124
    ethics, 68–9
    information system, 43–4
    mission, 33
    physical distribution, 174
    product planning, 141–2
    profit centre, 65
    sales, 132–3
    strategic decisions, 36–8
    values, 32
Margin, 160
Mark-up, 162
Market:
    auditing, 250–2
    development, 16
    growth rate, 143
    penetration, 16
    relative market share, 143–6
    share, 143
Marketing:
    business-to-business, 249–69
    charity, 227–33
    concept, 206–7
    ethics, 69
    global, 285
    industrial, 249–69
    information system, 44–5
    internal, 87–9, 231, 285
    international/multinational, 285
    internationally, 289–90
    non-business, 223–4
    not-for-profit, 223
    organization, 51–5
    planning, 4
    planning cycle, 48–51
    plans, 5, 45–51
    programme, 45
    relationship, 178–9
    role, 4–5
    social, 223–4
    societal, 223–4
    strategy, 5, 103–4

Marketing research:
    constraints, 238–40
    content research, 112
    copy testing, 112
    effectiveness research, 112
    focus groups, 112
    international, 291–3
    pre- and post-testing, 112
    promotional, 112–15
    sales research, 261
    tracking study, 112
Media, 104–8
    relations, *See* Public relations
Minimum total transactions, 174
Mission, 6
Morals, *See* Ethics
MOSAIC, *See* segmentation

Negotiation, 84
New product development, 150–3
Non-business marketing, 223–7
Not-for-profit marketing, 223–7

Objectives, 6
    price, 160–1
    promotional, 101, 110
    sales, 131
    sales promotion, 125
    service, 237–8
    SMART, 38
    strategic, 7
OECD, 283
Opportunities to see, 120
Organization:
    budgetary considerations, 42–3
    buying, 256–7
    decisions, 254
    demographics, 264–5
    departmentalism, 55
    environment, 257–9
    international, 286–7
    marketing, 51–5
    matrix, 53
    relationships, 258–9
    selling to, 260–3
    service, 197–8
    structures, 52–3
    task force, 152–3
    upside down, 198
Outsourcing, *See* Relationships

Package, benefits, 139–40
Packaging, 176–7
Perishability, 196
Personal selling, *See* Selling
PEST, *See* STEEPLE
Physical distribution management,
    73–4
    logistics, 297
    strategy, 174–5

Planning:
  Ansoff, 16–17
  audit, 34, 54
  campaign, 118–20
  control, 7
  corporate, 5
  corporate plan, 10–11
  cycle, 48–51
  framework, 11
  gap analysis, 35–6
  goals, 32
  hierarchy, 6
  internationally, 290–1
  marketing, 5, 45–51
  mission, 32–3
  objectives and strategy, 33–4
  process, 30–7, 49
  product, 141–2
  SWOT, 11
  system, 49
  tactics, 7
  terminology, 6–7
  tools, 11
Policy
  corporate, 7
  ethical, 70
Positioning, 17–24, 103–4
  and life cycle, 164
  statement, 104
Power, 178
Pre- and post-testing, *See* Marketing
  research
Price:
  bonus, 167
  ceiling, 164–5
  differential, 159
  discount, 167
  elasticity, 163
  goods or cash, 168
  importance, 159
  lining, 162
  morality based, 68
  objectives, 160–1
  promotions, 168
  psychology, 161–2
  reduction, 126
  sale or return, 167
  strategies, 161, 163
  tactics, 162, 167–8
  tenders, 84–7
  transfer, 73, 168–9, 289
  uniqueness, 159
  value, 84, 159
  wars, 162
Product:
  benefits, 4, 139–40
  Boston Matrix, 142–6
  components, 139
  development, 16
  differential advantage, 104
  industrial, 249–50
  international, 294–6
  life cycle, 140–1
  mix, 146–7
  orientation, 141
  planning, 141–2

portfolio, 140–7
  and services, 138–40
  7Ps and 7Cs, 4
Profit, 160
  centre, *See* Management
Promotion:
  brand, 149
  budgeting, 110–1
  business-to-business, 266–9
  campaign planning, 118–20
  creative brief, 119
  evaluation, 109–13
  objectives, 110
  personal and non-personal, 118
  research, 112–13
  synergy, 117–18
  USPs, 119
Public relations, 121–4
  costing and budgetary control, 124
  lobbying, 123–4
  media relations, 122–3
  publicity, 121–2
  target publics, 121
Purchase decision process, 256–7

Quality:
  chain, 65–6
  circles, 76
  Just in time, 67–8
  service, 234–6
  TQM, 65–7

Regional trading groups, 279–81
Regionalization, 279
Relationship marketing, 65, 178–9
Relationships, 64–5
  complaints, 183–4
  managing, 81
  organizational, 258–9
  outside resources, 73–4
  outsourcing, 74–80
Relative market share, 143–6
Research, *See* Marketing research
Risk, 43

Sale or return, *See* Price
Sales engineers, *See* Selling
Sales promotion, 124–7
Scheduling, 120–1
Scripting, 194
Segmentation:
  charities, 229
  consumer, 19
  forms, 17–19
  geodemographic, 21–3
    costs, 23
  industrial, 19
  lifestyle, 21
  motive, 20–1
  personality, 20
  personalized, 21

Selling:
    effectiveness, 130–1
    evaluation, 130–1
    literature, 132
    management, 132–3
    objectives, 131
    to organizations, 259–61
    overseas, 283–5
    sales engineers, 132
    sales force size, 129–30
    sales force types, 128–9
    sales support, 131–2
    use of time, 130
Services, 192–7
    elements, 205–6
    objectives, 237–8
    operations, 208–13
    organization, 197–8
    packaging, 176
    people, 207–8
    quality, 234–6
    see also Products
7Cs, 4
7Ps:
    business-to-business, 265–6
    consumer, 4
    international, 296–303
7Ss, 197–8
SLEPT, *See* STEEPLE
SMART, *See* Objectives
Social/societal marketing, 223–4
Split-run, 112
Sponsorship, 133–4
STEEPLE, 13
Stock-turn, 160
Strategy:
    after market, 181–2

decisions, 36–8
marketing, 103–4
new product development, 152
objectives, 7
PDM, 174–5
price, 161, 163
role, 5
service, 198
Suppliers, internal, 65
Supply and demand, 199
SWOT, 11–13

Tactics, 7
Tailor-mades, 126
Tangibility, 192–4
Targeting, 17–24
Tendering, 85–6
3As, *see* Communication
Time bombs, *See* Sales promotion
TQM, *See* Quality
Tracking study, *See* Marketing research
Transfer pricing, *See* Pricing
Turnover, 160

Unique selling points, 119

Value, 84, 148–9, 159, 178
Variability, 197
Variance, *See* Budget
Voluntary controls, 72

World Bank, 283

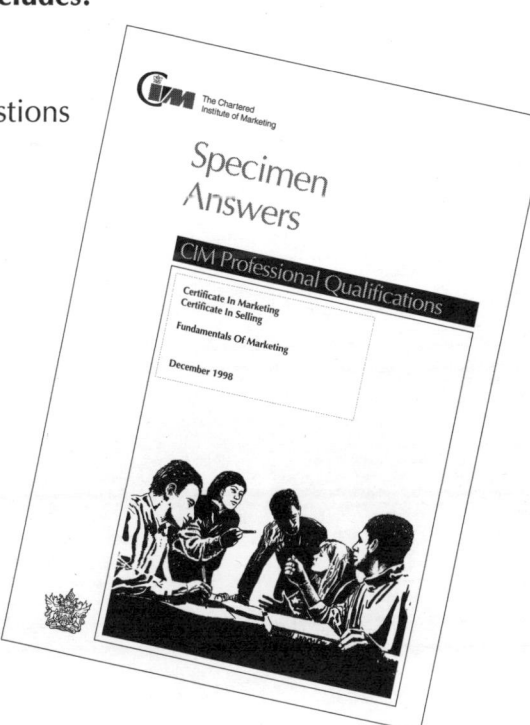